DISCRIMINATION LAW: TEXT, CASES AND MATERIALS

Richard Townshend-Smith, BA, BCL
Senior Lecturer in Law
University of Wales, Swansea

Cavendish
Publishing
Limited

London • Sydney

First published in 1998 by Cavendish Publishing Limited, The Glass House, Wharton Street, London WC1X 9PX, United Kingdom.

Telephone: +44 (0) 171 278 8000   Facsimile: +44 (0) 171 278 8080

E-mail: info@cavendishpublishing.com

Visit our Home Page on http://www.cavendishpublishing.com

Townshend-Smith, Richard
Discrimination Law: Text, Cases and Materials
1. Discrimination – Law and Legislation – Great Britain

I. Title
344.1'041'133

ISBN 1 85941 228 9

Printed and bound in Great Britain by
Biddles Ltd, Guildford and King's Lynn

FOREWORD BY CHERIE BOOTH QC

As a practising lawyer in the field of discrimination law for over 20 years, I welcome this scholarly book for its placing of the law in its economic and social context. I share Richard Townshend-Smith's conclusion that 'Discrimination and inequality are moral issues ... a study of discrimination law and its effects which is politically and ethically neutral is unattainable and pointless'.

The task that the author set himself is at once formidable and important. Most legal textbooks on discrimination law do not even attempt to address the social and economic assumptions underlying the legislation, and some of the most thoughtful and provoking areas of this book are those which address these very issues.

It is as well to remember, some 50 years after the European Convention on Human Rights and Fundamental Freedoms was first drawn up, that the distinguished authors of that text did not include a free standing right not to be discriminated against as one of those fundamental rights and freedoms. Yet today it was regarded as self-evident in Beijing that 'Women's rights are human rights'. In the field of sex discrimination, at least, progress has been made, and the law has contributed to that progress.

In the first part of this book, the author sets out to provide a historical and socio-economic background to the legislative material whose legal analysis forms the second part of the book. To provide such a context is not only refreshing but also vital to a true understanding of the legislation not only for students but also for practitioners. The changing patterns of both social and economic conditions brought about by the changing role of women in our society, and by the increasing importance of ethnic minorities in Britain today, are admirably and comprehensively set out in the first two chapters of the book. The author then raises and answers the vital question of whether the law can and should intervene in this area at all. Most practitioners in this area would share Richard Townshend-Smith's conclusion, both that there is a real role for the law and that its role should not be over-exaggerated.

What is clear is that British law concepts, based as they are on the common law notions of individual rights, can be strained to the limits by legislation whose aims go beyond that of remedying individual grievances to providing a remedy for historical, and social and economic, inequities. This is particularly so in relation to the remedies provided for breaches of the Acts. For many, monetary compensation based on an individual's loss does not truly compensate for grievances which are communal, rather than individual, and which have non-monetary consequences which are difficult to compensate by damages alone. There is no doubt that there is a weakness in the discrimination law of this country arising from the fact that it does not easily lend itself to class actions or, indeed, class remedies.

The author grapples with a fundamental question about the law against discrimination. Is discrimination unlawful because of the harm caused to the individual? This is the traditional tort base/compensatory focus of the common law. Alternatively, is the aim to promote the wider valuing of people as individuals entitled to our respect as a matter of human rights? This less traditional approach could justify extending the law to other groups who are disadvantaged. The present focus of our law is firmly in the former and more traditional tort base approach. This, in turn, has frustrated the efforts of those who have tried to extend discrimination law beyond the historically disadvantaged groups, such as homosexuals, older people and those who are excluded from our society because of their economic and social circumstances.

The author is surely right to highlight the concept of indirect discrimination as a new and interesting development of British law. It is the area of most creativity for the practitioner. Apart from the perennial questions of pregnancy and sexual and racial harassment discussed in detail in this book, direct discrimination is a relatively straightforward concept. Most of the current developments of the law of discrimination centre around the socio-economic issues raised by claims of indirect discrimination. The traditional harm based tort concepts are of less use here, where an employer may have had no intent to discriminate at all but to be swayed by socio-economic factors over which he or she has no immediate control. This is shown most clearly in the interesting discussion about the position of part time workers, whose previous exclusion of rights, benefits and opportunities in their employment has gradually come under attack by use of the law of indirect discrimination. These parts of the book, which are based on a real understanding of the legal arguments as well as their socio-economic concept, make this book a different yet very necessary read for those practitioners in this area who are seeking to use the law as a creative source of equality.

This book is also valuable for bringing together not only the employment areas of the legislation, which are the areas most commonly litigated, but also the related areas of discrimination in education, goods, facilities and services, housing and equal pay. Its focus on the religious discrimination position in Northern Ireland is very welcome to those of us who practise on the mainland. Disability discrimination is also reviewed, although necessarily in less detail than discrimination based on race or sex. It is particularly useful to view this relative new-comer to the scene in its socio-economic context.

By the end of the book, the author has well established his conclusion that, whilst law reform by itself can never transform society, it can indeed be a significant first step in such a transformation. No one can deny the real progress that has been made since the mid 1970s when the current legislation was first introduced. Neither can anyone deny that there is still a long way to go before we create a truly equal and just society. The proposal for reform and strengthening of the law should be studied by all those interested in this field. But in the end I share the author's view that law reform is just one small part of a general need to transform our society into one that is truly equal, fair and empowering. That lawyers have as role in such an agenda I have no doubt. I am certain that the author's expressed wish – that this book will help encourage lawyers to use the law in a positive and proactive way in the interests of all who are disadvantaged – will be achieved.

Cherie Booth QC
4–5 Grays Inn Square
Grays Inn
London WC1R 5AY

PREFACE

Twenty years ago issues of discrimination and inequality received very little attention either in academia or in political life generally. The issues are now seen as of fundamental importance in social and political life. It is hardly possible to read a serious newspaper without coming upon an item which relates to issues of discrimination and inequality. The position of women in our society and the degree to which it is changing is a constant subject for discussion, as is epitomised by the growing awareness of sexual harassment and the need to work for its elimination; the Stephen Lawrence inquiry has once more concentrated attention on racism in society and the best means of tackling it; disability discrimination and age discrimination, virtually ignored ten years ago, have entered public consciousness and are likely to continue to do so to an ever greater extent; the outlawing of discrimination on the ground of sexual orientation, while remaining very controversial, is openly discussed and considered in a way which would have seemed surprising even a decade ago; religious discrimination, especially in Northern Ireland, continues to represent a very obvious blot on equality, while at the same time is a clear indication that the mere passing of legislation can only be a small part of attempts to secure lasting social change.

The roots of all these developments can all be traced to the passing of the Sex Discrimination Act in 1975 and the Race Relations Act a year later. These pieces of legislation continue to provide the bulk of the case law in the field of anti-discrimination, and thus provide the bulk of the legal analysis contained in this book. Indeed, the anti-discrimination statutes form the basic boundary to the subject matter of this book. There is no question that this is a limited focus, for one of the criticisms of the legislation is that areas of social life are excluded from its ambit, such as immigration and family law. Nevertheless, to consider issues of discrimination and inequality, in all their manifestations, across the whole field of law would have expanded this book beyond a manageable scope. It has also been decided to exclude detailed consideration of social security issues; the justification is that the book is primarily aimed at students, and that the case law on social security is impossible to grasp without fairly extensive description and discussion of the way the social security system operates.

The book is primarily aimed at students. The author firmly believes – it is surely self-evident – that it is impossible to understand discrimination law without a grasp of the historical, social and economic situation in which the law operates. All anti-discrimination law is designed, to a greater or lesser degree, to change society. It is part of the task of this book to encourage students to consider how successful the law is likely to be in this aim, and what are the pitfalls that stand in the way. It is also hoped that the book will be of use to practitioners and others concerned with the provision of legal advice.

As will be apparent, my approach has been to cite extensive extracts from other works, especially those concerned with the social and economic aspects of discrimination and inequality, and those concerned with how the law actually operates in practice. My thanks go to those publishers and authors who have granted me permission to refer to their works. I apologise if anyone has been allowed to slip through the net.

Many people have provided invaluable assistance in the preparation and writing of this book. Ruth Costigan, Ursula Kilkelly, Claire Kilpatrick, Jane Lawson, Jenny Levin and Helen Power each read and commented on earlier drafts. Simon Hoffman and Rhianydd Lewis were excellent research assistants, the former at an early stage in helping to pull together the case law material, and the latter doing a great deal of checking and proofreading work. Sean Barr, our law librarian, was a constant source of new materials and references, always supplied in a helpful and supportive manner. Jo Reddy and the other staff at Cavendish Publishing were unfailingly helpful and provided constant support. Last, I am, of course, deeply indebted to Cherie Booth QC for her willingness, in the midst of all other commitments, to write a foreword to this book. Naturally, I remain solely responsible for any remaining errors and inadequacies. The law is stated as of 10 July 1998.

My previous book was dedicated to my wife, Lesley. I am delighted to accede to the pressure from my children, Hannah and Nathan, to dedicate this book to them. Whether I can persuade them to read any of it is another matter. I trust, though, that issues of inequality and discrimination will affect future attitudes and decisions made in their lives, whether from a legal or a wider social perspective.

Richard Townshend-Smith
Swansea
July 1998

ACKNOWLEDGMENTS

Adkins, L, *Gendered Work: Sexuality, Family and the Labour Market*, 1995, Buckingham: Open University.

Anon, 'Adjusting the workplace: employers' duty under the Disability Discrimination Bill' (1995) 61 EOR 11, published by Industrial Relations Services, Eclipse Group Ltd, 18–20 Highbury Place, London N5 1QP.

Anon, 'Age discrimination – no change!' (1993) 48 EOR 21, published by Industrial Relations Services, Eclipse Group Ltd, 18–20 Highbury Place, London N5 1QP.

Anon, 'Bargaining for equality' (1990) 29 EOR 22, published by Industrial Relations Services, Eclipse Group Ltd, 18–20 Highbury Place, London N5 1QP.

Anon, 'Compensation awards up' (1997) 74 EOR 13, published by Industrial Relations Services, Eclipse Group Ltd, 18–20 Highbury Place, London N5 1QP.

Anon, 'Coping with work and eldercare' (1997) 73 EOR 23, published by Industrial Relations Services, Eclipse Group Ltd, 18–20 Highbury Place, London N5 1QP.

Anon, 'Disability Discrimination Act' (1996) 65 EOR 31, published by Industrial Relations Services, Eclipse Group Ltd, 18–20 Highbury Place, London N5 1QP.

Anon, 'EOC sexual harassment guide' (1994) 58 EOR 35, published by Industrial Relations Services, Eclipse Group Ltd, 18–20 Highbury Place, London N5 1QP.

Anon, 'Equal pay law: paradise for lawyers – hell for women' (1991) 35 EOR 30, published by Industrial Relations Services, Eclipse Group Ltd, 18–20 Highbury Place, London N5 1QP.

Anon, 'Equality for lesbians and gay men in the workplace' (1997) 74 EOR 20, published by Industrial Relations Services, Eclipse Group Ltd, 18–20 Highbury Place, London N5 1QP.

Anon, 'Life after the tribunal: the CRE and follow-up work' (1997) 76 EOR 13, published by Industrial Relations Services, Eclipse Group Ltd, 18–20 Highbury Place, London N5 1QP.

Anon, 'Limited positive discrimination allowed' (1998) 77 EOR 38, published by Industrial Relations Services, Eclipse Group Ltd, 18–20 Highbury Place, London N5 1QP.

Anon, 'Making the invisible visible: rewarding women's work' (1992) 45 EOR 23, published by Industrial Relations Services, Eclipse Group Ltd, 18–20 Highbury Place, London N5 1QP.

Anon, 'Maternity arrangements 95: part 1' (1995) 63 EOR 9, published by Industrial Relations Services, Eclipse Group Ltd, 18–20 Highbury Place, London N5 1QP.

Anon, 'Minimum wage benefits women and ethnic minorities' (1997) 73 EOR 13, published by Industrial Relations Services, Eclipse Group Ltd, 18–20 Highbury Place, London N5 1QP.

Anon, 'Racial harassment at work' (1993) 49 EOR 17, published by Industrial Relations Services, Eclipse Group Ltd, 18–20 Highbury Place, London N5 1QP.

Applebey, G and Ellis, E, 'Formal investigations: the Commission for Racial Equality and the Equal Opportunities Commission as law enforcement agencies' [1984] PL 236.

Bartholet, E, 'Application of Title VII to jobs in high places' (1982) 95 Harv L Rev 947.

Beechey, V, *Unequal Work*, 1987, London: Verso.

Beechey, V, 'Women's employment in contemporary Britain', in Beechey, V and Whitegg, E (eds), *Women in Britain Today*, 1986, Milton Keynes: OU Press.

Beechey, V and Perkins, T, *A Matter of Hours: Women, Part-Time Work and the Labour Market*, 1987, Cambridge: Polity.

Bertin, J, 'Reproductive hazards in the workplace', in Cohen, S and Taub, N (eds), *Reproductive Laws for the 1990s*, 1989, Clifton, New Jersey: Humana.

Bourn, C and Whitmore, J, *Anti-Discrimination Law in Britain*, 3rd edn, 1996, London: Sweet & Maxwell.

Bramwell, R and Davidson, M, 'Reproductive hazards at work', in Firth-Cozens, J and West, M (eds), *Women at Work: Psychological and Organizational Perspectives*, 1991, Buckingham: Open University.

Brown, C, 'Ethnic pluralism in Britain: the demographic and legal background', in Glazer, N and Young, K (eds), *Ethnic Pluralism and Public Policy*, 1986, Aldershot: Gower.

Brown, C, 'Same difference: the persistence of racial disadvantage in the British labour market', in Braham, P, Rattansi, A and Skellington, P (eds), *Racism and Anti-Racism: Inequalities, Opportunities and Policies*, 1992, London: Sage.

Browne, N, 'The fundamental tension between market wages for women and comparable worth' (1984) 2 Law and Inequality 473.

Buck, T, 'Ageism and legal control', in Hepple, B and Szyszczak, E (eds), *Discrimination: The Limits of Law*, 1992, London: Mansell.

Cockburn, C, *In the Way of Women: Men's Resistance to Sex Equality in Organisations*, 1991, Basingstoke: Macmillan.

Collinson, D and Collinson, M, 'Sexuality in the workplace: the domination of men's sexuality', in Hearn, J, Sheppard, D, Tancred-Sheriff, P and Barrell, G (eds), *The Sexuality of Organisation*, 1989, London: Sage.

Collinson, D, Knights, D and Collinson, M, *Managing to Discriminate*, 1990, London: Routledge.

Conaghan, J, 'Pregnancy and the workplace: a question of strategy' (1993) 20 JLS 71.

Coussey, M, 'The effectiveness of strategic enforcement of the Race Relations Act 1976', in Hepple, B and Szyszczak, E (eds), *Discrimination: The Limits of Law*, 1992, London: Mansell.

Craig, C, Garnsey, E and Rubery, J, *Payment Structures and Smaller Firms: Women and Employment in Segmented Labour Markets*, 1984, London: Department of Employment.

Davies, P and Freedland, M, *Labour Legislation and Public Policy*, 1993, Oxford: Clarendon, by permission of Oxford University Press.

Doyle, B, *New Directions towards Disabled Workers' Rights*, 1994, London: Institute of Employment Rights.

Fenwick, H, 'Special protections for women in European Union law', in Hervey, T and O'Keeffe, D, *Sex Equality Law in the European Union*, 1996, Chichester: John Wiley.

Finley, L, 'Transcending equality theory: a way out of the maternity and the workplace debate' (1986) 86 Columbia L Rev 1118.

Fitzpatrick, C, 'How long is a piece of string? European regulation of the post-birth period', in Hervey, T and O'Keeffe, D (eds), *Sex Equality Law in the European Union*, 1996, Chichester: John Wiley.

Flynn, L, 'Case-note: *P v S and Cornwall CC*' (1997) 34 CML Rev 367, with the kind permission of Kluwer Law International.

Flynn, L, 'Gender equality laws and employers' dress codes' (1995) 24 Industrial LJ 255, by permission of Oxford University Press.

Fredman, S, 'A difference with distinction: pregnancy and parenthood re-assessed' (1994) 110 LQR 106.

Fredman, S, 'The poverty of equality: pensions and the ECJ' (1996) 25 Industrial LJ 91, by permission of Oxford University Press.

Fredman, S, 'Reversing discrimination' (1997) 113 LQR 575.

Gardner, J, 'Liberals and unlawful discrimination' (1989) 9 OJLS 1, by permission of Oxford University Press.

Gardner, J, 'Section 20 of the Race Relations Act 1976: "facilities" and "services"' (1987) 50 MLR 345.

Gooding, C, *Disabling Laws, Enabling Acts*, 1994, London: Pluto.

Hearn, J and Parkin, W, *Sex at Work: The Power and Paradox of Organisation Sexuality*, 1987, Brighton: Wheatsheaf.

Holterman, S, 'The costs and benefits to British employers of measures to promote equality of opportunity', in Rubery, J (ed), *The Economics of Equal Opportunities*, 1995, Manchester: EOC.

Hunter, R and Leonard, A, 'Sex discrimination and alternative dispute resolution: British proposals in the light of international experience' [1997] PL 298.

Jenkins, R, 'Equal opportunity in the private sector: the limits of voluntarism', in Jenkins, R and Solomos, J (eds), *Racism and Equal Opportunity Polices in the 1980s*, 1987, Cambridge: CUP.

Jenkins, R, *Racism and Recruitment: Managers, Organisations and Equal Opportunity in the Labour Market*, 1986, Cambridge: CUP.

Jewson, N and Mason, D, 'Monitoring equal opportunities policies: principles and practice', in Jenkins, R and Solomos, J (eds), *Racism and Equal Opportunity Polices in the 1980s*, 1987, Cambridge: CUP.

Jones, T, *Britain's Ethnic Minorities: An Analysis of the Labour Force Survey*, 1996, London: Policy Studies Institute.

Kenney, S, 'Reproductive hazards in the workplace: the law and sexual difference' [1986] International Journal of the Sociology of Law 393, by permission of the publisher, Academic Press Ltd, London.

Lacey, N, 'Legislation against sex discrimination: questions from a feminist perspective' (1986) 14 JLS 411.

Lacey, N, 'From individual to group', in Hepple, B and Szyszczak, E (eds), *Discrimination: The Limits of Law*, 1992, London: Mansell.

Lester, A and Bindman, G, *Race and Law*, 1972, Harmondsworth: Penguin.

Lustgarten, L, 'Racial inequality and the limits of the law' (1986) 49 MLR 68.

McColgan, A, 'Legislating equal pay: lessons from Canada' (1993) 22 Industrial LJ 269, by permission of Oxford University Press.

McCrudden, C, 'Equal pay for work of equal value: the Equal Pay (Amendment) Regulations 1983' (1983) 12 Industrial LJ 197, by permission of OUP.

McCrudden, C, 'Equal treatment and occupational pensions: implementing European Community law in the United Kingdom following the post-*Barber* decisions of the European Court of Justice' (1995) 46 Northern Ireland LQ 376.

McCrudden, C, 'Rethinking positive action' (1986) 15 Industrial LJ 219, by permission of Oxford University Press.

MacEwan Scott, A, 'Gender segregation and the SCELI research', in *Gender Segregation and Social Change*, 1994, Oxford: OUP, by permission of Oxford University Press.

Miles, R, *Racism*, 1989, London: Routledge.

Moore, S, 'Justice doesn't mean a free lunch: the application of the principle of equal pay to occupational pension schemes' (1995) 20 EL Rev 159.

O'Donovan, K and Szyszczak, E, *Equality and Sex Discrimination Law*, 1988, Oxford: Blackwells.

Phizacklea, A and Wolkowitz, C, *Homeworking Women: Gender, Racism and Class at Work*, 1995, London: Sage.

Pitt, G, 'Can reverse discrimination be justified?', in Hepple, B and Szyszczak, E (eds), *Discrimination: The Limits of Law*, 1992, London: Mansell.

Rubery, J and Fagan, C, *Social Europe: Wage Determination and Sex Segregation in Employment in the European Community*, 1995, Luxembourg: Office for Official Publications of the European Communities.

Rubery, J, Horrell, S and Burchell, B, 'Part-time work and gender inequality', in MacEwan Scott, A (ed), *Gender Segregation and Social Change*, 1994, Oxford: OUP, by permission of Oxford University Press.

Rutherglen, G, 'Discrimination and its discontents' (1995) 81 Virginia LR 117.

Rutherglen, G, 'Disparate impact under Title VII: an objective theory of discrimination' (1987) 73 Virginia L Rev 1297.

Rutherglen, G, 'From race to age: the expanding scope of employment discrimination law' (1995) 24 JLS 491.

Sacks, V, 'Tackling discrimination positively', in Hepple, B and Szyszczak, E (eds), *Discrimination: The Limits of Law*, 1992, London: Mansell.

Sawyer, M, 'The operation of labour markets and the economics of equal opportunities', in Rubery, J (ed), *The Economics of Equal Opportunities*, 1995, Manchester: EOC.

Skellington, R with Morris, P, *'Race' in Britain Today*, 2nd edn, 1986, London: Sage.

Solomos, J, *Race and Racism in Britain*, 2nd edn, 1993, London: Macmillan.

Solomos, J and Back, L, *Racism and Society*, 1996, London: Macmillan.

Sullivan, K, 'Sins of discrimination: last term's affirmative action cases' (1986) 100 Harv L Rev 78.

Stockdale, J, 'Sexual harassment at work', in Firth-Cozens, J and West, M (eds), *Women at Work: Psychological and Organizational Perspectives*, 1991, Buckingham: Open University.

Sunstein, S, 'Three civil rights fallacies' (1991) California L Rev 751.

Townshend-Smith, R, 'Economic defences to equal pay claims', in Hervey, T and O'Keeffe, D (eds), *Sex Equality Law in the European Union*, 1996, Chichester: John Wiley.

Townshend-Smith, R, 'Justifying indirect discrimination in English and American law: how stringent should the test be?' (1995) 1 IJDL 103.

Townshend-Smith, R, *Sex Discrimination in Employment: Law, Practice and Policy*, 1989, London: Sweet & Maxwell.

Vogler, C, 'Segregation, sexism and the labour supply', in MacEwan Scott, A (ed), *Gender Segregation and Social Change*, 1994, Oxford: OUP, by permission of Oxford University Press.

Walby, S, *Gender Transformations*, 1997, London: Routledge.

Ward, T, 'Beyond sex equality: the limits of sex equality in the new Europe', in Hervey, T and O'Keeffe, D (eds), *Sex Equality Law in the European Union*, 1996, Chichester: John Wiley.

Wasserstrom, R, 'Racism, sexism and preferential treatment: an approach to the topics' (1977) 24 UCLA Rev 581.
Copyright 1977, the Regents of the University of California. All rights reserved, and by permission of the author.

Webb, M, 'Sex and gender in the labour market', in Reid, I and Stratta, E (eds), *Sex Differences in Britain*, 2nd edn, 1989, Aldershot: Gower.

Whiteford, E, 'Lost in the mists of time: the ECJ and occupational pensions' 1995 CML Rev 801, with the kind permission of Kluwer Law International.

Whiteford, E, 'Occupational pension schemes and European law: clarity at last?', in Hervey, T and O'Keeffe, D (eds), *Sex Equality Law in the European Union*, 1996, Chichester: John Wiley.

Willborn, S, 'The disparate impact model of discrimination: theory and limits' (1985) 34 American UL Rev 799.

Wintemute, R, 'Recognising new kinds of direct sex discrimination: transsexualism, sexual orientation and dress codes' (1997) 60 MLR 334.

Wintemute, R, 'Sexual orientation discrimination', in McCrudden, C and Chambers, G (eds), *Individual Rights and the Law in Britain*, 1995, Oxford: Clarendon, by permission of Oxford University Press.

Wood, R, 'Psychometrics should make assessment fairer' (1996) 67 EOR 27, published by Industrial Relations Services, Eclipse Group Ltd, 18–20 Highbury Place, London N5 1QP.

CONTENTS

Contents

Contents

Contents

TABLE OF CASES

TABLE OF STATUTES

TABLE OF ABBREVIATIONS

AC	Appeal Cases
All ER	All England Law Reports
American UL Rev	American University Law Review
Anglo-Am LR	Anglo-American Law Reports
Boston UL Rev	Boston University Law Review
California L Rev	California Law Review
Chicago ULR	Chicago University Law Reports
CLP	Current Legal Problems
CMLR	Common Market Law Reports
CML Rev	Common Market Law Review
Columbia L Rev	Columbia Law Review
Conn LR	Connecticut Law Reports
ECR	European Court Reports
EHRR	European Human Rights Reports
EL Rev	European Law Review
EOC	Equal Opportunities Commission
EOR	Equal Opportunities Review
Harv L Rev	Harvard Law Review
Human Rights LJ	Human Rights Law Journal
ICR	Industrial Court Reports
IJDL	International Journal of Discrimination and the Law
Industrial LJ	Industrial Law Journal
Iowa LR	Iowa Law Reports
IRLR	Industrial Relations Law Reports
JLS	Journal of Law and Society
LQR	Law Quarterly Review
Minn LR	Minnesota Law Reports
MLR	Modern Law Review
Northern Ireland LQ	Northern Ireland Law Quarterly
Ohio State LJ	Ohio State Law Journal
OJLS	Oxford Journal of Legal Studies
Penns UL Rev	Pennsylvania University Law Review
PL	Public Law
QB	Queen's Bench Law Reports
UCLA L Rev	University of California Los Angeles Law Review
US	US Supreme Court Reports
Virginia L Rev	Virginia Law Review
WLR	Weekly Law Reports
Yale LJ	Yale Law Journal

THE BACKGROUND TO RACE DISCRIMINATION LEGISLATION IN THE UNITED KINGDOM

This chapter will examine the background to the issues of racial discrimination, racial inequality and consequent legislation in the UK. We will highlight key statistics and the way in which they have been changing and developing in recent years. Consideration will briefly be given to the causes of racism and racial disadvantage. Finally, we will examine the history of race discrimination legislation in the UK.

THE BRITISH ETHNIC MINORITY POPULATION

The population of Great Britain (excluding Northern Ireland) is about 60.5 million.[1] 'There were 616,000 adults [over 16] in the Indian ethnic group, 1.4% of the adult population. Within this group, 20% were born in the United Kingdom. The Afro-Caribbean ethnic group was only slightly smaller; at 583,000 it accounted for 1.3% of the adult population, but over one-third were born in the United Kingdom. Overall, the ethnic minority population constituted 4.9% of the total population of Great Britain aged 16 or over, at 2.1 million; just over a quarter were born in the United Kingdom ... Results from the 1991 census ... showed that 33% of the ethnic minority population in Great Britain was under 16 compared with 19% of the white population. Overall, just over three million people, 5.5% of the population of Great Britain, described themselves as belonging to an ethnic minority group in the 1991 Census.'[2] People whose origin is in either the Caribbean or the Indian subcontinent will be the main focus of attention as, first, the other minority groups are small and varied, and secondly because the Afro-Caribbean and Asian communities have been at the forefront of pressure for legal, political and social change. This is not to say, however, that similar problems may not arise for members of other minority ethnic groups, who are of course equally protected by the race discrimination legislation.

It is very important to stress the diversity between the backgrounds and experience of Britain's minority ethnic groups. This manifests itself in

---

[1] *Social Trends*, 1995, London: HMSO, Table 1.2, p 16.
[2] *Ibid*, Table 1.8, p 19.

numerous ways. First, the pattern of geographical distribution is complex.[3] There may be high levels of local segregation between different ethnic groups, and between those whose origins lie in different parts of the Indian subcontinent or the Caribbean. Secondly, there is a distinction of great significance between those groups whose first language is English, that is, those from the West Indies and some Asian groups, and those who had little or no knowledge of English on arrival. Thirdly, those of Afro-Caribbean origin are very likely to come from a notionally Christian background, while Asians are predominantly Muslims, Hindus and Sikhs. The nature of religious affiliation may profoundly affect both relationships between different groups and the ability and willingness of people to embrace what may be seen as a more 'Western' way of life. Fourthly, there may be significant cultural differences between older people, for whom the ideas and values of the land they left may continue to loom large, and younger people, born and brought up entirely in the UK. These and other factors influence the experience of racism and inequality, and may also influence the ability of the law to tackle it in a meaningful way.

Immigration into Great Britain is not simply a recent phenomenon.[4] There was a large influx of Irish people, especially in the 19th century. 'In purely numerical terms the number of Irish immigrants to Britain over the last two centuries has been far in excess of any other immigration.'[5] Yet, this does not imply an absence of racism on the part of the indigenous population. 'Images of the racial or cultural inferiority of the Irish were based not only on particular ideological constructions of the Irish but on a self-definition of Englishness or Anglo-Saxon culture in terms of particular racial and cultural attributes. In later years, such images of the uniqueness and purity of Englishness were to prove equally important in the political debate about black migration and settlement.'[6]

The next main wave of immigration, from the late 19th century onwards, was of Jews. There is also a significant and long standing history of black communities in Britain, often associated with seaports, such as in Liverpool and Cardiff. 'By the Second World War there was already a long historical

---

[3] 'People of Indian and Pakistani origin are characteristically found in nearly all towns [where immigrants have settled], but the population of West Indian origin is not nearly as widespread, being heavily concentrated in London and the West Midlands.' Brown, C, 'Ethnic pluralism in Britain: the demographic and legal background', in Glazer, N and Young, K (eds), *Ethnic Pluralism and Public Policy*, 1986, Aldershot: Gower, pp 34, 38. See, also, Skellington, R, with Morris, P, *'Race' in Britain Today*, 2nd edn, 1996, London: Sage Publications, pp 52–62.

[4] Solomos, J, *Race and Racism in Britain*, 2nd edn, 1993, London: Macmillan, pp 38–51.

[5] *Ibid*, p 42.

[6] *Ibid*, p 43.

experience of political debate and mobilisation around issues of ethnicity, race and religion.'[7]

Brown, C, 'Ethnic pluralism in Britain: the demographic and legal background', in Glazer, N and Young, K (eds), *Ethnic Pluralism and Public Policy*, 1986, Aldershot: Gower, p 34:

[T]he period of [black] immigration of any scale begins after the Second World War. An initially small migration increased during the 1950s to a substantial flow from the West Indies, India and Pakistan. This peaked sharply in the years before the introduction of immigration control in 1962, and since then there has been an overall downward trend in black immigration ...

[T]here have been substantial changes in the pattern of that immigration. First, the peak period of West Indian immigration was before the first immigration controls: in the 1950s there were migrants from both sending areas, but West Indians predominated. Since then, the position has been reversed, and throughout the 1960s and 1970s migrants from the Indian subcontinent [were] in the majority. Secondly, the earlier stages of the migration were characterised by a predominance of adult males, and these were later to be outnumbered by women and children. More than 90% of New Commonwealth citizens accepted for settlement on arrival in 1979 were women, children or elderly men.

In the period 1988–92, an average of 243,000 people entered the country each year to stay for a least a year (compared with 134,000 who left the country). Of these, 62,000 came from the EU, 80,000 from other non-Commonwealth countries, 44,000 from the 'white' Commonwealth, and 38,000 from the New Commonwealth.[8] By all logic, black immigration should long since have ceased to be a serious political issue; tighter immigration control could make no more than a very minor impact on the size of the ethnic minority population of Great Britain.

Jones, T, *Britain's Ethnic Minorities: An Analysis of the Labour Force Survey*, 1996, London: Policy Studies Institute, p 61:

A number of factors led to the migration of people to Britain from its former colonies ... Perhaps the most important was the contrast in terms of economic well being between Britain and many of the countries it had colonised. People were attracted by the prospect of a higher standard of living, and more developed education and health systems. Because of specific labour shortages affecting jobs then considered undesirable in some of the main conurbations, the early immigrants had very good prospects of finding work. Two further developments boosted immigration. First, the partition of India, which created a population of political and religious refugees who had a high incentive to emigrate. Second, from the late 1960s onwards the political persecution of South Asians living and working in East Africa created a new class of migrants

---

7   *Op cit*, Solomos, fn 4, p 51.
8   *Social Trends*, 1995, London: HMSO, Table 1.14, p 23.

... There is a great deal of evidence that the life chances of [migrants] were powerfully constrained by widespread racial discrimination. They tended to be in the more poorly paid jobs which the indigenous population did not want, and had to live in cheap, low quality housing.

RACE AND RACISM

The social significance of this immigration cannot be understood without some consideration of the concepts of 'race' and 'racism'.

Solomos, J and Back, L, *Racism and Society*, 1996, London: Macmillan, pp 34, 59:

[O]nly in the late 18th century and early 19th century does the term race come to refer to supposedly discrete categories of people defined according to their physical characteristics ... [T]he concept as we understand it today came into being relatively late in the development of modern capitalist societies. Although usages of the term race have been traced somewhat earlier in a number of European languages, the development of racial doctrines and ideologies begins to take shape in the late 18th century, and reached its high point during the 19th and early 20th centuries ... [9]

Although racial ideologies often appeal to primordial notions of kinship and myths of common ethnic origins to support their arguments, it is worth emphasising that the notion that there are races and racial relationships is relatively new ... This means breaking with the view that sees race and racism as transhistorical categories and as unchanging.

The concept of 'race' is thus historically and scientifically problematic.

Skellington, R with Morris, P, *'Race' in Britain Today*, 2nd edn, 1996, London: Sage, p 25:

[T]he ethnic or racial categories used in a census or survey are not fixed or given ... but have to be decided upon and have to be constructed. It is important to note that 'race' and ethnicity are generally conceptualised as interchangeable categories in the various areas of data collection. Indeed the category 'white' is a good example of this, in that it is regarded as a fixed and unchanging category, whereas 'black' is generally broken down into different 'ethnic' groups. The only truly objective category in this respect is that of legal nationality ... A woman who is a Pakistani national living in Scotland, for example, may think of herself as black or Asian or Muslim or Scottish. A British-born black girl may think of herself as West Indian or black or British or Afro-Caribbean. Probably such people would think of themselves as each of these things at different times and in different situations.

---

[9] See Miles, R, *Racism*, 1989, London: Routledge, pp 11–30.

Each country has a separate and unique history in respect of racial issues. Thus the American experience of slavery has a significant and continuing impact upon current argument and opinion. The different histories in the USA and the UK suggest that the drawing of social and legal analogies in the field of race relations and anti-discrimination legislation should be done only with the greatest of care. What is distinctive about British history is the colonial experience which, while in some regards paralleling slavery, was fundamentally different from it. The form colonial racism took related more to an ideology of national, cultural, religious and economic supremacy.

Lester, A and Bindman, G, *Race and Law*, 1972, Harmondsworth: Penguin, p 13:

The opposition to Jewish immigrants – European in physical appearance and culture – might have led us to expect that the ... immigration from Asia and the Caribbean of people with an unfamiliar culture and a different skin colour would meet a strong tide of racial feeling. Still more predictable is this reaction when one recalls the salient chapters of British imperial history: the vast and lucrative trade in African slaves in the 17th and 18th centuries and the encouragement of a brutal system of servitude in the colonies; the replacement of that system by Asian indentured labour in the 19th century; and the creation of rigidly segregated societies, dominated by white settler minorities, in British Africa in this century. In several senses, post-war immigration from the new Commonwealth has transplanted to the old mother country prejudices and patterns of behaviour which could be conveniently ignored or righteously condemned so long as they flourished only within an Empire beyond our shores.

Even if one accepts that there are such things as racial differences, the issues so far as race and racism are concerned focus more on supposed social, cultural and perhaps religious differences. They are therefore more contingent on the experiences of a particular society than are gender issues.[10]

In examining the causes of racism and racial inequality in Britain, we will first consider something of the ideology of race and racism, and then examine how such assumptions are translated into real employment decisions which may operate to the disadvantage of minority ethnic groups.

Solomos, J, *Race and Racism in Britain*, 2nd edn, 1993, London: Macmillan, pp 8–9, 183–85, 193:

[I]t has long been recognised that, notwithstanding the long history of debates about this category, races do not exist in any scientifically meaningful sense.

---

[10] For that reason, I do not intend to deal with 'critical race theory', a doctrine which has in recent years informed much of the discussion about racism and racist thought in the USA. That theory builds on the view that racism can only be understood in the light of the particular historical and cultural experience of any particular society. For a helpful introduction to the theory, see Caldwell, V, 'Review of *Critical Race Theory: The Key Writings that Formed the Movement*' (1996) 96 Columbia L Rev 1363.

Yet it is also clear that in many societies people have often acted and continue to act as if race exists as a fixed objective category, and these beliefs are reflected in political discourses and at the level of popular ideas. Common sense conceptions of race have relied on a panoply of classificatory variables such as skin colour, country of origin, religion, nationality and language to define different groups of people ... [11]

[R]acism is broadly defined in the sense that it is used to cover those ideologies and social processes which discriminate against others on the basis of their ... different racial membership. There is little to be gained from seeing racism merely as a signifier for ideas of biological or cultural superiority, since it has become clear in recent years that the focus on attributed biological inferiority is being replaced in contemporary forms of racist discourse by a concern with culture and ethnicity as historically fixed categories ... [R]acism is not a static phenomenon. In societies such as Britain racism is produced and reproduced through political discourse, the media, the educational system and other institutions. Within this wider social context racism becomes an integral element of diverse social issues, such as law and order, crime, the inner cities and urban unrest.[12]

By the 1980s ... the language ... used to describe the politics of race in contemporary Britain had as much to do with a definition of Englishness or Britishness as it did with characteristics of the minority communities themselves ...

[N]ew-right racial discourses increasingly present black people as an 'enemy within' that is undermining the moral and social fabric of society. In both popular and elite discourses about immigration and race, black communities as a whole, or particular groups such as young blacks, are presented as involved in activities which are a threat to social order and political stability. Such ideological constructions do not necessarily have to rely on notions of racial superiority in the narrow sense ...

Commonly held images of black people include assumptions about differences between the culture, attitudes and values of black people compared with the white majority. Additionally the attempts by black people to assert their rights and lay claim to social justice have often been presented in the media as a sign of the failure of the majority communities to adapt to British society, and not as a sign that racial injustice is deeply embedded.

This ... amounts to the claim that the demands of black minorities are not legitimate, that they are in fact the product of attempts to claim special privileges and thus a threat to the majority. Because such claims are presented as coming from groups which are outside the traditions of culture of British political life they are more easily portrayed as a challenge to the values of the majority communities, and by a twist of logic as unjust ...

---

[11] See, also, *op cit*, Miles, fn 9, pp 30–40, 70–71.
[12] See, also, *op cit*, Miles, fn 9, pp 41–50.

[O]ne important aspect of contemporary racial ideologies in Britain is the tendency to obscure or deny the meaning and implications of the deployment of race categories. This fits in with the wider tendency (a) to deny the importance of racism in British society and (b) to deny that hostility to the presence of black communities in Britain is a form of racism. According to this line of argument it is only natural that, given the choice, people should prefer to live with their own kind and not become a multiracial society. Such a wish is not seen as the manifestation of racialist attitudes, but as a natural response to the presence of people of a different cultural and racial background.

Miles, R, *Racism*, 1989, London: Routledge, p 119:

[I]t is now clear that the problematisation of the migrant presence occurred through the signification of both biological and cultural characteristics, and that the working class played an active role in what was a process of racialisation.[13] This process, and the related articulation of racism, was a significant political force before the onset of major economic crisis and it was a form of partially autonomous resistance from below in that it derived from the experience of competition for scarce resources and of localised economic decline ... But ... the British State has been ... an active agent of racialisation by, *inter alia*, passing exclusionary immigration legislation which has institutionalised racism and identifying young people of Caribbean origin as a threat to 'law and order'. In so doing, the economic and political consequences of the crisis of capital accumulation have been expressed in part through the idea of 'race' ...

But this process of racialisation has articulated intimately with nationalism ... [T]he issue is not whether or not people of Asian and Caribbean origin were inferior 'races', but rather one of reconstructing a positive sense of Englishness ...

The representational content ... is classically nationalist, but it is neatly lined, and therefore sustained, by racism. This articulation depends, in part, upon a simultaneous signification of cultural differences and somatic features: the Other is differentiated by skin colour as well as by clothing, diet, language and religion, for example. The presence of the Other is represented as problematic by virtue of, for example, its supposed use of the resources and facilities of 'our own people', its propensity to violence or its stimulation of the 'natural prejudice' of 'our own people' against those whose 'natural home' ... is elsewhere in the world.

Solomos, J and Back, L, *Racism and Society*, 1996, London: Macmillan, pp 210, 216:

[A]lthough at its root racism may involve clear and simple images, it is by no means uniform or without contradictions. Indeed, what is really interesting about racism as a set of ideas and political practices is that it is able to provide images of the 'other' which are simple and unchanging and at the same time to

---

[13] See Phizacklea, A and Miles, R, 'The British trade union movement and racism', in Braham, P, Rattansi, A and Skellington, R (eds), *Racism and Anti-Racism: Inequalities, Opportunities and Policies*, 1992, London: Sage, pp 30–45.

adapt to the changing social and political environment. Thus contemporary racist ideas are able to retain a link with the mystical values of classical racism and to adopt and use cultural and political symbols which are part of contemporary society ... It is precisely this combination of the mystical and the scientific that lies at the heart of the attempts by contemporary racist movements to reinvent their ideas as those which are attempting to protect the cultural and ethnic boundaries of race and nation.

Simplistic and monolithic accounts of racism ... do little to enlighten us as to why it is that in particular social and political contexts millions of people respond to the images, promises and hopes which are at the heart of mass racist movements.

Racism may be reproduced at both a national level, such as through the media, and at a micro level, such as through the actions of individual employers.

Solomos, J and Back, L, *Racism and Society*, 1996, London: Macmillan, pp 19, 26:

The role of the press and other popular media in shaping social images about racial and ethnic minorities has been a particular focus [of research]. A number of detailed studies have looked at how press coverage of racial questions can help to construct images of racial minorities as outsiders and a threat to racial cohesion ... One important example of this was the furore about Salman Rushdie's *The Satanic Verses* and the response of some Muslim political leaders to its publication ... The attempt by some ... to use the affair as a means of political mobilisation received wide coverage in the media and led to a wide-ranging debate about the future of race relations in British society ... Sections of the press used the events ... to question the possibility of a peaceful transition towards a multiracial society. Hostile media coverage of the events surrounding the political mobilisations around the Rushdie affair thus served to reinforce the view that minorities who do not share the dominant political values of British society pose a threat to social stability and cohesion.

In a very real sense the question of how to conceptualise racism has never been purely an academic matter. From its very origins the study of racism has been intimately connected to issues such as the rise of fascism, the holocaust, and the destructive consequences of racist political mobilisations. In this sense the analysis of racism cannot be easily separated from the wider political culture ... Indeed it is clearly the case that the manipulation of racial symbols and the development of racist movements has involved a politicisation of racist signifiers through political discourse and State policies.

POST-WAR POLITICAL AND LEGAL RESPONSES

Lester, A and Bindman, G, *Race and Law*, 1972, Harmondsworth: Penguin, p 13:

The growth of racial feeling in Britain was both ignored and condemned during the first decade of immigration from the Commonwealth. In the next decade, the existence of a problem was reluctantly recognised; and, once more echoing earlier history, the initial governmental response was entirely defensive and negative. In 1962, after another ugly racist campaign, legislation was passed with the aim of limiting further coloured immigration. Since that date, public attitudes have become increasingly ambivalent. It is now conventional wisdom that Britain is too small and overcrowded to absorb fresh newcomers – unless they are white. At the same time, it is also widely accepted that racial discrimination is economically wasteful, socially divisive, harmful to international relations, or morally wrong (according to one's particular standpoint). The approach of successive governments has therefore been that Commonwealth citizens should therefore be excluded from this country because they are coloured, but that Commonwealth citizens who are already here should be treated equally, regardless of their colour. Understandably, few people have grasped the distinction. The more obvious conclusion that has generally been drawn is that if coloured immigration presents a threat to Britain's well-being, so does the coloured minority living in Britain.

Solomos, J, *Race and Racism in Britain*, 2nd edn, 1993, London: Macmillan, pp 82–84:

From the 1950s the question of what to do to counter racial discrimination emerged as a major dilemma in debates about immigration and race relations. Even in the early stages of black immigration there was an awareness that in the longer term the question of racial discrimination was likely to become a volatile political issue. In the early stages of post-war black immigration, political debates about race were centred upon the question of immigration controls. However, an underlying concern, even at that stage, was the future of race relations. The notion that the arrival of too many black immigrants would lead to problems in relation to housing, employment and social services was already widely articulated ...

Two problems were usually seen as in need of urgent attention. First, the negative response of the majority white population to the competition of black workers in the housing and labour markets ... Second, the frustration of black workers who felt themselves excluded from equal participation in British society by the development of a colour bar in the labour and housing markets, along with related processes of discrimination ...

The first attempts to deal with potential racial conflict and tackle racial discrimination can be traced back to the 1960s and took two basic forms. The first involved the setting up of welfare agencies to deal with the problems faced by black immigrants and to help the white communities understand the immigrants. The second stage of the policy response began with the passage of the 1965 and 1968 Race Relations Acts, and was premised on the notion that the State should attempt to ban discrimination on the basis of race, colour or ethnic origin through legal sanctions and public regulatory agencies charged with the task of promoting equality of opportunity ...

The notion that immigration was essentially an issue of race was consistent with the view that: (a) the growing number of black citizens resident in Britain was either actually or potentially the source of social problems and conflicts, and (b) that it was necessary for the State to introduce measures to promote the integration of immigrants into the wider society and its fundamental institutions.

The linking of immigration controls with integrative measures was a significant step since it signalled a move towards the management of domestic race relations as well as legitimising the institutionalisation of firm controls at the point of entry ... [S]ince the 1960s the two sides of State intervention have been seen as inextricably linked. According to Roy Hattersley's famous formula, 'integration without control is impossible, but control without integration is indefensible'.[14] The rationale of this argument was never articulated clearly, but it was at least partly based on the idea that the fewer immigrants there were, the easier it would be to integrate them into the English way of life and its social cultural values.

Brown, C, 'Ethnic pluralism in Britain: the demographic and legal background', in Glazer, N and Young, K (eds), *Ethnic Pluralism and Public Policy*, 1986, Aldershot: Gower, p 51:

The 1965 Race Relations Act outlawed discrimination in specified places of public resort, such as hotels, restaurants ... and made it a criminal offence deliberately to stir up racial hatred by publishing or distributing written matter or by speaking in public. The Act set up the Race Relations Board ... which co-ordinated seven regional conciliation committees to deal with complaints of discrimination ... Although the number of complaints was small (690 in the year 1967–68), a large majority of them fell outside the scope of the Act, the most frequent of these being complaints about employment, the police and housing.

[As a result of reports confirming the continued existence of racial discrimination, the] Race Relations Act 1968 widened the coverage of the law to housing, employment, and the provision of goods and services. The Race Relations Board was given the power to investigate cases where there was reason to believe that discrimination had taken place but no complaint had been received; the Board was also given the power to bring legal proceedings when attempts to conciliate failed ...

The more public indications of discriminatory practices, such as advertisements specifying 'no coloureds', and outright statements of racist job recruitment policies, all but disappeared ... But there were still high levels of discrimination, on a scale far greater than would have been judged from the still small number of complaints to the Race Relations Board. In addition, it had become apparent that direct discrimination was not always at the heart of racial disadvantage: regulations, policies and practices of organisations often discriminated indirectly against ethnic minorities, and the Act lacked any provision for dealing with these cases.

---

[14] *Hansard*, Vol 789 Cols 378–85.

Davies and Freedland, *Labour Legislation and Public Policy*, 1993, Oxford: Clarendon, p 229:

Perhaps the most significant aspect of the remedial provisions of the 1968 Act ... was its exclusion of the individual from direct access to the courts. Unlike the individual complaining of unfair dismissal or unequal pay, the complainant in a race relations case had to channel his or her complaint through the Board ... Even if these machineries failed to produce a settlement, the decision on taking proceedings in the courts lay exclusively in the hands of the Board, to whom indeed any award of damages was made, although the Board had to account to the individual for the money received. This procedure had two consequences. First, the resources of the Board were overwhelmingly deployed in the handling of individual complaints, so that it had very little opportunity to initiate independent investigations into situations which suggested that deep-seated patterns of discrimination had become established ... Second, from the point of view of the individual, the remedies against discrimination appeared rather ineffective. Especially in the employment field, where the voluntary machinery, if established, operated first, the procedures were cumbersome and slow, whilst the monopoly of the Board deprived the individual of control over the handling of the grievance. In fact, before 1975, only one employment case had reached the courts.

Pressure for more effective legislation came from a number of sources, concerned both with the apparent ineffectiveness of the legislation and the evidence of continued racial discrimination in practice. The 1967 Political and Economic Planning Report on Racial Discrimination demonstrated empirically what had until then been largely anecdotal evidence of the extent of discrimination. In addition, campaigning monographs by leading lawyers coherently and persuasively argued the case for more powerful legislation, which arrived in the shape of the 1976 Race Relations Act.[15]

Further pressure for more effective legislation came from evidence of what has come to be known as 'institutional discrimination',[16] factors which entrench patterns of social disadvantage within minority ethnic communities, although this was often attributed to the relatively recent arrival of the bulk of the black population. As the White Paper which preceded the 1976 Race Relations Act put it:

There is at work in this country ... the familiar cycle of cumulative disadvantage by which relatively low paid or low status jobs for the first generation of immigrants go hand in hand with poor and overcrowded living conditions, and a depressed environment. If, for example, job opportunities, educational facilities, housing and environmental conditions are all poor, the

---

[15] Eg, Lester, A and Bindman, G, *Race and Law*, 1972, Harmondsworth: Penguin; Hepple, B, *Race, Jobs and the Law in Britain*, 1968, Harmondsworth: Penguin. The fact that both were published by Penguin helped the debate to reach the public domain rather than being confined to the academic domain.

[16] McCrudden, C, 'Institutional discrimination' (1982) 2 OJLS 303.

next generation will grow up less well equipped to deal with the difficulties facing them. The wheel then comes full circle as the second generation find themselves trapped in poor jobs and poor housing. If at each stage of the process an element of racial discrimination enters in, then an entire group of people are launched on a vicious downward spiral of deprivation. They may share each of the disadvantages with some other deprived group in society, but few groups in society display all their accumulated disadvantages.[17]

There is no doubt that racial disadvantage was and remains prevalent in our society. Whether such institutional disadvantage should properly be referred to as discrimination is less clear cut.

Miles, R, *Racism*, 1989, London: Routledge, pp 54–60:

[Institutional racism offers] a very different concept of racism from that used by [earlier] writers ... who defined it exclusively and specifically as an ideology. First, the concept has a generalised rather than a specific referent: it identifies as racism all those beliefs, actions and processes which lead to, or sustain, discrimination against and the subordination of 'black' people. Second, it denies that intentionality or motivation are measures of the presence or absence of racism. Whilst an explicit motive or intention to subordinate may be evident, it is not considered to be a necessary condition for the identification of racism. Third, by definition, racism is a prerogative of 'white' people. Fourth ... it asserts or assumes a theory of stratification in which the terms 'white' and 'black' have analytical status. The social formation under analysis is identified as constituted by the presence of two (homogeneous) groups, 'whites' and 'blacks', which have a hierarchical relationship with each other ...

[T]he concept is inseparable from a theory of stratification that is simplistic and erroneous because it states or assumes that the sole or primary division within a society is between 'white' people and 'black' people ... [T]his suppresses and denies the existence of class divisions and conflict, and the distribution of 'white' and 'black' people to different class positions ... Evidence of the extent of racist belief and sympathy for Fascist politics among sections of the 'white' unskilled working class ... is therefore more accurately understood as a response ... to powerlessness rather than the possession of power ...

It is ... simplistic and misleading to argue that the specific disadvantage [of higher unemployment rates] faced by people of Asian and Caribbean origin is a consequence of what 'white' people do. This is no single explanation for comparatively higher rates of unemployment amongst people of Asian and Caribbean origin, despite the impression so created by attributing the origin of the fact to racism. Additionally, it is simplistic and misleading because in a capitalist economy undergoing rationalisation and reorganisation, 'inefficient' sectors ... are likely to be closed down irrespective of who has the power to make decisions and of who is employed in them. In this sense defining the employers as 'white' ... could be irrelevant to the determination of the actual outcome ... Explanations which refer solely to racism ignore or deny [the] structural precondition and determinant of unemployment ...

---

[17] *Racial Discrimination*, Cmnd 6234, 1975, London: HMSO, para 11.

If disadvantage is the consequence of intentionality and of a belief in the existence and inferiority of certain 'races', rather than being the unintentional outcome of certain decisions or taken-for-granted processes by people who do not hold such beliefs, distinct interventionist strategies will need to be employed in each case ... Moreover, where there is no logical connection between ideas and actions, an analysis of the prevalence of racist beliefs may prove to be a very unreliable guide to the extent of discriminatory behaviour, and vice versa. By defining racism broadly by reference to consequences, use of this inflated concept absolves the analyst (and political activist) from the often difficult task of identifying the particularities of the processes that create and reproduce disadvantage ...

There are many forms and determinants of disadvantage. The claim that the concept 'racism' identifies all those actions that have 'black' disadvantage as their consequences includes a very large number of actions and processes.

Solomos, J and Back, L, *Racism and Society*, 1996, London: Macmillan, pp 77–79:

[T]he processes which help to structure racialised inequalities are by no means static. In the present economic and social climate racialised inequalities are being constantly transformed. A case in point is the relationship between the spatial restructuring of industries and jobs ... and its impact on employment opportunities for minorities ... [S]uch patterns of restructuring may end up having a major impact on those sections of racial and ethnic minorities who are most vulnerable and least likely to be able to benefit from equal opportunities policies.

[T]here has been a hardening of racial and ethnic cleavages among lower class groups. This is borne out by the evidence of racial disadvantage in the major urban conurbations and by what some have defined as the 'racialisation of poverty'. But at the same time we have seen a noticeable growth of a black professional middle class and of ethnic minority small businesses with an impact at all levels of society ... This has led to much greater emphasis in recent studies on the role of economic and social processes which have helped to transform the class position of sections of minority communities.

Solomos, J, *Race and Racism in Britain*, 2nd edn, 1993, London: Macmillan, p 241:

[T]he basic problem confronting any account of the complex relations between race, class and the State is to be found in the very nature of racism in contemporary capitalist societies ... [T]here are at least two problems which have so far defied resolution. First, the question of the interplay between racial and ethnic categorisations and economic and class determinations. Second, the role of the State and political institutions of capitalist societies in the reproduction of racism, including the complex role of State intervention in many countries to control immigration, to manage race relations, and, more broadly, to integrate racial and ethnic groupings into the wider society ...

If evidence of serious social disadvantage is accepted, anti-discrimination legislation should be only one strand of a wider policy aimed at remedying social disadvantages, a policy which would require considerable expenditure of public money for it to have any chance of success. It is even possible to argue that passing legislation appears to take an activist stance while involving little or no expenditure of public funds, whereas real social change is more likely to result from appropriately targeted financial resources.

We have seen why the 1968 Act was considered inadequate and why further legislation was considered necessary. In fact, the Race Relations Act 1976 was passed a year after the Sex Discrimination Act 1975, and is substantially identical to it.[18] It follows that it makes more sense to consider why it appeared in that form after examination of the social position of women up to that time.[19] Current statistics suggest strongly that, despite legislation, racial discrimination and disadvantage remain a serious social issue.

THE CURRENT EMPLOYMENT POSITION OF MINORITY ETHNIC GROUPS[20]

Jones, T, *Britain's Ethnic Minorities: An Analysis of the Labour Force Survey*, 1996, London: Policy Studies Institute, pp 69–71, 112–13, 121:

[A] complex pattern is developing, with some minority groups having similar (or higher) job levels than white male employees, whereas other groups have substantially lower ones. In general, African Asian, Indian and Chinese male employees have similar or better job levels than white male employees. In fact, there are more of the Chinese in the top category (professional, managerial, employer) than there are of whites: 30% compared with 27%. African Asians have the same proportion of whites in the top category, and Indians have a similar proportion (25%) ... [But] the proportion of Afro-Caribbean, Pakistani and Bangladeshi male employees in the top category is ... 12% for each of the three groups ... Afro-Caribbeans and Pakistanis are the most likely to be found in skilled manual work, with 39% and 34% respectively of their male employees in such jobs. A very high proportion of Bangladeshi men are employed in semi-skilled or unskilled manual jobs (70% of Bangladeshi men compared with 19% of whites) ...

[H]ighly qualified male employees of all ethnic groups except the Afro-Caribbeans are more likely than whites to be in professional jobs. Afro-Caribbean men with highest qualifications ... are in lower jobs than men of other ethnic groups. (23% of Afro-Caribbeans compared with 37% of whites) ... Of those male employees with no formal qualifications, Afro-Caribbeans and

---

[18] For the reasons for this identity, see *op cit*, McCrudden, fn 16, p 337.

[19] See below, pp 100–01.

[20] See, also, Modood, T *et al* (eds), *Ethnic Minorities in Britain: Diversity and Disadvantage*, 1997, London: Policy Studies Institute.

Bangladeshis are found more often at lower level jobs than employees of other ethnic groups ...

[W]hite people are still much less prone to unemployment than ethnic minorities. Compared to a white rate of 7% for 1988–90, the overall rate among ethnic minorities was 13%. Unemployment is higher among men and people aged 16–24 than among women and the older age group. The overall figures hide substantial differences within the ethnic minority population ... Whilst African-Asians and Indians have unemployment rates closest to that of the white population, people of Pakistani and Bangladeshi origin suffer from higher rates of unemployment than any other racial group. The Afro-Caribbean rate is higher than that of Indians and African-Asians, but not as high as for Pakistanis or Bangladeshis.

Among those aged 16–24 these differences are magnified. Young Pakistanis have a particularly high unemployment rate, which at 30% is about three times the rate for young whites. The rate for young people of African origin is nearly as high (27%) and that for young Afro-Caribbeans (23%) is over double the white rate. The lowest rate of unemployment in this age group is found among African Asian men, who with a rate of just 9% have a similar likelihood to young white men of being unemployed.[21]

[The study controlled for job level, as workers in lower level jobs are more vulnerable than other workers to unemployment. This explained some but by no means all of the varying unemployment rates between the different groups.]

[The findings on unemployment] cannot be explained in terms of a gradual process of adaptation among groups of immigrant origin. The more recently arrived groups – African Asians and Bangladeshis – are ones with starkly contrasting unemployment rates. Also, the differences between specific ethnic groups are most marked among young people aged 16–24, and in all ethnic groups most of the young people will have spent their formative years in Britain. These findings suggest that the differences in vulnerability to unemployment between specific ethnic groups are likely to persist.

'Minimum wage benefits women and ethnic minorities' (1997) 73 EOR 13, pp 20–22:

Ethnic minority employees as a whole are marginally more likely to be in low paying jobs than white employees ... For example, in 1996, 10% of ethnic minority employees earned less than £3 an hour compared with 7% of whites, and 15% earned under £3.50 compared with 14% of whites.

Across all wage levels however, Indian and Pakistani/Bangladeshi employees are more likely to experience low pay than their white counterparts ... One in 10 Pakistani/Bangladeshi employees earn less than £2.50. Over a quarter earn less than £3.50 and around three in five, double the rate for white employees, earn less than £4.50.

---

[21] A recent report suggests that the true figure for black unemployment is twice the official figure of 222,000. See (1997) 73 EOR 9.

However, not all ethnic minorities fare proportionately worse than whites. There are proportionately fewer black employees and employees of mixed/other origins at each hourly pay level than white employees.

Reliable statistics on ethnic minority pay are only available for [certain] occupations ... [E]thnic minorities as a whole are significantly more likely to be low paid than their white counterparts in craft and related occupations. Over half of ethnic minorities in this occupation earn less than £4.00 compared with 16% of whites. In the other occupations the proportions earning low pay are similar but in sales, over half of the white employees earn less than £4.00 compared with just under a third of ethnic minorities.

The largest proportion of any ethnic minority group employees on low pay is to be found in craft and related occupations and personal and protective occupations. In both these, all Pakistani/Bangladeshi employees are employed on less than £4.00 and £4.50 an hour compared with 16% of white employees in craft, rising to 23% earning less than £4.50, and 39% in personal and protective occupations rising to 52% under £4.50.

The growing diversity in economic performance between different ethnic groups, especially the relative success achieved by Indians, has implications for future policy and strategy. Modood argues that it is wrong to assume that 'being white or not is the single most crucial factor in determining the sociological profile of any non-white group in contemporary Britain, dwarfing class, employment, capital assets, skills, gender, ethnicity, religion, family, geography and so on'.[22] To some extent, the example of Indian success renders the simple divide between 'white' and 'black' increasingly outmoded. It is not denied that such problems may be true for many if not most ethnic groups; it is the assumption that economic underperformance is always directly traceable to racism which is questionable, as is any belief in the universality of purported solutions or policy interventions.

THE REPRODUCTION OF RACISM

Racial disadvantage is partly attributable to direct or overt racism, which itself has different meanings or values. In addition, racial disadvantage is compounded by structures and institutions which operate to the detriment of black people. As the focus of this work is substantially on employment, it is necessary to examine how such attitudes are reproduced.

---

[22] Modood, T, 'The Indian economic success: a challenge to some race relations assumptions' (1991) Policy and Politics 177, p 178. He further argues that it is wrong to assume, first, that until 'racial prejudice and discrimination in all its forms is eliminated, though some non-white individuals will be allowed to succeed, all non-white groups will share a below-average socio-economic profile; they will form a racial under-class' and, secondly, that the 'only way "black" people can improve their condition *as a group* is through political militancy and/or substantial State action.'

Solomos, J and Back, L, *Racism and Society*, **1996, London: Macmillan, pp 67–69:**

[W]e need to understand forms of racial inequality at levels on which decisions are taken which, consciously or not, either increase or decrease such inequalities. 'It is necessary to understand the workings of social institutions, such as those which socialise children, which channel jobseeking and employee selection so that particular sorts of people end up in particular jobs' ... Such detailed investigations have highlighted the complex processes which have helped to shape racialised inequalities in both an institutional and an everyday context.

Migrants to Britain of the 1950s and 1960s came to find work primarily in those sectors experiencing labour shortages. Workers from the Caribbean, India and Pakistan were recruited for employment in foundries in the Midlands, textile mills in the North, transport industries in major cities, and the health service. In common with migrant workers across Europe, these workers experienced a high degree of exploitation, discrimination and marginalisation in their economic and social lives. Despite the need for their labour, their presence aroused widespread hostility at all levels ... Employers only reluctantly recruited immigrants where there were no white workers to fill the jobs; white workers, through their unions, often made arrangements with their employers about the sorts of work immigrants could have access to ... At this time the preference for white workers was seen to be quire natural and legitimate – immigrant workers were seen as an inferior but necessary labour supply.

Over time these workers remained in a relatively restricted spectrum of occupational area, over-represented in low paid and insecure jobs, working anti-social hours in unhealthy or dangerous environments. Although by the 1970s African-Caribbean and Asian people worked in a broader range of occupations than before, these were still jobs that were 'deemed fit' for ethnic minorities rather than white workers. In 1984 the Policy Studies Institute published a major survey of the state of black people in Britain, covering housing, education and employment, showing that black people are still generally employed below their qualification and skill level, earn less than white workers in comparable job levels, and are still concentrated in the industries they were 25 years earlier.

Miles, R, *Racism*, **1989, London: Routledge, pp 124–25:**

The vast majority of the migrants of the 1950s arrived with little or no capital and therefore had no choice but to sell their labour power for a wage ... Because only a small proportion were specifically recruited before their migration to particular jobs, most arrived to fill positions either found for them by kin and friends or by themselves ... [T]hese were positions that were the result of the movement of indigenous labour into 'new jobs' characterised by higher rates of pay and better conditions of work ... [C]ertain economic sectors faced acute shortages of labour, and in conditions of relative full employment, these positions could not be filled from the population within Britain. Thus, structural circumstances defined a demand for labour in certain sectors of the economy, and it was these positions that Caribbean and Asian migrants filled ...

[T]hose present in the labour market are ranked by employers. Where that hierarchy is constructed in such a way that the qualities of individuals are perceived to be representative of a wider collectivity, and if the individual is deemed to possess the criteria that designate membership of that collectivity, the question of suitability may be determined by reference to the perceived qualities of the collectivity rather than to the perceived qualities of the individual applicant. In such circumstances, the processes of inclusion and exclusion are effected by signification and group categorisation. Where such a process is effected by reference to phenotypical characteristics, the recruitment of labour is racialised. That is, the labour market is perceived to include members of different 'races', each of which is seen to possess a different range of skills and abilities which distinguish that group as a supposed 'race'.

The strength of the next extract is to show how, at a micro level, these attitudes and stereotypes may be translated into real employment decisions. It does not make for comfortable reading, as it suggests how difficult it will be for the law to have an impact on the racial dimension of such decisions.

Jenkins, R, *Racism and Recruitment: Managers, Organisations and Equal Opportunity in the Labour Market*, 1986, Cambridge: CUP, pp 46, 74–78, 92–97, 102–05, 108:

In making selection decisions, recruiters are attempting to do two things: first, to satisfy themselves that the candidate is capable of carrying out the practices entailed in the ... job in question, and second, to predict whether or not the candidate will integrate smoothly into the managerial procedures and social routines of the employing organisation ... Selection criteria ... can be broadly divided into two categories, the *functionally specific*, such as educational qualifications, training or physique, which relate to job performance and competence, and the *functionally non-specific*, which relate to the organisational context and are much less easy to delineate. [The author refers to these as suitability and acceptability respectively] ...

[The author shows how the concept of acceptability may be overlaid with conscious or unconscious assumptions which may disadvantage black people.]

[I]t is necessary to have regard to those non-verbal and largely unselfconscious aspects of communication such as facial expression, eye contact, physical proximity and body contact (ie, shaking hands, etc.). Psychological research has indicated that these are all significant in determining the outcome of selection interviews ... they are also evaluated in different ways in different cultures. Thus, to take the example of the maintenance of eye contact, a white English recruiter might well interpret an avoidance of direct eye contact by a candidate as indicative of anything from 'shiftiness' to a lack of self-confidence. For many jobseekers with cultural backgrounds deriving from the Indian subcontinent, however, the refusal of eye contact might well be a respectful attempt to avoid being rude. It is only to be expected that, in inter-ethnic selection interviews, non-verbal communicative behaviour may be systematically misinterpreted by both sides of the exchange. This kind of miscommunication is particularly important inasmuch as the evaluation of manner and attitude, appearance, speech style and the ability to 'fit in' are all at stake here, not to mention the manager's 'gut feeling'. Job candidates whose cultural repertoire, and understanding, of non-verbal communicative behaviour is the same as the interviewer's will clearly be at an advantage, albeit an unconscious one ...

Selection decisions which rely heavily on implicit criteria are likely to be more opaque than those involving explicit criteria ... Unsuccessful job applicants in such a situation are not necessarily going to understand the reason for their rejection – which will make it difficult for them to enhance their acceptability in the future – and decisions are going to be difficult for bodies such as Industrial Tribunals to investigate convincingly after the fact. Furthermore ... the implicitness of much selection decision making will, by virtue of the ambiguity and lack of definition of many of these implicit criteria, allow *direct*, ie, deliberate racist and sexist discrimination, scope to operate with relative impunity ...

The ethnocentrism of many of the components of acceptability is of relevance to the discussion of *indirect* discrimination. None of these criteria are necessarily racially *prejudiced*, nor do they involve the *intent* to discriminate against black workers ... In their unintended consequences, however, there is good reason to suppose that they will systematically place many black jobseekers at a disadvantage ...

[C]riteria such as 'gut feeling', speech style, and the ability to 'fit in', which are both ethnocentric and implicit, are, by virtue of their taken-for-grantedness and lack of definition, extremely elusive ...

One of the most interesting aspects of this material is the relatively low level of definition of the category 'white' or 'English' ... There are, I suspect, two reasons for this. In the first place the notion of 'Englishness' is largely taken for granted; it is a background common-sensical assumption which managers assume that 'everybody knows about'. Second, it is equally the case that one of the pervasive themes of ethnocentric categorisations ... is that 'we're all different, but they're all the same'. This is the proposition which lies at the heart of many ethnic stereotypes. As a result, there is a very real sense in which 'we' don't constitute an ethnic group at all. As a result, it seems likely that there may be a greater predisposition on the part of white managers to regard white job candidates as individuals, as opposed to their black counterparts, who may be more likely to be treated as representatives of a stereotypical category ...

[T]he stereotype might best be regarded as a model of *probability*, not a statement of *certainty*. Thus, when faced with job candidates of any particular ethnic identity, the manager may choose to discriminate against them simply because he or she feels that there is a degree of *likelihood* that the worst predictions of the stereotype may be fulfilled.

[Having demonstrated the 'racism of acceptability', the author establishes the other side of the coin, which he refers to as 'the acceptability of racism'.]

[A]lthough ... managers may recognise that it is 'wrong' for other managers or workers to resist the recruitment of black workers, their principles do not usually extend to counteracting that resistance. Putting up with racism is definitely the lesser of the two evils, when compared with the organisational and industrial relations problems which moving against it might precipitate.

Clearly there are some managers who do respect the 'customs and habits' of their workforce. It is likely that many more do not, however. For this group of managers, there is a 'right' way of doing things: this is the white, 'British' way. In this profoundly ethnocentric world-view, cultural difference is viewed as alien and distasteful, and racism is merely the upholding of 'normal standards'. Discrimination, by this token, vanishes; in its place one finds people insisting that they are not prejudiced, but simply defending what is 'right and proper', upholding the maintenance of 'acceptable' standards.

There are two related themes ... In the first place, the problem is seen to be created by black workers, not by discrimination or other racist behaviour by managers or other white workers ... Second ... the root of the problem is seen to lie in the prejudice of black workers ... Once again the problem of white racism is not even considered by most of these managers: 'I've got no colour prejudice, of course I've not'. Since there is, therefore, not a problem of this nature, the reaction of black workers becomes defined as irrational and unreasonable.

Even where ... the manager does admit the existence and force of racism, black workers 'often look for prejudices where there aren't any', and, because of this, they 'use their race or their colour against the company'. Thus, in one move, racism is either ignored or underestimated, on the one hand, or defined away as a problem of 'their' making, on the other. Viewed from within this logic, equal opportunities policies, or any other attempts to deal with the problem of racism in the workplace, become unfair and 'lopsided'.

[T]he perception by managers of these problems undoubtedly *does* have an influence, and possibly a major one, on the selection process. This influence is to the systematic detriment of black workers ... [M]ost of the perceived problems relate in one way or another to the issue of acceptability ... [I]t is equally clear that, to use the word in another context, racism, whether on the part of colleagues, subordinates or self, is acceptable to a great many of these managers. It is ... not a problem so long as the routines of the organisation continue to run smoothly, defined as simply to do with personalities, unrecognised except as a reflection of the unreasonable prejudice of black workers, or, in some cases, positively approved of. There is very little evidence of managers choosing to oppose discrimination or racism on moral or political grounds. Depressing though this conclusion may be, this is perhaps only to be expected, given that managers are paid to manage in the interests of the goals of the organisation, among which is not usually numbered opposition to racism.

[T]he clearest thread which runs through [the research] is the notion that black workers are not British, they are alien. Put very simply, black workers do not belong in Britain in the eyes of these managers, and admission into the UK should not be, nor should it ever have been, theirs by right. A second, and perhaps equally strong theme, is that black migrants are somehow taking without giving, whether it be welfare benefits, health care, or sending home remittances to their families.

It is unlikely that recruiters will either consciously or deliberately relate their stereotypical notions of acceptability to their repertoire of ethnic stereotypes and decide the fate of individual jobseekers accordingly. The process is likely to be more subtle and less obvious than that.

The ambiguity of many selection criteria, and the tacit taken-for-grantedness of many of the decisions which are made, do not lead one to have much confidence in the accountability of recruitment.

Cockburn, C, *In the Way of Women: Men's Resistance to Sex Equality in Organisations*, 1991, Basingstoke: Macmillan, pp 174, 182:

The purchase of labour power is ... a purchase for the services of a certain kind of person, someone with a perceived social status (it may be high or low), certain cultural attachments and certain looks, to all of which ethnicity and skin colour are germane. The system of male power which operates in and through major employing organisations in Britain is specifically *white* male power and the culture of management is almost solidly a white monoculture, identifying and excluding other groups ...

What appeared to be appearing in all four organisations [researched] was a split in white intentions. Some, characteristically the equal opportunity officers and a few enlightened senior managers, wanted to encourage black recruitment and promotion. Other white people did not want to see any dilution of the white workforce by black incomers. The deal that was struck between the two white positions and between whites and incoming blacks cohered around the issue of cultural *assimilation*. Non-white ethnic groups would be 'acceptable' if as nearly as possible indistinguishable from the host group. '*If you want equality you must forego difference.*' It is the same theme we saw invoked in resistance to sex equality and will see again in the case of homosexuals and people with disabilities. It is of course a condition impossible for most members of out-groups to fulfil, even if a minority of individuals is able and willing to adopt protective colouring.

The importance of these analyses is the implication that legal rules are unlikely to bring about a significant reduction in either discrimination or disadvantage. Recent research confirms that the improvement, if any, has been no more than minor.

Brown, C, 'Same difference: the persistence of racial disadvantage in the British employment market', in Braham, P, Rattansi, A and Skellington, R (eds), *Racism and Anti-Racism: Inequalities, Opportunities and Policies*, 1992, London: Sage, pp 60–63:

There was no evidence during the 1980s to suggest that the extent of discrimination fell at all. Repeats of the applications trials ... in 1984 and 1985 produced figures for the minimum level of employer discrimination that were no lower than in 1973 and 1974 ... [T]he research ... showed that at least one-third of private employers discriminated against Asian applicants, Afro-Caribbean applicants, or both ...

In addition to ... reports on direct, deliberate discrimination there has been research ... detailing the disadvantage still suffered by ethnic minorities in employment because of both direct and indirect discrimination ...

The lack of substantial improvement in the general position of blacks and Asians within the labour market is all the more disappointing because the past decade has been a period of apparent political breakthrough for Britain's minorities. The number of elected local councillors from the minority communities has risen steeply; race equality became a real issue in local politics in urban areas and, occasionally, a national issue ... the provisions of the Race Relations Act 1976 have facilitated 'positive action' by employers on race equality; and some large employers – particularly in the public sector – have openly paid a good deal of attention to reviewing policy and practice to eliminate direct and indirect discrimination. The small progress that has taken place has therefore involved an enormous expenditure of effort by ethnic minority organisations and by others campaigning and working alongside them ...

The patterns of employment among blacks and Asians are shifting, and there is now greater diversity among them than before. Examples of success in business, in the professions and in politics are now easier to point to; in particular, business and commerce seems to have reached a 'critical mass' within some sections of the Asian communities, sufficient to sustain its own growth and to insulate itself partially against discrimination. But these achievements have been in spite of the general experience of hostility, stereotyping and exclusion, and they should not blind us to the other realities of minority employment. Considering the years that have passed and the work that has been put in, the surprising fact is not that some people have hewn a niche in the business world or become professionally qualified, but that so few have been allowed to succeed ... [P]rogress has been most evident where the acceptance, endorsement and help of white employers has been least required: in self-employment and in the professions. Even the contrast between business and the professions is illuminating in this respect. Although entry to the professions has been achieved by many ... progress within them has been restricted because it relies on the decision making of white superiors ...

Prospects for the future cannot be expected to rest on this circumvention of racial discrimination. It is unrealistic to expect the whole black and Asian population to develop strategies of dealing with racism by avoiding it. We therefore have to turn to the reduction of discrimination as a priority for public policy. As a nation we have to confront the fact that racial hostility underlies the persistence of racial discrimination, and that it is unlikely to wither with time ... In the absence of any vigorous action from central government, the chances of any real reduction in the extent of racism and discrimination are slim.

These authors look to the future with considerable pessimism. Jenkins pins many of his hopes on the formalisation of recruitment procedures. This is an issue to which we will return when considering the possible impact of equal opportunities policies. Brown considers that voluntary efforts will come to naught without a vigorous, active lead from government. This is unlikely to be forthcoming, at least to the extent considered desirable. What is notable is that neither considers that the law has the capacity to make a significant dent in the social disadvantages experienced by minority ethnic groups.

CHAPTER 2

THE BACKGROUND TO SEX DISCRIMINATION LEGISLATION IN THE UNITED KINGDOM

The history of women's inequality is well documented. Politically, legally, socially and economically, even partial freedom for women arrived only relatively recently.[1] Social disadvantages remain, if judged by the proportion of women in high political or judicial office, or senior professional or management positions, and by the stubbornly persistent gap in average pay levels between men and women. As with race issues, the causes of continuing inequality are complex and difficult to dislodge, throwing into doubt the capacity of any law to deal with them adequately, let alone laws drafted with the inadequacies of the Equal Pay Act 1970 and the Sex Discrimination Act 1975.

However, this century, and especially the years following the Second World War, has seen a social transformation in the economic and social position of women. Not all the changes are necessarily beneficial, and few would suggest that complete equality has been achieved, but it is undeniable that the changing expectations and opportunities for many women has been one of the major social changes experienced in the last 50 years by 'Western' societies.

The task of this chapter is to trace the changes in the employment position of women through the 20th century. It is then necessary to examine the causes of employment inequalities, both historically and presently. It is by examining such causes that we can begin to appreciate whether the law has contributed to any reduction in gender inequality, and whether it has the capacity to bring about any further reduction in the future.

PARTICIPATION IN EMPLOYMENT[2]

The distinction between paid work, performed outside the home, and unpaid work, usually at home, developed its modern clarity following the Industrial Revolution. Before that, the distinction was largely concealed by the prevalence of subsistence agriculture and craft work. It was the concentration of labour in factories necessitated by the Industrial Revolution which marked the shift towards the distinction which remains so significant today. It has

---

1   See Fredman, S, *Women and the Law*, 1997, Oxford: Clarendon, Chapter 2.
2   See 'Women in the labour market' (1998) 79 EOR 30.

been argued that it was a social choice that women should remain at home and that men should work in the factories – not a result which was in any sense inevitable. The proportion of married women in paid employment outside the home actually declined between 1851 and 1921 from 25% to 8.7%.[3] This ideology – for that is what it was – was also manifested in that women were excluded from certain jobs requiring physical strength, and from night work. The assumption was that women could not and *should not* perform such jobs.[4] In addition, women were often required to leave paid employment on marriage.

Walby, S, *Gender Transformations*, 1997, London: Routledge, pp 27–34:

There has been a massive growth in the number of women who are in formal waged employment since the Second World War. There are now nearly as many women as men who are employees in employment – 49.6% were women in 1995 ... Since the 1950s women have moved from being around one-third to one-half of employees ... The changes are most marked among married women, whose economic activity rate has increased from 26% in 1951 to 71% in 1991.[5] This is now little different from that of unmarried women ...

This is a tremendous change in gender relations in paid employment. It suggests the possibility of rapid and substantial changes in the typical life experiences of women in this period.[6] However, there is a series of caveats which place some qualifications on this picture including: the implications of the particular definition of work and employment used; that most of the increase is in part time rather than full time work; that there are significant patterns of difference and inequality between women ...

Much of the narrowing of the differences and inequalities between men and women in employment has taken place among full time workers only. There are very significant inequalities and differences between full time and part time work. For instance, part time work is on average paid significantly less than full time work, and typically has fewer fringe benefits. Since almost all of the growth in women's employment in the post-war period has been in part time work, this acts as a serious qualification to any picture of the improvement in the position of women ...

The increase in full time women workers from 1971 to 1995 is less than 200,000, a rise of only 3%. During the same period the number of women working part

---

3   Atkins, S and Hoggett, B, *Women and the Law*, 1984, Oxford: Robertson, pp 18–19.

4   See *op cit*, Fredman, fn 1, pp 67–74.

5   Male economic activity rates have declined from 93% in 1973 to 86% in 1993. The decline has been especially significant as regards men over 50. Walby, S, *Gender Transformations*, 1997, London: Routledge, pp 28–29.

6   The proportion of married women in the female workforce rose from 13% in 1901 to 40% in 1951 to 64% in 1971. See Hakim, C, *Occupational Segregation*, 1979, London: Department of Employment, p 11. Since then, the rising divorce and cohabitation rate may make these particular figures unhelpful. It is noteworthy that this dramatic change occurred before the passing of the Sex Discrimination Act 1975.

time has increased by over 2 million, that is 75%, and as a percentage for total employment has risen from 13% to 23%. Women are now almost as likely to be working part time as full time, that is, 47%.[7]

Male part time employment has been growing, but not on the same scale, rising to 11% of male workers in 1994. Most of this is concentrated among young people, often students, and among older workers, while that among women is more widely spread among various age groups ...

The extent of part time working among women means that the proportion of total working hours performed by women as compared with men has not risen as rapidly as the proportion of women holding jobs ... [But] part time work should be ... recognised as a distinctive form of employment with its own significance for the position of women in society ...

The legal definition of part time work formerly gave workers rights if they amassed two years' continuous employment and normally worked for 16 hours per week, while if they normally worked for a minimum of eight hours a week, five years were needed.[8] This hours requirement was held, in *R v Secretary of State for Employment ex p Equal Opportunities Commission*,[9] to be indirectly discriminatory against women. While it has often been suggested that the absence of legal protection causes more jobs to be created, the fact that the growth in part time employment occurred, even though the majority of such employees were protected, casts doubt on this argument, and there is no indication of a reduction in part time employment since the abolition of the hours threshold.

The effect of children on female labour force participation is changing. 'The economic activity rate for women aged 25–34 years rose by 25 percentage points between 1971 and 1993, a greater increase than for any other group.'[10]

---

7   'Over twice as many men as women work full time, while more than five times as many women as men work part time. In 1994, there were one and a half million more women working, either full or part time, than there were 10 years earlier.' *Social Trends*, 1995, London: HMSO, p 69 and Table 4.12.

8   'The majority of part time workers worked more than 16 hours per week, while only 10% of part time workers ... worked under 8 hours per week ... About two-thirds of working women [full time and part time] were covered by employment protection legislation ... Among those women not covered, insufficient length of service, rather than insufficient hours, was the main reason.' Martin, J and Roberts, C, *Women and Employment: a Lifetime Perspective*, 1984, London: HMSO, p 41. The government is proposing to reduce the qualifying period from two years to one. See *Fairness At Work*, Cm 3968, 1998, London: HMSO, para 3.9.

9   [1995] 1 AC 1; [1994] ICR 317; [1994] 1 All ER 910; [1994] IRLR 176. The case was followed by the Employment Protection (Part Time Employees) Regulations 1995 SI 1995/31 which abolished the hours requirement altogether, such that any employee with a contract of employment is potentially protected. However, for unfair dismissal legislation, unlike the SDA 1975 and RRA 1976, two years' continuous employment is still required. A challenge that this requirement was also indirectly discriminatory was made in *R v Secretary of State for Employment ex p Seymour-Smith and Perez* [1997] ICR 271; [1997] 2 All ER 273; [1997] IRLR 315, HL, where the issue was referred to the European Court.

10   *Social Trends*, 1995, London: HMSO, p 66.

The following table compares the participation rate for women between 1984 and 1994, based on the age of the youngest dependent child.

		0–4	5–9	10+
Working full time	1984	6	12	27
	1994	16	20	34
Working part time	1984	22	41	41
	1994	30	45	40[11]

It remains common, though less common than previously, for women who worked full time before starting a family to return on a part time basis either after maternity leave or some time later. This pattern is associated with downward occupational mobility – such women frequently return to a lower level job than they previously occupied. Furthermore, the longer the period out of the labour market, the greater the likelihood that return will be to a lower level job.[12] In Britain there are very few high grade part time jobs. This forces many women to choose between working full time in a career or part time in a low skilled job, and has the result of increasing the divergence in women's labour market experience, even in the case of women with similar qualifications.

Walby, S, *Gender Transformations*, 1997, London: Routledge, pp 52–54:

The higher the woman's level of education and the higher her occupational level the more likely she is to be in paid employment while looking after young children. In 1994, among women who are in the professional, employer or manager group with pre-school children, 64% are economically active, 33% with full time employment, as compared with 50% among the unskilled manual group, where only 2% are working full time ... Possible reasons for this difference ... could include: that the cost of childcare is more within the reach of professionals[13] ... [and] the relative balance of attractiveness of the activities of paid work and homework ... between these groups.

Women who are in full time employment do less housework than those who are non-employed or work part time ... The case that paid employment enhances women's position in the household is ... supported by comparative analysis of time budget studies, which shows that the proportion of housework done by men has increased over time, and particularly so in the

---

11 The number of children significantly affects the likelihood of economic activity. '[I]n Spring 1994, 66% of women with four or more dependent children were economically inactive, compared with only 32% of women with only one child.' *Social Trends*, 1995, London: HMSO, p 66. See, also, *op cit*, Walby, fn 5, p 51 for a similar but more detailed table.

12 *Op cit*, Martin and Roberts, fn 8, p 137.

13 Only 16% of female workers incurred any direct childcare costs. *Op cit*, Martin and Roberts, fn 8, p 42.

case of the partners of full time employed women ... However, the contrary case, that paid work is merely an additional burden to women, is supported by ... studies which suggest that married women who have full time employment do more hours of work (housework plus paid work) than do women who do solely housework, with women who do part time paid work and housework being in between.

People who were sick, elderly or disabled either inside or outside the household were reported to be looked after or given special help by 17% of women or 12% of men in the adult population in 1991 ... The women who provide this care are disproportionately aged between 45 and 64, while the most typical age of men carers is over 75.

For all married women with dependent children, in the period 1992–94, 22% were working full time and 42% were working part time.[14] For single mothers, 13% were working part time and 16% working part time.[15] As in 1991, 19% of families with dependent children were single parent families,[16] these figures are of considerable numerical and social significance. The Government is attempting to increase the number in work, partly, it seems, in order to reduce the overall social security bill. The obstacles faced include the cost of childcare,[17] but also, probably more significantly, the absence of a partner with whom to share childcare duties. It is, to say the least, most unlikely that sex discrimination laws or the particular form that they take will have any appreciable impact on the proportion of single mothers in paid employment. Other social and perhaps legislative changes are likely to be far more significant.

EXPLAINING THE CHANGE IN WOMEN'S PARTICIPATION RATES

The reasons for the change are numerous and it is impossible to determine the precise degree to which each separate cause has contributed. The labour market factors which are relevant are the increased demand for female labour and the increased qualifications of women in the labour market.

---

14 *Op cit*, Martin and Roberts, fn 8, p 42, found that of working mothers with a child under five, 38% worked in the evenings and 6% at night.

15 *Op cit*, Walby, fn 5, p 54.

16 *Social Trends*, 1995, London: HMSO, p 33 and Table 2.9.

17 Under the Budget proposals unveiled on 17 March 1998, a 70% rebate on childcare costs will be available to families with one child where income does not exceed £14,000, and to families with more than one child where income does not exceed £17,000, up to a maximum of £100 and £150 per week respectively.

Webb, M, 'Sex and gender in the labour market', in Reid, I and Stratta, E (eds), *Sex Differences in Britain,* **2nd edn, 1989, Aldershot: Gower, pp 136–37:**

[T]he increase in the 'supply' of women workers was partly connected with changes in women's role and the decision of women to remain in gainful employment for longer before having a child. However, the changes in the pattern of childbearing may merely have resulted from, rather than caused, the increase in women's labour market participation. Childbearing patterns cannot be a complete explanation of the labour market changes, for the increase in paid work took place at all stages in the lifecycle including the period of childrearing ...

A better explanation of the increase in the proportion of women in work lies not on the 'supply' side but involves looking at economic 'demand'. During the 1950s and 1960s the economy was booming, whereas there was a recession after the mid 1970s and particularly after 1979. These periods match quite closely the periods of fastest and slowest rise in female employment. Therefore a key explanation of the rise in women's activity lies in the increased demand in the economy for people to undertake paid work; in recent years this has mainly been in the form of part time work.

Walby, S, *Gender Transformations,* **1997, London: Routledge, pp 41–49:**

One of the most important reasons for the changes in employment has been the increased educational qualifications gained by young women. Girls now achieve more educational qualifications than boys at school ... Women are much more likely to be in paid employment if they have received higher levels of education. This relationship is particularly acute among the younger age groups, but holds for all ages. In 1994, among women aged 20–29 with higher educational qualifications, 89% are working and only 4% economically inactive, while among the same age group with no qualifications only 33% are working and 56% are economically inactive ...

In the youngest age group, 16–24, men and women have similar levels of qualifications. In the oldest age group, 50–59, there are considerable differences, with women being significantly less likely to hold a formal educational qualification and indeed 54% of such women, as compared with 33% of men, have no qualifications at all.

Thus we have age-specific patterns of gender inequality. There can be no sweeping statement about women catching up with men ... The fact of very significant gender inequality in qualifications among people over 40 is not affected by the changes discussed for younger people ... We see a new form of inequality – that between women of different age cohorts.

The significance of these changes depends on the significance of educational qualifications for access to social and economic opportunities. If employment chances are primarily structured by qualifications, then these changes in education will have dramatic consequences for gender relations in employment. If, however, employment chances are determined by other factors than this type of merit, then the consequences will be less important. Other intervening variables include: structures of sex segregation; work commitment; discrimination. The correlation between educational qualifications and employment ... makes it clear that, whatever the remaining structures of disadvantage or differences in work commitment, educational changes are making a significant impact on gender relations in employment, at least for younger women.

The implications of this are highly significant. It is becoming less true to talk of patterns of disadvantage affecting women in general and more necessary to focus attention on particular groups of women. Secondly, and perhaps more controversially, the growth of families where both partners are in permanent well paid jobs might be thought to be increasing *overall* inequality in society, as alongside this growth many households have no earner, or one part time earner on a low wage.

But examining the demand for female labour and the increased supply of qualified women workers is far from the whole answer. Availability for work is affected both by the greater control which women have over their own fertility, and by the greater availability of domestic labour-saving devices – and the greater need of money to pay for them! The fact that women can work more has resulted in a greater investment in human capital on the part of many women. But this hardly seems an adequate explanation of the huge increase in the number of women with young children who work.

Webb, M, 'Sex and gender in the labour market', in Reid, I and Stratta, E (eds), *Sex Differences in Britain*, 2nd edn, 1989, Aldershot: Gower, pp 168–69:

One survey found that 50% of the women questioned said that money was the overriding reason for working. The Women and Employment Survey [1984] found that 67% of working married mothers worked to earn money for basic essentials or extras.

Despite the importance of money, work may be performed out of a mixture of motivations, such as a desire to escape domestic drudgery ... and isolation ... and a desire for job satisfaction.

That it has become expected that most women work may itself be a factor in explaining why more women work. Isolation will be greater if one's peers work, and that will reinforce the belief that work is necessary, expected and desirable. Such reactions are, of course, dependent on the availability of such work, and so we are driven back to the position that the root cause of the increase in female employment, especially in the part time sector, is the increased demand for such employees; indeed, many employers have chosen to organise their whole labour policy around part time employment, in the confident expectation that the supply of such employees will be maintained.[18] Furthermore, the dramatic rise in the participation rate of women with young

---

[18] The measurement of female unemployment is notoriously problematic, because availability for work is partly dependent on knowing that there are available jobs. On whether women experience unemployment disproportionately to men, see, eg, Webb, M, 'Sex and gender in the labour market', in Reid, I and Stratta, E (eds), *Sex Differences in Britain*, 2nd edn, 1989, Aldershot: Gower, pp 157–61.

children has occurred without any significant corresponding improvement in childcare provision.

WOMEN'S PAY LEVELS

It is commonplace to point out and bemoan the fact that the gap between women's pay levels and those of men has not declined rapidly since the Equal Pay Act 1970 (which actually came into force in 1975). To ensure that like is compared with like, the usual comparison is of hourly pay rates. When that is done, it is seen that in the early 1970s women full time workers were paid, on average, between 63% and 67% as much as men. As a result of the Act, that figure increased to 72% in 1975. It had only reached 74% by 1986, but since then there has been a significant reduction in the gap.[19] The figures were 78% in 1991 and 80% in 1995.[20]

Perhaps not surprisingly, there is no possible room for complacency when the pay levels of part time women are concerned. The average hourly pay of part time female employees, as a percentage of the hourly pay of full time men, has varied from 54% in 1974 to 60% in 1977 and 1995.[21] The gap is far larger than between full time men and full time women, but there is no evidence that it is declining. In fact, the earnings of part time women, as a percentage of the earnings of full time women, has actually *declined* from 82% in 1974 to 75% in 1995.[22] The reason may not be the *fact* of part time working as such, but that the occupations which are largely performed by part time women employees tend to have significantly lower hourly rates of pay than those organised around full time employees.[23]

We have thus seen some increase in the relative pay of full time workers. However, much of that increase has been achieved by women at the top end of the earnings curve. These gains are largely due to a change in the distribution of employment towards higher paid non-manual work. Within the categories of non-manual and manual work the increase in women's pay has been no more than marginal. Furthermore, those at the bottom of the earnings distribution curve have seen no relative improvement in relation to male earnings.

There is thus a greater fragmentation and diversification in female labour market experience, largely due to changes in the nature of the labour market

---

[19] *Op cit*, Walby, fn 5, pp 30–31.

[20] The hourly figure tells only part of the story, as men are more likely than women to have overtime opportunities and to receive bonus payments. In 1987, 38.6% of men received overtime payments, compared with 18.2% of women. *Op cit*, Webb, fn 18, p 139.

[21] *Op cit*, Walby, fn 5, p 32.

[22] *Op cit*, Walby, fn 5, p 32.

[23] *Op cit*, Martin and Roberts, fn 8, p 58.

itself. Factors contributing to this development include deregulation and the removal of labour standards, as industry-wide collective agreements became a thing of the past, the abolition of Wages Councils, which provided some measure of protection for lower paid workers, predominantly women,[24] and the use of subcontracting in the public sector.

'Minimum wage benefits women and ethnic minorities' (1997) 73 EOR 13, pp 15–18:

Though part time workers make up a quarter of the labour force, they are disproportionately represented among the low paid ... 32% of all part time employees earn less than £3.50 [per hour], compared with 8% of full time employees. Over half of all part timers earn less than £4.50, compared with a fifth of full time employees.[25]

Around two-thirds of low paid employees are concentrated in four industries – wholesale, retail and motor trade; hotels and restaurants; manufacturing; and social work. Of the 3 million employees earning less than £3.50, around 30% are employed in the wholesale, retail and motor trade, 17% in hotels and restaurants, 15% in manufacturing, and 12% in health and social work.

Women workers are almost twice as likely to be low paid than male employees. Almost 10% of women earn less than £3.00 an hour, compared with just over 5% of men; 30% of women earn less than £4.00 and 40% less than £4.50 compared with 14% and 20% of male employees ... Overall, if a minimum wage was set at £4.00 an hour, over 3 million female employees and 1.6 million male employees would benefit.

The national minimum wage will be set at £3.60 per hour, which the government calculates will benefit 1.4 million women, 1.3 million part time workers, 110,000 homeworkers, 175,000 working lone parents, and 130,000 workers.[26] Of course, these figures assume 100% compliance with the legislation.

---

24 *Op cit*, Fredman, fn 1, pp 264–67.

25 It has been observed that 'women's wage labour plays a crucial role in supporting the low-wage economy in the UK. Women are so poorly supported in their attempts to work through public provision of childcare, and wages are so low [that the majority cannot afford private childcare]. In addition, the low-wage economy in the UK has made use of women as a cheap labour force, as reflected in downward mobility after childbirth, even at the expense of under-utilising the skills and experience that women do have from their previous experience and training.' Fine, B, *Women's Employment and the Capitalist Family*, 1992, London: Routledge, p 161.

26 See Department of Trade and Industry Press Release P/98/489, 18 June 1998.

THE JOBS WOMEN DO

The issue here is the extent to which women perform, as a whole, different jobs from men, a phenomenon often referred to as occupational segregation, and the extent to which this segregation may be in decline. A comparison here must be made not only with the actual jobs performed by men and women, but with whether such jobs have the same or different socio-economic status.[27]

Walby, S, *Gender Transformations*, 1997, London: Routledge, pp 34–36:

There has been a decline in the extent to which top jobs in the upper socio-economic levels were monopolised by men ... Women have increasingly entered top positions, especially those managerial, administrative, and professional jobs for which university degrees are the effective entry qualifications ... Between 1975 and 1994, the percentage of economically active women who were in the upper [socio-economic groups] ... increased significantly, from 5% to 13%. This compares with a parallel male shift from 20% to 28% in the same period ...[28]

There has been a very significant change in the distribution of women across the occupational orders between 1981 and 1991 ... Whilst most occupations still show that they are staffed predominantly by one sex or the other, indeed seven occupational orders are still over 80% male in 1991[29] (though there are none which are 80% female),[30] there has been a marked reduction in the extent of segregation. In particular, women have increased their participation in the upper occupational orders and reduced them in the lower ones – the higher the order, the more likely an increase in both the absolute and relative numbers of women. The largest proportionate increase is women in the top occupational order, 'professional and related supporting management; senior national and local government managers', where the number of women has increased by

---

27 'A not wholly inaccurate caricature of women's occupations is provided by the list of the '10 deadly Cs': catering, cleaning, clerking, cashiering, counter-minding, clothes-making, clothes-washing, coiffure, childminding and care of the sick.' *Op cit*, Webb, fn 18, p 145.

28 '[T]he proportion of women working full time (44%) who are in the top two social classes is higher than that for men (41%). However, women still account for just over one-third of all those working full time in the top two social classes. And, although the number of women employed in many managerial and professional organisations has increased, they still only represent 32% of managers and administrators.' *Op cit*, 'Women in the labour market', fn 2, p 31.

29 The largest three are: (a) processing, making, repairing and related (5% female); (b) transport operating, material moving, storing and related (6%); and (c) construction, mining and related (1%). Of course, the larger the groups that are put together to form one composite group, the less likely that extreme segregation will be shown. Put another way, the narrower the definition of an occupational group, the more likely it to be performed disproportionately by either men or women.

30 The highest are clerical and related (74% female); catering, cleaning, hairdressing and other personal services (74%); and professional and related in education, welfare and health (65%).

155% as compared with 33% among men, shifting the gender composition from only 21% women to 30% ... In the lower occupational orders, largely manual jobs, where there have been some significant overall reductions in employment, the reduction in women is largely in absolute numbers and their relative proportions have remained largely stable ...

In 1974, the jobs that were 90% or over female were: hand and machine sewers and embroiderers; nurses; maids and valets; canteen assistants; and typists, shorthand writers and secretaries. The jobs that were 90% or over male were more numerous but included miners and quarry workers; butchers and meat cutters; painters and decorators; postal workers and mail sorters; and the armed forces.[31]

It remains the case that women are crowded into a relatively narrow range of occupations. In 1991, 30% of women worked in clerical and related jobs; 20% in catering, cleaning, etc; and 15% in education, welfare and health. Thus 65% of women worked in three occupational bands; for men, the three dominant occupations comprised only around 40% of total male employment. Many of the subgroups from among these broad groups are likely to be even more segregated, and, given that very many women work in small enterprises, it will be the norm rather than the exception for a female employee to have no male counterpart doing the same job for the same employer.[32]

THE CAUSES OF WOMEN'S INEQUALITY[33]

It is self-evident that explanations for differences and inequalities experienced by women in relation to work are connected with the division of labour in the household. After the Industrial Revolution led to a more general separation of work and home, women's primary responsibility for children impacted on working opportunities. This operated both ideologically – what was perceived

---

31 See, also, *op cit*, Webb, fn 18, p 146.

32 Martin and Roberts, *op cit*, fn 8, p 33, found that, of women working with others doing the same job, 63% worked only with other women, and that women were much more likely to work only with other women if they worked part time. Furthermore, 'the pattern of career segregation over the lifetime ... is highly variable by sex and class. For men, career segregation is more accentuated at the top of the occupational hierarchies, both manual and non-manual, whereas for women it is more accentuated at the bottom of these hierarchies ... Many men in positions of power and influence ... will have had little experience of working with women in the same occupations, but women cannot reach such positions without working with men. The situation is reversed at the bottom of the occupational hierarchy where the men are more likely to have worked with women but the women are more likely to have worked only with other women.' MacEwan Scott, A and Burchell, B, 'Gender segregation and work histories', in MacEwan Scott, A (ed), *Gender Segregation and Social Change*, 1994, Oxford: OUP, pp 151–53.

33 For an excellent straightforward introduction to the subject specifically aimed at students, see Reskin, B and Padavic, I, *Women at Work*, 1994, Thousand Oaks: Pine Forge.

as appropriate for women to do, and practically – what in the real world could be done. The evidence suggests that these two factors or approaches continue to operate to the detriment of women. There are two major issues which need to be considered: first, the reasons why women perform the jobs that they do, and, secondly, why on average women receive lower pay than men. However, many of the factors are so interrelated that it becomes extremely difficult to determine which is the primary or most important explanation, or even if there is one. It is important to appreciate that the social situation we are attempting to explain is in a permanent state of flux, so any explanations need both to be grounded in the history of women's employment, and to be able to take account of changing conditions. The aim is to provide a foundation for consideration of the degree to which legal intervention is likely to make a significant impact on continuing gender inequality.[34]

Neo-classical economics

However, the first issue is whether there is even a *problem* which needs to be explained. Those who believe in the primacy and the efficacy of the free market as the allocator of jobs and resources would argue that both the pay which women receive and the jobs which they perform are the result of market economics mediated by the free choices of the individuals concerned. On this view, the price of labour is determined in precisely the same way as the price of any other product, namely supply and demand. Wage levels are the lowest which the employer can pay while at the same time maintaining the ability to attract employees.

This approach implies that discrimination is irrational and that the discriminating employer would face higher labour costs than his non-discriminating counterpart. In particular, the fact that women are apparently willing to work for lower wages than men would predict that employers would replace men with cheaper women. This would break down segregation and contribute to the reduction of the pay differential. The statistics considered earlier are only consistent with this happening to a very limited extent in the case of full time workers. The problem is to account for the persistence of the pay gap and occupational segregation.

The first answer is to deny the analogy between product markets and labour markets: the supposedly 'simple' laws of supply and demand do not operate at all simply when dealing with labour. 'Opportunities for the marginal substitution of labour ... are severely constrained by the widespread

---

[34] The whole area continues to be a very fertile field of study for sociologists and others, many of whose answers vary diametrically from each other. It is not my task or within my capability to resolve these disputes; rather, the task is to outline the various different approaches.

acceptance by employers [and] workers of three key principles: the rate for the job, no money wage cuts and the right of all existing employees to retain their job in relation to all other potential recruits.'[35] The rate for the job means that it is normal practice, though becoming less so, to pay the same to everyone doing the same job irrespective of their productivity. Unlike the product market, oversupply of workers very rarely leads to wage cuts, which, if they are occur, are more likely to result from lack of profitability. Equally, current employees are almost never displaced by a cheaper alternative – unless that alternative is mechanical rather than human. In the absence of redundancies, the social function of employment has led to the assumption that a competent employee will retain a job. In any event, the *external* job market has only a limited influence on pay levels. Large employers may lack effective competition and so set their own pay levels; many firms operate an *internal* market where there is progression through the hierarchy; and there is very considerable variation in pay between people doing the same job for different employers. The conclusion must be that social factors are more significant explanations of pay levels than the economic laws of supply and demand.

Furthermore, the *assumptions* of neo-classical economic theory are far removed from the way in which labour markets operate in practice.[36]

Browne, N, 'The fundamental tension between market wages for women and comparable worth' (1984) 2 Law and Inequality 473, pp 473, 476, 480–83:

It is argued that the market automatically and accurately determines the relative worth of individual male and female workers ... In part, the market defence achieves its intellectual appeal because of an unstated belief that a free and fair market is already dispensing incomes. Additionally, people who advocate the superiority of market mechanisms necessarily adopt certain assumptions describing the characteristics of the setting in which markets function.

Defenders continually describe markets as impersonal. Such a characterisation is highly convenient for those who have a disproportionate influence on the determination of relative wages. Market defenders cite 'the laws of supply and demand' as the determinants for what the proper gap between the income of a surgeon and a nurse both is and should be. These laws supposedly result from objective forces beyond individuals' control. Consequently, income differentials are calibrated not by a person who could conceivably be a misogynist, racist, homophobe or ignoramus, but by forces that would mysteriously and automatically make appropriate monetary distinctions ... Market proponents also argue that legislative or judicial intervention in resulting wage decisions is a clumsy and burdensome interference with impersonal processes.

---

[35] Craig, C, Garnsey, E and Rubery, J, *Payment Structures in Smaller Firms: Women's Employment in Segmented Labour Markets*, 1984, London: Department of Employment, p 5.

[36] For an attack on the primacy of economic values in current social decision making, see Fredman, *op cit*, fn 1, pp 403–11.

A [further] belief held by those who defend market outcomes is that the *rational* employer and employee will each shape wage and employment decisions by calculating the net pecuniary benefit to herself. That economic actors might be motivated by altruism, community well being, or moral principles is dubbed 'remote' by market advocates. In neo-classical economic theory, human nature is not necessarily devoid of moral content; instead, moral actions are defined in terms of efficient and individualistic calculations. The moral employee or seller of labour acts to maximise her income; the moral employer or purchaser of labour acts to maximise her profit ... Supposedly, the employer always searches for the most productive employee, and the employee readily leaves a job when the wage lags behind the market value of her marginal output.

[Four assumptions underlie neo-classical theory.]

(1) [T]hat product and factor markets are competitive ... If an employer pays employees less than their worth, higher wages elsewhere will lure the employees away. If the employer pays employees more than their worth, the employer will realise no profit. [In other words, no worker is forced to accept a wage lower than marginal productivity would dictate. Given the alternatives to paid employment, this assumption is totally unrealistic.]

(2) Rational economic calculations depend on the existence of necessary information. Both the employer and the employee must have considerable information about a particular job to match precisely the employee's wages with the value of the employee's marginal output and simultaneously to provide the employer with the optimal bargain consistent with the profit maximisation objective. Many types of information, including the productivity of all pertinent potential employees, quality of alternative jobs in other geographic regions, and the market value of an employee must be considered prior to such wage setting. Without this data, market defenders' characterisation of a wage decision as objective and rational is absurd ...

(3) Neo-classical labour market theory ascribes powerful efficiency effects to the market mechanism because it presumes that the market wage cannot exist below the value of an employee's output. Discrimination can exist temporarily, but soon some other profit-hungry employer will lure the justifiably dissatisfied employee to a workplace where her true value is appreciated. In reality, this may not be the case. Many employees will not abandon a job that pays less than the value of marginal output. Cultural or pecuniary reasons, as well as an employee's failure to perceive the discrimination, cause this immobility ... [Furthermore] in a period of high unemployment and persistent recession ... workers move from job to job less often than under more prosperous macroeconomic conditions. Macroeconomic conditions have a definite effect on the amount and degree of mobility that can realistically be expected from workers. Yet, no worker controls the macroeconomic conditions affecting her. Mobility, therefore, is not simply a matter of individual choice in society ...

(4) For wages to serve as an accurate measure of the value of an employee's output, the individual must have a particular productivity that both the

employer and the employee can measure and then compare to the productivity of other employees ... Measuring an individual's productivity would provide a meaningful yardstick of worker value only if discrete marginal output were attributable to each individual worker ...

Neo-classical economic theory attempts to treat the market as impersonal, separate from its participants. In reality, the market is no more than a sum of the attributes and behaviours of its participants, including what may be a propensity to discriminate. If we reject the purity of the market mechanism, we need to consider how discrimination continues to operate.

Becker asserted that some employers had a 'taste' for discrimination, though where these tastes originated, and in particular the extent to which society was responsible for their development, was never explained.[37] Whether a theory developed in the context of racial issues in the USA can satisfactorily translate to race *or* gender issues in the UK must be a matter of some doubt. In any event, the hiring of cheaper female or black labour should increase profits and thus rapidly lead to a change of heart, for commercial reasons, among those who are continuing to discriminate. The theory implies a personal contact between discriminator-employer and victim-employee which seems far removed from the impersonal reality of most employment situations. Finally, the theory cannot explain extremely stable patterns of job segregation in an era of very rapid social change.

Human capital theories

So the labour market devotees shifted to another approach: the human capital theory. Here, women's lower wages are said to result from a decision to invest less in education and skills training than men, coupled with the fact that skills and experience decline during the period when women are absent from the labour market for family reasons. Women may choose to make a lower investment than men because they anticipate significant periods of absence from the labour market. The conclusion from the theory is that women are, on average, less productive than men.

There is no doubt some validity in this approach: evidence has shown that the average pay of women declines for each year of absence from the labour market. Furthermore, it is clear that the reduction in the pay gap for full time workers is due in substantial part to the fact that women are obtaining more and better qualifications, although whether the decline is in proper proportion to the level of women's improvement is open to serious doubt. But attempting to demonstrate a close correlation between women's pay levels and their qualifications and experience is fraught with problems. For example, pay rates are higher in jobs requiring scientific and technical qualifications, more often

---

37 Becker, G, *The Economics of Discrimination*, 2nd edn, 1971, Chicago: Chicago UP.

held by men. It is not clear from the theory why some investments should be valued more highly than others. Again, it may be questioned whether experience is as essential for jobs as is often made out; to reward those with long periods of continuous employment may be done for social more than managerial reasons. The evidence suggests that not all absences from work have the same consequences so far as pay and job position are concerned. It is the first return to work, usually after the birth of the first child, which is associated with declining earnings and status, and this is even more true if the return to work is on a part time basis. So the reduction in earnings is not linear for each year of absence, as the theory predicts. The decline on first return suggests instead that institutional factors are at work, and that, if choice is involved, the choice is made by employers, not employees.[38]

The above criticism of the theory is the technical one, that it fails to explain the pay gap. The second and more fundamental defect with the human capital approach is that it implies that all decisions about how much to invest in human capital are freely and rationally made. Many decisions are made without full information as to the human capital consequences. More importantly, if women know or suspect that they are less likely to be hired for particular jobs, then they will not invest in the human capital training necessary for such jobs. The theory passes responsibility to the individual rather than blaming the discriminator. In addition, it simply assumes that women are more likely than men to take time out of the labour market for childrearing reasons. Why that should be is not considered, nor is the fact that the provision or lack of childcare may have significant influence on the working patterns of mothers. If employers act on the basis of stereotypes, it becomes rational from a human capital perspective to act as if the stereotype were true, for otherwise the investment is in danger of being wasted. This perpetuates a vicious circle whereby employers assume that women will not be qualified or be able to perform a particular job, and thus women are not given the opportunity to do so.

The most persistent and damaging stereotypes concern the interaction for women between work and home. One is that women will leave work, at least temporarily, to have children. It is thus argued to be economically rational for employers not to hire women for jobs which require extensive on the job training. Another stereotype is that women employees with young children are more likely to prove unreliable than men with young children; indeed, for a man, having young children may be regarded as a plus factor, for such men are assumed to be reliable employees for domestic and financial reasons. A further stereotype is that women have higher turnover rates than men and thus overall training costs can be controlled by hiring only men. But turnover is a function of job status; the lower the status of a job, the higher the

---

[38] See England, P, 'The failure of human capital theory to explain occupational segregation' (1982) 17 Journal of Human Resources 356.

employee turnover tends to be. Thus women's higher turnover rate may be because of the jobs they do, not because of supposed personal failings. Many of these approaches to hiring and training developed when a job for life was commonplace. Men may also be liable to move jobs, even though they may often do so for different reasons from women. The old-fashioned stereotypes may retain a hold in today's quite different labour market.

Segmented labour market theories

The explanations so far considered have concentrated on the attributes women bring to the labour market and thus imply that the actions of employers are not responsible for any marketplace inequality; they might thus be regarded as 'blaming the victim'.[39] These fail to provide an adequate explanation of why men and women behave differently in the labour market. It is necessary to seek to explain why women are employed in particular jobs and why on average such jobs receive lower pay.

The first such approach argued that there are different labour markets operating in the economy.

Beechey, V, *Unequal Work*, 1987, London: Verso, pp 32–36:

Essential to the notion of the dual labour market is the assumption that the labour market is segmented into a number of structures ... Primary sector jobs have relatively high earnings, good fringe benefits, good working conditions, a high degree of job security and good opportunities for advancement, while secondary jobs have relatively low earnings levels, poor working conditions, negligible opportunities for advancement and a low degree of job security ... The difference between the opportunities for advancement offered by jobs in the primary sector and those in the secondary sector is usually related to the existence of structured internal labour markets to which primary jobs are attached. A highly structured internal labour market contains a set of jobs organised hierarchically in terms of skill level and rewards, where recruitment to higher positions in the hierarchy is predominantly from lower positions in the same hierarchy and not from the external labour market. Only the lowest's positions in the firm's job hierarchy are not filled from within the organisation by promotion. Secondary jobs, on the other hand, are not part of a structured internal market; recruits to these jobs tend to come from outside the organisation ... Furthermore, because of the low skill requirement for most

---

[39] 'In explaining the characteristic features of women's position in the labour force in terms of characteristics of women themselves, the common sense explanations are all individualistic forms of explanation ... They explain the position of women in the organisational structure in terms of assertions about women's nature, or capabilities or temperament, rather than social structures. Individualistic explanations very often implicitly or explicitly involve biologically determinist claims, that is, claims that women's capabilities are determined by their biological attributes.' Beechey, V, 'Women's employment in contemporary Britain', in Beechey, V and Whitegg, E (eds), *Women in Britain Today*, 1986, Milton Keynes: OU Press, p 103.

secondary jobs, training is non-existent or minimal, so that secondary workers rarely acquire skills which they can use to advance their status on the open market ...

[It has been argued] that there are five major attributes which make a group likely to be a source of secondary workers, and that women possess each of them. These are:

(1) workers are easily dispensable, whether voluntarily or involuntarily;

(2) they can be sharply differentiated from workers in the primary labour market by some conventional social difference;

(3) they have a relatively low inclination to acquire valuable training and experience;

(4) they are low on 'economism' – that is, they do not rate economic rewards highly;

(5) they are relatively unlikely to develop solidarity with fellow workers ...

There is no doubt that the distinction between primary and secondary jobs has some useful insights as to the differences between work typically done by men and that typically done by women.[40] However, the neat distinction into two categories of jobs is impossible to substantiate empirically.[41]

Beechey, V, 'Women's employment in contemporary Britain', in Beechey, V and Whitegg, E (eds), *Women in Britain Today*, 1986, Milton Keynes: OU Press, p 111:

Dual labour market theory has little to say about horizontal occupational segregation – that is, the segregation of women into jobs like clerical work and selling, and men into jobs like security and protective services. It does, however, throw some light on the process of vertical occupational segregation, since it is centrally concerned with the question of hierarchy and privilege within the workforce, and with the strategies used by employers to privilege certain groups of workers in order to keep them within the firm ...

[M]any kinds of women's jobs do not fit easily into the category of secondary sector work. Some women's work in manufacturing industry is skilled work which is integral to the production process, for example, work in the textile industry. Although this may be low paid in comparison with men's work, it is not marginal or insecure as secondary sector work is. Much secretarial work throughout all sectors of the economy requires considerable training, and secretaries are an integral part of the workforce. Although secretarial work may not be well paid in comparison with men's work, and although it may not actually be defined as skilled, it is not marginal and insecure. Finally, a good

---

40 The distinction is between primary and secondary jobs, not primary and secondary employers. Many employers, of which the NHS is a good example, employ large numbers of workers in both categories.

41 '[S]ome areas of employment such as agriculture where men form the vast majority of workers and other areas of predominantly male employment such as construction where employment is highly insecure, show characteristics normally associated with the secondary sector.' Joseph, G, *Women at Work: The British Experience*, 1983, Deddington: Philip Allan, pp 223–24.

number of women are employed in professional and technical jobs, especially in the public sector ... Dual labour market theory's conception of women being a secondary sector workforce cannot adequately account for these kinds of women's work ... [Furthermore the theory] does not explain why so many occupations have been constituted as 'women's work' – why, for instance, secretarial work is done almost exclusively by women, and why women predominate in sales work, domestic work, teaching and nursing.

Craig, C, Garnsey, E and Rubery, J, *Payment Structures and Smaller Firms: Women and Employment in Segmented Labour Markets,* **1984, London: Department of Employment, pp 92, 97:**

Contrary to the early labour market segmentation models, many 'secondary type' workers (that is, those drawn from relatively disadvantaged groups and in receipt of low wages) have considerable levels of skill and experience acquired through informal on-the-job training, and undertake work which makes heavy demands on the workers ...

Many of the apparently semi-skilled or unskilled jobs in the survey industries carried out by women require fairly long periods of on-the-job training and experience. Moreover, many of the jobs carried out by non-qualified men were often equally tedious, so that it was the difference in pay and grading of the jobs rather than differences in the content and nature of the jobs themselves that was the main cause of women's inferior employment status.

The dual labour market approach was the jumping off point for more sophisticated theories arguing that the labour market was indeed divided into different segments, which at a practical level tended to operate to the disadvantage of women.

Craig, C, Garnsey, E and Rubery, J, *Payment Structures and Smaller Firms: Women and Employment in Segmented Labour Markets,* **1984, London: Department of Employment, p 6:**

[A] structured or differentiated labour supply is created through the interaction of the employment system and the system of social organisation ... [D]ifferentiation of the labour supply arises through four main but interrelated causes. In the first place, even if workers enter the labour market with similar characteristics and opportunities, they will acquire different work histories, experience and skills which subsequently limit their mobility and restrict them to particular firms and industries. Secondly, workers enter the labour market with unequal access to jobs due to differences in their social characteristics: these range from their different educational qualifications, which do not necessarily directly affect their productivity in the labour market but which are nevertheless used as screening devices by employers, to their different access to jobs because of their family connections.

Thirdly, workers are not usually independent individuals who rely entirely on their own wage or State-provided income but are members of social and family groups in which income is pooled or at least partly shared ... Firms make general assumptions about the relative income needs of specific demographic groups in structuring their pay and employment practices, and members of these groups may have to adjust to conventional assessments of their relative needs even if this does not correspond to their own specific family circumstances.

Fourthly, individuals accept different responsibilities for family or domestic commitments which restrict their availability in the labour market. These domestic commitments may in some cases make the employee less productive from the point of view of the employer, but they also provide a means by which firms can differentiate between different types of labour and take advantage of groups with limited access to the wage labour market by paying them wages which do not necessarily reflect their relative productivity.

The relatively disadvantaged position of women in the labour market can be seen to stem from the interaction of these four factors. Women are not only assumed to require less income, but they are also expected to take on the major share of family responsibilities, a division of responsibilities reinforced by unequal opportunities in the labour market. Expectations of limited commitment to wage labour and discrimination within the education system may result in women entering the labour market at a relative disadvantage even when young and single; this disadvantage can become reinforced through work experience as women are excluded from training or promotion through discrimination or as the result of an interrupted work history.

Ideology and practice

The final extract epitomises a move from concentrating on the supposedly abstract qualities of labour markets to the importance of human agency and choice in the reproduction of women's employment disadvantage. It argues that jobs have been 'gendered' or 'sex-typed' – a process whereby it comes to be regarded as appropriate or natural for a job to be performed only or mainly by persons of one sex. The quest is to determine historically how this occurred and if, how and why it is reproduced in today's conditions.

There is no doubt that there is a link between women's position in the family and women's position at work. The way in which the link operates is, however, controversial. Some argue that it is the domestic division of labour which causes employment disadvantage; others argue that the causal factors largely operate the other way round. A further source of disagreement concerns the extent to which the primary cause of women's disadvantage has been capitalism or patriarchy. The former approach emphasises the inferior position of all workers, accepting that the manifestations of that inferiority may operate differently between men and women. The latter argues that society has been systematically structured by men in order to oppress and control women.[42] Resolution of these disputes is beyond the scope of this work; rather, the task is to identify, in relation to a number of different

---

[42] Walby, S, *Patriarchy at Work*, 1986, Cambridge: Polity.

themes, the interlocking role of theory and practice in contributing to women's employment disadvantage.

The definition of skill

Historically, especially where pay has been determined by collective bargaining, there has been a distinction of great significance for levels of pay between work classified as 'skilled' and that classified as 'unskilled.' The notion of skill has been manipulated in the interests of men.

Beechey, V, 'Women's employment in contemporary Britain', in Beechey, V and Whitegg, E (eds), *Women in Britain Today*, 1986, Milton Keynes: OU Press, p 121:

The first reason why women's jobs are often not classified as skilled is because they generally involve quite short periods of formal training ... A further important point is that many women's jobs use skills which women learn informally within the home ... This informal training, however, never counts as training in the more formal sense ... and is not generally considered a significant variable in the determination of women's pay.

A second reason why women's jobs are not defined as skilled is that women have frequently been unable to get their jobs defined as skilled through trade unions. Trade unions have fought to get jobs defined as skilled or to maintain their definition as skilled in the face of employers' endeavours to define jobs as unskilled or semi-skilled, and they have often tried to impose restrictions on entry into apprenticeships so that the number of skilled workers can be restricted.

[T]he concept of skill is socially constructed, and an adequate account of the exclusion of women from skilled jobs has to take account of this.

Beechey, V and Perkins, T, *A Matter of Hours: Women, Part Time Work and the Labour Market*, 1987, Cambridge: Polity, p 137:

[T]he notions of skill and training are absolutely central to the ways in which the distinction between primary and secondary sector workers is drawn, and the theory assumes that what counts as skilled work can be treated positivistically – as an objective phenomenon which is unaffected by employers' conceptions or by the bargaining power or the social status of those who characteristically do it. It is quite clear, however ... that gender enters into the definition of skilled work and that it also plays a part in what counts and what does not count as training. That women's skills and training are systemically downgraded and undervalued is well documented.[43]

---

[43] See, also, Phillips, A and Taylor, B, 'Sex and skill: notes towards a feminist economics' (1980) 6 Feminist Review 79.

Gender-typing of jobs

This refers to processes, whether informal or informal, by which certain jobs come to be associated with women employees. The evidence suggests that this has happened by design rather than by accident.

Cockburn, C, *In the Way of Women: Men's Resistance to Sex Equality in Organisations*, 1991, Basingstoke: Macmillan, pp 38–41:

People have a gender, and the gender rubs off on the jobs they do. The jobs in turn have a gender character which rubs off on the people who do them. Tools and machinery used in work are gendered too, in such a way that the sexes are expected to relate to different kinds of equipment in different ways ... In a training workshop where I have been doing fieldwork, it is impossible to get a teenage lad to wipe the floor with a mop, though he may be persuaded to sweep it with a broom. Any woman lifting a crowbar is likely to have some gender-conscious thought as she does so.

When a new invention arrives in the workplace it is already gendered by the activities and expectations of its manufacturers and owners. It may even be ergonomically sex-specific, scaled for the average height or anticipated strength of the sex that is to use it. Even if it arrives apparently gender-neutral it quickly acquires a gender by association with its user or its purpose. The computer was the brainchild of male engineers and was born into a male line of production technology. The fact that it has a keyboard rather like a (feminine) typewriter confuses no one for long. When a computer arrives in a school, for instance, boys and girls are quick to detect its latent masculinity ...

The many technologists and technicians I have interviewed (almost all male) have expressed time and again their identification as men with technology and of technology itself with masculinity ...

There are good reasons for women's reluctance [to enter technical work]. It is not that women are set against the idea of non-traditional fields of work ... They are simply aware, however, of the high social costs that we all pay if we disobey gender rules. The gendering of jobs ... advertises loudly where women are not to enter. If we ignore the message we are made to feel silly, pushy, unnatural ... There is a relentless background noise of harassment. We become unlovable ...

The dichotomies, separations and power inequalities that occur at home and those that occur at work are related and mutually reinforcing.

Beechey, V, 'Women's employment in contemporary Britain', in Beechey, V and Whitegg, E (eds), *Women in Britain Today*, 1986, Milton Keynes: OU Press, pp 125–26:

Familial ideology asserts that men are primary breadwinners and that women are their dependants. It proclaims that a woman's primary role is that of housewife and mother. Familial ideology has in fact changed historically in Britain. In the 19th century it was thought to be unacceptable for married women to engage in paid employment outside the home at all, and single women's employment was only grudgingly accepted ... Today women's paid work is becoming more recognised and acceptable. Nevertheless, it is still assumed that a woman's work outside the home should not interfere with her domestic responsibilities in caring for her husband and particularly in caring for her children and other dependent relatives.

Despite the fact that fewer and fewer families correspond to the nuclear model with male breadwinner, non-working wife and dependent children, familial ideology remains pervasive. It is a crucial element of the dominant ideology. It plays an important role in structuring women's participation in the labour market and in restricting opportunities for paid work. It affects her participation in the labour market, deeming it unacceptable for her to work when she should be caring for others. It enters into the construction of certain jobs as 'women's jobs' and other jobs as 'men's jobs', with women's jobs frequently involving caring for and servicing others ... [I]t is embedded in the concept of the family wage – the notion that a man's major responsibility is as family breadwinner and that he should provide for a dependent wife and children – which is still prevalent in employers' and trade unions' ways of thinking about wages. When ideologies make differentiations among people on the basis of ascriptive characteristics such as age, sex or race they tend to be particularly pervasive because they represent social relations as though they were natural. Familial ideology, which assumes that women are primarily wives and mothers, plays an important role in the organisation of paid employment, while simultaneously portraying the sexual division of labour and women's position in the labour market in quasi-naturalistic terms.

Collinson, D, Knights, D and Collinson, M, *Managing to Discriminate*, 1990, London: Routledge, pp 131–35:

[There are] at least four common and recurrent rationalisations for sex discrimination ... First, managers were found to deny their responsibility for sex-discriminatory practices, while simultaneously exaggerating the choice and power of jobseekers. By emphasising supply side factors, recruiters tended to slip into 'blaming the victim' ... [W]hen managers required male breadwinners, it was often argued that women were 'their own worst enemy' because they were: too emotional; likely to leave for marriage or children; unreliable workers (particularly if they had children); lacked ambition, confidence, toughness and assertiveness; were not geographically mobile; were inflexible because they could not work nights or weekends and were not prepared to study in the evenings and sit professional examinations. Equally, when managers wished to appoint temporary or less ambitious staff they looked to appoint female homemakers since it was believed that these workers would accept highly routinised and controlled jobs which offered only poor pay and conditions.

Another way in which managers denied responsibility for their own practices and economic vested interests was by claiming to be the victim of 'tradition', 'history', 'culture', 'society', 'customers', 'other workers', 'clients/intermediaries', and other managers. Blaming other workers for the exclusion of one sex from a particular job was invariably interrelated with the concern of selectors to appoint candidates who are seen to 'fit in' with the organisation. Against the social conditioning and values of the wider society, recruiters claimed to be powerless to intervene ...

[A] recurrent explanation by personnel managers for the perpetuation of practices which have sex discriminatory effects was that change could be destabilising for production and control ...

It is precisely because of the 'common sense' plausibility that gender and managerial ideologies are routinely taken for granted and reproduced through the rationalisations and practices of personnel and line managers.

Cockburn, C, *In the Way of Women: Men's Resistance to Sex Equality in Organisations*, 1991, Basingstoke: Macmillan, pp 96, 100–02:

Many women experience the same conflicts. Ambitious women without children, some of whom are unmarried besides, know full well that having all these 'mother's privileges' serves to confirm men's beliefs that women as a sex are unreliable employees who have their mind half the time on domestic matters. Though part timing, jobsharing and career break schemes are now sometimes available to women to help them through the childrearing years, they know full well that this route is a succession of career impediments.

Women find the requirement of mobility hard to meet. This is because their husbands often require their own job to take precedence – he earns more, his career 'matters' more. Men, for their part, find mobility hard to sustain. Their wives and children often complain at being uprooted from their communities ... [M]en must discourage their wives from developing attachment to a job so as not to add to this family inertia.

There is a vicious circle ... Women's relatively low pay prevents men giving up their salary to care for the home, while women's domestic confinement limits their chance of earning a salary on which they could, wholly or partly, support man and child.

We are in a time of significant social change in which it might be argued that the above assumptions and ideologies are outdated – in the sense that they no longer influence behaviour. While there might be limited change, especially for women with high educational qualifications, evidence suggests that the impact of such changes should not be overestimated.[44]

MacEwan Scott, A, 'Gender segregation and the SCELI research', in *Gender Segregation and Social Change*, 1994, Oxford: OUP, pp 34–35:

Despite the economic changes of recent years, women's increased labour market participation, and changes in family structure, such as increases in divorce and single parenthood, there appears to be enormous stability in women's and men's domestic roles and the value system that underpins them ... [W]omen's role as primary childcarers causes severe disruption to their long term labour market position. This is mirrored in the fact that male breadwinners increase their career opportunities over their lifetime and enjoy a substantial earnings premium in the process ...

---

[44] Thus, eg, anecdotal evidence suggests that female solicitors may have greater difficulty than men in obtaining partnerships because male partners are concerned that a woman partner may leave in order to raise a family.

The primacy of the male breadwinner role continues to structure the labour market in a variety of ways, mainly through the material and ideological differentiation of labour supply. In many cases, this is translated into employment structures and payment systems, which further rigidifies segmentation (for example, part time work). However, gender segregation is not based solely on primary or secondary earner status. There is much evidence that naturalistic beliefs about gender, embodied in notions of strength, dexterity, sensitivity and so on, play a fundamental role in the sex-typing of jobs. These beliefs seem to be much more enduring than economic and family structures. Finally, there is substantial inertia in the labour market; traditional employment practices persist despite pressure for change. Patterns of gender segregation are sustained by 'tradition' as much as by the rational strategies of individual employers and employees. All in all, despite marginal changes within specific occupations, there is much less evidence of desegregation than might have been expected given the extent of social and economic change during the 1980s.

Vogler, C, 'Segregation, sexism and the labour supply' in MacEwan Scott, A (ed), *Gender Segregation and Social Change*, 1994, Oxford: OUP, pp 59–63:

Constraints resulting from an unequal division of labour within the home may force people into highly segregated or part time work regardless of their attitudes ... It is therefore important to ask how far those working in segregated or part time jobs were also living in households characterised by a traditional domestic division of labour and how attitudes mediated this linkage ...

[T]he data show that men living in households with a more traditional division of labour were more likely to be working in segregated jobs, whereas women's domestic tasks and responsibilities were related to gender segregation indirectly through their effects on part time work ...

[A] partner's attitude and the presence of children were as important in explaining the pattern of women's labour market participation as their own attitudes, if not more so. These findings are consistent with the hypothesis that women's sexist attitudes are likely to be constrained by inequalities in the division of labour within the home. It cannot therefore be assumed, as human capital and cultural theorists have tended to do, that households are egalitarian consensual units in which both partners are free to realise their 'choices' on the labour market. Moreover, men's sexist attitudes had implications for women. By influencing the length of time women had spent out of employment, husbands were able to impose their sexism on women within the household as well as in the labour market, and this in turn affected the latter's chances of working in a segregated job.

Gender-typing of jobs occurs because of the attitude and behaviour of employers and because of the domestic circumstances of women. However, the role played by other employees must not be ignored. This operates in two main ways: the role historically played by trade unions in seeking to secure benefits for men, and the role played by notions of male sexuality in impacting upon the different opportunities and experiences for men and women at work.

Beechey, V, 'Women's employment in contemporary Britain', in Beechey, V and Whitegg, E (eds), *Women in Britain Today,* **1986, Milton Keynes: OU Press, pp 117–18:**

It has been argued that the *basis* of labour market segmentation lies in the fact that new supplies of wage labour have been introduced into the economy at different historical periods. Thus, in the UK, Commonwealth immigrants, blacks and married women have all entered the labour force more recently than men, and they have all been confined to the lowest strata of the labour market. They are often prepared to work at lower wage levels than white male workers, and this ... leads to hostility of white male workers towards these groups. If employers try to substitute any of these groups for white male workers ... this may well lead to a decline in relative wages within a given occupation, and reduce employment opportunities for men. This, in turn, may lead trade unions to try and confine them to a particular sector of the labour force by using a variety of mechanisms, ranging from union-organised apprenticeship schemes to promotion lines based upon strict seniority provisions ...

Hartmann argues that the development of capitalism threatened men's power over women. It threatened to bring all women and children into the labour force, and hence to destroy the family and the basis of men's power over women (which lay in control over men's labour power within the family). Men, she argues, therefore developed strategies to retain their power within the developing wage-labour system. One of these strategies was the development of techniques of hierarchical organisation and control within the labour market. Hartmann identifies a number of factors that partly account for the existence of job segregation by sex, and for women's lower wages: the exclusionary power of the male unions, the financial responsibility of men for their families, the willingness of women to work for less ... and women's lack of training. Most important of all, she argues, is the ability of men to organise in trade unions, which has played such an important role in maintaining job segregation and differentials and excluding women.

A further way in which male control over women may operate is through the construction of women's sexuality in the workplace.

Beechey, V, 'Women's employment in contemporary Britain', in Beechey, V and Whitegg, E (eds), *Women in Britain Today,* **1986, Milton Keynes: OU Press, p 125:**

Women are constructed within the ideology of femininity in relation to men throughout their lives ... Some white feminists have emphasised the importance of notions of glamour and sexuality in the construction of young women's jobs, especially jobs like secretarial work, telephone/receptionist work, hairdressing, and flight attendant, which represent women as being visibly attractive to men. Other have emphasised the servicing aspect of women's work which frequently underlie these glamorous representations ... Black women are frequently excluded from more glamorous jobs, it is suggested, precisely because it is white femininity which is required to be visible. The dominant representations which exist for black women are those of nurses, cooks, domestics and machinists, and their servicing role is often invisible 'below stairs.'

Adkins, L, *Gendered Work: Sexuality, Family and the Labour Market,* **1995, Buckingham: Open University, pp 147–55:**

At the two tourist workplaces [in her research], the labour market was shown to be gendered *prior* to occupations being differentiated. Specifically, women workers had to fulfil the condition of being sexualised workers regardless of their occupations. Men and women were constituted as different kinds of workers within these workplaces.

The gendering of production means that men and women within the two workplaces ... are different sorts of workers. They do different sorts of work even when working alongside each other, and have different relationships of and to production. Moreover, the gendering of production means that men occupy a structurally more powerful position in all these various areas of employment, a position from which they can control and appropriate some of the products of the work of women.

Women producing and maintaining a sexualised identity is both required and appropriated. Presenting a certain appearance and a sexualised way of being ... is part of their job ... Men, on the other hand, are not required to produce and maintain a particular sexual 'self' as part of their jobs.

[R]ather than being an intrusion into the workplace and unrelated to labour market practices, the sexual harassment and sexualisation of women is deeply embedded in such practices ... [S]exual harassment and the sexualisation of women is the outcome of the organisation of (gendered) relations of production.

PARTICULAR GROUPS OF WORKERS[45]

It must not be assumed that all the various influences operate evenly throughout the labour market. There are three groups of workers who face particular problems: part time workers, female minority group workers, and homeworkers.

Part time workers

The rapid growth in part time employment in recent years has been almost entirely female. It is more than a decade since writers began to analyse this sector of the labour market as possessing its own peculiar characteristics and as resulting in particular problems. We have seen that relatively low levels of

---

[45] See, also, Dickens, L, *Whose Flexibility? Discrimination and Equality Issues in Atypical Work*, 1992, London: Institute of Employment Rights.

pay are characteristic of part time work. Despite that, the growth in demand for part time labour is partly due to the fact that, in the British labour market, part time work suits many women with strong domestic commitments. Surveys consistently indicate a high level of job satisfaction among workers in this group.

Rubery, J, Horrell, S and Burchell, B 'Part time work and gender inequality' in MacEwan Scott, A (ed), *Gender Segregation and Social Change*, 1994, Oxford: OUP, pp 228–31:

Part time jobs are differentiated from full time jobs along a range of different dimensions. This differentiation cannot be explained solely in terms of gender as often the differences are more between full and part time jobs than between female and male jobs, especially when male and female full timers are compared. The main areas where there are strong differences ... are in job content and skills, in promotion prospects, access to benefits, and in types of working-time flexibility required. Thus part time jobs appear to require less training, experience, and fewer qualifications, to involve relatively few responsibilities (especially those associated with supervisory duties), and to require relatively few attributes or talents for the job to be performed well. Part timers are very unlikely to consider themselves to be in a job with promotion prospects and they have limited access to a wide range of employment benefits. Part timers are also extensively used to provide unsocial and flexible working hours, involving weekend working, variable days, and evening and some nightwork ... All these characteristics taken together provide strong evidence for the view that part timers constitute a distinct segment of the labour market ...

The evidence that part time jobs are both low quality ... and are associated with long term career downgrading suggests the need to develop and promote new forms of part time working which will enhance the quality of part time jobs and integrate them better into career ladders and promotion chains. Without such a development it is likely that the female labour market will become increasingly polarised between those pursuing a continuous career in full time jobs, and those who suffer permanent downgrading after leaving the labour market for childbirth and re-entering via part time employment.

Cockburn, C, *In the Way of Women: Men's Resistance to Sex Equality in Organisations*, 1991, Basingstoke: Macmillan, pp 81–83:

[I]t is not so much women's need as employers' labour force strategies which have led to this massive increase in part time working. The cost benefits of employing part time workers are many. They can be applied to more intensive work than a worker who has to sustain her energies for an eight hour shift. Mothers offer a special attraction of being a kind of seasonal worker, paid for in school term time ... laid off without pay in school vacations ... [W]hole occupations and sectors of the economy are now organised on a part time basis ...

[T]his growth in the significance of women in the paid labour force has occurred through two quite contrasted economic movements – the economic growth and stability of the fifties and sixties, followed by the turmoil, economic crisis and restructuring of the seventies and eighties.

Beechey, V and Perkins, T, *A Matter of Hours: Women, Part Time Work and the Labour Market,* **1987, Cambridge: Polity, pp 8–9, 117–19, 145–149:**

[E]mployers have gender-specific ways of organising their labour forces. Where the labour force is female ... employers use part time workers as a means of attaining flexibility. On the other hand, where men are employed, other means of attaining flexibility are used. Thus ... many of the characteristics of part time work do not stem from some generally defined economic process like de-skilling or the segmentation of the labour force into primary and secondary or core and peripheral workers, but from employment strategies which are related to gender ... [T]he division between full time and part time jobs is one crucial contemporary manifestation of gender within the sphere of production ... We take issue with theories which see part time work as some kind of 'natural' outgrowth of relations within the family ... Cross-national comparisons show that part time working is not always as closely correlated with married women's employment as it is in Britain ...

It is the need for flexibility which seems to be most central to people's conceptions of part time workers. The part timer is seen to be a woman with young children, who does not want full time work but wants a job which gives her a bit of money, gets her out of the house, and which is compatible with her maternal/wifely role. The managers whom we interviewed talked about part timers as if they were representative of *all* women. They spoke of women as having divided loyalties, requiring flexible hours ... And the employers often implied that they were doing women a favour by giving them part time work.

The domestic responsibilities of women who were employed on a full time basis were, by contrast, rarely mentioned ... The possibility that these women might like more flexible or shorter hours was never countenanced ...

[P]art time women workers are defined by their domestic responsibilities. Thus, when their labour is needed, employers seem prepared to recognise these and sometimes even prepared to accommodate them. In other circumstances, however, their domestic circumstances become a reason not to employ women on a part time basis, and at times not to employ them at all ... [P]art timers are not generally seen as wishing to do interesting work, or as wanting training or promotion ... Promotion invariably entailed becoming full time. And when they work full time, the recognition of their domestic responsibilities, and their need for flexibility, seems to disappear ...

[I]t was simply not the case that employers used sex-blind criteria in their hiring practices, or in selecting people for training schemes, or in their definitions of what constitutes 'skill' or appropriate qualifications, but that they had very definite conceptions relating to gender. So did many trade unionists. Certain jobs ... had been constructed as part time jobs because they were seen to be women's jobs. Various things followed from this. Part time jobs were invariably low graded, they were rarely defined as skilled even when they involved a range of competencies and abilities, women doing them lacked opportunities for promotion and training ... Whether their work was central or marginal to particular production processes, part time workers were regarded as marginal, their work was not defined as skilled, and they were badly paid ... [T]here is nothing *inherent* in the nature of particular jobs which makes them full time or part time. They have been constructed as such, and such constructions relate closely to gender ...

[T]he domestic division of labour is clearly an important part of the explanation of why women work part time because it imposes real constraints upon women's participation in the labour market ... We do, however, wish to counter the view that this is the only way in which gender enters into the organisation of work relations ... In order to analyse why married women ... so often work part time, it is necessary to analyse not only the domestic division of labour within the family, but also the ways in which this has been shaped through the operation of State policies ... [I]t is only in certain countries, of which Britain is a prime example, that high levels of women's activity rates are associated with high levels of part time employment ... [I]t is the absence of adequate facilities for caring for children and for the elderly and the handicapped that is one of the crucial determinants of the fact that most married women with dependants work part time ...

From the time of the industrial revolution, if not before, women have been constructed as marginal workers ... No matter what jobs they have done, however, their position has been defined as marginal because of a powerful form of gender ideology – the ideology of domesticity – which was deeply rooted in the emergence of bourgeois society and, indeed, became a defining characteristic of bourgeois class relations ...

It is certainly not the case that all women workers, nor even all part time workers, are marginal to the production processes in which they work. Nor is it the case that all women have interrupted work histories in order to care for their families, or that all women have spells of part time working. It is the case, however, that all women are defined as if there were a conflict between their paid work and their domestic responsibilities, and all women working part time are defined as marginal workers, no matter what they actually do. Similarly, all men (with the possible exception of young men ...) are defined as if they have families to support, no matter what their actual situations may be.

Ethnic minority women in the labour market[46]

Ethnic minority women often have a double handicap in the labour market, being vulnerable to economic inequalities on the basis of their race as well as their gender. It seems clear that they form distinctive groups within the labour market, with patterns which differ both from white women and from ethnic minority men.

---

[46] See Fredman, S and Szyszczak, E, 'The interaction of race and gender', in Hepple, B and Szyszczak, E (eds), *Discrimination: The Limits of Law*, 1992, London: Mansell.

Jones, T, *Britain's Ethnic Minorities: An Analysis of the Labour Force Survey,* **1996, London: Policy Studies Institute, p 63:**[47]

[W]omen's economic activity rate varies according to whether or not they have dependent children in quite a different way for different ethnic groups. This suggests that a large part of the variation in economic activity rates ... is due to differences in culture concerning the role of women in home-making and childrearing. Afro-Caribbean women have relatively high rates of economic activity whether or not they are married or cohabiting or have dependent children. Pakistani and Bangladeshi women have much lower rates of economic activity than women of other groups, and this is true of both married and unmarried women.[48]

Webb, M, 'Sex and gender in the labour market', in Reid, I and Stratta, E (eds), *Sex Differences in Britain,* **2nd edn, 1989, Aldershot: Gower, p 179:**

The differences in participation between the different ethnic minority groups are partly a reflection of their different age structures: all 'New Commonwealth' ethnic groups are relatively young, but the proportion of women in the childcare age ranges will vary. These ethnic minorities also have few persons over retirement age ... as a result it is likely that a smaller proportion of women's time is spent in the care of elderly relatives than is the case with the white population ...

The likelihood of women's participation in paid work may also be affected by the length of time individuals have spent in this country. Female immigrants may have followed their husbands to the UK after a considerable time lag, and so have had less opportunity to enter the employment networks, thus depressing their participation rate. The tendency for individuals to have a job may also increase as the ethnic group to which they belong becomes established. This is clearly relevant in the case of the West Indian community, and indeed the long standing recruitment of West Indian women by one employer (the NHS) may have contributed to their above average participation rate.

While ethnic minority women face specific labour market problems, it certainly should not be assumed that such problems are the same for each ethnic group and in every geographical location.

Phizacklea, A and Wolkowitz, C, *Homeworking Women: Gender, Racism and Class at Work,* **1995, London: Sage, p 7:**

[A]ll recent analyses of women in the labour market indicate that ethnic minority women are not sharing in [the] gains. Quite the reverse, not only are they over-represented in areas of occupational decline and under-represented in the growth sectors, but they are also likely to be working longer hours, in

---

[47] See, also, Bruegel, I, 'Sex and race in the labour market' (1989) 32 Feminist Review 49.

[48] '[W]ork participation rates for black mothers with young children ranged in different towns from 13% to 33%, whereas the rate for white mothers was only from 20% to 23% ... The variations ... partly reflect the balance of ethnic groups ... of each town.' *Op cit,* Webb, fn 18, p 177.

poorer conditions for lower pay than white women. Ethnic minority women are also twice as likely to be unemployed than white women ...

Cockburn, C, *In the Way of Women: Men's Resistance to Sex Equality in Organisations*, 1991, Basingstoke: Macmillan, pp 185–86:

The fact that white women share the racism of white men does not mean that there is no gender dimension to the race issue. There is a particularly intense relation of domination and resistance binding white men to black men. In fact, when black individuals were problematised in the discourse of either sex I found it was almost always a black *man* that was referred to. Black women were largely invisible ... It seemed that if a black woman was problematised it was more likely to be because she was a woman than because she was black. The reason race issues invoke in white men more anger and fear than do gender issues is because a *male* protagonist is involved. Black men are menacing in the eyes of white men in a way that women, white or black, can never be.

The sexual contract ... gives white and black men some common ground. Black men in my study shared with white men a resistance to the women's movement and a distaste for positive action for sex equality.

Changes in women's cultural expectations may be particularly significant in some Asian communities.

Walby, S, *Gender Transformations*, 1997, London: Routledge, pp 62–63:

There is some evidence of very rapid changes in the gender relations in some of the ethnic minority communities ... [T]he highest rate of economic activity [in the Pakistani/Bangladeshi community] is found among those aged 16–24, 32% [despite full time education for many], falling to 23% for those aged 25–44. Whilst it might be argued that this is simply indicative of a settled pattern of pre-marital employment which ceases or is reduced on marriage and childbirth, it is also open to the interpretation that it reflects rapid change among younger South Asian women towards a more public gender regime ... [It has been argued] that access to education for young South Asian women in Britain is transforming their ability to gain employment and independence. However ... tensions between identities articulated through both Islam, modernity and locality mean that such processes are likely to be contested.

Homeworkers

This category of worker literally includes many relatively privileged workers such as authors and those utilising information technology to work at home. However, the bulk of homeworkers are those, almost exclusively female, engaged in jobs such as sewing, making Christmas crackers, or filling envelopes. This group of workers is often considered to be among the most disadvantaged in the labour market.[49] Problems of definition, such as whether to include all homeworkers of whatever socio-economic status, and practical counting problems, mean that it is exceptionally difficult to determine the number of homeworkers.[50]

While it is clear that many women work at home because of the need to look after young children, that is only one factor among many. 'The existence of the homeworking labour force cannot be understood without reference to women's position in the labour market. For instance, differences in the relative amount and kinds of training received by women and men, the over-concentration of women's work opportunities within a vary narrow range of low paid, often part time, and the differential impact of unemployment are also part of the explanation.'[51] Homeworking highlights in a very direct and physically immediate way the conflicts between home and work which are part of the lives of so many women. 'Husbands, children and elderly relatives are free to interrupt her paid work, and this may account for the preference by families that the woman work at home. Popular images of working at home – flexible working hours, more time to spend with one's children, a reduction of work pressure, a less stressful day – have nothing to do with the experience of homeworking ... [I]t is very far from being a boon to women, for instead of liberating them from or reducing the burden of the 'double day', it intensifies the pressures of both waged work and unpaid domestic labour.'[52]

In addition, research has established a clear racial dimension to the pattern of homeworking.

> **Phizacklea, A and Wolkowitz, C, *Homeworking Women: Gender, Racism and Class at Work*, 1995, London: Sage, pp 28–30, 45–46, 54–55:**
>
> [There is a] contradiction between the ways in which homework is represented according to the dominant ideology, such as 'pin money', 'turning a hobby into an additional source of household income', 'increased autonomy' and so on, and the reality of homework for many ... long hours, punctuated by strict deadlines from employers, demanding family members and the reliance on homework for a regular family income ...
>
> [T]he sexual division of labour [is] the key factor producing a homeworking labour force ... [A] division in the female labour force between those women who put their families first, and those who develop lifetime careers, is now quite central to the organisation of production and reproduction in Western

---

[49] See Allen, S and Wolkowitz, C, *Homeworking: Myths and Realities*, 1987, Basingstoke: Macmillan Education.

[50] *Ibid*, pp 30–52.

[51] *Ibid*, p 74.

[52] *Ibid*, p 134.

societies and simply cannot be seen as the result of women's own choices; the work of reproducing labour still has to be done and no one can point to an influx of men into this kind of work. Although it may be true that no one forces women to do this kind of work in the way that the concept of 'patriarchy' perhaps implies ... women will continue to do it for their families not only because they have internalised these responsibilities but because there is no alternative given the persistence of segregated low paid work and the high price of childcare and domestic services.

[O]ur explanation of the role of homeworking in [Coventry] suggests that within the shared constraints that all women with children experience, there are racialised differences in levels of employment that force families into a situation where inadequate benefits have to be supplemented by low-wage, home-based work. Unlike white women, Asian women in Coventry were not represented at all in the better paid, less onerous clerical homework available in the city.

For the manual workers in the sample the issues which arise out of racialised segregation are not only differences in hourly earnings but also differences in hours, regularity and intensity of work. This is particularly acute in the Coventry clothing industry, a major employer of Asian women, because of the extent to which their predominantly Asian employers are themselves in a 'master-servant' relationship in the subcontracting chain of production. Some Asian men may have found an escape route from unemployment through clothing entrepreneurship, but with meagre start-up capital and with initially no history of clothing manufacture, they have had to start on the bottom rung of the production chain. This is where profit margins are slim, where the ability to meet rush orders on short runs is imperative, and where the most flexible production methods become a necessity: enter homeworking women.

[H]ourly earnings in manual employment are extremely poor, and there is relatively little difference in average hourly earnings between white manual (£1.31) and Asian manual (£1.26) homeworkers. They compare badly with women's earnings in manual employment outside the home, which averaged £3.23 in the West Midlands in 1990; even among part time women manual workers, only 11% earned less than £2.20 per hour ... Within this overall situation, however, the distribution of levels of earnings by ethnic group is distinctive, especially once clerical homework is included ... [H]ourly earnings for Asian homeworkers in the sample are concentrated in a narrow range; two-thirds earn between 75p and £1.50 per hour. In contrast, earnings for white homeworkers are more spread out across the wages span. The proportion of white homeworkers who earn very low wages (below 75p) is slightly higher, but nearly half earn £2 or more.

Discrimination law has little role to play in improving the lot of homeworkers. The national minimum wage will apply, and is potentially by far the most significant legal protection for homeworkers, but there will be problems of enforcement to overcome. The reduction in the hours threshold for the purposes of employment protection legislation is of some benefit. However, these protections are only available to those classed as 'employees' and thus homeworkers may be excluded. This group of workers demonstrates the relative powerlessness of the law in seeking to overcome multiple employment disadvantages.

THE REPRODUCTION OF DISCRIMINATION

Just as we saw in connection with race, discriminatory attitudes and stereotypes are reproduced at the level of individual decision making, often with no real awareness of the disadvantage and discrimination which women suffer in consequence.

Collinson, D, Knights, D and Collinson, M, *Managing to Discriminate,* **1990, London: Routledge, pp 60–61, 67:**

Curran[53] ... found that [selector]s tended to prioritise highly informal acceptability criteria that, in turn, required subjective evaluations which were very susceptible to both intentional and unintentional sex discrimination. The most common required attribute overall was that of 'personal qualities' which covered such intangibles as common sense, confidence and liveliness. Relevant experience and family and domestic circumstances were also revealed to be high priorities of selectors ... 70% of the gender preferences discovered by Curran were for women. These preferences were closely linked to job characteristics such as low pay, poor promotion prospects and female-dominated workforces and supervisory grades. They were also usually based on employers' 'common sense stereotypes' about male breadwinners and female homemakers. This was particularly the case where selectors attributed importance to the criteria of 'family commitments, married status and dependants' ...

[D]omestic responsibilities are viewed *positively* for men because they are believed to indicate stability and motivation, but *negatively* for women since they suggest divided loyalties between home and work. Resting on the assumption that domestic work is primarily women's responsibility, these gender stereotypes were seen to inform the criteria of recruitment acceptability. It is precisely because of such vague, impressionistic and non-job-related criteria of acceptability that conventional gender stereotypes continue to be so prevalent and influential ...

[I]nterviews may be self-reproducing in perpetuating class and sex inequality even where procedures are relatively systematic and standardised ... [W]here judgments are shaped by informal criteria and are heavily circumscribed by selectors' evaluation of the extent to which candidates either contrast, compare or identify with their own experience and perception of themselves, they almost inevitably reproduce the prevailing employment profile.

---

[53] Curran, M, *Stereotypes and Selection: Gender and Family in the Recruitment Process,* 1985, Manchester: EOC.

It is, therefore, appropriate to consider whether increased formalisation of the recruitment process can reduce the scope for such unacknowledged discrimination.[54]

Collinson, D, Knights, D and Collinson, M, *Managing to Discriminate*, 1990, London: Routledge, pp 72–75, 108, 209:

[There is] a strong compatibility between the equal opportunity interests of the [Commission for Racial Equality] and [the Equal Opportunities Commission] and personnel managers' commitment to the 'professional model of selection', for the welfare and technicist traditions in personnel work dovetail with the formalised meritocratic liberalism in which the EOC and CRE have their origins. This is partly why these equal opportunities agencies have concentrated their promotional efforts on reinforcing the commitment of personnel specialists to formalisation. Yet despite this, informality continues to pervade much of the recruitment process. This, in turn, indicates that there might be significant barriers in the form of internal opposition and resistance to the formalisation of selection ...

The danger of formalisation ... is that managers seeking to discriminate informally may be furnished with a formal alibi which is very difficult to penetrate.

[M]anagement cannot be treated as a homogeneous, monolithic and omniscient force ... [It] is characterised by heterogeneity, defensiveness and fragmentation, the politics of which can often militate against the achievement of equal opportunity. Attempts by corporate and local personnel to implement formal, accountable and lawful recruitment practices often failed because of these managerial divisions. In particular, line management resisted the intervention of personnel, resulting in the latter's marginalisation in precisely those areas – that is, recruitment – where it might have expected to be most influential. *Age* and *gender* differentials often reinforced the marginal and subordinate status of personnel managers. This was particularly so at the local level where recruitment was often perceived to be a mundane task ... While line managers tended to be older, with extensive knowledge of the production process ... local personnel specialists involved in routine recruitment were often younger and/or women, which made it difficult to challenge the authority of male line managers ... As the self-appointed organisational breadwinners, line managers typically dismissed formalisation as a bureaucratic encumbrance impeding their ability to recruit and manage production effectively. Formal procedures were seen as unnecessary, time consuming and costly.

[F]ormalisation can only ever be a *necessary* framework for the elimination of sex discrimination in recruitment. It is not, in itself, *sufficient*. Formalisation can facilitate recruitment by rendering practices more structured, visible and accountable. It cannot predetermine in a mechanical and uniform fashion the implementation of consistent recruitment practices at local level. The need to judge and evaluate candidates will always afford selectors a substantial

---

[54] See below, pp 326–30, 557–61.

element of discretion, regardless of the degree of bureaucracy and formality present in the selection process. The interactional nature of the interview, in particular, is not fully amenable to formalisation.

The issues considered in this chapter reveal only too clearly the difficulties faced by legal intervention. The deep structural causes of male and female working patterns and family life patterns inevitably limit the scope and ability of the law to transform the social and economic position of women. For more radical change, a radical shift in attitudes to work may be needed. 'What in the long run has to change is the pattern of men's lives. A 45 hour week, a 48 week year and a 50 year wage earning life cannot be sustained by both sexes. It should be worked by neither.'[55] Even without such dramatic change '[p]rogress towards sex equality may in practice depend more on the spread of unionisation and collective bargaining to industries and jobs in which women are concentrated than on specific legislation designed to deal with inequality between men and women within firms'.[56]

[55] Cockburn, C, *In the Way of Women: Men's Resistance to Sex Equality in Organisations*, 1991, Basingstoke: Macmillan, p 104.

[56] Craig, C, Garnsey, E and Rubery, J, *Payment Structures and Smaller Firms: Women and Employment in Segmented Labour Markets*, 1984, London: Department of Employment, p 99.

CHAPTER 3

THE AIMS OF ANTI-DISCRIMINATION LEGISLATION

INTRODUCTION

We are concerned in this chapter with ideas about what the aims of anti-discrimination both are and should be. There is a distinction between equality of opportunity, which seeks to enable all people to compete equally, in particular, in the employment market, and equality of outcome or results, a notion which pays at least some regard to the distribution of outcomes between the various different groups. A further question is whether the law can and should take account of group rights, as opposed to the more traditional approach which focuses on individual rights. Consideration of these issues also requires analysis of rather broader questions concerning the nature of discrimination and why it is unlawful – at least in certain contexts; why racial groups and women have been isolated as groups most worthy of the benefits of anti-discrimination legislation; and whether the ideas lying behind such legislation are appropriate for extension to other groups. Finally, it is necessary to consider whether the law is a suitable weapon or forum for remedying the disadvantages caused by discrimination, or whether it should be abandoned in favour of a more overtly political stance.[1]

It is first essential to distinguish clearly between what might be perceived as the actual aims of the current legislation – though it is naive to believe that it is possible to isolate one sole aim – and ideas as to the aims which an ideal or model legislative regime might seek.

---

[1] I have consciously avoided too lengthy an excursion into jurisprudential theory, partly because of a desire to include material relevant to both race and gender.

In relation to race, see: Crenshaw, K, 'Race, reform and retrenchment: transformation and legitimation in anti-discrimination law' (1988) 101 Harv L Rev 1331; Delgado, R, 'The ethereal scholar: does critical legal studies have what minorities want?' (1987) 22 Harv CR CL LR 301; Freeman, A, 'Legitimating race discrimination through anti-discrimination law' (1982) 62 Minn LR 96; Freeman, A, 'Racism, rights and the quest for equality of opportunity: a critical legal essay' (1988) 23 Harv CR CL LR 295; Bell, D, 'Racial realism' (1992) 24 Conn LR 363; Caldwell, V, 'Review of *Critical Race Theory: The Key Writings that Formed the Movement*' (1996) 96 Columbia L Rev 1363.

In relation to gender, see: Barnett, H, *Sourcebook on Feminist Jurisprudence*, 1997, London: Cavendish Publishing; Rhode, D, *Justice and Gender*, 1989, Cambridge, Mass: Harvard UP; MacKinnon, C, *Feminism Unmodified*, 1987, Cambridge, Mass: Harvard UP; MacKinnon, C, *Towards a Feminist Theory of the State*, 1989, Cambridge, Mass: Harvard UP; Olsen, F, 'The family and the market: a study of the ideology of legal reform' (1983) 96 Harv L Rev 1497; Littleton, C, 'In search of a feminist jurisprudence' (1987) 10 Harvard Women's LJ 1; Lacey, N, 'Feminist legal theory beyond neutrality' [1995] CLP 1; Bartlett, K, 'Feminist legal methods' (1990) 103 Harv L Rev 829.

Wasserstrom, R, 'Racism, sexism and preferential treatment: an approach to the topics' (1977) 24 UCLA L Rev 581, pp 583–84:

There are three different perspectives within which the topics of racism, sexism and affirmative action can most usefully be examined. The first of these perspectives concentrates on what in fact is true of the culture, on what can be called the social realities. Here the fundamental question concerns the way the culture is: what are its institutions, attitudes and ideologies in respect to matters of race and sex?

The second perspective is concerned with the way things ought to be ... Here the fundamental question concerns ideals: What would the good society ... look like in respect to matters involving race and sex?

The third perspective looks forward to the means by which the ideal may be achieved. Its focus is on the question: what is the best or most appropriate way to move from the existing social realities ... to a closer approximation of the ideal society? ...

[W]hat might be an impermissible way to take race or sex into account in the ideal society, may also be a desirable and appropriate way to take race or sex into account, given the social realities.

Sunstein, C, 'Three civil rights fallacies' (1991) 79 California L Rev 751, p 751:

From the early 1950s until the present day, three propositions have permeated the arguments of lawyers and others interested in advancing the cause of civil rights.

The first proposition is that the target of the civil rights movement is discrimination, which is always or usually a product of irrational hatred, fear, or prejudice. In this view, the purpose of civil rights law is to eliminate these forms of irrationality from the public and private realms.

The second proposition is that the principal function of civil rights law is compensatory. Just as an injured person in a tort action has a right to be made whole, so victims of a history of discrimination (including slavery) are entitled to be put into the place they would have occupied if discrimination had never occurred ...

The third proposition is that the judiciary is the appropriate institution for the making and enforcement of civil rights law. Reliance on the courts, principally though interpretation of the Constitution, has been a distinctive feature of the civil rights movement ...

The issues of discrimination and group inequality can never be understood in isolation from the particular society in which it is alleged to be occurring. Historically, in America black people – a minority – were excluded from economic and political power. In other countries, notably South Africa, minorities have oppressed majorities. The same legal and/or political solutions may not be appropriate for different societies. While Wasserstrom's questions are of universal relevance, it does not follow that the answers will be the same in all countries. For example, it is clear that slavery necessarily leads to a different understanding of the American black experience from that of black people in Britain. At the same time, Sunstein's arguments concerning the role of and faith in the law, while powerful and relevant, are probably too strongly stated to be directly transferable to Britain, especially as the absence of a written constitution and a tradition of judicial activism in support of individual rights means that few would have the faith in the British judiciary's capacity for the creative law making that might on occasion emanate from the United States Supreme Court.

WHAT IS MEANT BY DISCRIMINATION

We need to examine the very concept of discrimination and its relationship with the concept of equality. This involves consideration of the sense, if at all, in which patterns or practices which give rise to group economic disadvantage ought properly to be included within the term 'discrimination', and whether race- or gender-conscious remedies are equally within its boundaries. It will be argued that the concept derives its strength from moral arguments,[2] but that these are necessarily contingent and variable.[3] While the first and most obvious meaning of discrimination emphasises hostility or prejudice, it is important that a wider definition be adopted because, first, the evidence has shown that disadvantageous differential treatment frequently does occur in the absence of prejudice or hostility, and, secondly, because of the difficulty in defining or proving prejudice or hostility.

Sunstein, C, 'Three civil rights fallacies' (1991) 79 California L Rev 751, pp 752–53:

For present purposes, perhaps we can understand 'prejudice' to encompass three sorts of mistakes. The first consists of a belief that members of a group have certain characteristics when in fact they do not. Here the relevant belief has no basis in reality and its irrationality is especially conspicuous. The second consists of a belief that many or most members of a group have certain characteristics when in fact only a few of them do. Here the error is an extremely over-broad generalisation. The third mistake consists in reliance on fairly accurate group-based generalisations when more accurate (and not especially costly) classifying devices are available. Here the members of a group actually have an undesirable characteristic in fairly large numbers ... but it is possible and more rational to use other, more direct devices to filter out

---

2   It has been argued that, as has occurred in America, Britain should pass an Age Discrimination in Employment Act. But, a general prohibition against discrimination on the ground of age, whatever the arguments in favour, surely has less moral force than a prohibition on racial discrimination. See below, pp 129–34.

3   There is a strong argument for not making all discrimination unlawful, even where it is immoral. 'For example, a person who, in choosing a spouse ... excludes members of a particular race solely because of a bias, may be acting within her moral rights even if she is acting immorally.' Alexander, L, 'What makes wrongful discrimination wrong? Biases, preferences, stereotypes and proxies' (1992) 141 Penns UL Rev 149, p 201.

that characteristic. The failure to use those more direct devices reflects a kind of prejudice ...

The theory of civil rights law has often identified 'discrimination' with prejudice, and defined an act as discriminatory when it is caused by prejudice ... For present purposes, I will understand discrimination to include a decision to treat a black person or a woman differently from a white person or a man, regardless of the motivation.

Rutherglen, G, 'Discrimination and its discontents' (1995) 81 Virginia L Rev 117, pp 127–28:

'Discrimination', as it is ordinarily used, refers to a process of noticing or marking a difference, often for evaluative purposes. The two most common synonyms for the verb 'discriminate' are 'distinguish' and 'differentiate', which in turn denote recognising, discerning, appreciating or identifying a difference ... The phrase 'intentional discrimination' is a redundancy according to the ordinary sense of 'discrimination'. All discrimination is intentional in the sense that anyone who discriminates acts on the ground for the discrimination. It is conceptually impossible to discriminate on the ground of race without taking race into account. Conversely, most forms of affirmative action explicitly require consideration of race or sex. They plainly involve discrimination in the ordinary sense: they require race or sex to be taken into account in awarding benefits or advantages. From the perspective of common usage, the typical liberal position is therefore doubly paradoxical: it insists that non-discriminatory actions with 'discriminatory effects' are nevertheless discriminatory just as it maintains that affirmative action plans that plainly take account of race or sex are not ...

[This] is not a conceptual point about what 'discrimination' must mean, for a term can have a technical legal sense in addition to its ordinary sense, but it is a point about how the term is understood by ordinary citizens. And it is the understanding of ordinary citizens that is crucial in a democracy ...

[T]he technical legal usage invites the question whether it is similar enough to ordinary usage to support a different sense of the same term. And it is in these controversial cases, when understanding of the issues is most needed in a democracy, that misunderstanding is most likely. Lawyers are likely to use the term in its technical sense while ordinary citizens understand it in its usual sense. Yet it is the ordinary citizens whose support is necessary for the enactment and enforcement of civil rights law.

We saw from consideration of the statistics and the causes that in many situations the focus is not so much on discrimination as is commonly understood but on processes that lead to social and economic disadvantage – that is, to inequality. The introduction into British and American anti-discrimination law of the concept of indirect discrimination – which is clearly intended in some more or less limited sense to reduce inequality – might be thought to confuse the issue: whether indirect discrimination ought to be called discrimination is one question; whether it is appropriate for the law to seek to provide a remedy for disadvantage is quite another. It seems that the unlawfulness is easier to accept if it is called 'discrimination', for that builds upon the stigma implied by that term, but arguably at a cost of introducing some intellectual sleight-of-hand.

The basis of this strand of the argument is, therefore, that discrimination is wrong because it leads to inequality. But most economic and social inequality is not the result of discrimination in the narrow sense. Why should discrimination leading to racial or gender inequality be a focus of attention? What precisely is wrong – in the moral sense – with discriminating against women and black people? In particular, is it wrong to discriminate against people because in so doing we are harming them, or is it because we are treating them unfairly – not according to their own individual merit or worth? In broad terms, the latter approach utilises a human rights perspective, the former more of a group economic rights perspective. The perspective which is adopted makes a difference, for reliance on the harm principle would imply that only members of historically disadvantaged groups would be able to utilise the law, while the unfairness principle would allow claims by white males and, potentially, by *anyone* who has been unfairly or inappropriately rejected for employment.[4]

Gardner, J, 'Liberals and unlawful discrimination' (1989) 9 OJLS 1, pp 2–8:

For those who subscribe to ... liberalism, it immediately matters whether we classify some social event, circumstance or practice as an injustice or as a harm ... The harm principle operates ... to implicate individual members of society. Citizens may be held personally responsible for those harms which take place under their control, and may be subject to enforced treatment of some kind in the light of their personal blameworthiness. By contrast, the injustice of a distribution is attributed to no one but the society as a whole.

Given the similarities between direct discrimination and more conventional crimes and torts, it is hardly surprising that theorists frequently opt for the ready assumptions that direct discrimination is unlawful because it is harmful ... [T]he fact that otherwise indirectly discriminatory processes may be 'justified' indicates that what is at stake is not a harm, but a redistributive goal which must be balanced against some other interests which citizens are at liberty to pursue ... Unlike the direct discriminator, it appears that the indirect discriminator is not marked off as a wrongdoer, but is implicated in our collective responsibility for social injustices ...

It is not the large *amount* of stigmatisation and denied opportunity which brings discrimination within the harm principle, but the *quality* of the stigmatisation and rejection. We respond, in our classification of harms, to the cultural context of our subject matter. Taking this line, there seem to be two

---

4   The unfair dismissal provisions already provide such a remedy for those who have been *dismissed from* employment, at least after two years' continuous employment, a period soon to be reduced to one year. A universal right not to be unfairly rejected for a job would involve very substantial control over what have traditionally been regarded as private decisions.

broad ways in which cultural context might allow intentional acts of discrimination to count as harms.

The first of these points to a strong relationship between stigma and denied opportunity on the one side, and their historical significance as instruments of wholesale disenfranchisement and disadvantage on the other. We might say that, in the classification of ethnic groups as unworthy, or women as inferior, a set of momentous and enduring collective disadvantages has been inflicted ... and that our willingness to treat continuing disparate treatment as a harm is a product of its close historical significance with distributional injustice ...

The other way of isolating a harm involves pointing out a rather weaker relationship between stigma, denial of opportunities and the historical facts of disadvantage. In this weaker connection, we have developed an historically informed view that race- and gender-dependent decisions are *unfair*, and this claimed *unfairness* is sufficient to turn stigmatisation and denial of opportunities into harms of the required sort ...

If we trace a strong link between the history of disadvantage and our present view that intentional discrimination is harmful, we can really only include discrimination which compounds that disadvantage among the activities which we count as harmful. If we make the strong connection, then the only sort of discrimination which falls within the harm principle is discrimination against certain sorts of people – primarily blacks and women. It would then be difficult to see the exclusion of a white male from some sort of opportunity as a relevant 'harm' ... If, on the other hand, we trace the rather weaker link between disadvantage and harm, through the mediating principle of 'unfairness', then we perceive the whole business of taking race and gender into account as a harm ...

Once the 'unfairness' takes over from the harm in this way, we risk identifying the wrongness of sexual subjugation or slavery with the failure of those invidious and enduring historical traditions to be perfectly meritocratic, and we start, illiberally, to treat all non-meritocratic preferences as being on all fours with slavery. So in the liberal tradition, the harmful unfairness must ... be narrowly tied to the degradation of those whose race or gender have been devalued, and the cultural meanings which race and gender have, on that account, assumed for us ...

The importance of Gardner's view is that he shows how the harm principle may be the prime justification for anti-discrimination legislation even for those who adopt a liberal world view based on individual human rights. For those of a more radical persuasion, who are sceptical of the rights-based approach to law, the harm analysis takes on a more overtly political tinge.

Lacey, N, 'From individual to group', in Hepple, B and Szyszczak, E (eds), *Discrimination: The Limits of Law*, 1992, London: Mansell, p 104:

[A]nti-discrimination legislation ... picks out certain features or categories only in order to prohibit their operating as reasons for certain kinds of decisions. This represents the liberal notion that all have *the same right* not to be discriminated against. It opens up the possibility of white male legal actions which exploit the vulnerability of any legal recognition of race or gender difference ... It can do so precisely because the legislation is framed in terms of difference rather than disadvantage: it constructs the problem to be tackled as race and sex discrimination, rather than as discrimination against and disadvantage of women and certain ethnic groups. Quite apart from the fact that this seriously misrepresents the social problems to which the legislation purports to respond, it means that any kind of protective measure addressing disadvantage is suspect. In particular, it rules out affirmative action, even of a moderate kind, as objectionable in principle ...

Wasserstrom, R, 'Racism, sexism and preferential treatment: an approach to the topics' (1977) 24 UCLA L Rev 581, pp 591–93:

[R]acism and sexism consist in taking race and sex into account in a certain way, in the context of a specific set of institutional arrangements and a specific ideology which together create and maintain a *system* of unjust institutions and unwarranted beliefs and attitudes ...

The primary evil of the various schemes of racial segregation against blacks that the courts were ... called upon to assess was not that such schemes were a capricious and irrational way of allocating public benefits and burdens ... The primary evil of such schemes was instead that they designedly and effectively marked off all black persons as degraded, dirty, less than fully developed persons who were unfit for full membership in the political, social and moral community ...

Sunstein, C, 'Three civil rights fallacies' (1991) 79 California L Rev 751, pp 770–71:

[O]ne who claims discrimination does not seek the prevention of certain irrational acts ... but asks instead for the elimination, in places large and small, of something like a caste system. Instead, a large mistake of civil rights policy has been to treat the issue as one of discrimination at all, since the term tends to connote irrational differentiation – an unacceptable practice to be sure, but not an appropriate description of the problem at hand, which is second-class citizenship ... A systemic disadvantage is one that operates along standard and predictable lines, in multiple important spheres of life, and that applies in realms like education, freedom from private and public violence, wealth, political representation, and political influence, all of which go to basic participation as a citizen in a democratic society ... In the areas of race and sex discrimination, and of disability as well, the problem is precisely this sort of systemic disadvantage ...

Wasserstrom, R, 'Racism, sexism and preferential treatment: an approach to the topics' (1977) 24 UCLA L Rev 581, pp 617–18:

The racial quotas and practices of racial exclusion that were an integral part of the fabric of our culture ... were pernicious. They were a grievous wrong and it was and is important that all morally concerned individuals work for their eradication from our social universe. The racial quotas which are a part of contemporary affirmative action programmes are, I think, commendable and right. [But even if they are wrong] they are wrong for reasons very different from those which made quotas against blacks wrong ... [They] were wrong both because of the direct consequences of these programmes on the individuals most affected and because the system of racial and sexual superiority of which they were part was an immoral one in that it severely and without any adequate justification restricted the capacities, autonomy and happiness of those who were members of the less favoured categories.[5]

Whatever may be wrong with today's affirmative action programmes and quota systems, it should be clear that the evil, if any, is not the same. Racial and sexual minorities do not constitute the dominant social group. Nor is the conception of who is a fully developed member of the moral and social community one of an individual who is either female or black. Quotas which prefer women or blacks do not add to the already relatively overabundant supply of resources and opportunities at the disposal of white males. If racial quotas are to be condemned or if affirmative action programmes are to be abandoned, it should be because they will not work well to achieve the desired result. It is not because they seek either to perpetuate an unjust society or to realise a corrupt ideal ...

Many of these writers are concerned to demonstrate that affirmative action – however defined – designed to benefit women and black people should not be judged by the same standards as direct discrimination *against* women and black people. The point is perhaps clearest when the issue of disability is considered. It is common sense that many disabled people will not be able to perform a job until some specific accommodation is made to their needs. The Disability Discrimination Act 1995 recognises this reality both by mandating employers to make such reasonable accommodation and by preventing a non-disabled person from claiming discrimination in respect of such accommodation.[6] There is no logical reason why such an approach could not have been taken in respect of race and gender. It is, however, true that the approach taken in respect of disability marries more easily to an individual rights focus, because of the great variety of disabilities of which the law must take account, whereas accommodation for black people and women would of necessity focus more on the needs of the group as a whole.

The next question is whether the focus on harm can also be used to explain why indirect discrimination is wrong. The task is harder here: for one thing, an employer may be liable for indirect discrimination without knowledge of the fact that such discrimination is occurring; for another, the inequality on which a claim of indirect discrimination is based may be the result of factors over which the individual employer or employers in general have no immediate control.

Gardner, J, 'Liberals and unlawful discrimination' (1989) 9 OJLS 1, pp 10–11, 18–20:

Waldron [has argued that] '[I]n the case of indirect discrimination, the wrongness of the employers' actions is nothing more than that they are not

---

5   See, also, *op cit*, Alexander, fn 3, pp 162–63.
6   See below, Chapter 16.

doing their bit to promote racial or sexual equality' ... [T]he duty not to discriminate indirectly seems to be imposed on citizens in a way that is partly arbitrary from the point of view of relative advantage. Employers, in other words, seem to be required by the State to do more than that which is entailed by their ordinary share of collective responsibility for disadvantage ...

At least two factors about the employment relationship give it a special institutional role in our culture. First, whether or not I am employed, and in what capacity, plays in our culture an absolutely decisive role in the relative advantages which I may enjoy throughout my life; secondly, the formation and preservation of the employment relationship involves a peculiarly large amount of control for one of the parties ... The employer finds himself in a special privileged position in the distributive mechanics of society, which makes him, for every individual employee or applicant, every bit as strong and as peremptory a distributive agency as the State itself ... When the employer's social significance is realised, requiring him not to discriminate indirectly is merely a proper response to current patterns of advantage and disadvantage, coupled with an understanding of the distribution of effective social power ...

Raz suggests that the harm principle does indeed set the boundaries of the use of State power, but that the harm principle is a wide harm principle: it allows governments 'to use coercion both in order to stop people from actions which would diminish people's autonomy and in order to take actions which are required to improve people's options and opportunities' ... So understood, distributive justice is not a principle which competes with the harm principle, but is rather a concomitant of it. 'Sometimes failing to improve the situation of another is harming him' ... [A]n employer who fails to provide opportunities to a woman, because his criterion of selection disadvantages women, harms her in the sense required by the wide harm principle – he fails to enhance her opportunities in the way that respect for her autonomous agency requires. We are all involved in a participative enterprise of protecting autonomy, an enterprise which carries with it obligations of mutual life-enhancement ...

For Raz, we are pursuing a culture in which the value of personal autonomy is understood to be the core value. Since the value of personal autonomy requires a culture of toleration and competitive pluralism, one of the reasons for precluding certain institutional structures in our society is that they fail to contribute to the ideals of toleration and competitive pluralism.

This argument is both complex and controversial.[7] It argues that even indirect discrimination is wrong, primarily because it is harmful rather than because it is unfair or anti-meritocratic – such employment practices might lead to inefficiencies but that hardly represents the gist of their undesirable social effects. It treats employment as more than a relationship between private parties – and employment law as having a deeper function than merely

---

[7] It is not my purpose to explore all the details of the controversy. See Morris, A, 'On the normative foundations of indirect discrimination law: understanding the competing models of discrimination law as Aristotelian forms of justice' (1995) 15 OJLS 199, and the reply by Gardner, J, 'Discrimination as injustice' (1996) 16 OJLS 353.

holding the fort between such parties. Employment becomes a semi-public state, the absence of which in a real sense produces harm, especially if the effects on the group are such that the harmful consequences are reproduced extensively or from generation to generation. Thus the harm is still linked with membership of and identity in a particular group. The harm, however, is contingent on the particular circumstances of the group against which the bias is manifest. It is impossible to understand discrimination without some grasp of the history of the group's experience under the particular regime at issue.

This raises a number of subsidiary questions. First, what is characteristic about the experiences of women and black people which have resulted in their being selected for specially favourable legislation? Secondly, are their experiences sufficiently similar as to warrant a fundamentally identical legislative approach? Thirdly, how does this approach respond to the fact that inequalities *between* women and between and within minority ethnic groups are increasing; is it still plausible to treat women as one single group and so entitled to benefit from anti-discrimination legislation? Fourthly, does this socio-historical approach apply equally to other groups which claim the right to have anti-discrimination legislation extended to them?

Lacey, N, 'From individual to group', in Hepple, B and Szyszczak, E (eds), *Discrimination: The Limits of Law*, 1992, London: Mansell, pp 109–12:

[I]t is implicit in the feminist project that some features of ... subordination are common to all women in a particular society, at least at some level – although the forms and nature of women's oppression are recognised to be historically and culturally specific ... [But] not all women's oppression, even in one society, is just the same. Since the subordination experienced by Afro-Caribbean women, Asian women, working class women, lesbian women, women who are single mothers and so on is qualitatively different, the feminist claim must be that gender is always *one factor*, and a fundamentally important one, in constituting the social position and experience of all women and men, but it is overlaid by many other factors, most notably in our society by race and class ...[8]

---

[8]   Posner's response to this kind of reasoning claims that because of the 'heterogeneity of women as an economic class and their interdependence with men, laws aimed at combating sex discrimination are more likely to benefit particular groups of women at the expense of other groups rather than women as a whole. And to the extent that the overall effect of the law is to reduce aggregate social welfare because of the allocative and administrative costs of the law, women as a group are hurt along with men. Sex discrimination has long been on the decline, for reasons unrelated to law, and this makes it all the more likely that the principal effect of public intervention may have been to make women as a group worse off by reducing the efficiency of the economy ...'. Posner, R, 'An economic analysis of sex discrimination laws' (1989) 56 Chicago ULR 1311, pp 1334–35. His argument is that sex discrimination laws are economically inefficient and are unnecessary as the operation of the free market is itself causing discrimination to decline. Even if he is correct on the economics, which is highly controversial, he fails, rather typically of the law and economics school, to give weight to other objectives of law such as justice and the vindication of rights. The only non-economic gain which is mentioned in the article is a gain in self-esteem which law might induce, thus propelling more women into the marketplace. Posner's underlying position seems to be that the sum total of human happiness will not be advanced [cont]

As social institutions, sexism and racism clearly exhibit certain important differences. The centrality of naturalistic and biologistic arguments in constituting and maintaining racism and sexism, at least in the UK, is arguably different; membership of particular racial groups is significantly correlated with social class and poverty, as conventionally understood, in a way which is not so obviously true of gender; the experience of racial oppression is arguably more diverse than that of sexism given the variety of stereotypes about different racial groups ...

There are also similarities between racism and sexism. Both are strongly associated with a variety of forms of political and social disadvantage ... and both rely to a significant extent on stereotyped views about what is normal to, appropriate for or to be expected of members of that group simply by virtue of that membership. Perhaps most importantly, both have been recognised as social institutions – parts of the structure and patterning of social relations – rather than as merely cumulations of individual prejudices, actions and decisions ...

THE OBJECTIVES OF LEGAL INTERVENTION

We might legitimately reach the conclusion that discrimination is harmful and that the history of the oppression or disadvantage experienced by black people and women provides sufficient justification for legal intervention. The next question which must be faced is what should be the overall aim of such intervention. Here, Wasserstrom provides some challenging ideas.

Wasserstrom, R, 'Racism, sexism and preferential treatment: an approach to the topics' (1977) 24 UCLA L Rev 581, pp 585–89, 603–14:

It is even clearer in the case of sex than in the case of race that one's sexual identity is a centrally important, crucially relevant category within our culture. I think, in fact, that it is more important and more fundamental than one's race ...

But to be female, as opposed to being black, is not to be conceived of as simply a creature of less worth. That is one important thing that differentiates sexism from racism: the ideology of sex, as opposed to the ideology of race, is a good deal more complex and confusing. Women are both put on a pedestal and deemed not fully developed persons ... Because the sexual ideology is complex, confusing and variable, it does not unambiguously proclaim the lesser value attached to being female ... nor does it unambiguously correspond to the existing social realities. For these, among other reasons, sexism could plausibly

---

8   [cont] if more women work. It is curious that as economic beings we are entitled and indeed virtually required by the theory to act in accordance with individual self-interest, but when it comes to the social consequences of legal intervention, no account is apparently taken of individual rights and liberties. See, further, Epstein, R, *Forbidden Grounds: The Case against Employment Discrimination Laws*, 1992, Cambridge, Mass: Harvard UP.

be regarded as a deeper phenomenon than racism. It is more deeply embedded in the culture and thus less visible. Being harder to detect, it is harder to eradicate. Moreover, it is less unequivocally regarded as unjust and unjustifiable ...

What would the good or just society make of race or sex, and to what degree, if at all, would racist and sexist distinctions even be taken into account? Indeed, it could plausibly be argued that we could not have an adequate idea of whether a society was racist or sexist unless we had some idea of what a thoroughly non-racist or non-sexist society would look like ...

[O]ne picture of a non-racist society is that which is captured by what I call the assimilationist model. A non-racist society would be one in which the race of an individual would be the functional equivalent of the eye colour of individuals in our society today ... The assimilationist ideal is not, however, the only possible, plausible ideal. There are two others that are closely related, but distinguishable. One is the ideal of diversity; the other, the ideal of tolerance. Both can be understood by considering how religion, rather than eye colour, tends to be thought about in our culture. According to the ideal of diversity, heterodoxy in respect to religious belief and practice is regarded as a positive good. In this view there would be a loss – it would be a worse society – were everyone to be a member of the same religion. According to the other view, the ideal of tolerance, heterodoxy with respect to religious belief and practice would be seen more as a necessary, lesser evil. In this view there is nothing intrinsically better about diversity in respect to religion, but the evils of achieving anything like homogeneity far outweigh the possible benefits ...

My view is that the assimilationist ideal may be just as good and just as important an ideal in respect to sex as it is in respect to race. But many persons think there are good reasons why an assimilationist society in respect to sex would not be desirable ... [T]o make the assimilationist ideal a reality in respect to sex would involve more profound and fundamental revisions of our institutions and our attitudes than would be the case in respect to race ... [I]n that event, for example, marriage, all sex-role differentiation, and any kind of sexually exclusive preference would be treated either as anomalous or as statistically fortuitous.

It may be that in respect to sex (and, conceivably, even in respect to race) something more like the ideals in respect to religion – pluralistic ideals founded on diversity or tolerance – is the right one. But the problem then ... is to specify with a good deal of precision and care what that ideal really comes to. Which legal, institutions and personal differentiations are permissible and which are not? Which attitudes and beliefs concerning sexual identification and difference are properly introduced and maintained and which are not? Part, but by no means all, of the attraction of the assimilationist ideal is its clarity and simplicity ...

Race as a naturally occurring characteristic is also a socially irrelevant category. There do not in fact appear to be any characteristics that are part of this natural concept of race and that are in any plausible way even relevant to the appropriate distribution of any political, institutional or interpersonal concerns in the good society. Because in this sense race is like eye colour, there is no plausible case to be made on this ground against the assimilationist ideal ... [But] it may be ... that one could argue that a form of the pluralist ideal ought to be preserved in respect of race, in the socially created sense, for reasons similar to those that might be offered in support of the desirability of some version of the pluralist ideal in respect to religion ...

It is sex-role differentiation, not gender *per se*, that makes men and women as different as they are from each other, and it is sex-role differences which are invoked to justify most sexual differentiation ... Even though there are biological differences between men and women in nature, this fact does not determine the question of what the good society can and should make of these differences ... [T]here appear to be very few, if any, respects in which the ineradicable, naturally occurring differences between males and females *must* be taken into account ... [T]he only fact that seems required to be taken into account is the fact that reproduction of the human species requires that the foetus develop *in utero* for a period of months ...

I think it important to see ... that the case against the assimilationist ideal ... must rest on arguments concerned to show why some other ideal would be preferable; it cannot plausibly rest on the claim that it is either necessary or inevitable ... If it is true, as I think it is, that the sex-role differentiated societies we have had so far have tended to concentrate power in the hands of males, have developed institutions and ideologies which have perpetuated that concentration and have restricted and prevented women from living the kinds of lives that persons ought to be able to live for themselves, then this says far more about what may be wrong with any non-assimilationist ideal than does the conservative premise say about what may be right about my non-assimilationist ideal ...

Equality of opportunity and equality of outcome

The concepts of discrimination and disadvantage are intimately linked with concepts of equality. Equality of opportunity implies that all people should be treated as individuals in the sense of having the opportunity to compete on equal terms for the goods which society has to offer. The problem, though, is that reliance on equal opportunity alone provides no guarantee that, in practice, those goods will not remain disproportionately in the hands of white males. Equality of outcome implies an equitable division of the economic cake between different groups in society.

Lacey, N, 'Legislation against sex discrimination: questions from a feminist perspective' (1986) 14 JLS 411, pp 413–17:

[T]he limitations of formal equality as a feminist goal are now widely recognised: it has little bite in view of the disadvantages which women suffer in private areas such as family life, untouched by the sex discrimination legislation. No concept of discrimination which is based exclusively on formal equality can take proper account of aspects of women's different position resulting from prior discrimination and disadvantage in spheres which fall outside the relatively limited ambit of the legislation ... Given the history and structure of sex discrimination, merely ruling out sex as a reason for action in certain areas promises little progress in terms of dismantling women's disadvantage. It may even be counterproductive in ruling out sex as remedially relevant reason in the context, for example, of affirmative action programmes ...

[T]he discourse of equality of opportunity presupposes a world inhabited by autonomous individuals making choices. These choices may differ along gender lines, resulting in a very different distribution of jobs or other goods as between women and men ... An equal opportunity principle is inadequate to criticise and transform a world in which the distribution of goods is structured along gender lines ... Differential treatment and unequal impact, even within the ambit of *prima facie* discrimination, may be legitimated subconsciously by Industrial Tribunal[9] members who believe that women and men just do typically make different choices. Different finishing points are not seen as problematic. In this way, the very stereotypes which the legislation is presumably meant to undermine inevitably and invisibly affect the tribunal's reading of legal issues ... [By] conceptualising the problem as *sex discrimination* rather than *discrimination against women*, the legislation renders invisible the real social problem and deflects away a social ideal or goal which would identify and address it ...

[T]he comparative approach ... presupposes (yet suppresses) the idea of a norm with which the scrutinised behaviour is compared. In the case of claims brought by women, that norm is the treatment usually accorded to men: thus, in so far as the sex discrimination legislation prescribes equality, it is *equality in terms of a norm set by and for men* – the logic of discrimination allows no challenge to *general* practices in any area. By definition, sex discrimination cases do not provide a jumping off point for criticism of general social practices or real debate about what kind of equality is worth having, and with whom. At best, the legislation promises some dismantling of practices restrictive of access to goods and resources which present (that is, male-dominated) culture has determined as valuable. It may go some way towards reducing the overt significance of sex in the allocation of certain goods, but it has no cutting edge against the significance of gender in setting them up as goods in the first place.

Ward, T, 'Beyond sex equality: the limits of sex equality in the new Europe', in Hervey, T and O'Keeffe, D (eds), *Sex Equality Law in the European Union*, 1996, Chichester: John Wiley, pp 370, 375:

The pervasive argument in sex equality, until recent years at least, has been that of sameness and difference ... [This approach] gives women just two choices; they can either aspire to be the same as men, and to enjoy the same rights, or they can campaign to have their difference from men recognised in

---

[9] Under the Employment Rights (Dispute Resolution) Act 1998, s 1(1), Industrial Tribunals are re-named Employment Tribunals.

law.[10] Either way, women are compared with a male norm, and by presenting women with these two choices, and these two choices only, the debate immediately establish parameters.

Any ... rights-based approach tends to be founded on a 'claim to similarity'. A collateral argument here is that the formal enactment of rights for women ... will not in reality address the myriad of substantive inequalities that women face. In other words, a liberal rights-based approach ... actually serves to entrench the real inequalities that women encounter, and does more harm in practice, than good. Thus, as MacKinnon concludes, the phrase 'sex equality law' contains three particular preconceptions. First, it assumes a particular determination of sex as denoting difference. Second, it then presumes that any 'inequalities' must be the result of 'mistakes' in addressing difference. Third, 'law' explicitly assumes that the problem is something that can somehow be resolved by law ...

Lacey, N, 'From individual to group', in Hepple, B and Szyszczak, E (eds), *Discrimination: The Limits of Law*, 1992, London: Mansell, pp 103–04, 106–07:

[T]he standard or treatment of the outcome which represents the point of comparison and hence the Acts' conception of what is normal or legitimate is necessarily a norm set by (and generally by) men. This poses particular problems in areas such as pregnancy ... [T]he legislation ... cannot provide any platform for litigants to criticise the formulation of the 'normal' standard: they must content themselves with arguing for assimilation to it. Complaints about formal difference rather than substantive critique is the name of the game ...

Feminists have criticised this ahistorical, pre-social view of human nature which underlies liberal rights theory and legal individualism, and have pointed out the ways in which the need to frame legal arguments in terms of individual claims systematically obstructs the project of revealing and dismantling structures and institutions which disadvantage women. These arguments have developed into a more general critique of the discourse of rights, which are seen as not only inherently individualistic, but also competitive and hence anti-socialistic. They are also seen as tied in with the notion of formal equality – hence the need to ascribe equal rights to all and the inevitable obscuring of real social problems and disadvantages. In a world in which white, male and middle class people both have more effective access to legal forums and meet a more sympathetic response when they get there, the ascription of formally equal rights will in effect entrench the competitively asserted rights of these privileged people. Far from dismantling the disadvantage of women, people from ethnic minorities and socio-economically underprivileged groups, it may even have the opposite effect ...

---

[10] 'The negative, narrow and exclusive features of the concept of discrimination, no doubt, made it an effective weapon against segregation. They have made it much less effective, if not entirely ineffective, in breaking down barriers to equality which are now both less obvious and more pervasive.' Rutherglen, G, 'Discrimination and its discontents' (1995) 81 Virginia L Rev 117, p 130.

Thus equality of opportunity is primarily concerned with formal equality under the law rather than with substantive or material equality. It may have no regard to the fact that women or black people may have difficulty in obtaining the relevant qualifications or experience. The equality of opportunity approach is based upon the notion of individual merit as supposedly the chief criterion for success in the labour market and in society as a whole. Certainly, the availability of the defence of 'justification' to a claim of indirect discrimination implies both that merit is an acceptable – and perhaps almost mandatory – basis for hiring and that employers are in a position to be able accurately to assess the merit of the potential employees. These assumptions fly in the face of evidence as to the unprincipled and unspoken criteria which are in fact utilised in making such decisions. In fact, one strand of arguing for equal opportunities is to argue for greater objectivity and clarity in such decision making to ensure that such decisions really are made on merit. Yet even apparently objective criteria, such as seniority and educational qualifications, may be only weakly correlated with successful job performance; they are utilised not because they predict success or reward merit but because they are cheap, convenient, and acceptable by long standing tradition. While persons may have built up or relied upon reasonable expectations concerning performance and admission criteria which they anticipate will be applied to them, and which have led to investment in human capital, it is certainly not obvious that these claims of desert are any stronger or more compelling than competing claims based upon the needs of or advantages to women or blacks.

O'Donovan, K and Szyszczak, E, *Equality and Sex Discrimination Law,* **1988, Oxford: Blackwells, pp 3–4:**

In liberal discourse the notion of equality of opportunity ... is employed to deal with perceived inequalities. Competition on merit is what equal opportunity is all about. To overcome the question of the relationship between need and merit liberal writers advocate minimal State provision for need, after which all compete on merit. Thus intervention because of need or inequality is a justification for State action ... Thereafter the role of the State is to hold the ring for free competition.

Wasserstrom, R, 'Racism, sexism and preferential treatment: an approach to the topics' (1977) 24 UCLA L Rev 581, pp 619–20:

Affirmative action programmes almost always make sex or race a relevant condition, not a conclusive one. As such, they function the way all other classificatory schemes do. The defect, if there is one, is generic, and not peculiar to programmes such as these. Part of what is wrong with even talking about qualifications and merit is that the argument derives some of its force from the erroneous notion that we would have a meritocracy were it not for affirmative action ...

To be at all persuasive, the argument must be that those who are the most qualified deserve to receive the benefits ... because they are the most qualified

... But why do the most qualified deserve anything? ... Most of what are regarded as the decisive qualifications for higher education have a great deal to do with things over which the individual has neither control nor responsibility: such things as home environment, socio-economic class of parents, and of course the quality of the primary and secondary schools attended. Since individuals do not deserve having had any of these things vis à vis other individuals, they do not, for the most part, deserve their qualifications. And since they do not deserve their abilities they do not in any strong sense deserve to be admitted because of their abilities ...

Townshend-Smith, R, *Sex Discrimination in Employment: Law, Practice and Policy,* **1989, London: Sweet & Maxwell, pp 25–26:**

The extent to which one is personally responsible for job performance is ... problematic. Many required abilities are innate; others are learned in a culture where there is no guarantee of equal opportunities to engage in such learning.

Success at work may be measured by factors to which men and women have unequal access. Ability to work long hours is a clear example, so is the ability to remain for a very long period with the same employer. Most difficult is the manifestation of characteristics such as aggression or dynamism which may be considered, rightly or wrongly, to be associated with being male. If women are conditioned to be submissive and to consider other people, how can they later be said to deserve less at work for failure to possess [other] characteristics?

[I]t is important to see how deep-rooted is the notion of merit in our society, and that merit has historically been determined in [white] male terms. The danger is that the law will accept male definitions of what is meritorious in employment, and that this will not correspond with the desires or best interests of many or most women.

There is little doubt that, in the narrow sense so far considered, equality of opportunity has severe limitations as a remoulder of society. However, it does have very great importance as a legal slogan or political rallying cry which arguably should not be entirely jettisoned. But some have contended that a thoroughgoing conception of equality of opportunity itself produces many of the advantages of an approach based on equality of results, as long as it is adequately concerned to ensure that opportunities truly are equal.

O'Donovan, K and Szyszczak, E, *Equality and Sex Discrimination Law,* **1988, Oxford: Blackwells, pp 4–5:**

Other writers contrast equality of opportunity with equality of outcome. For example, socialist feminists argue that equal opportunity is procedural and formal whereas equality of outcome is substantive. Equal opportunity as a concept is criticised for being concerned merely to ensure that the rules of entry into competition are the same for all. Equality of outcome as a concept looks to the results of competition and then raises questions about the rules of entry ...

[I]n discussions of anti-discrimination legislation it is often assumed that once barriers to competition are removed, women, who have historically been discriminated against, will show their prowess and compete equally. But this conception of equality is limited, for it abstracts persons from their unequal situations and puts them in a competition in which their prior inequality and its effects are ignored ... Williams explains [that] equal opportunity 'requires not merely that there should be no exclusion from access on grounds other than those appropriate or rational for the good in question, but that the grounds considered appropriate for the good should themselves be such that people from all sections of society have an equal chance of satisfying them'.

Equality of opportunity in its full sense requires a fair, rational and appropriate competition for goods and benefits. This means that competitors must have an equal starting point, where possible. It goes further than lowering barriers to education, services and the labour market. For women to compete equally with men, both sexes must start equally.

Lacey, N, 'Legislation against sex discrimination: questions from a feminist perspective' (1986) 14 JLS 411, p 414:

Equality of opportunity represents only one among many of the more programmatic conceptions of equality described and defended in modern political theory. Equality of welfare, results, resources and consideration of interests, to name but a few, have been energetically and ably defended. Any of these conceptions *might* be easier to extend beyond a liberal world-view or more susceptible of being given a distinctively feminist content than is equality of opportunity ... [T]he idea [of equality of opportunity] provided a crucially important campaigning slogan for the legislation, but ... by the same token, it was not discussed or analysed in any open or rigorous way. Had it been, it seems likely that both its ambiguity and its potentially radical implications would have come to the surface and it would have lost its capacity to unite diverse political groups. How many liberal supporters of the current legislation, for example, would have been content to reflect on the implications of a thorough-going commitment to equality of opportunity in terms of socialisation of childrearing or even genetic engineering? Thus, we should not expect to find that the legislation conforms to a unitary or coherent ideal of equality. We should rather recognise equality of opportunity as a crucial piece of political rhetoric which also provides guiding and limiting principles ...

Much of the criticism of the approach based on equality of opportunity focuses on the nature of the rights which are protected – or the rights which are excluded – under a doctrine of equality of opportunity. But even a more thorough and realistic approach designed to foster *genuine* equality of opportunity may founder on the problem of remedies. For the *legal* model of equality of opportunity is closely bound up with the view that the law's function is to compensate the victims of wrongdoing. This may have a number of unfortunate consequences. First, the political association of anti-discrimination law with wrongdoing is so strong that defendants resist all efforts to have them classified in this way, and this may hinder the promotion of out-of-court settlements with the potential to improve the position of disadvantaged groups. Secondly, the levels of compensation awarded are unlikely in most cases to be sufficient to act as a deterrent against repetition of such behaviour.[11] Thirdly, in a variation of the previous point, the assumption is that there is no entitlement to a remedy *unless* the claimant can prove that measurable financial loss has been suffered.

Sunstein, C, 'Three civil rights fallacies' (1991) 79 California L Rev 751, pp 762–64:

In important respects ... the model of compensatory justice inadequately captures the nature of the problem and is therefore a recipe for confusion ... For example, the requirement of 'discriminatory intent' might well be understood as an effort to adhere to compensatory principles ... The question, thus conceived, is whether an identifiable actor has harmed an identifiable person in an identifiable way. To abandon the touchstone of intent would lead courts far from the compensatory model. It would lead courts to require redress of social wrongs committed by third parties in the distant past, which would involve conspicuous social re-ordering and harms to innocent persons, rather than a restoration of some well defined *status quo ante* ... In this more expansive view, the redress of harms other than those created by the particular practice in question would be the goal of the equality principle. The notion of compensation would remain, but it would require public and private employers to ensure that the distribution of benefits and burdens between blacks and whites would be roughly what it would have been without the legacy of discrimination.

The general problem is that the compensatory model, in any form, is based on notions of causation, injury and restoration to the status quo ante that are well adapted to the tort or contract setting, but singularly ill-suited to the problem of discrimination ...

Many people have concluded that equality of opportunity is inadequate as a fundamental philosophy for anti-discrimination legislation. But there are also problems with the more radical approach based on equality of outcome.[12]

---

[11] The absence of creative remedies may not flow as a logically necessary consequence of an equality of opportunity frame of reference, although it certainly seems to have done so in the British context. In the American context, however, where, again, equality of opportunity has been the dominant rhetoric, class actions and patterns and practice suits have led in some instances to very substantial awards of compensation. See below, p 535.

[12] It is sometimes argued that the philosophy of direct discrimination is equality of opportunity, while the philosophy of indirect discrimination is equality of results. For many reasons, this is too radical a view of the way indirect discrimination law operates. First, the way the group comparison must be made focuses only on the particular employer rather than the wider society. Secondly, the defence of justification means that equality of result may sometimes be trumped by other values, including the defendant employer's own economic well being. Thirdly, the remedial framework for indirect discrimination remains firmly wedded to an individualistic equality of opportunity model. These points will be developed further in Chapter 9; the aim of this chapter is to consider not whether current legislation does aim at equality of results, but at whether ideal legislation should do so.

O'Donovan, K and Szyszczak, E, *Equality and Sex Discrimination Law,* **1988, Oxford: Blackwells, p 6:**

Another answer to perceived limitations of equal opportunity is to propose equality of outcome or results ... It is evident that the creation of outcome equality would require a major social revolution ... Whilst liberal political theory advocates equality of opportunity in an unspecified way, equality of outcome is characteristic of radical and socialist society. Liberals object that 'equality of outcomes could be maintained only at a substantial cost to liberty'. The argument is that maintenance of strict equality would require coercive interference to maintain an egalitarian distribution pattern ...

Recognition of differences

To move to an approach based fairly and squarely on equality of results is theoretically and practically problematic, as taken literally it would appear to require equality of distribution between black and white, male and female, over a whole range of economic goods. Given that redistribution of wealth is conceptually intertwined with the relief of poverty, it is entirely unclear why certain victims of poverty and not others should be entitled to relief under the doctrine. Far more appropriate is an approach based on pluralistic political philosophies, which argues that equality can only be attained if appropriate recognition is given to the factors which render formal equality inadequate or ineffective.

O'Donovan, K and Szyszczak, E, *Equality and Sex Discrimination Law,* **1988, Oxford: Blackwells, pp 7–9:**

The question of whether equality is viewed as a competition between men and women starting from the same point, or as a pluralistic recognition of different qualities and needs, is fundamental to theories of sex equality ... If the model for whom the competition ... is designed is male then women may find it difficult to fit ... Economic and social institutions, willing to admit women under a policy of equality, will not necessarily adapt to accommodate them.

If treatment as an equal implies respect for others, avoidance of stereotypes and viewing the world from another's point of view, then pluralism goes further than equal treatment. For it allows for differences in persons, their situations, their needs ... In this guise equality does not mean giving or receiving the same treatment, but rather giving or receiving equal concern ... Pluralism goes further than equal treatment because it allows the dissimilarities between the sexes to enter in. A focus on inequality puts differential treatment to the forefront. This is a deeper perspective which enables the standpoint or perspective of those, unequal in social reality, to emerge. But instead of women's difference from men being a signal for unequal treatment to follow, as it has done in the past, it would be a sign for suspicion of the existing inequality ...

The argument, therefore, is that, in the name of equality, the law must take account of the differences between groups which affect their capacity for equal competition in the marketplace. The argument has been in the forefront of feminist thinking concerning the way in which the law should seek to reconcile tension between work life and family life. Such an approach should inform the way the law deals with pregnancy, which is a biological difference between men and women. The same approach may be applied to social differences, and thus the law may allow for the fact that women continue to have prime responsibility for care of children and other dependants. It may do this by protecting part time workers, giving rights to time off and by encouraging or permitting a more flexible pattern of work. It is far less clear what the recognition of differences approach has to say about racial discrimination in the labour market,[13] though it has plenty to say about the recognition of differences, primarily cultural, outside the labour market.[14]

The issue of ensuring the appropriate legal response to pregnancy has, as we will see in Chapter 7, caused serious problems for British – and American – anti-discrimination law. The reason is that the non-discrimination principle depends on a comparison, a comparison which in the case of pregnancy is either impossible or inappropriate. English law – with more than a little help from the EC – has now largely resolved the debate by the direct provision of employment rights which do not depend on the concept of discrimination.

Rutherglen, G, 'Discrimination and its discontents' (1995) 81 Virginia L Rev 117, p 141:

On the one hand, discrimination on the basis of pregnancy is formally equivalent to discrimination on the basis of sex ... On the other hand, this way of looking at the issue systematically underestimates the barriers to employment of women created by the traditional division of labour within families ... The question whether an employer should be required to take account of these burdens led to the more general debate among feminists whether women have the right to be treated the same as men or the right to be treated differently. However this debate over sameness and difference should be resolved, the concept of discrimination leaves no room for it to arise in the first place. It pre-empts the debate in favour of sameness.

The issue of childcare, which many regard as essential for any move towards genuine workplace equality, has, in Britain at least, largely escaped regulation by law. This may reflect the ideological position that the family, the domestic, are private matters and thus the concern of the parties rather than the State.

---

[13] Cultural pluralism might require, eg, employers to permit employees to take time off for celebration of religious festivals.

[14] See Poulter, S, 'The limits of legal, cultural and religious pluralism' and Montgomery, J, 'Legislating for a multi-faith society: some problems of special treatment', in Hepple, B and Szyszczak, E (eds), *Discrimination: The Limits of Law*, 1992, London: Mansell, Chapters 10 and 11 respectively.

Townshend-Smith, R, *Sex Discrimination in Employment: Law, Practice and Policy,* **1989, London: Sweet & Maxwell, p 28:**

Neither the State nor employers have provided childcare adequate to enable most women to exercise a real choice as to whether they wish to continue working ... Even where childcare is available, school holidays and illness may cause problems, and a woman employee who is absent during such periods has no legal or collectively negotiated protection. Her absences may be treated as personal failings.

In this social context equality of opportunity is insufficient ... The purpose even of indirect discrimination law is to improve women's integration into the labour market ... If women's family commitments prevent such integration then the law will provide no help, though if limited accommodation can be made at no serious cost to efficiency then individual employers may be required to alter their practices. It may, for example, sometimes be discriminatory not to allow a jobshare.[15]

Indirect discrimination law cannot overcome the inherent labour market disadvantages facing many women. Equality theory has been useful in gaining some limited access to male preserves, but is problematic in other areas where there are real biological or social differences between men and women. True equality can only occur both when employers are obliged to take such differences into account and when the social differences are of less significance.

THE ROLE OF LAW

Some would argue that it is misconceived to rely on the law to bring about improvements in the social position of women and minority ethnic groups. Passing legislation may create the false impression that the problem of discrimination and disadvantage has been tackled and perhaps even solved, as ordinary people often assume that laws necessarily achieve their purpose. This criticism fails to take adequate account of the symbolic function of the law; in particular the message that would accompany any decision, for whatever reason, to repeal anti-discrimination legislation is hardly likely to be welcomed by the prior beneficiaries of such legislation. The strength of the argument, however, lies in its clear recognition that law can only ever be one strand in what is effectively a political campaign concerning the allocation of resources, in which legal victories may themselves have symbolic importance at the political level – as may legal defeats!

O'Donovan, K and Szyszczak, E, *Equality and Sex Discrimination Law,* **1988, Oxford: Blackwells, p 12:**

The State, through anti-discrimination legislation, affirms its interest in the quality of citizens. It recognises individuals as members of the polity and the

---

[15] See below, pp 304–06.

wider social interest in social solidarity. It makes a legal statement prohibiting discrimination as wrong. That the statement may be limited, that the means may be ineffective, should not cause us to overlook the importance of such a statement in official discourse.

Lacey, N, 'Legislation against sex discrimination: questions from a feminist perspective' (1986) 14 JLS 411, pp 418–20:

[D]oubts must arise as to whether the legal forum really represents a useful place in which to attempt to advance arguments for women's liberation, or to seek concrete improvements in the position of women in our society The more specific features relevant to these doubts would include the male domination of the legal forum in terms of its personnel; the male domination of the legal system in terms of the composition of the legislature and powerful interest groups; and the construction of disputes in individual terms and their resolution through a closed system of reasoning. It is hardly surprising that many feminists see the 'equality' legislation as a sop intended to promote false consciousness; it enables women to think that things are getting better or enables men to resist women's further claims, while actually making no real contribution to the dismantling of sexism in our society.

[W]e should acknowledge the limitation of legislation designed to give individual remedies ... [P]rimacy should rather be given to action at the policy level such as contract compliance; changes in the practice of education; adequate provision of childcare facilities and parental leave [and] revaluation of women's work.

We must continue to struggle for a proper emphasis on changes to material conditions which both reflect and consolidate sexism and women's disadvantage ... And we must campaign for policies which reach a much broader range of women – particularly those such as black women, working class women, and single mothers – who suffer specific disadvantages and discriminations ...

[I]f we are to exploit the ideal of equality, our focus must be equality not in terms of opportunity within the liberal model, but in terms of welfare, power resources and goods ...

[W]e could argue for the abandonment of formal equality legislation and the adoption of a specific Act of Parliament prohibiting discrimination against women ... This would not, of course, be to imply that discrimination against men on grounds of sex is morally unproblematic, although it certainly does imply that non-discrimination on grounds of sex conceived in formal equality terms is not a moral absolute. But the main thrust of such a strategy would be to acknowledge that sex discrimination against men is not a social phenomenon of the same order, does not involve comparably damaging and oppressive effects as does sex discrimination against women, and that this clear social difference justifies, and indeed calls for, a totally different legal response ...

[I]f we are to minimise both the dangers attaching to the legislation and its limitations, I would argue that we must abandon equality of opportunity as an important underlying principle. The images it conjures up in both political and legal discourse are closely associated with a minimal and atomistic libertarian vision which fails to address the factors implicated in women's oppression. The opportunity ideal's presupposition of a world of autonomous individuals starting a race or making free choices has no cutting edge against the argument that men and women are simply running different races. And it poses the real danger of actually serving to legitimate existing differences: inequality of impact or results can just be defined as to do with different 'free' choice – or natural sex difference! ... [W]e would be better advised to aim for a determinate measure of equality of results (as through affirmative action programmes) than to run the risks presented by the manipulable notion of equality of opportunity ...

We should neither abandon anti-discrimination legislation just because of its inherent limitations nor regard it as the *only* appropriate *legal* response to women's oppression ... The reform of anti-discrimination law *can* form part of a genuinely feminist political strategy, but it cannot be more than a minor part.

Sunstein, C, 'Three civil rights fallacies' (1991) 79 California L Rev 751, pp 765–68:

The courts' insulation – from an electoral process that is often said to have produced civil rights violations in the first place – is considered a comparative virtue, allowing the judges to implement anti-discrimination principles without being affected by political biases. There can be no question that because of their insulation, judges have often been in an unusually good position to elaborate and implement principles of anti-discrimination. But for several reasons, reliance on the judiciary may have been a mistake. It may have diverted attention from more productive alternatives and at the same time disserved the very causes at issue. In any case, such reliance seems a poor strategy for the future. Three considerations are relevant here.

(a) Efficacy

Judicial decisions are of limited efficacy in bringing about social change. Study after study has confirmed this basic conclusion ... [T]he evidence suggests that judges are less effective than the elected branches of the government in attempting to reform systems of discrimination.

(b) Democracy, citizenship, compromise and legitimacy

For achieving sensible and effective reform, political channels are often far better than the courts. The resort to politics can produce a kind of citizen mobilisation that is a public and private good, and can inculcate political commitments, broader understanding, feelings of citizenship and dedication to the community ... [R]eliance on the courts has large and hidden disadvantages. It may divert energy and resources from political processes, and the substitution effect imposes large costs on these processes. And if questions of morality tend to become questions of constitutional law, their resolution before nine judges can harm the practice of citizenship.

(c) The narrowing focus of adjudication

[L]egal thinking and legal procedures are most suited to ideas growing out of the tradition of compensatory justice, which is poorly adapted to the achievement of serious social reform. Adjudication is ill-suited to undertaking the necessary changes. Many of the important problems in current civil rights policy are systemic and complex. The lack of adequate schools, job training, or jobs creates a cycle of poverty, vulnerability to drugs and to crime, teenage pregnancy and single-parent households. Courts simply lack the tools to respond to these problems.

Lacey, N, 'From individual to group', in Hepple, B and Szyszczak, E (eds), *Discrimination: The Limits of Law*, 1992, London: Mansell, pp 106–08, 114–20:

The liberal legal world is one in which legal rules are applied and enforced in a politically neutral and formally equal way; the legal sphere is seen as relatively autonomous from the political sphere; all are equally subject to the law and formally equal before it. There are stringent limits on the proper ambit of State intervention by means of law, which is seen as positively protecting individual rights and interests against political encroachment, and negatively as protecting a sphere of private life in which public regulation is inappropriate and indeed oppressive ...

One possible strategy ... is for feminists and anti-racists to attempt to intervene in the legal forum, reworking legal concepts and definitions so as to reflect Afro-Caribbean, Asian, female and other perspectives. A notable example of such a strategy is law defining and making actionable sexual harassment – a concept which reconstructs, from a feminist perspective, behaviour conventionally regarded as acceptable and even favourable to women as unacceptable, oppressive and illegal. This kind of social and legal reconstruction is one of the most important potential contributions of critical social theory, and in the anti-discrimination area it raises a number of possibilities for reform. One example might be the recognition of groups' rather than individuals' claims, combating the notion of the legal subject as an abstract individual and putting the position and experience of an oppressed group explicitly on the legal agenda ...

Could a move to the recognition of group rights and/or collective remedies help to overcome the problems of legal individualism or to deconstruct the notion of the abstract legal subject in acknowledging as subjects entities recognised precisely because of their substantive political position? ...

I want to assess the potential of a ... conception of group rights which I shall call 'remedial' rights. These rights would apply to groups which were suffering disadvantage as a result either of present oppression or the present effects of past oppression. The essence of the right would be that positive and effective steps be taken to combat and overcome that disadvantage within a reasonable period of time ...

The assertion of group rights would be met with remedies not only of the traditional legal kind ... but also with a wide range of radically different remedies ... This feature would be crucial in breaking the conceptual link between loss and remedy which characterises the individual legal form. Hence contract compliance, quota systems and affirmative action programmes, urban development programmes, educational reforms and money to set up community projects of various kinds would be possible responses to the legal assertion of the violation of a group right ...

A more serious problem for the notion of group rights seems to be the fact of fragmentation and diversity of individual and group identity. People in any social world are members of a number of different communities and groups, and suffer or enjoy a number of overlapping and interacting identities, advantages and disadvantages as a result ... [W]e certainly cannot assume any kind of identity of interest among members of a group just because of one shared oppression, nor can we assume that, for example, racial oppression will have had the same kind of impact on the experience, consciousness and life chances of all members of that group. A recognition of this kind of diversity, and a commitment to recognition of a plurality of oppression, experiences and interests, seems to bring with it a nightmarish vision of a potential explosion of overlapping groups defined along different lines all competing with other (and implicitly with parts of themselves) for the resources or changes necessary to dismantle their specific disadvantages ... [T]he practical and conceptual difficulties raised by the diversity of social oppression and the consequent fragmentation of group identity cannot be underestimated.

On the present construction of the boundary between law and politics, remedial decisions with the kinds of significant resource implications likely to be effective in tackling racial and sexual disadvantage could only come from government institutions. As things stand at the moment ... I suspect that effective recognition of group-based remedial rights would have to be at a political rather than a legal level ...

Concepts such as equality of opportunity and equality of results are only a means to an end. That is why their usefulness is as much symbolic as purely philosophical. The law and the legal system are also a means to an end, rather than a closed system with a life and a rationale of their own. From this standpoint, it is perfectly consistent to be at the same time cynical and sceptical about the usefulness of the law and yet to seek to have it strengthened and to make use of it to its full capacity. What is essential for anyone concerned with the economic and social position of disadvantaged groups is that the law is never seen as the only way forward for tackling the problems.

CHAPTER 4

THE SOURCES OF ANTI-DISCRIMINATION LAW

The primary sources of domestic anti-discrimination legislation are the Equal Pay Act 1970, the Sex Discrimination Act 1975, and the Race Relations Act 1976.[1] As is well known, European Community law provisions on gender equality operate alongside domestic provisions, in many instances granting more extensive rights. In addition, incorporation into domestic law of the European Convention on Human Rights will affect domestic anti-discrimination law, though in what ways and to what extent is at this stage very speculative.

This chapter will first outline the basic principles of European law in order to show why it has had such a dramatic impact in the field of discrimination law; secondly, consideration will be given to the origin and form of current anti-discrimination law, both domestic and European, and, thirdly, the potential impact of incorporation of the European Convention on Human Rights will be briefly examined.

It should also be noted that there is a strong case to be made for consolidating legislation. At present, sex and race discrimination law comprises a large number of domestic statutes, to which must be added the implications of European Community and Human Rights law. Disability discrimination is somewhat similar to but different in certain key respects from sex and race discrimination law. In addition, there are arguments that discrimination law should be extended to cover discrimination of the basis of sexual orientation, religion, and age.

EUROPEAN LAW

Supremacy

As is well known, the basic legal foundation of the European Community is the Treaty of Rome, although its subsequent amendment means that it is now more accurate to refer to it as the European Community Treaty. European law has supremacy over domestic law.

---

[1] The 1975 Act excluded Northern Ireland, but the almost identical Sex Discrimination (Northern Ireland) Order 1976 followed a year later. Remarkably, race discrimination legislation was absent from Northern Ireland until the Race Relations (Northern Ireland) Order 1997.

Costa v ENEL Case 6/64 [1964] ECR 585[2]

Judgment (p 586):

By contrast with ordinary international treaties, the EEC Treaty has created its own legal system which, on the entry into force of the Treaty, became an integral part of the legal systems of the Member States and which their courts are bound to apply ... [T]he Member States have limited their sovereign rights, albeit within limited fields, and have thus created a body of law which binds both their nationals and themselves ...

The transfer by the States from their domestic legal system to the Community legal system of the rights and obligations arising under the Treaty carries with it a permanent limitation of their sovereign rights, against which a subsequent unilateral act incompatible with the concept of the Community cannot prevail.[3]

Community law gives rights to, and creates obligations on, individuals as well as Member States, unlike treaties governed by conventional international law doctrine, such as the European Convention on Human Rights, which tend only to bind the State Parties.

Amministrazione delle Finanze v Simmenthal Case 106/77 [1978] ECR 629[4]

Judgment (pp 643–44):

[The Treaty provisions are] a direct source of rights and duties for all those affected thereby, whether Member States or individuals, who are parties to legal relationships under Community law ...

Furthermore, in accordance with the precedence of Community law, the relationship between provisions of the Treaty and directly applicable measures of the institutions on the one hand and the national law of the Member States on the other is such that those provisions and measures not only by their entry into force render automatically inapplicable any conflicting provision of current national law but ... also preclude the valid adoption of new national legislative measures to the extent to which they would be incompatible with Community provisions ...

It follows ... that every national court must ... apply Community law in its entirety and protect rights which the latter confers on individuals and must accordingly set aside any provision of national law which may conflict with it, whether prior or subsequent to the Community rule.[5]

---

2   See, also, [1964] CMLR 425.
3   This principle forms part of UK domestic law as a result of the European Communities Act 1972, ss 2 and 3.
4   See, also, [1978] 3 CMLR 263.
5   See, also, *Van Gend en Loos v Niederlandse Administratie der Belastingen* Case 26/62 [1963] ECR 1; [1963] CMLR 105.

Direct effect of Treaty provisions

The doctrine of the supremacy of Community law makes it necessary to determine the precise mechanism by which provisions of the Treaty take effect within the domestic law of the Member States.

Defrenne v SABENA Case 43/75 [1976] ECR 455[6]

An air hostess with the Belgian national airline claimed compensation for the low pay she received in comparison with male workers. The claim was based on Art 119 of the Treaty of Rome, which obliges the Member States to ensure and maintain the 'application of the principle that men and women should receive equal pay for equal work'. The case is the foundation for subsequent European Community sex equality law because of the decision that Art 119 was directly applicable.[7]

Judgment (pp 473–75):

For the purpose of the implementation of these provisions a distinction must be drawn within the whole area of application of Art 119 between, first, direct and overt discrimination, which may be identified solely with the aid of the criteria based on equal pay and equal work referred to in the article in question and, secondly, indirect and disguised discrimination, which can only be identified by reference to more explicit implementing provisions of a Community or national character.[8]

Among the forms of direct discrimination which may be [so] identified must be included in particular those which have their origin in legislative provisions or in collective labour agreements ...

This applies even more in cases where men and women receive unequal pay for equal work carried out in the same establishment or service, whether public or private ...

[I]n such a case the court is in a position to establish all the facts which enable it to decide whether a woman worker is receiving lower pay than a male worker performing the same tasks.

In such a situation ... Art 119 is directly applicable and may thus give rise to individual rights which the courts must protect ...

---

6   See, also, [1976] 2 CMLR 98; [1976] ICR 547.

7   The Treaty of Amsterdam amends Art 119 so as specifically to include 'the principle of equal pay for equal work or work of equal value'. Moreover, a new numbering system for Treaty articles is put in place. Article 119 becomes Art 141. In addition, it is now technically correct to refer not to the Treaty of Rome but to the EC Treaty. However, both as the Treaty of Amsterdam is not yet ratified and to make it easier to follow the case law, this work will continue to refer to the Treaty of Rome and to use the old numbering system.

8   This paragraph might be interpreted as deciding that equal pay claims based on indirect discrimination were excluded from the scope of the direct effect of Art 119. This limited interpretation of *Defrenne* did not prevail; see, especially, *Bilka-Kaufhaus v Weber von Hartz* Case 170/84 [1986] ECR 1607; [1986] 2 CMLR 701; [1987] ICR 110; [1986] IRLR 317.

[T]he fact that certain provisions of the Treaty are formally addressed to the Member States does not prevent rights being conferred at the same time on an individual who has an interest in the performance of the duties thus laid down

...

Thus, Art 119 is directly effective, requiring no implementation by Member States. It can therefore be utilised by individuals – against employers in both the public and the private sector. The rights thereby conferred may be enforced by individuals despite there being no equivalent right under domestic legislation. In such a case, the applicant will be relying on the precise wording of the Treaty which itself becomes part of domestic law. It follows that in the event of a conflict between domestic law and Art 119, the latter must prevail. Thus, the direct effectiveness of Art 119 necessarily implies that in some cases the provisions of domestic law are overridden and cannot be applied, because of the overriding principle that EC law is supreme.[9]

The legal effect of directives

Directives are not part of the Treaty of Rome and their legal effect is thus fundamentally different from Treaty provisions. They are addressed to governments of Member States rather than to individuals, requiring each government, within a specified time period, to amend domestic law so as to ensure that the requirements of the directive are complied with. The precise way in which that is done is a matter for each Member State. It logically follows that an individual should not expect to be able to enforce a directive before a national court or the European Court. Despite this, some early cases appeared to suggest the contrary.[10] Such a view did not prevail.

Marshall v Southampton and South West Hampshire AHA **Case 152/84 [1986] IRLR 140**[11]

The complainant was dismissed at age 62 when a man doing her job would have not had to leave until 65. Such differentiation was then lawful under the SDA 1975, but it was argued to be in breach of the Equal Treatment Directive 76/207. That Directive clearly applied to the facts of the case, but it had not been implemented in the UK, and the question was whether she could rely on the Directive in an individual claim before an English court.

---

9   See, eg, *Macarthys Ltd v Smith* Case 129/79 [1980] ECR 1275; [1981] QB 180; [1981] 1 All ER 11; [1980] IRLR 210, in which the claim was brought by an individual. In *R v Secretary of State for Employment ex p Equal Opportunities Commission* [1995] 1 AC 1; [1994] ICR 317; [1994] 1 All ER 910; [1994] IRLR 176, the EOC obtained a declaration that British unfair dismissal legislation was contrary to Art 119 and the Equal Treatment Directive because it was indirectly discriminatory against part time workers. The decision thus disapplies domestic legislation. See below, pp 302—04.

10   *Van Duyn v Home Office* Case 41/74 [1974] ECR 1337; [1975] 1 CMLR 1; *Pubblico Ministero v Ratti* Case 148/78 [1979] ECR 1629; [1980] 1 CMLR 96.

11   See, also, [1986] ECR 723; [1986] 1 QB 401; [1986] ICR 335.

Judgment (p 149):

[W]herever the provisions of a directive appear, so far as their subject matter is concerned, to be unconditional and sufficiently precise, those provisions may be relied on by an individual against the State where that State fails to implement the directive in national law by the end of the period prescribed or where it fails to implement the directive correctly ...

[T]he binding nature of a directive, which constitutes the basis for the possibility of relying on the directive before a national court, exists only in relation to each Member State to which it is addressed. It follows that a directive may not of itself impose obligations on an individual and that a provision of a directive may not be relied on as such against such a person.

[W]here a person ... is able to rely on a directive as against the State he may do so regardless of the capacity in which the latter is acting, whether employer or public authority. In either case it is necessary to prevent the State from taking advantage of its own failure to comply with Community law.

Actions are thus permitted against organs of the State because it would be unjust to permit such organs to rely on the State's own failure to implement the directive in question. Of course, the disadvantage of this approach is that whether there is a remedy depends entirely on the nature of the defendant. It was thus not surprising that the Sex Discrimination Act was amended in 1986 to ensure that the right which Ms Marshall had against organs of the State should henceforth be available against *all* employers.

Another consequence of the ECJ's limiting of the direct effectiveness of directives to vertical direct effect against the Member State is a natural tendency to construe the notion of 'the State' widely. In *Foster v British Gas*,[12] the issue was whether the pre-privatised British Gas Corporation was or was not an organ of the State. The European Court held that any body, 'whatever its legal form, which has been made responsible, pursuant to a measure adopted by the State, for providing a public service under the control of the State and has for that purpose special powers beyond those which result from the normal rules applicable to relations between individuals is included in any event among the bodies against which the provisions of a directive capable of having direct effect may be relied upon'.

There are three subsequent English domestic cases on the point. In *Doughty v Rolls-Royce Ltd*,[13] the Court of Appeal held that Rolls-Royce, even when in public ownership, was not part of the State as, even though it was under State control, it was neither a public service nor dependent on special powers granted by the State in the same sense as British Gas had been. In *Griffin v South West Water Services Ltd*,[14] the High Court held that a privatised water company was an emanation of the State, as it provided a particular

---

[12]   Case C-188/89 [1990] 3 All ER 897; [1990] IRLR 353; [1990] ECR I-3133.
[13]   [1992] IRLR 126, CA.
[14]   [1995] IRLR 15; High Court, ChD.

service under the control of the State which derived from special statutory powers granted to it. Finally, in *National Union of Teachers v Governing Body of St Mary's Church of England (aided) Junior School*,[15] the Court of Appeal considered that the concept of an emanation of the State was very broad, embracing all organs of administration; there was no one exclusive formula to resolve the issue and the approach of the ECJ in *Foster* had not suggested otherwise. Furthermore, the estoppel rationale of *Marshall* itself supports a wide view. Voluntary aided schools rely significantly on the State, which has considerable control and influence over them, and thus they are sufficiently closely tied to the State education system to be regarded as an emanation of it.[16]

Construing domestic law to conform with Community law[17]

The problem in *Marshall* arose because of a conflict between the relevant directive and English domestic law. If it can be concluded that there is no such conflict and that the wording of the directive in question is in accordance with domestic law, the practical consequence will be to apply the directive in all situations, not simply against emanations of the State, not in a formal sense, but because domestic law reaches the same outcome.

Von Colson and Kamann v Land Nordrhein-Westfalen Case 14/83 [1984] ECR 1891[18]

Judgment (p 1909):

[T]he Member States' obligation arising from a directive to achieve the result envisaged by the directive and their duty under Art 5 of the Treaty to take all appropriate measures ... to ensure the fulfilment of that obligation, is binding on all the authorities of Member States ... including the courts. It follows that, in applying the national law and in particular the provisions of a national law specifically introduced in order to implement [a directive], national courts are required to interpret their national law in the light of the wording and the purpose of the directive in order to achieve the [required] result ...[19]

---

15 [1997] ICR 334; [1997] IRLR 242, CA.

16 For comment, see Eady, J (1997) 26 Industrial LJ 248.

17 See Craig, P, 'Directives: direct effect, indirect effect and the construction of national legislation' (1997) 22 EL Rev 519.

18 See, also, [1986] 2 CMLR 430.

19 For leading examples of the way in which domestic courts have reacted to the *Von Colson* imperative, see *Litster v Forth Dry Dock and Engineering Co* [1990] 1 AC 546; [1989] ICR 341; [1989] IRLR 161 (a case on the Transfer of Undertakings Regulations 1981); *Pickstone v Freemans plc* [1989] AC 66; [1988] ICR 697; [1988] IRLR 357 (an equal pay case – see below, p 414), and *Webb v EMO Air Cargo (UK) Ltd* Case C-32/93; [1994] ECR I–3537; [1994] QB 718; [1994] ICR 770; [1994] IRLR 482, and [1995] ICR 1021; [1995] IRLR 645, HL (a pregnancy case – see below, pp 187–90).

Duke v GEC Reliance **[1988] IRLR 118, HL**[20]

The issue was whether the exclusion concerning provisions relating to retirement which was contained in the SDA 1975 could or should be interpreted so as to conform with the requirements of the Equal Treatment Directive. It was argued for the applicant that, in the light of *Marshall*, the exception should be interpreted narrowly so as to refer only to the consequences of retirement but not to the age of retirement.

Lord Templeman (pp 122–23):

Of course a British court will always be willing and anxious to conclude that United Kingdom law is consistent with Community law. Where an Act is passed for the purpose of giving effect to an obligation imposed by a directive or other instrument, a British court will seldom encounter difficulty in concluding that the language of the Act is effective for the intended purpose. But the construction of a British Act of Parliament is a matter of judgment to be determined by British courts and to be derived from the language of the legislation considered in the light of the circumstance prevailing at the date of enactment ... [The EqPA 1970 and the SDA 1975] were not passed to give effect to the Equal Treatment Directive and were intended to preserve discriminatory retirement ages ... [T]he words of s 6(4) [of the unamended SDA] are not reasonably capable of being limited to the meaning ascribed to them by the appellant. Section 2(4) of the European Communities Act 1972 does not ... enable or constrain a British court to distort the meaning of a British statute in order to enforce against an individual a Community directive which has no direct effect between individuals.

This case lays down the principle that domestic legislation, especially that passed before the directive in question, should only be construed so as to conform to the directive if capable of being interpreted in that way. The following case casts doubt on that limiting principle, holding that there is an obligation on national courts to construe national legislation so far as possible so as to ensure conformity with a directive.[21]

Marleasing SA v La Comercial Internacional de Alimentacion SA **Case C-106/89 [1990] ECR I-4135**[22]

Judgment (p 4159):

[T]he Member States' obligation arising from a directive to achieve the result envisaged by the directive and their duty under Art 5 of the Treaty to take all appropriate measures ... to ensure the fulfilment of their obligation, is binding on all the authorities of Member States including ... the courts. It follows that, in applying national law, whether the provisions in question were adopted before or after the directive, the national court called upon to interpret it is

---

[20] See, also, [1988] AC 618; [1988] ICR 639.

[21] See Docksey, C and Fitzpatrick, B, 'The duty of national courts to interpret provisions of national law in accordance with Community law' (1991) 20 Industrial LJ 113.

[22] See, also, [1992] 1 CMLR 305.

required to do so, as far as possible, in the light of the wording and the purpose of the directive in order to achieve the result pursued by the latter ...

Actions against the State

An individual may suffer financial loss as a result of a State's failure to implement a directive or implement it correctly. In such a case, there may be a remedy against the State.[23]

Francovich and Others v Italian State **Cases C-6/90 and C-9/90 [1992] IRLR 84**[24]

Judgment (p 88):

The full effectiveness of Community rules would be impaired and the protection of the rights which they grant would be weakened if individuals were unable to obtain redress when their rights are infringed by a breach of Community law for which a Member State can be held responsible.

It follows that the principle whereby a State must be liable for loss and damage caused to individuals as a result of breaches of Community law for which the State can be held responsible is inherent in the system of the Treaty.

[T]he full effectiveness of that rule of Community law requires that there should be a right to reparation provided that three conditions are fulfilled.

The first of those conditions is that the result prescribed by the directive should entail the grant of rights to individuals. The second condition is that it should be possible to identify the content of those rights on the basis of the provisions of the directive. Finally, the third condition is the existence of a causal link between the breach of the State's obligation and damage suffered by the injured parties.

Brasserie du Pêcheur SA v Federal Republic of Germany **Case C-46/93**

R v Secretary of State for Transport ex p Factortame Ltd **Case C-48/93 [1996] IRLR 267**[25]

The first case concerned the alleged failure of the German Government to comply with EC law on the marketing of beers with the effect that the French plaintiffs were unable to export to Germany. The second case concerned UK legislation on fishing rights, which discriminated on the basis of nationality. The European Court expanded on the *Francovich* principles of State liability for damages.

---

[23] In *Secretary of State for Employment v Mann* [1997] ICR 200, CA, it was held that such claims had to be instituted in the High Court and could not be made before an Industrial Tribunal, as the latter's jurisdiction was entirely governed by statute.

[24] See, also, [1991] ECR I-5357; [1995] ICR 722.

[25] See, also, [1996] QB 404.

Judgment (pp 295–98):

[T]he principle of State liability for loss and damage caused to individuals as a result of breaches of Community law for which it can be held responsible is inherent in the system of the Treaty.

It follows that the principle holds good for any case in which a Member State breaches Community law, whatever be the organ of the State [including the legislature] whose act or omission was responsible for the breach ...

Community law confers a right to reparation where three conditions are met: the rule of law infringed must be intended to confer rights on individuals; the breach must be sufficiently serious; and there must be a direct causal link between the breach of the obligation ... and the damage sustained ...

[T]he decisive test for finding that a breach of Community law is sufficiently serious is whether the Member State ... manifestly and gravely disregarded the limits of its discretion.[26]

The factors which the competent court may take into consideration include the clarity and precision of the rule breached, the measure of the discretion left by that rule to the national ... authorities, whether the infringement and the damage caused was intentional or involuntary, whether any error of law was excusable or inexcusable, the fact that the position taken by a Community institution may have contributed towards the omission, and the adoption or retention of national measures or practices contrary to Community law ...[27]

While the imposition of [national] restrictions may be consistent with the requirement that the conditions laid down should not be less favourable than those relating to similar domestic claims, it is still to be considered whether such restrictions are not such as in practice to make it impossible or excessively difficult to obtain reparation ...

[A]ny condition that may be imposed by English law on State liability requiring proof of misfeasance in public office, such an abuse of power being inconceivable in the case of the legislature, is also such as in practice to make it impossible or extremely difficult to obtain effective reparation for loss or damage resulting from a breach of Community law where the breach is attributable to the national legislature ...

The obligation to make reparation for loss or damage caused to individuals cannot ... depend upon a condition based on any concept of fault going beyond that of a sufficiently serious breach of Community law ...

[I]n order to determine the loss or damage for which reparation may be granted, the national court may inquire whether the injured person showed reasonable diligence in order to avoid the loss or damage or limit its extent and

---

[26] In *Dillenkoffer v Federal Republic of Germany* Case C-178/94 [1997] QB 259; [1997] IRLR 61, it was held that failure within the period laid down to implement in national law the provisions of a directive was by definition a sufficiently serious breach of Community law so as to entitle a *Francovich* claim to be brought.

[27] In *R v HM Treasury ex p British Telecommunications plc* Case C-392/93 [1996] QB 615; [1996] IRLR 301, it was held that a *Francovich* claim could not succeed, as the directive in question was imprecisely worded and was reasonably capable of bearing the interpretation which the UK Government had in good faith given to it.

whether, in particular, he availed himself in time of all the legal remedies available to him.

Recommendations, Codes, etc

In *Grimaldi v Fonds des Maladies Professionelles*,[28] the Court stated that 'national courts are bound to take ... recommendations into consideration in order to decide disputes submitted to them, in particular, where they clarify the interpretation of national provisions adopted in order to implement them or where they are designed to supplement binding Community measures'. The 1992 Council Recommendation on Childcare[29] has recently been supplemented by guidance on good practice in relation to work and childcare.[30]

As under domestic legislation, Codes of Practice may assist in the interpretation of European equality legislation. The two most significant, which will be considered in more detail subsequently, concern sexual harassment and equal pay.

The European Community is also very active in the promotion of equal opportunities. For example, there have been regular five year action programmes, the fourth such programme, covering the years 1996–2000, having been adopted in December 1995.[31]

Enforcement and interpretation of EC law

Many key sex discrimination cases have arisen where a national court has referred a case to the European Court of Justice under Art 177 of the EC Treaty for clarification of EC law.[32] Such cases, from whichever Member State they originate, become precedents which an English court is bound to apply.[33]

A further way in which EC law develops is through the procedure under Art 169, which enables the European Commission to bring a Member State before the European Court alleging failure to comply with a Treaty

---

[28] Case 322/88 [1989] ECR 4407; [1991] 2 CMLR 265; [1990] IRLR 400.

[29] 92/241/EEC.

[30] 'Work and childcare: implementing the Council recommendation on childcare – a guide to good practice' (1998) 77 EOR 33.

[31] For the details, see (1996) 67 EOR 34. For comment, see Szyszczak, E (1996) 25 Industrial LJ 255.

[32] See Ellis, E and Tridimas, T, *Public Law of the European Community: Text, Materials and Commentary*, 1995, London: Sweet & Maxwell, pp 466–92.

[33] Eg, in *Bilka-Kaufhaus v Weber von Hartz* Case 170/84 [1986] ECR 1607; [1986] 2 CMLR 701; [1987] ICR 110; [1986] IRLR 317, it was held to be unlawful to exclude part time workers from occupational pension schemes unless the employer could demonstrate that such exclusion was justified.

obligation.[34] There are numerous cases where the UK has been found wanting under this provision. From the sex equality perspective, the most important is *Commission of the European Communities v United Kingdom*[35] which held that the then existing British equal pay law failed to comply with Art 119 and the Equal Pay Directive in that it had no provision for a woman to allege that her work was of equal value to that of a man.[36] A finding of breach under this procedure does not automatically change domestic law, but both the political pressures and the likelihood of claims based on *Francovich* are likely to bring about such change. In this instance the law was changed by the Equal Pay (Amendment) Regulations 1983.[37]

European law and race discrimination legislation

The final issue concerns the interrelationship between European law and race discrimination legislation. This subdivides into, first, the effect of the sex equality jurisprudence on domestic race discrimination law, and, secondly, the prospects and arguments for Community legislation on race discrimination.

The British SDA 1975 and RRA 1976 are, for most practical purposes, identical. The SDA 1975 must of course be interpreted in the light of decisions of the European Court of Justice. To ensure consistency of interpretation, it follows that in practice the RRA 1976 is also interpreted in the light of those self-same European cases. If that is not done, there will be confusion in that identical words in statutes will be interpreted differently, and a sense of injustice that women receive the benefit of the more favourable, 'European', interpretation. Thus, for example, the Court of Appeal in *Ojutiku and Oburoni v Manpower Services Commission*[38] interpreted the defence of justification to claims of indirect discrimination in a manner considered to be relatively favourable to employers. The European Court in *Bilka-Kaufhaus v Weber von Hartz*[39] interpreted the equivalent defence to Art 119 in a significantly more stringent fashion, an approach which the Court of Appeal in *Hampson v*

---

[34] *Op cit*, Ellis and Tridimas, fn 32, pp 340–60.

[35] Case 61/81 [1982] ECR 2601; [1982] ICR 578; [1982] IRLR 333. See, also, *Commission of the European Communities v United Kingdom* Case 165/82 [1983] ECR 3431; [1984] 1 All ER 353; [1984] ICR 192; [1984] IRLR 29, which concerned three allegations of failure to comply with the Equal Treatment Directive and was one of the progenitors of the Sex Discrimination Act 1986.

[36] The draft Treaty of Amsterdam (which will only come into effect when formally ratified by all the EU Member States) amends Art 119 so that it now specifically refers to work of equal value.

[37] SI 1983/1794.

[38] [1982] ICR 661; [1982] IRLR 418.

[39] Case 170/84 [1986] ECR 1607; [1986] 2 CMLR 701; [1987] ICR 110; [1986] IRLR 317.

Department of Education and Science[40] held to be applicable to cases under the RRA 1976. The second example is, if anything, even stronger. Both Acts originally had provided a maximum limit on compensation. The European Court held in *Marshall v Southampton and South West Hampshire AHA (No 2)*[41] that such a limitation contravened the Equal Treatment Directive. As a result the limitation was abolished for gender cases by the Sex Discrimination and Equal Pay (Remedies) Regulations 1993.[42] This provision clearly had no direct effect so far as race cases were concerned, but the continuance of a maximum limit in such cases would have appeared both anomalous and unjust. In consequence, the limit in race cases was abolished by the Race Relations (Remedies) Act 1994.

The second issue concerns the likelihood of European initiatives in the area of race discrimination.[43] Despite the strong belief in many quarters that action is needed, a belief manifested in the fact that 1997 was the European Year Against Racism,[44] there has until recently been no clear legal basis for European legislation. It was, however, argued that there was some legal foundation for such action, first in the preamble to the Social Charter, which refers to 'discrimination on the ground of sex, colour, race opinions and beliefs ...' and also on the basis of the general principle of non-discrimination contained in Art 7 of the Treaty.[45]

The legal authority for legislation is now clear. The Treaty of Amsterdam amended the Treaty of Rome to enable action to be taken 'to combat discrimination based on sex, racial or ethnic origin, religion or belief, disability, age or sexual orientation'. This amendment is not capable of being directly effective; rather, it provides a statutory basis for future legislation which is far wider than any previous Community measure in the area. However, such legislation will require unanimity, which may not be forthcoming, given the different traditions of Member States especially as regards the use – exploitation? – of foreign workers, and the greater influence of far right political movements in some Member States. However, in March 1998, the European Commission set out a comprehensive Action Plan for

---

[40] [1989] ICR 179; [1989] IRLR 69, reversed by the House of Lords on other grounds, [1991] 1 AC 771; [1990] ICR 551; [1990] IRLR 302.

[41] Case C-261/91 [1993] ECR I-4367; [1994] AC 530; [1994] ICR 242; [1993] 4 All ER 586; [1993] IRLR 445.

[42] SI 1993/2798.

[43] See Szyszczak, E, 'Race discrimination: the limits of market equality', in Hepple, B and Szyszczak, E (eds), *Discrimination: The Limits of Law*, 1992, London: Mansell, Chapter 8; Docksey, C, 'The principle of equality as a fundamental right under Community law' (1991) 20 Industrial LJ 258, p 261; Bourn, C and Whitmore, J, *Anti-Discrimination Law in Britain*, 3rd edn, 1996, London: Sweet & Maxwell, pp 34–35.

[44] Council Resolution 96/C 237/01; see (1997) 71 EOR 5.

[45] See below, pp 105–06.

combating racism, one strand of which seeks to prepare the ground for legislation on racial discrimination to be adopted before the end of 1999.[46]

SOURCES OF GENDER DISCRIMINATION LAW

The Equal Pay Act 1970

One of the main consequences of the history and sources is that the British Equal Pay Act was passed separately from the Sex Discrimination Act.[47] This still has unfortunate consequences, both in determining which of the two acts is involved in a given case, and also in determining the precise relationship between domestic and European law.

Davies, P and Freedland, M, *Labour Legislation and Public Policy,* **1993, Oxford: Clarendon, pp 123, 211–13:**

[T]he TUC had passed as early as 1888 a resolution in favour of the proposition that 'it is desirable in the interest of both men and women that in trades where women do the same work as men they shall receive the same payment'. [After the Second World War] the TUC was ... prepared to press more vigorously for governmental action to help achieve selected TUC objectives. In the case of equal pay, the TUC's main demand of government was that it ratify [the International Labour Organisation] Convention 100 of 1951, which provided that 'each member shall, by means appropriate to the methods in operation for determining rates of remuneration, promote and, in so far as is consistent with such methods, ensure the application to all workers of the principle of equal remuneration for men and women workers for work of equal value' ...

In January 1955 a major part of the campaign for the public sector was achieved when the Government agreed through the Civil Service National Whitley Council to the introduction of equal pay (for like work) in the non-industrial civil service ... [S]imilar developments took place in local government, the nationalised industries and the health service.

[G]overnments throughout the 1960s (Labour as well as Conservative) took the view that the TUC demand put the cart before the horse, and that the UK should stick to its traditional policy of not ratifying any particular ILO Convention unless it was thought that British practice was already broadly in conformity with it. So from government's point of view the question became, not whether Convention 100 should immediately be ratified, but what, if anything, government should do to bring about a situation in which

---

[46] *Communication from the Commission – an action plan against racism,* COM(1998) 183 final.

[47] The fact that there are two pieces of legislation can lead to problems in determining which is relevant, especially as in some situations the detailed rules differ. The Equal Opportunities Commission has long sought a single consolidating statute; see below, pp 390–91.

ratification became possible. The Conservative administrations of the early 1960s were unwilling to undertake any commitment in this direction. The crucial change occurred when, in its 1964 election manifesto, the Labour Party ... put forward the notion of a seven point 'Charter of Rights for all employees' one of the heads of which was 'the right to equal pay for equal work.' ... [At the end of the 1960s the Government turned to equal pay and secured the passing of the Equal Pay Act 1970 as a means of repairing the fissures that had opened up in relations between the Labour Government and the union movement over incomes policy and the Government's proposals for reform of collective labour law ...

The strength and significance of this explanation is that it shows how the origins of equal pay legislation are to be found firmly in the context of collective labour relations. The legislation itself marked a major shift away from the British tradition of voluntarism in industrial relations, whereby workplace issues – with some significant exceptions, in particular health and safety – were left to be resolved by the parties without legal intervention. As we will see later, the collective dimension of the equal pay legislation has been swamped, both by the interpretation given to the law in the courts[48] and by the individual rights focus of other legislation, most notably of course the SDA 1975 and the RRA 1976 – as well as the individual rights approach which has dominated the European Court in its interpretation of Art 119. Given the decline in trade union membership in the last 20 years, such a shift in emphasis is understandable, but many would take the view that equal pay legislation cannot be truly effective in the absence of a parallel commitment by trade unions to place the issue at the centre of their collective bargaining agenda.[49]

The Sex Discrimination Act 1975 and the Race Relations Act 1976[50]

The historical genesis for this legislation is completely different from that of the Equal Pay Act 1970. Rather than arising largely from pressure from within the trade union movement, that which led to the SDA 1975 was strongly influenced by the concept of equal rights for women which was a key aim of

---

[48] *R v Central Arbitration Committee ex p Hy-Mac* [1979] IRLR 461, DC.

[49] The basic principle of equal pay law is that a woman may claim pay equality with a man where she is employed on like work with him, where she is employed on work which has been rated as equivalent to his under a job evaluation scheme, or where she is employed on work which is of equal value to his. There is a defence to a claim of equal pay if the employer can prove that the difference in pay is genuinely due to a material factor which is not the difference of sex, such as seniority or merit payments. See below, Chapter 12.

[50] Both the SDA 1975 and the RRA 1976 have subsequently been amended, but their basic structure and philosophy remain intact. It makes sense, therefore, to examine the amendments as they relate to the appropriate issues of substantive law.

the feminist movement in the USA – where the notion of individual rights was far stronger than in the UK and where, by the 1970s, the ability of trade unions to achieve their aims via legislation had declined virtually to nil. Similarly, the Race Relations Act 1976 followed lobbying which had focused on the perceived inadequacies of the previous legislative attempts in the area.[51] Unlike the Equal Pay Act, both the Sex Discrimination Bill and the Race Relations Bill came under the general control of the Home Office, rather than the Ministry of Labour – the predecessor of the Department of Employment. This naturally led to a greater focus on individual rights than collective strategies.

It was a deliberate policy decision that the Sex Discrimination Act 1975 and the Race Relations Act 1976 should contain largely identical provisions. One reason for the parallelism is that the American Civil Rights Act 1964 dealt with issues of race and gender in one piece of legislation. Furthermore, a visit to the USA by the then Home Secretary, Roy Jenkins,[52] convinced him that the Sex Discrimination Bill, which was then going through Parliament, needed amendment so as specifically to cover indirect discrimination, which had relatively recently been held by the United States Supreme Court[53] to be covered by the Civil Rights Act.

While the main objective was to benefit women and minority ethnic groups, the legislation adopts a symmetrical approach in that men and white people may also claim to be victims of unlawful discrimination. The basic definition of discrimination divides into direct and indirect discrimination. Direct discrimination is where a person is treated less favourably than another on the basis, for example, of race or gender. Indirect discrimination is where a rule is applied which has the effect of excluding disproportionately more black people or women, such as a rule requiring someone to be a full time worker or to have lived in the UK for 10 years. The defendant will only lose an indirect discrimination claim if it cannot be shown that the challenged rule is justifiable. For example, a requirement to have an engineering degree would often be justifiable, even though it is a qualification attained by far fewer women than men. Discrimination is unlawful in the fields of employment, education, and the general provision of other benefits and services, such as housing, financial services, restaurants, etc. In practice, the vast majority of claims concern employment.

---

[51] See above, Chapter 1.

[52] For the details, see McCrudden, C, 'Institutional discrimination' (1982) 2 OJLS 303, pp 337–38.

[53] *Griggs v Duke Power Co* 401 US 424 (1971). In fact, the Civil Rights Act made no mention of any distinction between direct and indirect discrimination. To hold that the Act nevertheless extended to the latter was thus a bold stroke of, in effect, judicial law making. See *ibid*, McCrudden, pp 329–36.

European sex equality law

There is a sense in which the origin of Art 119 is far more controversial than anything in the domestic legislation.[54]

Defrenne v SABENA Case 43/75 [1976] ECR 455

Judgment (p 472):

Article 119 pursues a double aim. First, in the light of the different stages of the development of social legislation in the various Member States, the aim of Art 119 is to avoid a situation in which undertakings established in States which have actually implemented the principle of equal pay suffer a competitive disadvantage in intra-Community competition as compared with undertakings established in States which have not yet eliminated discrimination against women workers as regards pay.[55] Secondly, this provision forms part of the social provision of the Community, which is not merely an economic union, but is at the same time intended, by common action, to ensure social progress and seek the constant improvement of the living and working conditions of their peoples, as is emphasised by the Preamble to the Treaty. This aim is accentuated by the insertion of Art 119 into the body of a chapter devoted to social policy whose preliminary provision, Art 117, marks 'the need to promote improved working conditions and an improved standard of living for workers so as to make possible their harmonisation while the improvement is being maintained'. This double aim, which is at once economic and social, shows that the principle of equal pay forms part of the foundations of the Community.

There is no doubt that market integration and economic growth were uppermost in the minds of the Community founding fathers, even if part of the rationale for such an objective was political in the sense of aiming to avoid future armed conflict in Europe. The role of the social provisions within this aim is not altogether clear. The remainder of the social provisions of that part of the Treaty in which Art 119 appears are more aspirational in nature, not expressed in a way likely to give rise to individual rights. The wording of Art 119 is largely based on International Labour Organisation Convention 100, and it may simply be the fact of a precedent on which to draw that explains the much greater precision of wording of this particular article.

In this context, it is impossible to overstate the importance of the decision in *Defrenne v SABENA*. The holding that Art 119 was directly effective was central to all subsequent European jurisprudence which gave individually enforceable rights to sex equality. It also contributed to the high profile which

---

[54] See Barnard, C, 'The economic objectives of Article 119', in Hervey, T and O'Keeffe, D (eds), *Sex Equality Law in the European Union*, 1996, Chichester: John Wiley.

[55] It is well known that France was here uppermost in the mind of the Court; see, eg, Ellis, E, *European Community Sex Equality Law*, 1991, Oxford: Clarendon, pp 38–39.

sex equality has had at a political level in the EC, epitomised, for example, by the various action programmes on equal opportunities for women. Ellis concludes that 'even though it may be more due to political chance rather than conscious planning that sex equality has emerged as such an important issue in the Community, the issue is now firmly on the legal and political agenda and those committed to its practical realisation would be foolish to ignore the potential offered by EC law ...'.[56]

And yet the whole basis for the judgment as expressed in *Defrenne* has been fiercely attacked for its attachment to market solutions at the same time as social objectives are espoused.[57] The issue will be considered in more depth in the chapter on equal pay but the main strands of the argument are as follows:

(a) that equal pay is seen as an issue of ensuring that people get what their work is worth in the marketplace; the assumption that market solutions are appropriate is taken as read and not subjected to critical examination. Another strand to this criticism is that equality is seen almost entirely in employment terms rather than viewed from a more general perspective of overall equality in all areas of society;

(b) the Court has sought to conceal the inevitable tensions between market solutions and social solutions to issues of unequal and low pay. For example, it is assumed that market forces may in certain situations amount to a defence to a claim based on Art 119, though the precise situations when this will occur are left to national courts;[58]

(c) the Court, even when granting substantive rights which *appear* to be far reaching, has used numerous procedural and remedial devices to ensure that the economic costs to employers of seemingly adverse decisions are drastically minimised. Examples include the ruling that equal benefits in occupational pension schemes should only apply as from the date of the judgment in the case, where the Court sanctioned a rare departure from the normal rule that its judgments have retrospective effect;[59] the ruling that retrospective membership of such pension schemes was dependent on the employee's paying the backdated contributions which should have been paid in the period when membership should have been made available;[60] and the ruling that substantive European law rights are

---

[56] *Op cit*, Ellis, fn 55, pp 40–41.

[57] See, eg, Fredman, S, 'European Community discrimination law: a critique' (1992) 21 Industrial LJ 119.

[58] See, eg, *Bilka-Kaufhaus v Weber von Hartz* Case 170/84 [1986] ECR 1607; [1986] 2 CMLR 701; [1987] ICR 110; [1986] IRLR 317; *Enderby v Frenchay AHA* Case C-127/92 [1993] ECR I-5535; [1994] ICR 112; [1994] 1 All ER 495; [1993] IRLR 591.

[59] *Barber v Guardian Royal Exchange Insurance Group* Case C-262/88 [1990] ECR I-1889; [1991] 1 QB 344; [1990] ICR 616; [1990] IRLR 240.

[60] *Fisscher v Voorhuis Hengelo BV* Case 129/93 [1994] ECR I-4583; [1995] ICR 635; [1994] IRLR 651. The Court was especially keen to restrict employer costs in pensions schemes because of the high potential cost of changes to pension rules.

dependent on *domestic* rules for limitation of action, which may be very unfavourable for applicants.[61]

The origins of the relevant EC directives can be dealt with more briefly. The Equal Pay Directive 75/117[62] was passed largely because of Commission dissatisfaction with the rate of progress made by the Member States towards the implementation of the principle of equal pay. As it turned out, the decision the following year in *Defrenne v SABENA* that Art 119 was directly effective had, as one of its consequences, that national legislation which conflicted with Art 119 was, so to speak, directly *ineffective*. Furthermore, as it has generally been held that it adds nothing to the substantive rights conferred by Art 119, but simply serves to make its meaning clearer,[63] the question of the direct effectiveness of the Equal Pay Directive is not an issue which has needed to trouble the court.

Of much greater significance so far as both domestic and European law are concerned is Directive 76/207 EEC, the Equal Treatment Directive.[64] If Art 119 parallels the British Equal Pay Act, then the Equal Treatment Directive parallels the SDA 1975. The Directive arose from the 1974 Social Action Programme, which 'included among the priorities action for the purpose of achieving equality between men and women as regards access to employment and vocational training and promotion, and as regards working conditions, including pay'.

These are the two general directives relevant to European Community anti-discrimination law. Others deal with particular issues and will be considered at the appropriate place. Directive 79/7[65] covers matters of State social security; Directive 86/378[66] covered occupational pensions. Its practical impact following the *Barber* decision was rather slight and it was amended by Directive 96/97, which came into force on 1 July 1997; Directive 92/85[67] gives added protection for the protection of women in connection with pregnancy and childbirth, the provisions of which were incorporated into British domestic law by the Trade Union Reform and Employment Rights Act 1993. Finally, following the British Government's decision to end its opt-out from the Social Charter, three further directives will impact upon anti-

---

61 *Emmott v Ministry of Social Welfare and AG* Case C-208/90 [1991] ECR I-4269; [1993] ICR 8; [1991] IRLR 387.

62 OJ L45/19, 1975.

63 *Defrenne v SABENA* Case 43/75 [1976] ECR 455, pp 478–79. See, also, *Jenkins v Kingsgate (Clothing Productions) Ltd* Case 96/80 [1981] ECR 911; [1981] 1 WLR 972; [1981] ICR 592; [1981] IRLR 228; *Commission of the European Communities v United Kingdom* Case 61/81, [1982] ECR 2601; [1982] ICR 578; [1982] IRLR 333.

64 OJ L39/40, 1976.

65 OJ L6/24, 1979.

66 OJ L225/40, 1986.

67 OJ L348/1, 1992.

discrimination law and gender equality issues: directives on parental leave,[68] on equal rights for part time workers,[69] and on the reversal of the burden of proof in sex discrimination cases.[70]

EUROPEAN LAW, DOMESTIC LAW AND HUMAN RIGHTS LAW[71]

The interaction between European Community law, domestic law, and individual human rights law is an under-developed but potentially highly significant area. It may operate in four ways. The first is the suggestion that there is in European law a fundamental principle of non-discrimination based on sex; the second that there is likewise a fundamental principle of equality; the third concerns the Charter of the Fundamental Social Rights of Workers; and the fourth looks forward to the impact on UK law of incorporation of the European Convention on Human Rights.

The principle of non-discrimination based on sex[72]

In *Defrenne v SABENA*,[73] the third Defrenne case, it was stated that '[t]he Court has repeatedly stated that respect for fundamental personal human rights is one of the general principles of Community law, the observance of which it has a duty to ensure. There can be no doubt that the elimination of discrimination based on sex forms part of those fundamental rights.'[74] The impact and influence of the general principles of Community law is a matter of considerable uncertainty. The very fact that there is detailed legislation on *some* aspects of gender equality implies that there is less space for a broad general principle to operate. But the principle has great potential and significance in the eyes of those who wish to see a refocusing and expansion of Community equality law.

---

68 Directive 96/34/EEC. The Government has announced that this Directive will be implemented by December 1999. See *Fairness at Work*, Cm 3968, 1998, London: The Stationery Office, para 5.11.

69 Directive 97/81/EEC. See (1997) 74 EOR 38. To be implemented by April 2000. *Ibid, Fairness at Work*, para 5.4.

70 Directive 97/80/EEC.

71 See Foster, N, 'The European Court of Justice and the European Convention for the Protection of Human Rights' (1987) 8 Human Rights LJ 245.

72 See Docksey, C, 'The principle of equality between women and men as a fundamental right under Community law' (1991) 20 Industrial LJ 258; *op cit*, Ellis, fn 55, pp 117–34.

73 Case 149/77 [1978] ECR 1365; [1978] 3 CMLR 312.

74 There has never been any equivalent declaration that the elimination of discrimination on the ground of race forms a fundamental principle of Community law.

The general principle of equality

The above principle is concerned solely with gender equality. The further suggestion is that there is in Community law a general principle of equality. The concern here is more with eliminating arbitrariness than with unjust outcomes.[75]

Neither of these principles can themselves normally establish a right or provide a remedy. Rather, in much the same way as recommendations, they can act as a spur or an aid to reaching a particular decision.

The Community Charter of the Fundamental Social Rights of Workers[76]

Yet another example of this process is the Charter of the Fundamental Social Rights of Workers.[77] 'The Charter has no legal status as a legislative instrument, but is more in the nature of a solemn declaration of the direction of policy intended by the signatories.'[78] Relatively little of the Charter is concerned with gender equality. However, Art 16 provides that '[m]easures should also be developed enabling men and women to reconcile their occupational and family obligations'. The problem with this approach is that it implies some degree of positive action, which will in many circumstances be incompatible with the Equal Treatment Directive.[79] Furthermore, the specific Community initiatives in such fields as childcare suggest that few, if any, developments in the area of gender equality are likely to be based on the Social Charter.

---

[75] It has been particularly utilised in the rather specialised group of cases concerning the employment of Community staff. See, eg, *Sabbatini v European Parliament* Case 20/71 [1972] ECR 345; [1972] CMLR 945; and *Razzouk and Beydoun v European Commission* Cases 75/82 and 117/82 [1984] ECR 1509.

[76] See Bercusson, B, 'The European Community's Charter of Fundamental Rights of Workers' (1990) 53 MLR 674; Bercusson, B, *European Labour Law*, 1996, London: Butterworths, Chapter 37.

[77] As is well known, this document was signed at the Maastricht summit, where the British Government, by Protocol, was allowed to opt out of its provisions. The Labour Government acceded to the Charter on 7 November 1997, but has not yet ratified it.

[78] *Op cit*, Bourn and Whitmore, fn 43, pp 35–36.

[79] *Kalanke v Freie und Hansestadt Bremen* Case C-450/93 [1996] ICR 314; [1995] IRLR 660. See below, pp 543–45.

Incorporation of the European Convention on Human Rights[80]

The Human Rights Bill will incorporate into domestic law the provisions of the European Convention on Human Rights, a document which emanates from the Council of Europe, a body which must not be confused with the European Community. Such rights are already part of UK international obligations and may be enforced via the European Human Rights Commission and the European Court of Human Rights.[81] In that sense, the substantive obligations will not change. But as a matter of practice it will be far easier, cheaper and speedier to allege a breach of the Convention, and the obligation on domestic courts so far as possible to interpret domestic legislation[82] so as to accord with the Convention[83] will enormously increase the profile of the Convention both with the judiciary and the general public. For these reasons, more domestic cases are to be expected, with a concomitant growth in domestic human rights jurisprudence.

The impact of the ECHR is a matter for speculation, not least because the jurisprudence emanating from the Commission and the Court is itself developing.[84] There is no protection for economic, social and cultural rights, which means that many of the issues relating to the discrimination in employment are thereby excluded. However, Art 9 grants a right to 'freedom of thought, conscience and religion', issues which might be relevant to both gender and race discrimination. Furthermore, Art 6 gives a right to a 'fair and public hearing' which may be relevant to the way in which decisions affecting employment are taken. This may be particularly significant as both the Commission and the Court have been especially concerned to protect this right to 'natural justice' or 'due process of law'. Both of these rights have the potential for development in the field of employment.

Furthermore, the employment contexts in which the rights may arise are also unclear. While the ECHR is primarily addressed to the State signatories, Art 1 requires that they 'shall secure to everyone within their jurisdiction' the

---

[80] The Universal Declaration of Human Rights 1948, Art 2, states: 'Everyone is entitled to all the rights and freedoms set forth in this Declaration without distinction of any kind, such as race, colour, sex, language, religion, political or other opinion, national or social origin, property, birth or other status.'

[81] Furthermore, the European Court of Justice has held that the ECHR is an unwritten source of Community law norms, such that, so far as possible, the latter should be interpreted so as to conform with the former. See *Internationale Handelsgesellschaft v Einfuhr- und Vorratstelle Getreide* Case 11/70 [1970] ECR 1125.

[82] This rule of construction is to apply to past legislation as well as to future legislation.

[83] There will be no power to *override* domestic legislation; rather, a court which cannot reach an interpretation which is so as to accord with the Convention may make a declaration that the legislation is incompatible with the Convention. Amending legislation would presumably follow.

[84] This chapter is concerned with the basic framework of the ECHR. The following chapter will consider some of the specific grounds of discrimination which might be actionable under the Convention.

rights and freedoms guaranteed by the Convention, thereby providing at least some degree of responsibility for rules applicable to private employment.[85] In addition, the extent to which the State in its capacity as employer thereby has greater duties and responsibilities than private employers is unclear.

The articles with perhaps the most potential significance so far as discrimination is concerned are Art 6, the right to a fair trial, mentioned above, Art 8 and Art 14. Article 8(1) provides that '[e]veryone has the right to respect for his private and family life, his home and his correspondence'. Article 14 provides that 'the enjoyment of the rights and freedoms set forth in this Convention shall be secured without discrimination on any ground such as sex, race, colour, language, religion, political or other opinion, national or social origin, association with a national minority, property, birth or other status'.[86] Article 14, however, does not provide a stand-alone right to be free from discrimination; rather, the right is to be free from discrimination as regards the enjoyment of the *other* rights and freedoms under the Convention. As employment is not such a protected right, employment matters will in most situations fall outside the scope of the Convention. It might be different, though, in the case of a declared policy affecting a group of employees which contravenes Art 14.

The effect is that allegations of sex and race discrimination in employment are unlikely to benefit from incorporation, both because they will not normally attach to another of the protected rights under the Convention, and because of the relative breadth of the current domestic law. But arguments that another article is violated are of potential significance, especially in relation to sexual orientation and religion. Article 8 guarantees 'the right to respect ... for private and family life' which may encompass issues of sexual orientation and gender identity. Article 9 protects freedom of religion, which may be especially relevant to race relations in employment where it concerns the observance of religious duties which may entail a conflict with obligations under the contract of employment.[87]

The impact of incorporation may be greatest as a symbol. The judiciary at every level will be exposed to new forms of reasoning. Whether and in what way this impacts on the public perception of the law and legal system may depend significantly on the types of cases that are brought and the way in which they are reported. In the USA there is a twin-track system of anti-discrimination law, the private law model based on the 1964 Civil Rights Act, and the public law model, based on the 14th amendment to the Constitution,

---

[85] In *Young, James and Webster v UK* (1981) 4 EHRR 38, it was held that, the circumstances of the case involving employment by British Rail, compulsory trade union membership violated the Art 11 right to freedom of association.

[86] See Arai, Y, 'The ECHR and non-discrimination' (1998) 7 *Amicus Curiae*: the Journal of the Society for Advanced Legal Studies 6.

[87] See below, pp 135–36.

which guarantees to everyone the equal protection of the law. This area has been especially significant in the law on affirmative action. For example, cases on the admissions policies of universities[88] and on the policy of a city to allocate at least 30% of its contracting work to minority businesses[89] have been argued under the Equal Protection clause rather than the specific provisions of the Civil Rights Act 1964. In the UK the private law model is, with rare exceptions, the only game in town. It is a matter for speculation whether, in 10 or 20 years time, incorporation of the European Human Rights Convention will have increased the scope for public law rights and remedies to be at least one of the jurisprudential models around which discrimination cases are resolved.

---

[88] *Regents of the University of California v Bakke* 435 US 265 (1978).
[89] *City of Richmond v JA Croson* 488 US 469 (1989).

CHAPTER 5

THE PROHIBITED GROUNDS OF DISCRIMINATION

The Race Relations Act 1976 prohibits discrimination on 'racial grounds'; the Sex Discrimination Act 1975 covers discrimination on the basis of sex and marital status, although the latter is only unlawful in the context of employment. This chapter will also consider the extent to which discrimination on the basis of sex extends to discrimination against transsexuals and discrimination on the basis of sexual orientation. In addition, it is necessary to consider the advantages and disadvantages of extending anti-discrimination legislation to cover discrimination on the basis of other prohibited criteria, such as age and/or religion.[1]

RACE

As we saw in Chapter 1, the origins and causes of what has come to be known generically as racial discrimination are complex. The history of slavery and colonialism rested substantially upon an ideology of the superiority of the white man, overladen with notions of religious and cultural superiority. In the 1950s and 1960s, as the issues became more prominent, 'colour' prejudice was the main focus of attention. Subsequently, the focus shifted somewhat to consideration of nationality, it being argued that, whatever their passports might say, members of minority ethnic groups were not truly 'British'. In any event, the concept of 'race' has little or no scientific credibility: few people are in any sense racially pure, whatever that might mean, and fewer still could begin to prove it to the satisfaction of a court; it is the social meaning of race which is significant, rather than its biological meaning.[2] Furthermore, as the prohibition against unlawful discrimination depends on the motivation of the discriminator, it makes no difference that the victim does not, in a technical or scientific sense, fall within a particular group. For example, a person who is racially harassed may claim, even if of mixed race or if mistakenly considered to be a member of an ethnic minority.

It was essential that the prohibited grounds of discrimination be widely defined, the more so as, for most people, it is impossible to disentangle

---

1   The definition of disability is dealt with in Chapter 16. This book does not deal with discrimination on the basis of being, or not being, a member of a trade union under the Trade Union and Labour Relations (Consolidation) Act 1992, s 137; see Townshend-Smith, R, 'Refusal of employment on grounds of trade union membership or non-membership: the Employment Act 1990' (1990) 20 Industrial LJ 102.

2   See Wasserstrom, R, 'Racism, sexism and preferential treatment: an approach to the topics' (1977) 24 UCLA L Rev 581, above, pp 71–72.

whether the discrimination was on the basis of race, nationality, colour or ethnicity. The width of the definition in the Act reflects this social reality. In addition, the primary purpose of the legislation is to identify prohibited conduct rather than require victims to identify with precision the particular group to which they claim to belong.[3]

As it was always recognised that there would be marginal cases requiring judicial elucidation, the Race Relations Act 1976, s 3(1), provides that 'racial group' means 'a group of persons defined by reference to colour, race, nationality,[4] or ethnic or national origins, and references to a person's racial group refer to any racial group into which he falls'.[5] Three questions have troubled the courts: the line between race and religion, the extent of separateness needed to qualify for the statutory protection, and the application of the legislation to the different national groups within Great Britain.

Mandla v Dowell Lee [1983] IRLR 209, HL[6]

The headmaster of a private school refused to admit a pupil who followed the Sikh religion unless the pupil removed his turban and cut his hair. One of the issues was whether Sikhs as a group were protected by the Race Relations Act 1976. The House of Lords were unanimous that they were.

Lord Fraser of Tullybelton (pp 211–12):

It is not suggested that Sikhs are a group defined by reference to colour, race, nationality or national origins. In none of these respects are they distinguishable from many other groups, especially those living, like most Sikhs, in the Punjab. The argument turns entirely on whether they are a group defined by ethnic origins ...

I recognise that 'ethnic' conveys a flavour of race but it cannot, in my opinion, have been used in the 1976 Act in a strict racial or biological sense. For one thing it would be absurd to suppose that Parliament can have intended that membership of a particular racial group should depend on scientific proof that

---

3   'I ... would insist upon the principle that each individual retains the right of self-definition about group membership or identity: it is not a matter of external characterisation by some outside body. Many people will not wish to be regarded as members of any ethnic group and many more will be of mixed parentage or otherwise have dual attachments that lead them to want to retain what they see as good or desirable elements within each. They must be permitted to choose for themselves.' Lustgarten, L, 'Racial inequality, public policy and the law: where are we going?' in Hepple, B and Szyszczak, E (eds), *Discrimination: the Limits of Law*, 1992, London: Mansell, p 457.

4   By s 78(1) this is defined to include citizenship.

5   The legal definition may therefore be more straightforward than the definition for the purposes of ethnic monitoring. Eg, a Tamil originally from Malaysia could be protected under the RRA 1976 either as a Tamil, a Malaysian or an Asian, but may be forced to tick the 'Other' box if the only possible choices are Indian, Pakistani or Bangladeshi. Similar problems face the children of mixed marriages. Such problems potentially arise in indirect discrimination cases, where the performance of one racial group is being compared with that of another.

6   See, also, [1983] 2 AC 548; [1983] ICR 385.

a person possessed the relevant distinctive biological characteristics (assuming that such characteristics exist). The practical difficulties of such proof would be prohibitive, and in the clear that Parliament must have used the word in some more popular sense. For another thing ... within the human race, there are very few, if any, distinctions which are scientifically regarded as racial ...

For a group to constitute an ethnic group ... it must, in my opinion, regard itself, and be regarded by others, as a distinct community by virtue of certain characteristics. Some of these characteristics are essential; others are not essential but one or more of them will commonly be found and will help to distinguish the group from the surrounding community. The conditions which appear to me to be essential are these:

(1) a long shared history, of which the group is conscious as distinguishing it from other groups, and the memory of which it keeps alive;

(2) a cultural tradition of its own, including family and social customs and manners, often but not necessarily associated with religious observance. In addition to those two essential characteristics, the following characteristics are, in my opinion, relevant;

(3) either a common geographical origin, or descent from a small number of common ancestors;

(4) a common language, not necessarily peculiar to the group;

(5) a common literature peculiar to the group;

(6) a common religion differing from that of neighbouring groups or from the general community surrounding it;

(7) being a minority, or being an oppressed or a dominant group within a larger community ...

A group defined by reference to enough of these characteristics would be capable of including converts, for example, people who marry into the group, and of excluding apostates. Provided a person who joins the group feels himself or herself to be a member of it, and is accepted by other members, then he is, for the purposes of the 1976 Act, a member ... In my opinion, it is possible for a person to fall into a particular racial group either by birth or by adherence, and it makes no difference ... by which route he finds his way into the group ... A person may treat another relatively unfavourably 'on racial grounds' because he regards that other as being of a particular race, or belonging to a particular racial group, even if his belief is, from a scientific point of view, completely erroneous ...

Lord Templeman (p 214):

[T]he statutory definition of a racial group envisages that a group defined by reference to ethnic origin may be different from a group defined by reference to race, just as a group defined by reference to national origins may be different from a group defined by reference to nationality. In my opinion, for the purposes of the 1976 Act a group of persons defined by reference to ethnic origins must possess some of the characteristics of a race, namely group descent, a group of geographical origin and a group history. The evidence shows that Sikhs satisfy these tests. They are more than a religious sect, they are almost a race and almost a nation. As a race, the Sikhs share a common colour, and a common physique based on common ancestors ... They fail to qualify as a separate race, because in racial origin prior to the inception of Sikhism they cannot be distinguished from other inhabitants of the Punjab ... [T]hey fail to qualify as a separate nationality because their kingdom never achieved a sufficient degree of recognition or permanence. The Sikhs qualify as a group defined by ethnic origins because they constitute a separate and distinct community derived from the racial characteristics I have mentioned.

As, by the same logic, Jews qualify for the statutory protection, it is clear that the Act may apply to people who are not visually different from others in the community. Furthermore, the Act clearly applies if a member of one minority group discriminates against a member of another.

The next problem concerned the degree of separateness which was needed. It arose in two cases.

Commission for Racial Equality v Dutton [1989] IRLR 8, CA[7]

The licensee of a pub was concerned about trouble from residents of a nearby caravan site, and so put up signs saying 'Sorry. No travellers'. The CRE brought an action alleging that the notice constituted racially discriminatory advertising under the RRA 1976, s 29. One issue was whether gipsies constitute a racial group.

Nicholls LJ (pp 10–12):

[I]n my view the word 'gipsy' has ... more than one meaning. The classic 'dictionary' meaning can be found as the primary meaning given in the Oxford English Dictionary (1933):

> A member of a wandering race (by themselves called Romany), of Hindu origin, which first appeared in England about the beginning of the 16th century and was then believed to have come from Egypt ...

Alongside this meaning, the word ... also has a more colloquial, looser, meaning ... a nomad ...

[Used in the narrow sense] it is clear that such gipsies are a minority, with a long shared history and a common geographical origin. They are a people who originated in Northern India. They migrated thence to Europe through Persia in mediaeval times. They have certain, albeit limited, customs of their own, regarding cooking and the manner of washing. They have a distinctive, traditional style of dressing ... They also furnish their caravans in a distinctive manner. They have a language or dialect ... which consists of up to one-fifth of Romany words in place of English words. They do not have a common religion, nor a peculiar, common literature of their own, but they have a repertoire of folk tales and music passed on from one generation to the next. No doubt ... gipsies are no longer derived from what, in biological terms, is a common racial stock, but that of itself does not prevent them from being a racial group ...

---

7   See, also, [1989] QB 783; [1989] 1 All ER 306.

I do not think that there was [before the judge] any evidence justifying his conclusion that gipsies have been absorbed into a larger group, if by that he meant that substantially all gipsies have been so absorbed. The fact that some have been so absorbed and are indistinguishable from any ordinary member of the public, is not sufficient in itself to establish loss [of a historically determined social identity]. In my view, the evidence was sufficient to establish that, despite their long presence in England, gipsies have not merged wholly in the population, as have the Saxons and the Danes, and altogether lost their separate identity. They, or many of them, have retained a separateness, a self-awareness, of still being gipsies.

Taylor LJ (p 14):

There may well be individuals on the borderline between membership and assimilation whom it might be difficult to classify, but that does not deny the existence of the group. Likewise, the fact that some of these within the group prefer to call themselves travellers rather than gipsies is not indicative of whether a discrete racial group has ceased to exist.[8]

Dawkins v Department of the Environment [1993] IRLR 284, CA

The applicant was rejected for a job as a van driver after indicating that, as a Rastafarian, he was unwilling to cut his hair and thereby comply with the requirement that drivers have short hair. The Court of Appeal held that Rastafarians did not constitute an ethnic group within the meaning of the Race Relations Act 1976.

Neill LJ (p 288):

It is clear that Rastafarians have certain identifiable characteristics. They have a strong cultural tradition which includes a distinctive form of music known as reggae music. They adopt a distinctive form of hairstyle by wearing dreadlocks ... But the crucial question is whether they have established some separate identity by reference to their ethnic origins ...

It is at this stage that one has to take account of both the racial flavour of the word 'ethnic' and Lord Fraser's requirement of a long shared history. [It was] submitted that if one compared Rastafarians with the rest of the Jamaican community in England, or indeed with rest of the Afro-Caribbean community in this country, there was nothing to set them aside as a separate ethnic group. They are a separate group, but not a separate group defined by reference to their ethnic origins. I see no answer to this submission ...

In my judgment it is not enough for Rastafarians now to look back to a past when their ancestors, in common with other peoples in the Caribbean, were taken there from Africa. They were not a separate group then. The shared history of Rastafarians goes back only 60 years or so.

The fact that in all these cases the history of the group was crucial to the decision shows that the decision on ethnic origin is a socio-historical one rather than in any sense a scientific one. Whether there is a sufficient shared

---

8   The Race Relations (Northern Ireland) Order 1997 specifically includes the Irish traveller community within its definition of protected groups, though in Great Britain travellers who are not gipsies are unprotected.

history, whether there has been more-or-less complete assimilation, must in the end be matters of fact and impression.

Nationality will usually be a more concrete concept. Normally it will refer to nationality as shown in a passport, but whether a 'nation' has a historic existence may still require judgment.[9]

Northern Joint Police Board v Power [1997] IRLR 610, EAT

The applicant claimed that he was rejected for a Chief Constable position in Scotland because he was English.

The EAT upheld the decision of the Industrial Tribunal[10] that it had jurisdiction to hear the complaint.

Lord Johnston (p 613):

Nationality, we consider, has a juridical basis pointing to citizenship, which, in turn, points to the existence of a recognised State at the material time. Within the context of England, Scotland, Northern Ireland and Wales the proper approach to nationality is to categorise all of them as falling under the umbrella of British ... Against that background, therefore, what context should be given to the phrase 'national origins'? It seems to us ... what has to be ascertained are identifiable elements, both historically and geographically, which at least at some point in time reveals the existence of a nation ... [W]hat cannot be in doubt is that both England and Scotland were once separate nations ...

[I]t is for each individual to show that his origins are embedded in such a nation ... [The case was remitted to the Industrial Tribunal] for consideration of the questions whether 'the respondent can establish that he has national origins based upon his assertion that he is English and ... that in fact he was discriminated against ...'.

[Having held that the applicant could bring a case based on discrimination on the basis of national origins, the EAT went on to hold that a claim could not be maintained on the basis of different ethnic origins. There was no sufficient common racial element within the group characterised as Scottish.][11]

The conclusion that the English, Scots, Irish and Welsh[12] have separate national origins seems clearly correct in terms of the policy of the law, even though no doubt the underlying historical premises will not please everyone. Other 'nations' may, on the same logic, be entitled to protection: for example, Walloons (French-speaking Belgians), Catalans and Basques would, it is submitted, all be entitled to protection if they were the victims of

---

9   On the specific issue of 'national' minorities within the UK, see MacEwen, M, 'Racial grounds: a definition of identity' (1998) 3 IJDL 51.

10 By the Employment Rights (Dispute Resolution) Act 1998, s 1(1), industrial tribunals are renamed employment tribunals.

11 See *ibid*, MacEwen, fn 9, pp 59–60.

12 *Griffiths v Reading University Students Union* (1996), unreported, Case No: 16476/96, see 31 DCLD 3.

discrimination in Great Britain; on the other hand, perhaps Sicilians, Bretons and Cornish people would not, on the basis that their identity may no longer be sufficiently distinct for them to be regarded as a 'nation'.

The further holding that the English and the Scots are not separate ethnic groups is also correct. The different ethnic origins of at least some of the various constituent parts of the UK are clear: at one time, for example, Celts, Saxons and Danes would probably have satisfied the modern definition. But assimilation, if not total, has proceeded so far that claims to separate ethnic identity, while in some contexts still having an emotional appeal, are far too flimsy to be accepted in law, a conclusion of course made easier by the fact that such discrimination is covered on the basis of nationality. As the court implied in *Dutton*, there may come a time when gipsies are no longer sufficiently separate to be entitled to protection under the Act.

SEX AND GENDER

The legislation covers discrimination on the basis of sex or, in the employment field only, discrimination on the ground of being married. Until a few years ago two statements seemed clear as a matter of law. First, *White v British Sugar Corporation Ltd*[13] had held that a person who had undergone a sex change operation remained with their biological sex as determined at birth. This meant that transsexuals were not protected and ignored the problem where there was an element of uncertainty concerning birth sex. Secondly, it was *assumed* that 'sex' did not include sexual orientation, and thus gay men and lesbians were not protected *per se*, although it would have been possible to challenge a rule which, for example, excluded gay men but not lesbians from consideration for employment.

Until very recently a contrary assumption was being made – that gender anti-discrimination law, with European law at its forefront, was moving inexorably towards a situation where transsexuals and gay people were within its protection. The decision of the European Court in *Grant v South West Trains Ltd*,[14] that a lesbian partner of an employee is not entitled to the fringe benefits to which she would have been entitled had they been married, has rendered that assumption inaccurate. We need to consider how the law has developed, and the arguments for including transsexuality and sexual orientation within the concepts of gender discrimination.

Arguments for change have come about for a number of reasons. First, there has been a growing understanding that transsexuality and same-sex attraction are, at least in many cases, states which are not necessarily freely

---

[13] [1977] IRLR 121, IT.
[14] Case C-249/96 [1998] IRLR 206.

chosen and can thus be seen as analogous to being black or female. Secondly, the higher public profile of gay men and lesbians has contributed to greater tolerance and social acceptability, while at the same time greater awareness has developed of the extent of discrimination on these grounds. Thirdly, the human rights approach to anti-discrimination legislation seems naturally to encompass discrimination on the basis of sexual orientation.

Wintemute, R, 'Sexual orientation discrimination', in McCrudden, C and Chambers, G (eds), *Individual Rights and the Law in Britain*, 1995, Oxford: Clarendon, pp 493–97, 528:

In asking how sexual orientation discrimination can be conceived of an issue of human rights, one is asking what the right to be free from such discrimination has in common with other human rights, and particularly the right to be free from other kinds of discrimination. Is there any general principle which can explain why certain kinds of discrimination are considered *prima facie* wrongful ... ?

[T]hree possibilities will be considered here: (1) prohibited grounds of discrimination are initially unchosen and currently immutable statuses over which a person has no control; (2) prohibited grounds of discrimination are fundamental rights or freedoms or choices which should not be interfered with; and (3) prohibited grounds of discrimination protect politically, economically, or socially disadvantaged groups that have historically been subjected to prejudice, stereotyping or discrimination ...

[A] fourth approach is possible. It involves arguing that sexual orientation discrimination is nothing more than a kind of sex discrimination ... Essentially, it maintains that whether or not a law ... restricts a person's choice of the direction of their emotional-sexual conduct depends entirely on that person's sex ...

What advocates of sexual orientation discrimination must be persuaded to do is to *accept* and *respect* this extremely difficult and deeply personal choice, whether or not they *understand* or *approve* of it. Most would be willing to do so in the case of persons who choose minority religious beliefs, and would not see the teaching of the existence of and respect for those beliefs as 'promoting' them. A similar view of minority sexual orientations would permit progress beyond the current state of 'limited tolerance'. The rejection of such a view, given the emptiness of the arguments about 'negative effects', amounts to the same kind of fear of difference that underlies much discrimination based on sex, race or religion.

'Equality for lesbians and gay men in the workplace' (1997) 74 EOR 20, pp 20–21:

In 1992, the Labour Research Department ... carried out a questionnaire survey ... Of the 362 respondents, 61% were lesbians, gay men or bisexual. A key finding was that nearly a quarter of respondents had personally experienced, or knew cases of, harassment or victimisation of lesbian or gay workers. Although 90% said that there was an equal opportunities policy at their workplace, only 62% of this group said that the policy covered sexuality ...

A survey of nearly 2,000 lesbians, gay men and bisexuals at work ... was conducted ... in 1993 ... The report found that one in six respondents (15%) had at least one experience of discrimination; a further 21% suspected that they had; and 8% had been dismissed because of their sexuality. But the findings indicated that 'discrimination by employers is only part of the problem. Harassment is a much bigger problem, and discrimination avoidance, including the closet, is the biggest problem of all' ... Almost half the respondents (48%) considered that they had been harassed because of their sexuality. A high proportion concealed their sexual orientation at work to avoid discrimination or harassment. Only 11% said they had never concealed their sexuality at work, compared with over half (56%) who had concealed it in some jobs, and 33% in all jobs ...

As in the LRD survey, the majority (79%) said that their employer had an equal opportunities policy. But just over a quarter of private sector employees said that the policy covered sexual orientation, compared with nearly two-thirds of public sector employees, and around nine out of 10 voluntary sector employees.

Until very recently, it was still assumed that 'sexual orientation' fell outside the definition of 'sex' in the SDA 1975, a view adopted by the EAT in *Smith v Gardner Merchant*.[15] Similarly, in combined appeals concerning the armed services, the Court of Appeal took the view that discrimination on the ground of sexual orientation was not in contravention of the Equal Treatment Directive.[16] Until the last two years the thrust of the argument has been more that the law needed changing specifically to cover sexual orientation; more recently, the view has gained ground that the concept of discrimination on the ground of sex necessarily includes discrimination on the ground of sexual orientation and transsexualism. The European Court first encouraged and then clamped down on this argument.

P v S and Cornwall County Council Case C-13/94 [1996] IRLR 347[17]

When the applicant was hired as a general manager, he was male. A year later the employers learned that the employee intended to undergo gender reassignment. The employee was dismissed, though there was a dispute as to whether this was because of redundancy or because of the proposed operation.

The Industrial Tribunal held that this case fell outside the scope of the Sex Discrimination Act 1975 but referred the case to the ECJ for consideration of whether the Equal Treatment Directive applied.

---

[15] [1996] ICR 740; [1996] IRLR 342. By focusing on the question of whether a gay man would have been treated differently from a gay woman, the Court of Appeal ((1998) *The Times*, 23 July) avoided having to decide this issue.

[16] *R v Ministry of Defence ex p Smith and Grady* and *R v Admiralty Board of the Defence Council ex p Lustig-Pream and Beckett* [1996] QB 517; [1996] ICR 740; [1996] IRLR 100. Nor was judicial review available, on the basis that the policy was, at the time, irrational.

[17] See, also, [1996] ECR I-2143; [1996] ICR 795.

Judgment (p 314):

[T]he right not to be discriminated against on grounds of sex is one of the fundamental human rights whose observance the Court has a duty to ensure ...

Accordingly, the scope of the [Equal Treatment] Directive cannot be confined simply to discrimination based on the fact that a person is of one or other sex. In view of its purpose and the nature of the rights which it seeks to safeguard, the scope of the Directive is also such as to apply to discrimination arising ... from the gender reassignment of the person concerned.

Such discrimination is based, essentially if not exclusively, on the sex of the person concerned. Where a person is dismissed on the ground that he or she intends to undergo, or has undergone, gender reassignment, he or she is treated unfavourably by comparison with persons of the sex to which he or she was deemed to belong before undergoing gender reassignment.

To tolerate such discrimination would be tantamount, as regards such a person, to a failure to respect the dignity and freedom to which he or she is entitled, and which this Court has a duty to safeguard.

Advocate General (p 352):

I am well aware that I am asking the Court to make a 'courageous' decision. I am asking it to do so, however, in the profound conviction that what is at stake is a universal fundamental value, indelibly etched in modern legal traditions and in the constitutions of the more advanced countries: *the irrelevance of a person's sex with regard to the rules regarding relations in society.* Whosoever believes in that value cannot accept the idea that a law should permit a person to be dismissed because she is a woman, or because he is a man, or because he or she changes from one of the two sexes ... by means of an operation which – according to current medical knowledge – is the only remedy capable of bringing mind and body into harmony. Any other solution would sound like a moral condemnation – a condemnation, moreover, out of step with the times – of transsexuality, precisely when scientific advances and social change in this area are opening a perspective on this problem which certainly transcends the moral one.

I am quite clear ... that in Community law there is no precise provision *specifically* and literally intended to regulate the problem; but such a provision can readily and clearly be inferred from the principles and objectives of Community social law, the statement of reasons for the Directive underlining 'the harmonisation of living and working conditions while maintaining their improvement', and also the case law of the Court itself, which is ever alert and to the fore in ensuring that disadvantaged persons are protected.

This decision first reflected an apparent willingness of the Court to engage in judicial activism and, secondly, encouraged the view that the next step on grounds of logic and policy was to extend the law to cover discrimination on the ground of sexual orientation more generally.

Wintemute, R, 'Recognising new kinds of direct sex discrimination: transsexualism, sexual orientation and dress codes' (1997) 60 MLR 334, pp 340–41:

Can *P* be explained ... as entirely consistent with a comparative approach to explaining direct sex discrimination? If so, who is P's comparator? At least three different comparisons are possible. The first is one the ECJ may have implicitly proposed: between a transsexual chromosomal male intending to undergo gender reassignment ... and a non-transsexual male not intending to undergo gender reassignment. This 'intra-sex' comparison shows that a chromosomal male who acquires or intends to acquire ... female physical sex characteristics is treated less favourably than a chromosomal male who complies with the aspect of his social sex role that requires retention of male physical sex characteristics. The second comparison is one I would propose: between a transsexual chromosomal male intending to undergo gender reassignment ... and a non-transsexual chromosomal female not intending to undergo gender reassignment. This 'inter-sex' comparison shows that a chromosomal male who acquires or intends to acquire female physical sex characteristics ... is treated less favourably than a chromosomal female who already has female sex characteristics and is permitted to retain them.

The third comparison is one proposed by P herself before the Industrial Tribunal: between the employer's treatment of P when she was perceived to be a non-transsexual man and the employer's treatment of P once she was known to be a male-to-female transsexual person who would be adopting female sex characteristics ...

Flynn, L, 'Case note: *P v S and Cornwall CC'* (1997) 34 CML Rev 367, pp 375–84:

Whether [the decision] is to be regarded as the principled stand of a body entrusted with a constitutional task requiring it to ensure the protection of human rights, or as the activism of individuals who are creating rights which the legitimate legislator has for its own reasons chosen not to grant, must rest on the commentator's vision of the Community legal order ...

[T]he Court ... states that a person dismissed for undergoing or proposing to undergo gender reassignment is treated unfavourably 'by comparison with persons of the sex to which he or she was deemed to belong [beforehand]'. As P was male under English law at all times and the Court does not seem to suggest that she was legally female as a matter of Community law, it appears that the 'comparison' is between persons of the same sex ... The comparison between P and other male employees is not a comparison based on biological sex but between persons, all of the same sex, of whom one has a feminine gender identity while the others have stable masculine gender identities.

Transsexuals effectively ask to be treated as the woman (or man) that they consider themselves to be, and whose external physical features they possess after surgery and hormonal treatment. They move from belonging to one sex to the other but do not call into question the social roles and expectations imposed on men or women as such. By contrast, for many people, lesbians and gay men offer a more fundamental challenge to the social meaning assigned to what it is to be a 'woman' or a 'man' precisely because they do not wish in any way to be less of a woman or a man by reason of their sexual orientation. On the other hand, compared with the legal arguments adopted by the Court in *P*, recognition that dismissal of a lesbian because she is a lesbian is 'discrimination on grounds of sex' is considerably easier to see than it was in the case of transsexuals ...

[A] far more liberal approach is taken by the Court [than in the past] to discover if a human rights' matter falls within its jurisdiction. The operative part of the Court's reasoning starts with the declaration that fundamental human rights include the principle of equality and that this non-discrimination principle extends to transsexuals. On this basis the Court concludes that the scope of the Directive must be read in the light of this principle. The traditional approach would have been to have first looked at the scope of the Directive and then to find that the principle of equality applied within its scope. The reasoning of the Court quite literally overturns its earlier perspective on this point ...

The logic of *P v S* was rapidly and inevitably accepted by English courts.

Chessington World of Adventures Ltd v Reed [1997] IRLR 556, EAT

In 1991, the applicant announced a change of identity from male to female. For the next three years she was subjected to a campaign of harassment by some of her male colleagues. Eventually, she took sick leave and five months later was dismissed on the ground of lack of capability.

The EAT upheld the decision of the Industrial Tribunal that the Sex Discrimination Act could, in the light of *P v S*, be construed so as to cover unfavourable treatment following a person's statement of intention to undergo gender reassignment.

Judge Peter Clark (pp 518–19):

[W]here, as in this case, the reason for the unfavourable treatment is sex based, that is, a declared intention to undergo gender reassignment, there is no requirement for a male/female comparison to be made. In these circumstances we interpret the 1975 Act consistently with the ruling of the European Court in *P v S*.

While as a matter of strict law this decision only covers discrimination against transsexuals, there is a strong argument that both policy and logic should indicate extension of the decision to cover discrimination on the ground of sexual orientation. The traditional view was that it is not sex discrimination to dismiss a gay man if the same treatment would have been meted out to a lesbian woman; *P v S* supported the view that the comparison could with a person of the same birth sex who had not undergone gender reassignment. By this logic, the comparator in a sexual orientation case might be a person of the same gender who was attracted to people of opposite gender. On this basis, it is discrimination to dismiss a man on the ground of his sexual attraction towards other men, as a woman who was sexually attracted to men would not have been dismissed.

There are two theoretical bases for arguing that discrimination on the basis of sexual orientation comes within the concept of discrimination on the ground of gender. Wintemute argues that an individual's sexual orientation can only be defined in relation to the sex of the individual. Distinctions based on sexual orientation necessarily involve distinctions based on the sexes of individuals.[18] An alternative is that the real basis for discrimination on the basis of sexual orientation is that gay people do not fit in with the stereotype about the way 'normal' men or women should behave.[19] Discrimination on the basis of gender stereotyping is unlawful discrimination, as people have the right to be judged on the basis of their individual characteristics which do not affect their work performance.[20]

The legal and policy arguments were a key reason why the following case was referred to the European Court.

R v Secretary of State for Defence ex p Perkins [1997] IRLR 297, QBD

The applicant brought judicial review proceedings contending that the decision to dismiss him in accordance with the policy of the armed forces to dismiss anyone of homosexual orientation contravened Art 2(1) of the Equal Treatment Directive. The High Court referred the issue to the European Court.

Lightman J (pp 303–04):

If, as the Advocate General [in *P v S*] indicates, transsexuals' right to sexual identity embraces the right to marry persons (according to English law) of the same sex, to allow discrimination against transsexuals on ground of sexual orientation would undermine, if not totally defeat, the protection to which the Court in *Cornwall*'s case held them entitled, namely discrimination on the ground of their transsexuality. The proper way to regard the decision in *Cornwall*'s case may well be that transsexuals are equally protected on the ground of sexual orientation. And if transsexuals, even before and without any gender reassignment operation, are entitled to protection against discrimination on grounds of sexual orientation, it is difficult to see how such protection can be withheld from those of homosexual orientation generally.

'Homosexual orientation' is ... a state of mind relating to sex ... [I]n many cases the distinction [between transsexualism and sexual orientation] (most particularly between transsexuals before any gender reassignment and persons of homosexual orientation) may not be easy to draw: at the least, there is likely

---

18 Wintemute, R, 'Recognising new kinds of direct sex discrimination: transsexualism, sexual orientation and dress codes' (1997) 60 MLR 334, pp 344–45.

19 See 'Gay rights claim fails' (1998) 78 EOR 48, p 49.

20 This is similar to the logic which concludes that discrimination on the ground of pregnancy is automatically sex discrimination because it takes into account a gender-related characteristic. To the argument that the drafters of the Equal Treatment Directive did not at the time intend to include discrimination on the basis of sexual orientation, the riposte is that the same point could be made as regards pregnancy discrimination. The argument did not trouble the Court in *Dekker v Stichting* Case C-177/88 [1990] ECR I-3941; [1992] ICR 325; [1991] IRLR 27 and, until *Grant*, rarely found favour in sex discrimination cases.

to be ... a substantial degree of overlap. It is perhaps difficult to see how the Directive can be directed to outlaw discrimination based on the one state of mind, but not the other, or at least there must be a prospect that like protection will be afforded to both.

The entire social policy reasoning of the Advocate General, as it seems to me, is equally applicable to those of homosexual orientation as it is to transsexuals. Homosexual orientation is a reality today which the law must recognise and adjust to, and it may well be thought appropriate that the fundamental principle of equality and the irrelevance of a person's sex and sexual identity demand that the Court be alert to ensure protection to them and ensure that those of homosexual orientation are no longer disadvantaged in terms of employment, save and unless the discrimination is justified under Art 2(2).

After the decision in the *Cornwall* case, it is scarcely possible to limit the application of the Directive to gender discrimination, as was held in the *Smith* case, and there must be a real prospect that the European Court will take the further courageous step to extend protection to those of homosexual orientation, if a courageous step is necessary to do so. I doubt, however, whether any courage is necessary, for all that may be required is working out and applying in a constructive manner the implications of the Advocate General's opinion and the judgment in the *Cornwall* case ...

The English law approach of concentrating on what may have been in the mind of the draftsmen of the legislation at the time it was passed and the social attitudes and concerns when the legislation was in gestation is not appropriate. The concern of the European Court is to ensure that the law adapts itself to meet new problems which were unconsidered, even if they had not yet revealed themselves at the date of the Directive but which emerged later, and to resolve them according to the fundamental principles or values underlying the Directive and ensuring that the law reflects, not outdated views, but current values.

The hope and expectation that the European Court would accept the logic and policy arguments proved to be in vain.

Grant v South West Trains Ltd Case C-249/96 [1998] IRLR 206

Male partners of female employees were granted travel concessions, whereas female partners of female employees were not. An Industrial Tribunal referred the case to the European Court for determination of whether this policy contravened the Equal Treatment Directive.

Judgment (pp 218–19):

[The] condition, the effect of which is that the worker must live in a stable relationship with a person of the opposite sex in order to benefit from the travel concessions, is ... applied regardless of the sex of the person concerned. Thus travel concessions are refused to a male worker if he is living with a person of the same sex, just as they are to a female worker if she is living with a person of the same sex.

Since the condition ... applies in the same way to male and female workers, it cannot be regarded as constituting discrimination directly based on sex ...

The European Commission on Human Rights ... considers that despite the modern evolution of attitudes towards homosexuality, stable homosexual relationships do not fall within the scope of the right to respect for family life[21] under Art 8 of the Convention ... and that national provisions which, for the purpose of protecting the family, accord more favourable treatment to married persons and persons of opposite sex living together as man and wife than to persons of the same sex in a stable relationship are not contrary to Art 14 of the Convention, which prohibits, *inter alia*, discrimination on the ground of sex ...

It follows that, in the present state of the law within the Community, stable relationships between two persons of the same sex are not regarded as equivalent to marriages or stable relationships outside marriage between persons of opposite sex. Consequently, an employer is not required by Community law to treat the situation of a person who has a stable relationship with a partner of the same sex as equivalent to that of a person who is married to or has a stable relationship outside marriage with a partner of the opposite sex.

In those circumstances, it is for the legislature alone to adopt, if appropriate, measures which may affect that position.

The Court [in *P v S*] considered that [the] discrimination [in that case] was in fact based, essentially if not exclusively, on the sex of the person concerned. That reasoning, which leads to the conclusion that such discrimination is to be prohibited just as is discrimination based on the fact that a person belongs to a particular sex, is limited to the case of a worker's gender reassignment and does not therefore apply to differences of treatment based on a person's sexual orientation.[22]

It could be argued that *Grant* is distinguishable from *Perkins*.[23] In *Grant*, the plaintiff was involved in an active lesbian relationship, whereas Perkins was dismissed on the ground of homosexual orientation rather than homosexual activity. Secondly, *Grant* concerned the issue of travel facilities for the employee's same-sex partner; it is arguable that discrimination against a gay employee should be unlawful under a human rights framework as it concerns a matter which has no effect on capacity to perform a job; the same principle may not apply to benefits to partners on the basis that it might be lawful or

---

[21] No mention is made of the fact that the article specifically refers to respect for *private* life as well as to *family* life.

[22] In *Dudgeon v United Kingdom* (1981) 4 EHRR 149, the European Court of Human Rights held that the then Northern Irish laws, which criminalised homosexual behaviour between consenting adults, contravened Art 8. The 1997 decision of the Commission in *Sutherland v United Kingdom* Application No 25186/94, where it was held to be in contravention of Art 8 for the UK to maintain a higher age of consent for homosexual as opposed to heterosexual activities, might suggest a greater willingness to move towards equivalent rights, at least in some areas.

[23] In *B v Secretary of State and others* (1998), unreported, IT, a claim was brought by a member of a pension scheme whose partner was transexual and thus could not lawfully marry the employee, in circumstances where survivor's benefits were only paid to spouses. The Tribunal held that there was no discrimination, either direct or indirect, as there was no differentiation between men and women. In effect, *Grant* was preferred to *P v S*.

appropriate to discriminate in favour of traditional heterosexual family units. However, the breadth of the reasoning of the *Grant* Court hardly permits an argument that it could be restricted in such a way, and it would be a major surprise were the applicant to prevail in *Perkins*.[24]

The Court of Appeal, in *Smith v Gardner Merchant* ((1998) *The Times*, 23 July), could have concluded that the SDA 1975 is wider than European law and should be interpreted to cover sexual orientation discrimination. After *Grant*, it would have taken a particularly bold court to reach such a conclusion. Instead, the Court remitted the case for consideration of a much narrower question, whether the applicant, as a gay man, was treated less favourably than a gay woman would have been. The broader question was thereby put off until another day.

So far as future legislation is concerned, the Treaty of Amsterdam provides the legal basis for Community legislation in relation to sexual orientation discrimination. But the prospects for such legislation are slender. Not only must the Treaty itself be ratified by each Member State before the power can arise, but, more importantly, such legislation requires unanimity, a unanimity which in relation to such a sensitive issue seems no more than a pipedream. There has been pressure, which will no doubt continue, for the UK Government to introduce legislation. My own view, for what it is worth, is that the political risks which such action would carry make it unlikely for the next few years at least. The strongest argument against such a view is that the Government *has* issued a consultation document concerned with proposed legislation to outlaw discrimination in employment on the grounds of transsexualism.[25] It is proposed that the new regulations will protect from discrimination 'someone who has *formally recorded* with a relevant medical practitioner or qualified psychiatrist that he or she has a settled intention to achieve a new gender identity; is *in the process* of doing so; or *has* achieved a permanent new sexual identity'.[26] There will be no exception based on the feelings of fellow employees, customers or clients; most of the proposed

---

[24] *Grant* was an equal pay claim and so would have applied automatically to all employees whoever their employer. *Perkins* is a claim under the Equal Treatment Directive and thus a successful claim would in the first instance only give protection where the employee concerned worked for an organ of the State. Legislation would become almost inevitable to avoid differential protections according to the status of one's employer, and to avoid a continuing breach of EC law. The exact form of such legislation would pose potential treacherous political problems for a Government.

[25] *Legislation Regarding Discrimination on Grounds of Transsexualism in Employment*, 1998, London: Department for Education and Employment.

[26] *Ibid*, para 11.

exceptions relate to matters of privacy and decency,[27] though a distinction will be drawn between exceptions applicable *during* the process of gender reassignment and those which will be applicable after the process is complete.[28] Defences which have no direct parallel with current SDA defences are 'where the employment has to comply with the doctrines of an organised religion' and, in some cases, where the applicant seeks to return to work with vulnerable people who 'could be disturbed by the fact of gender reassignment in someone they know'. The Government is seeking views on whether there should be a further exception in relation to employment with children.[29]

On the issue of sexual orientation generally, progress in the immediate future is more likely to come through voluntary measures than legal intervention.

'Equality for lesbians and gay men in the workplace' (1997) 74 EOR 20, pp 25–26:

Over 60% of private sector schemes can provide pensions to a dependant other than a partner or children, and 31% of public sector schemes can do so. Just over 20% of private sector schemes and nearly 10% of private sector schemes will consider making provision for same-sex relationships ... All pension schemes are subject to Inland Revenue rules which provide that pensions may be paid to widows and widowers as of right, but in other cases can only be made where the beneficiary is 'financially dependent' on the member. After discussions with Stonewall, the Inland Revenue revised their previous restrictive definition of financial dependence to include 'interdependence' ...

Some organisations provide employees with private health insurance cover ... According to ... BUPA, the issue of whether same-sex partners are covered by the scheme is entirely at the discretion of the employer ... There is no reason why same-sex partners should not be covered, but it is up to the company to specify who, and how many people, are covered ...

Among [other] benefits that may be provided for employees are free or concessionary travel for staff of public transport companies and discounts on products in retail organisations. Where these benefits exist, they may be extended to employees' partners. In these cases, equal treatment requires that same-sex partners be included.

It is now relatively commonplace for equal opportunities policies to cover sexual orientation. However, in this case statistical monitoring and the use of targets will be both impracticable and inappropriate. The concept of under-

---

[27] For the operation of these defences under the SDA 1975, see below, pp 345–47. In *M v Chief Constable of the West Midlands Police* (1996), unreported, Case No: 0864/96, see 31 DCLD 5, the tribunal held that the rejection of an application by a male-to-female transsexual to join the police was justified under Art 2(2) of the Equal Treatment Directive, which provides a defence where 'the sex of the worker constitutes a determining factor', on the ground that the applicant would be unable legally to conduct intimate body searches of females.

[28] *Op cit*, fn 25, paras 13–16.

[29] *Op cit*, fn 25, para 18.

representation of minorities cannot be utilised in the same way as with race and gender; an employer who sought to monitor the sexual orientation of individual members of the workforce would be asking for trouble. For that reason, the emphasis of equal opportunities policies is more on issues concerned with the workplace culture. 'Liverpool City Council's central policy unit has developed a 'lesbian and gay equality checklist' to be used for monitoring the action taken by individual directorates across the council. The questions cover areas including: action plans; resources specifically dedicated to lesbian and gay equality; training of employees on the implementation of lesbian and gay equality in their area of work; monitoring of employment, harassment and discrimination; implementation, policy and procedures; and service delivery issues ...[30] 'In addition, efforts can be made to recruit from within the gay community, both by advertising in particular publications and by stating that applications are welcome from, among others, people who are gay or lesbian.

DISCRIMINATION ON THE GROUND OF BEING MARRIED

Sex Discrimination Act 1975

3 (1) A person discriminates against a married person of either sex in any circumstances relevant [to the employment provisions of the Act] if:

(a) on the ground of her marital status he treats that person less favourably than he treats or would treat an unmarried person of the same sex ...

Section 3(1)(b) outlaws indirect discrimination against married people. There are two key points in the definition. First, while s 3(1)(a) refers to marital status, which could be thought to include the status of being single, it is clear that only discrimination against a married person is covered; discrimination against a single person is lawful under the SDA 1975. Secondly, the comparison is with an unmarried person *of the same sex* as the complainant, so that the provision applies even where the workforce is wholly female. It follows that it is irrelevant that male married people are treated in the same way as female married people if a female married person is treated less favourably than a female single person.

The drafting appears to require that the complainant be married at the time of the action of which complaint is made. This excludes those intending to be married, those about to be married, those living together who are not formally married, and those who have once been married. Article 2(1) of the Equal Treatment Directive is more extensive, covering discrimination, as well

---

[30] 'Equality for lesbians and gay men in the workplace' (1997) 74 EOR 20, p 25.

as on the ground of sex, 'in relation to marital or family status'. While the Court has not ruled on the extent of this provision, the context would appear to support a wide interpretation. This may be important if, for example, someone is dismissed having announced their intention of marrying or divorcing, although the rights would only be against organs of the State. In any event, there is no groundswell of pressure that domestic law needs reforming. Discrimination on the basis of family status may refer to one's position in the family; if one is discriminated against as a parent or a child it would be highly likely that discrimination on the basis of sex would also have occurred.

AGE

The possible extension of anti-discrimination legislation to cover age discrimination – ageism – depends on two things: the prevalence of discrimination on the basis of age, and the extent to which it is possible to analogise between racism and sexism on the one hand and ageism on the other.[31] While discrimination against older people may be more prevalent, younger people may also suffer discrimination on account of their age, perhaps due to a stereotype concerning unreliability. The setting of the national minimum wage for 18 to 20 year olds at £3.00 per hour rising to £3.20 per hour in 2000 will, of course, enshrine in law discrimination against younger workers.

'Age discrimination – no change!' (1993) 48 EOR 21, pp 21–24:

[W]e found that 30% of the job advertisements stated an age preference or requirement ... the vast majority in the private sector; less than 1% were in the public sector. Three-quarters of the advertisements specifying an age preference were placed on behalf of employers by recruitment agencies ... Overall, four out of five job advertisements giving an age preference required someone aged 45 or under ... Around half of the advertisements mentioning age gave a limit of 35 or under ... [32]

[M]any of the age-based assumptions are stereotypes having little basis in fact. Three main conclusions can be drawn from the growing body of research:

(a) age-related declines in productivity, mental efficiency and reaction time are small and many of the losses can be, and are, compensated for by experience;

---

[31] See, generally, Bytheway, B, *Ageism*, 1995, Buckingham: Open University. To illustrate the point, the author shows how ageist birthday cards are socially acceptable in a way that sexist and racist cards are not (pp 75–78).

[32] The survey found that age is commonly used as a form of screening where there is a large number of applicants, and that older people may be denied the opportunity to go on training courses. There is some evidence of a decline in overtly ageist job advertising, although it may be replaced by wording such as 'Don't read this unless you want to join a young team'. See 'Drop in ageist job ads' (1997) 76 EOR 10.

(b) older workers are more satisfied with their jobs than are younger workers, are less likely to leave their jobs than are younger workers, are less likely to leave the organisation for another job and have lower rates of absenteeism and accidents; and

(c) there is considerable variation in age-related losses. It is more meaningful to look at differences between individuals, which are far greater than differences between age groups.

The basis of the argument that ageism is analogous to racism and sexism is that the anti-discrimination principle rests on a human rights argument that one has a right to be considered on merit for a position for which one applies. On this view the argument in favour of a law to deal with age discrimination could be said to be almost self-evident. If the anti-discrimination principle depends more on a history of stigmatised characteristics and economic disadvantage, the arguments for extension to cover age appear far more flimsy.

Buck, T, 'Ageism and legal control' in Hepple, B and Szyszczak, E (eds), *Discrimination: The Limits of Law*, 1992, London: Mansell, pp 246–54:

[T]here are some immediately apparent similarities between [ageism] and sexism and racism. All three identify negative attitudes and stereotypes ascribed to a person by virtue of nothing more than belonging to one of these categories ... [T]hese pejorative attitudes have been, to a greater or lesser extent, institutionalised, although one has to say that the empirical evidence in relation to ageism in the UK is still at a formative stage. The problem in relation to ageism, certainly in the UK, is that it has not fully emerged in the public consciousness.

There are perhaps four qualifications to be made to the latter proposition. First, 'youth culture' has on occasion been a significant social and political entity ... Second, on the personal and psychological plane, individuals persist in being acutely aware of their age ... indeed many individuals could be described as being obsessed with their chronological age. Third, in public affairs, sporadic outbursts from politicians and the press may be occasioned by firms refusing to employ anyone over 35 or 40. Finally, there would appear to be an increasing interest among feminists in the particular position of older women ...

The balance of evidence relating to the use of age limits in job advertising ... would suggest that age is frequently a marginal factor in the decision. Furthermore, employers frequently breach their own age limits in recruitment. Of course, the difficult question here is whether ageism is more covert precisely because age consciousness is generally low or whether it is the nature of the phenomenon that it operates in a less potent fashion than either sexism or racism?

[It has been argued] that men are 'allowed' to age without the same penalties as women. Men's ageing crisis is often linked to pressures on them to be 'successful', while women's ageing crisis relates to their sexual attractiveness and loss of reproductive function ...

The relationship between racism and ageism is also problematic. Each ethnic group imposes its own distinctive social meaning on the individual's experience of ageing. Some commentators have argued that black Americans do not suffer the same discontinuities in their lives as their white peers. Other argue that the 'triple jeopardy' of being old, poor and belonging to a racial minority has an additive discriminatory effect ...

The obvious difference about being old compared with being female or a member of a racial minority is that it is an attribute achieved over a long period of time and ... it is achieved by most members of society. The experience of ageing can, therefore, claim to have a more universal application. If equality legislation can be made wide enough to accommodate some rational model of equality between age cohorts, it is arguable that all members of such a society will have a direct interest in supporting the equality principle ...

It may ... be the case that one of the strongest arguments in support of age discrimination legislation ... is that it is (potentially) a protection for all workers.

Arguably, a clear, simple measure is required, perhaps predominantly as a public relations exercise. A law making age-discriminatory advertising unlawful has much to recommend it in this respect. There is ample evidence to show that age limits in employment advertising are fairly widespread ... Such a law would 'bite' in a clearly defined area and cause many employers, for the first time perhaps, to pause and reconsider their opportunities policies in the age context.

The obvious legislative model is the USA, which in 1977 passed the Age Discrimination in Employment Act (ADEA). The basic legal model adopted reflected existing law on race and sex discrimination.[33] The impact of the law has been less in terms of granting significant legal or political rights to a disadvantaged group, and more in terms of granting certain legal rights to individuals which were not previously available.

Rutherglen, G, 'From race to age: the expanding scope of employment discrimination law' (1995) 24 JLS 491, pp 495–501, 509, 520:

With several exceptions, the [Age Discrimination in Employment Act] covers all employees at or above the age of 40, regardless of race or sex.[34] Although Title VII nominally has equally broad coverage, it was intended to protect mainly racial minorities, women and other traditional victims of discrimination ... What the reported cases reveal, and what the empirical evidence confirms, is that white males have been the principal beneficiaries of the ADEA. Whatever be the justification for protecting white males aged 40 or over, it cannot be that they have been excluded from political and economic

---

[33] Procedurally, there were originally significant differences, especially as regards the ability of age discrimination plaintiffs to obtain trial by jury. Since the 1991 Civil Rights Act, trial by jury is now more frequently available in race and gender cases.

[34] It follows that affirmative action *in favour* of those over 40 is permissible. Any proposed British legislation would have to resolve the issue of whether to extend protection to younger workers where there is discrimination in favour of older workers.

power. The justification for the ADEA must therefore be based on entirely different grounds. These turn out to have a surprising resemblance to the justification for recognising claims for wrongful discharge [or unfair dismissal in British terms] ...

ADEA cases usually concern a discharge from employment, or less frequently, denial of promotion or refusal to hire. These cases are decided under the same structure of proof as claims of racial or sexual discrimination ...

In constitutional law, there is no need to protect the old from the rest of the population, most of whom will live to the same age. So too, in employment, there is no evidence that older workers on the whole are worse off than younger workers, although the earnings of unskilled workers do tend to decrease before retirement.

Nor can discrimination against older workers be condemned as an inefficient form of statistical discrimination ... A statistical theory of age discrimination would have to establish that the balance of efficiency lies with prohibiting generalisations on the basis of age. This conclusion is implausible for several reasons: first, everyone's physical and mental abilities decline at some point with age, more steeply for some individuals than others and more steeply in some jobs than others; second, the countervailing benefits of age, such as experience and judgment, do not invariably outweigh the loss of these abilities; third, the period over which older workers can gain and utilise new skills necessarily is shorter than for younger workers; and fourth, more accurate methods of evaluation, such as individualised testing, may cost enough to outweigh the gain in accuracy that they achieve ...

[Claims have been] mainly concerned with protecting the investment that long term employees have made in developing skills specific to their jobs ...

[T]he average recovery for each ADEA action ... was two-and-one-half times the average recovery in each Title VII case ...

By every measure, plaintiffs in ADEA cases are better off than plaintiffs in other employment discrimination cases ... [T]hey are much more likely to be managerial and professional employees ... They are, of course, likely to be older than other plaintiffs and to have a longer tenure on the job ... It is therefore not surprising to find that the average salary of ADEA plaintiffs is almost twice the average salary of other plaintiffs ...

Claims under the ADEA bear a far stronger resemblance to wrongful discharge claims than other claims of employment discrimination precisely because they are not claims on behalf of a discrete and insular group in our society. Like wrongful discharge claims, they are usually brought by white males, and they can usually be avoided by employers who establish general safeguards against unjust dismissal. The institutional reform stimulated by the ADEA, apart from changes in retirement and benefits policies, is indistinguishable from the reform caused by the law of wrongful discharge.

The logic of this argument is that age discrimination law is unlikely to be used frequently by those who are denied job opportunities. Even if it were, it is arguable that compensation levels would be lower than in race and gender cases; if ageism is less stigmatising than racism or sexism, the degree of injury to feelings and thus compensation will consequently be lower. The law would be used in some promotions cases, although problems of proof and the difficulty of establishing the level of loss of earnings may depress awards and thus reduce claims.

Proof of discrimination on the basis of age would often be difficult. It was pointed out in *Laugesen v Anaconda Co*[35] that, even without discrimination, a dismissed older worker will normally be replaced by someone younger. 'This factor of progression and replacement is not necessarily involved in cases involving the immutable characteristics of race, sex and national origins. Thus, while the principle thrust of the Age Act is to protect the older worker from victimisation by arbitrary classification on account of age, we do not believe that Congress intended automatic presumptions to apply whenever a worker is replaced by another of a different age.' On the other hand, even though the American legislation only protects those over 40, it is perfectly possible that the Act could be violated where, for example, a 55 year old was replaced by a 45 year old.

It may be contended that reaction time declines with age and that in consequence there may be safety issues involved in continuing to employ older workers. The following case concerns an American attempt to face up to the issue.

Hodgson v Greyhound Lines Inc 499 F 2d 859 (7th Cir 1974)

The bus company had a policy that no one over 35 could be hired for a job as an inter-city bus driver.

Greyhound had to establish that the essence of its operations would be endangered by hiring drivers over 40 years of age.

Swygert CJ (pp 864–66):

[I]t is not necessary that Greyhound show that all or substantially all bus driver applicants over 40 could not perform safely ... Greyhound must demonstrate that it had a rational basis in fact to believe that the elimination of its maximum hiring age will increase the likelihood of risk of harm to its passengers. Greyhound need only demonstrate, however, a minimal increase in risk of harm ...

Greyhound contends that even though an applicant between age 40 and 65 may satisfactorily perform on the driver qualification examinations so that at the outset he would be entitled to employment, there is no way of telling how safely he will perform for a sustained period of time given the fact that he will be assigned to the arduous tasks involved [which may involve being on call 24 hours a day, seven days a week with as little as two hours' notice to take runs that the more senior regular drivers do not operate] at a time when his body begins to undergo degenerative changes due to the ageing process. The statistical evidence produced by Greyhound lends support to its belief that

---

35   510 F 2d 307 (6th Cir 1975).

elimination of the maximum hiring age will increase the risk of harm to passengers ... [D]espite the offsetting benefits derived through increased experience as a Greyhound driver, the driver accident rate begins to increase at age 55 ... Greyhound's safest driver is 55 years of age and has 16 years of experience as a Greyhound driver – two qualities which newly hired drivers between ages 40 and 65 would never be able to attain during their tenure at Greyhound ...

Greyhound need not establish its belief to the certainty required by the Government and the district court, for to do so would effectively go so far as to require Greyhound to experiment with the lives of passengers in order to produce statistical evidence pertaining to the capacities of newly hired applicants aged 50 to 65 years of age. Greyhound has amply demonstrated that its maximum hiring age policy is founded upon a good faith judgment concerning the safety needs of its passengers and others. It has established that its hiring policy is not the result of an arbitrary belief lacking in objective reason or rationale.

The Government has stated its belief that at present there is no proven need for a law on age discrimination. Rather, there is to be a Code of Practice aimed at persuading employers to take voluntary steps towards the avoidance of age discrimination and at encouraging diversity of ages within the workforce.[36]

RELIGION

Discrimination on the basis of religion is not unlawful in Great Britain, though it is in Northern Ireland, where issues of discrimination against Catholics and Protestants are clearly more significant than in Great Britain.[37] Discrimination against those who practise non-Christian religions is extremely hard to disentangle from discrimination on the ground of ethnic origin, overt *religious* discrimination will very often constitute covert *racial* discrimination.[38] Given the wide range of different circumstances which such a law might cover, the close connection between religion and lifestyle which would give rise to issues as to when discrimination on the basis of lifestyle was justifiable, and the well known and largely intractable problem of arriving at a satisfactory definition of religion – the spectre of groups such as Scientologists utilising a religious discrimination law is potentially problematic – it is unsurprising that the

---

[36] See 'Government pledges age code' (1998) 78 EOR 2.

[37] Fair Employment (Northern Ireland) Act 1989. The interest of this legislation lies more in its remedial structure than in the concept of religion which it employs. See below, p 557.

[38] *JH Walker Ltd v Hussain* [1996] ICR 291; [1996] IRLR 11, EAT, below, p 512.

Government has decided that there is no proven need for legislation outside Northern Ireland.[39]

The counterargument focuses more on the symbolic and educative message that such a law would send.[40] The current law may not always cover converts or situations where, for example, Muslims are merely a small minority within a larger racial group. More importantly, such a law 'would convey the important message that religious identities are valued and respected throughout British society'.[41] In the USA, where the Civil Rights Act 1964 does include religious discrimination, there is an exception 'with respect to the employment of individuals of a particular religion to perform work connected with the carrying on ... of its activities'. The boundaries of such an exception, such as the range of jobs which it covers, and the extent to which, for example, a group may discriminate against women on the basis that it believes that women should not hold certain positions, have given rise to considerable litigation.[42]

It may well be that the developing European Human Rights jurisprudence has a role to play here. Article 9 protects freedom of religion,[43] while Art 14 includes discrimination on the basis of religion, which gives scope to argue that public authorities unjustifiably favour a particular religion over another. This would of course not avail victims of religious *employment* discrimination, but such victims are unlikely to fall outside the provisions of the Race Relations Act 1976. It is in the public domain, which largely falls outside the scope of this work, that legislation may be most needed.[44] It remains to be seen to what extent Art 14 will prove adequate. The following case, though decided 20 years ago, is not an encouraging precedent.

---

[39] See (1997) EOR 10. On the Northern Ireland legislation, see Yarrow, S, 'The individual pursuit of fair employment' (1998) 78 EOR 25; 'Sectarian harassment guidelines' (1997) 71 EOR 32.

[40] See, eg, *Islamophobia – A Challenge to us All*, 1997, London: Runnymede Trust.

[41] *Ibid.*

[42] See Boyle, J, 'Religious employers and gender employment discrimination' (1986) 4 Law and Inequality 637.

[43] Harris, D, O'Boyle, M and Warbrick, C, *Law of the European Convention on Human Rights*, 1995, London: Butterworths, Chapter 9.

[44] See Poulter, S, 'The limits of legal, cultural and religious pluralism' and Montgomery, J, 'Legislating for a multi-faith society: some problems of special treatment', in *op cit*, Hepple and Szyszczak, fn 3, Chapters 10 and 11 respectively; Poulter, S, 'Minority rights', in McCrudden, C and Chambers, G (eds), *Individual Rights and the Law in Britain*, 1995, Oxford: Clarendon.

Ahmad v Inner London Education Authority **[1978] 1 All ER 574, CA**[45]

The applicant teacher was a devout Muslim who felt it was his religious duty to attend a Mosque each Friday afternoon. The authority terminated his full time contract and offered him a contract for four-and-a-half days each week, excluding Friday afternoon. He refused to accept the offer, resigned and claimed constructive unfair dismissal. One of the issues was whether the actions of the authority infringed Art 9.

The claim failed, with Scarman LJ dissenting.

Denning MR (p 578):

I think that Mr Ahmad's right to 'manifest his religion ... in ... practice and observance' must be subject to the rights of the education authority under the contract and to the interests of the children whom he is paid to teach. I see nothing in the European Convention to give Mr Ahmad any right to manifest his religion on Friday afternoons in derogation of his contract of employment, and certainly not on full pay.

Scarman LJ (p 585):

A narrow construction ... would mean that a Muslim, who took his religious duty seriously, could never accept employment as a full time teacher ... In modern British society, with its elaborate statutory protection of the individual from discrimination arising from race, colour, religion or sex, and against the background of the European Convention, this is unacceptable, inconsistent with the policy of modern statute law, and almost certainly a breach of our international obligations.[46]

There was no argument based on indirect racial discrimination. Such a claim would have been problematic, as the employers' evidence was that the applicant was the only person who had complained among many hundreds of Muslim teachers. To come within indirect discrimination, the employer's policy must have an adverse impact on a significant proportion of people. A right to be free from religious discrimination, on the other hand, would, assuming the belief was genuine, apply however many adherents held the same views.

Ahmad suggests that it will be difficult to utilise the ECHR where one's religious convictions prevent one from performing the duties of the job. There may be a stronger case where, for example, employers attempt to prevent workplace proselytising or the wearing of badges with religious slogans.[47] It would be difficult to deny that a breach had occurred if, for example, an employer required employees in some sense to participate in religious activities while at work.

---

[45] See, also, [1978] QB 36.

[46] In *X v UK* (1981) No 8160/78, 22 DR 27, where the issue was similar, the Commission held that the employers who refused to release him had given 'due consideration' to his right in that they had attempted to reach a reasonable accommodation with him.

[47] See *Kokkinakis v Greece* (1993) A 260; see *op cit*, Harris *et al*, fn 43, pp 366–68.

THE EUROPEAN CONVENTION ON HUMAN RIGHTS[48]

Article 14 uses extremely wide language.[49] It covers discrimination 'on any ground such as sex, race, colour, language, religion, political or other opinion, national or social origin, association with a national minority, property, birth or other status'. Not only are the specific examples far wider than current domestic or European anti-discrimination legislation, it is clear that the use of the words 'such as' mean that other unstated grounds for discrimination might contravene the article. 'The Strasbourg authorities have characterised a large number of "other statuses", including sexual orientation, marital status, illegitimacy, status as a trade union, military status, conscientious objection, professional status and imprisonment as falling within this residual category.'[50]

The width of this provision does not mean that there is great scope for expanding domestic jurisprudence. Article 14 does not provide for a free standing right, but only protects persons from discrimination in relation to one of the other rights guaranteed under ECHR.[51] As the vast majority of rights protected by the Sex Discrimination Act 1975 and the Race Relations Act 1976 are economic, social and cultural rights which fall outside the protection of ECHR, the overlap between these two sources of anti-discrimination law is likely to prove very limited. Furthermore, the Court has shown a marked disinclination to utilise Art 14 where it is possible to establish breach of a different article. This caution is the result not of the wording of Art 14 itself but a 'policy of judicial abstention'.[52]

The way in which the Court has interpreted the concept of discrimination shows similarities to domestic and EC jurisprudence, but is less fully developed. In particular, it is unclear whether indirect discrimination falls within Art 14; if it does, the burden on the applicant to establish its existence is a heavy one.[53] In order to establish discrimination, the applicant has to show less favourable treatment than of another person in an analogous situation. The State defendant then has the opportunity to justify the differentiation. In other words, direct discrimination is potentially justifiable. In the *Belgian Linguistic*[54] case, the Court held that the non-discrimination principle was

---

[48] See Aras, Y, 'The ECHR and non-discrimination' (1998) 7 *Amicus Curiae*, the Journal of the Society for Advanced Legal Studies 6.

[49] See *op cit*, Harris *et al*, fn 43, Chapter 15.

[50] *Op cit*, Harris, fn 43, p 470.

[51] This does not mean that a violation of Art 14 can *only* occur where there is a violation of one of the other rights. Rather, Art 14 only applies to situations within the *ambit* of one of the other rights. See *op cit*, Harris *et al*, fn 43, pp 464–69.

[52] *Op cit*, Harris, fn 43, p 469.

[53] *Op cit*, Harris, fn 43, fn 43, pp 477–79.

[54] (1968) A 6.

only violated if the distinction had 'no reasonable and objective justification. The existence of such a justification must be assessed in relation to the aim and effects of the measure under consideration'. The objective of the differentiation must be legitimate, and the means chosen must be both appropriate and proportionate to that objective. While the criteria appear relatively stringent, the manner of their interpretation has been less so. It is normally not difficult for States to show that the policy under challenge has a rational aim. As regards the means chosen, the Court is relatively deferential to what is termed the 'margin of appreciation', that is, the State's discretion as to the appropriate manner in which to achieve its policy objectives. In evaluating the issue, the Court has held that race, gender and illegitimacy are what are called 'suspect categories', which operate to place a higher burden on the State to justify a policy of differentiation. This means that the highest standards of review are in areas where UK domestic legislation is already at its strongest.

The scope for development in areas not at present covered by UK anti-discrimination legislation – and, for that matter, in areas which are – is probably limited. Cases may be most likely to concern a more or less explicit policy rather than the outcome of individual employment decisions. In such cases, a rational explanation of the objective will normally be forthcoming. As human rights jurisprudence is concerned with the setting of supra-national standards, any argument that a situation is peculiar to one State will be treated seriously. The Court's conception of its role as 'subsidiary' to national legal systems is a further reason why deference to State decision making is likely to be manifest.

Two further, more general points may be made. First, the ECHR is concerned with individual and not with group rights. The Convention is not primarily concerned to protect minority rights, though this may be a side effect of its jurisprudence. It follows that there can be no *redistributive* thrust to Art 14. Secondly, a holding that a State has violated ECHR imposes an obligation on that State to ensure non-repetition, often via a change in domestic law. It does not, in itself, provide a remedy for the individual whose rights have been violated. This will frequently act as a disincentive to the bringing of individual claims. It may be more promising to argue that domestic legislation should be interpreted in the light of ECHR rather than simply alleging a breach of the Convention. All in all, it is probably unwise to anticipate that incorporation of the European Convention will lead to any significant or rapid widening of the scope of the anti-discrimination principle as it operates in the UK.

CHAPTER 6

DIRECT DISCRIMINATION

There are two stages in the successful proof of unlawful discrimination. The first is to show that an act has occurred which satisfies the definition of discrimination. This may be either direct discrimination, indirect discrimination or victimisation. If this is achieved, the second stage is to establish that discrimination occurred in one of the prohibited contexts. These are, respectively, employment, education and the provision of services. The definition of discrimination is the same in each context, though what is prohibited in each of the contexts clearly differs. This means that, for example, a non-employment case may be authoritative on the meaning of discrimination in the employment context. The vast majority of reported cases, though, do stem from employment.

Most claims of unlawful direct discrimination involve an allegation that the aggrieved person has been refused a job, or not promoted, or dismissed because of their race or gender. Occasionally, though less frequently than in the past, some specific reference will have been made to race or gender. Most employers are now sufficiently aware of the legislation to avoid such an obvious error, even if possessed of a deliberate intention to discriminate. Yet discrimination may occur even without such hostility. The case law is now clear that no ill-will or prejudice need be shown in order to prove unlawful direct discrimination. This chapter will first consider the definition of direct discrimination; the specific issue of discrimination in dress and appearance codes will be analysed; and the range of difficulties involved in proving direct discrimination will be examined. Issues of pregnancy discrimination, and claims based on harassment, are dealt with in separate chapters.

Sex Discrimination Act 1975

Section 1(1):

A person discriminates against a woman ... if:

(a) on the ground of her sex he treats her less favourably than he treats or would treat a man ...[1]

Race Relations Act 1976

Section 1(1):

A person discriminates against another ... if:

---

[1] SDA 1975, s 3, prohibits discrimination on the ground of being married, this prohibition being restricted to the field of employment. Here the comparison is with how an unmarried person of the same gender as the applicant was or would have been treated. See above, pp 128–29.

(a) on racial grounds[2] he treats that other less favourably than he treats or would treat other persons ...

It will thus be seen that neither act specifically utilises the phrase 'direct discrimination', though this has become the accepted shorthand. Such shorthand may be misleading as it may wrongly convey an impression – especially to those not versed in the intricacies of the legislation – that such discrimination need necessarily be deliberate and motivated by ill will.

LESS FAVOURABLE TREATMENT

There are two parts to the definition of direct discrimination: that the applicant was treated less favourably[3] than her comparator, and that such treatment was on ground of sex, or race, as the case may be.

Most instances of less favourable treatment will be obvious: the applicant will not have been appointed, or promoted, etc. As long as the treatment is less favourable, the definition is satisfied – what some might regard as relatively trivial may still be covered. Early cases suggested that minor distinctions were not covered by the legislation; thus, in *Peake v Automotive Products Ltd*,[4] the Court of Appeal held that allowing women employees to leave the factory five minutes earlier than the male employees was not actionable partly because the court considered that the degree of differentiation or discrimination was too minor. This approach was effectively overruled in *Gill v El Vino Co Ltd*[5] where it was held to be unlawful to refuse to serve women in a bar even though the degree of upset or insult might to many people not be worth the bother of complaining. If there is less favourable treatment, it is irrelevant how much less favourable that particular treatment may be.

There is a difference between race and gender on the question of whether different treatment *necessarily* constitutes less favourable treatment. Under s1(2) of the Race Relations Act 1976 it is stated that to segregate a person from other persons on racial grounds is to treat him less favourably than they are treated.[6] This is a clear recognition of the historical fact that segregation on

---

2 'Racial grounds' is defined by s 3(1) to mean 'colour, race, nationality or ethnic or national origins'. See above, pp 111–17.

3 In America, direct discrimination is known as disparate treatment. See *McDonnell Douglas v Green* 411 US 792 (1973).

4 [1978] QB 233; [1978] 1 All ER 106; [1977] IRLR 365.

5 [1983] QB 425; [1983] 1 All ER 398; [1983] IRLR 206. See, also, *McConomy v Croft Inns Ltd* [1992] IRLR 561, High Court of Northern Ireland.

6 RRA 1976, s 26, provides a limited exception to the principle of non-discrimination for the benefit of certain clubs, societies, etc, which aim to benefit members of a particular nationality or racial group, although such organisations may not discriminate on the basis of colour. See below, p 377.

ground of colour has been a central plank in the ideology of racial inferiority, and is essential to render unlawful the provision of, for example, separate but equivalent toilet and washing facilities. Of course, in the USA, the provision of 'separate but equal' facilities, especially in the field of education, were usually nothing of the kind.

The problem with this provision concerns the meaning of 'segregate'. In *FTATU v Modgill, Pel Ltd v Modgill*,[7] one of the grounds of the applicant's complaint was segregation based on the high numbers of Asians who performed his particular job. The EAT held that the racial separation resulted from the actions of the employees themselves who introduced their friends and acquaintances whenever a vacancy arose. A distinction was drawn between deliberate racial segregation brought about by the employer, which is unlawful, and the situation where the fact that all the workers are of a particular racial group arises from the actions of the employees. In the latter case, the failure by the employer to intervene and to insist on workers of other racial groups going into the shop does not amount to an act of segregation.[8]

Where gender is concerned, it is not the case that segregation *necessarily* entails less favourable treatment. This clearly reflects the cultural reality that men and women should sometimes be separate, especially, but not only, as respects washing and bathroom facilities. The other area where segregation occurs is in the field of education, where there is some evidence to suggest that girls do better – or at least achieve better exam results – where they are educated in an all-female environment. The provision of single-sex schools is specifically permitted by s 26 of the SDA 1975, but the way in which such provision was forthcoming led to problems in the following case.

Birmingham City Council v Equal Opportunities Commission [1989] AC 1155, CA and HL[9]

Selective single-sex education was provided in grammar schools for about 5% of Birmingham children – such selection being based on exam results. There were more grammar school places available for boys and thus girls required higher marks to gain a grammar school place than did boys. The EOC succeeded in the contention that this constituted unlawful discrimination.

Dillon LJ (p 1176):

The loss, because of sex, of the chance of getting something which is reasonably thought to be of value is enough to constitute sex discrimination. It is not necessary for the Commission, in order to establish less favourable

---

7 [1980] IRLR 142, EAT.

8 The result might thus have been different had a claim been brought by someone of a different racial group who wished to work in that shop; such a claim would not be based on segregation, but on the indirectly discriminatory requirement that to be employed there one had to be a relative or friend of a current employee.

9 See, also, [1989] 1 All ER 769; [1989] IRLR 173, HL.

treatment, to prove ... that selective schools are, either generally, or in the case of particular pupils, objectively better or more suitable than comprehensive schools.

Lord Goff of Chieveley (p 1193):

It is enough that, by denying the girls the same opportunity as the boys, the council is depriving them of a choice which (as the facts show) is valued by them, or at least by their parents, and which ... is a choice obviously valued, on reasonable grounds, by many others ...

The specific legislative protection for single-sex education is required because not all providers of education operate both boys' schools and girls' schools. The *Birmingham* case, however, demonstrates that where separate facilities are provided, they must be equal as between males and females. Thus the provision of as many places for girls as boys in single-sex grammar schools would not have been unlawful. As segregation on the ground of sex is not automatically unlawful, it may be permissible to provide separate facilities or teaching for boys and girls even within the confines of a mixed school – as long, of course, as the facilities so provided are equal. It is not equal to offer boys metalwork classes and girls needlework classes but it would be permissible for boys' metalwork classes and girls' metalwork classes to take place at different times. Nor is the argument limited to schools: separate leisure centre gymnastic or trampolining classes for boys and girls are not unlawful because there is no element of less favourable treatment.[10] It is clear and of fundamental importance that the same arguments are totally impermissible as regards race; the deliberate segregation of the races for whatever reason is always conclusively regarded as constituting less favourable treatment.

It is possible that differentiation between the sexes may involve less favourable treatment of both men and women. *Birmingham* established that denial of a perceived opportunity is sufficient for less favourable treatment.[11] This is particularly significant when considering the issue of retirement ages. To require men to work until they are 65 whereas women must retire at 60 may be discriminatory against men who would like to retire at 60 and also against women who would like to work until they are 65.

---

[10] See below, pp 384–85, for discussion of the provision of facilities, especially sport, known to be more likely to be attractive to men than women.

[11] In *Burrett v West Birmingham HA* [1994] IRLR 7, EAT, it was held that the fact that the applicant herself considered that she was being treated less favourably was insufficient. The question of whether there is in fact less favourable treatment is an objective one for the tribunal to determine. In *Birmingham*, there was an objective denial of an opportunity to attend grammar school.

... ON GROUND OF SEX OR RACE

When it has been established that there has been less favourable treatment, it must be established that it was *on ground of* sex or race. There is here a difference between the two pieces of legislation. Under the SDA 1975, the less favourable treatment must be on the ground of the sex of the complainant.[12] Under the RRA 1976, on the other hand, the less favourable treatment may be on the ground of the race of a third party. In *Showboat Entertainment Centre Ltd v Owens,*[13] the applicant, a white male, was dismissed from his job as entertainment centre manager for refusing to obey instructions to prevent black customers from entering the centre. He claimed he had been dismissed on racial grounds. The EAT held that the legislation applied where the race of a third party is the effective cause of the complainant's detriment. Browne-Wilkinson J said that 'the words "on racial grounds" are perfectly capable in their ordinary sense of covering any reason for an action based on race, whether it be the race of the person affected by the action or others'.[14]

Weathersfield Ltd v Sargent [1998] IRLR 14, EAT

The applicant obtained a job as a receptionist for a van rental company. She was instructed that she should inform ethnic minority inquirers that no vehicles were available. The following day she decided that she could not carry on in the job and resigned. The question whether she was a victim of racial discrimination was decided in her favour.

Morison J (p 16):

> [It is contended that] she had two options only available to her, either to accept the racially discriminatory instruction; or to reject it. If she had elected to continue with it ... there would have been no proceedings. If she decided to reject it, then either she was going to be dismissed, or she might have been required to continue in her employment in knowing breach of the implied term of trust and confidence which is a fundamental term of the contract of employment. [It is submitted] that discrimination in the form of a compulsion or requirement to carry out an unlawful racially discriminatory practice occupies ... a peculiar or special position ...

> [T]he actual or hypothetical comparator to be used under s 1 was someone who was prepared to go along with the employer's unlawful instruction.

> In those circumstances it is not difficult ... to say that Mrs Sargent has been unfavourably treated by comparison with such another person, because she,

---

[12] But action taken against someone on the basis of the sex of a third party may be actionable under s 4, the victimisation provision. In addition, where an employee discloses unlawful discriminatory behaviour to the employer or other person, there may in some circumstances be protection under the Public Interest Disclosure Act 1998, the Act designed to protect whistleblowers. See below, pp 366–67.

[13] [1984] 1 WLR 384; [1984] 1 All ER 836; [1984] IRLR 7, EAT.

[14] See, also, *Zarcznska v Levy* [1979] 1 WLR 125; 1979 1 All ER 864; [1978] IRLR 532, EAT.

unlike the comparator, did not regard herself as being able to continue to work with an employer who operated such a policy ... Accordingly, therefore she regarded herself as a victim of the treatment meted out to her by the employers.

It follows that, for example, a person who complains in general terms about the racial harassment of a fellow employee will be protected against subsequent retaliation, whereas if the complaint is about sexual harassment the complainant must rely on the victimisation provisions, though the latter do potentially include situations where the employee simply protests to the employer about the latter's behaviour.[15]

The need to show that the less favourable treatment was on ground of sex or race is essentially a comparative exercise, comparing how a man or a white person in the same situation would have been treated. So much is obvious, but it was thought necessary to spell it out in the legislation. It is provided that such a comparison 'must be such that the relevant circumstances in the one case are the same, or not materially different, in the other'.[16] It is clear that this requires a comparison of, for example, how a similarly qualified and experienced white person would have been treated. Unlike equal pay legislation, where a female applicant, in order to bring a claim, normally has to be able to point to an actual male employee employed by her employer, under both RRA 1976 and SDA 1975 a claim may be based on how a comparable man, or white person, etc, was treated or *would have been* treated. Of course, a case is likely to be much easier to prove – not that discrimination cases are ever easy to prove – if the complainant can point to actual treatment rather than having to rely on hypothetical treatment. Where the provision has caused problems is in situations where, arguably, the relevant circumstances cannot be the same, such as in cases involving pregnancy or sexual harassment, which is one of the reasons why these topics require treatment in separate chapters.

The phrase 'on ground of' is ambiguous. The crucial question has arisen whether it is sufficient that the less favourable treatment is the result of the applicant's race or gender, or whether it must be shown that, from a subjective viewpoint, race or gender motivated the defendant in treating the plaintiff less favourably. This is a key question because, if the second alternative be correct, it will, first, be very hard to bring unconscious racism or sexism within the ambit of the legislation; secondly, it may be very hard to prove such subjective motivation in the absence of a 'smoking gun'; and, thirdly, there would

---

[15] See below, pp 362–63.
[16] SDA 1975, s 5(3); RRA 1976, s 3(4).

potentially be a defence if the defendant were able to establish a good motive for the alleged discrimination.[17]

James v Eastleigh BC [1990] IRLR 208, HL[18]

The council policy of providing free swimming for those who had reached the State pensionable age meant that women received this benefit when they were 60, whereas men had to wait until 65. The motive was to provide free swimming to those who were less likely to be able to afford it. The Equal Opportunities Commission, recognising the importance of the claim, supported the man's case all the way to the House of Lords, even though only 75p was at stake on each occasion. The claim was upheld by a bare majority of 3–2, with Lords Griffiths and Lowry dissenting.

Lord Bridge of Harwich (pp 291–92):

[T]he statutory pensionable age, being fixed at 60 for women and 65 for men, is itself a criterion which directly discriminates between men and women ... [A]ny other differential treatment of men and women which adopts the same criterion must equally involve discrimination on the ground of sex ... The expression 'pensionable age' is no more than a convenient shorthand expression which refers to the age of 60 in a woman and to the age of 65 in a man. In considering whether there has been discrimination against a man 'on the ground of his sex' it cannot possibly make any difference whether the alleged discriminator uses the shorthand expression or spells out the full meaning ...

The Council in this case had the best of motives for discriminating as they did. They wished to benefit 'those whose resources were likely to have been reduced by retirement' and 'to aid the needy, whether male or female'. The criterion of pensionable age was a convenient one to apply because it was readily verified by the possession of a pension book or a bus pass. But the purity of the discriminator's subjective motive, intention or reason for discriminating cannot save the criterion applied from the objective taint of discrimination on the ground of sex.[19]

Lord Goff of Chieveley (pp 294–95):

I do not read the words 'on ground of sex' as necessarily referring only to the reason why the defendant acted as he did, but as embracing cases in which a gender-based criterion is the basis upon which the complainant has been

---

17 The absence of a defence based on good motive is one of the reasons why positive discrimination in favour of women or black people is normally unlawful in Great Britain; see below, pp 542–43. In this respect, the Disability Discrimination Act 1995 is different; the fact that no complaint may be brought by a non-disabled person means that positive action in favour of disabled people is permissible, although care must be taken not to discriminate in favour of some groups of disabled people, but against others.

18 See, also, [1990] 2 AC 751; [1990] 2 All ER 607.

19 Lord Bridge also held, p 292, that this was not a case of indirect discrimination: 'Pensionable age cannot be regarded as a requirement or condition which is applied equally to persons of either sex precisely because it is itself discriminatory between the sexes.'

selected for the relevant treatment ... [T]he present case is no different from one in which the defendant adopts a criterion which favours widows as opposed to widowers.

I incline to the opinion that, if it were necessary to identify the requisite intention of the defendant, that intention is simply an intention to perform the relevant act of less favourable treatment ... [I]t is not saved from constituting unlawful discrimination by the fact that the defendant acted from a benign motive. As I see it, cases of direct discrimination ... can be considered by asking the simple question: would the complainant have received the same treatment from the defendant but for his or her sex?[20]

The most important consequence of this decision is to rule out a range of defences based on the alleged good motives of the defendant.

Defences based on chivalry or etiquette

In *Peake v Automotive Products Ltd*,[21] the Court of Appeal accepted this as a good reason for allowing women to leave the factory five minutes before the men. Such an approach is clearly wrong. In *Ministry of Defence v Jeremiah*,[22] the reason that women doing overtime were not required to work in the dirty part of the factory related to the greater discomfort to a woman in having her hair and clothes dirtied. This is a classic example of gender stereotyping which is unlawful. In *Greig v Community Industry*,[23] a woman was denied access to a training scheme on the basis that, as the only female trainee, she might expect problems from the male trainees. Again, such reasoning is clearly unlawful: it is the policy of the law to leave such choices to the individual women and, in consequence, it is becoming recognised that it is the employer's responsibility to protect such women from problems at the hands (or mouth) of fellow employees.[24]

Bain v Bowles [1991] IRLR 356, CA

The plaintiff, a man, wanted to advertise in *The Lady* for a resident housekeeper/cook. He was told that it was magazine policy only to accept advertisements for employment outside the UK when the employer is a

---

[20] This decision confirmed the previous House of Lords' decision in *Birmingham CC v EOC* [1989] AC 1155, CA and HL, the case involving the provision of fewer grammar school places for girls than for boys. There, Lord Goff had stated ([1989] AC 1155, p 1194) that the 'intention or motive of the defendant to discriminate ... is not a necessary condition of liability ... [I]f the council's submission were correct, it would be a good defence for an employer to show that he discriminated against women not because he intended to do so but (for example) because of customer preference, or to save money, or even to avoid controversy'.

[21] [1978] QB 233; [1978] 1 All ER 106; [1977] IRLR 365, CA.

[22] [1980] QB 87; [1979] 3 All ER 833; [1979] IRLR 436, CA.

[23] [1979] ICR 356; [1979] IRLR 158, EAT.

[24] See below, pp 247–56.

woman resident in the household concerned. The reason was stated to be to prevent sexual harassment and molestation of young girls.

Dillon LJ (pp 357–58):

[SDA 1975, s 5(3)] seems to be a fairly obvious statement that if you are carrying out a comparison you must compare like with like. [Here] there was discrimination because they would have allowed a woman to place the advertisement. But the 'relevant circumstances' do not, in my judgment, extend to including what might happen to a person who answered the advertisement and obtained the job. They are limited to the placing of the advertisement and they cannot include the motive of the defendant in refusing to place the advertisement because motive is not a valid justification for discrimination.

Cost defences

These may include the argument that the employer did not wish to discriminate, but only did so because of the wishes of the victim's fellow workers or the employer's customers. In *R v CRE ex p Westminster CC*,[25] vacancies for council refuse workers had previously been filled through friends or family of current employees, as a result of which no black people were hired. The employer introduced a new system, but the workforce insisted on the continuation of the former procedure, and even backed up the demand with the threat of industrial action, yet it was clear that the resulting discrimination was unlawful. In principle, you may never discriminate because of the preferences of others.[26] In *Smyth v Croft Inns Ltd*,[27] where a Catholic worked in a 'Protestant' bar, it was held to amount to discrimination where nothing specific was done to protect the employee from implied threats against the applicant; the case was no different from any situation where discrimination occurred to satisfy the demands of the employer's customers.

Employers frequently utilise stereotypes, partly to reduce the costs of hiring and partly based on perceptions as to the average cost or productivity of particular groups of employee. The evidence is clear that such stereotyping remains commonplace, yet it is clearly unlawful. Basing a decision in an *individual* case on stereotypes or averages about women or a particular racial group will amount to unlawful discrimination. An obvious example concerns the exclusion of women from jobs requiring physical strength on the ground

---

[25] [1985] ICR 827; [1985] IRLR 426, CA.

[26] There is a particular problem where it is alleged that attractive women are required for a job because of customer expectations. We will deal with this as part of the more general question of grooming and clothing codes; see below, pp 151–59.

[27] [1996] IRLR 84, NICA.

that women, on average, are less strong than men. This is clearly unlawful.[28] Other such stereotypes relate to the social reality of the lives of many women, such as being a single parent or having a partner who works or seeks to work in another part of the country.[29]

Hurley v Mustoe [1981] IRLR 208, EAT[30]

The applicant was rejected for a waitressing job because she had four young children; it was the employer's policy not to employ women with young children because in his experience they were unreliable.

Browne-Wilkinson J (p 210):

Even if ... one concedes that *some* women with small children are less reliable than those without, it does not follow that it is necessary in order to achieve reliability to exclude all women with children ... In general, a condition excluding *all* members of a class from employment cannot be justified on the ground that *some* members of that class are undesirable employees ... Parliament has legislated that women with children are not to be treated as a class but as individuals. No employer is bound to employ unreliable employees, whether men or women. But he must investigate each case and not simply apply a rule of convenience, or a prejudice, to exclude a whole class of women or married persons because some members of that class are not suitable ...

Three comments are needed on this important case:

(a) The claim of direct discrimination succeeded, as there was no evidence that the employer would have applied the same criterion to *fathers* with young children. Had he done so, the policy could still have been attacked as being unjustifiable indirect discrimination. A claim may be brought under either theory of discrimination: the applicant does not have to opt for one or the other and indeed it may not become apparent until relatively late in the proceedings which is the more appropriate theory.

(b) The claim succeeded even though economists might argue that the policy was efficient and rational in a profit-maximising sense. For this reason, the law's attempt to change behaviour, while not by any means doomed to failure, clearly faces formidable obstacles.

---

[28] *FM Thorn v Meggit Engineering Ltd* [1976] IRLR 241, IT. What the employer must do is to decide what level of strength is required for the job and how it is to be measured. On the assumption that fewer women can meet the requirement than men, there will be a *prima facie* case of indirect discrimination, but the employer may very well be able to justify the requirement.

[29] In *Effa v Alexandra Healthcare NHS Trust* (1997), unreported, Case No: 45390/95, see 33 DCLD 9, the dismissal of a locum doctor was held to be on racial grounds because the assumption that someone of his age and position must have little ability was based on the standards of a 'white' career, which assumes that everyone who practises medicine in the UK wishes to become a consultant.

[30] See, also, [1981] ICR 490.

(c) It is still a case of unlawful sex discrimination even though the employer did not discriminate against all women, but only against a subset of women,[31] in this case women with young children. In such a case the appropriate comparison is with how a man possessed of the same characteristic would have been treated, and of course the employer would have almost certainly shown no interest in whether such an applicant had children.

Horsey v Dyfed CC [1982] IRLR 395, EAT[32]

The applicant began employment as a trainee social worker in 1979. The job involved starting in work but she was required to start a social work course within one year. She was also required to undertake that after completing the course she would return to work for the county for at least two years. She wanted to attend a course in Kent as her husband lived in London. The county refused to allow her to attend that particular course as they considered that she would probably not return afterwards.

Browne-Wilkinson J (pp 397–98):

The Act covers generalised assumptions in relation to particular characteristics. Most discrimination flows from generalised assumptions of this kind and not from a simple prejudice dependent solely on the sex or colour of the complainant. The purpose of the legislation is to secure equal opportunity for individuals regardless of their sex, married status or race. This result would not be achieved if it were sufficient to escape liability to show that the reason for the discriminatory treatment was simply an assumption that women or coloured persons possessed or lacked particular characteristics and not that they were just women or coloured persons ...

Mr Evans assumed that Mr Horsey would not give up his job to join his wife, but that Mrs Horsey would give up her job to join her husband, ie, he had made a general assumption on the basis of her sex ... [even though] on two occasions previously Mr Horsey had followed his wife.[33]

CAUSATION

Lord Goff said in *James* that the essential question is whether the complainant would have received the same less favourable treatment *but for* his or her sex

---

[31] In the USA, this is known as 'sex-plus' discrimination, as the treatment is based on gender *plus* the particular characteristic. See *Phillipps v Martin Marietta Corp* 400 US 542 (1971).

[32] See, also, [1982] ICR 255.

[33] See, also, *Alexander v Home Office* [1988] 1 WLR 968; [1988] 2 All ER 118; [1988] ICR 685; [1988] IRLR 190, CA, where an Afro-Caribbean prisoner was described in his report as showing 'the anti-authoritarian arrogance that seems to be found in most coloured inmates'.

or race. That a man or a white person was treated more favourably does not necessarily prove the case; there must be a causal connection between the less favourable treatment and the race or gender of the complainant. In *Bullock v Alice Ottley School*.[34] teachers and domestic staff retired at 60, gardeners and maintenance staff, who were difficult to recruit, at 65. The complaint was by a woman domestic who had to retire at 61. All the domestic staff were female apart from the caretaker, whereas all seven gardeners and maintenance staff were men. The claim of direct discrimination failed.[35] Neill LJ said there was 'nothing in s 5(3) or in any other provision of the Act of 1975 which prevents an employer from having a variety of retiring ages for different jobs, *provided* that in the system which he uses there is no direct or indirect discrimination based on gender. In the case of alleged direct discrimination the question is: would a man in the same job have been treated differently?'.[36] It was accepted that the same rule was or would have been applied in the case of a male domestic or a female gardener.[37] The principle was articulated by Browne-Wilkinson J in *Showboat Entertainment Centre Ltd v Owens*,[38] where he said that 'although one has to compare like with like, in judging whether there has been discrimination you have to compare the treatment actually meted out with the treatment which would have been afforded to a man having all the same characteristics as the complainant except his race [or gender] ... Only by excluding matters of race can you discover whether the differential treatment was on racial grounds'.[39]

It was established in *Owen and Briggs v James*[40] that race or gender need not be the sole factor leading to the less favourable treatment, as long as it is a contributory cause. On the other hand, in *Seide v Gillette Industries Ltd*[41] the EAT said that it was insufficient that race was merely part of the background which led to the treatment in question. Here, anti-Semitic remarks made to the

---

[34] [1993] ICR 138; [1992] IRLR 564, CA.

[35] The facts nevertheless gave rise to a *prima facie* case of indirect discrimination against the women who wished to continue working until age 65. However, the requirement was held to be justified on the grounds of business and administrative efficiency, based on the difficulties in hiring adequately qualified gardeners and maintenance staff.

[36] [1993] ICR 138, pp 146–47.

[37] In *Dhatt v McDonalds Hamburgers Ltd* [1991] 1 WLR 527; [1991] 3 All ER 692; [1991] IRLR 130, CA, the employers required the applicant to produce evidence of his right to work in the UK. They did not accept the stamp in his passport as adequate evidence and dismissed him. He claimed that they had unlawfully discriminated against him on the basis of his nationality as they would not have so investigated the status of a UK or EEC national. The Court of Appeal held that this was not the true comparison; rather, his case should be compared with that of a national from any other country who did not have an automatic right to work in the UK and on that basis there was no discrimination. See Ross, J (1991) 20 Industrial LJ 208.

[38] [1984] 1 WLR 384; [1984] 1 All ER 836; [1984] IRLR 7, EAT.

[39] *Ibid*, p 10.

[40] [1982] ICR 618; [1982] IRLR 502, CA.

[41] [1980] IRLR 427, EAT.

complainant led to his transfer (about which no complaint was made). He subsequently sought to involve another employee in the dispute, which led to a further transfer in order to minimise disruption, this transfer entailing loss of wages. The question was whether this second transfer was on racial grounds. While it was clear that the train of events would not have occurred had he not been Jewish, the EAT said that was insufficient. 'It does not seem to us to be enough merely to consider whether the fact that the person is of a particular racial group ... is any part of the background ... [T]he question which has to be asked is whether the activating cause of what happens is that the employer has treated a person less favourably than others on racial grounds.'[42] The finding that the second transfer was not on racial grounds was undoubtedly made easier by the acceptance that the second employee involved had no anti-Semitic views.[43] This approach should be contrasted with *Din v Carrington Viyella Ltd*,[44] in which the EAT correctly observed that it will normally be unlawful to remove the victim from the source of the discrimination, whether or not any loss of pay or status is involved, and even if the motive is simply the avoidance of future unrest.[45]

Such cases on causation and 'mixed motives' are potentially very problematic; disentangling causes leads to conceptual and practical problems in many areas of law, and may be accentuated here if more than one person is involved in an allegedly discriminatory decision; different people may have different states of mind and reasons for acting. The danger is that tribunals will too easily resort to a finding that prejudice or discrimination somewhere in an organisation played no part in a decision. Whether or not the above cases are technically reconcilable may matter little; what is of far greater importance is the ability and willingness of fact-finders to delve into and be sensitive to unlawful attitudes at different levels of an organisation.

GROOMING AND APPEARANCE CODES

The question is the extent to which the anti-discrimination legislation constrains the ability of an employer to regulate the appearance or clothing of

---

[42] *Seide v Gillette Industries* [1980] IRLR 427, EAT, p 431.

[43] See, also, *Simon v Brimham Associates* [1987] IRLR 307, CA, where a claim of racial discrimination was rejected in circumstances where an applicant, who, unknown to the defendants, was Jewish, withdrew his application for a position which involved working with Arab employers. He refused to answer a direct question about his religion and was then informed that being Jewish might prejudice his application. In a narrow interpretation of the law, it was held that there was no less favourable treatment, as the employers were simply explaining why they felt a need to inquire about the religion of applicants.

[44] [1982] ICR 256; [1982] IRLR 281, EAT.

[45] See, also, *Kingston v British Railways Board* [1984] ICR 781; [1984] IRLR 146, CA.

employees. In principle, the SDA 1975 comes into play if the employer's rules involve unequal treatment between men and women. The difficulty is that, for most people, social convention dictates that men and women do present themselves differently. It could be argued that it is discriminatory to require them so to do; it could also be argued to be discriminatory to require men and women to look the same when conventionally they appear different. At one level, these issues might seem comparatively trivial; however, they go to the heart of a male view of woman as a sexual object whose responsibility is to appear attractive to men. In addition, it is dangerous to refer in this context to the view taken by society. Grooming and appearance codes are enormously moulded by one's racial, religious and cultural background, and may alter rather rapidly with the passage of time. The law has to tread a fine line between accepting what has traditionally been the norm – such traditions are likely to be relatively recent and in any event the anti-discrimination legislation aims to challenge tradition and stereotyping – while on the other hand avoiding outcomes which might be thought by many people to bring the law into disrepute.

Schmidt v Austicks Bookshops Ltd [1977] IRLR 360, EAT[46]

The plaintiff complained that her employers required her to wear a skirt and not trousers while serving the public and also to wear overalls. Her claim of sex discrimination failed.

Phillips J (p 361):

[T]he rules were plainly designed to assist in creating what to the employers was a satisfactory image and to assist in relations with the public ... [T]he restriction applied only when she was working with and in sight of the public ...

[T]he evidence showed that although there was less scope for positive rules in the case of the men, in that the choice of wearing apparel was more limited, there were restrictions in their case, too. For example, they were not allowed to wear tee-shirts ... [T]here were in force rules restricting wearing apparel and governing appearance which applied to men and also applied to women, although obviously, women and men being different, the rules in the two cases were not the same ...

[A]n employer is entitled to a large measure of discretion in controlling the image of his establishment, including the appearance of staff, and especially so when, as a result of their duties, they come into contact with the public.

Flynn, L, 'Gender equality laws and employers' dress codes' (1995) 24 Industrial LJ 255, pp 257, 260:

As a result of its dual function, identifying both what the subject is and what she should be, dress has a significance beyond the conventional; aspects of

---

[46] See, also, [1978] ICR 85.

personal appearance which are regarded as feminine ... not only indicate that, in general, one is looking at a woman but also serve to identify a deviation from social norms if one knows that the person one is observing is male. This equation of the habitual with the normal means that any move by some members of one sex to take up the elements of dress associated with the other sex are initially treated as a major transgression. That spectre of cross-dressing may, in turn, provoke a panicked defence of masculinity (or femininity) which sometimes spills over into the courts ...

The reasoning of the EAT [in *Schmidt*] rests on a questionable assumption, namely that it is not open to men to wear certain items of apparel which are open to women. This premise removes the possibility of strict comparability between the sexes in matters of dress and necessitates the use of a modified, equivalence analysis. Neither of these elements in the EAT's reasoning ... stands up to scrutiny ... The boundaries of acceptable male and female dress can, and have, shifted significantly over the centuries and have altered with dramatic speed in the last few decades. Efforts to fix the process through an ascription of natural limits to 'female' and 'male' apparel cannot be reconciled with the basic philosophy of anti-discrimination legislation.

In *Schmidt*, the court attempted to reconcile the need to apply the non-discrimination principle with a belief that dress codes cannot be identical. The problem is that women were far more constrained by the employer's code than men were – women were presumably not allowed to wear tee-shirts either – and thus the rules could not be said to have operated even-handedly. No objective reason for the no-trousers rule was put forward; the EAT was content to hold that the such a rule lies within the scope of the employer's discretion to regulate his business.

McConomy v Croft Inns Ltd [1992] IRLR 561, High Ct of NI

Men with earrings were not allowed admission to a particular pub in Belfast. The complainant was asked to leave when it was noticed that he was wearing two small stud earrings in one ear. No objection was raised to women with earrings.

The claim of unlawful sex discrimination was brought under the Northern Ireland equivalent of s 29 of the SDA 1975, concerning the discriminatory provision of services to a section of the public.

The lower court said what is required is equal rather than identical treatment, applied *Schmidt* and rejected the claim. The applicant's appeal was allowed.

Murray LJ (pp 563–64):

[W]hile I can see that in comparing like with like one would have to take account of certain basic rules of human conduct – such as the ordinary rules of decency ... which might permit or require different dress regulations as between men and women, I find it difficult to see how in today's conditions it is possible to say that the circumstances are different as between men and women as regards the wearing of personal jewellery or other items of personal adornment ...

[The judge was clearly unhappy with the decision he felt bound to reach, as he commented that] there are people about who would take a robust view of this, would regard it with some scorn as effeminacy, and could, under the influence of drink, be moved to violence towards the wearers of such things. [If this be the employer's position] their motive in wishing to avoid disorder in their premises is entirely laudable.

This is not an employment case, and it may be that courts are instinctively prepared to give employers greater discretion in regulating the appearance of employees than bar owners the appearance of customers. However, if regard is had, as surely it must be, to changing social convention, it is very hard to defend *Schmidt* 20 years after it was decided. Nevertheless two recent cases have reinstated and approved the *Schmidt* approach, with no recognition that times have changed and are continuing to change. The first, *Burrett v West Birmingham Health Authority*,[47] concerned a requirement to wear a cap that some departments imposed on female but not on male nursing staff. The applicant was disciplined and transferred for refusing to wear a cap on the ground that she found it demeaning and undignified and that it stereotyped nurses, an action she claimed breached the SDA 1975. While a majority of the female staff appeared to favour the practice, it was clear that it could not be justified for any operational reason such as hygiene. The EAT rejected her claim on the basis that *Schmidt* was the appropriate authority; the fact that men and women were each required to wear uniforms, albeit not identical, was sufficient to show that less favourable treatment had not occurred.

The following case is the first case on the issue to reach the Court of Appeal; it is notable for the clear difference of approach and philosophy between the EAT and the Court of Appeal.

Smith v Safeway plc [1995] IRLR 132, EAT[48]

A delicatessen assistant was dismissed because his pony-tail became too long to be contained under his hat. The applicable rule for male employees insisted on: 'Tidy hair not below shirt collar length. No unconventional hair styles or colouring.' For women the equivalent provision stated: 'Shoulder-length hair must be clipped back. No unconventional hair styles or colouring.' There was no suggestion that the rule was based on considerations of hygiene.

The Industrial Tribunal[49] said it that was lawful to have different lengths of hair for men and women. They applied *Schmidt*, reasoning that the law permits different standards to be applied to men and women provided they enforce a common standard of smartness if read as a whole.

---

[47] [1994] IRLR 7, EAT.

[48] See, also, [1995] ICR 472.

[49] By the Employment Rights (Dispute Resolution) Act 1998, s 1(1), industrial tribunals are re-named employment tribunals.

By a majority the EAT allowed the appeal.

Pill J (pp 134–35):

[The applicant argued that hair length] could not be equated with dress. Dress can be changed on leaving work whereas hair is worn into public life. Hair length is not a function of any physiological difference between men and women. Differences are a question only of custom or fashion. Unlike differences in dress, there is no counterbalancing feature; the rule discriminates against men ...

The lay members of this tribunal have no difficulty in holding that the treatment was less favourable and self-evidently so. The requirements ... with respect to hairstyle are capable of being applied to both men and women in such a way as to take account of convention (and therefore be compatible with *Schmidt*) without placing the restriction they do on hair length for men only ...

[According to the chair] *Schmidt* [is] concerned with appearance. Employers are entitled to lay down reasonable requirements as to the way employees present themselves at work, if, for example, they come into contact with the public. Employers can have regard to current conventions and decline to accept what is 'out-of-the-way' ... What is conventional and what is out-of-the-way for men will often be different [than] ... for women.

If the employer is entitled to require an appearance which is not out-of-the-way, it is difficult to distinguish between dress and other aspects of personal appearance including hairstyle. Provided requirements for men and women can reasonably be related to current perceptions of what is a conventional appearance for men and for women, the requirements do not treat one sex less favourably than the other. The sexes are treated differently but equally by the standards of what is conventional.

[1996] IRLR 456, CA[50]

The Court of Appeal reversed the decision of the EAT and restored the decision of the Industrial Tribunal.

Phillips LJ (pp 458–59):

[It was submitted] that the principle to be derived from *Schmidt* ... has become unsound in law as a result in changes in society [and that it does not apply to these facts] ...

In my judgment, a package approach to the effects of an appearance code necessarily follows once one accepts that the code is not required to make provisions which apply identically to men and women ... [O]ne has to consider the effect of any [one] item in the overall context of the code as a whole ...

Appearance depends in part on ephemera: clothes, rings and jewellery worn; but it also depends on more permanent characteristics: tattoos, hairstyle, hair colouring and hair length. The approach adopted in *Schmidt* can in my judgment properly be applied to both types of characteristic ...

---

[50] See, also, [1996] ICR 868.

I can accept that one of the objects of the prohibition of sex discrimination was to relieve the sexes of unequal treatment resulting from conventional attitudes, but I do not believe that this renders discriminatory an appearance code which applies what is conventional. On the contrary, I am inclined to think that such a code is likely to operate unfavourably with regard to one or other of the sexes unless it applies such a standard ... A code which applies conventional standards is one which, so far as the criterion of appearance is concerned, applies an even-handed approach between men and women, and not one which is discriminatory ...

[We do not] lay down a rule of law that it can never be discriminatory to require men to wear their hair short, but is simply to say that in this case it was not perverse for the Industrial Tribunal to hold that a code containing the requirement that men's hair should be collar length was not discriminatory on the facts of the case.

Wintemute, R, 'Recognising new kinds of direct sex discrimination: transsexualism, sexual orientation and dress codes' (1997) 60 MLR 334, pp 354–55:

The 'package approach' adopted in *Safeway* is clearly inconsistent with the House of Lords' decision in *James v Eastleigh Borough Council*. 'But for' his sex, Mr Smith would not have been dismissed. The Court of Appeal reasoned that the dress code 'as a whole' treated men and women equally by applying different, but somehow equivalent and compensating, restrictions to their freedom to choose their clothing, make up, jewellery and hairstyles. But there was clearly 'less favourable treatment' if individual items of the code are examined. In particular, men could not have hair below shirt-collar length, whereas women could have shoulder length hair so long as it was clipped back. The Court of Appeal attempted to escape a finding of 'less favourable treatment' by using direct sex discrimination against women in individual items of the code to justify the direct sex discrimination against men in individual items of the code. It is unlikely that the House of Lords in *James* would have found no 'less favourable treatment' and therefore no direct sex discrimination, if the Council's admission prices 'as a whole' had treated men and women aged 60–64 equally: for example, swimming (75p for men, free for women); badminton (free for men, 75p for women). Sex distinctions applying to different choices cannot be lumped together and their net effect examined. Courts must look instead at their net effect on the ability of individuals to make each specific choice. For the woman who wants badminton at the same price as a man, free swimming is no consolation. For the man who wants to wear a pony-tail or a skirt, it is no consolation that women are prevented from wearing short hair or trousers.

Even if courts come to accept the view of the EAT in *Safeway*, the limits of that approach should be noted. A full blown anti-discrimination standard was only applied to those aspects of appearance which necessarily spill over from the workplace into other aspects of the applicant's life, and thus can be viewed as relating to freedom of expression and personal autonomy. This approach would continue to permit, for example, differential rules concerning clothing, jewellery and make up, all of which may be altered on leaving work. But these are all aspects of appearance where there have in recent history been conventional differences between men and women, differences which in some small ways are being reduced. Even the approach of the EAT in *Safeway*, let alone that of the Court of Appeal, permits the employer to insist on maintaining such differences amongst his employees. The main reason given for such a view is the need to allow employers discretion in controlling staff appearances. This is an assertion, not an argument, and comes close to permitting discrimination because that policy would be favoured by customers or fellow employees, arguments normally rejected. The argument that, were the law otherwise, any man would be able to insist on wearing a skirt, is simply wrong. The courts have adopted a view of convention as allowing for only one convention, rather than many different conventions among different groups. People should have a right to whatever appearance they choose as long as their choice is that made by a reasonably sized *group* from within their gender; sex discrimination law does not and should not protect the whims of individuals. If the man who wishes to wear a skirt is a transsexual, protection should depend on the larger question whether transsexuals *as a group* come within the SDA 1975 or some other human rights legislation.

Wintemute's approach, however, is somewhat wider, based on individual human autonomy.

Wintemute, R, 'Recognising new kinds of direct sex discrimination: transsexualism, sexual orientation and dress codes' (1997) 60 MLR 334, pp 356–57:

If it is accepted that dress codes containing items which are different for men and women ... constitute direct discrimination, how can that discrimination be eliminated? One alternative would be to choose a single 'male' or 'female' uniform and require all employees to wear it (for example, all employees must wear skirts or dresses and lipstick, or all employees must wear jackets, ties, trousers and very short hair). But a single uniform that is closely associated with one sex would discriminate indirectly against members of the other sex, because they would be far more likely to feel unable to wear it ... A second alternative would be a single 'unisex' uniform (for example, overalls, or a 'genderless' shirt and trousers) that might be acceptable to roughly equal proportions of both sexes. A third alternative would be two uniforms, one 'male' and one 'female', which any employee of either sex would be free to choose. Even if 99% of men chose the 'male' uniform and 99% of women chose the 'female' uniform, it would be important that there was freedom to choose regardless of one's sex.

The third alternative would accommodate the needs of transsexual and transvestite employees, but a rigid insistence on uniforms or acceptable combinations of clothing, make up, jewellery and hairstyle would present a problem for non-conformist partial and full 'gender blenders' who would like to 'mix and match' items from the lists of acceptable 'male' and 'female' clothing, etc. An employer could say that any employee may wear trousers or short hair, but only in combination with a 'male' jacket, tie, shirt and shoes. Any employee may wear long hair, make up, or one or more earrings, but only in combination with a dress or skirt and high-heeled shoes ... [But] either men or women could be disproportionately excluded from a 'female' or 'male' uniform or combination because they might be unwilling to adopt it in its entirety, and might prefer to select individual items from it ... Under [the fourth] alternative, any employee would be free to wear any individual item of clothing or jewellery, kind of make up, or hairstyle that would be acceptable either for a man or a woman, and would be free to combine these elements of their appearance in any way they saw fit. Although individual elements considered acceptable neither for a man nor for a woman could be excluded (perhaps ripped jeans or purple hair in a company's head office), they would be excluded for both sexes.

There are problems with such an extreme approach. First, it treats all conventionally gendered items in the same way. Is a man's freedom to wear lipstick or a bra really the same as his freedom to wear long hair or earrings? Secondly, it reduces almost to nothing the ability of employers to exercise any control over employee appearance, as virtually all appearance rules have some gender implications. Thirdly, it appears to imply that there is no alternative between almost complete individual autonomy in the name of gender equality and the upholding of wide employer discretion as the court did in *Safeway*. This is a counsel of despair. The problem is difficult both conceptually and as a matter of detail, but it should not be beyond the wit of employers and tribunals to reach a definition of, for example, 'smartness', which neither assumes that for men only short hair can be smart, nor which requires absolute identity of uniform. For such approach to be acceptable, however, it would be essential that fact-finders were sensitive to the possibility – likelihood? – that employers will seek to use smartness as a proxy for an appearance requirement designed in the interests of purported sexual attractiveness.

Supposed sexual attractiveness may operate to exclude men from consideration for a job. If so, and it can be proved, that would amount to direct sex discrimination; it would also be direct sex discrimination against a class of women if a job were open to all men but only attractive women. However, many such jobs are conventionally defined as female and so attract few if any male applicants; such rare applicants as there are, even if unsuccessful, may be particularly unwilling to bring a claim of unlawful discrimination. Attractiveness may also be used as a criterion which operates to disadvantage supposedly less attractive female applicants. Such a criterion may utilise a white, female view of attractiveness and may therefore potentially be racially discriminatory. The exclusion of older women, in the absence of legislation dealing with age discrimination, remains lawful, so long as the same age requirement is applied to any male applicants there might happen to be.[51] Furthermore, it is impossible to disentangle notions of sexuality from notions of what is an appropriate personality for a position, especially one entailing contact with the public. It is considered unlikely that tribunals will be willing to hold that a decision which the employer claims to be based on personality was in reality based on unlawful gender considerations.[52]

PROOF OF DIRECT DISCRIMINATION

It is rare, and probably becoming rarer, for employers to do or say something to the victim which reveals that discrimination has occurred – except, that is, in cases of racial and sexual harassment which raise rather different problems. It is more likely that the discriminator will give away what has occurred to a third person; such action may both lead to a realisation that a claim may be possible, and be the chief evidence in support of such a claim. However, this presupposes a willingness to blow the whistle and give the evidence, a willingness which, in the case of employees, even employees totally out of sympathy with what has occurred, cannot be taken for granted.[53]

But most direct discrimination is covert, resulting from a state of mind which, by its very nature, is not likely to be susceptible to direct proof. A claim may develop from a feeling, whether based on instinct or a certain amount of knowledge, that the best person has not been appointed. Defendants will almost always put forward an alternative explanation for their behaviour, in some cases because they have every incentive to do so, and also as it is possible to be unaware that one is engaging in discriminatory behaviour. Discrimination often results from stereotypes, assumptions and the like which may lead an employer to behave in a particular manner. Furthermore, the law must counter the fact that almost all the information as to what did occur is within the employer's control. The law will be seriously weakened if tribunals are unwilling to appreciate the practical problems faced by applicants in providing direct proof of discrimination. It is important that tribunals are prepared to draw *inferences* of discrimination in cases where direct evidence is not and cannot be forthcoming.

---

51 See Buchanan, P, 'Title VII limits on discrimination against television anchorwomen on the basis of age-related appearance' (1985) 85 Columbia L Rev 190.

52 For an extensive discussion of the role played by women's sexuality in many employment situations, see Adkins, L, *Gendered Work*, 1995, Buckingham: Open University. The issue is considered further in Chapter 8.

53 For discussion of the provisions on victimisation, see below, pp 362–67.

As discrimination is a civil matter, the burden of proof is satisfied if the applicant proves the case on a balance of probabilities.[54] Thus the burden lies on the party making the allegation, although there will be some limited modification if and when the proposed European Community Burden of Proof Directive comes into effect.[55] Whatever be the formal burden of proof, defendants, who normally have at their disposal greater information about what happened than applicants, are almost invariably required to provide their version of events.[56]

It has been argued that the more formalistic approach to the ordering of proof which is characteristic of American law would ease the task of tribunals in knowing when to draw adverse inferences and, perhaps not incidentally, make it more likely that complainants will win their cases. According to the United States Supreme Court in *McDonnell Douglas Corp v Green*,[57] the applicant has to show:

(a) that he belongs to a racial minority;

(b) that he applied and was [minimally] qualified for a job for which the employer was seeking applicants;

(c) that ... he was rejected; and

(d) that after such rejection the position remained open.

The burden then shifts to the employer to articulate some legitimate non-discriminatory reason for the employer's rejection.

Thirdly, the applicant has the opportunity to establish that the employer's stated reason for rejection was a pretext for the real reason.[58]

English law has not adopted such a formal approach. The strength of the American approach is in its assumption that if facts are established which call for an answer from the employer, and if the answer which is forthcoming fails to satisfy the fact-finder, the plaintiff should win. Under English law, the current position, that in such circumstances the plaintiff may win rather than *must* win, is less clear-cut.

---

[54] It is sometimes suggested that tribunals see an allegation of discrimination as very serious, almost quasi-criminal in nature, and as a result may, consciously or subconsciously, demand a rather higher standard than the normal balance of probabilities test. See Bourn, C and Whitmore, J, *Anti-Discrimination Law in Britain*, 3rd edn, 1996, London: Sweet & Maxwell, p 116.

[55] See below, p 174.

[56] See *Oxford v DHSS* [1977] ICR 884; [1977] IRLR 225, EAT.

[57] 411 US 792 (1973).

[58] Clearly, the same logical principles can be applied to gender cases and to other cases of discrimination not involving a failure to hire.

Khanna v Ministry of Defence [1981] IRLR 331, EAT[59]

Mr Khanna was repeatedly turned down for promotion, on the final occasion despite being better qualified than the successful applicant. The tribunal dismissed the claim on the ground that the applicant failed to discharge the burden of proof required.

The EAT allowed the appeal and remitted the case to another Industrial Tribunal.

Browne-Wilkinson J (p 332):

> [W]e think Industrial Tribunals may find it easier to forget about the rather nebulous concept of the 'shift in the evidential burden' ... The right course in this case was for the Industrial Tribunal to take into account the fact that direct evidence of discrimination is seldom going to be available and that, accordingly, in these cases, the affirmative evidence of discrimination will normally consist of inferences to be drawn from the primary facts. If the primary facts indicate that there has been discrimination of some kind, the employer is called upon to give an explanation and, failing clear and specific explanation being given ... an inference of unlawful discrimination from the primary facts will mean the complaint succeeds.[60]

The danger of a relatively informal approach to the ordering of proof is that it may lead tribunals to assess the facts in too broad and insufficiently rigorous a fashion. There is evidence that this used to be true of far too many tribunals.[61] In particular, too much weight was placed on evidence that employers were not motivated by hostility towards the applicant, and this may have been true in *Khanna* itself. However, it may be that greater experience has lead tribunals to appreciate that hostile motivation is not required, that direct discrimination may originate in unconscious stereotyping, and thus that a claim may succeed without proof that the employer was overtly racist or sexist.

Noone v North West Thames RHA [1988] IRLR 195, CA[62]

The appellant, who was originally from Sri Lanka, applied for a vacancy as a consultant microbiologist. Despite superior qualifications, experience and

---

59 See, also, [1981] ICR 653.

60 Browne-Wilkinson J took the same approach in *Chattopadhyay v Headmaster of Holloway School* [1981] IRLR 487, [1982] ICR 132, EAT, observing (p 490) that if 'an applicant shows that he has been treated less favourably in circumstances which are consistent with the treatment being on racial grounds, the Industrial Tribunal should draw [such] inference unless the respondent can satisfy the Industrial Tribunal that there is an innocent explanation'. The suggestion that in such cases tribunals must draw adverse inferences was repudiated by the same judge in the House of Lords' decision in *Glasgow CC v Zafar*, below, pp 165–66. The Court of Appeal in *Baker v Cornwall CC* [1990] ICR 452; [1990] IRLR 194 had also concluded that in such cases an Industrial Tribunal 'should be prepared' to draw an adverse inference, while the Northern Ireland Court of Appeal in *Dornan v Belfast CC* [1990] IRLR 179 had implied that such inference must be drawn.

61 Leonard, A, *Judging Inequality: The Effectiveness of the Industrial Tribunal System in Sex Discrimination and Equal Pay Cases*, 1987, London: The Cobden Trust, pp 38–51, 78–85.

62 See, also, [1988] ICR 813.

publications, she was not appointed. The tribunal concluded that the interview procedure was 'little more than a sham' and that the decision was made on subjective grounds which almost amounted to arbitrariness.

The EAT allowed the employer's appeal on the basis that there was no positive evidence to show the decision was on racial grounds, but the Court of Appeal restored the decision of the Industrial Tribunal.

May LJ (p 198):

The first step is to decide whether or not there has been an act of discrimination at all; the next is to decide whether or not there was a difference in race; then one must consider whether there is any positive evidence which supports an allegation of discrimination on racial grounds. The Appeal Tribunal correctly commented that this is notoriously difficult to find ... It is not often that there is direct evidence of racial discrimination, and these complaints more often than not have to be dealt with on the basis of what are the proper inferences to be drawn from the primary facts. For myself, I would have thought that it was almost common sense that, if there is a finding of discrimination and of difference of race and then an inadequate or unsatisfactory explanation by the employer for the discrimination, usually the legitimate inference will be that the discrimination was on racial grounds.

If there is no evidence or material from which an Industrial Tribunal can draw the inference of racial discrimination then, of course, they should not do so. On the other hand, one must not forget that it is the Industrial Tribunal who see and hear the persons actually involved. Perhaps more than in most cases the assessment by the Industrial Tribunal of the thinking of the person or persons against whom an allegation of racial discrimination is made is most important ... If in the circumstances of the instant case the discrimination is held to have been based on a personal bias or personal prejudice, it seems to me to be only a very small step to go on and conclude that the discrimination was racial.

Baker v Cornwall CC [1990] IRLR 194, CA[63]

Neill LJ (pp 197–98):

In the present case, submitted Mr Sedley, the correct approach was to examine the primary facts to see what inferences could properly be drawn from them. Any instructed examination would inevitably lead to the conclusion that Mrs Baker had been discriminated against. It was then necessary to consider whether the Council had produced any acceptable explanation for the discrimination. It was submitted that no satisfactory explanation had been put forward ...

It was submitted that a requirement to 'fit in' was a very productive source of unintended acts of discrimination because it tended to perpetuate historic patterns of employment and to ensure that existing segregated groups remained unaltered.

It is important to recognise:

---

[63] See, also, [1990] ICR 452.

(a) that a person who complains ... will almost always face great difficulties in proving the case because the alleged discriminator is most unlikely to admit the discrimination; and

(b) that discrimination can often result from a wish to preserve an existing pattern of employment ... which has worked well and harmoniously in the past, rather than from any deliberate wish to exclude the complainant as an individual.

This case is a helpful summary of the problems facing applicants and the way in which tribunals need to be sensitive to such problems. The conclusion that the tribunal was entitled to conclude that there was no discrimination is surprising, given the remainder of the judgment. But it is stressed that such decision could only be overturned if there was no evidence to support it. The judgment of the Court of Appeal is in no sense a ringing endorsement of the tribunal decision.

The principles established in the above line of cases were summarised in the following decision.

King v Great Britain-China Centre [1991] IRLR 513, CA[64]

The applicant was Chinese but had been educated in Britain. She applied for the post of deputy director of the centre, a government-sponsored organisation which aims to foster closer ties with China. She met the requirements of fluent spoken Chinese and personal knowledge of China. All eight shortlisted candidates were white and the appointee was an English graduate in Chinese.

The tribunal upheld her complaint on the ground that the employers had failed to demonstrate that she had not been treated unfavourably because of her race. The employers had admitted that none of the five ethnically Chinese applicants had been shortlisted and that no ethnically Chinese person had ever been employed in the centre. The majority concluded that it was entitled to draw the conclusion that she was discriminated against because she did not come from the 'same, essentially British, academic background' as the existing staff.

The EAT allowed the appeal on the ground that the tribunal had approached the case on the basis that there was a burden on the employers to disprove discrimination.

The Court of Appeal restored the decision of the Industrial Tribunal.

Neill LJ (p 518):

From [the] several authorities it is possible ... to extract the following principles and guidance:[65]

---

[64] See, also, [1992] ICR 516.

[65] These guidelines were approved by the House of Lords in *Glasgow CC v Zafar*, below, pp 165–66.

(1) It is for the applicant who complains of racial discrimination to make out his or her case. Thus if the applicant does not prove the case on the balance of probabilities he or she will fail.

(2) It is important to bear in mind that it is unusual to find direct evidence of racial discrimination. Few employers will be prepared to admit such discrimination even to themselves. In some cases the discrimination will not be ill-intentioned but merely based on an assumption that 'he or she would not have fitted in'.

(3) The outcome of the case will therefore usually depend on what inferences it is proper to draw from the primary facts found by the tribunal. These inferences can include, in appropriate cases, any inferences that it is just and equitable to draw in accordance with s 65(2)(b) of the 1976 Act from an evasive or equivocal reply to a questionnaire[66]

(4) Though there will be some cases where, for example, the non-selection of the applicant for a post or for promotion is clearly not on racial grounds, a finding of discrimination and a finding of a difference in race will often point to the possibility of racial discrimination. In such circumstances, the tribunal will look to the employer for an explanation. If no explanation is then put forward or if the tribunal considers the explanation to be inadequate or unsatisfactory it will be legitimate for the tribunal to infer that the discrimination was on racial grounds. This is not a matter of law, but, as May LJ put it in *Noone*, 'almost common sense'.

(5) It is unnecessary and unhelpful to introduce the concept of a shifting evidential burden of proof. At the conclusion of all the evidence the tribunal should make findings as to the primary facts and draw such inferences as they consider proper from those facts. They should then reach a conclusion on the balance of probabilities, bearing in mind both the difficulties which face a person who complains of unlawful discrimination and the fact that it is for the complainant to prove his case.

The process of reasoning [in the Industrial Tribunal] did not involve a reversal of the burden of proof but merely a proper balancing of the factors which could be placed in the scales for and against a finding of unlawful discrimination.

In most of the cases, the applicant appears to be better or at least as well qualified as the successful candidate, and the employer articulates a reason as to why the latter was chosen. There are a number of ways of showing that the employer's stated reason was a pretext, that the employer's reason had never been utilised before, that the applicant was treated unfairly, and by the use of statistics. It has been held in Northern Ireland, however, that no inference of any kind is raised by the mere fact that the members of the appointing panel were all of a different religion from a candidate.[67] This is correct as a general

---

[66] See below, p 168.

[67] *Armagh DC v Fair Employment Agency* [1994] IRLR 234, NICA.

rule, as otherwise an obligation would arise to ensure that the panel had a member of the same race and gender as each applicant. There is no recommendation in the Codes of Practice that attempts need be made to ensure that the panel is as representative as possible. But the membership must be relevant evidence, especially if normal procedures were not followed or there is evidence that the panel's composition was in some way manipulated.

Examples of proving pretext by relying on a reason which is not applied to everyone include pregnancy dismissals where the period of absence had never led to dismissal of a sick man, or applying different criteria of misconduct or satisfactory work performance. The evidence of unfair or prejudiced questioning at interview may be sufficiently powerful to prove the applicant's case. However, the more equal the candidates are on merit, the more difficult it will be to prove a case simply on the basis of such unfairness.[68] But unfairness in the sense of incompetence will not necessarily lead to a finding of unlawful discrimination. In *Qureshi v London Borough of Newham*,[69] it was held that failure to follow the employer's own equal opportunities policy was insufficient to establish discrimination. 'Incompetence does not, without more, become discrimination merely because the person affected by it is from an ethnic minority.' It was assumed, rather than for the employer to prove, that similar incompetence would also have affected any white applicant. As in most cases this would be hard to prove, in effect this case turns on the allocation of the burden of proof.

Glasgow CC v Zafar [1998] IRLR 36, HL

The applicant was dismissed after being found guilty of serious sexual harassment. The Industrial Tribunal found that procedure for dealing with the allegations had been so seriously defective as to constitute unreasonable treatment, and that such unreasonable treatment amounted to less favourable treatment which gave rise to a presumption that it had been on grounds of race. The tribunal further held that, as the presumption had not been rebutted, there was no choice but to conclude that discrimination was proved.

The EAT dismissed the appeal but the Court of Session allowed the employer's further appeal, a decision upheld by the House of Lords.

Lord Browne-Wilkinson (p 38):

[T]he conduct of a hypothetical reasonable employer is irrelevant. The alleged discriminator may or may not be a reasonable employer. If he is not a reasonable employer he might well have treated another employee in just the same unsatisfactory way ... in which case he would not have treated the complainant 'less favourably' for the purposes of the Act of 1976. The fact that,

---

[68] See, eg, *Saunders v Richmond upon Thames LBC* [1978] ICR 75; [1977] IRLR 362, EAT.
[69] [1991] IRLR 264, CA.

for the purposes of the law of unfair dismissal, an employer might have acted unreasonably casts no light whatsoever on the question whether he has treated the employee 'less favourably' for the purposes of the Act of 1976.

I cannot improve on the reasoning of Lord Morison ... who stated that it 'cannot be inferred, let alone presumed, only from the fact that an employer has acted unreasonably towards one employee, that he would have acted reasonably if he had been dealing with another in the same circumstances'.

The difficulty with this important case arises because the tribunal held that the employers failed to overcome the presumption of discrimination where in reality there was no evidence of less favourable treatment, only evidence of unfair treatment. Without a comparator, real or hypothetical, unfair treatment cannot give rise to any *prima facie* case of less favourable treatment, so that the issue of what, if any, evidence the employer need produce does not arise. But if there is such evidence, the emphasis – both here and in *King* – on the discretion of the tribunal to draw adverse inferences may mean that more direct positive evidence of discrimination will be required by tribunals before they are willing to conclude that discrimination is made out. That would be an unnecessary and an undesirable conclusion. In a case like *Zafar* there may be no precise comparator in relation to an exactly parallel disciplinary hearing, but failure to comply with normal disciplinary practices, especially if such departure is exceptional, should require employers to produce *some* evidence as to why this occurred. Yet, in *Martins v Marks and Spencer plc*,[70] it was held to be irrelevant that an interview panel was guilty of 'bias' against a black applicant, because it could not be shown that there would not have been similar bias against a white applicant. This imposes an almost impossible burden on an applicant, downplays the importance of fair and transparent procedures for the avoidance of discrimination, and would make it much more difficult to prove discrimination even if the clearly best candidate was not appointed. The *Zafar* unreasonableness was irrelevant to the issue of racial discrimination; that in *Martins* was not. The two cases are clearly distinguishable.

The unfair or prejudiced views of one member of an appointing panel need not necessarily have influenced the final outcome. There are potential problems, not at present reflected in the case law, where some members voted for discriminatory reasons but others voted against the same person for lawful reasons. If there is *any* evidence of such unfairness, the employer, the only party who can give evidence on why decisions were taken, must have the burden of showing that the result was not influenced by it – that should require more than merely proving that there was a majority against the complainant even if the unfairness was disregarded. It is not simply the

---

[70] [1998] IRLR 326, CA

numbers which matter; the process by which the decision was reached must be shown not to be tainted by discrimination.[71]

The extent to which the rules on the allocation of proof affect the outcomes of cases is unclear. They are less important than a willingness on the part of tribunals to understand the realities of situations in which intentional and unintentional discrimination may occur and, what is perhaps largely the same thing, a willingness to draw inferences adverse to the employer in appropriate circumstances.

Aids to proving discrimination

There are four ways in which claimants may be assisted with the task of proving discrimination.[72] The first is the use of the Codes of Practice issued by the Equal Opportunities Commission and the Commission for Racial Equality; the second the use of the statutory questionnaire procedure; the third is by reliance on statistical evidence; and the fourth is by obtaining relevant information from the employer via the discovery procedure.

Codes of Practice

Both the SDA 1975 and the RRA 1976 give the appropriate Commission power to issue a Code of Practice aimed at giving practical guidance as to the steps employers should take in order to avoid acts of unlawful discrimination.[73] Both Commissions have issued such Codes 'for the elimination of discrimination ... and the promotion of equality of opportunity in employment'. The details of the Codes will primarily be considered in the chapters dealing with discrimination in employment and with positive action. The issue here is the relevance of the Codes to proof of discrimination.

Section 47(10) of the RRA 1976 provides that a 'failure ... to observe any provision of a Code of Practice shall not of itself render him liable to any proceedings; but in any proceedings under this Act ... [the] Code of Practice ... shall be admissible in evidence, and if any provision ... appears ... to be relevant to any question arising in the proceedings it shall be taken into account ...'.[74] A failure to observe a provision of the Code should therefore

---

71 In *Robson v Comrs of Inland Revenue* [1998] IRLR 196, a case where an allegation of racial abuse was made by an Irish employee, the EAT held that it was an error for the Industrial Tribunal, in rejecting the complaint, to have taken into consideration the fact that two of the defendants were related by marriage to people from ethnic minorities.

72 What might be considered as a fifth, the actual provision of legal assistance by the EOC or the CRE, is considered below, pp 498–99.

73 SDA 1975, s 56A; RRA 1976, s 47.

74 See, also, SDA 1975, s 56A(10).

make it easier to establish that discrimination has occurred. The general impression, however, is that tribunals refer to the Codes only rarely.[75] The reasons for this are unclear. It may be that their substance forms the basis of an argument; it is only the explicit reference that is absent. It may be that their provisions, which are in rather general terms, are thought, rightly or wrongly, to lack the precision necessary to be relevant to individual cases. It does not follow that their overall impact has been minimal. They are among a number of developments which have raised the profile of equality issues and assisted in showing employers – perhaps primarily those who wished to know – steps that might be taken to avoid discrimination.

The questionnaire procedure

This procedure is designed to assist applicants to know if they have a genuine case and what the employer's response might be. Under s 74 of the SDA 1975 and s 65 of the RRA 1976 there are prescribed forms (though there is no legal requirement to use them) under which (a) 'the person aggrieved may question the respondent on his reasons for doing any relevant act ...' and (b) 'forms by which the respondent may if he so wishes reply to any questions ...'. The questions[76] and any answers are admissible in any subsequent hearing, and it is specifically provided that 'if it appears to the court or tribunal that the respondent deliberately, and without reasonable excuse, omitted to reply within a reasonable period or that his reply is evasive or equivocal, the ... tribunal may draw any inference from that fact which it considers just and equitable to draw'.[77]

Like so much else in the legislation, the procedure has not been as effective as was envisaged. Leonard found that only 16 cases from the 215 she studied had utilised the procedure.[78] She argued that 'the questions must be drawn effectively, and discrepancies skilfully pursued at the hearing'.[79] There is also a danger of alerting the employer to the nature and strength of the employee's case.[80] Overall, an attempt to overcome lack of legal expertise and encourage self-representation, while worthy in itself, is likely to founder in the face of the many other problems faced by such applicants.

---

[75] *Op cit*, Bourn and Whitmore, fn 54, p 115.

[76] The Commissions may assist potential claimants with the drafting of an appropriate questionnaire.

[77] SDA 1975, s 74(2); RRA 1976, s 65(2). For examples, see *Virdee v ECC Quarries Ltd* [1978] IRLR 295, IT; *King v Great Britain-China Centre* [1992] ICR 516; [1991] IRLR 513, CA.

[78] *Op cit*, Leonard, fn 61, p 63. It is unclear whether the proportion has changed since then.

[79] *Op cit*, Leonard, fn 61, p 66.

[80] *Op cit*, Bourn and Whitmore, fn 54, p 123.

Statistics

Unlike indirect discrimination, direct discrimination is fundamentally individualistic in concept. It follows that in most cases statistical evidence will be of no relevance. But the total numbers of women or black people who have been hired or promoted may be relevant. The assumption is that, if the employer were not discriminating, the numbers hired should be in approximate proportion to the number of applicants.[81] No one should expect a perfect match, so this kind of evidence should only carry significant probative weight if the mismatch is glaring, and the bigger the numbers in absolute terms, the more a mismatch becomes suspicious. The very concept of indirect discrimination is itself statistical, though a *prima facie* case is potentially justifiable; whereas here, statistics are being advanced as proof, conclusive in glaring cases, that direct discrimination has occurred.

Despite this compelling logic, it was held in *Jalota v Imperial Metal Industries (Kynoch) Ltd*[82] that the applicant could not force the employer to disclose the racial make up of the workforce as such evidence was irrelevant. This unsympathetic approach no longer represents the law.

West Midlands Passenger Transport Executive v Singh [1988] IRLR 186, CA[83]

The employers rejected the plaintiff's application for promotion. He sought discovery of statistics on the number of whites and non-whites who had applied for promotion to similar posts, and the numbers of each who had been successful. The employers kept such statistics in accordance with their equal opportunities policy.

The claim depended on whether the discovery ordered was 'necessary for disposing fairly' of the claim.

The Court of Appeal granted the order sought.

Balcombe LJ (pp 188–89):

Statistical evidence may establish a discernible pattern in the treatment of a particular group: if that pattern demonstrates a regular failure of members of the group to obtain promotion to particular jobs and of under-representation in such jobs, it may give rise to an inference of discrimination against the group. That is the reason why the Race Relations Code of Practice ... recommends

---

81 'By definition, discrimination is not a response to a given individual's character or behaviour, but rather a repeated and unthinking reaction to any person who possesses a particular trait. Thus if an employer does engage in direct discrimination, he is likely to do so against all non-whites, not just the particular complainant. Over time one would expect the result to be a demonstrable pattern of a low proportion of non-white employees and/or a high proportion of rejected applicants. Statistical data merely expresses this common sense observation in a convenient manner.' Lustgarten, L, *The Legal Control of Racial Discrimination*, 1980, London: Macmillan, p 209.

82 [1979] IRLR 313, EAT.

83 See, also, [1988] 1 WLR 730; [1988] 2 All ER 873.

ethnic monitoring of the workforce and of applications for promotion and recruitment ... Statistics obtained through monitoring are not conclusive in themselves, but if they show racial or ethnic imbalance or disparities, then they may indicate areas of racial discrimination.

If a practice is being operated against a group then, in the absence of a satisfactory explanation in a particular case, it is reasonable to infer that the complainant, as a member of the group, has himself been treated less favourably on ground of race. Indeed, evidence of discriminatory treatment against the group in relation to promotion may be more persuasive of discrimination in the particular case than previous treatment of the applicant, which may be indicative of personal factors peculiar to the applicant and not necessarily racially motivated.

If evidence of a non-discriminatory attitude on the part of an employer is accepted as having probative force, as being likely to have governed his behaviour in a particular case, then evidence of a discriminatory attitude on his part may also have probative effect.

The suitability of candidates can rarely be measured objectively; often subjective judgments will be made. If there is evidence of a high percentage rate of failure to achieve promotion at particular levels by members of a particular racial group, this may indicate that the real reason for refusal is a conscious or unconscious racial attitude which involves stereotyped assumptions about members of that group.

This important case shows how statistics may be *necessary* because of the absence of any other evidence, but are unlikely, in themselves, to be *sufficient* to prove discrimination. There are, however, a number of problems which may prevent the successful utilisation of such evidence. First, it may not be available. It is ironic that employers who, perhaps with the best of intentions, have conducted ethnic and gender monitoring exercises, are thereby rendered more vulnerable to discrimination claims based on the use of such evidence. Even though such monitoring is recommended by the Codes of Practice, it is unlikely that a tribunal would ever be prepared to regard a failure to monitor as in any way indicative of discrimination, at least until it appears that monitoring is the norm amongst employers. Secondly, the numbers involved may mean that more often than not the weight to be attached to such evidence is, in the absence of other supporting evidence, necessarily limited. On the other hand, it must be borne in mind that statistical significance is not required; the evidence is being used to persuade and indicate, rather than scientifically prove. In *King v Great Britain-China Centre*,[84] all the eight shortlisted applicants were white and no ethnic Chinese had ever worked there. There were only four employees in total, and no information was provided as to how many ethnic Chinese had ever applied for jobs at the centre, yet the figures were considered important, especially as the purported

---

[84] [1992] ICR 516; [1991] IRLR 513, CA.

reasons for her rejection failed to withstand scrutiny. Thirdly, the relevance of statistics depends on some notion of how many black people or women one might expect to find doing a particular job. Comparing proportions promoted with proportions at lower level may be relatively straightforward, as it might be reasonable to assume that promotions should be in proportion to applications from each group. Applying the same approach to entry-level jobs is more problematic. There is no guarantee that average qualifications among groups are the same, particularly in areas of past under-representation of women and minority ethnic groups. Applied correctly, the statistical approach requires information on those qualified for the particular job in the labour market from which the employer recruits.[85] Even if the figures are available, which is highly unlikely, their interpretation is complex, and in America, where expert statisticians become involved, very expensive. However, it should be for an employer who wishes to contend that a disparity in appointment rates is of low probative value to explain why this is the case; the burden of lack of information on the causes of a demonstrated disparity should fall on the employer. Such an approach would require the employer to articulate more explicitly his selection criteria, which may in itself reveal that he was operating criteria which *prima facie* were indirectly discriminatory.

Bourn, C and Whitmore, J, *Anti-Discrimination Law in Britain*, 3rd edn, 1996, London: Sweet & Maxwell, pp 127–28:

Suppose a black person applies for a job and is told that the job has gone, but disbelieves that explanation. One option open to him is, as soon as possible, to get white friends to make comparable applications to the same employer citing the same qualifications. Sometimes a local racial equality council can arrange such a test. If it is established by the testing that the job is still open to the white applicant, the inference that the employer's statement ... that the job had gone was a pretextual reason for a racially discriminatory decision is strong.[86]

The CRE commonly uses 'testing' evidence of this sort ... Other examples are cases of refusal of entry to a nightclub, or of a drink in a public house. In these situations the number of reasons other than race which can be offered by way of explanation are limited. In both cases age, dress or behaviour may be cited and therefore it is essential for the testers to be of the same age, wear comparable clothes and to behave similarly ...

In recent years, courts and tribunals have generally been happy to accept supporting evidence of the testing kind ... [T]esting depends for its efficacy on the simple nature of the situation. In more complex situations where the number of comparable features which have to be controlled increases, it is

---

85 Willborn, S, 'Proof of discrimination in the United Kingdom and the United States' [1986] Civil Justice Quarterly 321, p 325.

86 In *Hussein v (1) Harrison and (2) CD Bramall (Bradford) Ltd* (1997), rejected, unreported, IT, Case No: 1800810/97, see 35 DCLD 5, the applicant, after having been for a job, submitted an application from a fictitious white person with the same qualifications. That person was offered an interview, a fact which was both admissible and probative of racial discrimination.

decreasingly useful as a tool. This is particularly so where the actual presentation of people is called for ...

In some types of situations, testing may be decreasingly useful as the nature of discrimination changes in society. If discrimination takes the form not of a complete ban on women or members of ethnic minorities, but instead acceptance of only those who are way above their male or white counterparts who are being accepted with lower qualifications, then the level at which the qualifications are pitched in the test becomes all-important. If high, then all the applicants, male, female, white and ethnic minority will be accepted. If low, then all the female and ethnic minority applicants will be accepted.

Discovery

There are many instances where conduct can only be evaluated if the employer is forced to disclose certain information. Statistical information such as monitoring is one example. But many applicants will only establish less favourable treatment if they can show that they were better qualified than the successful candidate or that the interview procedure was different and unfair in a particular case. Unless the employer can be forced to disclose the criteria and procedures adopted, it may be impossible to make out a case, a fact which has been recognised by the House of Lords.[87]

Nasse v Science Research Council; Vyas v Leyland Cars [1979] IRLR 465, HL[88]

Mrs Nasse claimed discrimination on the ground of marital status in that she was not selected to appear before an interview panel, which was as essential step in the promotion procedure. Under the procedure, an annual confidential report is made on each candidate. She sought discovery of the annual reports on two of her colleagues and the minutes of the meetings where those two were considered for promotion and she was not recommended.

Mr Vyas's case was of failure to transfer on racial grounds. The tribunal chair ordered BL to provide information concerning the employment records of the four men interviewed, but not confidential information about them or the forms on which the interviewing panel had recorded their opinions.

The Court of Appeal set aside the orders for discovery.

The House of Lords allowed the appeals.

Lord Wilberforce (pp 467–68):

[My] conclusions are as follows:

---

[87] Unlike the questionnaire procedure, the discovery procedure is only available after proceedings have been instituted. It may be necessary to start proceedings, obtain discovery, and only then consider whether there is a valid claim. In *Nasse*, Lord Salmon observed that the questionnaire procedure was not 'intended to be a substitute for, but an addition to, the complainant's rights of discovery and inspection of documents'. [1979] IRLR 465, p 469.

[88] See, also, [1980] AC 1028; [1979] 3 All ER 673.

(1) There is no principle of public interest immunity ... protecting such confidential documents as these ...

(2) There is no principle in English law by which documents are protected from discovery by reason of confidentiality alone. But there is no reason why, in the exercise of its discretion to order discovery, tribunals should not have regard to the fact that documents are confidential ... In the employment field, the tribunal may have regard to the sensitivity of particular types of confidential information, to the extent to which the interests of third parties (including the employees on which confidential reports have been made, as well as those reporting) may be affected by disclosure, to the interests which both employers and employees may have in preserving the confidentiality of personal reports ...

(3) [R]elevance alone, though a necessary ingredient, does not provide an automatic sufficient test for ordering discovery. The tribunal always has a discretion ...

(4) The ultimate test ... is whether discovery is necessary for disposing fairly of the proceedings ... But where the court is impressed with the need to preserve confidentiality in a particular case, it will consider carefully whether the necessary information has been or can be obtained by other means, not involving a breach of confidence.

(5) [T]he tribunal should inspect the documents. It will naturally consider whether justice can be done by special measures such as 'covering up', substituting anonymous references for specific names, or, in rare cases, hearing *in camera*.

Lord Salmon (p 469):

[T]here is, particularly in large enterprises, an elaborate system for making and filing written reports and records in relation in each employee ... [T]hese reports are of special importance when it comes to decide which of the employees [will be promoted]. Suppose that one of the candidates who happened to be black had excellent written reports and records but failed to obtain the promotion or transfer for which he applied, whilst two other candidates who happened to be white did obtain promotion or transfer although their records and reports were well below those of the black man; this could well be regarded as establishing a strong *prima facie* case ... But without discovery and inspection of the relevant documents, the truth could not have been found nor justice done.[89]

Sometimes there may be so many candidates that a tribunal may regard an order for discovery on all of them to be oppressive. In *Perera v Civil Service Commission*,[90] there were 1,600 applicants; perhaps understandably, discovery was only ordered in relation to the 78 who were interviewed, though the complainant was no doubt interested in the criteria and process by which candidates were shortlisted. As the same discovery criteria apply to indirect as

[89] Discovery should not be ordered of information which may assist the employer's case. *British Railways Board v Natarajan* [1979] ICR 326, EAT.

[90] [1980] ICR 699; [1980] IRLR 233, EAT.

well as direct discrimination cases, determining the adverse impact of a criterion may well require discovery of information relating to a very large number of potential employees.

THE BURDEN OF PROOF DIRECTIVE[91]

The European Commission first proposed a directive on the burden of proof in discrimination cases in 1988. As unanimity was required, UK opposition caused the shelving of the proposal. Matters changed following the change of Government, and in July 1997 the Council of Ministers of the European Community adopted a common position on the proposal, which is likely to result in its passage within a relatively short time scale.[92] The key articles of the draft directive are as follows.[93]

Article 4

(1) Member States shall take such measures as are necessary ... to ensure that, when persons who consider themselves wronged because the principle of equal treatment has not been applied to them establish ... facts from which it may be presumed that there has been direct or indirect discrimination, it shall be for the respondent to prove that there has been no breach of the principle of equal treatment.

(2) This Directive shall not prevent Member States from introducing rules of evidence which are more favourable to plaintiffs.

Article 7

The Member States shall bring into force the laws, regulations and administrative provisions necessary for them to comply with this Directive by 1 January 2001.

The burden of proof will thus shift only when facts have been established from which discrimination may be presumed – it will remain for the complainant to establish such facts. It appears that there will be no choice for the fact-finder: if the employer fails to prove that there has been no discrimination the complainant will win. The tribunal must draw an inference of discrimination rather than merely being permitted to do so. The impact of the change, though, is unlikely to be substantial. The success of a discrimination claim will still depend more on the quality of the evidence and the ability and willingness of tribunals to respond to such evidence by drawing inferences adverse to the employer.

---

[91] See 'EC Burden of Proof Directive' (1997) 76 EOR 37.

[92] 97/C 307/02.

[93] Article 2(2) will make for easier for complainants to establish a *prima facie* case of indirect discrimination; see below, p 268.

CHAPTER 7

ANTI-DISCRIMINATION LAW, PREGNANCY AND CHILDBIRTH[1]

INTRODUCTION

The fact that women get pregnant and give birth, while men do not, raises issues of great theoretical and practical importance for those concerned with equality issues. This is because, first, pregnancy has historically been the cause and the occasion for the exclusion of many women from the workplace and, secondly, because of the practical difficulties which many women face in juggling the demands of work and family responsibilities. There is no logical reason why the fact that women give birth to children should necessarily lead to prime responsibility for childcare. However, it is clear that the traditional division of labour within the home continues to exert a major effect on gender equality issues, both at home and at work.

There are two areas pertaining to anti-discrimination legislation which are specifically concerned with the fact that women and not men get pregnant, the offspring develops inside the female uterus, and the woman then gives birth, the birth itself giving rise to after effects which vary enormously in their duration and intensity. The first area of concern is the employment rights of pregnant women and women who have recently given birth. The second area concerns issues of health and safety, both of the mother and the unborn or new-born baby. This may manifest itself, first, in purported attempts to 'protect' all women or pregnant women from certain jobs or work at certain times – in particular, at night – where it is considered to be inappropriate or dangerous for women to work and, secondly, where it is suggested that continuing to work may, usually because of some product or discharge associated with the work process, risk damaging the health of the unborn child. In addition, it is appropriate in this chapter to consider the issue of rights to parental leave associated with looking after a very young child and, by extension, the wider issue of reconciling domestic life and work life, such as where responsibilities for the care of dependent relatives may affect attendance and performance at work, even leading to loss of a job.

The first two of these issues arise because of the fact of women's physical difference from men. This raises conceptual problems for anti-discrimination legislation; such legislation may be predicated on the assumption that those in similar positions should be treated equally, with the inference being that those

---

[1] See Fredman, S, *Women in Labour: Parenting Rights at Work*, 1995, London: Institute of Employment Rights; Palmer, C, *Maternity Rights*, 1996, London: Legal Action Group.

in different situations may be treated unequally. If a woman cannot compare herself with a similarly situated man, how can adverse treatment of a pregnant woman amount to discrimination? Indeed, pregnancy is perhaps the starkest example of the perceived inadequacies of the comparative approach. The answers to the problem have varied: some purported solutions have emphasised an approach whereby failing to take account of the disadvantages in which pregnancy may result itself amounts to discrimination; other approaches have abandoned a discrimination model in favour of an approach which gives direct rights to women. Some such rights may be specifically job-related; others place greater emphasis on the health and safety issues surrounding pregnancy.

British law has, in the last few years, been transformed by European developments, both legislative and case law, though in some respects the law remains in a state of considerable uncertainty. In addition, the premises and objectives of the law are not free from controversy. The law on pregnancy rights may be seen as a stepping stone for those who wish to see the law foster, first, a more equitable division of domestic responsibilities between men and women and, secondly, greater possibilities to take temporary absences from the workplace without experiencing significant employment disadvantages in consequence.

The plan of this chapter will be, first, to examine why pregnancy and related matters have historically disadvantaged women at work; secondly, to consider what should be the aims of the law; and, thirdly, to examine the law in the light of the various frames of reference and objectives which have been identified.

WHY HAVE PREGNANT WOMEN BEEN DISCRIMINATED AGAINST?

Finley, L, 'Transcending equality theory: a way out of the maternity and the workplace debate' (1986) 86 Columbia L Rev 1118, pp 1118–19, 1126, 1129–35:

There is a persistent, deeply entrenched ideology in our society ... that men and women perform different roles and occupy different spheres. The male role is that of worker and breadwinner, the female role is that of childbearer and rearer. The male sphere is the public world of work, of politics and of culture – the sphere to which our legal and economic systems have been thought appropriately to be directed. The female sphere is the private world of family, home, and nurturing support for the separate public activities of men. Traditionally, in our culture, legal intervention in this private sphere has been viewed as inappropriate or even dangerous. The notion that the world of remunerative work and the world of home ... are separate has fostered the economic and social subordination of women in two interrelated ways. First, the values necessary for success in the home world, such as nurturing, responsiveness to others' needs, and mutual dependence, have been viewed as unnecessary, even incompatible with the work world. Since the work world is assigned economic importance, the traditionally 'female' tasks and qualities of the home world have come to be generally devalued in our society. Second, the separateness of the public and private worlds, and the consignment of women to the home world, is seen as natural, based on unquestioned assumptions stemming from the apparent immutability of roles derived from different reproductive capacity.

The fact that women bear children and men do not has been the major impediment to women becoming fully integrated into the public world of the workplace. The lack of integration of women into the public world has made the workplace unresponsive to values such as interconnectedness and concern for the needs of others. This unresponsiveness not only perpetuates barriers to the participation of women in the economically valued work world, it also denies men the opportunity to participate more meaningfully in the home world ...

Despite the changed composition of the workforce, the structures of the workplace remain built either around the needs of male management, or the assumption that the typical worker is a man with a wife at home to worry about the demands of the private sphere. Thus, when women return to work, they often find that workplace structures are utterly insensitive to the reality of a worker with both home and job responsibilities. Childcare arrangements are generally regarded as a woman's private problem, of no concern to the employer ... Flexible job scheduling ... is still far from common. Most workplaces remain structured around an eight hour day, five days a week, even though such a schedule conflicts with employees' needs to do shopping and errands, to attend children's school functions or doctor's appointments, to be available to children when they are out of school, or to meet similar needs of other dependants. There is nothing inevitable or natural about this particular workplace structure ... Employers have too readily assumed that only the existing way of doing things can satisfy their needs.

Assumptions underlying pregnancy policies

(1)   The natural roles ideology

The ideology of separate spheres built upon natural roles has fostered both penalisation of and paternalism towards women. Underlying both the burdens and the protections has been an assumption that women's biological destiny incapacitates them as workers in the public sphere. This assumption of incapacity goes deeper than the view that mother and worker are inherently clashing roles, or that woman's primary responsibility is to the home world. It has caused women to be viewed as either especially vulnerable, in need of protection from the rigours and dangers of work for the good of the human race, or as unsafe and unreliable workers who must be excluded from certain jobs lest they endanger others ...

The premise that women's natural role makes them unsafe or unreliable as workers is reflected in policies that deny leaves or benefits on the assumption that women will not return full time or with full commitment to the workforce after having children. This assumption also underlies the tendency to call into question a woman's job commitment when she seeks some accommodation between her dual roles ...

(2)   Aesthetic and moral qualms

The twin problems of ignorance and failure to consider women's perspective are closely related to another set of values ... aesthetic and moral queasiness triggered by the sight of pregnant women. These qualms stem from our society's deeply ambivalent attitude towards female sexuality ... Because many of us, especially men, do not understand what it is like to be pregnant and are stirred by conflicting and complicated feelings of envy, fear and uncertainty about how the condition is actually affecting the woman, the sight of a pregnant woman can arouse either discomfiting protective impulses or disgust ... It is hard to treat [a pregnant woman] just like any other worker. Consequently, employers have sometimes feared that male workers would be distracted from their duties if they had to work alongside pregnant women ...

While proclaiming female sexual activity, pregnancy can simultaneously serve as a denial of sexual attractiveness or availability. The prevalent view in our culture is that to be sexually attractive a woman must be slim and should confine her curves to places other than her belly. A pregnant woman is often thought of as fat and sexually unattractive. It is no coincidence that the airlines, which fired or grounded women when they became pregnant, also had stringent attractiveness qualifications for flight attendants, including weight guidelines.

This important article was written more than a decade ago. It sought to explain the exclusion of pregnant women from the workforce and their consignment to the domestic sphere; with the rapid increase in the number of women – including pregnant women and women with small children – in the workforce, attention has shifted to the practical problems involved in combining domestic and workplace responsibilities, and the way these tend to impinge more severely on women than on men.

Conaghan, J, 'Pregnancy and the workplace: a question of strategy?' (1993) 20 JLS 71, pp 71–72:

While most women exercise whatever rights are available, the reality is that the limited income replacement and right to return to work which British law provides, combined with the enormous gap between supply and demand in terms of the availability of decent and affordable childcare, leaves women with children in a significantly disadvantaged position in relation to the terms upon which they return to the workplace. The 'working mother' is still vulnerable to job loss during the period of her pregnancy and thereafter. She is still more likely to work part time, and part time work continues to be economically disadvantaged. She is also more likely to experience downward vertical mobility leading to lower pay and poorer working conditions. The constraints imposed by motherhood in an essentially unsympathetic working environment become another resource for employers to use in their increasing search for flexibility. A woman's lack of bargaining power, directly consequent upon the absence of significant legal protection of her economic position during pregnancy and thereafter, makes her economic vulnerability easy to exploit.

THE OBJECTIVES OF LEGAL INTERVENTION

The law must deal with a number of issues: the treatment of pregnant women while they are pregnant and in the aftermath of the birth, and the broader issue of responsibility for childcare and the domestic division of labour. It is the former which has thrown into sharp focus the issue of what is meant in this context by equality and equality of treatment.

Conaghan, J, 'Pregnancy and the workplace: a question of strategy?' (1993) 20 JLS 71, pp 75–77:

In [the American] context pregnancy, as a biologically constituted difference between men and women, had historically been used to justify discrimination *against* women. Feminists, espousing an 'equal treatment' position, were understandably wary about calling attention to this difference in order to gain particular benefits, pointing to where arguments about women's 'difference' had got them in the past. They also argued that emphasising the special or unique nature of pregnancy risked reinforcing stereotypical notions of women's 'natural' role as mothers ...

Advocates of 'special' treatment, by contrast, insisted that pregnancy was neither a disability or an illness and that it did not benefit women to characterise it as such, serving also to reinforce the damaging association of pregnancy with illness and vulnerability. Moreover, to subject pregnancy to the same conditions as disabilities generally was to fail to recognise that pregnancy *was* a unique and *enabling* condition requiring specially tailored policies. Furthermore, it failed to acknowledge the social *value* of pregnancy and childbearing. Finally, it was contended that differential treatment was not inconsistent with equality ... To require pregnant workers to conform to standards laid down without taking account of pregnancy was to require women to conform to a male norm, to assimilate to established male working patterns rather than to forge new ones.

MacKinnon argues for an approach to sexual equality which focuses primarily on power and dominance and only derivatively on questions of sameness and difference. More important than identifying difference or justifying differential treatment is the need to ask why it is *women* who are perceived to be different and who, on account of their difference, are accorded unequal treatment. Why is it that women who at one and the same time must assert their sameness to men (and thereby their entitlement to equal treatment) and their difference from men (and thus their need for special treatment), inevitably inviting the accusation that they want to have it both ways. Ultimately, this is a question of hierarchical ordering, a question of who gets to define the standard by which difference is measured.

Close analysis reveals that the concept of equality is perfectly consistent with either the equal/special treatment position, depending on how difference is defined. If equality requires that like cases be treated alike, the position of feminists who espouse equal treatment is to assert that men and women are, for all relevant purposes, alike and entitled to equal treatment. Hence the tendency to equate pregnancy with other 'similar' disabilities. Those arguing for special treatment, on the other hand, assert that pregnancy constitutes a significant difference between men and women. Equality does not require similar treatment because men and women are in fact differently situated.

Either position is supportable. If pregnancy is perceived in terms of its immediate financial and administrative consequences in the workplace, then it is arguably 'similar' to other disabilities. On the other hand, characterised as a normal, natural, often voluntary condition, pregnancy is distinguishable from disability resulting from disease or injury ... What is crucial is the power to decide what counts as difference, and how the difference counts. This suggests that the important issues in the equality debate are those of power, not philosophy ...

Fredman, S, 'A difference with distinction: pregnancy and parenthood re-assessed' (1994) 110 LQR 106, pp 110–11, 118–19:

In the pregnancy context, the equal treatment principle presents some intractable problems. Five central limitations will be dealt with here. First, the equal treatment principle requires an answer to the question 'Equal to whom?' The answer supplied by anti-discrimination legislation is, generally, 'equal to a man' ... In the pregnancy context, this central reliance on a male norm leads straight into the awkward question of who the relevant male comparator should be. Secondly, the reach of the equal treatment principles is necessarily restricted to those who are held to be similarly situated. It requires no explanation for the type of treatment meted out to those who are not equal in the relevant ways. Thus, no justification is required for detrimental treatment of women in cases in which there is no similarly situated male. In the pregnancy context, if no relevant comparator can be found, detrimental treatment is in effect legitimated. The third limitation of the equality principle is that it requires only consistency of treatment between men and women, not minimum standards. In the pregnancy context, this means that a woman's rights are entirely dependent on the extent to which comparable rights are afforded to comparable men [such as the rights afforded to sick men] ... Fourthly, the equal treatment principle leads to an inadequate consideration of the question of who should bear the social cost of pregnancy and childbearing. Because the principle translates into an obligation placed upon the individual employer, the courts are prompted to require justification for placing the cost of pregnancy on that employer. But this ignores the fact that sparing an 'innocent' employer leaves the whole cost with the woman and prevents any consideration of the potential cost-spreading role of the State. Finally, the equal treatment principle tends to operate symmetrically, striking down inequalities between men and women regardless of whether differential treatment favours women or men ... [Thus] maternity leave policies might be challenged on the grounds that they constitute a benefit which is not available to men.

The rights approach has at least four advantages over the equal treatment approach. First, there is no need for a male comparator. Secondly, minimum rights exist independently both of a finding of equality and a finding that a relevant man has the protection sought. Thirdly, the question of cost can be dealt with explicitly ... Arguments that greater maternity rights merely result in lower employment for women can be countered by allowing the employer to recoup the costs from the State ... The final and possibly most significant advantage of the specific rights approach is that it constitutes an explicit acknowledgment of the social value of pregnancy and parenthood. This percolates through to judicial attitudes ...

[T]he rights approach is controversial in at least three respects. The first is political. It may be difficult or impossible to persuade a legislature to enact pregnancy rights, whereas a general equal treatment right may already exist as a constitutional or statutory guarantee ... Secondly, legal enforcement may be problematic, frequently requiring each individual to find her way to a court or tribunal, and to prove her case on its own merits. Moreover, remedies may be too limited to make such effort worthwhile.

Thirdly, rights are only as good as their content. The decision to grant rights is only the first stage: there remains much difficult and controversial territory to cover in deciding the strength of the rights. One implication of this is that the impression given by the existence of specific rights may be quite misleading, particularly where other elements of the system operate to undermine those rights.

Conaghan, J, 'Pregnancy and the workplace: a question of strategy?' (1993) 20 JLS 71, pp 84–86:

[T]he consideration of *context* – political, legal and economic – is crucial to any strategic evaluation of the likely effects of a particular legal engagement. An approach which relies on 'workers' rights' may be of value in the British political climate of the 1970s but is less likely to produce results in the post-Thatcherist 1990s. Likewise, an approach which relies on liberal 'entitlements' such as the 'right' to equality, may be more in keeping with the legal tradition in the United States of America than the social welfarist approach implicit in British maternity law ...

[Furthermore], the equality approach should be regarded as valuable in so far as it produces results, *not* because it conforms to scholarly standards of logic and/or coherence. Equality is better viewed as a *means* than an end ... [E]quality has little fixed meaning except that which those with the power to define choose to allot it. This is not to say that equality is valueless in the struggle to achieve a just society (both for men and women) but rather to suggest that its value is tactical rather than inherent, pragmatic rather than principled ...

[P]ractical political concerns raise a host of broader questions about the regulation of the workplace ... Chief among these is who pays for such policies: parents, employers or the State? Who should assume the primary financial responsibility for childbearing – the individual or society?

> Those who oppose the introduction of maternity and parental leave arrangements have very definite answers to these questions. Invoking the rhetoric of individual freedom and market efficiency [it is claimed that] maternity policies furnish employers with a disincentive to employ women.

This argument can to some extent be countered empirically. It is quite clear that more and more employers are introducing maternity polices which go beyond the minimum requirements established by law. The reasoning is economic: it is likely to cost more to hire and train a replacement for a well qualified and experienced female employee who leaves a job because of what are perceived to be inadequate leave arrangements. It is also clear that the women left behind by these developments are those who have little or no market clout: it is they who have inadequate employment rights and are likely to remain confined to the low pay, usually part time, secondary sector of the economy. The assumption that it is the primary role of women to be responsible for family and childcare is largely responsible for that continued confinement.

THE LAW

Since 1975, there have been two strands to the law. In that year the Employment Protection Act was passed,[2] which gave pregnant women three main rights: the right not to be dismissed on the ground of pregnancy (this took effect as part of the general unfair dismissal provisions); the right to maternity pay; and the right to cease working 11 weeks before the baby was due and return to work within 29 weeks of the baby being born. These rights undoubtedly benefited considerable numbers of women, and were, it is contended, instrumental in the fostering of social attitudes which accept the normality of women returning. In fact, given the narrowness and limitations of the rights created, it is probable that the symbolic significance of the new legal regime was as important as its practical significance.

That regime had significant limitations and weaknesses. First, its beneficiaries were confined to those employees who had two years' continuous employment with their current employer. At a stroke, large numbers were excluded. Secondly, to acquire the rights after two years necessitated a normal working week of at least 16 hours, while those who worked 8–16 hours only won the rights after five years.[3] Thirdly, the bulk of

---

[2]   These rights were first consolidated in the Employment Protection (Consolidation) Act 1978 and now appear in Pts VIII and X of the Employment Rights Act 1996.

[3]   The requirements to work minimum weekly hours, however, were swept away as a result of the decision of the House of Lords in *R v Secretary of State for Employment ex p Equal Opportunities Commission* [1995] 1 AC 1; [1994] ICR 317; [1994] 1 All ER 910; [1994] IRLR 176, which held that the existence of hours thresholds was indirectly discriminatory against women as so many more women than men failed to meet them. See below, pp 302–04.

the maternity leave was unpaid. What became statutory maternity pay was only payable for six weeks out of a total permissible leave period of around 40 weeks, although many employers made more generous provision. Fourthly, the drafting and the interpretation of the right to return provisions seems at times almost designed to cause women to lose their rights through an oversight, as if neither the legislature nor the judiciary really believed in the value of these rights, considering them to be an unwarranted intrusion upon the freedom of employers to manage their business and as imposing too great an economic burden on such businesses.[4] Fifthly, parental leave was not on the agenda and thus the legislation, at the same time as giving inadequate rights to women, only served to reinforce stereotyped assumptions that responsibility for childcare was the woman's. Finally, and arguably most importantly, the legislation said nothing about childcare responsibilities once the 29 week post-birth period had elapsed; this was assumed to remain the private responsibility of the family or the woman herself, with no direct State or employer involvement being mandated.

These rights, such as they were, applied to all women who met the qualifying conditions. They were entirely separate from rights under the Sex Discrimination Act 1975, passed in the same year, and thus in no sense required proof of discrimination – no comparison with how a similarly situated man would have been treated was required, nor, in many situations, could one have been made. But rights under the SDA 1975 are not, and never have been, dependent on qualifications such as two years' continuous employment or 16 hours' work per week. It follows that women who were unprotected under maternity rights legislation nevertheless had a claim if they could establish sex discrimination, and it was in this way that the early claims of pregnancy discrimination arose.[5]

Meanwhile, EU law has also adopted this twin track approach. The first track asks whether disadvantageous treatment of pregnant women is sex discrimination in contravention of the Equal Treatment Directive (76/207/EEC).[6] The second track, manifested especially in Commission Directive (92/85/EEC),[7] the Pregnant Workers Directive, grants direct rights to such workers irrespective of discrimination. That Directive was incorporated into English law by the Trade Union Reform and Employment Rights Act 1993 and re-enacted in the Employment Rights Act 1996. The relationship between the two different tracks may become problematic: in

---

4   Employment Rights Act 1996, ss 71ff, especially ss 74 and 82; see Pitt, G, *Employment Law*, 3rd edn, 1997, London: Sweet & Maxwell, pp 131–35.

5   The SDA 1975 makes no specific mention of discrimination claims by pregnant women; however, to avoid claims by men that rights granted to pregnant women discriminate against men, s 2(2) provides that the definition of discrimination shall not apply to 'special treatment afforded to women in connection with pregnancy or childbirth'.

6   OJ L39/40, 1976.

7   OJ L348/1, 1992.

particular, may an employee choose whichever track is likely to give her a more favourable outcome, or is the track based on the Directive and subsequent legislation to take precedence over the case law established under the anti-discrimination principle?

In addition, the approach based on health and safety sits uneasily alongside the other two approaches. Both in domestic and European law, women sometimes receive *additional* health and safety protection because of pregnancy; and have sometimes received additional protections on the grounds that they are new mothers or simply or the grounds that they are women. What is permissible under this heading is still somewhat unclear.

There are four different areas of law which need to be considered: dismissal because of pregnancy; pay and other benefits consequential on being pregnant; rights in respect of maternity – and paternity – leave; and finally, health and safety issues connected with pregnancy.

Dismissal

Given that a man cannot get pregnant, remorseless logic unaffected by consideration of the purpose of the law would suggest that the dismissal of a woman because she is pregnant cannot therefore amount to sex discrimination. It was precisely this reasoning which prevailed in *Turley v Allders Department Stores Ltd*,[8] the first such case to reach an appellate court. This 'no comparison possible' approach fell on exceptionally stony critical evaluation and proved very short lived. The next approach, the 'sick man' standard, provided the first mechanism by which protection was granted, and may still today be relevant in contexts other than dismissal.

Hayes v Malleable Working Men's Club and Institute [1985] IRLR 367[9]

The applicant was dismissed after telling her employers that she was pregnant; she lacked sufficient service to be able to claim unfair dismissal, so any claim had to be under the SDA 1975.

Waite J (pp 368, 370):

[T]he Industrial Tribunal[10] applied *Turley v Allders* to hold that dismissal because of pregnancy was incapable, as a matter of law, of amounting in any circumstances to discrimination between the sexes. The logic appears flawless ... If you dismiss a woman on the ground of her pregnancy, no one can say that you have treated her less favourably than you would treat a man, because nature has ensured that no man could ever be dismissed upon the same ground ...

---

8   [1980] ICR 66; [1980] IRLR 4, EAT.

9   See, also, [1985] ICR 703.

10 As a result of the Employment Rights (Dispute Resolution) Act 1998, s 1(1), industrial tribunals are re-named employment tribunals.

To say of someone that she has been dismissed 'on the ground of pregnancy' can never be more than at best a half-told tale, because it begs too many questions. It must in practice be extremely rare these days for anyone to be dismissed simply because they were going to have a baby, and for no other reason ... It will usually be the consequences of pregnancy rather than the condition itself, which provides the grounds for dismissal: the general effect, that is to say, upon the employee's performance at work of the need to take time off for confinement and for periods of rest both before and afterwards. Those consequences will vary greatly in importance and significance from case to case ...

[W]e have not found any difficulty in visualising cases – for example, that of a sick male employee and that of a pregnant woman employee, where the circumstances, although they could never in strictness be called the same, could nevertheless properly be regarded as lacking any material difference.

Thus, the comparison mandated was with how the employer would have treated a similarly situated sick man; there appeared no necessity to postulate that the illness had to relate to a man's reproductive system unless there was evidence that such illnesses were treated differently from other male illnesses. This approach is open to criticism on four grounds. First, pregnancy is not an illness but a normal, natural and necessary event which should be celebrated. While the approach may give practical protection, its theoretical foundation is thus demeaning to women. Secondly, in any event, the amount of time off which results even from a normal pregnancy is far in excess of typical examples of sick leave and allows for the possibility that men requiring long absences would not receive generous provision. Thirdly, the approach means that pregnant women must not be treated worse than sick men. If a sick man with less than two years service would be instantly dismissed, or if the employer made no provision for sick pay, he would be free to treat pregnant women in the same way. Fourthly, given that so many women have no male colleagues doing the same job, or that the organisation may lack formalised personnel policies, it may be impossible to rebut an employer's assertion that a hypothetical sick man would have been treated just as unfavourably as the applicant was treated.

This approach was, in the absence of anything better from the English courts, accepted as law for a number of years. The transformation wrought by the European Court began with the next case.

Dekker v Stichting Vormingscentrum voor Jonge Volwassen (VJV-Centrum) Plus **Case C-177/88 [1991] IRLR 27**[11]

The complainant applied, when pregnant, for employment as a training instructor. She was told that she could not be employed; their insurer would not reimburse the sickness benefits which she would have to be paid because

---

[11]　See, also, [1990] ECR-I 3941; [1992] ICR 325.

the fact she was pregnant at the time of her application meant that such absences would be regarded as a foreseeable incapacity.

The claim was that this decision was in contravention of the Equal Treatment Directive.

Judgment (pp 29–30):

As employment can only be refused because of pregnancy to women, such a refusal is direct discrimination on grounds of sex. A refusal to employ because of the financial consequences of absence connected with pregnancy must be deemed to be based principally on the fact of pregnancy. Such discrimination cannot be justified by the financial detriment in the case of recruitment of a pregnant woman suffered by the employer during her maternity leave ...

[A]n employer is acting in direct contravention of the principle of equal treatment ... if he refuses to enter into a contract of employment with a female applicant found suitable by him for the post in question, where such refusal is on the ground of the possible adverse consequences for him arising from employing a woman who is pregnant at the time of the application, because of a government regulation concerning incapacity to work which treats inability to work because of pregnancy and confinement in the same way as inability to work because of illness ...

[T]he answer to the question of whether the refusal to recruit a woman constitutes direct or indirect discrimination depends on the motive for such a refusal. If this motive resides in the fact that the person concerned is pregnant, this decision is directly related to the applicant's sex ... [I]t is of no importance ... that there were no male applicants ...

[T]he Directive does not make the liability of the discriminator in any way dependent upon the evidence of fault or the absence of any grounds of legal justification ... [A] contravention of the prohibition of discrimination in itself should be sufficient in order for full liability of the discriminator to arise. No grounds for justification existing in national law can be accepted.

The European Court unequivocally stated that refusal of employment on the ground of pregnancy is direct discrimination on the ground of sex.[12] The reasoning is that pregnancy is a condition unique to women; in consequence, an adverse decision made on the ground of pregnancy is, *by definition*, a decision made on the ground of sex. That the employer had no male employees cannot affect the conclusion that the non-discrimination principle has been violated. The reason or motive that impelled the employer not to hire on ground of pregnancy, be it financial, social or whatever, cannot provide a defence.

It is not and cannot be argued that it is necessarily sex discrimination to dismiss a pregnant woman: for example, she might be made redundant or be guilty of gross misconduct. It must therefore be established that there is a

---

[12] It has been argued that pregnancy discrimination is better viewed as a species of indirect sex discrimination. See Wintemute, R, 'When is pregnancy discrimination indirect sex discrimination?' (1998) 27 Industrial LJ 23.

causal link between the dismissal and the fact of her pregnancy. However, this allows for the possibility of a defence that the pregnancy was the occasion, not the cause, of the dismissal, and courts who have seemed unable or unwilling to accept the breadth of the *Dekker* principle have sometimes grasped at this line of reasoning so as to deny the applicant's claim.

Webb v EMO Air Cargo (UK) Ltd [1993] IRLR 27, HL[13]

The firm had an import department of four people, including an import operations clerk. When the holder of that job became pregnant, Ms Webb was hired, as it was considered that she would need six months' training in order to be able to act on her own as a temporary replacement. It was nevertheless anticipated that Ms Webb would probably remain employed when Ms Stewart returned. Several weeks after starting work Ms Webb discovered she was pregnant, whereupon the employers dismissed her.

The Court of Appeal said that dismissal of a pregnant woman can be, but is not necessarily, direct discrimination. The question is whether a man with a condition as nearly comparable as possible which had the same practical effect upon his ability to do the job would, or would not, have been dismissed. *Dekker* was distinguished on the ground that that case was not concerned with whether a woman was incapable of doing her job.

[The House of Lords referred the case to the ECJ, but made certain observations in the process.]

Lord Keith of Kinkel (pp 29–30):

There can be no doubt that in general to dismiss a woman because she is pregnant or to refuse to employ a woman of childbearing age because she may become pregnant is unlawful direct discrimination. Childbearing and the capacity for childbearing are characteristics of the female sex. So to apply these characteristics as the criterion for dismissal ... is to apply a gender-based criterion ... In the present case, there was not any application of a gender-based criterion. If the appellant's expected date of confinement had not been so very close to that of Ms S she would not have been dismissed. It was her expected non-availability during the period when she was needed to cover ... which was the critical factor.

If [this] is not legitimate, then cases can be envisaged when somewhat surprising results would follow. For example, an employer might require to engage extra staff for an event due to take place over a particular period, such as the Wimbledon fortnight or the Olympic Games. [Is there direct discrimination if the employer refuses to hire a woman whose confinement is expected to be on the first day of the event?] ...

The circumstances in the case of a woman due to have a hysterectomy are different from the circumstances in the case of a man due to have a prostate operation. The question is whether they are materially different, and the

---

13 See, also, [1993] ICR 175; [1992] 4 All ER 929.

answer must be that they are not, because both sets of circumstances have the result that the person concerned is not going to be available at the critical time. Then it has to be considered whether there is something special about pregnancy which ought to lead to the conclusion that the case of a woman due to be unavailable for that reason is materially different from the case of a man due to be unavailable because of an expected prostate operation. In logic, there would not appear to be any valid reason for that conclusion ... [T]he correct comparison is not with any man but with a hypothetical man who would also be unavailable at the critical time ... The precise reason for the unavailability is not a relevant circumstance.

[It is hardly surprising that this opinion brought forth a torrent of criticism, since it appears to fly in the face of *Dekker* and to resurrect the supposedly discredited 'sick man' comparison. Moreover, it does so by quoting examples which are far removed from the typical experience of working women – a very small tail being made to wag a very large dog.]

Case C-32/93 [1994] IRLR 482[14]

Advocate General (p 491):

[I]t is ... difficult to separate and distinguish pregnancy from inability to work for a specific length of time which coincides, moreover, with the duration of maternity leave. In such cases, absence from work is determined by the pregnancy ... a condition which affects only women. While it may be true that the woman in question was engaged for the purpose of replacing for a short time another employee during the latter's maternity leave, the fact remains that she was engaged on the basis of a contract for an indefinite period and therefore her inability to carry out the task for which she was engaged affects only a limited period in relation to the total length of the contract ...

[T]he absence from work is the result ... of the employer's concern to avoid possible financial or in any event organisational burdens arising from the need to engage an employee to perform – on a temporary basis – the tasks which the female employee who was subsequently dismissed had been recruited to carry out ...

[I]t is of no significance whatever ... that the employer would not have recruited [her] if he had been aware of her pregnancy ... [T]he dismissal cannot in any case be considered lawful when the appellant herself ... was not aware of her condition.

Judgment (p 494):

[T]here can be no question of comparing the situation of a woman who finds herself incapable, by reason of pregnancy discovered very shortly after the conclusion of the employment contract, of performing the task for which she was recruited with that of a man similarly incapable for other reasons ...

[T]he protection afforded by Community law to a woman during pregnancy and after childbirth cannot be dependent on whether her presence at work during maternity is essential to the proper functioning of the undertaking in

---

[14] See, also, [1994] ECR I-3567; [1994] ICR 770; [1994] 4 All ER 115.

which she is employed. Any contrary interpretation would render ineffective the provisions of the Directive.

In [these] circumstances ... termination of a contract for an indefinite period on grounds of the woman's pregnancy cannot be justified by the fact that she is prevented, on a purely temporary basis, from performing the work for which she has been engaged.

The case was returned to the House of Lords for final resolution.

Webb v EMO Air Cargo (UK) Ltd (No 2) [1995] IRLR 645[15]

Lord Keith of Kinkel (pp 647–48):

The emphasis placed by the court upon the indefinite nature of the appellant's contract of employment suggests the possibility of a distinction between such a case and the case where the woman's absence due to pregnancy would have the consequence of her being unavailable for the whole of the work for which she had been engaged. [If the latter situation] does not fall to be distinguished, so that an employer who fails to engage a woman who, due to pregnancy, will not be available for any part of the period of the proposed engagement is to be made liable for wrongful discrimination, the result would be likely to be perceived as unfair to employers and as tending to bring the law on sex discrimination into disrepute ...

The ruling of the European Court proceeds upon an interpretation of the broad principles dealt with in Arts 2(1) and 5(1) of Directive 76/207. Sections 1(1)(a) and 5(3) of the 1975 Act set out a more precise test ... and the problem is how to fit the terms of that test into the ruling. It seems to me that the only way of doing so is to hold that, in a case where a woman is engaged for an indefinite period, the fact that the reason why she will be temporarily unavailable for work at a time when to her knowledge her services will be particularly required is pregnancy is a circumstance relevant to her case, being a circumstance which could not be present in the case of the hypothetical man. It does not necessarily follow that pregnancy would be a relevant circumstance in the situation where the woman is denied employment for a fixed period in the future during the whole of which her pregnancy would make her unavailable for work, nor in the situation where after engagement for such a period the discovery of her pregnancy leads to the cancellation of the engagement.

It therefore follows that, as a general principle, having regard to pregnancy in reaching a decision to dismiss constitutes the application of a sex-based criterion, and, according, to the European Court, the application of a sex-based criterion necessarily amounts to sex discrimination. It does not follow that the dismissal of a pregnant woman is automatically unlawful. It still has to be shown that the treatment she has received was on the *ground* of her pregnancy. The question which must be asked in order to satisfy the comparative approach is whether the woman would have received the same

---

15   See, also, [1995] ICR 1021; [1995] 4 All ER 577.

treatment had she not been pregnant. The employer thus remains free to argue that the pregnancy was irrelevant or no more than a background cause of the dismissal, and that the real cause is different.[16] The approach of the courts to these difficult causes of causation – as problematic here as in other branches of the law – will largely determine the width and the effectiveness of the protections proclaimed by the European Court in *Dekker* and *Webb*.[17]

Pregnancy or immorality

O'Neill v Governors of St Thomas More RCVA School and Bedfordshire County Council [1996] IRLR 372, EAT[18]

The applicant was a teacher of religious education expected to teach Catholic principles. She became pregnant as the result of a relationship with a Roman Catholic priest in the locality. Effectively she was forced to leave her post. It was accepted that the dismissal was unfair but the issue was whether it was also a case of sex discrimination.

The tribunal said it was a mixed motives case and that pregnancy *per se* was not the dominant motive for the dismissal.

The EAT allowed the appeal.

Mummery J (pp 376–78):

The consequence of [*Webb (No 2)*] is that the applicant's pregnancy is a circumstance relevant to her case, though it is not a circumstance which would be present in the case of a hypothetical man. The appellant's claim ... is not, therefore, to be determined by a comparison of her treatment with the treatment of a hypothetical male comparator proposed by the governors as a male teacher of RE ... who had fathered a child by a Roman Catholic nun and where there had been press publicity about that relationship. Such a

---

16 A harbinger of the appropriate approach had been seen in *Stockton-on-Tees BC v Brown* [1989] AC 20; [1988] 2 All ER 129; [1988] IRLR 263, where the applicant was selected for redundancy because she was pregnant. Here, the reason for the dismissal was not pregnancy but redundancy, so the general unfair dismissal provisions applied rather than the SDA 1975. It was held, though, that the same principles apply; if the pregnancy was a significant factor leading to the dismissal, that would be sufficient to make it unlawful. The 'but-for' test applies; she would not have been chosen for redundancy had she not been pregnant.

17 In the two consolidated cases of *Dixon v Rees; Hopkins v Shepherd and Partners* [1994] ICR 39; [1993] IRLR 468, decided before the decision of the ECJ in *Webb*, the EAT held in *Dixon* that the dismissal of a pregnant employee was acceptable as they had found an adequate replacement and did not wish to lose the opportunity to employ her; and in *Hopkins* that the dismissal of a veterinary nurse was acceptable as the employers took the view that it was unsafe to continue her employment because of health risks to the baby. It was stated that the employers would have treated a similarly situated man in the same way and thus the dismissals were not on ground of pregnancy. In the light of the first House of Lords' decision in *Webb*, the cases are probably wrong; after the decision of the European Court they are certainly wrong.

18 See, also, [1997] ICR 33.

comparison is not legally appropriate under the interpretation of the 1975 Act in the light of the ruling of the ECJ. Pregnant women in employment occupy a special position which attracts special protection ...

The basic question is: what, out of the whole complex of facts before the tribunal, is the 'effective and predominant' cause or the 'real and efficient' cause of the act complained of? ... [T]he event or factor alleged to be causative of the matter complained of need not be the only or even the main cause of the result complained of (though it must provide more than just the occasion for the result complained of) ...

In our view, the distinction made by the tribunal between pregnancy *per se* and pregnancy in the circumstances of this case is legally erroneous ... The concept of 'pregnancy *per se*' is misleading, because it suggests pregnancy as the sole ground of dismissal. Pregnancy always has surrounding circumstances, some arising prior to the state of pregnancy, some accompanying it, some consequential on it. The critical question is whether, on an objective consideration of all the surrounding circumstances, the dismissal or other treatment complained of ... is on ground of pregnancy. It need not be only on that ground. It need not even be mainly on that ground. Thus, the fact that the employer's ground for dismissal is that the pregnant woman will become unavailable for work because of her pregnancy does not make it any the less a dismissal on the ground of pregnancy ... [I]n the present case the other factors in the circumstances surrounding the pregnancy ... are all causally related to the fact that the applicant was pregnant – the paternity of the child, the publicity of that fact and the consequent untenability of the applicant's position ... Her pregnancy precipitated and permeated the decision to dismiss her ...[19]

Pregnancy or misconduct

Shomer v B and R Residential Lettings Ltd [1992] IRLR 317, CA

The applicant was a negotiator for the company and had a company car. In September she told the managing director that she was pregnant and would be leaving in January. Soon afterwards she arranged two weeks' holiday. She was informed that her car would be needed during that period. She took the car to the airport and left it there while on holiday. She was dismissed on her return.

The majority of the Industrial Tribunal said that this gross misconduct would not have resulted in dismissal had she not been pregnant. They had a

---

[19] This decision casts serious doubt upon the previous EAT decision in *Berrisford v Woodard Schools (Midland Division)* [1991] ICR 564; [1991] IRLR 247, where a matron at a Church of England school was dismissed after telling the head she was pregnant but had no immediate plans to marry. It was held that she was dismissed not because she was pregnant but because the pregnancy manifested extra-marital sex. It was concluded that a man acting in a similar way would also have been dismissed.

replacement lined up whom they were concerned not to lose. A male employee with long term incapacity may well not have been dismissed.

The EAT allowed the employer's appeal, a decision upheld by the Court of Appeal.

Glidewell LJ (p 322):

[Her argument was that a good male negotiator with long term illness would not have been dismissed.]

What is relevant is whether an employee who was going to suffer from a disability and was then guilty of misconduct would have been dismissed if he had been a man ... I, for my part ... can find no material on which [the tribunal] could conclude on the balance of probabilities that the hypothetical man guilty of misconduct would not have been dismissed ... If they would have dismissed the hypothetical man, then it cannot be said that there was discrimination within the meaning of the Act.

While it is possible to quibble with the outcome on the facts, the approach adopted by the court is legally correct. Pregnancy was the trigger for the misconduct, but was not its cause. Thus her only hope was to argue that a man would not have been dismissed for the same misconduct; it is not surprising that this argument was unsuccessful.

Pregnancy or illness

Pregnancy may itself disable an employee from continuing to work, and the effects of the pregnancy or the birth may lead to further periods of absence through sickness. These periods of illness may fall within the permitted maternity leave or may extend beyond it. In each situation the question arises whether the dismissal is on the ground of pregnancy, in which case the protected status will mean that the Equal Treatment Directive is contravened, or on the ground of sickness, in which case comparison with a man's treatment becomes appropriate. It is clear that a woman absent through illness arising because of and during her pregnancy – not extending afterwards – may not be dismissed even if a man absent for an equivalent length of time would have been dismissed. The pregnancy, at least while it lasts, confers a protected status. The position is less clear as regards illnesses which originate in pregnancy but continue after childbirth.

Handels-og Kontorfunktionaerernes Forbund i Danmark (acting for Hertz) v Dansk Arbejdsgiverforening (acting for Aldi Marked K/S) **Case C-179/88 [1991] IRLR 31**[20]

The applicant experienced a complicated pregnancy involving considerable periods of absence. Between when the child was one and two she was off

---

[20] See, also, [1990] ECR I–3979; [1992] ICR 332.

work for 100 days as a result of an illness arising from the pregnancy and childbirth. She was dismissed as a result of these absences and claimed that such dismissal was in breach of the Equal Treatment Directive. The ECJ rejected her claim.

Judgment (pp 32–33):

It is submitted on the one hand that the dismissal of a woman because of her pregnancy, confinement, or reported absence due to an illness which has its origin in a pregnancy or confinement, at whatever moment this illness may occur, is contrary to the principle of equal treatment in so far as such problems cannot affect a male worker and he could not, therefore, be dismissed for the same reason.

On the other hand, it is submitted that an employer cannot be forbidden to dismiss a female worker because of a large amount of sick leave simply for the reason that the illness has its origin in pregnancy or confinement ...

[T]he Directive does not deal with the case of an illness which has its origin in pregnancy or confinement. It does, however, allow for national provisions which ensure specific rights for women in respect of pregnancy and maternity, such as maternity leave. It follows that during the maternity leave from which she benefits under national law, a woman is protected from dismissal because of her absence.

In regard to an illness which appears after maternity leave, there is no reason to distinguish an illness which has its origin in pregnancy or confinement from any other illness. Such a pathological condition therefore falls under the general scheme applicable to an illness.

Female and male workers are in fact equally exposed to illness. Although it is true that certain problems are specifically linked to one sex or another, the only question is whether a woman is dismissed for absence due to illness on the same conditions as a man: if that is the case, there is no direct discrimination on grounds of sex.

Advocate General (p 37):

[On the applicant's argument] if the complications caused by a confinement are very serious, the female worker may be unable to work for long periods of time without her employer being allowed to dismiss her ... [T]he efficient operation of the company may be compromised by the difficulty of employing a replacement for that post immediately. But the most serious difficulties arise where the employer, prevented from dismissing his employee, is legally bound to contribute, even partially, directly or indirectly to the payment of social security payments which are due to the employee ...

It seems to me equally that the financial difficulties which confront an employer obliged to retain on his payroll a female employee who is incapable of work ... may lead numerous employers to refuse to employ pregnant

women (very probably under false pretext) or even women of childbearing age
... It must be considered how a solution which would protect those women
who have serious post-natal difficulties – [a small proportion] – carries dangers
for all women wishing to enter the labour market.

[There should be no protection for] medical conditions which do not arise from
the normal risks of pregnancy and which should therefore receive the same
treatment as illness under the normal law.[21]

The judgment appeared clear that dismissal for illness within the national
period of statutory maternity leave was unlawful. The following case
attempted to distinguish *Hertz* on the basis that there, the illness did not come
to light until after the statutory maternity leave period had ended. Here, her
illness began during the pregnancy and continued after the expiry of her
maternity leave.

Handels-og Kontorfunktion Aerernes Forbund i Danmark (acting on behalf of
Larson) v Dansk Handel and Service (acting on behalf of Fotex Supermarket)
Case C-400/95 [1997] IRLR 643[22]

During her pregnancy, she was on sick leave in August 1991 and from
November 1991 to March 1992 when her maternity leave commenced. That
finished in September 1992 after which she took four weeks' annual leave. She
again went on sick leave, after which her contract of employment was
terminated on the ground of 'your lengthy period of absence and the fact that
it is scarcely likely that you will at any time in the future be in a position to
carry out your work in a satisfactory manner'.

The European Court held that there was no breach of the Equal Treatment
Directive.

---

21 '[*Hertz*] gives us a non-medical, male view of what represents normal pregnancy,
childbirth and post-confinement recovery. For a woman who does not fit this normal
model (she and/or her baby may have post-confinement problems), the protection of
the law is partially removed. If we are beginning to recognise the special nature of
pregnancy and motherhood, what justification is there for protecting a mother only
before childbirth and not afterwards, when she and her new-born baby are equally as
vulnerable? ... [T]he rationale for distinguishing between the two [periods] can only be
on policy, that is, economic grounds – precisely those grounds rejected in *Dekker*.'
Szyszczak, E, 'Community law on pregnancy and maternity', in Hervey, T and
O'Keeffe, D (eds), *Sex Equality Law in the European Union*, 1996, Chichester: John Wiley,
p 54. In the same volume (pp 85–86), Fitzpatrick responds that 'although the *Hertz*
decision is heavily criticised, it is less clear what the Court should have done. Does it
mean that the length of the 'protected period' should have been extended by the Court
to cover Ms Hertz or that open-ended protection should be provided for pregnant
employees? ... [M]any feel that the anchoring of maternity rights in discrimination law
weds it to the sameness/difference debate in a way that involves the use of artificial
comparisons and makes pregnancy rights a derogation from equality, a special right or
preferential treatment ... [T]he critiques of *Hertz* are directed against not protecting the
pregnant woman *enough* by not recognising the realities of pregnancy complications,
which can continue long after the birth of the child and by providing a cut-off point for
protection after which she is thrown back into the comparative approach'.

22 See, also, [1997] ECR I-2757.

Judgment (p 650):

Outside the periods of maternity leave ... a woman is not protected against dismissal on grounds of periods of absence due to an illness originating in pregnancy ... [A]s male and female workers are equally exposed to illness, the Directive does not concern illnesses attributable to pregnancy or confinement.

[A]bsence during the protected period, other than for reasons unconnected with the employee's condition, can no longer be taken into account as grounds for subsequent dismissal.

After this decision the only clearly discriminatory dismissal is one which occurs during the period of maternity leave.[23] Dismissals arising after that period has ended should logically be compared with how a similarly situated sick man would have been treated. In making that calculation, policy demands that the whole of the period of illness during maternity leave be ignored – the illness clock will only begin to tick the day after the end of maternity leave; otherwise, dismissal might be permissible even if it only lasted a very short time after maternity leave had ended.

The problem that remained concerned the effect of illness in pregnancy *before* maternity leave commenced. *Fotex* had implied that pre-maternity leave absences could be added to post-maternity leave absences to determine whether a woman was treated less favourably than a comparable man. The European Court has now rejected that approach and held that *all* absences due to pregnancy must be disregarded.

Brown v Rentokil Ltd Case C-399/96, judgment delivered 30 June 1998

The applicant became unable to work some two months into her pregnancy because of various pregnancy-related disorders. She was dismissed after 26 weeks of absence in accordance with the company rule that sickness absence for 26 consecutive weeks would lead to dismissal. The Court of Session[24] purported to distinguish between pregnancy and illness arising from pregnancy and held that no breach of the Equal Treatment Directive had occurred.

Judgment:

[D]ismissal of a woman during pregnancy cannot be based on her inability, as a result of her condition, to perform the duties which she is contractually bound to carry out. If such an interpretation were adopted, the protection afforded by Community law to a woman during pregnancy would be available only to pregnant women who were able to comply with the

---

[23] It is unclear whether this protection applies only during the minimum period of maternity leave required by European law, during any further period of maternity leave introduced by legislation in a Member State (such as the UK), or whether it extends throughout any further period of leave which may be provided by the contract of employment.

[24] [1995] IRLR 211.

conditions of their employment contracts, with the result that the provisions of Directive 76/207 would be rendered ineffective ...

[P]regnancy is a period during which disorders and complications may arise compelling a woman to undergo strict medical supervision and, in some cases, to rest absolutely for all or part of her pregnancy. Those disorders and complications, which may cause incapacity for work, form part of the risks inherent in the condition of pregnancy and are thus a specific feature of that condition.

[T]he principle of non-discrimination ... requires ... protection throughout the period of pregnancy ... However, where pathological conditions caused by pregnancy or childbirth arise after the end of maternity leave, they are covered by the general rules applicable in the case of illness ... In such circumstances the sole question is whether a female worker's absences, following maternity leave, caused by her incapacity for work ... are treated in the same way as a male worker's absences of the same duration ...

Where a woman is absent owing to illness resulting from pregnancy or childbirth, and that illness arose during pregnancy and persisted during and after maternity leave, her absence not only during maternity leave but also during the period extending from the start of her pregnancy to the start of her maternity leave cannot be taken into account for computation of the period justifying her dismissal under national law ...

The effect of this decision is that the principle of non-discrimination protects a woman from the time she informs her employer she is pregnant until the time she returns from maternity leave. She is, however, not protected from all sickness dismissals in the period before the birth but only those connected with the pregnancy. Employers will therefore need to ensure that they are informed of the precise cause of each sickness absence during pregnancy.

Pregnancy or unavailability

Caruana v Manchester Airport plc [1996] IRLR 378, EAT

The applicant worked as an independent contractor as a researcher under a series of fixed term contracts, the final one being for a period of 12 months. When she became pregnant, she was told that her contract would not be renewed for a further period because she would not be available for work at its commencement.

As she was self-employed, she could not claim unfair dismissal (nor would she have any right to maternity pay). The EAT upheld her claim under the SDA 1975.

Buxton J (pp 380–81):

There is no doubt that although the employers decided not to offer Mrs Caruana a new contract because of her future unavailability, that unavailability was because of ... her pregnancy ... Since pregnancy was a circumstance relevant to her case ... and that circumstance could not be present in the case of a man, she ... was the object of unlawful discrimination.

The contention [that the principle does not apply to fixed term contracts] is not consistent with Lord Keith's limitation of a possible special rule for fixed term contracts to cases where the employee would be available for no part of the term. [All that Lord Keith is saying is that] it does not necessarily follow from the ECJ's ruling that pregnancy would be a relevant circumstance where the woman will be absent for the whole duration of the contract ... That approach gives little ground for confidence that there are other, entirely unstated, exceptions ...

To disqualify Mrs Caruana from the protection of the ECJ's ruling would be a positive encouragement to offer or to impose, not a continuous and stable employment relationship, but a series of short term contracts, with the object or collateral advantage of avoiding the impact of the discrimination laws. We are confident that neither the ECJ nor the House of Lords did or would support such an approach.

Thus, there *may* be an exception for one-off fixed term contracts, as opposed to renewed or renewable contracts as in *Caruana*. Lord Keith in *Webb* took pains to exclude from the scope of the protection an employee whose pregnancy caused her to be unavailable for the whole duration of the contract. Such a contract would perforce be relatively short. However, this exception does not appear in the Equal Treatment Directive, did not find favour with the Advocate General in *Webb*, runs contrary to the general policy of seeking to improve the legal position of atypical workers, and may indeed provide an incentive for employers to hire women on short term temporary contracts.[25]

Availability for work is premised on the assumption that the woman will, after the birth, return to the same job she was performing beforehand.

British Telecommunications plc v Roberts and Longstaffe [1996] IRLR 601, EAT

The two applicants decided they wanted to work on a jobshare basis when they both returned from maternity leave. Their plan was rejected on the basis that the operational needs of the job required Saturday working, which was only available if they worked part time. The Industrial Tribunal upheld their complaint of sex discrimination, purporting to follow *Dekker* and *Webb*.

The EAT allowed the employer's appeal in respect of direct discrimination, but remitted the case for an Industrial Tribunal to consider whether there had been indirect discrimination.

Tucker J (pp 602–03):

[T]he finding of direct discrimination arose solely from the tribunal's view that, since the requests and refusals followed directly from the pregnancy and maternity, there was automatically direct discrimination on the grounds of sex ...

In our opinion ... the situation did not arise because the respondents sought to exercise their statutory rights, but because they did not seek to do so, but rather sought to alter the terms of their employment ...

---

[25] See *op cit*, Szyszczak, fn 21, pp 54–57.

Once a woman returns to work after her [maternity] leave, the statutory protection finishes, and her work thereafter is to be considered in the same circumstances as if she was a man ... [W]hat happened to these two respondents had nothing to do with them being pregnant, but with them having children to look after ... They were not permanently entitled to rely on having had babies as a protecting feature.

There is thus no *automatic* right to return to work on a part time basis, or to be granted the benefit of other modifications to the contract of employment in order to reconcile work and parenthood. Refusal of such changes is likely to amount neither to direct discrimination nor to breach of the Employment Rights Act 1996. Such a refusal may, however, amount to indirect discrimination, as it is likely that such employer policies will disproportionately affect women as compared with men. In such situations, employers may argue that they were justified in refusing to permit such changes to be made.[26]

Section 99 of the Employment Rights Act 1996

We saw above that statutory protection against dismissal on the ground of pregnancy originally required two years' continuous employment. In addition, there were two exceptions to the protection: where the employee had become incapable of doing her work; and where it had become unlawful to continue to employ her – normally for health and safety reasons – as a result of her pregnancy, and there was no other suitable alternative work available. In no sense, therefore, was there a *guarantee* against dismissal during pregnancy or on the ground of pregnancy.

The UK became obliged to amend this law as a result of the Pregnant Workers Directive.[27] The consequent Trade Union Reform and Employment Rights Act – the provisions are now to be found in the Employment Rights Act – amended the law in two important respects. First, there is no longer any continuity or hours requirement; an employee is protected as from day one of her employment. Secondly, dismissal is automatically unfair if the principal reason for the dismissal is pregnancy or 'any other reason connected with her pregnancy'.[28] The effect of this provision is largely to supersede the dismissal

---

[26] See Cox, S, 'Flexible working after maternity leave: the legal framework' (1998) 78 EOR 10; see, also, below, pp 304–07.

[27] The proposed directive was opposed by the then UK Government. However, it had been brought forward under Art 118A of the Treaty of Rome as a health and safety measure which could pass by qualified majority voting with no possibility of a UK veto.

[28] The dismissal will also be unfair in the following circumstances, which are in effect specific instances of the general prohibition: when the dismissal is for childbirth or any reason connected with it; when it occurs during the maternity leave period; when it occurs because the employee concerned took up maternity rights and benefits; and when she would otherwise have been redundant, and there was a suitable alternative vacancy which was not offered to her: ERA 1996, s 99(1). In addition, under s 99(3), a dismissal within four weeks of the end of the maternity leave period is also [cont]

cases decided under the Equal Treatment Directive; it is clear, for example, that Ms Webb was dismissed for a reason *connected with* her pregnancy. The new approach will be easier for applicants to satisfy, as it sets a lower causal threshold.

However, three comments are needed. First, the dismissal can only be connected with the pregnancy if the employer knows the employee is pregnant. Pregnant employees who are absent or likely to be absent for extended periods need to ensure the employer is aware of the reason. In addition, a causal connection between the pregnancy and the dismissal must be shown and causal tests are notoriously difficult to pin down. For example, if an employer, within his contractual rights, orders a pregnant employee to move to a different office – for organisational reasons, not simply because she is pregnant – and she refuses because she is pregnant and does not want the additional hassle, it is unclear whether the dismissal would be connected with her pregnancy. The same problem might arise, as in *Shomer*, where misconduct is in some sense triggered by the pregnancy. The second problem is where pregnancy-related illness is long-lasting. Literally, if the illness was a complication of the pregnancy or childbirth it is surely covered, but the economic argument that this may potentially cause unfair economic hardship for employers may lead to the words being given a more restricted meaning. But, in *Caledonian Bureau Investment and Property v Caffrey*,[29] the EAT held that a dismissal for post-natal depression was automatically unfair under this provision, even though its effects continued after the protected period of maternity leave and even though, on a very narrow reading of the legislation, it could be argued that the condition was connected with childbirth rather than pregnancy. Whether this approach will stand the test of time remains to be seen. Finally, and most importantly, the different compensation rules in the UK mean that there may still be a strong incentive to allege breach of the SDA 1975. The new rights take effect as part of the general law on unfair dismissal, for which there is a maximum limit on compensation. Until the decision in *Marshall (No 2)*,[30] the same limit applied to the SDA 1975, but the decision of the European Court and resulting legislation means that there is now no limit in such cases.[31] Some sex discrimination cases may involve greater loss than may be awarded for an unfair dismissal; in such cases a claim under the SDA

---

[28] [cont] automatically unfair if the woman was covered by a medical certificate at the time. More lengthy absences, if resulting in dismissal, will need to be dealt with either under the general unfair dismissal provisions or under the Equal Treatment Directive cases considered earlier.

[29] [1998] IRLR 110.

[30] *Marshall v Southampton and South West Hampshire AHA (No 2)* Case C-271/91 [1993] ECR I-4367; [1994] AC 530; [1994] QB 126; [1993] IRLR 445.

[31] See below, pp 509–10.

1975 should also be brought.[32] However, this point would lose much of its significance if the proposed abolition of the maximum limit for unfair dismissal takes effect.[33]

Pregnancy, pay and benefits

The Pregnant Workers Directive[34] provides that Member States must establish a right to maternity pay for at least 14 weeks, for which a qualifying period of no more than one year is permissible. The amount of such pay must be at an adequate level, which is defined as at a level at least equal to the value of the minimum state sick pay in the Member State concerned, which is of course in many cases lower than employer-provided occupational sick pay.

Two recent cases have argued that, if pregnancy confers a protected status, there should be no loss of income during pregnancy and that an employer is obliged to treat absences for pregnancy in the same way as sickness absences are treated.

Gillespie v Northern Health and Social Services Board **Case C-342/93 [1996] IRLR 214**[35]

The provision of the relevant collective agreement on maternity leave provided for full pay for four weeks, nine-tenths for the next two weeks and then half pay for 12 weeks. This was slightly more generous than the then Statutory Maternity Pay. The gist of the claim was that a woman on maternity leave should suffer no disadvantage in terms of employment as compared with those continuing to work; in order words, that she should have continued to receive her normal pay throughout her maternity leave as otherwise she was being discriminated against on the ground of her pregnancy.

Judgment (p 224):

[Women on maternity leave] are in a special position which requires them to be afforded special protection, but which is not comparable either with that of a man or with that of a woman actually at work ...

---

[32] The abolition of the limit on compensation proved crucial in the cases where the armed forces admitted a long standing policy of dismissing those who became pregnant. As the claim was against an organ of the State, damages could be awarded for losses arising in respect of any period after the UK's failure to implement the Equal Treatment Directive. The Government was forced to concede the unlawfulness of its policy, so the litigation concerned the proper approach to compensation in such cases. See, eg, *Ministry of Defence v Cannock* [1994] ICR 918; [1995] 2 All ER 449; [1994] IRLR 509, EAT; Arnull, A, 'EC law and the dismissal of pregnant servicewomen' (1995) 24 Industrial LJ 215; and now the Sex Discrimination Act 1975 (Application to Armed Forces, etc) Regulations 1994 SI 1995/3276. See below, pp 361, 513–514.

[33] See *Fairness at Work*, Cm 3968, 1998, London: The Stationery Office, para 3.5.

[34] Directive (92/85/EEC).

[35] See, also, [1996] ICR 498.

Directive [92/85] does not apply *ratione temporis* to the facts of the present case. It was therefore for the national legislature to set the amount of the benefit to be paid during maternity leave ...

[A]t the material time neither Art 119 ... nor Art 1 of Directive 75/117 required that women should continue to receive full pay during maternity leave. Nor did those provisions lay down any specific criteria for determining the amount of benefit to be paid to them during that period. The amount payable, however, could not be so low as to undermine the purpose of maternity leave, namely the protection of women before and after giving birth ...

As to the question whether a woman on maternity leave should receive a pay rise awarded before or during that period, the answer must be 'yes' ...[36]

The reasoning in the case is thin; the outcome inevitable. The Pregnant Workers Directive in general, and, in particular, the levels of maternity pay which employers should be obliged to pay, was the outcome of a compromise among the Member States; for the ECJ to hold that, after all, *full* pay was payable *throughout* the pregnancy would have been politically unthinkable.

When the case was returned to the Northern Ireland Court of Appeal[37] it was held, inevitably, that there was no case for concluding that contractual maternity pay which was at a higher level than statutory sick pay was inadequate. The result of this is that European law in effect says that there must be maternity pay, but that its level is entirely a matter for individual Member States. No attempt is to be made ensure harmonisation or a properly adequate minimum level. In *Todd v Eastern Health and Social Services Board*, heard at the same time as *Gillespie*, it was contended that it was unlawful for her maternity pay provisions under her contract to be less generous than the sick pay provisions, as the latter covered all forms of disability which could be encountered by a man, but not all the forms which could be met by a woman, such as pregnancy. The argument was accepted by the Industrial Tribunal but rejected by the Northern Ireland Court of Appeal on the basis that the contractual maternity and sickness provisions could not be rolled up together into one term providing for disability; a healthy pregnancy fell outside the contractual provisions relating to sickness and disability as pregnancy cannot be compared with sickness. This reasoning is flawed. If a pregnant woman requires time off because of illness it seems clear that she should be treated the same as an employee off sick for any other reason. The argument is that the employer should have treated all disabling conditions in the same way, as

---

[36] This part of the judgment, which provides that the employee has the right to have taken into account any backdated pay increase used to calculate maternity pay, was implemented by the Statutory Maternity Pay (General Amendment) Regulations 1996 SI 1996/1335. Note that the protection is only in relation to backdated increases in relation to the period used to calculate the due amount of Statutory Maternity Pay. This is different from the period during which the SMP is actually paid; for this period there is no right to receive the benefit of pay increases.

[37] [1997] IRLR 410.

otherwise the woman is being treated worse than a similarly situated man. The fact that pregnancy is not an illness is irrelevant to a comparison of benefits for different periods of absence; even worse is to deny the claim on the basis that the courts had previously decided that to treat pregnancy as an illness was inappropriate and demeaning.[38]

Statutory maternity pay (SMP) is now available to women with 26 weeks' continuous employment by the 15th week before the birth is expected, as long as they earn more than a minimum figure (for 1998, £64 per week).[39] It comprises six weeks' pay at nine-tenths of usual pay, plus a further 12 weeks' pay at the same level as Statutory Sick Pay – £57.70 in 1998.[40] The woman's contract must still be in existence up to the 15th week (though she may not in fact be working for health reasons) but she may elect to work for a further period, in which case the maternity pay period will commence on work ceasing.[41] The right to maternity pay is not dependent on the woman intending to or actually returning to work after the birth.[42]

The effect of *Gillespie* is that the legislative provisions on maternity pay supersede the protected status or anti-discrimination approach to pregnancy. It has been decided that as a matter of pragmatism there should be no automatic right to full pay when the employee is not working. Not all benefits depend on the physical performance of a job and there is no reason why these should not continue unaltered while the employee is not at work because of pregnancy or childbirth. Examples might include the accrual of holiday or bonus entitlement, or social club membership. In *Caisse Nationale d'Assurance Vieillesse des Travailleurs Salaries (CNAVTS) v Thibault* Case C–136/95 [1998] IRLR 399 the European Court had to consider a rule that, to qualify for a merit assessment and possible consequential bonus payment, an employee had to have been present at work for at least six months of the year. It was held that the employee could not be deprived of the benefit of this provision if the reason for the absence was pregnancy or maternity leave. The UK Government is proposing legislation to provide that the contract of employment will continue 'during the whole period of maternity or parental

---

[38] For discussion of the complicated interaction between pregnancy rights and sickness benefits, see Cox, S, 'Maternity and sex discrimination law: where are we now?' (1997) 75 EOR 23, pp 26–28.

[39] It has been estimated that 20% of pregnant employees earn below the lower earnings threshold and are therefore excluded from the SMP scheme. It was argued, in *Banks v Tesco Stores Ltd*, unreported, Case No: 18985/95, see 33 DCLD 7, that the existence of the earnings limit was contrary to Art 119. The Industrial Tribunal rejected the claim on the ground that there was no sex discrimination as it was impossible to compare the applicant's position with any man or group of men.

[40] Social Security Benefits (Uprating Order) 1998 SI 1998/470.

[41] Employers receive no rebate in respect of the first part, but a 92% rebate – set off against National Insurance contributions – for the 12 week period.

[42] Workers who do not qualify for SMP may qualify for maternity allowance, which is a contributory State social security benefit.

leave, unless it is expressly terminated by either party ...'.[43] It would remain open to employers expressly to specify in the contract what terms would continue during the period of absence.

'Maternity arrangements 95: part 1' (1995) 63 EOR 9

[This was a survey to ascertain the extent to which employers were doing more than was required by law. Although 243 organisations were surveyed, the majority were subscribers to Equal Opportunities Review, and thus the sample was not representative.]

Seventy eight per cent of respondents gave pay in excess of the minimum. On average, employers paid the equivalent of full pay for 14.1 weeks during maternity leave – the statutory scheme pays 5.4 full weeks' pay. The contractual pay is usually made up of two elements. The first comprises 100% or 90% of full pay for a number of weeks. The second is at a reduced rate, often 50% of pay for a number of weeks.

Just under 75% of organisations that topped up SMP required that some or all of the excess be paid back if the employee did not return to work or returned for less than a specified period.

All women on maternity leave, even if unpaid, have the right to continue to build up pension rights for the first 14 weeks of their leave. Forty-seven per cent paid pension contributions during unpaid extended maternity leave, 53% did not. Where employers pay contributions, this may be subject to conditions. Usually the employee must agree to pay her contributions. In some cases, the employee is given the opportunity to pay arrears of contributions on return.

Leave provisions – maternity and paternity[44]

The 1975 legislation gave women with two years' continuous employment, who worked until the 11th week before the baby was expected, the right to return to work within 29 weeks of the birth.[45] The right is, in effect, one to unpaid leave, and for a period so much in excess of the normal period of recovery from childbirth itself that it can be assumed to incorporate an element of childcare leave. For that reason, the legislation can be criticised as perpetuating the stereotype that women have primary childcare responsibility. After 1980, there was no longer an *automatic* right to return to one's old job; it could be defeated if the employer proved that to allow such return was not reasonably practicable, in which case an offer of suitable

---

[43] *Op cit, Fairness at Work*, fn 33, para 5.21.

[44] Because of the complexity of the law, the government has announced that the law will be reformed so as to create a coherent package of rights. *Op cit, Fairness at Work*, fn 33, para 5.13.

[45] This right still exists and is now to be found in the Employment Rights Act 1996, s 79. The interaction with the more widely available 14 week right in ERA 1996, s 71, is complex.

alternative employment was required.[46] In addition, the way in which an employee must notify the employer that she wishes to exercise her right to return is so fearsomely complex that it is all too easy for employees to lose the right by accident.[47] In *Kwik Save Stores Ltd v Greaves; Crees v Royal London Mutual Insurance Society Ltd* [1998] IRLR 245, CA, the EAT had held that a woman lost her right to return to work when she was incapable of physically returning to work on the due day because of illness. In a purposive construction of the legislation, one with potential implications for significant numbers of women, the Court of Appeal held that such women had in effect 'returned' to work when notice was given of that intention. Her contract thus continues in existence even if she is ill on the day return should have occurred. Dismissal for failure to return will be potentially both unfair and discriminatory. *Caffrey* held that it will be automatically unfair if the illness is connected to the pregnancy or childbirth. It is also clear that, for the purposes of the normal law of unfair dismissal, periods of illness during maternity leave cannot be counted so that periods of absence only begin to accumulate on the first day of illness after maternity leave has finished.

The s 71 right to 14 weeks' leave, whose progenitor is the Pregnant Workers Directive, applies with no qualification period based on hours or length of service.[48] The period may begin at any time before the expected birth date, usually depending on when the employee stops work. However, to prevent employees claiming to be sick right up to the birth, such that the 14 weeks would only begin around the time of the birth, s 72 provides that any pregnancy-related sickness absence in the six weeks before the birth will automatically trigger the commencement of the 14 week maternity leave. Unlike the s 79 right, the employee must be permitted to return to her old job, the only exception being where it has become redundant in her absence, in which case she *must* be offered any suitable alternative employment – even, it seems, in preference to an employee with longer service, or the dismissal will be automatically unfair.

The right is for *maternity* leave. The European Court has decided that there need not be equivalence between the rights granted to mothers and to fathers.

Hoffman v Barmer Ersatzkasse **Case 184/83 [1984] ECR 3047**[49]

Under German law mothers enjoyed a compulsory period of eight weeks' leave after childbirth. A second, optional period of leave ran from the expiry

---

[46] Employers with fewer than five employees need not make *any* offer of alternative employment if it was not reasonably practicable to do so: ERA 1996, ss 96(2)–(4).

[47] *Op cit*, Pitt, fn 4, pp 133–34.

[48] Note that, to add to the complication, the maternity pay right is for 18 weeks' pay, while the maternity leave right is for 14 weeks' leave. Partly because of this confusion, the Government proposes to extend maternity leave to 18 weeks. *Op cit, Fairness at Work*, fn 33, para 5.14.

[49] See, also, [1985] ICR 731.

of the first period until the child was aged six months; mothers taking this leave were entitled to a State allowance.

Mr Hoffman, the child's father, took leave during the second period. He claimed that he should also have been paid the allowance on the basis that Art 2(3) of the Equal Treatment Directive, which provides an exception for special treatment of women particularly as regards pregnancy and maternity, could not be interpreted to cover the second leave period, which was for the benefit of the child, not the mother.

The ECJ rejected the claim.

Judgment (p 3075):

[T]he Directive is not designed to settle questions concerned with the organisation of the family, or to alter the division of responsibility between parents.

[It] recognises the legitimacy, in terms of the principle of equal treatment, of protecting a woman's needs in two respects. First, it is legitimate to ensure the protection of a woman's biological condition during pregnancy and thereafter until such time as her physiological and mental functions have returned to normal after childbirth; secondly, it is legitimate to protect the special relationship between a woman and her child over the period which follows pregnancy and childbirth, by preventing that relationship from being disturbed by the multiple burdens which would result from the simultaneous pursuit of employment.

In principle, therefore, a measure such as maternity leave granted to a woman on the expiry of the statutory protective period falls within the scope of Art 2(3) of Directive 76/207, inasmuch as it seeks to protect a woman in connection with the effects of pregnancy and motherhood. That being so, such leave may legitimately be reserved to the mother to the exclusion of any other person, in view of the fact that it is only the mother who may find herself subject to undesirable pressures to return to work prematurely.[50]

The case has been criticised for failing to appreciate the distinction between maternity leave, which is for the benefit of the mother and thus personal to her, and childcare leave, which is for the benefit of the child and according to principles of non-discrimination should be exercisable by either parent.[51]

---

[50] See, also, *Commission v Italy* Case 163/82 [1983] ECR 3273, where the ECJ held that there was no breach of the Equal Treatment Directive where only mothers were provided with adoption leave; in effect, adoption was treated as the same as birth so far as its impact on the family was concerned, and thus the rather cautious non-interventionist approach in *Hoffman* prevailed.

[51] Although the same critics who regard *Hertz* as not providing enough protection for women in the post-birth period may criticise *Hoffman* for providing too much protection in the same period. See Fitzpatrick, C, 'How long is a piece of string? European regulation of the post-birth period', in Hervey, T, and O'Keeffe, D (eds), *Sex Equality Law in the European Union*, 1996, Chichester: John Wiley, p 90.

Fitzpatrick, C, 'How long is a piece of string? European regulation of the post-birth period', in Hervey, T and O'Keeffe, D (eds), *Sex Equality Law in the European Union*, **1996, Chichester: John Wiley, pp 93–96:**

[A] long period of mother-only leave following the birth may be positively detrimental to women's chances on the labour market ... It furthermore has negative effects on male parents who wish to care for their young child and more generally on the facilitation or promotion of a re-partition of caring responsibilities between parents. This would suggest that maternity leave should not be extended beyond the period necessary for the physical recovery of the mother and all care periods thereafter should be packaged as parental leave periods. If maternity leave is seen as a positive action measure, the longer it is, and the more women benefit, the better. Similarly, from a health and safety perspective, the longer the female-specific post-birth period, the better ...

The [European] Court refuses to explore the content and implications of 'maternity leave', 'protected periods' and other legislation affecting the division of mothers' and fathers' time between care work and market work [saying these are matters for Member States to resolve] ...

[T]he Court is, in effect, doubly 'blind'. First, if a Member State decides to call or not call something maternity leave, the Court will not scrutinise the content or length of the leave. Secondly, if the Court has to make a decision on a particular rule, it will not examine the implications of the maintenance or modification of this rule for the organisation of the family or the division of responsibility between parents. Whatever we can say about this approach, the consistency of its application cannot be denied ... In *Bilka* ... [the Court] ruled that Art 119 does not have the effect of requiring an employer to organise its occupational pension scheme in such a manner as to take into account the particular difficulties faced by persons with family responsibilities in meeting the conditions for entitlement to such a pension ...

Bar the UK, the maximum length of post-birth, mother-only leave in the EC hovers around 14 weeks. Recognition of this by the Court would clarify considerably regulation of the post-birth period, allow situations such as that in *Hertz* to be regulated adequately but separately and give the Court a clearly defined operating space for the second area it has so far steadfastly refused to confront; the effects of leave packages and other legislative provisions on the division of responsibilities between parents ...

This is not to argue that equality laws or judicial rulings can (or should) be employed to create periods of maternity or parental leave or oblige employers or legislatures to build creches. It does mean, however, that equal treatment laws ... could, and should, play a central role in evaluating the equality effects of the particular packages adopted by Member States ... The terms 'maternity leave' and 'paternity leave' can cover a wide range of very different provisions. Thus, a fully remunerated and non-transferable period of parental leave is a completely different right from a lowly remunerated right to be absent from the labour market .... The ETD outlaws discrimination on grounds of family status and discrimination on grounds of sex. While the Court continues to abstain from using these provisions to regulate post-birth leave, a black hole exists at the centre of European equality law and critical assessment of the equality implications of current provisions or suggestions for future reform are less likely to take place.

Proper parental leave would give either parent the right to childcare leave, for whatever period the employer, the Member State or the European Union deemed appropriate. The Parental Leave Directive (96/34/EEC), implemented through the Social Chapter, goes a very limited way towards that end.[52] It gives all parents with one year's service[53] the right to at least three months' unpaid leave – it need not all be taken at the same time – after the birth *or adoption* of a child, and to have time off work for urgent family reasons. Protection is also provided against dismissal for exercising the right. It is a non-transferable individual right which may be exercised at any time up to when the child is eight.[54] Certain issues, in particular the issue of income during leave, are left to be decided at national level, and the British Government has made it clear that the leave will be unpaid.[55]

Paternity leave is conceptually different from parental leave, referring to time off at or around the birth (or adoption). At present in the UK, there is no *right* to paternity leave, so that a father who takes time off at or around the birth of a child will, when the Directive is in force, be using up his right to parental leave. However, most large employers provide some contractual or discretionary benefits, typically of around five days' paid leave. While in many cases it has to be taken at or around the time of the birth, others permitted the leave to be taken at any time in the 12 months after the birth. About one-quarter of the organisations surveyed provided that the leave could be taken by a 'nominated carer' who need not be of the same gender as the mother.[56]

Just as with maternity pay, it is commonplace for employers to offer maternity leave benefits in excess of the statutory requirements. It is especially

---

[52] OJ L145/4, 1996.

[53] The Government is also proposing to reduce the qualifying period for extended maternity leave from two years to one. *Op cit, Fairness at Work*, fn 33, para 5.19.

[54] It is backed up by provisions to protect workers from dismissal on the ground of applying for or taking parental leave; and the right to return to the same job or, if that is not possible, to an equivalent or similar job. See (1996) 65 EOR 3.

[55] 'It had been assumed that the application to the UK of any Directive brought under the Social Chapter, which now forms part of the main body of the new Treaty of Amsterdam, would be dependent upon the Treaty being ratified by all Member States, which could take up to 18 months. But, mindful of the delay, and the fact of the UK Presidency which commenced on 1 January 1998, the Council has indicated that a means will have to be found, in advance of the signature of the Amsterdam Treaty, to give legal effect to the UK Government's willingness to accept the Directives which have already been adopted under the Social Chapter and those which may be adopted prior to the new Treaty coming into force.' The government has announced that implementation will be by December 1999. *Op cit, Fairness at Work*, fn 33, para 5.11. 'Parental leave and part time rights for UK workers' (1997) 74 EOR 2.

[56] 'Paternity leave' (1994) 55 EOR 14.

common to offer 18 weeks' leave in order to dovetail with the maternity pay provisions. In addition, some employers offer more extensive leave beyond the 40 week period, or reduce the service qualification for the 40 week entitlement. Furthermore, in nine out of 10 organisations surveyed, women had the option to return on reduced hours, an arrangement which in 80% of the organisations could be permanent. It was found that the average return to work rate of women employed by organisations offering improved maternity provision was 15% higher than that of women employed by organisations which offer only the basic statutory provision. Costs were arguably not excessive: on average 1.8% of the workforce was on maternity leave each year, a figure amounting to 3.3% of female staff. Finally, 70% of organisations gave adoption leave and in the majority of cases some or all of it was paid.

Yet for many mothers, the key issue is childcare of somewhat older children and not simply maternity leave, even if that leave has a certain childcare element to it. One recent survey found that there was one childcare place for every nine children under eight.[57] In addition, the issue of care for other dependent relatives – especially the elderly – is increasingly a barrier to full time commitment to the labour market. Such care falls disproportionately on women, and the problem is exacerbated as the State attempts to reduce its commitment to the provision of care for the elderly. Evidence shows there are more women looking after elderly relatives than there are looking after pre-school age children, that 30% of carers are male, three-quarters of carers work full time and approximately 5% of UK employees take one day's sick leave each month in order to care for a dependent relative.

It is for these reasons that many have argued that real equality for women, in the workplace and more generally, cannot occur until, first, there is a more equitable division of domestic responsibility between men and women, and, secondly, there is greater opportunity for periods out of the workforce without pay and career prospects being thereby damaged. The Parental Leave Directive is no more than a modest first step towards the latter ideal.

Finley, L, 'Transcending equality theory: a way out of the maternity and the workplace debate' (1986) 86 Columbia L Rev 1118, pp 1165–66:

The problem is that the spheres of work and family have been viewed as separate in a way that has excluded the values, needs and perspectives of one from recognition in the other. This dichotomy of values has limited the ability of both women and men to become fully realised interdependent human beings, because it has tolerated the assumption by employers and the rest of society that workers can be dealt with as disembodied from the entire context of their lives ... We do not conceive of work roles and home roles as integrated, mutually reinforcing experiences, but rather see them in competition with each other. The benefits to be gained from working are not seen as enhancing a woman's contributions to her roles as wife, lover, friend or mother.

---

[57] For the proposals on childcare in the 1998 Budget, see above, p 27.

We need to focus on the falsity of the public-private dichotomy and the need to integrate the values and structures of both the public and home worlds accordingly. It is necessary to challenge openly certain assumptions about men and women that flow from the dichotomy, such as the definition of career commitment that allows work demands to crowd out other needs and the related assumptions that the career commitments of women are reduced by their family responsibilities or by their desire to give time to both worlds, and that men do not care as much as women about their families or human attachments.

Adoption of this approach would involve far more than simply more generous maternity and paternity leave provisions. It would involve, for example, dependant care leave, flexible scheduling or adjustments in break time for those who are breast feeding or have to pick up children. It might also involve flexibility in defining expected performance so that suitable types of work could be done at home or at untraditional hours. It is arguable that focusing on conceptions of equality could hamper these developments, because of the linguistic and practical problem that equality seems to presuppose a process of comparison.

Some employers are beginning to introduce some 'family-friendly' policies, although, as ever, those standing to benefit are the better paid, more experienced, better qualified women workers. In the maternity arrangements survey referred to above, just under two-thirds of employers provided at least one childcare-related benefit. Seventy one per cent provided career breaks, 43% nursery facilities, 25% out of school play schemes and 23% childcare allowances. Seventeen per cent of employers surveyed offered three of these benefits and 27% offered two.

Care of other dependants falls more frequently on women than men. An ageing population and a decline in State provision indicates an increasingly high profile for this issue, one which some employers are beginning, in a modest way, to take on board.[58]

'Coping with work and eldercare' (1997) 73 EOR 23, pp 23, 26:

The types of policies being introduced by employers committed to equal opportunities to deal with support for carers include career breaks, special leave, jobsharing, part time work, reduced hours, flexi-time, home and teleworking coupled with other support measures such as counselling services, carers' networks and fairs, and written and audio-visual material.

[For example,] Barclays introduced a range of flexible options:

(1) Emergency carers' leave where staff can take up to five days' unpaid leave, in addition to annual holiday entitlement, or they can take time as paid holiday, borrowed from the following year.

---

[58] The Government is proposing to introduce a right to reasonable time off for family emergencies, which will apply to all employees regardless of length of service. *Op cit*, *Fairness at Work*, fn 33, para 5.78.

(2) Holiday float, where holiday is accumulated from the previous year and brought over.

(3) Responsibility break, which allows those with a minimum of two years' service who have responsibility for an elderly sick or disabled person, to take a complete break from work or to work on a temporary part time basis for up to six months if longer term care suddenly becomes necessary. The break is unpaid but existing staff benefits are retained.

(4) Jobshare.

It is unrealistic to expect employers of lower paid, often part time workers to be active in this direction; any improvement in childcare or dependent provision can only come from the State.

Health and safety issues

There are three ways in which health and safety may interact with anti-discrimination principles. These concern, first, the health and safety of the pregnant women herself; secondly, the possibility of risks to an unborn child; and thirdly, more general concerns for the health and safety of women on the ground that certain work, or work at certain times, is not appropriate for women to perform.

Health and safety in pregnancy

Conaghan, J, 'Pregnancy and the workplace: a question of strategy?' (1993) 20 JLS 71, pp 82–83:

[F]rom a feminist perspective, there are reasons for feeling uncomfortable with a health and safety approach. First, it reinforces a social and legal tendency to associate pregnancy with ill health ... Secondly, a traditional concern for women's health and childbearing functions ... has, more often than not, produced and legitimated social and legal practices which exclude and disempower women ... The conception of women as the 'weaker sex', which has served to legitimate their oppression throughout history, is closely related to the idea that pregnancy confers upon women a particular vulnerability. Thirdly, a concern for health and safety during pregnancy encompasses the health of the foetus as well as the mother ... [C]oncern for the foetus has often justified the imposition of restrictions on women in the form of foetal protection policies. [Furthermore] the focus on maternal health makes the case for paternity leave more difficult to argue.

The law now derives mainly from the Pregnant Workers Directive. Article 8(2) of the Directive requires that all women must take two weeks' maternity leave before or after the birth. The method of implementation, contained in the Maternity (Compulsory Leave) Regulations 1994,[59] is that the two week

---

[59] SI 1994/2479.

period shall commence on the day birth occurs. In the rare cases where the 14 week maternity leave has already elapsed, that period will be extended until two weeks after the birth. As enforcement of this mildly paternalistic measure will be the responsibility of the Health and Safety Executive, it is possible that, if employer and employee agree, it will in practice sometimes be ignored, particularly, perhaps, where women work for family businesses. Secondly, under s 66 of the ERA 1996 it is unfair to dismiss a pregnant woman who becomes unable to carry on with her work for health and safety reasons. She must be offered suitable alternative employment or, if that is not available, has a right to be placed on paid suspension.

The Directive also mandated further steps requiring employers – the original draft of the Directive having placed the obligation on Member States – to assess the health and safety risks for pregnant women and new mothers, although these do little more than make explicit what was previously implicit in the general employer duties.[60]

Fenwick, H, 'Special protections for women in European Union law' in Hervey, T and O'Keeffe, D (eds), *Sex Equality Law in the European Union*, 1996, Chichester: John Wiley, pp 77–78:

[A]n employer might refuse to make an offer of employment to a pregnant woman on the ground that she would be exposed to a risk referred to in Arts 4 or 6. Moving a worker from one job to another might mean a demotion or loss of the opportunity of promotion or of access to training. At this point the relationship between the Pregnancy Directive and the Equal Treatment Directive is called into question, presenting the national courts with a difficult task in fulfilling their duty to interpret provisions of national law in accordance with Community law ...

[T]he judgments in both *Webb* and *Habermann-Beltermann* impliedly accept that adverse treatment flowing from pregnancy is susceptible to justification. Therefore an employer may be able to contend successfully that not only costs associated with unavailability, but also other costs ... were the 'cause' of the refusal to appoint or the demotion of a pregnant woman. This might include adjustment of working conditions or removal of hazardous substances from the working environment, or other measures of special protection for pregnant workers required by the Pregnancy and Maternity Directive ... The question now becomes, it seems: did the cost of the pregnancy cause the adverse treatment, thus undermining the express derogations from the equal treatment principle and introducing other justifications for direct discrimination under the cloak of causation?

---

[60] The changes are achieved by amending the Management of Health and Safety at Work Regulations 1992 SI 1992/2051; see 'New health and safety rights for pregnant workers' (1995) 60 EOR 35. In order to comply with the Directive, a civil action for breach of the new assessment of risk regulations is provided, even though absent from equivalent provisions not relating specifically to pregnant women.

Habermann-Beltermann v Arbeiterwohlfahrt, Bezirksverband Ndb/Opf Ev
Case C-421/92 [1994] ECR I-1657[61]

The complainant applied for a job as a night nurse in an old people's home. For family reasons she was only able to work at night, and the contract provided for night work only. When she became pregnant, the employers dismissed her, relying on a statutory prohibition on pregnant or breast-feeding mothers working at night.

Judgment (p 1667):

The first question which arises is whether the annulment or avoidance ... of an employment contract in a case such as this constitutes direct discrimination on grounds of sex. To that end, it must be established whether the fundamental reason for the annulment or avoidance of the contract applies without distinction to workers of both sexes ...

It is clear that the termination of an employment contract on account of the employee's pregnancy ... concerns women alone and constitutes therefore direct discrimination on grounds of sex ...

The question ... is whether the Directive precludes compliance with the prohibition on night time work by pregnant women, which is unquestionably compatible with Art 2(3), from rendering an employment contract invalid or allowing it to be avoided on the ground that the prohibition prevents the employee from doing the night time work for which she was engaged ...

[T]he article recognises the legitimacy, in terms of the principle of equal treatment, first, of protecting a woman's biological condition during and after pregnancy, and second, of protecting the special relationship between a woman and her child over the period which follows pregnancy and childbirth ...

[T]o acknowledge that the contract may be held to be invalid or may be avoided because of the temporary inability of the pregnant employee to perform the night time work for which she has been engaged would be contrary to the objective of protecting such persons pursued by Art 2(3) of the Directive and would deprive that provision of its effectiveness ...

The effect of the case is not to hold that the prohibition is itself invalid, but to hold that she may not be dismissed, as her incapacity to perform her contract because of pregnancy was purely temporary. The assumption that the German law was valid can only have been based on a generalised notion that night work is especially harmful for pregnant women, an argument which is far from clear cut.[62] It must follow that the exclusion of pregnant women from the workplace for health and safety reasons is thought by the ECJ to be at least

---

[61] See, also, [1994] IRLR 364.

[62] Fenwick, H, 'Special protections for women in European Union law' in Hervey, T and O'Keeffe, D (eds), *Sex Equality Law in the European Union*, 1996, Chichester: John Wiley, p 72.

potentially justifiable, so to that extent complete automatic protection is not forthcoming.[63]

Reproductive risks

At first sight, the chance that working in a dangerous environment may risk damaging a foetus would seem clearly to justify measures taken to avoid the risk. The problems, though, are numerous. The number of women exposed to the risk at one time is likely to be small, and, for many or most women, pregnancy is planned and so the potential risk is one that can be anticipated and dealt with in advance. However, the most dangerous period for the foetus may be in the period before the women is aware or is certain that she is pregnant – thus the foetus *might* be damaged before anyone is aware of its presence. Rigorous logic might impel employers to the conclusion that the only safe measure is the exclusion of all fertile women from such dangerous jobs – to which women might respond, out of economic need, by being sterilised. To rely entirely on the free choice of women in such a case might be problematic, not only because of the economic pressures under which such women might be placed, but also because the interests of the foetus may be viewed as distinct from those of the mother. A far safer approach would appear to be to place the employer under an obligation to ensure that no such risk is present in his working environment. Even this may not work, however: for one thing, some industrial processes which are regarded as being essential for industry are well known to carry risks; for another, the state of scientific knowledge is in many instances too sparse for there to be certainty about whether there is in fact any such risk. Finally, there have long been doubts as to whether employers have operated such exclusion policies in an even-handed manner; there is a suspicion that they have been used to exclude women from high-paying blue collar jobs by the application of stringent standards which are used neither where there is an all-female workforce nor where concerns are expressed about risks to the community in the neighbourhood of the operation.

Bramwell, R and Davidson, M, 'Reproductive hazards at work', in Firth-Cozens, J and West, M (eds), *Women at Work: Psychological and Organisational Perspectives*, 1991, Buckingham: Open University, pp 84–85, 93:

A reproductive hazard may be defined as an exposure which increases the probability of an adverse reproductive outcome. These cover a wide range, from pre-conception (that is, infertility), through adverse pregnancy outcomes (for example, miscarriage), to developmental abnormalities in children – both behavioural and physical – which may not manifest themselves for some years.

---

[63] *Op cit*, Fenwick, fn 62, p 78.

Furthermore, reproductive hazards do not only affect those wishing to have children – other adverse reproductive outcomes include menstrual problems and early menopause; and both male and female occupational exposures are of potential importance for reproductive harm. Mutational damage or interference with sperm production in men can induce sterility or affect the development of their children. Reproductive hazards may be mutagenic or teratogenic. Mutagenesis is damage to the genetic material of reproductive cells: teratogenesis refers to interference with the normal development of the embryo and foetus. These two processes are often difficult to distinguish in their effects and may interact ...

[T]here are many more suspected occupational reproductive hazards than proven ones. This is partly because of the difficulty of proving that a reproductive hazard exists, both by the nature of scientific inquiry itself and because of the practical difficulties involved in conducting and evaluating the results of epidemiological studies ...

Bertin, J, 'Reproductive hazards in the workplace', in Cohen, S and Taub, N (eds), *Reproductive Laws for the 1990s*, 1989, Clifton, New Jersey: Humana, pp 279–80, 295:

'Foetal protection' policies assume that the foetus is uniquely susceptible to injury from hazardous workplace exposures, or that it is susceptible at lower exposure levels than those which would threaten adult workers. Some companies have adopted policies solely on the basis of this unexamined assumption, rather than on the basis of an actual examination of the biological effects of specific chemicals or conditions. A review of the scientific literature on the reproductive and other health effects of occupational exposures reveals that the assumption of heightened or unique foetal risk, while sometimes ultimately validated, frequently relies more on stereotypes than on facts, and that the adverse health effects of toxic chemicals are rarely confined to the foetus *in utero* ...

The prevalent assumption is that an exposure is unsafe for the foetus unless and until its safety is conclusively proved. In most other contexts chemicals are presumed safe until proven otherwise.

Exclusionary policies exist because of cost considerations: because women are viewed both as marginal workers and as more physically vulnerable, and thus as more expensive employees. The costs may be those associated with cleanup, with voluntary temporary transfer systems, with compound substitution of non-toxic materials, with more sophisticated and wearable personal protective equipment protection, or with insurance.

Kenney, S, 'Reproductive hazards in the workplace: the law and sexual difference' (1986) 14 International Journal of the Sociology of Law 393, pp 393–98:

Should we, as feminists ... seek to minimise the differences between men and women and whenever possible draw analogies between men's and women's biological characteristics and social circumstances? Or should we seek to emphasise the differences between men and women in order to ensure that a male standard is not accepted as the norm and that women are not penalised to the extent that they diverge from it? Or should we demand that women's different needs be recognised and accommodated without disadvantage?

Is the goal of feminism to break down societal distinctions ... or is it about a revaluing of so called women's characteristics and activities done in women's sphere – or is it both? Is feminism about getting the best deal for women in the short term or is it about eradicating sex difference in the long run? How do feminists guard against the danger that equality is used as a ruse for treating women even worse than they are treated presently and lowering standards for everyone? Is feminists' primary goal on this issue to protect the foetus? To protect women's right to work? To reduce exposure for everyone? To eradicate differences between the sexes? To what extent are these goals in conflict with each other?

The TUC argues that that neither biological nor social differences ... justify differential standards while on the other, social differences between men and women justify differential treatment. Its position can best be understood as a demand for a high standard of protection for all workers while distinguishing between short term and long term strategies. It fears a demand for equality will be used as an excuse to lower standards ...

If our understanding of the tragic potential for malformations was clearly impressed on our minds by the thalidomide disaster, our knowledge of what reproductive hazards exist in the workplace is often restricted by what the media has chosen to focus on ...

The difficulty in determining the correct public policy on reproductive hazards is made more difficult because of the dismal state of current knowledge. Not only are few chemicals tested for possible reproductive harm, but often the tests that are done investigate only the potential reproductive effects to the female. There is also the difficulty in extrapolating human effects from animals as well as immense problems in epidemiological studies ... Thus, employers and policy makers will have to make decisions in a situation of uncertainty and unquantified risks rather than on the basis of conclusive evidence ... an exposure may affect one foetus but not another ... a safe threshold exposure may be difficult to establish, unless it is zero.

Legal developments

Unlike the UK, the American Civil Rights Act contains no specific defence in relation to health and safety. The two arguments which might be put to counter suggestions that differential treatment of pregnant women on the ground of reproductive risks is unlawful are, first, that it constitutes a justification to a claim of indirect discrimination, and, secondly, that in such cases the sex of the worker constitutes a *bona fide* occupational qualification for the job. The first approach[64] reasons that the employer applies a gender-

---

[64] See *Wright v Olin Corp* 687 F 2d 1172 (4th Cir 1982), and *Hayes v Shelley Memorial Hospital* 726 F 2d 1154 (11th Cir 1984).

neutral health and safety rule which has a disparate impact on women, but because it is disparate impact rather than disparate treatment the employer may justify the rule, which can then be examined on its merits. The approach may be understandable; the problem is that the fundamental premise is wrong. It is not a gender-neutral rule but a rule of specific application to women and thus the defence of justification can logically not be applied. This argument prevailed before the United States Supreme Court in the following case.

United Automobile Workers v Johnson Controls 111 S Ct 1196 (1991)

A primary ingredient in the defendant's battery manufacturing process is lead, occupational exposure to which entails health risks, including foetal risks. After eight of its employees became pregnant after maintaining blood levels exceeding that noted by [the Occupational Safety and Health Authority] as critical to a worker planning to have a family, they introduced a policy barring all women, except those whose infertility was medically documented, from jobs involving actual or potential lead exposure exceeding the OSHA standard.

The applicant's claim of unlawful sex discrimination succeeded.

It was held that the policy created a facial classification based on gender and explicitly discriminated against women on the basis of their sex ... The Court of Appeals erred in assuming that the policy was facially neutral because it had only a discriminatory effect on women's employment opportunities, and because its asserted purpose ... was ostensibly benign ... Good motive is not a defence in a disparate treatment as opposed to a disparate impact case ...

[Discrimination would only be permitted if] the reproductive potential prevents her from performing the duties of the job – [it] must actually interfere with job performance ...

Title VII, as amended by the Pregnancy Discrimination Act, mandates that decisions about the welfare of future children be left to the parents who conceive, bear, support and raise them, rather than to the employers who hire their parents or to the courts.

An employer's tort liability for potential foetal injuries and its increased costs due to fertile women in the workplace do not mandate a different result. If, under general tort principles, Title VII bans sex-specific foetal-protection policies, the employer fully informs the woman of the risk, and the employer has not acted negligently, the basis for holding an employer liable seems remote at best.

Blackmun J (pp 195–211):

The majority of the Court of Appeals emphasised that, in view of the goal of protecting the unborn, more is at stake than simply an individual woman's decision to weigh and accept the risks of employment ...

Posner said that the *bona fide* occupational qualification defence applied – the normal operation of the business encompasses ethical, legal and business concerns about the effects of an employer's activities on third parties.

Dissenting judge [below] said that the policy applied to all women ... although most women in an industrial labour force do not become pregnant, most of those who do become pregnant will have blood lead levels under 30 micrograms per decilitre, and most of those who become pregnant with levels exceeding that figure will bear normal children anyway ... 'Concerns about a tiny minority of women cannot set the standard by which all are judged.'

The policy is facially discriminatory because it requires only a female employee to produce proof that she is not capable of reproducing .... Respondent has chosen to treat all its female employees as potentially pregnant; that choice evinces discrimination on the basis of sex.

The most telling term in the BFOQ defence is 'occupational'; this indicates that these objective, verifiable requirements must concern job-related skills and aptitudes ... In effect the concurrence argues that sterility may be an occupational qualification for women because Johnson Controls has chosen to require it ...

This is not a customer or a third party case – the unconceived foetuses are neither customers nor third parties whose safety is essential to the business of battery manufacturing.

Expanding the law contradicts not only the language of the BFOQ and the narrowness of its exception but the plain language and history of the PDA.

[W]omen as capable of doing their jobs as their male counterparts may not be forced to choose between having a child and having a job.

Of the eight pregnancies reported among the female employees, it has not been shown that any of the babies have birth defects or other abnormalities .... Fear of pre-natal injury, however sincere, does not begin to show that substantially all of its fertile women employees are incapable of doing their jobs.

The tort liability argument reduces itself to two equally unpersuasive propositions. First, [the employer] attempts to solve the problem of reproductive health hazards by resorting to an exclusionary policy. Title VII plainly forbids illegal sex discrimination as a means of diverting attention from an employer's obligation to police the workplace. Second, the spectre of an award of damages reflects a fear that hiring fertile women will cost more [and extra cost is no defence to a charge of discrimination].

It is no more appropriate for the courts than it is for individual employers to decide whether a woman's reproductive role is more important to herself and her family than her economic role. Congress has left this choice to the woman as hers to make.

This casts the burden on the employer to protect the workforce and on the mother to decide what is best for herself and her foetus – even in a context where the risks are known. It will surprise no one that the only significant British case on the issue adopted a far more paternalistic and protectionist approach.

Page v Freight Hire (Tank Haulage) Ltd [1981] IRLR 13, EAT[65]

A 23 year old female lorry driver was engaged in the transport of chemicals. The manufacturers, ICI, told the employers that women should not be permitted to transport a particular chemical, DMF, which was said to be potentially harmful to women of childbearing age. The employers thereupon removed her from the job, causing her financial loss as she was hired on a casual basis to do the work when it was available.

Her claim of unlawful discrimination failed.

Slynn J (pp 14–16):

[S]he said she knew of the dangers of DMF but that she was prepared both to accept them and to provide the employers with some form of indemnity.

It is submitted that there is insufficient evidence here of the sort of hazard which could possibly justify barring her ... [and that] the proper approach is to ask whether it was necessary for the employer to do this in order to comply with the Health and Safety at Work Act 1974 – that it has to be shown that there is no other way of protecting a woman ... other than by debarring her ... from taking up a job.

It is important to consider all the circumstances of the case, to consider the risk involved and the measures which it can be said are reasonably necessary to eliminate the risk. It may well be that the wishes of the person whom it is desired to protect are a factor. Here it was said that she did not want a child and did not anticipate becoming pregnant as she was divorced ... In our judgment, where the risk is to the woman, of sterility, or to the foetus, whether actually in existence or likely to come into existence in the future, these wishes cannot be a conclusive factor.

It does not seem to us that an employer ... has to show that inexorably this was the only method open to him ... It seems to us that there may well be some cases where one course (which is suggested as being sufficient) may leave open some doubt as to whether it is going to achieve the desired level of protection. It such a case it may well be that an employer is complying with the requirements of the legislation if, in all the circumstances, he thinks it right not to allow an employee ... to do the particular job at all.

If there had been material which suggested that this was an act of excessive caution on the part of the employers, that it really was being used as a device to prevent Mrs Page from being employed, then the situation would be very different ... Since there was no evidence to suggest that any other course was a sufficient form of protection for Mrs Page (who was still clearly potentially of childbearing age despite the fact that she was, at the time, divorced) [the decision was lawful].[66]

---

65 See, also, [1981] ICR 299; [1981] 1 All ER 394.

66 The technical *ratio* of the decision in *Page* is that the employers had a defence under the then SDA 1975, s 51, in that the acts complained of were necessary to comply with the requirements of a statute passed before the SDA 1975, in this case the Health and Safety at Work Act 1974. That Act contained restrictions on women's work far more extensive than simply the type of situation at issue in *Page*, restrictions called into serious question by the decision of the European Court in *Johnston v Royal Ulster Constabulary* (see [cont]

The contrast between the approaches taken in *Page* and in *Johnson Controls* is stark. First, the attitude to employee choice is very different; there must be problems in elevating the value of free choice when knowledge about risks is so often uncertain. Secondly, it is arguable that in *Page* the court did not impose a stringent enough test on the employers to establish the degree and nature of the hazard.[67] That might have been understandable on the facts where the information was provided by a large multinational to a small road haulage firm which was clearly not in a position to test the evidence for itself. But in principle a standard needs to be set for establishing both the nature and extent of the risk which neither relies on the employer's say-so, nor imposes impossibly stringent standards of scientific proof. Thirdly, dismissal should not be the response even where a hazard is properly demonstrated; it is the employer's responsibility to create a safe working environment and, in those rare cases where that cannot be done for pregnant workers, they should not be the ones to carry the financial penalty.

A further issue concerns the way in which potentially conflicting goals are resolved in the policy-setting arena.

Kenney, S, 'Reproductive hazards in the workplace: the law and sexual difference' (1986) 14 International Journal of the Sociology of Law 393, pp 407–09:

Comparing events in Britain with the same process in America demonstrates the closed nature of the process, the scarcity of groups who campaign on this issue, and the unwillingness of the enforcement agency (the EOC) to launch a vigorous campaign ...

[For example, when the regulations concerning exposure to lead were being drafted], there appeared to be no organised demand for the setting of a single low standard either on the grounds that men would be damaged at high levels of exposure or that the different standards would be discriminatory. In fact, the issue of discrimination was never (so far as I can ascertain) seriously considered by the working party which drafted the regulations. In the United States, on the other hand, legal scholars debated the legality of setting a dual standard, a feminist group was set up to campaign on the issue, and feminist groups presented evidence to Congress advocating the establishment of a single low standard of exposure to lead.

---

66 [cont] below, pp 220–22. As a result, s 51 was amended by the 1989 Employment Act to provide a defence only for safety provisions which have 'effect for the purpose of protecting women as regards pregnancy or maternity ...'. This adds little or nothing to the approach adopted by the court in *Page*; it seems unlikely that the amendment will have any effect on the way subsequent similar cases are analysed and decided. The main import of the 1989 Act lies elsewhere.

67 '[It was argued that the employer should] have the burden of proving that removing her was necessary as the only course of action available to the employer. [The EAT] rejected this standard, claiming only that the employer's action need be reasonable. Yet even the standard of reasonableness was easily met. Apparently it was Page's responsibility to prove the substance harmed men as well, or that she was not being exposed. The tribunal provided almost no scrutiny ...' Kenney, S, 'Reproductive hazards in the workplace: the law and sexual difference' (1986) 14 International Journal of the Sociology of Law 393, p 405.

Knowledge is power – as *Page* demonstrated. The stumbling block to a satisfactory resolution of the issue is practical as well as theoretical – the absence of proper information as to the extent of risks, to men as well as women. Thus the problem may become who should bear the risk of ignorance, the woman worker or the unborn child. It is understandable that sympathy should be with the latter, especially as the comparison is between physical and economic well being. But such a comparison is too simplistic, for at least two reasons. First, exclusionary policies may harm very many women, while risks may materialise relatively infrequently. Secondly, it may benefit employers to remain in a state of relative ignorance: they should be required to demonstrate that reasonable efforts have been made to establish the scope of any potential hazards created by the materials with which they are dealing.

Protective legislation

Historically, a great deal of legislation was passed to 'protect' women, and thereby had the effect of restricting their hours of work, their opportunities to engage in night work, and the type of work they were legally permitted to undertake.[68] The effect of such provisions is to deny employment opportunities for women, so is of practical economic benefit to men as restricting the supply of labour in particular areas of the labour market. In addition, such legislation reflected and confirmed patriarchal assumptions that the appropriate place for women was in the home rather than in the male world of work.

The SDA 1975 threw down little or no challenge to this traditional view, which collapsed for two ideologically separate, though converging, reasons. First, the restrictions on female labour market participation were seen as an unnecessary and outdated fetter on the operation of the free market economy. Secondly, European law saw such restrictions as breaching the fundamental principle of equality between men and women, which was manifested in the Equal Treatment Directive. That Directive is subject to two relevant exceptions: first, by virtue of Art 2(2), in relation to occupational activities where 'the sex of the worker constitutes a determining factor' and, secondly, by virtue of Art 2(3), in relation to 'provisions concerning the protection of women, particularly as regards pregnancy and maternity'. The scope of these exceptions was considered in the following case.

Johnston v The Chief Constable of the Royal Ulster Constabulary **Case 222/84 [1986] IRLR 263**[69]

The applicant was a reservist with the Royal Ulster Constabulary on a full time, fixed term contract. Until 1980 she performed regular police duties,

---

68 Fredman, S, *Women and the Law*, 1997, London: Clarendon, pp 67–74.
69 See, also, [1986] ECR 1651; [1987] QB 129; [1986] 3 All ER 135.

although she was not armed when doing them. It was the policy of the RUC that women officers should not carry firearms or receive training in their use; it was considered that it would increase the risk that they would become targets for assassination, that armed women officers would be less effective in areas for which women are 'better suited' such as welfare work, and the public would regard women carrying firearms as a much greater departure from the ideal of an unarmed force.

In 1980, her contract was not renewed on the basis that a substantial part of the duties would involve the use of firearms. She claimed sex discrimination. The Secretary of State for Northern Ireland issued a certificate that the reason for the refusal was for the purpose of safeguarding national security and protecting public safety or public order, which was a conclusive defence to the claim.

It followed that she could not succeed under domestic legislation. However, as she contended that the Equal Treatment Directive applied, the Industrial Tribunal referred the case to the ECJ, before which the claim succeeded.

Judgment (pp 277–78):

The reasons which the Chief Constable gave for his policy relate to the special circumstances in which the police must work in the situation existing in Northern Ireland ...

[I]t must be recognised that the context in which the occupational activity of members of an armed police force is carried out is determined by the environment in which that activity is carried out. In this regard, the possibility cannot be excluded that in a situation characterised by serious internal disturbances the carrying of firearms by policewomen might create additional risks of their being assassinated and might therefore be contrary to the requirements of public safety.

In such circumstances, the context of certain policing activities may be such that the sex of police officers constitutes a determining factor for carrying them out ...

[The] principle [of proportionality] requires that derogations remain within the limits of what is appropriate and necessary for achieving the end in view and require the principle of equal treatment to be reconciled as far as possible with the requirements of public safety, which constitute the decisive factor as regards the context of the activity in question ...

It is clear from the express reference to pregnancy and maternity that the Directive is intended to protect a woman's biological condition and the special relationship which exists between a woman and her child. That provision of the Directive does not therefore allow women to be excluded from a certain type of employment on the ground that public opinion demands that women be given greater protection than men against risks which affect women and men in the same way and which are distinct from women's specific needs of protection ...

> A total exclusion of women from ... an occupational activity which, owing to a general risk not specific to women, is imposed for reasons of public safety is not one of the differences in treatment that Art 2(3) of the Directive allows out of a concern to protect women.

Thus, the national security defence was permitted to succeed on the very specific facts of the case, although the court held that the ministerial certificate to that effect could not be conclusive, as that would deprive the applicant of the right under Art 6 to a judicial hearing of a complaint. This aspect of the decision is clearly vulnerable to the criticism that it allows social attitudes as to what role is appropriate for women to justify their exclusion, thereby adopting a much less rigorous approach to equality than under Art 2(3). *Johnston* is the only example where the European Court has upheld a so called 'special protection' which does not relate to pregnancy or maternity issues; the decision is explicable only in relation to the situation in Northern Ireland at the time. Outside the context of national security, the Court decided that the *only* protective legislation which was permissible was that which related specifically to pregnancy and maternity. Generalised assumptions that women were unsuited to particular areas of work were outdated and unlawful.

The upshot was the 1989 Employment Act. The equality rationale relied on by the Court in *Johnston* dovetailed with the then Conservative Government's intention to sweep away unnecessary legislation restricting the operation of a free labour market, but by both routes the end result would be the same. Most of the restrictions on the employment of women were swept away, such as the restriction on the employment of women working underground in mines and the restrictions on women cleaning machinery in factories. It is, however still possible to justify a requirement – most obviously a height or strength requirement – if it can be shown to be necessary to comply with health and safety duties.[70]

The objectives of health and safety policies reflect theoretical and practical problems. If the goal is equality, it would be satisfied by a dangerous playing field but one which was level as between men and women: permitting women to work at night on the same terms as men is vulnerable to this criticism. If the goal is improving standards for all working people, the aim should be to extend to men those protections which had previously only be available to women. In this light may be seen the 1990 International Labour Organisation Convention on night work, which applies to both men and women, and requires measures to protect the health of night workers and also to assist reconciliation of domestic and employment responsibilities.[71] While there are

---

[70] See below, pp 313–14.

[71] The Working Time Directive (93/104/EC), OJ L307/18, 1993, p 18, to the extent that it restricts total working time, may, despite its numerous exceptions, be viewed in a similar light.

some features of health and safety which primarily affect women, the real questions, which cases such as *Johnson Controls* do nothing to illuminate, concern the cost society is prepared to impose on employers in order to improve the health and safety of all workers. The role of anti-discrimination law in advancing this debate is necessarily limited.

CHAPTER 8

SEXUAL AND RACIAL HARASSMENT

INTRODUCTION

When the 1975 Sex Discrimination Act was passed, the *concept* of sexual harassment, though not of course the experience of it, was almost unknown. Racial harassment was seen as an issue, perhaps without using that exact phrase, but here the focus was – and to a large extent remains – on violence and intimidation away from the workplace. Yet within 20 years, sexual harassment has become one of the most discussed and significant aspects of the anti-discrimination legislation,[1] one where the removal of the statutory limit on compensation had an immediate impact in some cases.[2] The change in awareness is startling, although of course it should certainly not be inferred that the problem of sexual harassment has somehow been solved.

The legal rules on harassment are decidedly muddled.[3] In the first place, there is no specific definition or outlawing of sexual or racial harassment in the anti-discrimination legislation. The courts and tribunals have had to fashion rules and definitions from the general principles of the legislation, and have not always done so in a coherent and comprehensive fashion. Not all instances of harassment are covered but only those which occur in the specific contexts with which the legislation deals. This means that harassment in a public place will, as a general rule, not be caught by the anti-discrimination legislation, nor will other particular instances of harassment, such as by one student on another. For the same reason, harassment not on the ground of race, gender or disability will not be caught by anti-discrimination legislation. But such legislation is not the only route available for dealing with harassment. The criminal law may be relevant. In extreme cases, sexual harassment may amount to rape or indecent assault, and both sexual and racial harassment may constitute criminal assault or other non-fatal offences against the person.

---

1   The publication in 1979 of Mackinnon, C, *Sexual Harassment of Working Women*, 1979, New Haven: Yale UP, is generally considered to have been a key development in this growth of consciousness.

2   Issues of compensation and other remedies for sexual and racial harassment will be considered below, in Chapter 14. See, also, Kelly, J and Watt, B, 'Damages in sex harassment cases: a comparative study of American, Canadian and British law' (1996) 16 New York Law School Journal of International and Comparative Law 79.

3   For an argument that discrimination law is the wrong legal home for sexual harassment, see Dine, J and Watt, B, 'Sexual harassment: moving away from discrimination' (1995) 58 MLR 343.

Furthermore, two recent statutes are potentially applicable to some cases of racial and sexual harassment. The Criminal Justice and Public Order Act 1994 controls some aspects of the public order issues involved. It creates a new offence of intentional harassment, which could cover racial and sexual harassment, as well as harassment on grounds of disability or sexual orientation or for any other reason. A person is liable if he causes harassment, alarm or distress by using threatening, abusive or insulting words or behaviour or displays any sign or writing which is threatening, insulting or abusive. The provision covers conduct in private as well as in a public place, although not in a dwelling house in relation to other people in that house.

The main limitation of this provision is that the harassment must be intentional. The Protection From Harassment Act 1997,[4] a provision primarily aimed at stalkers, contains no such limitation. This legislation provides no specific definition of what constitutes harassment; there is liability if 'a reasonable person in possession of the same information [as the defendant] would think the course of conduct amounted to harassment'.[5] It is specifically provided that references to 'harassing a person include alarming the person or causing the person distress'[6] and that conduct 'includes speech'.[7] To be unlawful, the behaviour must be repeated at least once. It is clear that many instances of workplace harassment would fall within the definition. Anonymous letters, abusive remarks, spreading unfounded rumours, as well as unwanted physical conduct, are liable to be caught by the section.

It will, in theory, be possible to bring proceedings under both the new statute and under anti-discrimination legislation. Under the former, the defendant will be the alleged harasser rather than the employer, as is the case under SDA 1975 and RRA 1976. Section 2 of the 1997 Act creates a new criminal offence with a maximum prison sentence of six months.[8] But the most significant remedy is likely to be s 3, which provides for civil remedies, which may be damages and, most significantly, an injunction. Damages may be awarded for anxiety caused,[9] which parallels the provisions in anti-discrimination legislation that damages may include compensation for injury to feelings,[10] a wider rule than the normal tort principles governing liability for emotional injury, which require proof of injury or illness flowing from the

---

4   See (1997) 73 EOR 32.

5   Protection From Harassment Act 1997, s 1(2).

6   Protection From Harassment Act 1997, s 7(2). It is arguable that anxiety is insufficient to amount to distress. What precisely will need to be shown will be for the courts to determine.

7   Protection From Harassment Act 1997, s 7(4).

8   Protection From Harassment Act 1997, s 4, creates a more serious criminal offence, with a maximum sentence of five years, of causing someone to fear that they will be the victim of violence.

9   Protection From Harassment Act 1997, s 3(2).

10 See below, pp 515–19.

emotional upset. Obtaining an injunction may be of crucial significance for victims of stalkers. How far the Act will be used to cover workplace harassment, only time will tell. At present, the focus of anti-discrimination law is on the liability of the employer; the new legislation is a timely reminder that the law can also be used against the actual harasser, an approach which many victims may feel is more appropriate.

Finally, while sex and race discrimination are treated by the legislation in effect as statutory torts, this does not prevent a claimant from pursuing a tort action in the ordinary courts.[11] Such a claim avoids the limitations of anti-discrimination legislation which may cause harassment to fall outside the scope of that legislation, as, for instance, where it is not based on race, gender or disability, and again allows for action against the actual harasser. Tort claims may be based on the intentional torts of assault and battery where there is actual physical contact between harasser and victim, and, arguably, on the tort of intentional infliction of emotional distress where there is not.[12] Claims against the employer of the harasser may either be based on vicarious liability – which is likely to prove problematic in respect of intentional torts – or on direct liability if there is a negligent failure to protect the health and safety of an employee. With the exception of intentional infliction of emotional distress, which as a tort remains under-developed, all these torts require personal injury to have been suffered, and as a result will exclude many harassment cases. Finally, employer action or inaction in respect of harassment may constitute a breach of the contract of employment, but enforcement normally requires the employee to quit and claim constructive unfair dismissal; such a claim is limited to employees with two years' continuous employment.[13]

THE DEFINITION, CAUSES AND EFFECTS OF HARASSMENT

The definition of harassment

There is no one universally accepted definition of sexual or racial harassment, and no legislative definition. The closest to a legal definition of sexual harassment comes from the European Commission Recommendation on the Protection of the Dignity of Men and Women at Work. This provides that:

---

11 On the advantages and disadvantages of utilising tort as a remedy for sexual harassment rather than anti-discrimination law, see Conaghan, J, 'Gendered harms and the law of tort: remedying (sexual) harassment' (1996) 16 OLJS 407.

12 See Townshend-Smith, R, 'Harassment as a tort in English law: the boundaries of *Wilkinson v Downton*' (1995) 24 Anglo-Am LR 299.

13 Employment Rights Act 1996, s 108. The government is proposing to reduce the period to one year. See *Fairness at Work*, Cm 3968, 1998, London:The Stationery Office, para 3.10.

... conduct of a sexual nature, or other conduct based on sex affecting the dignity of women and men at work ... is unacceptable if:

(a) such conduct is unwanted, unreasonable and offensive to the recipient;

(b) is used ... as a basis for an [employment] decision; and/or

(c) such conduct creates an intimidating, hostile or humiliating work environment for the recipient.[14]

This is supported by the EC Code of Practice, where sexual harassment is defined as:

... unwanted conduct of a sexual nature, or other conduct based on sex affecting the dignity of men and men at work. This can include unwelcome physical, verbal or non-verbal conduct.[15]

The Commission for Racial Equality defines racial harassment as:

... offensive or hostile behaviour which causes discomfort, distress, exclusion or withdrawal [such as] racist jokes, abuse, language, graffiti, posters, literature, shunning an ethnic minority employee, violence or threats of violence.[16]

Because of the difficulty of deciding the exact point at which unpleasant and offensive behaviour amounts to sexual harassment, there is a need to treat surveys as to how many people have been harassed with a certain degree of circumspection. Nevertheless, it is clear that the number of people who report harassment on the basis of gender or race is very considerable.[17] Women's experience may vary from everyday unpleasantness through to serious sexual assaults. In reality, such behaviour should be viewed as a continuum.[18] The exact point along that continuum at which the law should be prepared to intervene is both a matter for policy debate and a problem of legal definition. Discrimination law has never and perhaps can never deal with more than a tiny fraction of incidents that women may define for themselves as amounting to sexual harassment.

---

[14] Commission Recommendation on the protection of the dignity of men and women at work, 91/131/EEC, OJ L49/1, 1991. See above, p 96, for the legal effect of recommendations.

[15] See Rubenstein, M, *The Dignity of Women at Work. A Report on the Problem of Sexual Harassment in the Member States of the European Communities*, 1988, Luxembourg: Office for Official Publications of the European Communities, pp 12–14.

[16] *Racial Discrimination and Grievance Procedures*, 1989, London: Commission for Racial Equality.

[17] Stockdale, J, 'Sexual harassment at work', in Firth-Cozens, J and West, M (eds), *Women at Work: Psychological and Organisational Perspectives*, 1991, Buckingham: Open University, pp 54–55; Bakirci, K, 'Sexual harassment in the workplace in relation to EC legislation' (1998) 3 IJDL 3, fn 30.

[18] See, eg, Thomas, A and Kitzinger, S (eds), *Sexual Harassment: Contemporary Feminist Perspectives*, 1997, Buckingham: Open University, Chapters 2 and 4.

The causes of harassment

Although the legal principles are applicable both to sexual and racial harassment, it is clear that the causes and motivations for sexual and racial harassment may well differ. While sexual harassment is normally viewed as an exercise of power over women, it may lack the overt hostility that tends to accompany much racial harassment, and the harassers may even delude themselves that such behaviour is appreciated. Perhaps not too much should be made of this point, as offensive language and banter form such a significant proportion of harassment complaints. Nevertheless, the attainment of sexual favours which may be the object of sexual harassment has no counterpart in racial harassment. Racial harassment perhaps follows more obviously from a belief in racial superiority or at least difference. When coupled with the still-expressed view that members of minority ethnic groups are an economic threat to indigenous white people, that may come to reflect a feeling that ill-treatment is acceptable as a means of preserving economic benefits. Nevertheless, it seems unlikely that much racial harassment is explicable, at least overtly, on economic grounds. In addition, the concept of harassment surely requires intention or at least knowledge that what is being done is offensive. There may be many occasions where white people – or members of other groups – offend the cultural or religious sensitivities of members of particular groups without being aware of the consequences of their actions. Such people may be ignorant, but they are not harassers.

The following extracts summarise some of the main sociological theories on the causes of sexual harassment at work.

Stockdale, J, 'Sexual harassment at work', in Firth-Cozens, J and West, M (eds), *Women at Work: Psychological and Organisational Perspectives*, 1991, Buckingham: Open University, pp 56–59:

Gutek ... considers three classes of model which offer explanations of sexual harassment at work. The natural/biological explanation is used to argue that what has sometimes been called sexual harassment is really sexual attraction. According to this view such behaviour is neither sexist nor discriminatory and does not have harmful consequences. Most importantly, this approach admits the existence of the behaviour but denies the intent to harass ... This perspective is compatible with the individual deficit explanation ... which attributes sexual harassment to women's own deficiency in handling an approach or the deficiency of individual men in controlling their natural desires.

The organisational (or structural institutional) perspective assumes that sexual harassment is the result of opportunity structures created by organisational climate, hierarchy and specific authority relations. People in higher positions can use their power ... to coerce lower status individuals, who are usually women, into engaging in sexual interactions ... Socio-cultural or sex role models focus on the power differentials of men and women, the motivation of men to retain their dominance over women, and the socialisation of women to acquiesce in general or to specific female sex role ideals ...

Gutek proposes a model that incorporates elements of all three approaches, emphasising the effects of sex role expectations in an organisational context. This is known as sex role spillover ...

Sex role spillover refers to the carry-over onto the workplace of gender-based roles that are usually irrelevant or inappropriate to work ... Sex role expectations are carried over into the workplace for a variety of reasons. For example ... women may feel more comfortable with stereotypically female roles in some circumstances, especially if they feel men at work have difficulty accepting them in anything other than a traditional female role ... [Some research reports] women in non-traditional, male-dominated jobs ... reporting more sexual harassment than women in traditional female jobs ...

Occupational segregation and gendered working spheres are seen as playing an important role ... Gutek argues that sex segregation at work calls attention to gender ... and therefore facilitates sex role spillover, the assumption that people in particular jobs and the jobs themselves have the characteristics of only one gender ... According to Gutek's analysis, when the sex ratio of an occupation is significantly skewed, aspects of the sex role for the dominant gender spill over into the occupational work role, especially if the numerically dominant gender also occupies the high-status positions in the work group.

For example, the person in the minority – usually a woman – is seen as a role deviate, because of an incongruence between the sex role of the majority gender, which has spilled over onto the occupational sex role. The woman perceives the differential treatment she receives to be discriminatory, and to constitute harassment when the content is sexual. In contrast, a woman in an occupation which is female-dominated is expected to fulfil those aspects of the female sex role emphasised by the particular job, and there is substantial overlap between the work role and the female sex role. In this situation, although women may recognise that their job contains aspects of sexuality ... they are less likely to view and report sexual harassment as a problem at work, because it is 'part of the job'. Men in comparable situations do not encounter the same problems as women, because women do not focus on male sexuality in the same way that men choose to focus on female sexuality. Moreover, when men working in a female-dominated work group do encounter socio-sexual behaviour, they are less likely to perceive it as discriminatory or to label it as harassment because of the wider context of gender relations in society and the underlying issues of power and control.

Stanko ... argues that gendered working spheres provide the context but not the script for coercive sexuality at work. While concurring with Gutek that women's employment spheres, largely composed of care-giving and service jobs, contribute to the sexualisation of women in those positions, Stanko sees sexual harassment as another example of male domination in women's everyday lives. In her view, women's experiences of sexual harassment are not bound by traditional or non-traditional occupational spheres, but are bound by the wider spheres of male dominance, power and economic control ...

Sexual harassment serves to reinforce the status quo. The imposition of unwanted sexual attraction is a routine means of exercising the unequal power relations which exist between bosses – usually men – and workers – usually women. With its origins in polarised gender relations and inappropriate sex role expectations, sexual harassment makes it difficult for women to achieve equal working relationships and makes it unlikely that men will recognise the discrimination faced by women. The failure to initiate change and to eradicate sexual harassment reflects the pervasiveness of male power ... and men's understandable wish to retain this power by means of protectionist strategies, involving collusion and mutual support. Sexual harassment is a barrier to the full integration of women into the labour market, and its removal demands the degendering, both of work categories and of areas of responsibility and expertise in society as a whole ...

Adkins, L, *Gendered Work: Sexuality, Family and the Labour Market,* **1995, Buckingham: Open University, pp 58–66:**

[W]omen entering 'non-traditional' areas of employment, especially previously all-male occupations, are more likely to report sexual harassment than women in 'traditional' areas of employment, because the former may assume that they are employed on a par with men and that harassment will not be part of their experience. In contrast, women in traditional areas of employment, such as those in service and care-giving jobs, have less 'right' to complain of sexual harassment and in consequence are less likely to report harassing behaviour.

MacKinnon argues that the sexual harassment of women is both productive and reproductive of gendered labour market divisions ... a reciprocal enforcement of two inequalities, one sexual and the other material.

It occurs not only because women occupy inferior job positions and job roles, but also because harassment works to keep women in such positions ... Rigid gender divisions in the labour market should therefore be understood as both created and reinforced by sexual harassment ...

The power relations of sexuality and capitalism interlock in the context of the labour market to specify women's position, keeping women sexually in thrall to men, at the bottom of the labour market. Women become jointly exploited in the workplace through both their sexuality and their work, when the work demands placed on women become sexual requirements of work ... Sexual harassment acts as a key mechanism in this more general process, sedimenting women's second-class status both sexually and economically ...

The sexual harassment of women within the labour market thus works to systematically disadvantage women in employment, for it is an abuse of economic power by men, but it operates in a structural situation in which women can be (and are) systematically subordinated to men sexually and in other ways ...

[Stanko] suggests that sexuality may serve as an organising principle in the labour market, that it may promote solidarity between men through which men may organise to exclude and segregate women workers from and within the labour market. What this part of her analysis implies is that sexuality may play a significant part in the production of gendered 'economic' divisions. With this suggestion, she moves away from assuming that sexuality only operates within the labour market in relation to the sexual harassment of women workers. Instead, she opens up the possibility of sexuality operating in a far broader sense – as a principle or organisation. As an outcome of this break, the significance to be attached to sexuality in the production of gender divisions changes dramatically. Instead of merely maintaining these divisions, it becomes – to some extent at least – productive of them ... [T]his suggests that forms of control of women's labour within the labour market may be produced through aspects of sexuality.

The strengths of these approaches are to link the causes of sexual harassment with gender relations outside the workplace, especially in the family. It shows how harassment is linked with attitudes to female sexuality and to power relations in the workplace. This emphasis on power echoes explanations of sexual violence against women. MacKinnon considers that the only adequate response 'is to eliminate the social inferiority of one sex to the other, to dismantle the social structure that maintains a series of practices that cumulatively ... disadvantage women'.[19] For that reason she is sceptical about the appropriateness or effectiveness of the discrimination model based on the comparative approach, as what is 'unjust about sex discrimination [is not irrationality but that] it supports a system of second-class status for half of humanity'.[20]

To say that power of men over women explains sexual harassment is only part of the answer. There are two further issues which require consideration: why does the prevalence of sexual harassment vary from workplace to workplace, and how does the theory deal with the fact that harassment is often committed by employees who, at least in the workplace context, do not have power over their victims?

Certain features of particular workplaces make sexual harassment more likely. There are clearly many jobs in which women are hired to be attractive either to fellow employees or to customers. Much of the entertainment, travel and leisure industry comes into this category. It is in such contexts that the line between a requirement to dress in a particular way and unlawful sexual harassment may be especially difficult to determine. This approach may be extended into those positions where a secretary, typically female, is required to bring to the job – and to her boss – characteristics which supposedly epitomise those of the submissive, domestic housewife, and where the job requirements easily slide into an obligation to meet more personal needs of the boss, which will not necessarily be sexual. Another context where sexual harassment may be especially prone to occur is where women are attempting

---

[19] *Op cit*, MacKinnon, fn 1, p 103.
[20] *Op cit*, MacKinnon, fn 1, p 105.

to break in to what has traditionally been an all-male working environment.[21] Here the harassment will typically be from fellow workers rather than superiors, although the reaction of management may be crucial to its future pattern. Many of the most extreme examples of harassment – at least in the sense that they have resulted in the highest levels of compensation or settlement – fall into this category, perhaps because they often feature a campaign of harassment by more than one individual. A further issue, which links closely with the previous point, concerns whether the extent of sexual harassment will be reduced if management has in place a well-publicised and comprehensive anti-harassment policy. Again, there is some evidence that this is the case, especially if employees genuinely come to believe that the penalty for harassment may include loss of a job.

It is also important to consider the particular contexts in which harassment operates or is allowed to operate.

Collinson, D and Collinson, M, 'Sexuality in the workplace. The domination of men's sexuality', in Hearn, J et al (eds), The Sexuality of Organisation, 1989, London: Sage, pp 107–09:

In the first case study, manual workers subscribed to a male sexual drive discourse which was designed to establish their sense of power, dignity and masculine identity in conditions of its erosion. The men's preoccupation with sexuality as an expression of personal power, significance and autonomy reflects their concern to resist management control and the organisational control system and to deny the reality of their subordination within the organisation. The second case study also illustrated how men may draw on sexuality as a means of maintaining power and control within organisations. In this example, attempts were made to discredit and undermine the commitment of the first female executive member of the trade union. The very presence of a woman in a relatively senior position was treated as problematic by colleagues, who, in turn, promulgated rumours about her sexual life that were entirely unfounded. The men's association and indeed conflation of

---

[21] 'It [has been suggested] that the subordination of women in the workplace is sometimes related to the sense of disempowerment that male workers feel ... [If a man] compensates for the low status he holds in the company through an exaggerated identification with his own maleness (and, explicitly, with the male social roles of worker and subordinator of women) then the presence of a female co-worker in his workplace, by challenging both of these traditional lines between male and female, will deprive him of an important sense of his self-identity. Her presence will not only make him feel emasculated, but will also threaten his very sense of self.

If it is true, then, that sexual harassment is partly a reaction to a socio-economic structure that disempowers and devalues workers at many levels, making them feel inadequate and unable to control their lives, its eradication will be no simple matter. Rather, to the extent that the male worker's acquiescence in the hierarchical and regimented structuring of the capitalist workplace is 'bought' by allowing him to retain some sense of power by subordinating women, sexual harassment will be difficult to stop without changing the workplace structure itself.' Ehrenreich, N, 'Pluralist myths and powerless men: the ideology of reasonableness in sexual harassment law' (1990) 99 Yale LJ 1177, p 1228.

'woman' with 'sexuality' demonstrates how male-dominated labour organisations can be characterised by assumptions and practices which seek to discredit and exclude women ... [T]he final example highlights how a supervisor sought to manipulate his hierarchical position in order to sustain a sexual relationship. Moreover, even when the supervisor's abuse of his position was challenged and exposed, management adopted a protective approach towards him.

Together the three case studies provide detailed evidence of how men may seek to secure themselves and their identity by drawing upon conventional forms of masculine sexuality and organisational power. They illustrate how the domination of men's discourses and practices about sexuality can reflect and reproduce the male-dominated nature of contemporary organisations. Equally, they show how management may treat these expressions of men's sexuality as largely unproblematic ...

[But] women are not merely passive objects of men's attempts to maintain organisational and personal control. Women do recognise and resist some of the contradictions of men's conventional expressions of sexuality and power within organisations.

The final two case studies, in particular, provided strong evidence of women's resistance to the patriarchal assumptions of men's and women's sexuality. The women's resistance was constructed in the face of extensive pressure from managers and male colleagues to discontinue their action. In each case the women were labelled as 'troublemakers' by those whom they were resisting. Whilst in both cases the original organisational 'problem' was initiated by men's preoccupation with sexuality, it was subsequently redefined as a reflection of women's inability to adjust to men's discourses and practices about sexuality. Yet, despite this pressure, the women were not only willing to pursue their grievance, but were also effective in challenging men's patriarchal assumptions.

Hearn, J and Parkin, W, *Sex at Work: The Power and Paradox of Organisation Sexuality*, 1987, Brighton: Wheatsheaf, pp 74, 82–85:

In most ... organisations formal induction ... may consist merely of suggesting that a certain style of dress, self-presentation or polite talk is appropriate 'here'. Initiation rites and rituals among co-members can be severe, sometimes including pronounced sexual and/or physical assaults. We have numerous examples of these sexual initiations from the armed forces, from junior cadets, the fire brigade, hospitals, coal mining, and engineering, chemical and textile factories. These may involve the use of glue to stick and smear on genitals, use of rope to tie, perhaps symbolising the intimacy of the bonds. Usually they are led by men, are common in men-only organisations and often part of male culture in mixed organisations ... Formerly, men-only homosexual overtones may become complicated by the mixed-sex and indeed sexually harassing nature of the ceremonies, as with the entry of a woman into the London Fire Service.

Organisations are not neat, uniform, asexual structures; they are more usually amalgamations of groups of women workers and groups of men workers, under the same control system of men. In mixed organisations where heterosexuality is dominant, this allocation in 'blocks' of women and men inevitably defines possible sex and love objects by means of job. Where one gender is in a minority, those few individuals are likely to receive greater attention in reality and/or in fantasy as *scarce* potential objects.

These divisions are powerful determinants of gender roles ... The social production of the gender role includes numerous aspects of the person that bear on sexuality: appearance, dress, emotionality, desire for others. Managerial control of dress through division of labour is particularly clear with aircraft cabin staff, nurses, shopworkers, amongst many others, especially women workers ...

Sexual harassment, despite the problems of definition, is a pervasive form of explicit sexual behaviour in many organisations. It is performed by management on workers and vice versa, by organisational members on clients and vice versa, and so on. However, to see harassment as a *process*, rather than just as specific actions, is important because it forms such a significant part of the *visible routine* of many organisations ... Policies and grievance procedures are often designed to deal with the more blatant forms of harassment, that are persistent and more easily verifiable, and that are between organisational members. As harassment becomes 'less blatant', 'more ordinary' and regular, yet less persistent with a single recipient or with non-organisational members in occasional contact, official policy becomes less easy to formulate and less effective.

[W]hat may be sexually implicit or ambiguous behaviour in the eyes of some participants may be sexual harassment for others ... A similar complex relationship of the implicit, the ambiguous and harassment is applicable to some speech and joking ... Implicit sexual behaviour often *underwrites* explicit sexual behaviour by providing the taken-for-granted routine of organisational life, which itself is more explicitly sexual at certain times in the form of harassment, display and so on.

The effects of harassment

'Sexual harassment pollutes the working environment and can have a devastating effect upon the health and safety of those affected by it. It imposes costs upon employers impeding efficiency and reducing profitability. It distorts the operation of the labour market by depriving women of the opportunities that are available to men without sexual conditions.'[22] Women who experience sexual harassment have an unenviable choice as to whether or not to complain. 'That women "go along" is partly a male perception and partly correct, a male-enforced reality. Women report being too intimidated to

---

[22]   *Op cit*, Rubenstein, fn 15, p 19.

reject the advances unambivalently ...[23] Women's most common response is to attempt to ignore the whole incident, letting the man's ego off the hook skilfully by *appearing* flattered in the hope he will be satisfied and stop.[24] These responses may be interpreted as an encouragement or even as provocation.'[25] If complaint is made, that in itself will lead to pressures at work, which may include ridicule, disbelief, and so on.[26] Women who do not complain 'experience humiliation, self-blame, anger, loss of self-confidence, and a drop in job performance as a result of unwanted/imposed sexual attention ... There are very concrete effects and economic consequences: some women resign, others are transferred or demoted and some lose their jobs if they do not co-operate with sexual advances'.[27] Thus sexual harassment may contribute to absenteeism, high turnover, lower productivity rates and motivation, job dissatisfaction and unemployment. It thus may help to reinforce the stereotype that women are less effective as workers than men, and thus have effects on the initial decision as to who should be hired.

THE LEGAL DEFINITION OF HARASSMENT

As neither sexual nor racial harassment is specifically mentioned in the anti-discrimination legislation, the process by which it has been held to be unlawful and the boundaries of that unlawfulness are entirely judge made.

---

[23] 'On the one hand there is the fear that resisting sexual advances may provoke violent assault and rape so it is safer to comply; at the same time there is a feeling of thankfulness that this particular approach was not as bad as it might have been – a feeling which stops women from making a complaint.' Hadjifotiou, N, *Women and Harassment at Work*, 1983, London: Pluto, p 17.

[24] 'By far the most usual response is to ignore it in the hope that it will eventually go away ... In 75% of such cases, it eventually worsened.' *Ibid*, Hadjifotiou, p 19.

[25] *Op cit*, MacKinnon, fn 1, p 48.

[26] 'The reasons respondents gave for doing nothing about sexual harassment reflect the widespread difficulties both individuals and organisations experience in dealing with such behaviour. Victims commonly thought that their complaints would not be taken seriously or they were too stunned and embarrassed to do anything. Other reasons for inaction included: harassment being the norm at work; the seniority of the harasser; individuals wanting to avoid retribution; and feeling that they needed to prove themselves in the company. The finding that in some cases no action was taken because there was no procedure or union representative available, and in others because of the identity of the person to whom they would have to report the incident ... highlights the importance of having clear company policies and a sympathetic reporting procedure.' Stockdale, J, 'Sexual harassment at work', in Firth-Cozens, J and West, M (eds), *Women at Work: Psychological and Organisational Perspectives*, 1991, Buckingham: Open University, pp 59–60.

[27] Adkins, L, *Gendered Work: Sexuality, Family and the Labour Market*, 1995, Buckingham: Open University, p 57.

Strathclyde Regional Council v Porcelli **[1986] IRLR 134, Court of Session**[28]

The plaintiff was harassed as part of a campaign to try to get her to leave the school where she worked as a laboratory technician. The campaign included suggestive remarks and deliberate brushing against her, but no sexual favour was sought. Eventually she applied for a transfer and complained that the employers had discriminated against her in that they were vicariously liable for the acts of sexual harassment committed against her. The main argument for the defence, which was accepted by the Industrial Tribunal,[29] was that much of the behaviour was of a non-sexual nature and that they would have harassed a man they wished to get rid of in largely the same way, even though some specific instances would have differed.

The EAT, in a decision upheld by the Court of Session, allowed the applicant's appeal.

Lord Emslie, the Lord President (p 137):

Section 1(1)(a) [of the SDA 1975] is concerned with 'treatment' and not with the motive or objective of the person responsible for it. Although in some cases it will be obvious that there is a sex-related purpose in the mind of a person who indulges in unwanted and objectionable sexual overtures to a woman or exposes her to offensive sexual jokes or observations, that is not this case. But it does not follow that because the campaign ... as a whole had no sex-related motive or objective, the treatment ... which was of the nature of 'sexual harassment' is not to be regarded as having been 'on the ground of her sex' ... In my opinion this particular part of the campaign was plainly adopted ... because she was a woman. It was a particular kind of weapon, based on the sex of the victim ... which would not have been used against an equally disliked man.

The effect of this case is that the same questions have to be asked as in a direct discrimination claim based on, for example, non-appointment or non-promotion. The plaintiff has to show less favourable treatment on the ground of sex or race which is sufficient to constitute a detriment. In this case the detriment was obvious; the real question, which was answered in the affirmative, was whether it was on the ground of sex. There is sexual harassment if the victim is harassed and the sex of the victim is a factor in the harassment; there is no requirement that the harassment itself be in any sense sexual – though of course in many cases it will be. In the same way racial harassment depends on the racial identity of the victim. That the harassment itself be of a racial nature is not required; it could be almost any form of bullying.

It is frequently asked – sometimes, it seems, almost in an attempt to discredit sexual harassment law – whether it is unlawful to harass on the basis

---

[28] See, also, [1986] ICR 564.

[29] By the Employment Rights (Dispute Resolution) Act 1998, s 1(1), industrial tribunals are re-named employment tribunals.

of sexuality. A number of different situations need to be distinguished. First, it is contended that it *is* clearly unlawful for a gay or lesbian to harass another person. Just as in the case of heterosexual harassment, the action is taken on the ground of sex. However, it is arguable that the harassment *of* a gay or lesbian, rather than *by* a gay or lesbian, can only be unlawful if and to the extent that discrimination on the ground of sexual orientation is generally unlawful.[30] This would mean that the outcome may turn on the motivation of the harasser: if the motive is some form of gratification, the action will be unlawful, while if it is vindicative unpleasantness based on the sexual orientation of the victim it may not be. However, in *Oncale v Offshore Services Inc*,[31] the United States Supreme Court simply held that 'same-sex' sexual harassment was unlawful irrespective of the motives of the harassers. The problem with this attractive solution is that, under current British and European law, it would mean that harassment of a gay or lesbian person would constitute unlawful discrimination, but that dismissal or the imposition of any other detriment would not.

If a person harassed both male and female employees in a sexual way, it might be contended that, while the action in every such case would be on ground of sex, there would be no less favourable treatment of those harassed. This is wrong: the comparison is with those employees in the enterprise who are *not* harassed; any employee who is harassed on ground of sex receives less favourable treatment than any employee not so harassed. Thus if the harassment contains an element of a sexual nature it by definition constitutes sexual harassment, but if some hypothetical defendant were shown to have harassed male and female employees alike in a non-sexual way, that would not contravene the SDA 1975, although of course it may be unlawful for some other reason. That this is correct is shown by the analogy with race: an employee who harassed all employees, black or white, is clearly not liable for racial harassment *unless* in either case there is a peculiarly racial nature to the harassment.

Finally, what of the employees who, for example, are passed over for promotion because they have not slept with the boss, even if no sexual favours have ever been requested? Clearly, they have been treated less favourably than the successful candidate. Just as it no defence to argue that not all female employees are harassed, but only those whom the boss happens to find attractive, it should be no defence that those preferred *have* provided sexual gratification. This is not sexual harassment; rather, it is the making of employment decisions on the basis of sex and that constitutes unlawful discrimination.

---

[30] In *Chessington World of Adventures Ltd v Reed* [1997] IRLR 556, EAT, the harassment of a male-to-female transsexual was held to be unlawful.

[31] Case No: 96-568, decided 4 March 1998.

The kinds of detriment which can amount to unlawful harassment divide into two main groups.[32] First, what is usually termed *quid pro quo* harassment covers those situations where the employer makes an employment benefit in some sense conditional on a sexual favour. This clearly applies where promotion, or remaining in the job, is made conditional on sleeping with, or otherwise gratifying, the male boss. This extreme form of harassment is probably rather infrequent, at least in cases where the threat is sufficiently explicit as to be the potential subject of legal proof. It is also likely to be restricted to cases of sexual rather than racial harassment, and to apply only to harassment by superiors as opposed to fellow employees. The great advance of sexual harassment law in the United States was to extend the law to what is often termed 'adverse working environment' harassment. This recognises both the difficulty of proving the threat and the fact that the very fact of harassment is extremely likely to have damaging effects on the employee's ability to cope with the working environment. Under English law, this is unlawful if it constitutes a *detriment* under SDA 1975 or RRA 1976; this inevitably raises the question of how serious the harassment must be in order to amount to a detriment.

De Souza v Automobile Association [1986] IRLR 103, CA[33]

Mrs de Souza overheard a manager tell another to 'get his typing done by the wog'. Although the Court of Appeal applied the normal meaning of 'detriment' as simply meaning 'putting under a disadvantage' the claim of unlawful racial discrimination nevertheless failed.

May LJ (p 107):

Racially to insult a coloured employee is not enough by itself, even if that insult caused him or her distress; before the employee can be said to have been subjected to 'some other detriment' the court or tribunal must find that, by reason of the act or acts complained of, a reasonable worker would or might take the view that he had been thereby disadvantaged in the circumstances in which he had thereafter to work.

[The judge quoted from the judgment of the EAT in *Porcelli* where Lord MacDonald had appeared to hold that there was liability only] if the result of the sexual or racial discrimination complained of was either dismissal or some other disciplinary action by the employer, or some action by the employee such as leaving the employment on the basis of constructive dismissal, or seeking transfer to another plant ... I think that this was too limited an approach. Thus if in another case the ... reasonable employee could justifiably complain about his or her working condition or environment ... I think that this too could contravene the sub-section ...

---

[32] The distinction was authoritatively expounded by the United States Supreme Court in *Meritor Savings Bank v Vinson* 477 US 57 (1986). See 'Sexual harassment law in the United States' (1987) 12 EOR 18.

[33] See, also, [1986] ICR 514.

[E]ven though the use of the insulting word in respect of the applicant may have meant that she was being considered less favourably, whether generally or in an employment context, than others, I ... do not think that she can properly be said to have been 'treated' less favourably by whomsoever used the word, unless he intended her to overhear the conversation in which it was used, or knew or ought reasonably to have anticipated that the person he was talking to would pass on the insult or that the appellant would become aware of it in some other way.[34]

[The Court of Appeal also considered that there was no evidence that the remark in any way caused the applicant to be placed at a disadvantage in the circumstances and conditions in which she was working.]

The Court of Appeal clearly recognised that the concept of adverse working environment harassment *was capable of* contravening the SDA 1975 and RRA 1976. Arguably, however, the court applied an over-narrow interpretation of the concept of detriment. This is essentially a factual question, the case is an early one, and there is some evidence from sexual harassment cases that a more liberal and purposive approach is now likely to be utilised. In effect, the claim failed because the remark did not emanate from the boss, was not directed at the plaintiff, and, so far as we know from the evidence, was not repeated. It is contended that a change to any one of these facts may well have seen a different outcome. But the case is one of a number to highlight the conceptual problem of analysing 'harassment' within the greater rubric of 'discrimination'. Employment discrimination is normally and inevitably regarded as comprising actions by the employer. In a case like this, while it was accepted that the employer would have been vicariously liable, it still has to be shown that the acts of the employee responsible were themselves acts of discrimination. To require Mrs de Souza to show that the employee involved treated her less favourably than he would have done a white person is a highly artificial and contrived exercise. At a more conceptual level, the structure of the legislation fails to get to grips with the issue whether liability should focus on the employer in whose enterprise the harassment occurs or on the liability of the actual individual harasser. The answer to this question depends on whether the aim of the law is thought to be retribution, compensation or deterrence, or at least on what the combination of these aims should be.

---

[34] Racial abuse was held to be a detriment in *Sutton v Balfour Beatty Construction* (DCLD 12). The Industrial Tribunal rejected the argument of the employer that the use of words such as 'black bastard' should be regarded as camaraderie and were not intended to be insulting.

The conditions for liability

Insitu Cleaning Co Ltd v Heads **[1995] IRLR 4, EAT**

The victim was area supervisor for a contract cleaning firm. The harasser, who was the son of two directors and a manager, entered a room and said 'Hiya, big tits'. She said that she found the remark very embarrassing and distressing, especially as she was nearly twice his age. She received no internal support in making a complaint, and eventually resigned and successfully claimed sex discrimination.

Morison J (p 5):

[T]he defence argued the following points:]

(1) The remark was not sex-related and therefore could not amount to direct discrimination on the ground of sex. It is said that a similar remark could have been made to a man, for example in relation to a balding head or beard.

(2) On the facts the employee did not suffer any detriment ...

(3) On the facts ... the tribunal were perverse to conclude that the one incident was so serious that it could of itself amount to sexual harassment.

The first ground seemed to us to be absurd. A remark by a man about a woman's breasts cannot sensibly be equated with a remark by a woman about a bald head or a beard. One is sexual and the other is not.

Whether the employee suffered any detriment is largely a matter of fact for the tribunal. Detriment means no more than disadvantage. For the bosses' son to make a sexual remark to a female employee nearly twice his age was calculated to, and did, cause distress which no doubt was a mixture of rage, humiliation and genuine embarrassment. This is a form of bullying and is not acceptable in the workplace in any circumstances. The wrong done was compounded by B's status, the aggressive way he responded to the complaint, and his arrogant and dismissive manner at the Industrial Tribunal ... [S]uch conduct is likely to create an intimidating, hostile and humiliating work environment for the victim.

Whether a single verbal act of sexual harassment is sufficient to found a complaint is also a question of fact and degree[35] ... No one, other than a person used to indulging in loutish behaviour, could think that the remark used in this case was other than obviously unwanted.

Stewart v Cleveland Guest (Engineering) Ltd **[1994] IRLR 440, EAT**[36]

A female inspector had to go through the manufacturing area where calendars and pin-ups of nude and partially nude women were on display. She complained to the works manager that she was embarrassed and degraded by the pictures. His view and that of the managing director was basically that the

---

[35] See, also, *Bracebridge Engineering Ltd v Darby* [1990] IRLR 3, EAT.
[36] See, also, [1996] ICR 535.

pictures were acceptable as they did not show the genital area. They treated her complaint as so trivial as not to be worthy of a reply. After she complained to the union, an order was issued to take the pictures down, whereupon a deputation of women employees said they had no objection to the pictures. When she realised that everyone knew it was she who complained, she resigned, saying she had no confidence in the employers being prepared to protect her from embarrassment and distress caused by the other employees' attitude. She claimed sex discrimination and constructive dismissal.

The Industrial Tribunal upheld the complaint of constructive dismissal on the ground that the employers had broken the implied term of mutual confidence. There was no appeal from that decision.

The EAT upheld the decision of the IT and rejected the claim of sex discrimination.

Mummery J (pp 442–43):

The detriment relied on took two forms.

(1) Miss Stewart had to work in areas of the workplace where male fellow employees displayed pictures of naked and semi-naked women which she genuinely and reasonably found offensive.

(2) When Miss Stewart made a complaint about the display of the pictures ... [the management] failed:

    (a) to deal with the complaint properly and within a reasonable time; and

    (b) to deal with the hostility to and ridicule of Miss Stewart by the others when they knew about her complaint.

It is important to state what this case does *not* decide ... [It] does *not* mean that it is *never* an act of sex discrimination for a company to allow its male employees to display pictures of that kind ... A decision to allow this appeal would *not* mean that such an employer would in *every* such case be liable for sex discrimination.

[The basic reasons for dismissing the appeal were that the Industrial Tribunal correctly directed itself on the relevant law, and that the decision it reached on the evidence was not perverse. There was no error of law in finding that since the display of pictures of nude women was 'neutral' in that a man might have found the display as offensive as the applicant, she had not established that she had been treated less favourably than a man was or would have been treated.]

The key to this case was that the complainant had not been singled out as a target for obscene language or pictures. That would conclusively have demonstrated an unlawful purpose. But even without such targeting, conduct of this type may have the practical effect of poisoning the working environment for women in a way which does not apply to men.[37]

But the problem for the law is to determine at what point unwelcome behaviour becomes unlawful harassment.[38] Harassment which involves touching without consent will be unlawful, although of course defendants will argue that there was consent, express or implied. Repeated acts not involving touching, such as by word or gesture, are likely to be unlawful *if* the victim can prove that she made her objection known, which, as much harassment occurs without witnesses, may prove far from straightforward. But it is inescapable that the law may have to determine what are the limits of acceptable behaviour in the workplace, and the criteria for making such decisions are uncertain. For example, the law may have to determine whether it is unlawful for a boss to tell his secretary that he would like to sleep with her.[39]

It should not be sufficient for liability that the victim found the behaviour offensive or detrimental, for that could occur without the knowledge of the alleged harasser – though that may change if the objections are made clear. On the other hand, a subjective standard does have the advantage of focusing on the standards and values of the victim, rather than allowing standards to be determined by what continues to be an overwhelmingly male judiciary. If the standard were that of the reasonable man, that might allow arguments based on some spurious male notion of reasonableness which regards limited low-level harassment as acceptable, perhaps in the context of a particularly sexualised workplace. Rather, the standard should be that of the reasonable victim, which would permit arguments that an individual woman reacted in a way which was unforeseeable without being so subjective that all standards disappear. Another way of expressing this idea is that there should be liability

---

[37] There is 'an apparent sensitivity to the possibility that different perspectives can be brought to bear on events or images whose contents are not contested. However, this recognition of difference is immediately swallowed up by the assertion that the real distress of the applicant is the same as the hypothetical distaste of a hypothetical male employee. This supposedly sidesteps sex discrimination because of the postulated parity of detriment. However, that analysis is blind to the context which forms the way in which we view the world. [The complainant is] differently positioned from that hypothetical male employee because ... many women experience pornography as a direct assault on their self-worth, on their identity as women ...'. Flynn, L 'Interpretation and disputed accounts in sexual harassment cases: *Stewart v Cleveland Guest (Engineering) Ltd*' (1996) 4 Feminist Legal Studies 109, p 122.

[38] Whether something is sufficiently serious to constitute a detriment is a question of fact, and thus different Tribunals may reach different conclusions. This will be especially true where the act complained of is a one-off, or where the complaint is of a sexually poisoned atmosphere rather than having been directed at any particular victim.

[39] I am fully aware that the example has been totally decontextualised. For example, the way in which it was said and the history of their working relationship would need to be considered. In the end, however, a value judgment is inescapable, though the current structure of the law enables appellate courts to sidestep the issue by holding that the issue is one of fact for the tribunal to determine.

if the harasser knew or should have known that the victim found the conduct to be objectionable.[40] Such an approach is also appropriate to racial harassment cases, particularly those based on racial insults. It should be for the reasonable member of a racial group to determine what is offensive language.[41]

British Telecommunications plc v Williams [1997] IRLR 669

The complainant alleged that, during a counselling meeting with her manager to discuss an appraisal, at which only the two were present, the manager was sexually aroused, stared at her throughout the meeting, arranged the paperwork so as to ensure close physical proximity between the two, and caused the meeting to last for an excessive period of time.

The EAT allowed the employer's appeal against the finding of the Industrial Tribunal that there had been unlawful sex discrimination.

Morison J (p 670):

> My colleagues and I are sure that it is neither required by law nor desirable in practice that employers should have female supervisors for female staff or to see that male managers are chaperoned when dealing with female staff ... If, as would appear, the reason why the tribunal concluded that the interview was sexually intimidating was because there was no woman present and the interview took place in a confined space, we have to say their conclusion must be rejected.

> [As the tribunal rejected the allegation that the manager was sexually aroused and stared at the complainant throughout the interview, the only permissible conclusion was that the allegation was not made out.]

The EAT took the view that the rejection of the specific allegations necessarily led to the rejection of the complainant. There was no willingness to analyse the *overall* atmosphere created by the manager's actions, which together might understandably have been regarded as creating an atmosphere intimidating to a reasonable woman. As it is the *effect* of the behaviour which is determinative, the fact that the manager might not have been aware of the reaction he was creating should not be relevant.

---

[40] 'The assessment requires to be both objective and subjective, in the sense that the act complained of must at least be capable, on an objective test, of being categorised as offensive. In many cases, if that test is satisfied, nothing more need be considered; but, in cases where the conduct might be regarded as neutral or such as to be regarded by some people as offensive, if not by others, the subjective standard comes into the equation in order to assess the reaction of the victim.' *Scott v Combined Property Services Ltd*, unreported, EAT No: 757/96, see 32 DCLD 4.

[41] It has been argued that the concept of reasonableness can never have any objective meaning. '[I]n treating the resolution of sexual harassment cases as a matter of neutral decision making [judges obscure the fact that the standard] necessarily requires a court to make substantive judgments about what kind of conduct should be allowed in the workplace ... In short, the discourse of reasonableness can create a false sense of security, lulling one into believing that a result is inherently fair regardless of its specific content, and reinforcing the idea that legal analysis can be neutral and objective.' *Op cit*, Ehrenreich, fn 21, p 1218.

Unwelcomeness[42]

Part of the concept of harassment and therefore an essential part of the proof is to show that the conduct was indeed unwelcome. This may cause numerous problems, especially as women may feel uncomfortable about complaining and fear the consequences if they do. The issue is not the same as that of consent for the purposes of the criminal law. A woman who consents to sexual intercourse may nevertheless be able to claim sexual harassment if she can prove that the original advances were unwelcome, though this would be difficult unless the man was in a position of some power or control over the woman's employment position, and, in any event, this kind of case would inevitably lead to harsh cross-examination and perhaps unpleasant publicity.

Sexual harassment *can* be analogised to rape in that the defence may wish to cross-examine the complainant about her sexual attitudes in order to support an argument that the advances were not unwelcome or that there was little or no injury to feelings in consequence.

Snowball v Gardner Merchant Ltd [1987] IRLR 397, EAT[43]

The applicant complained of conduct by her district manager, which included requests for sex, sending her sexual material, and pestering her with phone calls. The defence wished to cross-examine her about her sexual attitudes in order to show that any sexual harassment had not caused injury to feelings.

The EAT ruled the evidence to be admissible.

Sir Ralph Kilner-Brown (pp 399–400):

Compensation must relate to the degree of detriment and in that context there has to be an assessment of the injury to the woman's feelings, which must be looked at not only subjectively with reference to her as an individual, but objectively with reference to what any ordinary reasonable female employee would feel.

[I]n order to challenge the alleged detriment and hurt to feelings, it is pertinent to inquire whether the complainant is unduly sensitive, or as in this case, if the proposed evidence is right, is unlikely to be upset by a degree of familiarity with a sexual connotation.

In the present case it could not be held that no reasonable IT would admit evidence of this nature so as to entitle the EAT to interfere with the tribunal's exercise of discretion ...

Wileman v Minilec Engineering Ltd [1988] IRLR 144, EAT[44]

The complaint was of sexual harassment over a period by a director, which was said to have included both salacious remarks and physical harassment.

---

[42] See *op cit*, Dine and Watt, fn 3, pp 355–57.
[43] See, also, [1987] ICR 319.
[44] See, also, [1988] ICR 318.

The Industrial Tribunal upheld her complaint, but awarded only £50 for injury to feelings on the basis that the harassment did not upset her and was a detriment to her only in the sense of being a minor irritation. They also took into account the fact that on occasion she wore to work clothes which were described as 'scanty and provocative'.

When the case reached the EAT the defence wished to include evidence that she had posed for a national newspaper in a flimsy costume subsequent to the IT hearing.

Popplewell J (pp 147–49):

Quite clearly the picture itself cannot affect, in any way, the question of physical harassment. Secondly, its probative value in relation to the comments made by the director seems to us to be almost minimal. A person may be quite happy to accept the remarks of A or B in a sexual context, and wholly upset by similar remarks made by C; the fact that she was upset to the extent which the tribunal have found by the remarks made by the director are not in our judgment vitiated in any way by the fact that she was willing to pose for the national newspaper ...

We think that the Industrial Tribunal were entitled to take into account as an element – not a decisive element but an element – in deciding whether the harassment really did constitute a detriment ... [I]f a girl on the shopfloor goes around wearing provocative clothes and flaunting herself, it is not unlikely that other work people – particularly the men – will make remarks about it ... If she then complains that she suffered a detriment, the tribunal is entitled to look at the circumstances in which the remarks are made ...

If this gentleman made sexual remarks to a number of people, it has to be looked at in the context of each person. All the people to whom they are made may regard them as wholly inoffensive; everyone else may regard them as offensive. Each individual has the right, if the remarks are regarded as offensive, to treat them as an offence under the Sex Discrimination Act ... The fact that on other occasions [he] is said to have behaved in this way ... does not affect the decision in relation to this applicant.

The issue of unwelcomeness invites the defendant to look for precisely the kind of evidence which may dissuade applicants from bringing claims. Evidence as to the way complainants behaved at work, while perhaps liable to be fabricated or exaggerated, is logically relevant to the question whether the conduct was unwelcome and thus a detriment, as is the question whether the alleged harasser has behaved similarly towards other women.[45] As the nature

---

[45] 'Where it is likely that evidence of a sensitive or salacious nature may be led, Industrial Tribunals have power to make a restricted reporting order under r 14, Sched 1 of the Industrial Tribunal (Constitution and Rules of Procedure) Regulations 1993, but not to clear the tribunal of the press and public, according to the EAT in *R v Southampton Industrial Tribunal ex p INS News Group and Express Newspapers plc* [1995] IRLR 247. In that case, the respondent and applicant both objected that a restricted reporting order made on the first day, which was intended to prevent the parties being identified, had been broken by a newspaper article and a radio broadcast. As the tribunal did not [cont]

and degree of any supposed encouragement must be balanced against the severity of the harassment, this argument can only be applicable to the very mildest forms of harassment. Furthermore, an employer who requires employees to wear what might be regarded as provocative clothing is arguably responsible for any subsequent harassment experienced at the hands of other employees. Again, though, this is better viewed as an issue of the employer's contractual duties rather than as an issue of anti-discrimination legislation.

In addition, the assumption, in *Wileman*, that sexual attitudes and experience are relevant in assessing the degree of detriment, is problematic both in principle and practice. It implies that people who are sexually active or comfortable in discussing sexual matters are likely to suffer less damage from sexual harassment than others. There is no theoretical basis for assuming this to be the case, and its practical effect is necessarily to permit cross-examination on intimate matters which may discourage the bringing of claims. Nevertheless, it should be possible to argue that the particular victim suffered *greater* injury to feelings than normal, perhaps because of religious beliefs or because of previous incidents of sexual harassment or violation. Such arguments should only be permissible to *increase* compensation rather than reduce it, as was done in *Wileman*.

Employer responsibilities

There are three issues which must be distinguished: the way in which complaints are investigated by the employer; the subsequent treatment of the complainant in relation to the harasser; and the responsibility of the employer to protect employees from harassment at the hands of fellow employees; in addition, the issue may arise of the employer's legal responsibility for the actions of the harasser.

Failure to deal adequately with a claim of sexual harassment is not in itself an act of sexual harassment or sex discrimination, but should be regarded in the same way as failure to deal with any other employment complaint would be regarded, assuming, of course, that the way the complaint was dealt with fell short of being an act of victimisation. As a matter of law this conclusion is

---

45 [cont] consider that in these circumstances it had powers to order that the proceedings be taken in private under r 8(3), the tribunal made its order to exclude the press under the general powers provided by r 9. The EAT was of the view that these wider powers could not be used to modify the specific powers set out to deal with the situation in r 14. The EAT advised that such restricted reporting orders should clearly specify what is meant in the circumstances by "the publication of identifying matter".' Bourn, C and Whitmore, J, *Anti-Discrimination Law in Britain*, 3rd edn, 1996, London: Sweet & Maxwell, p 161. There is also a case that tribunals should be granted power to hear cases in camera; see *op cit*, Rubenstein, fn 15, p 83.

probably correct, but it leaves the victim with the general problem of how to enforce this implied term in the contract of employment. Suing for damages is unlikely to be practical or beneficial; resigning and claiming constructive unfair dismissal is the ultimate step and, while it is a price victims may well feel they must pay, not all would wish to do so. In addition, unlike claims under the SDA 1975, constructive unfair dismissal claims are only open to employees who have acquired two years' continuous employment.[46] Thirdly, many cases reveal tension between the actions of the alleged harasser and those of the employer. Arguably, the claims in *Heads*, *Stewart* and *Balgobin* were only brought because of the employer's failure to respond adequately to the original complaint, thereby revealing the importance, from the employer's perspective, of having proper procedural mechanisms in place. Such procedural failure may be a breach of contract, even if the original action is insufficiently serious or detrimental on its own to amount to unlawful harassment.

In *Balgobin and Francis v London Borough of Tower Hamlets*[47] two female employees complained of sexual harassment by a cook. The cook was suspended during an investigation, but the complaints could not be substantiated. The women were then required to continue working alongside their alleged harasser, and they argued that to have to continue working in that way itself constituted sex discrimination. The argument was rejected, Popplewell J observing that 'is no doubt that the intolerable situation to which these ladies were exposed had a sexual context but the reason they were exposed to that intolerable situation which affected them because they were women was not on account of their being women; the consequence of working with Mr C was no doubt a detriment to them as women; but they were not required to work with Mr C because they were women ... We have to say that the employers did not require these applicants to work with Mr C because of their sex'.[48] Just as with complaints of failure to investigate, such behaviour might constitute a breach of contract, but it is not sex discrimination.

Balgobin was not a case where the employer knew or had reason to anticipate that the actions might be repeated. If the employer *knows* or *should know* that harassment may occur, that may entirely alter the outcome.

Burton and Rhule v De Vere Hotels Ltd [1996] IRLR 596, EAT[49]

The applicants were black casual waitresses at a dinner where the comedian Bernard Manning was guest speaker. He made jokes about the sexual organs

---

[46] The government is proposing to reduce the period to one year. See *op cit*, fn 13.

[47] [1987] IRLR 401, EAT.

[48] *Balgobin and Francis v London Borough of Tower Hamlets*, pp 303–04.

[49] See, also, [1997] ICR 1; for comment, see Mullender, R, 'Racial harassment, sexual harassment and the expressive function of law' (1998) 61 MLR 236.

of black men and their sexual abilities, and made offensive personal remarks about the waitresses. They carried on working while all this was occurring, and suffered some sexual harassment by guests.

The only possible complaint against Manning or the guests would have been under the general law of tort. Such a claim was not brought. Rather, they complained to the management for placing them in a prejudiced atmosphere, and a letter of apology was forthcoming. They nevertheless brought a claim of race discrimination which was rejected by the Industrial Tribunal on the ground that none of the managers had anticipated that Manning would behave like that.

The appeal to the EAT was allowed.

Mrs Justice Smith (pp 598–600):

The parties agree that the problem is to decide what an applicant must prove in order to decide that the employer 'subjected' the employee to the detriment of racial abuse or harassment, where the actual abuser or harasser is a third party and not a servant or agent of the employer ... Put another way, the problem is to decide the extent of the duty of an employer to protect the employee from racial harassment from third parties.

[I]n practice, where an employer is shown to have actual knowledge that racial harassment of an employee is taking place, or deliberately or recklessly closes his eyes to the fact that it is taking place, if he does not act reasonably to prevent it, he will readily be found to have subjected his employee to the detriment of racial harassment.

We do not think that the word 'subjecting' is a word which connotes action or decision ... Rather we think it connotes 'control'. A person 'subjects' another to something if he causes or allows that thing to happen in circumstances where he can control whether it happens or not. An employer subjects an employee to the detriment of racial harassment if he causes or permits the racial harassment to occur in circumstances in which he can control whether it happens or not.

[F]oresight of the events or the lack of it cannot be determinative of whether the event was under the employer's control. An employer might foresee that racial harassment is a real possibility and yet be able to do very little, if anything, to prevent it from happening or protect his employees from it. For example, the employer of a bus or train conductor may recognise that the employee will face a real risk of racial harassment at times. Yet the prevention of such an event will be largely beyond the control of the employer ... On the other hand, if the harassment occurs even quite unexpectedly, but in circumstances over which the employer has control, a tribunal may well find that he has subjected the employee to it.

The tribunal said that [the manager] ought to have warned his assistant managers to keep a look out for Mr Manning and withdraw the young waitresses if things became unpleasant. He did not do so because he did not give the matter a thought. He should have done. Events within the banqueting hall were under the control of [his] assistants. If they had been properly instructed by him, these two young women would not have suffered any harassment. They might possibly have suffered a few offensive words before they were withdrawn, but that would have been all.

This duty clearly arises in the employment context, whether the harasser be a fellow employee, a customer, a member of the public or anyone else who comes into contact with the employee while she is at work.[50] Furthermore, logic dictates that this obligation is not limited to harassment within employment. It imposes a duty on schools to protect both employees and students from harassment from whomever it might occur, and landlords to protect tenants from fellow tenants.

But merely stating that there is a duty does not delineate its precise scope. It is difficult to be more precise than to say that the employer must take reasonable steps to protect the employee from harassment at the hands of third parties. Tribunals must judge whether the employer's conduct was in all the circumstances reasonable. The impact of this new legal approach will depend crucially on the sensitivity of tribunals to particular fact situations and the extent that they will be prepared to require employers to be proactive in taking steps in *advance* by way of procedures and training to minimise the risk of harassment. Prior experience does not engender confidence that courts and tribunals will develop a sophisticated approach to what amounts to good industrial relations practice in this context.

Dealing with situations such as arose in *de Vere Hotels* is far from straightforward for employers, especially where problem situations arise unexpectedly. Employees who are deprived of the opportunity of working because of employer fears that they would be harassed will have a claim. The same is true if they are removed from the job when the employer became aware of the harassment and did not pay them for the period when they were not working. There is a further problem if the waitresses here were properly removed from the job, but were told later about the racist content of the jokes. Despite the fact that such outcome might be entirely predictable, the imposition of liability might be thought to be going too far.

Section 32(1) of the RRA 1976[51] provides that anything 'done by a person in the course of his employment shall be treated for the purposes of this Act as done by his employer as well as by him, whether or not it was done with the

---

[50] In *Jeffers v North Wales Probation Committee*, unreported, IT, Case No: 61385/93, see 31 DCLD 6, the probation service was held liable for failure to protect an employee from the racial abuse and antagonism of a client.

[51] See, also, SDA 1975, s 41(1).

employer's knowledge or approval'.[52] The meaning of that provision was at issue in the following case.

Jones v Tower Boot Co [1997] IRLR 168, CA[53]

The applicant was seriously racially harassed while working for the employers. Among other incidents, his arm was burnt with a hot screwdriver, metal bolts were thrown at his head, and he was repeatedly called racially abusive names. The EAT held that the employers were not liable for these acts of harassment. They applied the traditional and well known tort test of vicarious liability and concluded, not surprisingly, that the employers were not liable, as the acts of harassment were committed outside the course of employment.

The Court of Appeal allowed the appeal.

Waite LJ (pp 171–72):

A purposive construction ... requires s 32 of the Race Relations Act (and the corresponding s 41 of the Sex Discrimination Act) to be given a broad interpretation. It would be inconsistent with that requirement to allow the notion of the 'course of employment' to be construed in any sense more limited than the natural meaning of those everyday words would allow ... [T]here is no sufficient similarity between the two contexts to justify, on a linguistic construction, the reading of the phrase 'course of employment' as subject to the gloss imposed on it in the common law context of vicarious liability ... [If such a construction were adopted], the more heinous the act of discrimination, the less likely it will be that the employer will be liable.

The policy ... is to deter racial and sexual harassment in the workplace through a widening of the net of responsibility beyond the guilty employees themselves, by making all employers additionally liable for such harassment, and then supplying them with the reasonable steps defence ... which will exonerate the conscientious employer who has used his best endeavours to prevent such harassment, and will encourage all employers who have not yet undertaken such endeavours to take the steps necessary to make the same defence available in their workplace.

It would be particularly wrong to allow racial harassment on the scale that was suffered by the complainant in this case ... to slip through the net of employer responsibility by applying to it a common law principle evolved in another area of the law to deal with vicarious responsibility for wrongdoing of a wholly different kind. To do so would seriously undermine the statutory

---

[52] It was held in *UP and GS v N and RJ*, unreported, IT, Case No: 10781/95, see 35 DCLD 11, that this potential exclusion of employer liability was contrary to European law, as neither the Equal Treatment Directive nor the European Commission Code of Practice make any mention of such possibility.

[53] See, also, [1997] ICR 254; [1997] 2 All ER 406.

scheme of the Discrimination Acts and flout the purposes which they were passed to achieve.[54]

The tribunals are free, and indeed bound, to interpret the ordinary and readily understandable words 'in the course of employment' in the sense in which every layman would understand them ... The application of the phrase will be a question of fact for each Industrial Tribunal to resolve, in the light of the circumstances presented to it, with a mind unclouded by any parallels sought to be drawn from the law of vicarious liability in tort.

[The Court of Appeal restored the order of the IT, which had held the employers to be vicariously liable without making reference to that doctrine as it is applied in the tort context.]

The harasser can only be liable under the anti-discrimination legislation for aiding unlawful acts, which in turn depends on the employer being liable. The legislation does not permit action against the harasser to the exclusion of the employer. The law of harassment has been included within anti-discrimination law partly because that is what occurred in the USA and partly for want of a better alternative under English law. The issue, of which this case is a paradigm example, of whether the employer or the actual harasser is the more appropriate defendant, has been ignored by both judiciary and legislature. There are conceptual difficulties in applying a law based on comparative treatment on grounds of race or gender to a situation based on bullying, abuse, or misuse of sexuality. 'Furthermore, harassment may occur on grounds other than race or gender and in situations other than at the workplace. As the conceptual base of the law on sexual and racial harassment is so fragile, it is unsurprising that there are difficulties in attributing appropriate blame to either employer or employee. The law on vicarious liability [was] not responsible for [the decision of the EAT in] *Jones*; that should be laid at the feet of the failure by the judiciary and the legislature to deal adequately with harassment at a more conceptual level.'[55]

The approach taken by the Court of Appeal, that the claim here is of an entirely different nature from one in tort, is not at all convincing. The applicant suffered personal injuries and might well have brought a tort claim. It is unclear in policy terms why an employer should be liable for racial discrimination but not liable in tort. It is apparently now the case that the employer will be liable for any actions of harassment committed by employees against fellow employees while at work, as long as the harassment is on ground of race, gender or disability. Logic suggests that the same principle applies if the victim is a customer or client. The employer may

---

[54] *Irving and Irving v The Post Office* [1987] IRLR 289, EAT, was distinguished on the basis that there it was *assumed* rather than argued and decided that the common law test of vicarious liability was appropriate for use in the discrimination context.

[55] Townshend-Smith, R, 'Case note' (1996) 2 IJDL 137, pp 139–40. For development of the argument, see *op cit*, Townshend-Smith, fn 12; *op cit*, Dine and Watt, fn 3.

therefore be liable, and labelled as a discriminator, whether or not there was knowledge or means of knowledge of what was occurring, unless proper efforts had been made to prevent harassment from occurring.

Section 41(3) of the SDA 1975 states that in 'proceedings brought ... against any person in respect of an act alleged to have been done by an employee of his it shall be a defence for that person to prove that he took such steps as were reasonably practicable to prevent the employee from doing that act ...'.[56] This provision is particularly relevant to harassment cases, where employers may seek to argue that an equal opportunities policy or other management strategy had been precisely designed to prevent harassment from occurring. The question is what steps must employers take to avail themselves of this defence. In *Balgobin and Francis v London Borough of Tower Hamlets*,[57] it was conceded that the employers were vicariously liable for the acts of sexual harassment, but the employers argued that they had a defence under s 41(3). The Industrial Tribunal found that no one in authority knew what was going on, there was proper and adequate supervision, they had made known their policy of equal opportunities, and that in this light there were no other practicable steps they could have taken to stop the harassment from occurring. The EAT said that this was a finding which, on the evidence, the tribunal was entitled to reach, even though no evidence was given that any employees were given instruction or guidance on the operation of the equal opportunities policy, or that any particular efforts were made to combat sexual harassment. It took little to persuade the EAT that there was nothing more the employers could reasonably have done. This approach is dubious in law and on the facts. The section expressly places on the employer the burden of showing that all reasonable steps were taken, a burden which should require employers to show both that the policy was effectively implemented and communicated to the employees, and that under it, sexual harassment was a specific disciplinary offence. It cannot be enough merely to tell employees not to discriminate.[58]

If the employer is *not* responsible for the alleged harassment, for example, because it occurred outside working hours, there will be no protection under the victimisation provisions for the employee who makes a complaint.[59] This extremely narrow and technical reading of the legislation fails to provide the protection which is needed to employees who, at the time they are considering making a complaint, may be unaware or have no means of knowing whether the employer will be held liable for the acts of the actual harasser.

---

[56] See, also, RRA 1976, s 32(3).
[57] [1987] IRLR 401, EAT.
[58] See European Commission Code of Practice, ss 5–7.
[59] *Waters v Commissioner of Police of the Metropolis* [1997] ICR 1073; [1997] IRLR 589, CA. See below, pp 363–64.

PREVENTING HARASSMENT – THE ROLE OF LAW AND VOLUNTARY POLICIES

There have been some significant advances in the last 20 years and the law has played a role in bringing these about. The more glaring examples of sexual and racial harassment at work have been identified, defined, and outlawed. That degree of progress should be neither underestimated nor downplayed. Nor should the need for further developments. The law has, with limited exceptions, focused on the more extreme instances of harassment, where the causes can be more easily attributed to individual wrongdoing. The further task is to counter the insidious normality of harassment. The difficulty in so doing is apparent. To the extent that sexual harassment is a reflection of a masculinity whose values are largely socially acceptable, it is at least arguable that the removal of sexual harassment requires a fundamental reordering of gender values.[60] In the same way, removal of racial harassment requires a thoroughgoing alteration of racial consciousness and attitudes. The part the law can play in these social changes is necessarily limited. Nevertheless, the law operates as an educator, as a deterrent and as punishment. Its significance should not be underestimated, both as a provider of a remedy for victims and as a spur to voluntary action on the part of employers. The final section of the chapter will explore some of the benefits and pitfalls of the legal approach and the voluntary approach.

Most employers of any size now have anti-harassment policies, the majority of which cover sexual and racial harassment, and may well cover harassment on other grounds as well. The thrust and aim of policies may vary. There is a danger that the primary objective of employers might be to avoid the possibility of subsequent legal liability rather than to meet the needs of victims. Those needs themselves may vary: there may be tension between preventing future harassment on the one hand and providing support for current victims on the other. For example, victims might prefer counselling and the avoidance of publicity. Counselling of harassers might be introduced, but such approach could 'turn into a mechanism for protecting men from the serious consequences of their actions ... On the other hand, successful counselling could have a far greater long term impact on sexism at work than any number of verbal and written warnings.'[61] The way in which complaints are handled is of vital importance and, while this should not be the primary objective, it is clear that a sympathetic internal procedure may as a by-product make it less likely that victims will feel a need to resort to the courts. No doubt the motivations of victims vary, and generalisations are dangerous, but it appears that victims are primarily interested in vindication of their rights,

---

[60] See Thomas, A, 'Men behaving badly', in *op cit*, Thomas and Kitzinger, fn 18.

[61] *Op cit*, Hadjifotiou, fn 23, p 142.

getting the harassment to stop, and discipline of the harasser. The law can only provide the first, although the others may follow in the wake of a successful legal outcome. A monetary remedy, so often the focus of legal proceedings, while not unwelcome, is liable to be seen as very much second best.

It is not straightforward to design and implement a voluntary policy which will reduce the incidence of harassment. Some of the central practical issues are addressed in Codes of Practice.[62]

'EOC Sexual harassment guide' (1994) 58 EOR 35, pp 36–38:

What women can do

Make it clear to the harasser that you object to his behaviour.

- You should ask the harasser to stop what he is doing. You may want to take a colleague or a trade union representative with you ... If you are too embarrassed to confront the harasser yourself you could ask someone else to do it ... If you decide to tackle the problem by writing to the harasser, you should keep a copy of the letter or memo.

- You should ask the harasser to stop what he is doing even if you are the only woman who objects to his behaviour. Whatever other women's reactions may be, you have the right to ask him to stop.

Keep a record of the incidents.

Report the harasser to someone in authority.

- You should do this even though you have made it clear to him that his behaviour is unacceptable ... You may not be the only woman being harassed but, in any event, if your employers do not know what is going on, they cannot deal with the problem.

- If a colleague is harassing you, go to your boss. If your manager or supervisor is harassing you, go to someone higher up, as well as to your personnel officer and, if you are in a trade union, to your trade union representative.

- If the person harassing you is the owner or the senior manager, and you have no one in the workplace to turn to, go to your nearest Citizens Advice Bureau.

Follow up the complaint.

Remember that the person harassing you also has a right to a fair hearing.

What trade unions can do

If the complainant and the alleged harasser are both members of the same union, the union should consider whether both members could be entitled to union support. It is helpful if unions have an agreed procedure in place so as to be able to deal effectively with this situation, should it arise. The lack of an

---

62 For discussion of what should be contained in an employer's policy, see *op cit*, Rubenstein, fn 15, pp 57–62.

agreed procedure can sometimes give rise to claims of sex discrimination against the union either from the person alleging harassment or from the alleged harasser, depending upon which person feels that they have been denied union support on grounds of their sex.[63]

What employers can do

If no one is complaining about sexual harassment, or if you have an 'open door' policy on grievances, you may see no need to introduce a special procedure. If this is your view, think again. Lack of complaints may mean only that people are too embarrassed or too fearful to come forward.

Taking action now can help to prevent problems in the future and avoid legal liability; it will also help you to introduce the relevant legal procedures in a way which wins the support of your workforce. In our experience, rushing into a policy, particularly after a tribunal claim, is not a good idea. Male employees may, quite understandably, regard the imposition of a policy as an unjust accusation of sexual harassment and, where this is the reaction, the chances of that policy being effective are seriously reduced.

[Employers should] lay down a procedure for dealing with complaints of sexual harassment ... The procedure should:

- specify to whom a complaint should be made, and provide for an alternative;

- ensure that complaints are treated seriously and sympathetically;

- wherever possible, provide for a manager of the same sex as the complainant to hear the complaint;

- ensure that any complaint is dealt with promptly and with due care;

- ensure that any panel set up to investigate the complaint has at least as many women as men on it. Very often, such panels include only one women, who is often of lower status than the men. A woman in this position will find it difficult to be effective;

- ensure that procedures set out a timeframe for the investigation.

- ensure that, if it becomes necessary, either during the investigation or afterwards, to separate the complaint and the alleged harasser, no pressure is put on the complainant to transfer.

There is a great deal of practical sense in the details of the Code. But it has been criticised for 'its failure to recommend that policies should provide for informal methods of resolution or that employers should offer advice and

---

63 In *Fire Brigades Union v Fraser* [1997] IRLR 671, EAT, it was held, over the dissent of the EAT chair, that an Industrial Tribunal was entitled to find that the union had discriminated against a male union member on the ground of his sex by refusing to provide him with assistance and representation in respect of his disciplinary proceedings where allegations of sexual harassment had been made by an employee who was a member of the same union. The assumption that men are more likely to be harassers than women and that women victims are more in need of union assistance than males accused of harassment led to a gender-tainted decision which would have been different in the unlikely situation of the roles being reversed.

assistance to employees subjected to sexual harassment'.[64] Furthermore, the 'stance adopted by the EOC ... seems more focused on documenting a potential tribunal case than on resolving problems with the minimum of anxiety for the victim of sexual harassment. [T]here is no mention at all of the value of employers providing counselling services ... or of employer-facilitated networks of advice and assistance to help harassment victims decide which course they wish to take. Yet many large employers have invested a great deal of work in such services, not only because they help to resolve complaints, but also because they help build confidence that the organisation takes sexual harassment seriously'.[65]

The publicity and attention given to sexual harassment in recent years has to some extent deflected attention from issues of racial harassment and how to deal with it within a workplace.

'Racial harassment at work' (1993) 49 EOR 17, pp 18–19:

[There is a] trend towards the adoption by organisations of one general harassment policy rather than several separate policies ... The rationale for issuing a general harassment policy is that the same procedures are applicable to different forms of harassment ... Other organisations which have issued a separate racial harassment policy do so because they consider that racial harassment in the workplace is often not recognised or understood and that it is important to spell out in detail what it is ...

While it is widely acknowledged that a woman who has experienced harassment may wish to consult a woman counsellor or advisor, we found very little recognition that an ethnic minority victim of harassment might wish to consult someone of the same ethnic minority background, as well as of the same sex ...

It is possible that the ethnicity of the person handling the complaint may affect the willingness of an ethnic minority employee to make a complaint ... While it would be inconceivable that an all-male panel would investigate a sexual harassment case, only three policies in our survey address the issue of ethnic minority representation on a panel investigating a racial harassment case ... [The] Camden and Islington Health Authority ... policy ... recommends that the investigating panel ... should reflect the nature of the complaint as far as possible, eg, for a racism complaint ensure that a black member of staff is included in the investigation.

CHANGES TO THE LAW

Legislation is needed which deals specifically with harassment, rather than leaving it all to judicial interpretation. 'A clear and explicit formulation of such

---

[64] 'EOC sexual harassment guide' (1994) 58 EOR 35, p 35.
[65] *Ibid.*

a prohibition will focus attention on the problem. It will alert the victims of harassment to their legal rights and employers, who wish to comply with the law, to their legal duties. It will resolve judicial uncertainty as to whether, and in what circumstances, sexual harassment is unlawful sex discrimination.'[66] As with pregnancy, specific legislation removes the need for reliance on the comparative approach which is so often the focus of anti-discrimination law. While the EAT in *British Telecommunications plc v Williams*[67] has stated there is no place for the comparative approach in the context of sexual harassment, thinking comparatively is so much a part of discrimination logic that one *dictum* cannot guarantee its elimination.

It should not be expected that such legislation would automatically overcome the many disincentives to the instigation of legal proceedings. Many of the problems faced by victims of discrimination in utilising the law are not peculiar to harassment.[68] Issues of cost, emotional stress, the possibility of being victimised, and the difficulty of remaining an employee at the same time as taking legal action against the employer, have all been well documented. Some issues, especially the fear of publicity and potentially embarrassing cross-examination, are especially applicable to harassment. For that reason the possibility of alternative dispute resolution needs exploring,[69] despite the fact that it carries a risk that harassers will thereby be able to avoid publicity and thus victims will not be publicly vindicated.[70]

Furthermore, the 'principal objective [of the law] should not be to provide a monetary remedy for victims of sexual harassment. The principal objective should be to protect workers against the risk of sexual harassment at work by encouraging employers to establish and maintain working environments free of sexual harassment. This can best be done by empowering the competent judicial authority ... to require an employer found liable for sexual harassment to submit a plan for approval setting out the steps to be taken to minimise the chances of similar unlawful behaviour recurring'.[71] As with other areas of discrimination law, legal reform requires both a more creative regime of available remedies, and a more deliberate legal policy of encouraging and provoking voluntary action, including training, on the part of employers.

---

[66] 'EEC legislation needed on sexual harassment' (1987) 14 EOR 26.

[67] [1997] IRLR 668.

[68] See below, pp 504–06.

[69] Hunter, R and Leonard, A 'Sex discrimination and alternative dispute resolution: British proposals in the light of international experience' [1997] PL 298; see below, pp 506–08.

[70] That possibility exists under the current structure: it is fairly common for employers to offer to settle out of court on condition that the victim say nothing publicly about the facts of which the complaint was made. This places victims and their advisers in an invidious position: the understandable desire to avoid the trauma of a court case must be set against the fact that the law thereby loses much of its educative value.

[71] *Op cit*, Rubenstein, fn 15, p 72. See, also, pp 76–78.

CHAPTER 9

INDIRECT DISCRIMINATION

INTRODUCTION

Direct discrimination requires proof of an intention to treat the applicant less favourably. While this does not necessarily entail proof of prejudice or hostility, it does focus attention on the mind and the behaviour of the alleged discriminator. There are two severe limitations to this approach. First, if two candidates are *not* equal, whatever meaning be given to equality in this context, the employer is not liable for direct discrimination if the better qualified candidate is chosen. This remains true even if the vast majority of those qualified are white males. Direct discrimination law is unconcerned with the *reasons* why women and minority ethnic groups may not be as well qualified or have as much experience as their white counterparts. Secondly, direct discrimination is fundamentally individualistic in nature: it assumes a decision making process focused on two competing individuals rather than allowing for patterns or practices of conduct based on stereotypical responses to perceived shared characteristics. This shapes the remedies: direct discrimination law in the UK does not extend the remedy to others who might also be victims of the defendant discriminator.[1] This has a damaging effect both on the motivation for bringing a claim, and on the potential deterrent effect of any award of compensation which might ensue.

The focus of indirect discrimination, on the other hand, is on social inequality measured in particular by economic and employment achievement. The essence of the doctrine is that some criteria or conditions exclude women or black people at a higher rate than men or white people.[2] It compares the performances and achievements of groups rather than individuals and asks whether there is a significant difference in achievement between such groups.

---

1   This point is significantly less true of the law of direct discrimination in the USA, where the availability of class actions and suits based on a pattern and practice of direct discrimination has enabled the remedy to be extended beyond the immediate litigants. See below, pp 521–22, 535–36.

2   The approach is also applicable to discrimination on other grounds, eg, disability discrimination or age discrimination. Most buildings have not been designed to exclude those with problems with mobility, yet as a practical matter many such people will be excluded, a far higher proportion than in the general population. While the Disability Discrimination Act 1995 does not deal with indirect discrimination in the same explicit manner as the SDA 1975 and RRA 1976, the *practical* effect of the law is that indirect discrimination is covered. See below, p 597. Similarly, educational requirements may well have the effect of indirectly discriminating on the ground of age, as a significantly higher proportion of younger people possess certain educational qualifications than is the case with their older counterparts.

The doctrine is American is origin, though as it was not specifically spelled out in the statute, it needed judicial creativity to secure its position as part of American anti-discrimination law.

Griggs v Duke Power Co 401 US 424 (1971)

The defendant utility company, which had a history of segregation in employment, instituted a practice whereby all employees except those hired to the lowest paying jobs were required to have successfully completed high school, and to have achieved satisfactory scores on two professionally prepared aptitude tests. It was accepted that 'there was no showing of a racial purpose or an invidious intent ... and that these standards had been applied fairly to whites and [black people] alike'. Nevertheless the statistics showed that while 34% of white males had completed high school, only 12% of black males had done so, and that the use by a different employer of these aptitude tests had in one instance resulted in a pass rate of 58% for whites and 6% for blacks.

Chief Justice Burger (pp 429–32):

The objective of Congress ... was to achieve equality of employment opportunities and remove barriers that have operated in the past to favour an identifiable group of white employees over other employees. Under the Act, practices, procedures or tests, neutral on their face, and even neutral in terms of intent, cannot be maintained if they operate to 'freeze' the status quo of prior discriminatory employment practices ...

The Act proscribes not only overt discrimination but also practices that are fair in form but discriminatory in operation. The touchstone is business necessity. If an employment practice which operates to exclude [black people] cannot be shown to be related to job performance, the practice is prohibited ...

[N]either the high school completion requirement nor the general intelligence test is shown to bear a demonstrable relationship to successful performance of the jobs for which it was used. Both were adopted ... without meaningful study of their relationship to job performance ability.

Congress directed the thrust of the Act to the *consequences* of employment practices, not simply the motivation. More than that, Congress has placed on the employer the burden of showing that any given requirement must have a manifest relationship to the employment in question.

Educational requirements are on their face neutral, yet because of the history of educational provision or lack of it in the American Deep South, disproportionately more black people were excluded. The disparity in achievement was outside the employer's control, yet still gave rise to liability. Of course, indirect discrimination will equally apply where the challenged requirement is more directly the responsibility of the employer, such as a requirement to have attained a given number of years' service in order to be eligible for promotion.

Relatively few cases of indirect racial discrimination have been brought under the Race Relations Act 1976; those that have been have tended to concern either educational and language qualifications, issues more to do with culture and religion than race in the narrow sense; the law has failed to get to grips with the social factors underpinning the economic disadvantage experienced by many minority ethnic groups.[3] Many more cases have been brought under the Sex Discrimination Act 1975, and the vast majority of these relate in some sense to the different life patterns of many women which reflect the ideological and practical constraints in juggling work and home. For example, any employment benefit which is dependent on working full time rather than part time will proportionately disadvantage far more women than men; the requirement or assumption of continuous work experience, thus putting women who have had a career break at a disadvantage, will have a similar effect. Other potentially indirectly discriminatory practices include height and strength requirements, given that, on average, there are physical differences between men and women.

THE THEORETICAL BASIS OF INDIRECT DISCRIMINATION LAW[4]

There is a sense in which the law of direct discrimination parallels criminal law and the law of tort in its focus on individual responsibility and blameworthiness. The law is less certain in its justification for imposing liability for indirect discrimination: one approach focuses on the knowledge or conduct of the defendant employer, restricting liability to situations where the employer has a degree of responsibility for the particular instance of adverse impact; another approach imposes liability if the defendant fails to take adequate steps to remove barriers which have historically existed, even though the employer may in no way have been responsible for the existence of such barriers. There is a close parallel between the justification for imposing liability for indirect discrimination and the justification for requiring employers to engage in some form of positive action.

Rutherglen, G, 'Disparate impact under Title VII: an objective theory of discrimination' (1987) 73 Virginia L Rev 1297, pp 1310–11:

The prevailing economic theories of discrimination confirm the need for objective evidence of discrimination, because objective economic incentives, as much as an employer's state of mind, motivate employers to engage in discrimination. According to Gary Becker, employers engage in discrimination

---

3   This contrasts with the situation in the USA, where most of the leading Supreme Court decisions on indirect discrimination have concerned race rather than gender. Apart from *Griggs*, examples include *Albemarle Paper Co v Moody* 422 US 405 (1975); *Dothard v Rawlinson* 433 US 321 (1977); *Watson v Fort Worth Bank and Trust* 487 US 977 (1988); and *Wards Cove Packing Co v Atonio* 490 US 642 (1989).

4   See, also, above, pp 68–71.

in order to satisfy tastes for discrimination: their own desire or the desires of their employees, customers, or suppliers not to associate with members of a disfavoured group. If employers cannot engage in explicit discrimination because it is obviously illegal, they will use other means to minimise contact between the group with discriminatory tastes and the disfavoured group: for example, neutral selection procedures that disproportionately screen out members of the disfavoured group. Moreover, employers could adopt these procedures without any taste for discrimination themselves or any intent to discriminate on their part. They might seek to obtain the benefits of satisfying others' tastes for discrimination, and they might even be unaware that these benefits derive from tastes for discrimination.

Likewise, according to the theory of statistical discrimination, employers screen out members of a disfavoured group because of the difficulty of accurately assessing their productivity. Employers can minimise the cost of assessing productivity and making mistakes in so doing by minimising the number of employees that they hire from the disfavoured group. They can do so by adopting neutral employment practices with adverse impact on the disfavoured group. For example, by setting artificially high minimum standards with an adverse impact on the disfavoured group, the employer can be assured of hiring only those members of the group most likely to be productive. It can screen out other members of the group whose productivity is more uncertain. Again, the employer may take these steps without any explicit intent to discriminate but simply to improve the predicted productivity of its work force as evaluated according to neutral standards.

This is a useful if somewhat conservative approach. Its strength is that it provides a justification for the imposition of liability for criteria over the existence of which the employer has no direct control and even, it seems, no knowledge of their adverse impact. Its weakness is that it proceeds from a purely meritocratic and individualistic approach to the allocation of employment benefits and opportunities. Indirect discrimination law does have the potential to recognise the ethical demand that society should make some attempt to secure some degree of redistribution of wealth and opportunities from privileged groups to those who have been historically less privileged.

Indirect discrimination is concerned with group disadvantage – situations where the attainments of a particular group are, on average, lower than those of another group – usually white males. The concern is with group rights, but this fails to resolve the issue of precisely what status such rights are to have. The two most extreme positions are as follows. First, indirect discrimination applies where we suspect that the employer is guilty of direct discrimination but the evidence is inconclusive. For example, in *Griggs*, the direct discrimination claim failed – perhaps marginally – but the inequality in educational achievement was so well known that the employer could hardly deny knowledge. Secondly, the objective of indirect discrimination may be seen as equality of outcome, whereby the employer is not permitted to utilise any employment practice which significantly differentiates between different relevant groups. This would require employment benefits to be allocated regardless of merit and in proportion to group membership in the relevant population – in other words, quotas. The main argument of principle against quotas is that they depart from the accepted mechanism of distributing goods and benefits in society based on individual merit. But as a practical defence mechanism, quotas may be inevitable unless employers are permitted to justify or provide an explanation for an observed difference between groups.

Willborn, S, 'The disparate impact model of discrimination: theory and limits' (1985) 34 American UL Rev 799, pp 801–03:

A pure disparate impact model would find discrimination whenever there is a disparate impact. A pure model would apply to all protected groups, would apply to all types of employer action, and would recognise no defences. A pure model, therefore, proposes that disparate impact equals discrimination. That proposition has not been accepted. There is a generally shared intuition that employment decisions need not always affect various groups equally. There are both ideological and practical reasons for this intuition. Ideologically, a pure disparate impact model seeking group justice conflicts with fairness and meritocracy [in] a society accustomed to individual justice concepts. Practically, a proportional distribution of employment benefits on the basis of group characteristics seems, at best, uneconomical and, at worst, impossible ...

The disparate impact model, therefore, recognises a limitation – business necessity. An employer practice is illegal only if it creates a disparate impact and is not justified by business necessity. The inquiry into business necessity examines the relationship between the employment criterion that has a disparate impact and the skills that are required to perform the job. If the criterion, despite its disparate impact, distinguishes between persons who are capable of performing the job and persons who are not capable of performing the job, the criterion is not illegal under current disparate impact theory.

Rutherglen, G, 'Discrimination and its discontents' (1995) 81 Virginia L Rev 117, pp 136–39:

The theory of disparate impact has had its principal effects ... in causing employers to abandon facially neutral employment practices, such as general aptitude tests, that have been successfully attacked using the theory and in encouraging employers to adopt affirmative action plans to eliminate the most obvious forms of disparate impact ... The theory was not originally devised as an inducement to engage in affirmative action, or at least it was not justified in those terms. It derived instead from the need to prevent evasion of Title VII through pretextual forms of discrimination. Judicial development of the theory, however, soon went beyond this limited goal ...

In its weakest form, the theory imposes only a light burden of justification upon the employer; it only extends the central prohibitions against discrimination and segregation to root out hidden discrimination. In its strongest form, the theory moves beyond the concept of discrimination to force employees to justify non-discriminatory practices that deny equal opportunity ... Faced with ambiguous statutory language codifying previous ambiguous case law, employers have apparently continued to do what proved successful in the past: abandon practices which have been condemned under the theory of disparate impact and engage in more or less voluntary (sometimes much less than voluntary) affirmative action ...[5]

In both American and English law, an employer is permitted to argue that a *prima facie* indirectly discriminatory practice is nevertheless justifiable if it can be shown to be essential in the interests of the business, especially if it enables the employer to select employees who are the best on merit. Thus a requirement that a job applicant have a degree in engineering will no doubt have an adverse impact on women, but normally this type of requirement will be justified, as it is presumably essential for the job and leads to a higher quality of applicant. However, to assume that it is easy to determine whether one applicant would be better for a business than another is unrealistic. To assume that merit both is and ought to be the basis for all hiring and promotion decisions is problematic both practically and ethically.[6]

Many employment practices have an effect which is *prima facie* indirectly discriminatory. Defendants are allowed to attempt to justify any such practice. The key difference between direct and indirect discrimination is that, for the former, good motive is no defence, whereas for the latter, assessing the purpose and effect of the defendant's behaviour via the concept of justification is central to the operation of the doctrine. It follows that the effectiveness of indirect discrimination law is greatly affected by the rigour with which the employer is put to the proof of justification. In this way the balance is drawn between permitting legal challenges to employer practices which work to the statistical disadvantage of protected groups, while permitting an employer to justify such requirements if they assist in the selection of the most meritorious applicants or advance other legitimate employer objectives. This requires a comparison to be drawn between the degree of the exclusion under challenge and the validity of the employer objective. Which is the superior value may involve implicit or explicit judgments, leaving a great deal to the sensitivity of the court or tribunal, and requiring appreciation of the way in which disadvantage may be socially reproduced. Not only that: the statutory definition of indirect discrimination is exceedingly complex, and this has itself been a factor in the relatively disappointing performance of this branch of anti-discrimination law.

---

[5] If the objective of indirect discrimination law is to promote voluntary action, there is no doubt that the British law has utterly failed in this regard.

[6] See above, pp 75–77.

THE DETAILS OF INDIRECT DISCRIMINATION LAW

Unlike the USA, British indirect discrimination law is spelt out in detail in the statutes rather than being left to be developed by the judges. This typically British approach to drafting has the advantage that some of the uncertainties of the American law were conclusively resolved at the legislative stage, but at the cost of a rigidity of wording which may prevent judges from focusing on the broader policy objectives of the law. Whether they would have relished or even accepted such a task is another question.

The claimant is not required to elect before the tribunal hearing whether the claim is to be based on direct or indirect discrimination; indeed it may not be clear which is the correct category. The difference between them is that direct discrimination requires proof of different treatment between the applicant and her comparator; indirect discrimination requires proof that the *same* requirement or condition was applied to them.[7]

Race Relations Act 1976

Section 1(1)

A person discriminates against another if:

...

(b) he applies to that other a requirement or condition which he applies or would apply equally to persons not of the same racial group as that other but:

> (i) which is such that the proportion of persons of the same racial group who can comply with it is considerably smaller than the proportion of persons not of that racial group who can comply with it; and

> (ii) which he cannot show to be justifiable irrespective of the colour, race, nationality or ethnic or national origins of the person to whom it is applied; and

> (iii) which is to the detriment of that other because he cannot comply with it.

---

[7] Thus, in *Hurley v Mustoe* [1981] ICR 490; [1981] IRLR 208, EAT, where the female applicant was refused a job because she had young children, direct discrimination was established because *different* criteria were applied to male and female applicants. Had the employer refused employment to anyone with prime responsibility for young children, it would have been a case of indirect discrimination as the requirement would have excluded more women than men. Again, *Bullock v Alice Ottley School* [1993] ICR 138; [1992] IRLR 564, CA, where the male gardener could retire at 65, but the female domestic had to retire at 60, was not a case of direct discrimination as the employers established that male domestics would have had to retire at 60 and female gardeners could work until 65. *Prima facie*, indirect discrimination was established as the requirement operated to the detriment of more women than men who wished to work until 65, but the requirement was held to be justified.

The wording of the SDA 1975 is effectively identical. Section 1(1)(b) replaces references to persons not of the same racial group with references to 'a man'.[8] So far as the detailed rules are concerned, the wording of the two acts and the cases decided under them are largely interchangeable.

There are four stages to a claim of indirect discrimination. First, has a requirement or condition been applied equally to both sexes or all racial groups? Secondly, is that requirement or condition one with which a considerably smaller proportion of women or persons of the relevant racial group can comply than men or persons not of that group? Thirdly, is the requirement or condition justifiable? Fourthly, has the imposition of the requirement or condition operated to the detriment of the person because he or she could not comply with it? While this is the order in which the issues are presented in the statute, as a matter of principle, policy and logical analysis, it makes sense to deal with the issue of justification last, as the other three are all concerned with the establishment of a *prima facie* case of indirect discrimination.

Requirement or condition

The first element in the definition is that a requirement or condition was or would have been applied equally to the claimant and to others of a different gender or race. The question has arisen whether the need to show a requirement or condition is itself contrary to European law.

The claim in *Enderby v Frenchay AHA*[9] was based on the lower average pay of speech therapists, mainly women, as compared with pharmacists and psychologists, mainly men. It was not possible to point to any particular factor or cause which led to this difference. It was, in effect, an equal pay case based on indirect discrimination, but no equivalent to a requirement or condition could be found. Nevertheless, the European Court held that the difference in average pay was sufficient to establish a *prima facie* case which would need to be justified: the claimant did not need to identify a particular cause or condition leading to the difference.

The question then arose whether *Enderby* meant that the need to establish a requirement or condition under the SDA 1975 (as opposed to the EqPA 1970) was now contrary to European law.

---

8 Section 3(1)(b), the section which deals with discrimination on the ground of being married, provides that the comparison is between a married person and an unmarried person of the same sex.

9 Case C-127/92 [1993] ECR I–5535; [1994] ICR 112; [1994] 1 All ER 495; [1993] IRLR 591.

Bhudi v IMI Refiners Ltd [1994] IRLR 204, EAT[10]

Part time female cleaners worked outside normal office hours, while male general service cleaners worked full time in normal office hours. It was decided to contract out the part time cleaning on grounds that 'the amount of administration required was disproportionate in terms of management resource to the services provided'. All the women were made redundant.

At first instance, an Industrial Tribunal[11] rejected a claim that the employers had applied a requirement relating to hours of work. The EAT held that this conclusion was wrong, but it was also argued that it was no longer necessary to establish a requirement or condition.

Mummery J (pp 206–07):

[The Advocate General in *Enderby* considered that attention] 'should be directed less to the existence of a requirement or a hurdle by means of which women suffer a disadvantage, and more to the discriminatory result'. The crucial question is whether this tribunal, as a court in the UK, is under an obligation to construe s 1(1)(b) [of the SDA 1975] in such a way as to disregard the express provision relating to a requirement or condition. In our view there are at least two reasons why there is no such obligation.

(a) We accept that ... *Enderby* was solely concerned with the interpretation and application of Art 119 and the Equal Pay Directive ... Although the provisions relating to equal pay are an aspect of indirect discrimination, different considerations apply. The provisions relevant to equal pay have not been drafted so as to impose expressly the onus of establishing a requirement or condition ...

(b) According to the present state of the authorities in the House of Lords, there is no obligation on a national court to distort the meaning of a statutory provision in domestic legislation in order to enforce against an individual a Community directive which has no direct effect as between individuals. The UK courts are under an obligation to construe legislation covered by Community directives so as to accord with the interpretation of the directive as laid down by the European Court if that can be done without distorting the meaning of the domestic legislation. This is so whether the domestic legislation came before or after the directive. It is however clear that the court should only construe domestic legislation to accord with the directive *if it is possible to do so*. The domestic legislation must be open to an interpretation which is consistent with the directive. [The court concluded that the sub-section was not open to divergent interpretations].

It is strongly arguable that this approach to the interpretation of the SDA 1975 is contrary to the Equal Treatment Directive.[12] Furthermore, the EC Burden of

---

10 See, also, [1994] ICR 307.

11 By the Employment Rights (Dispute Resolution) Act 1998, s 1(1), industrial tribunals are re-named employment tribunals.

12 Directive 76/207/EEC, OJ L39/40, 1976; see '*Enderby* has no effect on SDA construction' (1994) 55 EOR 41, pp 42–43.

Proof Directive,[13] intended to come into force in 2001, applies to both equal pay cases and equal treatment cases. Article 2(2) defines indirect discrimination as covering any 'neutral provision, criterion or practice'.[14] The reference to a practice focuses attention on the result of the employer's conduct, which was the approach taken by the European Court in *Enderby*; implementation of the Directive will necessarily have the effect of reversing the outcome in *Bhudi*. The distinction between the approach to be taken in sex discrimination and equal pay cases is not utilised by the European Court; in reality, the fact that there are in Great Britain different statutes[15] drafted differently is largely due to historical accident;[16] furthermore, the apparent refusal even to attempt to conclude that the SDA 1975 could be interpreted to accord with the Equal Treatment Directive, especially in a case such as this, where the fact of adverse impact and its statistical significance were so self-evident, is decidedly narrow minded. It can hardly be contended that such an approach advances the policy of the law: the phrase 'requirement or condition' is merely the jurisdictional route chosen by the drafters to enable the plaintiff to reach the meat of the discussion – adverse impact in fact. In policy terms the phrase has not and should not have been allowed to have any independent life of its own. Furthermore, if *Bhudi* is inconsistent with the Equal Treatment Directive, the correct interpretation could be directly relied upon by an applicant in a claim against an organ of the State. The difference in meanings between domestic and European law is made worse in light of the particularly narrow interpretation of domestic law in the cases of *Perera* and *Meer*, discussed below.

The remainder of this section is based on the assumption that at present it remains necessary for an applicant under the RRA 1976 or the SDA 1975 to establish that a requirement or condition was applied.

Clarke and Powell v Eley (IMI) Kynoch Ltd [1982] IRLR 482, EAT[17]

In a redundancy situation, part time workers were dismissed first.

Browne-Wilkinson J (p 485):

> We see no reason why the words 'requirement' and 'condition' should have wholly separate meanings. In our view, although not wholly synonymous, there is a large degree of overlap between the two words ... In our view, it is not right to give these words a narrow construction ... If the elimination of such

---

13 Directive 97/80/EEC. See 'EC Burden of Proof Directive' (1997) 76 EOR 37.

14 For a more detailed proposed amended definition, see *Reform of the Race Relations Act: Proposals from the Commission for Racial Equality*, 1998, London: CRE, p 17.

15 The EOC has recommended that the legislation should be consolidated in one overarching statute, partly to avoid problems of this kind. *Equality in the 21st Century: a New Approach*, 1998, Manchester: EOC, paras 5–9.

16 See above, pp 99–101. As a result of *Bhudi*, a race discrimination equivalent of *Enderby* would have to be decided against the applicant. Unequal pay cases on the ground of race are dealt with under the RRA 1976, there being no race equivalent to the EqPA 1970.

17 See, also, [1983] ICR 165.

practices is the policy lying behind the Act ... it is in our view a powerful argument against giving the words a narrower meaning thereby excluding cases which fall within the mischief which the Act was meant to deal with.

Home Office v Holmes [1984] IRLR 299, EAT[18]

After the birth of her baby a woman applied to her employers (the Civil Service) to return to her previous full time post on a part time basis. The request was refused. The Industrial Tribunal upheld her claim of indirect discrimination.

Waite J (p 301):

> It appears to us that words like 'requirement' and 'condition' are plain, clear words of wide import, fully capable of including any obligation of service whether for full time or part time, and we see no basis for giving them a restrictive interpretation in the light of the policy underlying the Act ...[19]

Once it was accepted that the terms 'requirement' and 'condition' do not convey fundamentally different ideas, the problem arose whether the legislation covered criteria which it was *preferred* that employees should possess, rather than being essential.

Perera v Civil Service Commission (No 2) [1982] IRLR 147, EAT[20]

The complaint centred on three attempts to obtain employment as a legal assistant in the Civil Service, and other jobs.

Browne-Wilkinson J (p 150):

> [I]t is not enough to show that the Board took into account one or more factors which candidates of Mr Perera's racial group were less likely to possess, since the lack of any one of those factors by itself could be offset by a plus factor. Only if the evidence established that the combined lack of a number of those factors constituted an absolute bar to selection would it have been demonstrated that a condition or requirement had been applied.[21]

---

[18] See, also, [1985] 1 WLR 71; [1984] 3 All ER 549.

[19] In *Clymo v Wandsworth London BC* [1989] ICR 250; [1989] IRLR 241, EAT, a refusal to permit a jobshare was held to be unchallengeable under SDA 1975 on the basis that a *requirement* had not been applied. It was reasoned that the job entailed by its nature full time working and thus no requirement had been applied by the council. Such an approach enables employers to deny women a jobshare arrangement without needing to show that there were objectively justifiable reasons for so doing. It must be regarded as wrongly decided and was not followed in the Northern Ireland case of *Briggs v North Eastern Education and Library Board* [1990] IRLR 181, NICA, where Hutton LCJ said 'the consideration that the nature of the job requires full time attendance does not prevent there being a "requirement" ... [T]he fact that the employer requires the employee to carry out the job she is employed to do does not mean that the employer does not "apply" a requirement to her'.

[20] See, also, [1982] ICR 350. The judgment of the EAT was upheld by the Court of Appeal on other grounds. See [1983] ICR 428; [1983] IRLR 166.

[21] In *Meer v London Borough of Tower Hamlets* [1989] IRLR 399, the Court of Appeal considered it was bound by *Perera* and so the same outcome was reached, even though Balcombe LJ accepted that there were 'strong arguments for [the] submission that the absolute bar construction ... may not be consistent with the object of the Act'.

It is arguable that the more senior the job under consideration, the less likely it is that particular requirements will be essential rather than merely preferred. Furthermore, a significant proportion of indirect discrimination cases, especially those where the alleged discrimination has been between full time and part time workers, have been concerned not with the process of obtaining a job in the first place but with access to benefits attaching to the job. Indirect discrimination law has been utilised very little as a challenge to entry barriers. The *Perera* rule makes this situation worse, though other factors – both substantive and procedural – which have limited the effectiveness of indirect discrimination law are probably of greater significance.[22]

The EAT in Scotland has now refused to follow *Perera*.

Falkirk Council v Whyte [1997] IRLR 560

The issue concerned the use of two factors, managerial training and experience, utilised in the appointment to a prison managerial post. The Industrial Tribunal upheld the complaint of indirect discrimination, observing that while the challenged criteria were only stated to be desirable, 'it was very clear that in practice, in the way in which the interview panel operated, they were the decisive factors ...'.

The EAT dismissed the appeal.

Lord Johnston (pp 561–62):

[T]he tribunal were ... liberally interpreting what is meant by a 'requirement or condition' ... We consider that this approach was open to the tribunal and ... not one with which we feel able to interfere. We would observe in passing that if the case turned upon whether or not the relevant factors ... had to be an absolute bar ... we would not be inclined to follow ... *Perera*. We consider that each case has to be determined on its own merits, and the status of the factors in question relevant to the application for the post in question very much depends upon the circumstances of the particular case ... [I]f material, and it is shown otherwise that qualifying for the particular factor is more difficult for women than for men ... we do not see why that should not be a condition or requirement in terms of the legislation in relation to applications for the post ...

While the conclusion is correct, the fact that the decision is treated as one of fact for the Tribunal somewhat weakens the authority of this case. The primary conclusion appears to be that the tribunal was entitled to find that there was a requirement or condition. By itself, the case cannot be said to have conclusively achieved what is surely inevitable – the overturning of *Perera* – but it anticipates its reversal at the latest when the Draft Burden of Proof Directive becomes part of English law.

---

[22] In the context of redundancy selection criteria, *Perera* was recently followed in *Hall v Shorts Missile Systems Ltd*; see (1997) 72 EOR 39.

Even when this occurs, it will not be straightforward to apply indirect discrimination law to the commonplace situation, especially as regards senior positions, where hiring procedures are largely subjective in nature, that is, where multiple selection criteria are combined in a way where it is impossible to allocate exact weightings to different factors; indeed, different selectors may have been influenced by different factors.

Watches of Switzerland v Savell [1983] IRLR 141, EAT

The claim was of a failure to be promoted to branch manager. The applicant argued that there were serious defects in their procedure which meant that women were less likely to be considered for promotion.

The tribunal held that there was no direct discrimination, but that a claim of indirect discrimination was made out.

The EAT allowed the employer's appeal on indirect discrimination on the decidedly dubious ground that the procedure in question did not operate to her detriment. But the significance of the case lies in the holding that the employer had applied a requirement or condition.

Waterhouse J (pp 145–46):

[T]he relevant criticisms of the promotions procedure ... were as follows:

(1) Impending appointments were not advertised to staff and women were less likely than men to ask to be considered for promotion.

(2) Persons under consideration for promotion were not interviewed.

(3) There were no clear guidelines to branch managers about the criteria to be applied in the regular assessments and appraisals; and some appraisals, including those of Mrs Savell, were out of date.

(4) The criteria for promotion were not written; they were subjective and not made known to persons in line for promotion.

(5) The employers made a point of promoting their own staff and paid particular attention to training when searching for potential managers, but Mrs Savell was unaware of the importance attached to training for which she could have volunteered ...

[On appeal] the requirement or condition was phrased as follows:

'... that to be promoted to the post of manager ... one must satisfy the criteria of a vague, subjective, unadvertised promotion procedure which does not provide any or any adequate mechanisms to prevent subconscious bias unrelated to the merits of candidates ...'

[A] requirement or condition of the kind formulated on behalf of Mrs Savell is capable of being a requirement or condition to which the Act applies ...

There is clearly a strong argument that, in the light of *Perera* and *Meer*, this case should be regarded as wrong. But should those cases be overruled, the importance of cases such as *Savell* will need re-asserting. It is an instructive case as it illustrates how sloppy procedures can so easily work to the disadvantage of women. It is hardly surprising that the allegation of direct discrimination was not made out; the very subjectivity of the procedures may make such a task almost impossible. The danger is that indirect discrimination law will be held unavailable where it is especially needed to overcome the difficulty of proving that subjective procedures were operated in a directly discriminatory manner. At present it makes sense for a well advised employer to avoid essential requirements which might be challenged and rely more on preferences and guiding factors. But, if the law is to apply to subjective procedures, it should be sufficient for a *prima facie* case to show any significant disparity in success rates. This would throw the burden of justification on the employer. It will be argued later that such a burden should be within the reach of the average employer and should not require a highly technical and statistical approach to validating selection techniques.

In America, both academic argument and judicial authority supports the use of indirect discrimination law in this type of case.

Bartholet, E, 'Application of Title VII to jobs in high places' (1982) 95 Harv L Rev 947, pp 955–58, 978–80:

For candidates who satisfy minimum objective qualifications, the final decision making tends to be largely subjective, based on evaluations of the candidates' previous work and potential for future performance.

Selection systems of this sort are likely to have an adverse racial impact. Blacks as a group are far less likely than whites to have had the education and experience that have traditionally been the prerequisites for these jobs. Use of such credentials – either as minimum objective requirements or as part of a subjective evaluation process – seriously limits black access to upper level positions. Subjective systems ... allow for the expression both of conscious bias and of the unconscious bias that is likely to result in the exclusion of persons who are visibly different from those doing the selecting ...

[Disparate impact litigation in the United States] has helped destroy the notion that the meritocratic principle is the norm governing job allocation. The systems exposed have not been outlawed because employers could not meet an impossibly strict standard of validation; they have been outlawed because they were revealed to be inconsistent with merit selection ... The *Griggs* doctrine, with its demand for proof of business necessity, can and should serve a similar function with respect to upper level employment systems ...

Enforcement of *Griggs* at the upper level would generate pressure for racially proportionate hiring from among the pool of those with conceded minimum qualifications ... [This] is as it should be. Validation and other proof of business necessity are particularly difficult on the upper level, largely because we are unsure what we mean by effective performance in our most important jobs. Our notions of effective performance are necessarily value laden, reflecting what are often essentially political choices. These considerations militate in favour of opening such jobs to groups traditionally excluded from them ...

[A] differential standard is elitist. The courts distinguish between selection systems primarily on the basis of the social and economic status of the job involved. They have intervened freely in low-status jobs, even when poor performance in those jobs might have threatened significant economic and safety interests. But with high-status jobs, a hands-off attitude has prevailed.

Judges defer to the employers with whom they identify, and they uphold the kinds of selection systems from which they have benefited. When they deal with prestigious jobs, the courts show an appreciation of the apparent rationality of the employment procedures at issue and a respect for the decision makers involved that can only be explained by the fact that these confront the courts with their own world. Judges have a personal investment in traditional selection procedures on the upper level ...

Judges must develop ... analytic distance in looking at upper level selection systems. The *Griggs* doctrine encourages such detachment. By rejecting apparent common sense as a sufficient defence, it forces courts to analyse their own assumptions. By insisting that employers produce evidentiary justifications for their systems, the doctrine educates courts about the actual strengths and weaknesses of these justifications.

Watson v Fort Worth Bank and Trust 487 US 977 (1988), US Supreme Court

The black applicant was rejected for promotion to supervisory positions in the bank. The employers had no formal criteria for the position, but relied on the subjective judgment of white supervisors. The United States Supreme Court held that the doctrine of disparate impact could be applied to challenge such a subjective procedure.

Justice O'Connor (pp 989–91, 999):

We are persuaded that our decisions in *Griggs* and succeeding cases could largely be nullified if disparate impact analysis were applied only to standardised selection practices. However, one might distinguish 'subjective' from 'objective' criteria, it is apparent that selection systems that combine both types would generally have to be considered subjective in nature ... So long as an employer refrained from making standardised criteria absolutely determinative, it would remain free to give such tests almost as much weight as it chose without risking a disparate impact challenge. If we announced a rule that allowed employers so easily to insulate themselves from liability under Griggs, disparate impact analysis might effectively be abolished.

We are also persuaded that disparate impact analysis is in principle no less applicable to subjective employment criteria than to objective or standardised tests. In either case, a facially neutral practice, adopted without discriminatory intent, may have effects that are indistinguishable from intentionally discriminatory practices ... [E]ven if one assumed that any ... discrimination can be adequately policed through disparate treatment analysis, the problem of subconscious stereotypes and prejudices would remain ... If an employer's undisciplined system of subjective decision making has precisely the same effects as a system pervaded by impermissible intentional discrimination, it is difficult to see why Title VII's proscription against discriminatory action should not apply ...

In the context of subjective or discretionary employment decisions, the employer will often find it easier than in the case of standardised tests to produce evidence of 'a manifest relationship to the employment in question'. It is self-evident that many jobs, for example, those involving managerial responsibilities, require personal qualities that have never been considered amenable to standardised testing.

Establishing adverse impact

The statute requires the applicant to establish that the *proportion* of those in the applicant's group who can comply with the requirement is considerably smaller than the proportion not in that group. This is a complex task. It necessitates, first, deciding which groups should be compared with each other, and, secondly, deciding whether there is a significant difference in the statistics on the different groups being compared.[23]

The use and availability of statistics

What is here being considered is a statistical comparison between those who can comply with a requirement and those who cannot. There is an important distinction between race and gender discrimination, in that it can normally be assumed that women and men are equally distributed throughout the population. This means that, if such matters as average height or average educational achievement are being considered, it will usually be possible to obtain the figures and their interpretation will be straightforward.

The position as far as race is concerned is far less simple, for three reasons. First, the national distribution of black people and white people is extremely uneven. It may be realistic to aim at 50% of women in a particular position but it will not be possible to arrive at an appropriate figure for black people without consideration of the numbers of black people in the relevant local labour market. Secondly, there are only two genders, but there are many races. This raises the very complex statistical question of which race should be compared with which. Should it be whites against non-whites, whites against Asians, whites against Pakistanis, etc?[24] The particular basis for comparison which is chosen may determine whether disparate impact can be demonstrated. Thirdly, and following from the previous point, in many cases the statistics are simply unavailable. National census statistics may be too

---

[23] See Lustgarten, L, 'Problems of proof in employment discrimination cases' (1977) 6 Industrial LJ 212, pp 218–28.

[24] In *Orphanos v Queen Mary College* [1985] AC 761; [1985] 2 All ER 233; [1985] IRLR 359, HL, a case involving indirect discrimination against Cypriots, it was held that the proper comparison was not between Cypriots and British people, but between Cypriots and everyone else not of that nationality. This cannot be right: it makes the task of assembling statistics all the harder, and ignores the fact that the allegedly indirectly discriminatory requirement affected other non-British nationals and not simply Cypriots.

generalised to serve the needs of a potential litigant, while there is no obligation on employers to keep detailed statistics concerning their own workforce.[25] Even so, it is far easier to build a case of indirect discrimination when the statistical focus is simply the current workforce rather than the populace at large; thus a high proportion of such cases concerns promotions and dismissals rather than original appointments. Even here, there is certainly no guarantee that, for example, statistics on the success rate in promotions procedures broken down by race and gender will be available.

There has been a recognition both that statistics may be unavailable and that their interpretation and presentation to the tribunal may be beyond the means of an unrepresented applicant.

Perera v Civil Service Commission (No 2) [1982] IRLR 147, EAT[26]

In relation to the statistics concerning his application for the position of administrative trainee, Browne-Wilkinson J commented (pp 151–52):

> [T]here remains the root problem that, by any normal statistical standard, the only statistical evidence laid before the Industrial Tribunal is in fact inadequate. It is based on a very small sample from a very small number of non-typical offices. Is it therefore right to hold that the applicant has proved his case? ... On the one hand the burden is on the applicant to prove his case and, viewed in isolation, the statistics produced do not prove it. On the other hand, it is most undesirable that, in all cases of indirect discrimination, elaborate statistical evidence should be required before the case can be found proved. The time and expense involved in preparing and proving statistical evidence can be enormous, as experience in the USA has demonstrated. It is not good policy to require such evidence to be put forward unless it is clear that there is an issue as to whether the requirements of s 1(1)(b)(i) [of the RRA 1976] have been satisfied.

As long as *some* evidence is forthcoming, the burden will shift to the defendant to discredit the plaintiff's statistics. What is noticeable, certainly by contrast with the USA, is how few indirect discrimination cases have involved statistical evidence which is more than elementary. While understandable and in one sense commendable, it is clear that a more sophisticated approach to statistics may increase the reach of indirect discrimination law. By comparison, both in equal pay cases where many claims are heard together, and in cases where the EOC is seeking judicial review, the sophistication of the statistics is greatly enhanced.

A vital way in which the task of applicants is simplified is by the willingness of tribunals to take judicial notice of statistical truths which are

---

[25] As is the case with direct discrimination, employers who monitor their workforce by race and gender may thereby render themselves more vulnerable to a claim, especially as such statistics may be obtainable via the discovery procedure. See above, pp 169–71.

[26] See, also, [1982] ICR 350.

clear and well established. This is again far more straightforward in gender cases than in race cases. Examples of difference and disadvantage which affect women tend to do so evenly across the country in regular and predictable patterns, so the resultant disparities are likely to be significant and well known. Patterns of part time work are clear examples here. But there other instances. For example, in *Briggs v North Eastern Education and Library Board*[27] judicial notice was taken of the fact that fewer female married teachers would be able to take after-school activities than male married teachers; and in *Meade-Hill v National Union of Civil and Public Servants*[28] it was accepted that, in practice, mobility requirements had a greater impact on women than on men.

So far, so good. But this approach – coupled with the approach that says that the interpretation of statistics is primarily a matter of fact for the Employment Tribunal – exposes the parties to the risk of whimsical decisions. In *Kidd v DRG (UK) Ltd*,[29] a case of alleged marital status discrimination, the tribunal, referring to the changing nature of family and employment life, refused to take judicial notice that a requirement to be in full time employment was one with which a considerably smaller proportion of married women with children than unmarried women with children could comply. The EAT held that this approach was within the tribunal's discretion; the argument was rejected that 'any tribunal which declines to act on generalised assumptions which they regard as too unsafe for acceptance is acting unreasonably'.

A different and more principled approach was adopted in *London Underground Ltd v Edwards*,[30] a case concerning the effect of new rostering arrangements. Mummery J said that the 'correct question ... is whether the condition or requirement of availability for rostering was such that a considerably smaller proportion of women qualified to be train operators ... could comply with it [rather than the approach of the tribunal of asking whether] a considerably smaller proportion of *female single parents* than *male single parents* could comply with it ... The pool consisted of train operators, male and female, to whom the new rostering arrangements were applied ... The fact that lone motherhood is more frequent than lone fatherhood does not mean that the proportion of lone mothers able to comply with rostering is considerably smaller than the proportion of lone fathers able to do so, either among London Underground train operators or generally'.[31]

---

27 [1990] IRLR 181, NICA.
28 [1995] ICR 847; [1996] 1 All ER 79; [1995] IRLR 478, CA.
29 [1985] ICR 405; [1985] IRLR 190, EAT.
30 [1995] ICR 574; [1995] IRLR 355, EAT.
31 [1995] IRLR 355, EAT, pp 357–58.

The basis of comparison

The next question concerns who should be compared with whom – or, in more technical language, what is the appropriate pool for comparison. It is vital to grasp that we are dealing with proportions rather than numbers. To illustrate, suppose that a test is taken by 500 women and 200 men. Suppose further that the test is passed by 100 women and 100 men. It is clear that a *prima facie* case of indirect discrimination will have been made out. It is irrelevant that the same *numbers* of men and women pass the test; what matters is that only 20% of women pass while 50% of the men do so. It is also clear that on these figures any tribunal will find that there has been a significant disparity in outcome – the test was passed by a considerably smaller proportion of women than men.

The following cases demonstrate how the process operates.

Jones v Chief Adjudication Officer [1990] IRLR 533, CA

Mustill LJ (p 537):

As I understand it, the process for establishing [indirect] discrimination takes the following shape ...

(1) Identify the criterion for selection.

(2) Identify the relevant population, comprising all those who satisfy the other criteria for selection. (I do not know to what extent this step in the process is articulated in the cases. To my mind it is vital to the intellectual soundness of the demographic argument.)

(3) Divide the relevant population into groups representing those who satisfy the criteria and those who do not.

(4) Predict statistically what proportion of each group should consist of women.

(5) Ascertain what are the actual male/female balances in the two groups.

(6) Compare the actual with the predicted balances.

(7) If women are found to be under-represented in the first group and over-represented in the second group, it is proved that the criterion is discriminatory ...

Stage one involves identifying the requirement or condition, stages two to six involve selecting the appropriate pool for comparison and discovering the statistics appropriate to such pool, and stage seven asks the 'considerably smaller question'. To illustrate how this operates in practice, consider the following case decided under the Fair Employment (Northern Ireland) Act 1989, where a more sophisticated understanding of the statistical issues was manifested than perhaps in any other case.

McAusland v Dungannon DC [1993] IRLR 583, NICA

The post of chief works manager was filled by seeking applications only from local government staff in Northern Ireland. The Fair Employment Tribunal held that this was a requirement or condition which excluded anyone from outside the local government service from being appointed. The tribunal looked at the proportions from each community of local government employees in Standard Occupational Classifications 1, 2 and 3, as representing those with appropriate qualifications. It was held that the proportion of Catholics who could comply was 1.5% and of Protestants 2.1%, and that this was not a considerably smaller proportion.

A re-hearing reached a different conclusion on the last point, and that was the issue on appeal.

McDermott LJ (p 585):

(1) The relevant class of employee to be considered was comprised of those in the grades referred to as standard occupational classifications (SOC) 1, 2 and 3. [This is to ensure that the comparison is limited to those with the basic qualification for the job in question, and is the inevitably rough and ready means of satisfying step two in *Jones*, above.]

(2) The number of district council employees ... in SOC 1, 2 and 3 were Protestant: 1,039; Roman Catholic: 423 ... [Thus] 71% ... was Protestant and 29% Roman Catholic.

(3) In the total Northern Ireland workforce there were, in SOC grades 1, 2 and 3, Protestant: 50,170; Roman Catholic: 28,159 ... 64% Protestant and 36% Roman Catholic.

(4) [There must be] a comparison between the group fulfilling the condition or requirement (LGS – SOC 1, 2 and 3) and the appropriate comparable group, those in SOC grades 1, 2 and 3 in the general workforce in Northern Ireland; a formula had to be applied. That favoured by the tribunal and accepted by both parties before us was PY/PT compared to CY/CT. In it, P refers to Protestant, C refers to Roman Catholic, Y refers to those who can comply with the requirement, T refers to the total in the comparable class.

(5) Using that formula, the result was PY/PT = 0.0207 (say 0.021) and CY/CT = 0.015.

(6) Grossing up those figures, 1.5 (Roman Catholics) can be expressed as 71% of 2.1 (Protestants). Thus, it can be said that the success chance for Roman Catholics ... is 29% less ... than for Protestants ...

The approach expounded in *Jones* thus worked as follows: the criterion for selection was to be a current employee of the Northern Ireland local government service. It was agreed that the only such employees who would have the necessary skills and qualifications for the professional position at issue were those in Standard Occupational Classifications 1, 2 and 3. There is no suggestion that Catholics formed a lower proportion in those groups than in the population at large. Had they done so, that would have been a factor of crucial importance. The comparison must be with those who are otherwise qualified for the job in question apart from their membership of the protected group. This was stressed in *Jones* and in principle must be correct. The proportion of Catholics who could comply then had to be compared with the proportion of Protestants. For Catholics, 423 out of 28,159 could comply (0.15%); for Protestants, 1039 out of 50,170 (0.21%). It is these last percentage figures which must be compared in order to determine if one is considerably smaller than the other, bearing in mind that 0.15 is 29% lower than 0.21.

In order to determine who should be compared, it is essential to ensure that the comparison made is with those who are otherwise qualified for the job apart from the requirement being challenged.

Pearse v City of Bradford Metropolitan Council [1988] IRLR 379, EAT

The applicant was a part time lecturer in the department of applied and community services at Ilkley College. A vacancy arose for a full time post in student counselling. There was an agreement with the union that, in the first instance, only full time workers were eligible to apply. She claimed that the requirement to be a full time worker was indirectly discriminatory against women. She submitted statistics showing that 21.8% of the female academic staff employed in the college were female, compared with 46.7% of male academic staff. The employers contended that the appropriate comparison was between women and men who had appropriate qualifications for the vacant post, and that there was no evidence concerning the impact of the requirement on men and women within that pool.

Her claim failed.

Hutchison J (p 381):

What could be more sensible, when considering what selection to make for purposes of comparison in relation to a requirement or condition biting upon an application for a post requiring particular qualifications, to look to those qualified to apply ...

[She failed to show that the proportion of men from the appropriate pool who could apply for the post was greater than the proportion of women. However, a more lenient EAT might have remitted the case to another Industrial Tribunal to give her the opportunity to produce the statistics in question.]

Jones v University of Manchester [1993] IRLR 218, CA[32]

The employers wanted a graduate careers adviser aged 27–35; the desire was for a younger person, to have someone closer in age and outlook to the students. The applicant was 46 and claimed that the requirement was indirectly discriminatory against women who were mature students – she did not get her degree until she was 41. The essence of the claim was that female mature students are, on average, rather older than male mature students. Her claim failed.

---

[32] Criticised by Hervey, T, 'Structural discrimination unrecognised' (1994) 57 MLR 307.

Evans LJ (pp 228–29):

If the numbers of women and of men, respectively, remaining after the requirement is applied are to be compared as 'proportions' of something other than the total number of those who can comply, then the question arises, as proportions of what? One possibility is, as proportions of 'all men' and 'all women', even of 'all humanity' ... The other possibility is what Mustill LJ called 'the relevant population', meaning all persons who satisfy the relevant criteria apart from the requirement or condition which is under consideration ... In my judgment, [this approach] is much to be preferred ... It is, in effect, the total number of all those persons, men and women, who answer the description contained in the advertisement, apart from the age requirement. Here, that means all graduates with the relevant experience.

[D]iscrimination ... cannot be established; the statistics only support the applicant's case if comparison is limited to mature graduates aged between 25 and 29 ... years of age ...

I have wondered throughout this appeal whether Parliament can have envisaged the kind of detail which has been produced in this case. Even these figures involve a considerable amount of approximation; for example, the numbers and ages of those attending university are taken apparently as the numbers and ages of those who obtain degrees, and there are no precise figures for those who graduate and are able to acquire the relevant experience, before or after graduating, before the age of 35.

In *Pearse*, the statistics cited were too wide: her statistics dealt with all the college academic staff rather than just those qualified for the advertised post. In *Jones*, her statistics were too narrow, focusing on female mature students rather than female students in general. While female mature students may tend to be older than men, and thus less likely to meet the requirement in question, the requirement only required a graduate, mature or otherwise. There was no reason at all to suppose that women graduates as a whole were proportionately disadvantaged by that requirement.[33]

The selection of the appropriate pool may be a highly technical exercise fraught with difficulty both for litigants, as *Pearse*, in particular, demonstrates, and for tribunals. The EAT has attempted to deflect the problem by emphasising that the question of the appropriate pool is one of fact for the tribunal. In *Kidd v DRG (UK) Ltd*,[34] Waite J said that the 'choice of an

---

[33] A similar need to ask the right question is apparent from *Kirshammer-Hack v Sidal* Case C-189/91 [1993] ECR I-6185; [1994] IRLR 185. Under German law, firms employing fewer than five workers are exempt from unfair dismissal law, and in making that calculation those who work less than 10 hours per week are disregarded. The applicant, a woman who worked more than 10 hours per week, claimed that the law contravened the Equal Treatment Directive as being indirectly discriminatory. The appropriate issue was not whether disproportionately more women work part time, but whether disproportionately more women worked for employers employing less than five employees.

[34] [1985] ICR 405; [1985] IRLR 190, EAT.

appropriate section of the population is in our judgment an issue of fact ... entrusted by Parliament to the good sense of the tribunals ... [There was no] error in deciding that the proper section of the community for the purposes of making the statutory comparison ... was the section of the population living in households needing to provide home care for children to an extent that would normally be incompatible with the acceptance of full time employment ...' In *Greater Manchester Police Authority v Lea*[35] it was argued that using the economically active population as the pool was far too wide because it included those who could not, for intellectual and other reasons, realistically apply for the post and also people who would have been over-qualified and would not have been interested in applying for such a job. The EAT said that the 'underlying consideration [is] that this is an issue of fact and judgment and that this is a matter in which it has to be shown that the tribunal has adopted a course which is outside the range of selection for any reasonable tribunal ...'. Furthermore, while it was accepted that the applicant's statistics were not perfect, the employers had put in no statistics of their own and thus were in effect estopped from denying the applicability of the only statistics which were available.

There are two further problems with selection of the appropriate pool, both of which demonstrate how much easier it may be to utilise indirect discrimination law as regards intra-firm practices rather than original hirings. The first point is that to compare the success rate of black and white applicants to a firm may be misleading, as it leaves out of account any reasons which may dissuade people from applying in the first place. There may be many factors, some discriminatory and others not, which may prevent the applicant pool being in any sense a representative sample. 'Demarcating the qualified applicant pool is particularly difficult, an as accurate study must count the number of potential or "discouraged" qualified applicants who would have applied but for their knowledge of the employer's discriminatory practices. This must be achieved by engaging in a complex [and very expensive] economic and geographic analysis ...'[36]

The second problem concerns the issue of the appropriate labour market. The concern here is to delineate the proportion of qualified minorities in the labour market from which the employer might reasonably be expected to hire. This is not usually a problem in sex discrimination cases, as, without more detailed evidence, it can safely be assumed that women and men with any given qualifications are evenly distributed throughout the community. Similarly, the Court in *McAusland* regarded Northern Ireland as sufficiently small that it could be treated as one labour market. The issue is especially

---

35 [1990] IRLR 372, EAT.
36 Garaud, M, 'Legal standards and statistical proof in Title VII litigation: in search of a coherent disparate impact model' (1990) 139 Penns UL Rev 455, p 474.

acute with race: the different races are extremely unevenly distributed, and are likely to have very different proportions with appropriate qualifications. One possible explanation of why this issue has not troubled the courts is simply the unavailability of detailed local labour market statistics pertaining to race. In *Hazlewood School District v United States*,[37] the allegation was that the employers had engaged in a pattern and practice of direct discrimination. The case was largely built on the statistical evidence that few black teachers were employed compared with their number in the surrounding geographical area. The question, to which there is no logical answer, is what is the appropriate labour market for the purpose of comparison. It will often be the case that the smaller the market utilised, the higher will be the black population within it, and thus the easier the task to demonstrate significant statistical disparity.

The 'considerably smaller' question

The previous section has focused on the issue of what statistics are relevant: this section is concerned with how to interpret those statistics. It has to be shown that the proportion of women or black people who can comply is considerably smaller than the proportion of men or white people. If *any* disparity were sufficient to raise a *prima facie* case of adverse impact, then the only certain means of avoiding a claim would be to utilise quotas. The legislation does not mandate that each group should be represented in employment situations in proportion to its numbers in the population, even though some might regard that as the aim to be sought. One of the ways that this tension between ends and means is mediated is through the 'considerably smaller' requirement; the smaller the disparity which is accepted as significant, the greater will be the burden on the employer.

The issue also raises mathematical considerations – issues of statistical significance concerning the likelihood that a particular result arose by chance. If 10 people passed a test, seven men out of 10 applicants and three women out of 10 applicants, the male pass rate is 70% and the female pass rate 30%. While there appears to be a significant disparity, both common sense and statisticians would accept that the result may have arisen for other reasons. But if 100 had passed the test, 70 men and 30 women, the proportions and percentages would be identical, but we should now be suspicious. And if there were 1000 successes, 700 men and 300 women, we should be almost certain that a gender-related factor was involved so as to give rise to a *prima facie* case of discrimination.[38] It follows that a hard and fast approach, such as

---

[37]   433 US 299 (1977).

[38]   If there were 10,000 applicants, even a 1% difference might be regarded as statistically significant, but it is questionable whether it should carry any legal weight.

the four-fifths rule conventionally operated by the United States Equal Employment Opportunities Commission, is statistically flawed, even if it be regarded, for its simplicity, as having practical merit. Under that approach, if blacks or women pass at a rate less than 80% of the white or male pass rate, that would give rise to a *prima facie* case of discrimination. This simplistic approach has no regard for the total numbers involved. It might have some use as a guide to equal opportunities practitioners, but should not determine the outcome of litigation. In addition, one of the problems with indirect discrimination law in the UK is that the numbers involved in hiring and other employment decisions are rarely large enough for meaningful statistical conclusions to be drawn. It is important that if only small samples are available, they are not simply rejected, but considered with other evidence in the determination of whether adverse impact is shown.[39]

The issues of legal proof and statistical significance must be kept distinct. Statisticians may not accept that a given result is significant at less than the 95% significance – a less than 5% chance that the observed result occurred by chance. But such a high level of proof is unnecessary and inappropriate in a court of law.[40] The plaintiff's burden is to establish a *prima facie* case merely on a balance of probabilities; the defendant has the opportunity to justify the practice which leads to adverse impact, and the weight of the burden of establishing justification does and should vary according to the degree of adverse impact which is established. It is to the credit of the British courts – accidental, perhaps, as advocates have rarely invited them to do so – that they have not been drawn into the statistical technicalities which so bedevil this aspect of American discrimination law. As a result, the question of what is a considerably smaller proportion becomes a question of fact, as the following cases illustrate.[41]

Staffordshire County Council v Black [1995] IRLR 234, EAT

The case concerned benefits available to part time teachers made redundant compared with those available to full time teachers. The tribunal said there

---

[39] '[T]he fact that a disparity is not statistically significant does not necessarily mean that it is not "practically significant" in the sense that it may be of a size which is considered important and indicative of possible discrimination. Conversely, a small disparity which is of little or no practical significance may nevertheless be shown to be "statistically significant" if based upon a sufficiently large sample of cases.' Sugrue, T and Fairley, W, 'A case of unexamined assumptions: the use and misuse of the statistical analysis of *Castenada/Hazlewood* in discrimination legislation' (1983) 24 Boston College L Rev 925, p 933, n 39.

[40] *Op cit*, Garaud, fn 36, pp 468–69.

[41] It is arguable that the EAT misread the legislation in *Greater Manchester Police Authority v Lea* [1990] IRLR 372, EAT. There, 99.4% of women and 95.3% of men could comply with the requirement of not being in receipt of an occupational pension. It is unlikely that such disparity should have been regarded as significant. But the EAT focused on the failure rate: the requirement excluded 4.7% of men and 0.6% of women. This disparity is significant, but should not have been relevant, as the legislation, for correct statistical reasons, directs comparison to the proportions who can comply with the requirement in question rather than the proportions who cannot.

was a requirement or condition that in order to qualify for the maximum additional service credit, an employee had to be employed full time at the date of dismissal. While the proportion of women teachers over 50 who were full time (89.5%) was held not to be considerably smaller than the same proportion of male teachers (97.0%), the Industrial Tribunal upheld the complaint under Art 119 of the Treaty of Rome on the basis that the condition affected a far greater number of women than men.

The EAT allowed the employer's appeal.

Morison J (pp 237–38):

What is or is not a 'considerably smaller proportion' is a matter for the Industrial Tribunal. The figures speak for themselves. Overall there are more full time women teachers than men. No doubt for historical reasons there are proportionately slightly less women than men in the over-50 age range, although, again, in absolute terms there are more women than men doing full time work in that bracket. A difference of 7.5 percentage points, in the context, is very small ... It is not unhelpful to keep in mind that the European Court refers to 'a much lower proportion' or a 'considerably lower percentage'...

McAusland v Dungannon District Council [1993] IRLR 583, NICA

The applicant argued that the 'four-fifths' rule should be adopted.

McDermott LJ (pp 585–86):

[The words 'considerably smaller'] are words in daily usage and do not require definition. They were not defined by Parliament and we think no useful purpose would be served by any judicial definition or interpretation ... In our judgment, Parliament has chosen to leave these words undefined, relying on the good sense and experience of [the tribunal] to produce a fair and relevant conclusion ...

The introduction of [the four-fifths] rule, if considered wise or helpful, should be by Parliament and not by judicial decision. We think it would be unwise to introduce such a test without a real knowledge of American law, a true understanding of the application of the rule in practice and the benefit of in-depth research on the impact of such a rule on industrial relations in the UK ...

[I]t could be said that the success chance for Roman Catholics ... was 29% less than for Protestants and, having regard to this, the tribunal was entitled to reverse its decision on the 'considerably smaller' question.

London Underground Ltd v Edwards (No 2) [1997] IRLR 157, EAT

A single mother with a young child was employed as a train operator. Her rostering arrangements allowed her to be at home in the mornings and evenings. She normally worked from 8 am to 4 pm or 8.30 am to 4.30 pm, with Saturday as a rest day, and as a result she did not receive shift bonuses for working between 6 pm and 7 am.

In 1991, a new flexible shift pattern was announced – duties were to begin at 4.45 am and were to include Sundays. Although it was possible to change shifts so as to avoid early and late work, the trade-off was a longer shift for the same money. She was not prepared to work the new system and when negotiations between management and unions about special arrangements for single parents were unable to reach agreement, she resigned and claimed indirect sex discrimination.

The second industrial tribunal[42] found that 100% of the 2,023 male train operators could comply with the requirement. Mrs Edwards was the only one of the 21 female train operators who positively complained that she could not comply, so that the proportion of women who could comply was 95.2%. However, the tribunal had regard to the small number of female train operators, stated that it was common knowledge that females are more likely to be single parents with sole responsibility for a child than males, and held that this meant that a considerably smaller proportion of females could comply with the requirement.

This approach was upheld by the EAT.

Morison J (p 160):

[A]s a matter of principle it seems to us that, when weighing the extent of the disproportionate effect that a condition has upon men and women in the relevant pool, the tribunal can properly have regard to the number of female train operators as against the number of male train operators. The industrial tribunal is entitled to have regard to the possibility that, where the number of women as against the number of men is, in percentage terms, very slight, some kind of generalised assumption may exist at the workplace that the particular type of work is concerned is 'men's' and not 'women's' work. Further, the tribunal is also entitled to consider whether the number of women drivers is so small as to be statistically unreliable ... The impact is ... to be assessed at the date of the complaint. But in assessing the extent of the disproportionate impact, the tribunal is entitled to take account of a wider perspective. It is for this reason that statistics showing the percentage of women in employment who have primary care responsibility for a child, in contrast to the percentage of men in that position, are relevant. The disproportionate impact of the condition may be assessed by looking both at the picture as it was at the time, and as it may be, had the small pool of women been larger and statistically significant ... With such a small pool, the tribunal were right to recognise that the percentage proportion would be substantially larger if just one more woman were unable to comply with the requirement due to temporary or permanent childcare responsibilities.[43]

The EAT is saying that the whole ethos of the organisation may itself have contributed to the small number of women doing the job in question – and, no

---

42 [1995] ICR 574; [1995] IRLR 355, EAT.

43 The Court of Appeal [1998] IRLR 364 dismissed the appeal on this point, adopting largely the same approach as the EAT, and emphasised both that the issue is one of fact for Industrial Tribunals, and that it would be unwise to lay down a figure which would be of general application in determining the 'considerably smaller' question.

doubt, many other jobs. Thus the female workforce was self-selecting and, as a result, arguably more likely to be able to comply with the changed working arrangements than a more representative group of women might have been. Thus the absence of statistical significance was not conclusive against a finding of disparate impact, although if there is statistical significance, that will normally establish the *prima facie* case. This sophisticated and commendable approach still leaves two unanswered questions. First, there was still a 5% disparity in ability to comply. Would the tribunal have been so bold if she had been one woman among 50 who objected to the new arrangements? Secondly, and more importantly, the EAT emphasises that the tribunal was *entitled* to have regard to the wider perspective. It does not hold that the tribunal was *bound* to have done so. The issue remains one of fact for the Employment Tribunal. It is unlikely that the EAT would have held it to be an error of law if a different Employment Tribunal had failed to take such an enlightened approach. Until this happens, the interpretation of indirect discrimination law will remain at the mercy of individual tribunals and its overall impact remain largely straightjacketed.

R v Secretary of State for Employment ex p Seymour-Smith [1995] IRLR 464, CA[44]

This case involved a claim that British unfair dismissal law contravened the Equal Treatment Directive and/or Art 119 in that the two year qualification period – or more precisely the 1985 Unfair Dismissal (Variation of Qualification Period) Order[45] which increased the period to two years – was indirectly discriminatory against women. One of the issues considered by the Court of Appeal – though not by the House of Lords – was whether the statistics did in fact show a sufficient disparate impact.[46]

Neill LJ (p 476):

The ratio of the number of women who qualified as against 100 men varies between 88.4 in 1990 to 90.5 in 1991 ... [F]or every 100 men who qualify, 92.5 women qualified in 1992 and for every 100 men who qualified in 1993, 94.6 women had two or more years' service.

We are impressed by the consistency and persistency of the figures from 1985 to 1991 inclusive. It is true that there was some narrowing of the gap for the year 1992 and a more marked narrowing of the gap in the year 1993, but no reason has been given for this narrowing, and in the absence of a reason the cumulative effect of the figures is striking. We are also impressed by the fact

---

[44] See, also, [1995] ICR 889; [1996] All ER (E) 1.

[45] SI 1985/782.

[46] A further issue was whether European law requires the disparity to be 'considerable' or whether 'any' disparity will be sufficient, bearing in mind that Art 2(1) of the Equal Treatment Directive mandates that 'there shall be no discrimination *whatsoever* on grounds of sex either directly or indirectly ...' (emphasis added). The Court of Appeal examined eight decisions of the European Court before concluding that the test was the same under European law as under British law.

that, to take the year 1985 ... there were 370,000 fewer women in the advantaged group than predicted; this represents 5% of the total female working population.

It follows [from our decision] that any proposed legislation, particularly in the social field, *which may* have a disparate impact between the sexes will have to be examined before it is introduced to see whether any consequential disparity can be objectively justified.

The House of Lords referred the case to the European Court of Justice without commenting on the appropriate resolution of this issue.[47] While the difference may not have appeared huge, there is no doubt that in a *statistical* sense it was significant. *London Underground v Edwards* shows that there can be adverse impact *without* statistical significance; this case may answer the question whether statistical significance is sufficient on its own to prove adverse impact.

COMPLIANCE AND DETRIMENT

It first has to be shown that 'the proportion of women who *can comply* [with a requirement] is considerably smaller than the proportion of men who *can comply* with it ...'. In addition, the requirement has to be shown to be to the applicant's *'detriment because she cannot comply* with it'. Ability to comply with the requirement is thus relevant at two separate stages: the first stage focuses on the effect of the requirement on the group; the second stage focuses on the effect on the individual applicant, where in addition such inability to comply must be to her detriment.

Price v Civil Service Commission [1977] IRLR 291, EAT[48]

At the time the Civil Service had a requirement that to be appointed as an Executive Officer one had to be between 17 and a half and 28, a requirement which the applicant claimed was indirectly discriminatory against women on the basis that many women between those ages are unavailable for work for family reasons. The tribunal rejected the claim on the basis that 'can comply' meant physically able to comply, an argument overturned by the EAT.

Phillips J (p 293):

In one sense it can be said that any female applicant can comply with the condition. She is not obliged to marry, or to have children, or to mind children ... Such a construction appears to us to be wholly out of sympathy with the spirit and intent of the Act ... It should not be said that a person 'can' do something merely because it is theoretically possible for him to do so: it is

---

47 [1997] ICR 371; [1997] 2 All ER 273; [1997] IRLR 315.
48 See, also, [1977] 1 WLR 1417; [1978] 1 All ER 1228.

necessary to see whether he can do so in practice. Applying this approach to the circumstances of this case, it is relevant in determining whether women can comply with this condition to take into account the current usual behaviour of women in this respect, putting on one side behaviour and responses which are unusual or extreme ...

Knowledge and experience suggest that a considerable number of women between the mid twenties and the mid thirties are engaged in bearing children and minding children, and that while many find it possible to take up employment, many others, while desiring to do so, find it impossible.[49]

Mandla v Lee [1983] IRLR 209, HL[50]

The case concerned an allegation that a refusal to permit Sikh pupils to wear turbans to school was indirectly discriminatory.

Lord Fraser of Tullybelton (p 213):

[A] literal meaning of the word 'can' would deprive Sikhs ... of much of the protection which Parliament evidently intended the Act to afford to them. They 'can' comply with almost any requirement or condition if they are willing to give up their distinctive customs and cultural rules ... The word 'can' ... must ... have been intended by Parliament to be read not as meaning 'can physically', so as to indicate a theoretical possibility, but as meaning 'can in practice' or can consistently with the customs and cultural conditions of the racial group.

It follows from these cases that the reason for adverse impact is not to be investigated at this stage; that is a factor which may be relevant to whether the requirement or condition in question is justified. Furthermore, the question whether the applicant can or cannot comply with the requirement depends only on whether they can comply with it at the time when the requirement or condition is applied. In *Clarke and Powell v Eley (IMI) Kynoch Ltd*,[51] Browne-Wilkinson J stated that the relevant point in time at which the ability of a part time worker to comply with the requirement of being full time was at the date

---

[49] When the case was remitted, the Industrial Tribunal ([1978] IRLR 3) held that the requirement was not justified; it had been introduced for reasons of convenience, not necessity, and there were other ways of achieving the same objective. The exclusion of younger workers will often be indirectly discriminatory against women and will be very difficult to justify. (But see *Leavers v Civil Service Commission* (1986), IT, unreported – see 8 EOR 38 – where it was held that a relatively low age limit for entry into the Diplomatic Service was justifiable as, without it, entrants would be unlikely to achieve before retirement age sufficient years of experience to be appointed as an ambassador). While the absence of an Age Discrimination Act means that, in general, discrimination against older workers is unlikely to contravene equality legislation, an Industrial Tribunal has recently held in *Nash v Mark/Roe Group Ltd* [1998] IRLR 168, that the statutory exclusion from unfair dismissal protection of workers over 65 contravenes the Equal Treatment Directive as being indirectly discriminatory against men on the basis that men constitute a higher proportion of the over-65 workforce.

[50] See, also, [1983] 2 AC 548; [1983] 1 All ER 1062.

[51] [1983] ICR 165; [1982] IRLR 482, EAT.

the detriment was imposed – the date she was made redundant. It was irrelevant that she could previously have become a full time worker, in which event she might have been able to comply.

Raval v DHSS [1985] IRLR 370, EAT[52]

'O' level English was a requirement to become a Civil Service clerical officer. Her Kenyan qualification was not regarded as equivalent, even though there was no doubt that she had sufficient command of English to be able to carry out the job. She was unwilling to sit the exam because she felt it would be degrading for her to have to do so after many years' experience of teaching lessons in English. She claimed that the imposition of the requirement was indirectly racially discriminatory.

Waite J (p 374):

The view of the majority is that in the context of a job advertisement for which specified qualifications are required to support applications which have to be received by a closing date in the near future, the words 'can comply' can only sensibly be construed as denoting an ability to produce proof that the relevant paper qualification has already been obtained [as opposed to the view of the tribunal] that capability of compliance was in some way to be construed more broadly as including anyone with the inherent ability to acquire the relevant qualifications ... [T]he majority of us considers that the Industrial Tribunal was wrong in saying that there was no evidence that Asians were inherently less able to obtain [the qualification than white people] ... When the matter is looked at, however, from the narrower standpoint of the ability to pass a particular language examination, such ability is bound to be affected if the exam is set in and relates to a language that is not the language of the examinee's home ...

The word 'detriment' also appears in s 6 of the SDA 1975, where it is provided that it is unlawful to discriminate against a woman 'by dismissing her, or subjecting her to any other detriment'.[53] It has been held that the word simply means 'putting under a disadvantage'[54] and that it should bear the same meaning in s 1 as it does in s 6.[55]

Raval v DHSS [1985] IRLR 370, EAT

Despite the finding on ability to comply, discussed above, her claim nevertheless failed.

Waite J (p 374):

The tribunal concluded that ... her inability to comply ... did not operate in practice to her detriment because it would have been so easy for her in the

---

52 See, also, [1985] ICR 685.
53 See, also, RRA 1976, s 4.
54 *Ministry of Defence v Jeremiah* [1980] QB 987; [1979] 3 All ER 833; [1979] IRLR 436.
55 *Home Office v Holmes* [1985] 1 WLR 71; [1984] 3 All ER 549; [1984] IRLR 299.

future ... to obtain the necessary qualification simply by sitting an examination which she could pass with ease ... [T]he finding of no detriment ... being one of fact, is binding on us ...

As a matter of law, this conclusion is surely wrong. At the time that the requirement was applied to her, it operated to her detriment because she did not at that moment have the appropriate qualification. The fact that she might easily have been able to obtain it is not relevant because, first, the relevant time is the moment the condition was applied and, secondly, there would have been some financial and emotional cost to a person in her position being required to take the examination.[56]

The reason for needing to show that the requirement operated to the applicant's detriment is to ensure that only those with a direct personal interest in the issue are permitted to institute litigation. There is no justification for denying a claim even if, in the absence of the challenged requirement, the applicant still would not have been appointed,[57] or if the requirement might not have operated to the applicant's detriment in the past and may not do so again at some time in the future. The power to act against discriminatory practices given to the EOC and CRE by ss 37 and 28 respectively proves the point. Action may be taken against practices which would amount to unlawful indirect discrimination but for the fact that, for example, no women have applied for the job in question. The sections would be redundant if it were necessary to point to a *particular* female applicant who would have obtained the job but for the imposition of the challenged requirement.

The drafting of this part of the legislation is predicated on the assumption that an individual will be claiming to be the victim of unlawful indirect discrimination. Where the allegation is that a statutory qualification operates in an indirectly discriminatory manner contrary to European law, problems may arise. In *Seymour-Smith*, the statistics relating to the numbers of male and female employees who attained the two year qualifying period for unfair dismissal related primarily to the years 1985 to 1991, the year in which the two women were dismissed. But, if the case is that the legislation itself is unlawful, it is by no means clear that 1991 is the appropriate date for determining whether a considerably smaller proportion of women than men can comply; potentially the answer might be different from year to year if the statistics vary. As a result, one of the issues which the House of Lords referred to the ECJ was whether the relevant date is when the measure being challenged was

---

[56] In *Turner v The Labour Party* [1987] IRLR 101, CA, it was held that a pension rule requirement that one had to be married did not operate to the detriment of the applicant, a divorcee, because it could not be said of her that she could not marry. This is incorrect for similar reasons to *Raval*.

[57] This was the fallacious reasoning applied by the EAT in *Watches of Switzerland v Savell* [1983] IRLR 141.

adopted, when it was brought into force, or when the employee is dismissed. There is even a case for saying that the relevant date should be the date of the hearing – it may be that adverse impact would need to be justified if it arose at any time while a particular piece of legislation was in force. The difficulty with this approach is that it might be said to infringe against the principle of legal certainty, in that the lawfulness of a particular piece of social policy legislation might become unpredictable, an outcome which would almost certainly lead the Court significantly to reduce the burden of justification placed on the Member State concerned.

JUSTIFICATION

The issue of justification is the central policy question underlying the law of indirect discrimination. The concept derives from *Griggs* in the United States Supreme Court, which used slightly different verbal formulations to express the idea, with business necessity being the most often cited.[58] Under this approach, a practice which has an adverse impact is impermissible unless it can be shown it was *necessary* for the employer to use it; that it was merely convenient or traditional is insufficient. The formulation invites and requires tribunals to reach complex and sensitive decisions as to the ways in which employment polices operate in practice, and as to the cost society is prepared to impose on employers to eliminate practices with an adverse impact. Unless such decisions are taken with awareness of the causes and impact of discriminatory practices, they may well prove unsatisfactory and over-cautious.

> **Townshend-Smith, R, 'Justifying indirect discrimination in English and American law: how stringent should the test be?' (1995) 1 IJDL 103, pp 106–10:**
>
> The task of the law is to reconcile the competing interests of the employer in efficiency and profits with those of members of the group seeking economic advancement. The assumption is that the employer must be allowed to hire, promote and pay more to those who are truly better employees, while at the same time artificial and irrational barriers to the economic advancement of protected groups can be challenged. As it will already have been shown that the challenged condition has a disparate impact, it logically follows that the burden of proof is on the employer to show that it is justified. As the rationale for permitting justification is that the employer's economic and other business objectives must be respected, it further follows that the employer's argument is only worthy of respect if it can be shown that the employer's policy will indeed have the result claimed for it.

---

58 Townshend-Smith, R, 'Justifying indirect discrimination in English and American law: how stringent should the test be?' (1995) 1 IJDL 103, p 111.

This point is the heart of the requirement for objective justification. But even if the employer is successful in proving this causal connection, he may still fail on the basis of what has come to be known as the principle of proportionality. First, the plaintiff may win if it can be established that there was a means of achieving the same objective which had less of a disparate impact. Secondly, the employer may also lose if the court considers that the gain to the employer from being allowed to continue with the practice is outweighed by the discriminatory consequences to the protected group ... [T]he decision on this issue is at bottom an issue of competing social policy values, is a matter for the court and of course depends enormously on judicial sensitivity to the social objectives of the legislation.

[O]n the question of objective proof that there is a causal link between the challenged policy and the employer's objectives, the two competing policy objectives are ... clear. On the one hand, employers must not be permitted to utilise practices with an adverse impact which cannot be proved to achieve business objectives. On the other hand, the standard at which that proof is set must not be so stringent as to be virtually unattainable, for that would logically lead to the use of surreptitious quotas, contrary to legislative policy ...

The task of the law is to produce a standard of justification which is sensitive to both of these policy objectives ... While it is important to examine what courts have said on the matter, it is contended that too often judicial *dicta* have been uttered with no awareness of the practical problems of application, or of how employers are supposed to discharge the burden laid upon them ...

There are three interconnected reasons why a standard less than full objective justification must necessarily be applied by courts and tribunals. The first reason concerns the appropriate role for statistics in an indirect discrimination claim. The second reason is to ensure that subjective employment practices are potentially challengeable via indirect discrimination law. The third concerns the very notion of the concept of 'necessity'.

A standard of literal objective justification requires that the employer prove on a balance of probabilities that the challenged practice will have the effect claimed for it. Almost by definition, this entails statistical proof that the workers concerned manifest higher productivity or efficiency. To require proper statistical proof would demand of tribunals and, more importantly, applicants, a familiarity with statistical techniques which is inappropriate. I am not arguing that statistics are always irrelevant, either to the original establishment of adverse impact or to prove of justification; I am simply arguing that these matters should in appropriate cases be provable without elaborate statistical techniques ...

The second reason why statistical proof should not be essential follows on from the above ... It is appropriate that a *prima facie* case of indirect discrimination should be raised merely by a statistically significant numerical disparity ... If such procedures cannot be validated, courts and tribunals will not allow the *prima facie* case to be established. The process of justification must permit reliance on best practice even if such practice cannot be proved to be effective. As jobs increase in their complexity and as people are increasingly hired for what they are rather than what they can do, it is essential that indirect discrimination is not relegated to traditional low-level jobs. In many situations it is impossible to define good job performance in such a way as to permit its scientific measurement ... If such practices were immune from legal challenge based on indirect discrimination, that would be some incentive for employers to utilise subjective and therefore unchallengeable practices in preferences to more objective procedures ...

The third reason why a statistical numerical approach cannot by itself be adequate concerns the very concept of 'necessity'. Necessity is not an abstract concept; whether something is necessary requires consideration for what and to whom the requirement is said to be necessary. This means that necessity has to be decided in the light of the employer's objective ... The law rightly requires the employer to identify which objective is sought to be achieved via the challenged requirement, but has fought shy of evaluating the merits of the objective itself. There is a great deal of difference between saying that a requirement is necessary to achieve an objective, and saying that the objective is itself necessary. While the former is admittedly extremely difficult, the second is highly interventionist and judgmental ...

It is therefore appropriate that courts are relatively deferential to the objectives of the employer. They should be far less deferential to the means chosen. Even if it can be shown that the means chosen will achieve the objective, the employer's case is not proven. It is necessary ... to consider the degree of adverse impact and thus the amount of social harm in need of remedy, and whether there are any alternatives which might achieve nearly the same result in a less discriminatory way ... There is no escape from the need to make a value judgment evaluating the degree of the adverse impact ... the social benefit of the employer's objective, whether the objective is likely to be achieved by the requirement, and whether or not the objective can be achieved by an alternative method.

The way the test has been formulated in response to the policy issues has changed over time. In the first case, *Steel v Union of Post Office Workers and the Post Office*,[59] Phillips J quoted from *Griggs* and emphasised that the test was necessity, not convenience. The stringency of that test was weakened by three subsequent cases. In *Singh v Rowntree Mackintosh Ltd*,[60] it was said that the term 'necessary' had to be applied 'reasonably and with common sense'. In *Panesar v The Nestle Co Ltd*,[61] 'necessity' was said to import a practice which 'is

---

[59] [1978] 1 WLR 64; [1978] 2 All ER 504; [1977] IRLR 288, EAT. In this case, basing allocation of postal delivery rounds on seniority may in principle have been acceptable; the problem was that female seniority was only calculated back as far as the coming into force of the SDA 1975, rather than to the date of first employment, so that there was a continuing discriminatory effect. This was justifiable neither in policy terms, nor in terms of the wording of the statute, which requires that the condition must be 'justifiable irrespective of the sex' of the person to whom it is applied. It cannot be justifiable to perpetuate sex or race based distinctions.

[60] [1979] ICR 554; [1979] IRLR 199, EAT.

[61] [1980] IRLR 60, EAT; upheld by the Court of Appeal [1980] ICR 44 (note); [1980] IRLR 64.

justifiable in the sense of right and proper in the circumstances'. Finally, in *Ojutiku v Manpower Services Commission*,[62] the judges in the Court of Appeal used slightly different formulations, including 'good and adequate reason' and reasons which would be acceptable to 'right-thinking people as sound and tolerable reasons'. This test was based on reasonableness, on normal acceptable standards of behaviour. It was a test which failed to grasp that anti-discrimination law aims to *change* the traditionally accepted ways of doing things. It placed far too much weight on the employer's reason for acting. It failed to require objective discriminatory effects to be countered only by objective proof that the practice would achieve the effects claimed for it.

Whether the English courts would have corrected the error manifested by the easing of the test is debatable; the following decision of the European Court made the issue largely academic.

Bilka-Kaufhaus v Weber von Hartz Case 170/84 [1986] IRLR 317[63]

Full time employees automatically qualified for a non-contributory pension on retirement, while part time employees only qualified if they had been employed full time for at least 15 years.

Judgment (pp 319–21):

> Bilka ... argued that it was not guilty of any breach of the principle of equal pay since there were objectively justified economic grounds ... [I]t emphasised ... that in comparison with the employment of part time workers the employment of full time workers involves lower ancillary costs and permits the use of staff throughout opening hours ...

> Bilka argues that the exclusion of part time employees ... aims solely to discourage part time work, since in general part time workers refuse to work in the late afternoon and on Saturdays. In order to ensure the presence of an adequate workforce during those periods it was therefore necessary to make full time work more attractive than part time work ...

> It is for the national court, which has sole jurisdiction to make findings of fact, to determine whether, and to what extent, the grounds put forward by an employer to explain the adoption of a pay practice which applies independently of the employee's sex, but which in fact affects more women than men, can be regarded to be objectively justified for economic reasons. If the national court finds that the means chosen by Bilka correspond to a real need on the part of the undertaking, are appropriate with a view to attaining the objectives pursued and are necessary to that end, the fact that the measures in question affect a far greater number of women than men is not sufficient to show that they constitute an infringement of Art 119 ...

The three-stage test in the previous paragraph is the nub of the judgment. The employer must first establish that the objective the measure is designed to

---

[62] [1982] ICR 661; [1982] IRLR 418, CA.
[63] See, also, [1986] ECR 1607; [1986] 2 CMLR 701; [1987] ICR 110.

achieve is appropriate, secondly, that there is no other way of achieving the same objective with a lower adverse impact and that it is worth paying the social costs of achieving the objective in terms of the degree of adverse impact, and thirdly, that the means chosen will in fact achieve the objective claimed for them.

Bilka was a case under Art 119 – an equal pay case. It is therefore authoritative on the interpretation to be given to the equal pay equivalent to the justification defence, s 1(3) of the Equal Pay Act 1970, which provides a defence where the employer proves 'that the variation [in pay] is genuinely due to a material factor which is not the difference of sex ...' In *Rainey v Greater Glasgow Health Board*[64] – another equal pay case – Lord Keith stated that 'there would not appear to be any material distinction in principle between the need to demonstrate objectively justified grounds of difference for the purposes of s 1(3) ... and the need to justify a requirement or condition' under the SDA 1975. 'Thus *Bilka*, a European case, is authoritative for EqPA 1970 and SDA 1975 cases, a fact confirmed by the House of Lords in *R v Secretary of State for Employment ex p EOC*.[65] Where does this leave cases under the RRA 1976, where the wording of the justification section is for practical purposes identical to that under the SDA 1975? In *Hampson v DES*[66] the Court of Appeal approved *Rainey*. Balcombe LJ said that "justifiable" requires an objective balance to be struck between the discriminatory effect of the condition and the reasonable needs of the party applying the condition ...'. Perhaps over-conscious of the rules of precedent, and maybe a little disingenuously, he could 'find no significant difference between the test adopted by Lord Justice Stephenson in *Ojutiku* and that adopted by the House of Lords in *Rainey*'. The decisions in *Bilka*, *Rainey* and *Hampson* were within two years of each other; following its approval in the other cases, it is safe to assume that the *Bilka* approach is authoritative across the board.

It would be possible to analyse in turn each element of the *Bilka* test. That approach is not being adopted for three reasons. First, judgments tend to refer to the test as a whole rather than to its separate components. Secondly, it is my basic contention that, no matter what verbal formula is used, tribunals will be greatly influenced by the particular context and subject matter of a case. The approach is to examine the cases on justification under the various factual categories where the issue has arisen.[67] Thirdly, it has frequently been

---

[64] [1987] AC 224; [1987] 1 All ER 65; [1987] IRLR 26, HL.

[65] [1995] 1 AC 1; [1994] ICR 217; [1994] 1 All ER 910; [1994] IRLR 176.

[66] [1989] ICR 179; [1989] IRLR 69, CA; appeal allowed on other grounds [1991] 1 AC 771; [1990] ICR 551; [1990] 2 All ER 513; [1990] IRLR 302, HL, where the issue of justification was not considered. See below, pp 350–52.

[67] The first two issues, seniority and differentiation between full time and part time workers, are relevant to claims both under SDA 1975 and EqPA 1970; these are dealt with in this chapter. Issues which relate solely to pay differentiation are dealt with in Chapter 12.

emphasised that the ultimate question on justification is one of fact for the Employment Tribunal,[68] a tendency not resisted in *Bilka*, where it was emphasised that the application of the guidelines to the facts of individual cases was a matter for national courts.[69] There are three points to make about this tendency. First, there is a clear possibility that different tribunals will reach different decisions on identical facts. Secondly, in many indirect discrimination cases the real issue is whether the challenged practice may lawfully continue to be used. In such a context, to tell an employer that a different tribunal may reach a different result is profoundly unhelpful.[70] Thirdly, however, there is considerable scope for an interventionist EAT to define an issue as one of law where the judges consider it appropriate to do so.

Seniority

Seniority may be relevant to employment benefits in a number of different ways. For example, incremental pay systems mean that greater seniority may be associated with higher pay; total accumulated seniority profoundly affects pension entitlement; priority for promotion or other benefits may be dependent on seniority as may access to fringe benefits; and reverse seniority – last-in, first-out – remains an extremely common method of selecting employees for redundancy. In the USA, where employment benefits are even more dependent on seniority than in the UK, many indirect discrimination cases have arisen where a prior pattern of direct discrimination prevented black people from acquiring the seniority which at a later date might be crucial for the allocation of benefits, even though s 703(h) of the Civil Rights Act 1964 provides a specific defence for *'bona fide* seniority systems'.[71]

> **Rubery, J and Fagan, C,** *Social Europe: Wage Determination and Sex Segregation in Employment in the European Community,* **1995, Luxembourg: Office for Official Publications of the European Communities, pp 127–31:**
>
> Seniority pay is a very important element of the pay package in many countries. In Belgium, for example, many agreements allow for 30 or more increments by seniority ... In Greece, seniority pay is such an important part of pay structures that it is also used in the calculation of the national minimum wage. In contrast, in the UK, seniority pay has only been found in specific

---

[68] See, eg, *Home Office v Holmes* [1985] 1 WLR 71; [1984] 3 All ER 349; [1984] IRLR 299, EAT; *Raval v DHSS* [1985] ICR 685; [1985] IRLR 370, EAT.

[69] The then Chair of the EAT spoke out against this trend in *Clarke v Eley (IMI) Kynoch Ltd* [1983] ICR 165; [1982] IRLR 482, but his words have not taken root.

[70] For example, *Raval* concerned the lawfulness of a very widely used English language test for entry to the Civil Service. The implications of the decision were clearly far wider than the specific facts. The absence of clear and authoritative criteria may cause serious problems for future personnel planning.

[71] See *International Brotherhood of Teamsters v United States* 431 US 324 (1977); *California Brewers Association v Bryant* 444 US 598 (1980).

sectors and even in these sectors performance pay systems are taking over from seniority. These differences in practice certainly suggest that there are different social values associated with pay, and that in some countries seniority pay is an entrenched part of the social structure.

Seniority pay may contribute negatively to women's relative pay for several reasons. First, women may be more likely to have interrupted careers than men ... Secondly, women may be less likely than men to be employed in organisations with seniority allowances ... or they may be employed in sectors with high rates of labour turnover where seniority allowances are therefore rarely paid ... Thirdly, women may be in jobs where seniority allowances are less generous. Fourthly, they may learn their skills not in the organisation but in the home or in the informal economy, but this experience is not given any recognition by seniority systems. Finally, women are disproportionately concentrated in part time and temporary jobs, but part timers often have to work twice as many years to receive the same number of seniority points, and time spent as temporary workers may not count ...

However, there are powerful arguments that can be made in favour of seniority pay as a system that can benefit women. The two main arguments in favour are, first, that it is an objective system, so that women are just as likely to receive these payments as men if they stay with the organisation, a principle which does not apply, for example, to merit pay. Second, seniority allowances provide prospects for pay advancement for lower grade staff and may even provide the possibility of lower grade staff being paid more than some higher graded staff ... The alternative of a flat rate of pay ... would tend to confine the less qualified to low earnings over their lifetime.

There are also arguments that seniority pay is not always discriminatory against women. Seniority pay is probably even more common in white-collar than in blue-collar work ... Furthermore, in some countries women are showing similar degrees of seniority to men, and sometimes even higher levels of seniority ... [72] However, where women's participation rates are different from men, seniority pay may well pose more of a problem. Women may not only lose increments for the years they are out of the labour market, but may also have to start at the bottom of an incremental scale when they return, or where it is difficult to re-enter jobs which have a strong seniority hierarchy, they may be forced into sectors where pay is low and undifferentiated by seniority or experience.

There are also important policy issues around whether part time service should be counted as the same number of years as full time workers or if maternity leave should count as continuous service even when it extends perhaps over a number of years. The arguments in favour or against such

---

[72] Thus the 'current move against seniority [in favour of more individualistic payment systems] comes just at the point where women in some countries are beginning to benefit significantly from these payments, as the gap between male and female seniority levels closes ...', Rubery, J and Fagan, C, *Social Europe: Wage Determination and Sex Segregation in Employment in the European Community*, 1995, Luxembourg: Office for Official Publications of the European Communities, p 203.

treatment hinge upon several different issues. The first is the reason for seniority pay; if this is a reward for increased productivity with service then it is arguable that those not in continuous service, or possibly even those in part time work, have not achieved the same increase in productivity. However, it is equally plausible to argue that seniority pay is more a reflection of social values that older workers should receive higher income and that workers should have some pay advancement to look forward to, possibly compensating for underpayment when they were young. Under these conditions, paying women according to actual years of work or hours of work reinforces their disadvantaged position in the economy by not according them the same pay status as their male cohorts.

It has generally been assumed that the utilisation of seniority has an adverse impact on women, though the degree of that adverse impact is debatable and may be changing. Whatever the figures in *Seymour-Smith* demonstrated, the *percentage* adverse impact was not extreme in the specific context of national figures relating to a two year qualifying period for claims of unfair dismissal.[73] Other usages of seniority might have a greater adverse impact, especially where applied at the micro level of the individual employer.

There are positive advantages for women and black people in the use of seniority as a criterion; its presumed objectivity should reduce the scope for subjective, biased decisions; it guards against victimisation and is used by employers to encourage employees to remain with a particular firm.[74] These are legitimate employer objectives within *Bilka*, but they can hardly be described as necessary; other means to the same end could be utilised. It is, however, contended that the overall advantages of relying on seniority mean that, even if adverse impact could be established,[75] justification would be relatively straightforward. In *Clarke v Eley (IMI) Kynoch Ltd*,[76] Browne-Wilkinson J observed, *obiter*, that it 'is most undesirable ... that there should be a doubt as to the question whether or not the formula "last-in, first-out" is lawful ... [B]earing in mind that Parliament has encouraged the making of redundancy agreements between employers and unions and that "last-in, first-out" has for many years been far the most commonly used criterion for selection, it would be right for an Industrial Tribunal to hold that [its] adoption ... was a necessary means ... of achieving a necessary objective, that is, an agreed criterion for selection ...'.[77]

---

73 See above, pp 286–87.

74 A failure to use objective criteria may lead to a finding that selection for redundancy was unfair under the Employment Rights Act 1996, s 98(4). See Pitt, G, *Employment Law*, 3rd edn, 1997, London: Sweet & Maxwell, pp 207–10.

75 Because of the nature of the action in *Seymour-Smith*, the appropriate pool comprised the whole country. In an action against an individual employer, it would need to be shown that female (or black) employees of a particular grade spent, on average, less time with that employer than male or white employees.

76 [1983] ICR 165; [1982] IRLR 482, EAT.

77 [1982] IRLR 482, EAT, p 487.

The situation may be different, however, where the degree of adverse impact is greater than normal, perhaps because the numbers of women, black people or Catholics have recently increased because of a programme of positive action.

Brook v London Borough of Haringey [1992] IRLR 478, EAT

The council's public works service employed some 1,200 manual and craft workers, traditionally male jobs. A successful positive action programme had meant that by early 1989, 80 of the employees were female. When redundancies became necessary, the council planned initially to give no weight to length of service. But after consultation with the unions, the performance criterion was dropped on the ground that it could not be objectively measured and the service component was greatly increased. The proportion of women who could gain sufficient points for length of service to counterbalance the loss of points for injury, illness and conduct was considerably smaller than the number of men who could do so.

It was held, *inter alia*, that the use of this seniority criterion was justifiable.

Wood J (p 486):

[I]t seems to us that in the light of history, indeed the approach generally on both sides of industry, and in the light of the ACAS advice ... justification [of a seniority criterion] will be a fairly simple burden for an employer to undertake

...

To suggest that a local authority ... which had taken initiatives designed to increase the representation of women ... should then give them preference in a redundancy is to introduce positive discrimination or gender quota.

In *Hall v Shorts Missile Systems Ltd*,[78] the court was prepared to take a more creative approach. The *Brook* court had taken the easy option by holding that the positive action programme did not override the normal principle that last-in, first-out should apply; the court in *Hall* held that the employer was entitled *not* to use the same approach. The court was not required specifically to decide whether utilising seniority would have been justifiable, but it manifests an awareness of the benefits of not relying solely on seniority and the tenor of the judgment implies that they would have been prepared to find that any such exclusive reliance would not have been justifiable on the facts.

Redundancies may have an adverse impact because the department or grades in which they occur are predominantly female or black. For example, a decision to contract out catering or cleaning within a firm will almost certainly affect far more women than men. In unfair dismissal law, courts are unwilling to investigate the *reason* for a redundancy, contenting themselves with concern with the method of implementation.[79] It is contended that, unless there is

---

[78] (1997) 72 EOR 39, NICA.
[79] *Moon v Homeworthy Furniture (Northern) Ltd* [1976] IRLR 298; [1977] ICR 117, EAT.

evidence that the redundancies are a pretext for discrimination or not genuine in some other way, the same reluctance to investigate will be a feature of anti-discrimination law.

Where pay increases with seniority, employers may be required to justify their system as a genuine material factor defence to claims under the EqPA 1970. When the European Court first broached the issue, in *Handels-og Kontorfunktionaerernes Forbund i Danmark v Dansk Arbejdsgiverforening (acting for Danfoss)*[80] it was observed that 'since seniority goes hand in hand with experience which generally places a worker in a better position to carry out his duties, it is permissible for the employer to reward it without the need to establish the importance which it takes on for the performance of the specific duties to be entrusted to the worker'. Seniority payments were only one aspect of the payments at issue in that case, and the court assumes their justification rather than arguing for it. When the issue next came before the European Court, a more sceptical line was adopted.

Nimz v Freie und Hansestadt Hamburg Case C-184/89 [1991] IRLR 222

The claimant worked 20 hours per week as a university administrator. The relevant collective agreement made provision for employees in her grade to move automatically up the salary scale after six years' service, but whereas seniority was fully taken into account for employees working for at least three-quarters of the working hours of a full time employee, only half of the period of service was taken into account where employees worked between half and three-quarters of the normal full time working hours. She would thus have had to work for 12 years to receive the same increase in pay.

Judgment (pp 224–25):

[I]n the present case there is a quasi-automatic system of salary scales operating on the basis of rules based on seniority contained in a collective agreement. These rules determine the gradual increase in salary due to an employee who remains in the same position. [Such rules] fall, in principle, within the concept of 'pay' ...

A collective agreement such as this which allows employers to maintain a general difference in pay between those working for a minimum numbers of hours per week or per month and those who, although employed in the same capacity, do not work this minimum number of hours, leads to discrimination against female employees ... when it turns out that a considerably smaller percentage of men than women are employed part time ...

[T]he City of Hamburg essentially maintained during the hearing that full time or three-quarter time workers acquire the skills necessary to their employment more quickly than other employees. The German Government also stressed their greater experience.

---

[80] Case 109/88 [1989] ECR 3199; [1991] 1 CMLR 8; [1989] IRLR 532.

It must nevertheless be pointed out that such considerations, in so far as they are simply generalisations concerning certain categories of employee, cannot amount to objective criteria unrelated to any discrimination based on sex ... In fact, although seniority goes hand in hand with experience which, in principle, should allow the employee to carry out his tasks all the better, the objectivity of such a criterion depends on all the circumstances in each case and notably on the relationship between the nature of the duties performed and the experience afforded by the performance of those duties after a certain number of working hours have been worked. Nevertheless, it is for the national court, which is the sole judge of the facts, to determine in the light of all the circumstances whether and to what extent a provision of a collective agreement, such as that in question, is justified by objective factors unrelated to any discrimination on grounds of sex.

Gerster v Freistaat Bayern Case C-1/95 [1997] IRLR 699

Promotion criteria included length of service, but the relevant regulations provided that periods of employment where the employee worked for less than half normal working hours did not count for the accumulation of such seniority, and where the employee worked between one-half and two-thirds of normal working hours seniority accrual was at two-thirds of the full time rate. The claim was that this exclusion of periods of part time employment contravened Art 119 and the Equal Treatment Directive. The Court first held that the rule fell outside the concept of 'pay' in Art 119; *Nimz* was distinguished on the ground that there, progression to a higher salary grade was practically automatic, whereas here promotion was a mere possibility.

Judgment (p 709):

According to the Bavarian State, the discrimination is objectively justified since the system is based on the administration's need to establish a general yardstick in terms of length of service against which the professional experience of employees can be assessed before they can be regarded as eligible for promotion ... [It] maintains that civil servants who work part time need to complete longer periods of service than those who work full time, if they are to acquire the professional skills and duties necessary for duties at a higher level.

Mrs Gerster, on the other hand, argues that in her capacity as a part time employee she has performed, in the course of the last 10 years of her professional life, duties attaching to the grade to which she aspired to be promoted ...

[If the national court finds] that part time employees are generally slower than full time employees in acquiring job-related abilities and skills, and that the competent authorities are in a position to establish that the measures chosen reflect a legitimate social policy aim, are an appropriate means of achieving that aim, and are necessary in order to do so, the mere fact that the legislative provision affects far more women than men cannot be regarded as an infringement of Directive 76/207.

[But if the national court] concludes that there is no special link between length of service and acquisition of a certain level of knowledge and experience [this provision] must be regarded as contrary to Directive 76/207.[81]

The approach adopted by the European Court in these cases is sceptical of seniority as a criterion – but not that sceptical. It has to be justified on the facts of each case, but the decision is left for national courts. Given the different social meaning attached to seniority pay in different Member States, this is understandable. As a consequence, effective regulation will come to depend on the degree of sensitivity shown by courts and tribunals in each State.[82]

Part time workers and family issues

It is now a truism to say that any distinction between part time and full time workers is *prima facie* indirect discrimination. *Bilka* itself concerned access to occupational schemes; the *Equal Opportunities Commission* case concerned the number of hours worked per week to qualify for employment protection rights; *Clarke* concerned a redundancy situation where part time workers with greater seniority were made redundant before full time workers with less seniority. The degree of adverse impact in these cases is such that justification of differential treatment is almost unimaginable.

The first type of justification which has been advanced is that providing rights for part time workers will do women more harm than good, as it will have the effect of reducing the availability of part time work.

R v Secretary of State for Employment ex p Equal Opportunities Commission **[1993] IRLR 10, CA**[83]

Dillon LJ (pp 16–17):

[It is said] that the objective is that there should be as much part time work available for those who want to work part time ... and that to achieve that it is necessary that the qualifying period ... should be longer for part time workers.

That appears to me to be the surviving shadow of the thinking that was once prevalent ... that unless the basic rate of pay for part time workers was less than the basic rate of pay for full time workers, employers would engage full time workers rather than part time workers and there would be less part time work available.

---

81 A similar approach was taken by the European Court in *Kording v Senator für Finanzen* Case C-100/95 [1997] IRLR 710, where the applicant challenged a requirement that, to be exempt from the examination to qualify as a tax consultant, an employee required 15 years' full time service and that in the case of a part time employee the exemption was calculated on the basis of the number of hours actually worked.

82 In *Charles v Pembrokeshire County Council*, unreported, IT, Case No: 25695/96, see 34 DCLD 4, a teachers' incremental pay scheme gave the authority discretion to recognise years of experience outside the profession, paid or unpaid, which was considered to be relevant and of value. It was held to be unjustifiable to refuse to recognise experience of raising a family as relevant experience.

83 See, also, [1993] ICR 251; [1993] 1 All ER 1022.

I can see no *evidence* that abolishing [the hours threshold] will cause any significant reduction in the availability of part time employment. On the contrary, recent history in relation to other ... measures underlines that according women the equal status which is justly their due has not led to the dire results which was foretold by the prophets of doom. In addition, I am much impressed by the fact that no other Member State of the European Community has a comparable threshold.

[1994] IRLR 176, HL[84]

Lord Keith of Kinkel (pp 181–82):

The bringing about of an increase in the availability of part time work is properly to be regarded as a beneficial social policy aim and it cannot be said that it is not a necessary aim.

[Lower pay for part time workers would in principle achieve the same result] and could not possibly be regarded as a suitable means of achieving an increase in part time employment.

The evidence for the Secretary of State consisted principally of an affidavit by an official in the Department of Employment which set out the views of the Department but did not contain anything capable of being regarded as factual evidence demonstrating the correctness of these views.

This case is crucial to discrimination law for many reasons. First, it emphasised that justification requires more than mere assertion or belief – at least where the defendant's argument is in principle capable of objective verification. For example, that the Government may have believed that granting part time workers equivalent rights would overall be detrimental was totally irrelevant – there was no proper evidence to support that view. How the court would have approached the issue had there been some good but not conclusive evidence remains for speculation. My argument is that such evidence would in principle be admissible: demanding perfect scientific proof is unrealistic, but the court should still have decided that the benefits were outweighed by the huge disparity between the rights of full and part time workers which was caused by the rule. Secondly, the case takes the same basic approach when dealing with challenges to social policy laws of Member States as to the employment practices of individual employers.[85] Thirdly, the challenged rule had the practical effect that part time workers were, on average, receiving lower overall total pay than full time workers; it is here impossible to differentiate between sex discrimination and equal pay cases. However, the most important and immediate practical effect of the decision is that it forced the Government to abandon the hours threshold.[86] Of course,

---

[84] See, also, [1995] AC 1; [1994] ICR 317; [1994] 1 All ER 910.

[85] The European Court has recently appeared to take a more lenient approach to this type of case; see below, pp 316–318.

[86] Employment Protection (Part Time) Employees Regulations 1995 SI 1995/31, which took effect in February 1995 and is now contained in the Employment Rights Act 1996, s 212.

the significance of this change depends on the overall impact of the law of unfair dismissal and of redundancy payments. The cases only require that part time workers be treated in the same way as male full time workers *in a comparable situation*, usually doing the same job. The law is of little assistance where jobs are defined as being female or part time and no male comparator is available. Comparison is the essence of sex discrimination; where comparison cannot be made, the law cannot be utilised and part timers must continue to tolerate lower average pay, benefits and career opportunities. Where there are comparable full time workers, though, examples of unlawful differentiation will be to include only full time workers in a sick pay scheme or limiting overtime opportunities to full time employees.

Many employees would value the opportunity to work part time;[87] the question has arisen whether it may be indirectly discriminatory to deny women the opportunity to jobshare or work only part of a week.[88]

Home Office v Holmes [1984] IRLR 299, EAT[89]

After the birth of her baby a woman applied to return to her previous full time post on a part time basis. The request was refused. An Industrial Tribunal found this to be unlawful indirect discrimination and that the condition or requirement of full time work was not justified.

The EAT dismissed the appeal.

Waite J (pp 301–02):

The scheme of the anti-discrimination legislation involves casting a wide net throwing upon employers the onus of justifying the relevant requirement or

---

[87] Directive 97/81/EEC, the Part-Time Work Directive, enshrines the principle of non-discrimination whereby 'part time workers shall not be treated in a less favourable manner solely because they are part time. Article 5, dealing with opportunities for part time work, may prove to be the most significant in the British context. It provides:

(2) A worker's refusal to transfer from full time to part time work or vice versa should not in itself constitute a valid reason for termination of employment ... for other reasons such as may arise from the operational requirement of the establishment concerned.

(3) As far as possible, employers should give consideration to:

(a) requests by workers to transfer from full time work ...;

(b) requests by workers to transfer from part time to full time work or to increase their working time should the opportunity arise ...;

(d) measures to facilitate access to part time work at all levels of the enterprise, including skilled and managerial positions and, where appropriate, to facilitate access by part time workers to vocational training to enhance career opportunities and occupational mobility.

The Government has announced that the Directive will be implemented by April 2000. *Fairness at Work*, Cm 3968, 1998, London: The Stationery Office, para 5.5.

[88] See Cox, S, 'Flexible working after maternity leave: the legal framework' (1998) 78 EOR 10, esp pp 13–15.

[89] See, also, [1985] 1 WLR 71; [1984] 3 All ER 549.

condition ... One must be careful, however, not to fall into the error of assuming that because the net is wide, the catch will inevitably be large. [Counsel for the employers] eloquently invited us to consider the shock to British industry and to our national and local government administration which, he submitted, would be bound to be suffered if ... they had to face a shoal of claims by women full time workers alleging that it would be discriminatory to refuse them part time status. ... [W]e emphasise ... that this one case of the employee and her particular difficulties within her particular grade in her particular department stands very much upon its own ... There will be cases where the requirement for full time staff can be shown to be sufficiently flexible as arguably not to amount to a requirement or condition at all. There will be cases where a policy favouring full time staff exclusively within a particular grade or department is found to be justified. There will be cases where no actual or no sufficient detriment can be proved by the employee. All such cases will turn upon their own particular facts.

Greater Glasgow Health Board v Carey [1987] IRLR 484, EAT

A health visitor wanted to return to work following maternity leave on the basis that she would work full days for two and a half or three days a week. The employers were only prepared to let her work every day of the week, either mornings or afternoons. The employer's view was that this arrangement was necessary to avoid the need for patient sharing. The tribunal were not convinced that it was necessary for a health visitor to be available on each day of the week.

EAT upheld the employer's appeal.

Lord Mayfield (p 489):

[W]e do not think that [the tribunal] had the efficiency of the service at the forefront of their mind ... The reasons stated [for the policy] were that health visiting work was mainly on a personal contact basis with the patient and not task-oriented; that therefore the family would discuss their personal problems with the health visitor, which were not always suitable to be recorded on the records; personal observations of the home surroundings and relationships with other members of the family could not always be put in detail on the record ... with the increasing emphasis on health visiting in cases of child abuse and granny abuse, if the same health visitor was not available on each day of the week that led to poor communication with general practitioners, social workers and other agencies. That was one of the problems which had been highlighted in cases of child abuse which had proceeded to court.

While it must be a question of fact whether part time work or jobsharing will impair the efficiency of the organisation, the failure of the EAT in *Holmes* to give *any* guidance as to the appropriate criteria is dismal, especially as the facts were so typical. *Carey* shows, correctly, that the factors relevant to efficiency are not necessarily economic; there was not, and could not, be proof that the arrangements the employers favoured were strictly *necessary*; the concept of necessity seems inappropriate where the aim is for healthcare to be as effective as possible. As long as the employer's argument is plausible, is backed up by as much evidence as possible, and the system is not introduced for discriminatory reasons, some degree of deference to the employer is sensible. Whether an employer can justify a refusal to permit a female employee to work part time will depend on various factors, such as the size of the enterprise, whether there is shift working and any additional administration and supervision costs. Factors personal to the employee such as prior length of service must not be discounted. Given the variation of potential fact situations, tribunals need to be sensitive to the demands of women to be allowed to work part time and the potentially severe career consequences if permission is refused. It is also important to consider the degree of adverse impact: if the challenged policy is one with the potential to affect all female employees, it will be harder to justify than a policy, as in *Carey*, where the adverse impact is in part due to her individual situation and where the employer was prepared to countenance some degree of accommodation.

It is all too easy for employers to emphasise the costs and disadvantages of jobsharing, minor as they will be in most cases. There is evidence that not only is jobsharing potentially beneficial for many women, but that employers obtain two motivated and productive employees whose combined output may exceed that of one sole employee. In addition, the ability to jobshare or work part time may enable an employer to retain an experienced employee who would otherwise leave. Thus employers who insist on full time work should be required to submit clear and convincing evidence of why it is necessary. Very few jobs, even senior positions, require continuous attendance as a matter of necessity, though some jobs may have to be done by one person to ensure consistency of decision making. For other jobs, the recipients of the work may benefit if the job is done by one person – such as teaching children with special educational needs. But, unless applications specify that jobsharing is welcome, applicants who wish to jobshare are in a difficult position, as it will be all too easy for employers to contend that one or both was not the best person for the job. Cases are more likely to be brought where incumbents are denied the opportunity to go part time or jobshare.

Thus, the law can do relatively little to change the culture that assumes that important jobs can only be performed on a full time basis, in the same way as the law assumes that childcare is a matter for the parents, not the employer or the State, unlike sick pay or pension provision, which is routinely provided by the employer. The European Court in *Bilka* held that Art 119 'does not have the effect of requiring an employer to organise its occupational pension schemes in such a manner as to take into account the particular difficulties faced by persons with family responsibilities in meeting the conditions for entitlement to such a pension'. There is thus no obligation on employers to assist with childcare and no obligation to count periods out of the workforce towards seniority or pension entitlements. However, the following case shows that there may be an obligation to take account of the fact that women have primary responsibility for childcare.

London Underground v Edwards (No 2) [1997] IRLR 157, EAT[90]

Having concluded that the new rostering arrangement had an adverse impact on women (see above, p 285), the EAT also concluded that its imposition was not justified.

Morison J (p 161):

There was evidence to justify the conclusion that London Underground could – and, we would add, should – have accommodated [her] personal requirements. She had been working for them for nearly 10 years. Her family demands were of a temporary nature. There were no complaints about her work ... London Underground were, we think, probably fully justified in rejecting the idea of a creche which would be unsuitable as a solution for a parent working unsocial hours. But ... there was good evidence that London Underground could have made arrangements which would not have been damaging to their business plans but which would have accommodated the reasonable demands of their employees ...

Although there is no direct correlation between the two, we would anticipate that ... the less justification London Underground had for the way they treated [her], the less likely it is that a tribunal will conclude that she has failed to show that the disproportionate effect of the condition was considerable.

This case is significant in two respects. First, the court demonstrates a real sympathy for the problems working mothers may have in juggling home and work responsibilities. The employer must at least consider whether assistance or accommodation is possible. While this is a potentially major advance, much will depend on the willingness of tribunals and the EAT to follow through this relatively interventionist perspective. Secondly, the link made between the issues of adverse impact and justification mark a rejection of a mechanistic point by point analysis of indirect discrimination law and a willingness to focus on the overall merits of the case. The caveat must be that the merits here may be have been too one-sided for the case to be of great use as a precedent: there was evidence that the employers were originally willing to accede to her demands but changed their mind following pressure from the predominantly male workforce.

It is normally unjustifiable to pay part time workers at a lower rate than full time workers.

---

[90] The decision was upheld by the Court of Appeal [1998] IRLR 364, but there was no appeal on the justification issue.

Jenkins v Kingsgate **Case 96/80 [1981] IRLR 228**[91]

The employers paid full time workers 10% more than part time workers, who were mostly women. The EAT referred the matter to the ECJ, asking whether Art 119 and Directive 75/117 required parity of pay even where different hours were worked.

The ECJ held (p 234) that the difference in rates did not contravene Art 119 where 'the difference in pay ... is attributable to factors which are objectively justified and are in no way related to any discrimination based on sex.

Such may be the case, in particular, when ... the employer is endeavouring, on economic grounds which may be objectively justified, to encourage full time work irrespective of the sex of the worker'.[92]

Rinner-Kuhn v FWW Spezial-Gebäudereinigung GmbH and Co KG **Case 171/88 [1989] IRLR 493**[93]

German law required employers to pay sick pay for six weeks, but excluded from the entitlement those who worked less than 10 hours per week or 45 per month. Employers received an 80% rebate from the State on all payments made.

The European Court concluded that the payments constituted 'pay' under Art 119; there was clearly *prima facie* indirect discrimination; the further question was whether the exclusion of some part time workers could be justified.

Judgment (p 496):

[The employers' defence was] that workers who work less than 10 hours a week or 45 hours a month are not integrated in and connected with the undertaking in a way comparable to that of other workers.

However, these considerations only represent generalised statements concerning certain categories of workers and do not therefore admit the conclusion of objective criteria unrelated to any discrimination on grounds of sex. If, on the other hand, the Member State is in a position to establish that the means selected correspond to an objective necessary for its social policy and are appropriate and necessary for the attainment of that objective, the mere fact that the legislative provision affects a considerably greater number of female than of male workers cannot be regarded as an infringement of Art 119.

---

[91] See, also, [1981] ECR 911; [1981] ICR 592; [1981] 1 WLR 972.

[92] The parts of the judgment quoted appear to reflect the standard approach to indirect discrimination. Elsewhere in the judgment, though, the Court appears to suggest that such a pay policy would only be unlawful if it was 'in reality discrimination based on the sex of the worker'. When the case returned to the EAT ([1981] IRLR 388; [1981] 1 WLR 1485), Browne-Wilkinson J identified the contradiction at the heart of the judgment of the ECJ, but held that, whatever European law provided, English law required the employer to show that the difference in pay was 'reasonably necessary in order to obtain some result (other than cheap female labour) which the employer desires for economic or other reasons'. Subsequent European Court decisions show that the proper interpretation of *Jenkins* is the same as that given to English law by the EAT.

[93] See, also, [1989] ECR 2743.

Kowalska v Freie und Hansestadt Hamburg **Case C-33/89 [1990] IRLR 447**[94]

The applicant was a part time law clerk whose employment relationship was governed by a public sector collective agreement. That agreement provided for a severance payment where the employment was terminated for reasons not attributable to the person concerned, such as reaching retiring age. Entitlement to such payments was limited to those who worked at least 38 hours per week.

The European Court again held that the payment constituted pay and that there was *prima facie* indirect discrimination.

The Court held that the outcome of collective agreements was just as subject to Art 119 as other means of determining pay levels. To establish justification, the *Bilka* test would need to be satisfied.

These cases establish a number of basic principles.[95] First, it makes no difference what is the source for the pay discrimination – or any other form of discrimination – against part time workers. Whether it be employer fiat, collective bargaining or statutory regulation, the same principles of justification apply. The employer's argument must be tightly focused on the precise objective and whether the policy will achieve the objective. Generalised assumptions or traditions will not suffice. Given that it is the employers' choice to organise a workplace with part time employees, presumably because some benefit is perceived from such a system, it is hard to imagine that *any* employer-generated differentiation between part time and full time workers will be justifiable. A possible exception is a rule which excludes membership of pension schemes – and perhaps other fringe benefits – to employees who work very few hours per week; arguably the inevitably high turnover amongst such employees provides an adequate administrative justification for differentiating between full time and part time workers. However, the principles may be applied rather less rigorously where a social policy argument is advanced by the government for a statutory distinction whose primary focus is not to differentiate between full time and part time employees as regards terms and conditions of employment.[96]

---

[94] See, also, [1990] ECR I-2591; [1992] ICR 29.

[95] It is unclear how much additional protection will be provided by the Part Time Work Directive. Article 4 provides that:

(1) In respect of employment and conditions, part time workers shall not be treated in a less favourable manner than comparable full time workers solely because they work part time unless different treatment is justified on objective grounds.

(2) Where appropriate, the principle of *pro rata temporis* shall apply ...

(4) When justified by objective reasons, Member States ... may, where appropriate, make access to particular conditions of employment subject to conditions such as a period of service, time worked or earnings qualification.

The great merit of this proposal is not the rights themselves, but the fact that it will be – it is hoped – contained in legislation, attracting publicity, which will improve the likelihood that the practical rights of part time workers will equate to their theoretical rights.

[96] See below, pp 316–18.

But if the differentiation does not impact upon all part time workers, the employer's task may be easier.

Barry v Midland Bank plc [1998] IRLR 138, CA[97]

The case concerned the way in which severance payments were calculated. The applicant argued that to base the calculation upon the fact that, when she left the bank's employ, she worked part time, took insufficient account of the fact that 11 of her 13 years' service had been full time. She was arguing for a *pro rata* method of calculation rather than one based on final salary.

The Court of Appeal first held that the applicant had failed to prove adverse impact. It could not be said that all part time workers were treated less favourably than all full time workers. The claim failed on this point because she failed to produce statistics concerning the specifically disadvantaged group – part time workers whose hours of work at termination were less than the average of their hours of work throughout their period of service. It was possible that some employees, perhaps older women who had previously worked part time and then become full time, would have benefited from the arrangement.

The Court of Appeal held that in any event the arrangements under the scheme were justified.

Peter Gibson LJ (pp 144–45):

In our judgment it would be wrong to extrapolate [from *Bilka*] that an employer can never justify indirect discrimination in a redundancy payments scheme unless the form of the scheme is shown to be necessary as the only possible scheme. One must first consider whether the objective of the scheme is legitimate ... In our opinion, there can be no doubt that the primary objective of the scheme, to cushion the effect of the unemployment, as well as the secondary objective found by the Industrial Tribunal, to compensate the employee for the loss of her job and to reward her loyalty, are legitimate and non-discriminatory aims ... As for the means used, it seems to us plain that the form of the scheme was both appropriate and reasonably necessary to that end. That is demonstrated by the fact that the scheme could not be redrafted to correlate the severance payment with the hours served by the employee in the way suggested by Mrs Barry without detracting from the primary objective of the scheme. Contrary to the views of the Industrial Tribunal, the form which the scheme took, of basing the award on the pay at termination, was not a mere matter of convenience, but was designed to promote the primary objective. The scheme also had the merit of clarity and simplicity, which was beneficial to both the bank and its employees ... In our judgment, therefore, if there is indirect discrimination, it is objectively justified and involves no infringement of Art 119 and is due to a material factor not based on sex.

---

[97] See, also, [1998] 1 All ER 805. Appeal to the House of Lords has been granted.

Testing and educational qualifications

Many employers require success in public examinations or their own test procedures, such as an intelligence, aptitude or psychometric test, as a prerequisite for employment. Such tests, especially the privately administered ones, have been the subject of constant litigation in the USA, because of their widespread use coupled with the fact that blacks have tended not to do as well as whites.[98] Even in America, there has been little litigation alleging that such tests are indirectly discriminatory on ground of gender.

In Britain such cases have been scarce, which partly reflects the general scarcity of indirect race discrimination litigation. In *Raval v DHSS*,[99] the employers required 'O' level English for entry at clerical grade level. Her Kenyan qualification was not regarded as equivalent, although it was not disputed that she had sufficient command of English to be able to fulfil the job requirements.[100] The Industrial Tribunal held that on balance, the requirement had more to be said in its favour based on fairness than against it on the ground of arbitrariness. The EAT held that this was a conclusion that the tribunal was perfectly entitled to reach. The case is easily attacked. The lenient standard applied must fail to survive *Bilka* and its progeny. The employer virtually admitted that a less discriminatory alternative was available to test her skills, concerning which there were in any event no doubts. In no sense did they even attempt to demonstrate that the use of this particular qualification was necessary.[101] As most employers would no doubt argue, it is cheap and convenient to rely on such exams which are assumed to be correlated with job performance, as no doubt they are to a limited extent. But there are counterarguments concerning reliance on tests in general, although not the precise way they were utilised here. Tests are objective – at least compared with interviews and other subjective hiring criteria. It is impossible to prove scientifically that a particular test outcome is correlated with successful job performance.

The case does not touch on the alleged underperformance of ethnic minorities in the *British* educational system, which is a factor which

---

[98] Apart from *Griggs* itself, see, eg, *Albemarle Paper Co v Moody* 422 US 405 (1975); *Guardians Association v Civil Service Commission* 630 F 2d 79 (2d Cir 1980). See, also, *op cit*, Townshend-Smith, fn 58, pp 114–16.

[99] [1985] ICR 685; [1985] IRLR 370, EAT.

[100] In *Mecca Leisure Group plc v Chatprachong* [1993] IRLR 531, EAT, it was held not to be unlawful indirect discrimination for an employer to fail to offer special training to an employee whose native language was not English in order to bring that employee to the standard of English admittedly needed for the job aspired to.

[101] For the general problem of recognition of overseas qualifications see, also, *Hampson v Department of Education and Science* [1991] 1 AC 771; [1990] ICR 551; [1990] 2 All ER 513; [1990 IRLR 302, HL; and *General Medical Council v Goba* [1988] ICR 885; [1988] IRLR 425, EAT. If the quantity of litigation is a good yardstick, this issue is a major cause for concern in relation to indirect race discrimination.

contributes to disproportionately high unemployment rates. It is questionable how far the law of indirect discrimination has a role here. Much of the inequality arises in and through the education system rather than the labour market. To impose impossibly stringent standards of validation on the use of general qualifications is unlikely to benefit ethnic minorities. Efforts should be concentrated towards encouraging the *achievement* of such qualifications as a means of reducing inequality.[102]

Most of the American litigation has focused on the use of tests by employers rather than reliance on public educational qualifications. 'Courts in North America have been ready to rule as illegal testing arrangements which are at variance with the nature of the job, and the way in which it is performed. Here, Industrial Tribunals have been loath to get to grips with these issues.'[103] As a matter of law it is almost always impossible to establish that the use of a particular test was necessary, and that the test employed was a scientifically accurate predictor of job performance. This is true as a generalisation: it becomes truer as one moves from simple job content tests to personality type tests.

Tests are potentially beneficial from an equal opportunities standpoint. It is an inappropriate and dangerous strategy to insist on such high and expensive standards of validation that testing will be abandoned. In America, such abandonment sometimes led to the use of quotas. Whatever is felt about this development, it would not happen in the UK; more subjective and thus potentially discriminatory practices would be substituted. It is, however, perfectly consistent both to defend testing and to demand that tests follow best professional practice, with a potential indirect discrimination claim if they fail.[104] This imposes an appropriate standard which is capable of being met.

Wood, R, 'Psychometrics should make assessment fairer' (1996) 67 EOR 27, pp 32–33:

It is undeniable that certain kinds of ability tests, specifically those of the verbal reasoning variety, will tend to disadvantage people from ethnic minorities, the

---

[102] It is probable that, where there is an over-supply of labour, employers will use unnecessarily high educational requirements as an understandably practical means of distinguishing applicants, perhaps in deciding who to shortlist. This may have an adverse impact on ethnic minorities but, even if it could be discovered which criteria were applied and proved that there was indeed an adverse impact, it is quite probable that a tribunal would hold such practices to be justified. There is very little incentive to bring such claims.

[103] Wood, R, 'Psychometrics should make assessment fairer' (1996) 67 EOR 27, p 30.

[104] In *Guardians Association v Civil Service Commission* 630 F 2d 79 (2d Cir 1980), it was said that the requirements for an acceptable test were: a suitable job analysis, reasonable competence in the actual construction of the test, test content must relate to and be representative of job content, and the system of scoring must appropriately select those better at performing the job. On testing generally, see Pearn, M, Kandola, R and Mottram, R, *Selection Tests and Sex Bias: the Impact of Selection Testing on the Employment Opportunities of Men and Women*, 1987, Manchester: EOC; *Towards Fair Selection: a Survey of Test Practice and Thirteen Case Studies*, 1993, London: Commission for Racial Equality.

reason being – and this will vary within and between minorities ... – that their understanding of written English is less secure than that of the people from the majority group they are competing against ... [O]utlawing tests is not the answer ... You would only end up using something less valid and reliable, like an interview, and make worse hiring decisions ... In the *Brent Council* case ... the council allowed the test results to be overridden by interview results, which only worsened the position of many ethnic minority applicants ...

In these circumstances it is necessary to proceed carefully. When using test scores to exclude applicants, set the lowest pass score which is sensible given the numbers involved. This will tend to minimise the numbers of those who score poorly on the tests, but could do the job if hired ... As a result of employing [such] a conservative strategy, most of the people you have rejected will be people who are appropriately rejected. It is likely that there will still be a disproportionate number of people from ethnic minorities among this number but there is nothing you can do about this given that, as well as being historically rooted, the causes lie elsewhere.

What you can do is to make sure that minority people have access to practice materials and the opportunity to familiarise themselves with the tests, and with testing generally. [British Rail did this] for people already employed – doing it for people you are not yet employing is another matter altogether.

As for personality questionnaires, there is no body of evidence which would substantiate bias against people from ethnic minorities, but ... it could happen. There may also be bias against women in some circumstances. But ... we do not know very much about what happens when these questionnaires are used in a 'hard' way. Just because they seem harmless is not a good reason for rushing around using them.

Physical and health and safety justifications

While the decline in the proportion of jobs which require physical strength is a factor in the increasing proportion of women in the labour market, it remains the case that strength or other physical attributes continue to be job requirements in some areas of employment. No height, weight or strength requirement may be a genuine occupational qualification.[105] It is unlawful direct discrimination to exclude *all* women from a job on the basis that few will be able to meet the relevant strength requirement. Employers are required to impose a standard common to both male and female applicants and, on the assumption that fewer women than men meet the standard, that is potentially justifiable. How this is to be done will vary according to the circumstances. Employers may not, for example, be able to test ability to lift weights, because failure leading to injury might conceivably lead to a tort claim and a health and safety prosecution. It may thus be permissible to use a height or weight

---

[105] SDA 1975, s 7(2)(a).

requirement as a proxy for strength, or to require experience in the kind of work, a requirement which would clearly tend to exclude women. Moreover, machinery designed for the average man may make the job impractical for most women; a height requirement would be imposed not because the job intrinsically needs it but because of the machine used to do the job. A requirement to make adjustments to previously accepted ways of working might be appropriate, but tribunals might understandably be reluctant to impose such obligation on employers with few employees. Safety rules with an adverse impact will arguably be easier to justify than many other rules with an adverse impact. Many cases where a justification is alleged raise issues of competing social values; it is arguable that the avoidance of physical injury is a more fundamental value than the avoidance of discrimination.

In relation to gender, the focus of attention so far as health and safety is concerned has been on issues relating to pregnancy and reproductive risks, discussed earlier.[106] Here, the discrimination is likely to be direct rather than indirect. In relation to race, the issue has surfaced where a cultural norm in relation to clothing or appearance might carry a health and safety risk. Thus in *Singh v British Rail Engineering Ltd*,[107] it was held to be justifiable to insist that all employees, including Sikhs, wear protective headgear, and in *Singh v Rowntree Mackintosh Ltd*[108] and *Panesar v The Nestle Co Ltd*,[109] it was held to be justifiable to prohibit the wearing of beards in confectionery factories in order to reduce the risk of contamination by facial hair. It was held that the defence of justification was not defeated by the fact that the employers did not adopt the 'no beards' policy in each of their factories. Such argument might often be conclusive against the employers, but in the health and safety context it ought to be permissible to introduce new criteria, even if only as an experiment to determine whether safety might indeed be improved. But if there is a high degree of adverse impact, the employer should need to show a reasonable belief in a substantial safety improvement as a consequence of the policy.

Social policy justifications

It may happen that justifications are put forward which seek to advance a broader social policy than merely the efficient and profitable operation of the enterprise. For example, in *Greater Manchester Police Authority v Lea*,[110] the plaintiff was not appointed to a police job because he was in receipt of an occupational pension following his compulsory medical retirement. The

---

[106] See above, pp 213–20.
[107] [1986] ICR 22, EAT.
[108] [1979] ICR 554; [1979] IRLR 199, EAT.
[109] [1980] IRLR 60, EAT; upheld by CA [1980] ICR 44 (note); [1980] IRLR 64.
[110] [1990] IRLR 372, EAT.

policy was to exclude those in receipt of such pensions and to consider only those who were unemployed. However high-minded the policy might have been, it was not justifiable because the reason for the policy was not related to a particular need of the employer for workers who met the requirement. In *Board of Governors of St Matthias Church of England School v Crizzle*,[111] it was held that a requirement that the headteacher of a church school should be a 'committed communicant Christian' was justifiable despite its adverse impact on Asians. The EAT concluded that the school's objectives could legitimately be regarded as wider than the mere provision of an efficient education, and that the challenged requirement was appropriate bearing in mind the ethos of the school. This is a social policy justification, prioritising the right of religious groups to employ those whose beliefs accord with the employers. The EAT had no difficulty in finding for the employers, failing to grasp the competing policy issues at stake.

However, in some instances the effective cause of the adverse impact is not a policy or practice of the employer, but a legislative or other State-employed requirement. Here, the *Bilka* test must be applied in a modified form, first because it is the objective of the *policy*, not the employer, which must be considered, and, secondly, because it is arguable that a somewhat more lenient approach should be taken.[112] This is not at all to say that justifications in such cases will ever be straightforward. They will still require proper evidence. In *Rinner-Kuhn* the statutory policy of excluding some part time workers from sick pay was subject to *Bilka*, and in *Equal Opportunities Commission* the evidence provided by the Government as to why it was necessary to exclude part time workers from statutory protections was so inadequate as clearly to fail the test. These cases, however, concern part time workers, where the degree of adverse impact is so great that the operation of the proportionality test is likely to mean that any purported justification will fail.

Where the facts are less clear cut, there are now numerous examples of a less rigorous standard being applied.

Kirshammer-Hack v Sidal Case C-189/91 [1994] IRLR 185[113]

The German law on protection from unfair dismissal does not apply to small businesses – businesses with five or less than five employees. In determining

---

[111] [1993] IRLR 112, EAT.

[112] There is also a procedural problem in that, if the case does not proceed by way of judicial review, the employer will be the defendant in such a case and will theoretically be in the position of having to defend government social policy. It has argued that an 'amendment to the tribunal rules to enable or even require the State to be joined as a party to justify any *prima facie* indirectly discriminatory legislation is essential'. See Allen, R, (1997) 73 EOR 48.

[113] See, also, [1993] ECR I-6185.

this number, no account is taken of those who work less than 10 hours per week or 45 per month.

The applicant's complaint of unfair dismissal was inadmissible, not because of her lack of hours but because of those of some of the others who worked in her dental surgery.

Judgment (p 188):

[L]egislation like that in question forms part of a group of measures intended to alleviate the constraints on small businesses, which play an essential role in economic development and job creation within the Community ... [I]t should be stressed that by providing that directives adopted relating to the health and safety of employees shall avoid imposing administrative financial and legal constraints in a way which hold back the creation and development of small and medium-sized undertakings, Art 118A ... indicates that these undertakings can be the object of special economic measures.

This decision is out of line with the more rigorous approach adopted in other cases, and with British law as epitomised by the *EOC* case. However, the finding on justification followed a holding that no adverse impact was established. Again, the two issues run together to reach what is overall considered to be a fair result. Such arguments as were here successful are, in any event, inapplicable to a case against an individual employer.

There is some evidence that the European Court will be at its most lenient in relation to matters of social security; here, the policy decisions may most suitably be resolved by national courts and a finding of indirect justification in relation to one benefit would be very likely to have serious knock-on effects elsewhere.

Nolte v Landesversicherungsanstalt Hannover **Case C-317/93**
Megner v Innungskrankenkasse Vorderpfalz **Case C-444/93**
[1996] IRLR 225[114]

The first case concerned a challenge to German social security rules which classed employment for less than 15 hours per week as 'minor employment', on which contributions were not payable. In consequence, when she became ill, she received no benefits. In the second case the complainants sought a ruling that deductions should be made from wages for similar employment.

There is no doubt that such provisions were indirectly discriminatory. The Court, in effectively identical judgments in the two cases, concluded that the German Government had provided adequate justification.

Judgment (p 235):

[T]he German Government argues, in particular, that the exclusion of persons in minor employment from compulsory insurance corresponds to a structural principle of the German social security scheme.

---

[114] See, also, [1996] All ER (E) 212.

The German Government further explains that there is a social demand for minor employment, that it considers that it should respond to that demand in the context of its social policy by fostering the existence and supply of such employment and that the only means of doing this within the structural framework of the German social security scheme is to exclude minor employment from compulsory insurance.

In addition, the German Government contends that the jobs lost would not be replaced by full or part time jobs subject to compulsory insurance. On the contrary, there would be an increase in unlawful employment (black work) and a rise in circumventing devices (for instance, false self-employment) in view of the social demand for minor employment.

[I]n the current state of Community law, social policy is a matter for the Member States ... Consequently, it is for the Member States to choose the measures capable of achieving the aim of their social and employment policy. In exercising that competence, the Member States have a broad margin of discretion.

It should be noted that the social and employment policy aim relied on by the German Government is objectively unrelated to any discrimination on grounds of sex and that, in exercising its competence, the national legislature was reasonably entitled to consider that the legislation in question was necessary to achieve that aim.[115]

But, the more lenient approach is not restricted to matters of social security.

Kuratorium für Dialyse und Nierentransplantation Ev v Lewark Case C-457/93 [1996] IRLR 637

German legislation which gives members of staff committees a right to time off without loss of pay in order to attend relevant training courses provides that both full time and part time workers attending a course are compensated up to the limit of their normal working hours. In *Botel*, it was held that such a provision is indirectly discriminatory and requires objective justification.

---

[115] See, also, *Jones v Chief Adjudication Officer* [1990] IRLR 533, CA, where, in the context of a very complex claim alleging indirect discrimination in the operation of social security provisions, Mustill LJ observed: 'I think it is essential when considering proportionality in the context of the Directive to be very clear about the issue which the national court is called upon to decide. What the court does not have to decide is whether it represents a sensible and moderate way of giving effect to a general legislative policy. Those general questions fall within the purview of the national legislature and of the national constitutional court, if the Member State possesses one, and are not the concern of European law. What the national court must do is to identify with precision those features of the measure under attack which discriminate against members of one sex either directly by their terms or indirectly by their effect. The court must then consider whether *those features* are the unavoidable consequence of a justifiable policy, not in itself of a sexual discriminatory nature.

The task is not to assess the general merits of [the] regulation ... but to consider whether those features of it which are sexually discriminatory can be validated on the grounds of a sexually neutral social policy.'

The complainant in this case worked four days a week and attended a course in respect of a day when she would not otherwise have been working. She was not compensated for that day.

Judgment (p 646):

The German Government considers that ... it is justified by the principle that staff council members are not paid, which is intended to ensure their independence ... from both internal and external pressures.

Such a social policy aim appears in itself to be unrelated to any discrimination on grounds of sex [and in itself is a worthy aim].

[T]he legislation is likely to discourage part time workers from performing staff council functions or acquiring the knowledge necessary for performing them, thus making it more difficult for that category of worker to be represented by qualified staff council members.

Advocate General (pp 642–43):

A distinction can ... be drawn between economic grounds and social policy grounds. Where it is alleged that a difference in treatment between men and women is justified on economic grounds, it is usually necessary to evaluate the specific circumstances of the case, taking into account, *inter alia*, the requirements of the market and of the employer concerned. Where a difference in treatment arises directly from national legislation and it is alleged that it is justified by reasons of social policy, it is less likely that the specific circumstances of the employees and of the employer concerned will be of decisive influence. In such a case, it may be possible for this Court to give more detailed guidance to the national court.

[T]he difference in treatment of part time workers is inherent in the nature of part time work and any disadvantage which part time workers suffer as a result of the measures is only an accidental consequence of the principle of compensation for loss of earnings.

The tenor of the judgment is probably meant as an indication to the German courts that they will be safe in finding the policy is justified. The case shows again that, while for analytical purposes it is important to divide them into their component parts, it is also important to view indirect discrimination cases in the round. The employer's argument is undoubtedly strengthened by the fact that the challenged payment only came within Art 119 on a wide reading of that provision,[116] and that, while there was indirect discrimination, the impact on an individual part time employee was rather marginal.

Whether the European Court in *Seymour-Smith* will adopt such a relatively lenient approach to the issue of justification is a matter for speculation.[117] On

---

[116] See below, p 403.

[117] The same problem potentially arises in *Nash v Mark/Roe Group Ltd* [1998] IRLR 168, where it was held that prohibiting those above normal retiring age from claiming unfair dismissal was indirectly discriminatory against men over 60. In that case, no justification was advanced.

the one hand, it is arguable that the most lenient approaches have been taken in social security cases; on the other, that it is a recent shift in the political make up of the Court which has made it more likely that decisions will uphold the actions of governments of Member States.

CHAPTER 10

DISCRIMINATION IN EMPLOYMENT

The vast majority of litigation under the Sex Discrimination Act 1975 and the Race Relations Act 1976 concerns discrimination in employment. This reflects the importance attached to employment in our society, in financial terms and in terms of self-esteem and psychological well being, especially where that employment relationship is ongoing and, for many people, semi-permanent. It also reflects the fact that in many respects it is easier for applicants to bring proceedings before Industrial Tribunals[1] than before county courts.

To succeed in a claim of unlawful employment discrimination, it is first necessary to establish that there has been discrimination within the meaning of s 1, and secondly that the discrimination satisfied one of the particular forms of discrimination which are outlawed in the employment context.[2] Section 6 of the SDA 1975 and s 4 of the RRA 1976 set out the different forms of unlawful discrimination, in what are largely identical terms. The difference is that s 4(2)(a) of the RRA 1976 covers discrimination in the terms of employment, a matter which in relation to sex discrimination is covered by the EqPA 1970.

QUALIFYING REQUIREMENTS

Employment

An applicant must first show that he or she is employed at an establishment in Great Britain. Under s 82(1) of the SDA 1975 and s 78(1) of the RRA 1976, 'employment' means 'employment under a contract of service or of apprenticeship or a contract personally to execute any work or labour'. The definition is wider than most employment protection legislation, such as the law of unfair dismissal, which only covers employees – those who work under a contract of employment. Most self-employed workers are thus entitled to bring a complaint if they are rejected for work because of gender or

---

1   Re-named Employment Tribunals as a result of the Employment Rights (Dispute Resolution) Act, s 1(1).

2   In *Weathersfield Ltd v Sargent* [1998] IRLR 14, EAT, Morison J said that 'the tribunal should start with the activities which form the subject matter of the complaint which fall, or allegedly fall, within s 4 [of the RRA 1976]. Section 1 is a definition section which will only arise assuming that an activity has been identified falling within s 4'. This is because, from a practical point of view, it makes sense first to identify the action complained of.

race, such as the self-employed sales assistant in *Quinnen v Hovells*.[3] Waite J
said that 'those who engage, however cursorily, the talents, skills or labour of
the self-employed' must ensure there is no discrimination in their
appointment, terms or dismissal.[4] Purely commercial contracts are, however,
outside the scope of this part of the legislation,[5] though they may be covered
by the prohibition on discrimination in relation to goods, facilities and
services.[6] In *Mirror Group Newspapers v Gunning*,[7] the contract was between a
newspaper and an independent wholesale newspaper distributor. It was not
necessary under the terms of the contract that the distributor company should
itself necessarily execute the work; the purpose of the contract was not the
execution of any work or labour but the distribution of newspapers and
therefore it fell outside the definition.

Under s 85 of the SDA 1975 and s 75 of the RRA 1976, Crown employees
are protected on the same basis as other employees, although office-holders
such as magistrates fall outside the scope of the legislation.[8] While apprentices
are covered, it was held in *Daley v Allied Suppliers Ltd*[9] that a Youth
Opportunities Programme trainee was outside the legislation as there was no
contract of any description between the trainee and the employer who was
alleged to have discriminated.[10]

While an illegal contract, such as one where the tax and national insurance
authorities are defrauded, may well preclude a claim for unfair dismissal, it
was held in *Leighton v Michael and Charalambous*[11] that an employee under
such a contract was nevertheless entitled to sue for sexual harassment. It was
held that the rights arose under the statute rather than under the contract;

---

3 [1984] ICR 525; [1984] IRLR 227, EAT.
4 It was held in *Wadi v Cornwall and Isles of Scilly Family Practitioner Committee* [1985] ICR
   492, EAT, that no contract existed between a GP and a local family health services
   authority, and therefore no claim could be brought under anti-discrimination
   legislation.
5 In *Loughran and Kelly v Northern Ireland Housing Executive* [1998] IRLR 70, NICA, it was
   held that the engagement or non-engagement of a firm of solicitors to carry out work on
   behalf of the defendants fell outside the scope of the legislation, as such work was not
   'personally to execute any work or labour'. However, the result was different in the case
   of a one-person firm where the owner was, in effect, the personal contracting party.
6 See below, Chapter 11.
7 [1986] ICR 145; [1986] 1 All ER 385, CA. 'The CRE proposes that this limitation should
   be removed, and also that the legislation should be extended so as to cover volunteers.'
   See *Reform of the Race Relations Act: Proposals from the Commission for Racial Equality*, 1998,
   London: CRE, pp 22–23.
8 *Knight v Attorney General* [1979] ICR 194, EAT; *Department of the Environment v Fox* [1979]
   ICR 736, EAT.
9 [1983] ICR 90; [1983] IRLR 14, EAT.
10 Employers who provide training have now been designated as vocational training
   bodies and so are now within the legislation by that route. Furthermore, Training and
   Enterprise Councils, who are now responsible for programmes such as the one at issue
   in *Daley*, must have an equal opportunity policy in place as a condition of funding.
11 [1995] ICR 1091; [1996] IRLR 67, EAT.

reference to the contract was merely to establish that the complainant was 'employed'. It would appear to follow that a complaint of refusal to enter or discriminatory termination of such a contract would fail on the ground of illegality.

In Great Britain

A complainant must be employed at an establishment in Great Britain,[12] a condition which is satisfied 'unless the employee does his work wholly or mainly outside Great Britain'.[13] This is a question of fact. The specific problem areas have arisen in relation to seafarers. A claim may be brought by someone who works on a ship registered in Great Britain unless the work is done *wholly* outside Great Britain;[14] but if the ship is registered abroad, the normal 'wholly or mainly outside Great Britain' test applies. In *Haughton v Olau Line (UK) Ltd*[15] the employee could not claim because the ship was registered in [West] Germany and worked mainly outside British territorial waters. This was despite the fact that Germany is part of the EC and thus governed by the Equal Treatment Directive.[16] It was held that the British statute was unambiguous and could not be interpreted in the light of that Directive. This approach is now probably wrong. *Marleasing* tells us that domestic legislation must be interpreted in the light of the policy of European law, and there is a strong argument of principle that a person who works all or most of the time within the EC must be protected under EC law if the employer is subject to the law of any Member State.[17] A further example of primacy of EC law was shown in *Bossa v Nordstress Ltd*,[18] where an Italian national claimed that he had been discriminated against on ground of nationality contrary to the RRA 1976. Despite the fact that the job entailed working wholly or mainly outside Great Britain, it was held that the claim could proceed; Art 48 of the Treaty of Rome, which provides for free movement of workers and thus protects

---

12 In 1987, both statutes were extended so as to cover the off-shore oil industry: see the Sex Discrimination and Equal Pay (Off-Shore Employment) Order SI 1987/930; and the Race Relations (Off-Shore Employment) Order SI 1987/920.

13 SDA 1975, s 10; RRA 1976, s 8.

14 In *Deria v The General Council of British Shipping* [1986] ICR 172; [1986] IRLR 108, CA, the claim failed despite the fact that the ship unexpectedly docked in Southampton, on the ground that when the employment commenced it was contemplated that the work would be done wholly outside Great Britain. The justification was that the parties would know for certain at the outset of the voyage whether or not the legislation applied, an explanation which will work in favour of the employer far more often than vice versa.

15 [1986] ICR 357; [1986] 2 All ER 47; [1986] IRLR 465, CA.

16 Directive (76/207/EEC), OJ L39/40, 1976.

17 See *Murray v NAAFI*, unreported, IT, Case No: 3100459/96, see 34 DCLD 11.

18 [1998] IRLR 285, EAT.

against discrimination on the ground of nationality, meant that the territorial provision of the RRA 1976 had here to be disapplied. This approach only benefits EU citizens alleging nationality discrimination.

Section 9 of the RRA 1976 grants an exception for seafarers recruited abroad, who may thus be paid less than their British recruited counterparts. The industry successfully lobbied that an obligation to pay 'Western' rates to third world based workers would seriously damage the British shipping industry.

RECRUITMENT AND SELECTION

Section 6(1) of the SDA 1975 and s 4(1) of the RRA 1976 are effectively identical. The former provides that:

> It is unlawful for a person, in relation to employment by him at an establishment in Great Britain, to discriminate against a woman:
>
> (a) in the arrangements he makes for the purpose of determining who should be offered that employment; or
>
> (b) in the terms on which he offers her that employment; or
>
> (c) by refusing or deliberately omitting to offer her employment.

The Codes of Practice issued by the Commission for Racial Equality and the Equal Opportunities Commission provide guidance on how to comply with the law and how to promote equal opportunities. Much of the guidance concerns the actual processes of how to avoid discrimination in recruitment. Failure to observe a provision of the Codes is not in itself automatically unlawful, but is evidence which may be taken into account in determining whether discrimination has occurred.[19]

Advertising[20]

Section 29(1) of the RRA 1976 makes it unlawful to publish 'an advertisement[21] which indicates, or might reasonably be understood as indicating, an intention by a person to do an act of discrimination' even if in fact any subsequent act of discrimination would be lawful. The equivalent provision of the SDA 1975, s 38(1), is weaker, being limited to those

---

[19] See above, pp 167–68.

[20] See 'Job advertising and the SDA' (1993) 52 EOR 12.

[21] 'Advertisement' is widely defined and need not necessarily be to the public; internal staff communications are thus included. Other examples include postcards in shop windows and house-to-house circulars.

advertisements which 'indicate an intention' to do an unlawful act.[22] However, s 38(3) creates a presumption that job titles with a sexual connotation (postman, waitress, etc) indicate an intention to discriminate unless the contrary specifically appears in the wording of the advertisement. The test for determining intention is objective, based on what an ordinary reasonable person, without any special knowledge, would understand by the advertisement. What the employer intended is irrelevant.[23]

It is clear that both the publisher and the advertiser may be liable for discriminatory advertising. The right to take action is placed primarily in the hands of the Equal Opportunities Commission and the Commission for Racial Equality. All a person offended by a discriminatory advertisement who is not interested in the position advertised can do is to inform the relevant Commission of the facts. However, it was long thought that advertising forms part of the arrangements made under s 6(1) or s 4(1) for the purpose of determining who will be offered employment, and thus someone directly affected in such a way had a right to claim.[24] Furthermore, unlike actions instigated by the Commissions, individual actions are not limited to complaints about the wording. It might, for example, be argued that it was indirectly discriminatory to place an advert in a magazine predominantly read by women or a part of a factory predominantly frequented by men. While in such a case the disparate impact would be difficult if not impossible to establish, and an employer should not be liable if reasonable efforts have been made to ensure that the applicant pool is representative, it should in theory be possible for a claim to be brought by, for example, someone who never saw an advertisement because of where it was placed.

This view of the law was altered by *Cardiff Women's Aid v Hartup*,[25] where Smith J said that 'it is only the Commission for Racial Equality which can bring ... proceedings. We also accept the construction of s 29 ... that "an intention by a person to do an act of discrimination" should be contrasted with "an act of discrimination" itself ...' As a result, individuals may not sue if they are affected by a discriminatory advertisement; they have to rely on the appropriate Commission to take action. The individual right to sue is dependent on the *individual* being discriminated against; thus the person must apply, wait to be rejected, and then sue, when presumably the wording of the

---

22 An advertisement to discriminate in a lawful way is protected by s 38(2), enabling an employer to specify that a female is wanted in circumstances where being female is a genuine occupational qualification for the job being advertised.

23 In *Equal Opportunities Commission v Robertson* [1980] IRLR 44, the Industrial Tribunal held that the words 'craftsman', 'ex-policeman or similar', 'bloke', 'manageress' (but not 'manager' and 'carpenter/handyman') all had sexual connotations and so it would need to be specifically stated in the advertisement that the job was open to people of either sex.

24 *Brindley v Tayside Health Board* [1976] IRLR 364, IT.

25 [1994] IRLR 390, EAT.

advert may be used as part of the evidence that discrimination has occurred. The incentive for individuals to go through such a process is decidedly limited. Such a restriction is particularly inappropriate where it concerns internal company advertisements: there is no fear of intermeddlers commencing litigation, and the effect on excluded individuals more likely to be immediate and significant.

The Code of Practice on racial equality recommends that 'employers should not confine advertisements unjustifiably to those areas or publications which would exclude or disproportionately reduce the numbers of applicants of a particular racial group' and that '[i]n order to demonstrate their commitment to equality of opportunity it is recommended that where employers send literature to applicants, this should include a statement that they are equal opportunity employers'.[26]

Cases on discriminatory advertising have been few; the Commissions have preferred to proceed by way of advice and explanation and have sought as much voluntary co-operation as possible. The cases themselves have usually involved flagrant and obvious breaches of the law, which have understandably become less common, though non-discriminatory advertising in no way guarantees that the remainder of the recruitment process will be free from direct or indirect discrimination. In practice, the greater problem with discriminatory advertisements concerns keeping the wording of a positive action advert within the boundary of what the law permits.

Hiring employees

Section 6 of the SDA 1975 and s 4 of the RRA 1976 are concerned with all aspects of the recruitment process, from the drawing up of the job specification to the actual decision on who will be offered a job and on what terms.[27] If the *effect* of the procedures is discriminatory, it is irrelevant that they are not intended to operate in such a fashion. In *Brennan v JH Dewhurst Ltd*,[28] a manager was responsible for the filtering out of some applicants even though he would not be involved in the final selection; his role was clearly part of the arrangements. Those filtered out would have had a claim whether or not they would have been offered the job if the procedures had operated in

---

[26] Paragraphs 1.6, 1.7; see, also, EOC Code of Practice, paras 19 and 20. Advertising may be very important as part of a strategy of positive action, as will be seen in Chapter 15. It is not unlawful to target a particular group in the hope of attracting applicants, for that in itself does not discriminate against members of the non-targeted group, assuming, of course, that actual applicants are judged solely on merit.

[27] It was held in *Ministry of Defence v Fair Employment Agency* (1988), Belfast Recorder's Court, unreported, see 355 IRLIB 14, to be discriminatory to require references only on Catholic candidates. All arrangements concerned with the taking up of references are clearly covered by the legislation.

[28] [1993] IRLR 357, EAT.

a non-discriminatory fashion or even if no one had been appointed. There is a right not to be discriminated against even if the plaintiff was unlikely to have been appointed.[29]

The Codes of Practice demonstrate how recruitment and interview practices may operate in a discriminatory manner and give examples of good practice.

Equal Opportunities Code of Practice

13 It is ... recommended that:

(a) each individual should be assessed according to his or her personal capability to carry out a given job. It should not be assumed that men only or women only will be able to perform certain kinds of work;

(b) any qualifications or requirements which are applied to a job which effectively inhibit applications from one sex or from married people should be retained only if they are justifiable in terms of the job to be done;

(c) any age limits should be retained only if they are necessary for the job. An unjustifiable age limit could constitute indirect discrimination ...

19 It is ... recommended that: ...

(b) where vacancies are filled by promotion or transfer, they should be published to all eligible employees in such a way that they do not restrict applications from either sex;

(c) recruitment solely or primarily by word of mouth may unnecessarily restrict the choice of applicants available. The method should be avoided in a workforce predominantly of one sex, if in practice it prevents members of the opposite sex from applying;

(d) where applicants are supplied through trade unions and members of one sex only come forward, this should be discussed with the unions and an alternative approach adopted.

21(a) If selection tests are used, they should be specifically related to job and/or career requirements and should measure an individual's actual or inherent ability to do or train for the work or career;

(b) tests should be reviewed regularly to ensure that they remain relevant and free from any unjustifiable bias, either in content or in scoring mechanism.

23 It is ... recommended that:

(a) employers should ensure that personnel staff, line managers, and all other employees who may come into contact with job applicants, should be trained in the provisions of the SDA, including the fact that it is unlawful to instruct or put pressure on others to discriminate;

(b) applications from men and women should be processed in exactly the

---

[29] For discussion of compensation in such cases, see below, pp 513–14.

same way. For example, there should not be separate lists of male and female or married and single applicants. All those handling applications and conducting interviews should be trained in the avoidance of unlawful discrimination and records of interviews kept, where practicable, showing why applicants were or were not appointed;

(c) questions should relate to the requirements of the job. Where it is necessary to assess whether personal circumstances will affect performance (for example, where it involves unsocial hours or extensive travel) this should be discussed objectively without detailed questions based on assumptions about marital status, children and domestic obligations. Questions about marriage plans and family intentions should not be asked, as they could be construed as showing bias against women. Information necessary for personnel records can be collected after a job offer has been made.

Code of Practice: Racial Equality

1.13 In order to avoid direct or indirect discrimination it is recommended that selection tests and criteria are examined to ensure that they are related to job requirements and are not unlawfully discriminatory ... For example:

(a) a standard of English higher than that needed for the safe and effective performance of the job or clearly demonstrable career pattern should not be required, or a higher level of educational qualification than is needed;

(b) in particular, employers should not disqualify applicants because they are unable to complete an application form unassisted unless personal completion of the form is a valid test of the standard of English required for safe and effective performance of the job;

(c) overseas degrees, diplomas and other qualifications which are comparable with UK qualifications should be accepted as equivalents, and not simply assumed to be of an inferior quality;

(d) selection tests which contain irrelevant questions or exercises on matters which may be unfamiliar to racial minority applicants should not be used (for example, general knowledge questions on matters more likely to be familiar to indigenous applicants);

(e) selection tests should be checked to ensure that they are related to the job's requirements, that is, an individual's test markings should measure ability to do or train for the job in question.

1.14 In order to avoid direct or indirect discrimination it is recommended that:

(a) gate, reception and personnel staff should be instructed not to treat casual or formal applicants from particular racial groups less favourably than others. These instructions should be confirmed in writing:

(b) in addition, staff responsible for shortlisting, interviewing and selecting candidates should be:

- clearly informed of selection criteria and of the need for their consistent application;

- given guidance or training on the effects which generalised assumptions and prejudices about race can have on selection decisions;

- made aware of the possible misunderstandings that can occur in interviews between persons of different cultural background;

(c) wherever possible, shortlisting and interviewing should not be done by one person alone, but should at least be checked at a more senior level.

Word of mouth hiring may give rise to discrimination, although one suspects that it is still commonplace, especially where there is an urgent need to fill a vacancy. It is a cheap and convenient method, often thought to be at least as reliable as more formal methods, whereas complying to the letter with the Codes of Practice imposes costs on the employer.[30] It is very important to ensure that recruitment knowledge is widely and generally available; even sports clubs and other networks may be a source of job information, sources which could work to the disadvantage of women and black people.

We have seen that many selection criteria may be indirectly discriminatory: mobility, experience, ability in English, education in the UK, etc. The Codes recommend – and the law may insist – that employers ensure that such requirements are actually necessary.[31] The combined impact of the law, the Code of Practice and more general pressure on behalf of women has certainly contributed to a reduction in the utilisation of criteria seen to disadvantage women. For example, it is probable that the use of mobility requirements is declining as employers fear that their utilisation has reduced the ability of employers to recruit and retain well qualified women.

However, the ability of the Codes and the law to counter direct discrimination is problematic; stereotypes may be unspoken or unacknowledged. It is safe to assume that discriminatory attitudes and behaviour may flourish more easily where employers do not operate their recruitment procedures with any degree of formality; it would *not* be safe to assume that formal procedures can necessarily prevent discriminatory attitudes and behaviour from being manifested. This is especially true for jobs

---

[30] Two CRE formal investigations castigated employers who adopted word of mouth recruitment. A policy of requiring drivers to be recommended by an existing employee had the result that the only black employee was the brother-in-law of one of the drivers; see *F Broomfield and London Drivers Supplied Services Ltd, Employment Agency,* 1980, London: CRE; Massey Ferguson in Coventry did not advertise for vacancies, but relied on unsolicited applications. This benefited those who could obtain information from current employees, and, as a result, there were six black employees in a total workforce of 5,500. This is precisely the type of case where a formal investigation is potentially so valuable, as an individual is unlikely to be able to make a successful claim for a failure to advertise; see *Massey Ferguson Perkins Ltd,* 1982, London: CRE.

[31] See above, pp 291–314.

where recruitment is based on attitude rather than ability – where decisions are based on subjective rather than objective criteria.[32] In addition, the subjective criteria themselves may be affected by racial or gender issues. These may range from ideas that women do not want to build a career; that some jobs such as sales require an aggressive personality women do not possess; for other jobs that 'femininity' will give a more effective job performance; that members of a particular racial group might antagonise clients or fellow employees or would not 'fit in';[33] or take long periods of leave to visit relatives. In many such cases, discrimination remains concealed and impossible for applicants to prove, especially where these and other similar criteria are used to distinguish between candidates who, on paper, appear relatively equally qualified. The impact of the law in these marginal and subjective cases is extremely difficult to determine.[34]

It may be possible to establish discrimination purely from the way in which an interview was conducted. In *Saunders v Richmond BC*,[35] amongst other questions put to a female golf professional was: 'Do you think men respond as well to a woman golf pro as to a man?' It was clear that such a question would not have been put to a man; the question whether she could teach men really meant whether they could accept being taught by her, but it was held that asking such gender-related questions was not of itself discriminatory and that on the facts discrimination had not been established. Such questions, though, usually reflect discriminatory attitudes and are strongly discouraged by the Code of Practice. Thus, it may be that nowadays not a great deal more evidence will be needed to support a finding of discrimination where an interview panel has persistently and intrusively questioned a female candidate about family responsibilities and childcare arrangements. The EAT also expressed the rather more controversial view that such questions may be entirely appropriate if related to capacity to do the job. The facts of *Saunders* have some parallels to those concerning jobs entailing the counselling of people of a different sex, and here questions to establish appropriate empathy – which may not be asked in precisely the same way of both genders – are justified. However, such argument is less convincing as regards questions designed to establish empathy with the needs of members of a different race.

---

[32] See Jenkins, R, *Racism and Recruitment: Managers, Organisations and Equal Opportunity in the Labour Market*, 1986, Cambridge: CUP, above, pp 18–21.

[33] See, eg, *Noone v North West Thames RHA* [1988] ICR 813; [1988] IRLR 195, CA, where a Sri Lankan consultant microbiologist, who was by far the best candidate on paper, was rejected for this reason.

[34] On the problems involved in proving discrimination, see above, pp 159–74.

[35] [1978] ICR 75; [1977] IRLR 362, EAT. See, also, *Adams v Strathclyde Regional Council* (1989), unreported, EAT, Case No: 456/88; *Woodhead v Chief Constable of West Yorkshire Police* (1990), unreported, EAT, Case No: 285/89.

Discriminatory terms of employment

Offers which are on different terms are potentially caught by s 6(1)(b) of the SDA 1975 and s 4(1)(b) of the RRA 1976. Once the offer becomes part of the contract, any sex discrimination claim must then be under the EqPA 1970 rather than the SDA 1975; the complex interrelationship between the two pieces of legislation will be dealt with in Chapter 12.[36] One point must be noted here though: under the EqPA 1970 a female applicant must normally point to an actual male comparator with whom to compare her terms and conditions of employment, whereas an equivalent claimant under RRA 1976 need only point to a hypothetical comparator of a different racial group.

Discrimination within employment

Under s 6(2)(a) of the SDA 1975, it is unlawful for an employer to discriminate against a woman 'in the way he affords her access to opportunities for promotion, transfer or training, or to any other benefits, facilities or services, or by refusing or deliberately omitting to afford her access to them ...'. Section 4(2)(b) of the RRA 1976 is effectively identical. Sections 6(2)(b) and 4(2)(c) respectively render unlawful discrimination by dismissal, or by subjection 'to any other detriment'. The concept of detriment within employment is potentially very wide. According to Brandon LJ in *Ministry of Defence v Jeremiah*,[37] it simply means 'putting under a disadvantage'. The fact that this clearly includes disadvantages which are not immediately measurable in financial terms explains how sexual and racial harassment are brought within the concept of detriment. The notion of disadvantage is sufficiently wide to cover situations falling short of amounting to a breach of contract, let alone a fundamental breach entitling the employee to resign and claim constructive unfair dismissal.[38]

EOC Code of Practice

25 It is ... recommended that:

(a) where an appraisal system is in operation, the assessment criteria should be examined to ensure that they are not unlawfully discriminatory and the scheme monitored to assess how it is working in practice;

(b) when a group of workers predominantly of one sex is excluded from an appraisal scheme, access to promotion, transfer and training and to

---

[36] See below, pp 390–91.
[37] [1980] QB 87; [1979] 3 All ER 833; [1979] IRLR 436, CA.
[38] Employment Rights Act 1996, s 95(1)(c).

other benefits should be reviewed, to ensure there is no unlawful indirect discrimination;

(c) promotion and career development patterns are reviewed to ensure that the traditional qualifications are justifiable requirements for the job to be done ...;

(d) when general ability and personal qualities are the main requirements for promotion to a post, care should be taken to consider favourably candidates of both sexes with differing career patterns and general experience;

(e) rules which restrict or preclude transfer between certain jobs should be questioned and changed if they are found to be unlawfully discriminatory. Employees of one sex may be concentrated in sections from which transfers are traditionally restricted without justification;

(f) policies and practices regarding selection for training, day release and personal development should be examined for direct and indirect discrimination. Where there is found to be an imbalance in training as between sexes, the cause should be identified to ensure that it is not discriminatory ...

30 It is ... recommended that:

(a) particular care is taken to ensure that an employee who has in good faith taken action under the Sex Discrimination Act or the Equal Pay Act does not receive less favourable treatment than other employees, for example, by being disciplined or dismissed;

(b) employees should be advised to use the internal procedures, where appropriate, but this is without prejudice to an individual's right to apply to an Industrial Tribunal ...;

(c) particular care is taken to deal effectively with all complaints of discrimination, victimisation or harassment. It should not be assumed that they are made by those who are over-sensitive.

The guidance on promotion is especially significant where an organisation operates an internal labour market (which places added weight on the original recruitment decision). It is not uncommon for there to be favoured pathways to promotion, whether by accident or design benefiting those hired to certain lower level entry jobs. If these are predominantly male, women will be disadvantaged. Just as with initial hiring, the Code works on the assumption that there is less scope for discrimination if there is open competition through advertising rather than promotion by simple selection; if the latter is the case, formal appraisal procedures should be in place.[39]

---

[39] Even objective promotion criteria may be indirectly discriminatory, especially if dependent primarily on length of service. However, it is arguable that women stand to gain more by the use of objective criteria, such as seniority, than they stand to lose because they have lower average lengths of service. Such criteria, after all, remove the need for subjective decision making where unspoken discriminatory assumptions may operate to women's disadvantage. See above, pp 44–47, 57–59.

It is clear that many women and black people are working in jobs from where there are no promotion pathways. An assumption that part time employees are unsuitable for promotion may be unjustifiable indirect discrimination. It is possible to argue that lack of promotion opportunities in lower, predominantly female or black grades, is indirectly discriminatory.[40] In *Francis v British Airways Engine Overhaul Ltd*,[41] the EAT said that a claim could be formulated that to be eligible for promotion on the basis of service and experience one would have to be a member of a particular grade or class of employee. The potential radicalism of this ruling, which implies that employers might need to reorganise their structure to ensure that promotion opportunities are more equitably distributed, has not been followed up in subsequent cases.

As promotion opportunities need to be open to all, irrespective of race or gender, it follows that there is no *obligation* on employers to give special training to women or minorities to equip them for promotion.[42] However, such special training may be *permissible* as being positive action to remedy situations where there is under-representation of women or minorities.[43] Where this is done, the actual decision on who to hire must continue to be made solely on the basis of merit.

The Codes emphasise that all training opportunities should be checked to ensure the absence of direct or indirect discrimination. Length-of-service requirements, exclusion of part time employees and preference to those with technical qualifications are examples of criteria which may disadvantage women. Day release has often only been available in the immediate post-school years, which may disadvantage women returners to the labour market and limit retraining opportunities.

Discrimination is also prohibited as regards access to fringe benefits. The most important of these is pension provision,[44] but discrimination could occur in access to sick pay schemes, mortgage subsidy, company car arrangements and so on, especially against part time employees. The effect of *Bilka-Kaufhaus v Weber von Hartz*[45] is that any provision which disadvantages part time

---

[40] Such a claim is subject to any limitations existing under the general principles of indirect discrimination law. Eg, few claims will be possible if it continues to be the law that the requirement or condition under attack needs to be an absolute bar, as was decided in *Perera v Civil Service Commission (No 2)* [1983] ICR 428; [1983] IRLR 166, CA, than if the more flexible approach adopted by the EAT in *Falkirk Council v Whyte* [1997] IRLR 560 is accepted. See above, p 270.

[41] [1982] IRLR 10, EAT.

[42] *Mecca Leisure Group Ltd v Chatprachong* [1993] ICR 668; [1993] IRLR 531, where the EAT held that there was no obligation to provide special language training which would have better equipped the plaintiff for the relevant promotion examination.

[43] See below, pp 266–71.

[44] See Chapter 13.

[45] Case 170/84 [1986] ECR 1607; [1986] 2 CMLR 701; [1987] ICR 110; [1986] IRLR 317.

employees will need to be justified according to objective criteria which by definition will not include long standing traditional arrangements. Recreational benefits are within the definition, so it might be possible to argue that the employer discriminates by providing facilities and subsidy for predominantly male sports rather than female, or predominantly white or European cultural activities rather than those more likely to be of interest to minority employees.

DISCRIMINATORY DISMISSALS

These are made unlawful by s 6(2)(b) of the SDA[46] and s 4(2)(c) of the RRA.[47] There is overlap with the general unfair dismissal provisions now contained in the Employment Rights Act 1996. The two key differences between unfair dismissal and discriminatory dismissal[48] concern qualifying conditions and compensation. The House of Lords in *R v Secretary of State for Employment ex p Equal Opportunities Commission*[49] held that the weekly hours threshold which used to exist for unfair dismissal,[50] and other, purposes was contrary to European law as being indirectly discriminatory against women. Employees who normally worked for at least 16 hours per week needed two years' continuous employment; those who normally worked between eight and 16 hours needed five years. As a result, the weekly hours requirement was abolished.[51] Unfair dismissal is thus brought into line with anti-

---

[46] Article 3 of the Equal Treatment Directive outlaws discriminatory dismissals on ground of gender.

[47] It was held in *Adekeye v The Post Office (No 2)* [1997] ICR 110; [1997] IRLR 105, CA, that there was no jurisdiction to hear a complaint of racial discrimination in the hearing of the internal appeal which followed dismissal for gross misconduct as the applicant was not a 'person employed' at the date of the appeal hearing. The Act does not protect persons previously employed by the defendant employer. The reasoning would not apply where a 'dismissed' employee retains employment status pending appeal. There is no suggestion by the Court of Appeal that a purposive approach to statutory construction would have been in keeping with statutory policy and, because of the equivalent wording of SDA 1975, in keeping with European law.

[48] There is no definition of dismissal in the anti-discrimination legislation. It was held in *Weathersfield Ltd v Sargent* [1998] IRLR 14, EAT, that the same definition is applicable as in the general part of employment law, thereby enabling an employee who resigns because of some highly detrimental treatment at work, such as severe harassment, to claim that she had been constructively dismissed and could thus claim that her 'dismissal' was discriminatory. In any event, action falling outside the statutory definition of dismissal might still involve the imposition of a detriment.

[49] [1995] 1 AC 1; [1994] ICR 317; [1994] 1 All ER 910; [1994] IRLR 176.

[50] In *Jesuthasan v Hammersmith and Fulham London BC* [1998] IRLR 372, CA, in relation to a dismissal after the *EOC* case but before the amending regulations, it was held that a man who previously would not have had sufficient hours of service could also rely on the House of Lords' decision to enable an unfair dismissal claim to proceed, even though the basis of that decision had been the indirectly discriminatory effect of the requirements against women.

[51] The Employment Protection (Part Time Employees) Regulations SI 1995/31.

discrimination law, which has never imposed an hours threshold. *R v Secretary of State for Employment ex p Seymour-Smith and Perez*[52] concerned a similar attempt to argue that a statutory instrument which increased the unfair dismissal qualifying period from one year to two years was indirectly discriminatory against women, as disproportionately fewer women obtained two years' continuous employment. The case was referred to the ECJ, but at the time of writing the qualifying period remains part of unfair dismissal law[53] but not anti-discrimination law.[54]

Unfair dismissal compensation remains subject to a statutory maximum limit on compensation.[55] An equivalent statutory maximum limit in both race and sex discrimination cases was swept away as a result of the decision of the European Court in *Marshall (No 2)*.[56] A plaintiff, therefore, may have significant advantages if she can establish that the dismissal was discriminatory, but it is often more difficult to do so than to establish unfairness under the general provisions. It is possible to combine the two allegations in one statement of claim.[57]

The impact of redundancy may not operate in a gender-neutral fashion. Assuming that the decision to impose redundancies is not tainted by discriminatory considerations, it is contended that no challenge can be mounted simply because there is a disproportionate number of women or minorities in the employees on whom redundancies will be imposed.[58] There may also be adverse impact between men and women in relation to offers of alternative employment, as it may be easier for men than women to move house or travel further to work. Such an effect is not unlawful: it is part of

---

[52] [1997] ICR 371; [1997] 2 All ER 273; [1997] IRLR 315, HL.

[53] In *Davidson v City Electrical Factors* [1998] IRLR 108, the EAT in Scotland held that all allegations of unfair dismissal where the complainant had been employed for between one and two years should be stayed pending the decision of the European Court in *Seymour-Smith*. The Government is proposing to reduce the qualifying period to one year. See *Fairness at Work*, Cm 3968, 1998, London: The Stationery Office, para 3.10.

[54] Under the Employment Rights Act 1996, s 99, there is no qualifying period where the allegation is that the dismissal is unfair because it was connected with pregnancy. See above, pp 198–200.

[55] As from 1 April 1998, the limit is £12,000; see Employment Rights (Increase of Limits) Order 1998 SI 1998/524. It is now proposed that the limit should be abolished. *Ibid, Fairness at Work*, para 3.5.

[56] *Marshall v Southampton and South West Hampshire AHA* Case C-271/91 [1993] ECR I-4367; [1994] AC 530; [1994] QB 126; [1994] ICR 242; [1993] IRLR 445. See below, pp 509–10.

[57] The EAT pointed out in *Clarke v Eley (IMI) Kynoch Ltd* [1983] ICR 165; [1982] IRLR 482, that an indirectly discriminatory dismissal will not automatically be unfair as the facts which made it discriminatory might not have been known to the employer at the time of the decision to dismiss; whether or not the dismissal is unfair will depend on the employer's knowledge and purpose at that time.

[58] Cf *Moon v Homeworthy Furniture Ltd* [1977] ICR 117; [1976] IRLR 298 where the EAT held, in an unfair dismissal case, that it is not possible to argue that the employer was wrong to decide that redundancies had to be made.

structural discrimination and cannot be laid at the feet of an individual employer.

Equal Opportunities Commission Code of Practice

32 It is ... recommended that:

(a) care is taken that members of one sex are not disciplined or dismissed for performance or behaviour which would be overlooked or condoned in the other sex;

(b) redundancy procedures affecting a group of employees predominantly of one sex should be reviewed, so as to remove any effects which could be disproportionate and unjustifiable;

(c) conditions of access to voluntary redundancy benefit should be made available on equal terms to male and female employees in the same or not materially different circumstances;

(d) where there is downgrading or short time working ... the arrangements should not unlawfully discriminate on grounds of sex;

(e) all reasonably practicable steps should be taken to ensure that a standard of conduct or behaviour is observed which prevents members of either sex from being intimidated, harassed or otherwise subjected to unfavourable treatment on the ground of their sex.

PERMISSIBLE DISCRIMINATION WITHIN EMPLOYMENT

This section brings together a range of situations where discrimination in employment on the ground of race or gender continues, to a greater or lesser extent, to be permissible. It does not consider discrimination in pension provision or permissible discrimination within the non-employment context, which are considered elsewhere. In addition, a number of exceptions or possible exceptions relating to issues of pregnancy, maternity and paternity leave have been specifically considered in Chapter 7.

The most significant general exception in both the SDA 1975 and the RRA 1976 is what is known as a genuine occupational qualification. The choice of language closely parallels the United States Civil Rights Act which uses the phrase 'bona fide occupational qualification'. However, there is an important distinction in that, under American law, the scope of the defence has been left for judges to develop, whereas, under English law, its scope is spelt out in great detail; the defence is confined to those genuine occupational qualifications specifically included in the relevant statute. Furthermore, Art 2(2) of the Equal Treatment Directive provides that the scope of the Directive is subject to the right of Member States to exclude from its scope occupational activities 'for which, by reason of their nature or the context in which they are carried out, the sex of the worker constitutes a determining factor'. The British domestic legislation must, of course, be construed in a manner consistent with European law.

There are many more GOQs concerning sex than race. This reflects the underlying social and moral reality that segregation of the sexes is, in many circumstances, regarded as appropriate and necessary, whereas segregation of the races is seen, because of its historical connotations, as a moral evil and a practice which was used to reinforce white power over other races.

While not specifically stated in either statute, it must be the case on grounds of both logic and policy that the employer has the burden of proving the existence of a GOQ. The defence can be raised where only some of the job duties fall within the scope of the exception.[59] This is subject to two limits. First, the defence will fail if the duties of the job were reorganised with the express purpose of bringing it within the scope of the defence.[60] Secondly, under s 7(4) and 5(4), the defence will fail where other employees are 'capable of carrying out the duties', that it would be reasonable to employ them on such duties, and where this can be done without undue inconvenience. In *Lasertop Ltd v Webster*,[61] it was held that these 'other employees' to whom the duties may be re-allocated must already exist at the time, so s 7(4) did not apply where the employer was hiring for a job in a health club which was not yet open. Thus the GOQ applied even though it might well not do so once other employees had been hired.[62] In *Etam plc v Rowan*,[63] the defence of GOQ in relation to a job in a ladies' clothing shop failed because reorganisation was possible. The only parts of the job which fell within the defence involved work in the fitting room and measuring customers. But there were some 16 employees normally in the shop – all women. A man would have been able to carry out the bulk of the job and the remainder could easily have been done by other sales assistants without causing any inconvenience or difficulty for the employers. It follows that, to an extent at least, the tribunal in effect has power to require the employer to reorganise the business, or at least to conclude that the defence will fail unless such reorganisation has been carried out.

---

59 SDA 1975, s 7(3); RRA 1976, s 5(3); see *Tottenham Green* below, pp 342–44.
60 *Timex Corporation v Hodgson* [1982] ICR 63; [1981] IRLR 530, EAT.
61 [1997] IRLR 498, EAT.
62 Such a construction may well be contrary to the Equal Treatment Directive; again, no attempt was made to apply the *Marleasing* principle in order to avoid such a conflict.
63 [1989] IRLR 150, EAT. A different result was reached in *Lasertop Ltd v Webster* [1997] IRLR 498, EAT, where it was held to be permissible to restrict to women a job of selling membership of a women-only health club, as the man would have to hand over to a woman whenever the changing area was reached. The IT found this aspect of the job did not involve a great deal of time and that arrangements could have been made without undue inconvenience. The EAT, accepting the employer's argument rather easily and reversing a finding largely of fact, held that the defence was made out.

Where the defence applies, it is lawful for the employer to discriminate in the arrangements made for determining who should be offered a job, in determining that someone may not be offered a job, or in denying opportunities for promotion or transfer. These all concern aspects of management pertaining to the obtaining of employment. But the defence is not available in relation to the terms on which employment is offered, to dismissal or to the imposition of any other detriment on an employee. The defence is only concerned with the process of offering employment in situations where jobs may legitimately be restricted to one race or gender; if members of more than one race or gender are performing a job, there is no logic or policy justification for allowing the defence. Thus an employer may not, after an employee has been hired, retrospectively decide that a GOQ applies to a job in question. It is, however, permissible, to dismiss someone following a reorganisation if the new job involves a GOQ where the incumbent's previous job did not do so. According to *Timex Corporation v Hodgson*,[64] the GOQ defence is permissible because in such circumstances it affixes to the failure to offer the reorganised new job rather than dismissal from the old job.

Section 5(2) of the Race Relations Act 1976 spells out the four GOQs which appertain to race.

> Being of a particular racial group is a genuine occupational qualification for a job only where:
>
> (a) the job involves participation in a dramatic performance or other entertainment in a capacity for which a person of that racial group is required for reasons of authenticity; or
>
> (b) the job involves participation as an artist's or photographic model in the production of a work of art, visual image or sequence of visual images for which a person of that racial group is required for authenticity; or
>
> (c) the job involves working in a place where food or drink is (for payment or not) provided to and consumed by members of the public or a section of the public in a particular setting for which, in that job, a person of that racial group is required for authenticity; or
>
> (d) the holder of the job provides persons of that racial group with personal services promoting their welfare, and those services can most effectively be provided by a person of that racial group.

In addition, s 4(3) provides an exception where the employment is for the purposes of a private household. Within the structure of the legislation, this is not a GOQ, although it directly parallels one of the GOQs relating to gender.

The provisions of the Sex Discrimination Act 1975 which directly match these are in s 7(2):

---

[64] [1982] ICR 63; [1981] IRLR 530, EAT.

Being a man is a genuine occupational qualification for a job only where:

(a) the essential nature of the job calls for a man for reasons of physiology (excluding strength and stamina) or, in dramatic performances or other entertainment, so that the essential nature of the job would be materially different if carried out by a woman ...;

(e) the holder of the job provides individuals with personal services promoting their welfare or education, or similar personal services, and those personal services can most effectively be provided by a man ...

Physiology and authenticity

At first sight it appears that there are, in these provisions, two types of GOQ, one based on *physical* differences between the races or the genders, and the other based on *social* or *cultural* expectations of what is most appropriate or beneficial. However, the first category, based on physical differences, is itself entirely based on a conventional social or cultural response to such differences.

It is permitted to hire a black person or a white person in all branches of the entertainment industry, if this is read widely to include modelling in all its forms, and in the catering industry. For example, it is permitted to restrict applications for the role of Hamlet to white people and Othello to black people. Such action is *permissible*; it is not *mandatory*. Directors may cast a white person as Othello. The suspicion may be that the practical result of the law does little to enhance opportunities for minority group members working in the performing arts.[65] While the RRA 1976 is more detailed than the SDA 1975, it appears that the same criteria as to authenticity will apply when restricting candidates to members of one sex. However, it does have to be shown that the essential nature of the job would be *materially* different if carried out by a woman. This gives scope to tribunals to make value judgments about what is appropriate or necessary. The problems are epitomised by advertising, as certain types of commercials are normally cast with women or with men – washing powder and beer, for example. It is highly likely that opportunities are restricted by gender, yet it is perhaps unlikely that tribunals, even if it could be demonstrated that such practices exist, would hold them to be unlawful, even though it could hardly be argued that the job of 'starring' in a soap powder commercial would be materially different if performed by a man.

---

[65] See Pitt, G, 'Madam Butterfly and Miss Saigon: reflecting on genuine occupational qualifications', in Dine, J and Watt, B (eds), *Discrimination Law: Concepts, Limitations and Justifications*, 1996, Harlow: Addison Wesley Longman, Chapter 15.

The physiology exception – the more appropriate word would be anatomy – seems restricted to wet-nurses and those working in the sex industry.[66] Male complainants are unlikely to be numerous! 'There is a thin but important line between sex as a GOQ where the essential nature of the job requires a woman, and the case where the job can more effectively be performed by a woman because of customer reaction.'[67]

Personal services

This defence raises directly the issue of when customer reaction or customer preference may provide a defence; the very existence of the defence is based on the assumption that in some limited circumstances these factors may justify discrimination. It has to be shown that the relevant services can 'more effectively' be provided by a person of the same race or gender as the recipient. The main difference between the two statutes is that the SDA 1975 refers to 'welfare or education', while the RRA 1976 is restricted to 'welfare'. The line between the two may be hard to distinguish, (see *Tottenham Green* below) as university tutors could no doubt testify, but it contended that it is very unlikely that a court would accept that, in a normal case, education could most effectively be provided by someone of the same sex as the pupils. Only if the education has a significant welfare component might the defence apply. As a general rule, therefore, teaching jobs in single-sex schools must be open to both men and women. In Muslim schools, however, it may be regarded as appropriate that girls should only be taught by female teachers, though if this GOQ were interpreted strictly, it is arguable that such a restriction would be unlawful.

The services provided must be 'personal'.

London Borough of Lambeth v Commission for Racial Equality **[1990] IRLR 231, CA**[68]

The council advertised two jobs in the housing benefit department, one for the assistant head and the other for group manager. More than half of tenants dealt with by the department were of Afro-Caribbean or Asian origin. The council therefore decided that the employees should also be Afro-Caribbean or Asian. The advertisement specifically referred to s 5(2)(d) of the RRA 1976 – the personal services defence.

The CRE considered that these were managerial and administrative posts not covered by the defence. The council argued that the restriction was

---

[66] In *Cropper v UK Express Ltd*, unreported, an Industrial Tribunal held that sex was a GOQ for working on a telephone sex chat-line.

[67] Pannick, D, *Sex Discrimination Law*, 1985, Oxford: OUP, p 238.

[68] See, also, [1990] ICR 768.

justified so as to ensure that housing benefit officers trained by the jobholders would have a particular empathy with black claimants.

The defence failed.

Balcombe LJ (p 234):

I am wholly unpersuaded that one of the two main purposes of the Act is to promote positive action to benefit racial groups ... It is true that ss 35, 37 and 38 do allow for limited acts of positive discrimination which would otherwise be unlawful, but that does not constrain us to give to s 5(2)(d) a meaning which its words do not naturally bear. If s 5(2)(d) had been intended to provide for positive action in the particular field to which it relates, one would have expected to find it grouped together with ss 35, 37 and 38 ...

I agree with the EAT when they say that the Act appears to contemplate direct contact between the giver and the recipient – mainly face to face or where there could be susceptibility in personal, physical contact. Where language or a knowledge and understanding of cultural and religious background are of importance, then those services may most effectively be provided by a person of a particular racial group.

[The tribunal also held that the racial group of the jobholder and of the recipient were not sufficiently identified so as to establish that the holder and the recipient were of the same racial group. The IT took the view that an advertisement which purported to designate persons from at least two racial groups was not consistent with the statutory language.]

If a person is providing persons of a racial group defined by colour (for example, black people) with personal services promoting their welfare ... it will be open to an Industrial Tribunal ... to find that those services can most effectively be provided by a person of that colour, from whatever ethnic group she (or he) comes, and even though some of her (or his) clients may belong to other ethnic groups.

Three points arise from this decision. First, the Court of Appeal was surely correct to interpret the phrase 'personal services' narrowly and as requiring direct contact between provider and client. Secondly, these provisions cannot be used as a substitute for the provisions on positive action in order to ensure that a team of workers have a balanced representation of races and sexes. Maintaining such a balance, while it probably happens rather frequently, is *never* a defence to discrimination. This reflects the individualistic focus of the legislation; each and every act of hiring has to be individually justified under the GOQ provisions. Thirdly, the EAT rejected the argument that the defence under RRA 1976 can only apply if the provider of the defence is from precisely the same racial group as the recipient. This is realistic given the range of ethnic backgrounds from which a particular clientele may originate. One may surmise, however, that rather more will be needed to convince a tribunal that the services can more effectively be provided by someone from a *different*, albeit minority, group than by a white person. In a sense, such a tribunal will be required to take judicial notice of common aspects of discrimination and stereotyping experienced by members of minority ethnic groups.

Tottenham Green Under Fives' Centre v Marshall [1989] IRLR 147, EAT[69]

The policy of a day care centre was to maintain a balance between ethnic backgrounds both among the children and the staff. When an Afro-Caribbean nursery worker left it was decided to replace her with another Afro-Caribbean. At the time the centre had four white staff, one Greek Cypriot and one other Afro-Caribbean. The advertisement stated that the post was for an Afro-Caribbean worker and said that the successful applicant would need 'a personal awareness of Afro-Caribbean culture' and 'an understanding of the importance of anti-racist and anti-sexist childcare'.

The complainant was a white male and the issue was whether the GOQ defence under s 5(2)(d) of the RRA 1976 applied. The centre contended that the personal services related to four areas: maintaining the cultural background link for children of Afro-Caribbean background; dealing with the parents and discussing those matters with them; reading and talking where necessary in dialect; and generally looking after their skin and health, including where necessary plaiting their hair.

The Industrial Tribunal said that save for the requirement of reading a book in West Indian patois there was 'no evidence that a nursery worker of any ethnic origin would not be able to carry out the requirements of caring for the child at the nursery equally well'.

The EAT allowed the appeal.

Wood J (p 149):

We would make the following points:

(a) The particular racial group will need to be clearly and, if necessary, narrowly defined because it will have to be that of the holder of the post and also that of the recipient of the personal services.

(b) The holder of the post must be directly involved in the provision of the services – to direct others so to do is insufficient as the service must be personal. It does not seem to us that it need necessarily be on a one to one basis.

(c) If the post holder provides several personal services to the recipient, then provided one of those genuinely falls within the sub-section, the defence is established.

(d) 'Promoting their welfare' is a very wide expression. The facts of each case are likely to vary enormously and different considerations will apply. It would be undesirable to seek to narrow the width of those words.

(e) [T]he words are not 'must be provided' nor 'can only be provided'. The Act assumes that the personal services could be provided by others, but can they be 'most effectively provided?' Would they be less effective if provided by others? Welfare of a child will include the broad

---

[69] See, also, [1989] ICR 214.

understanding and handling of a child, and in the present circumstances an understanding of the background of the culture and the ways of the family. This is a matter of fact for the tribunal, and in so deciding the tribunal will need to carry out a delicate balancing exercise bearing in mind the need to guard against discrimination and the desirability of promoting racial integration. However, it seems to us that if a tribunal accepts that the conscious decision of a responsible employer to commit an act of discrimination and rely upon s 5(2)(d) is founded upon a genuinely held and reasonably based opinion that a GOQ will best promote the welfare of the recipient, then considerable weight should be given to that decision when reaching a conclusion whether or not the defence succeeds.

[The case was sent back to an Industrial Tribunal as too high a fence had been placed in the path of the appellants.]

(No 2) [1991] IRLR 162, EAT[70]

It was again held that the defence failed. The tribunal accepted that one of the personal services required for the post was reading and talking where necessary in dialect and that an Afro-Caribbean would most effectively provide this service. But they concluded: 'this particular requirement was the least emphasised of the four. We believe than an applicant who fulfilled the other requirements listed and who had no ability to speak or read the dialect would not have been precluded from getting the post ... Also this requirement is not mentioned in the advertisement or in the job description. It is in the nature of a desirable extra and no more.'

The EAT allowed the appeal and held that the defence succeeded.

Knox J (p 165):

[I]t is not the correct view of the meaning of this paragraph that the Industrial Tribunal can make an evaluation of the importance of the duty in question and disregard it although it is satisfied that it is something that is not so trivial that it can properly be disregarded altogether. It seems to us that sub-s (3) indicates clearly that one of the duties of the job, if it falls within any of the relevant paragraphs ... will operate to make the exception available.

[Reading and talking in dialect is] one of the duties of the job and in those circumstances, it not being trivial and it being genuine, it seems to us that the exception necessarily did apply.

The principles underlying the defence are clearly and correctly stated in this case – until the final point. The EAT *assumes* that only an Afro-Caribbean will be able to read and talk in the appropriate dialect. This is a stereotype which is no different from assuming that men are stronger than women. A white person who had the necessary abilities should have the right to be considered for such a job. That a higher proportion of Afro-Caribbean applicants would have been able to satisfy the requirements goes to justified indirect discrimination and not to the existence of a GOQ.

---

[70] See, also, [1991] ICR 320.

Neither of these cases, important as they are, do much to explore the key issue of what kinds of service are potentially within the scope of the defence. Examples often given include rape crisis centres, refuges for battered women, and birth control clinics on the one hand, and dealing with the victims of racial attack or abuse on the other. It is contended that, strictly speaking, most legal and other advice centres for minority ethnic groups would not come under this section unless specifically concerned with the experience of being black or a victim of discrimination. However, it may well be that, by analogy with *Tottenham Green*, the section will not be interpreted so rigidly. This may be all very well where the issue is of providing services to a member of a minority group. But when, if ever, can a white person argue that personal services can most effectively be provided by another white person? Given that discrimination against white people is dealt with in exactly the same way as discrimination against black people, a wide reading of this defence is potentially problematic. Tribunals have to balance two arguably conflicting approaches to discrimination law: first, that the law should aim to be colour-blind and gender-blind, under which approach the characteristics of the provider of the service should be irrelevant; secondly, the approach based on recognition of differences, under which an assumption is made that there are differences which arise from culture,[71] background and experience, and of which the law should take note. The personal services defence is a limited acceptance of the latter approach. The extent to which such a defence *ought* to be accepted is very controversial. Of course, the strategy whereby as much as possible is left to be decided on the facts by tribunals means that issues of principle and theory are unlikely to be resolved in litigation.

There is also here a potentially complex interaction of race and gender. For example, it is contended that most cases of medical treatment do not fall within the sections, because the cultural norm allows and expects medical treatment to be carried out by members of either sex. This becomes progressively less true as the medical treatment involves a greater element of counselling, as with birth control clinics. But some racial and religious groups, especially Muslim women, may object to medical examination and treatment, not necessarily intimate, by a man. If a school or a factory which was predominantly Muslim hired a female nurse, it is probable that the defence would apply. It is contended that all medical treatment comes within the meaning of the term 'personal services'; whether the services can most effectively be provided by a woman will then turn on the tribunal's evaluation of the depth and appropriateness of the objection. Furthermore, there is a clear overlap between the issue under this section of whether the services can more effectively be provided by a woman and the issue under s 7(2)(b) of whether a

---

[71] These are not necessarily based on race. The definition of racial group allows for reference to be made to what are in effect cultural differences. See above, pp 111–17.

woman might reasonably object to such procedures on the grounds of privacy or decency.

The remainder of the GOQs apply only to gender.

Privacy or decency

Section 7(2)(b) provides a defence:

... where the job needs to be held by a man to preserve privacy or decency because:

(i) it is likely to involve physical contact with men in circumstances where they might reasonably object to its being carried out by a woman; or

(ii) the holder of the job is likely to do his work in circumstances where men might reasonably object to the presence of a woman because they are in a state of undress or are using sanitary facilities ...

Examples of physical contact[72] include measurements for clothing,[73] medical procedures and perhaps instruction in sports such as gymnastics. The nature of the physical contact must potentially involve an issue of privacy or decency – dentistry or shoe fitting are outside the section. No guidance is given as to when objections are to be regarded as reasonable. The section states that it is enough if men or women *'might'* reasonably object. The question arises at the point of hiring; the employer will be refusing employment on the basis of anticipated objections and whether they will be regarded as reasonable. Given the wide variety of attitudes in society, and the fact that norms may be changing, it is impossible to be definitive on what objections will be accepted as reasonable, and, just as important, what evidence employers will be required to produce to demonstrate their belief in the existence of such objections.

This GOQ also applies to the provision of goods, facilities and services, where admitting both sexes to certain facilities simultaneously would be likely to cause serious embarrassment.[74] The EOC is concerned that the provision of women-only sports and leisure sessions does not clearly fall within this defence, as the degree of embarrassment may be insufficiently substantial, yet many women might be unwilling to participate in mixed sessions. The reason for the embarrassment may vary as between women of different cultural and religious traditions, though male sexism may cause difficulty for all different groups of women. The law needs to be clarified and perhaps widened.[75]

---

72 The IT, in *Sisley v Britannia Security Systems Ltd* [1983] ICR 628; [1983] IRLR 404, EAT, in an aspect of the decision which was not appealed, correctly held that physical contact means what it says and that proximity is insufficient.

73 *Etam plc v Rowan* [1989] IRLR 150, EAT.

74 SDA 1975, ss 35(1)(c), 35(2)

75 See *Equality in the 21st Century: a New Approach*, 1998, Manchester: EOC, paras 64–65.

The second limb of the defence is where the jobholder is in a state of undress or is using sanitary facilities.

Sisley v Britannia Security Systems Ltd [1983] IRLR 404, EAT

The employers operated a security control station. The employees worked in shifts, the longest of which was 12 hours, in a part of the premises described as 'a building within a building'. When the unit was opened, it was felt that there would be problems if men and women worked together and shared the facilities provided in such a confined space. Therefore only women were hired.

Tudor Evans J (p 408):

We read [s 7(2)(b)(ii)] as dealing with the situation where the holder of a particular job is likely to do his work, and all matters reasonably incidental to it, in circumstances where the holder might reasonably object ... because the holder is ... in a state of undress ... We do not read the sub-section as being confined to cases where the job itself requires the holder to be in a state of undress ... We think that the sub-section covers the situation where the employer says that he has to have a man (or a woman) to do the job because working conditions are such that if the holder is in a state of undress or is using sanitary facilities, he or she might object to the presence of a member of the opposite sex at the place of work ... We construe the reference to 'the duties of the job' as encompassing not only the duties of the job but all matters reasonably incidental to it ... It seems to us to be reasonably incidental to that necessary part [of taking a rest] for the women to remove their clothing.

The EAT held that, literally, the section only applied where the jobholder is in a state of undress, but that there were good policy arguments for not so restricting it and that it should also cover situations where members of the public, customers or fellow employees are in a state of undress. Otherwise the section would not cover the cleaning of showers or work in a sauna because the actual jobholder may not be undressed while performing the duties. However, the decision is problematic in that the EAT went beyond work in a state of undress to cover rest periods. There is no warrant for this, and, in addition, no consideration was given as to whether the women had to be undressed during the rest periods and whether there were alternative methods available to preserve decency.

If an employer refuses to employ both men and women on the ground that it is impracticable to provide separate toilet facilities, two questions will arise. First, is it truly impracticable? This raises similar issues to that of the provision of separate sleeping accommodation and will be considered there. Secondly, when will objection be considered reasonable? There are different tribunal decisions on whether a unisex lockable lavatory ensures enough privacy.[76] Equally, it may be contended that it is not reasonable to object to a lavatory cleaner of a different sex as long as individual cubicles are private, though some would argue that there is a difference between female cleaners in male facilities and vice versa. Who can predict what objections a tribunal would view as reasonable?

Work in a private home

Section 6(3) of the original SDA 1975 provided exceptions in all cases where the number of employees did not exceed five, and also where the employment was for the purposes of a private household. These wide exceptions were held to be contrary to the Equal Treatment Directive in *Commission of the European Communities v United Kingdom*.[77] The Court reasoned that as regards small undertakings with not more than five employees, it was not the case that in any undertaking of that size the sex of the worker would be a determining factor for the purposes of Art 2(2) of the Directive. But it was recognised that the law must reconcile the principle of equal treatment with the fundamental principle of respect for private life. The 1986 SDA therefore repealed the provisions held unlawful by the European Court and introduced a new s 2(ba) to the 1975 Act which is couched in far more restrictive terms. It provides a defence where:

> ... the job is likely to involve the holder of the job doing his work, or living, in a private home and needs to be held by a man because objection might reasonably be taken to allowing to a woman:
>
> (i) the degree of physical or social contact with a person living in the home; or
>
> (ii) the knowledge of intimate details of such a person's life,
>
> which is likely, because of the nature or circumstances of the job or of the home, which is allowed to, or available to, the holder of the job ...

For example, personal companions and nurses may be the same sex as the client; those working outside the home are not covered. For those with a large coterie of domestic servants, most, such as butlers or cooks, surely do not provide a sufficiently personal or intimate service.[78] Actual physical contact is not required; a very close working relationship may suffice as long as it provides intimate knowledge of the client's life, knowledge which must be personal rather than, say, financial.

---

[76] See 'Genuine occupational qualification' (1988) 18 EOR 24, p 28.

[77] Case 165/82 [1984] ECR 3431; [1984] ICR 192; [1984] 1 All ER 353; [1984] IRLR 29.

[78] The employee covered need not be working for the actual employer; she could be working directly with a parent or children. It is, however, unlikely that employment as a nanny, governess or private tutor will be covered, though in *Neal v Watts* (1989), IT, unreported, the rejection of a professionally qualified male nanny was held not to be unlawful because the job duties would include bathing the child and the mother liked to bath with her baby.

Section 4(3) of the RRA 1976 provides a blanket exception where the employment is 'for the purposes of a private household'. This exception is far too wide, even though it is arguable that the words 'for the purposes of' are narrower than 'in'. Many would argue that there should be no exception even where there is close and intimate proximity between employer and employee. Others, more mindful of human autonomy, would concede that there should be an exception, but drawn no more widely than that under the amended SDA 1975.

Live-in jobs

Section 7(2)(c) provides a defence where:

> ... the nature or location of the establishment makes it impracticable for the holder of the job to live elsewhere than in premises provided by the employer, and:
>
> (i) the only such premises which are available ... are lived[79] in, or normally lived in, by men, and are not equipped with separate sleeping accommodation for women and sanitary facilities which could be used by women in privacy from men; and
>
> (ii) it is not reasonable either to equip those premises with such accommodation and facilities or to provide other premises for women ...

This defence applies to jobs such as on oil rigs or building sites. It is contended that there is no need to provide separate sleeping *blocks*. Just as the provision of individually separate toilet facilities should suffice, so should the provision of individually separate rooms or separate dormitories. Such an interpretation would greatly limit the scope for a successful defence under this section. This is important as many such jobs, often short term and moving from place to place, are in areas where the proportion of women workers is extremely low. While it is not suggested that this interpretation will cause an influx of women into such jobs, the law should not make it easier for employers to resist *any* female entrants at all. The section is a rare example under the legislation of a cost defence being admissible. Clearly, what is reasonable expenditure will depend on the total size of the workforce, the numbers of men and women, and the likely duration of the work in that location. Tribunals will have to balance the right to be free from discrimination against a plea of financial hardship, which places them in what is potentially an uncomfortable position.

---

[79] In *Sisley*, this was interpreted as requiring actual residence rather than the mere provision of rest facilities.

Hospitals, prisons, etc

Section 7(2)(d) provides a defence where:

> ... the nature of the establishment, or the part of it within which the work is done, requires the job to be held by a man because:
>
> (i) it is, or is part of, a hospital, prison, or other establishment for persons requiring special care, supervision or attention; and
>
> (ii) those persons are all men (disregarding any women whose presence may be exceptional); and
>
> (iii) it is reasonable, having regard to the essential character of the establishment or that part, that the job should not be held by a woman.

This defence is additional to, and not dependent on, the provision of personal services or issues of privacy or decency. Certain jobs in prisons and hospitals may well come within one or both of those defences, but it must be assumed that some jobs are covered by this and only this GOQ. The emphasis here is on the essential character of the establishment rather than simply on the particular job being performed. The section is based on the assumption that it is permissible for staff in an all-female hospital or prison to be female – medical or custodial staff dealing with patients or inmates, not support or domestic staff. In the case of hospitals, this may provide a defence for a medical job which would not be within any other GOQ. The emphasis on the nature and function of the establishment rules out an argument that, for example, women prison staff would be more vulnerable to attack by male prisoners than their male counterparts.[80]

Duties to be performed abroad

Section 7(2)(g)[81] provides a defence where a job involves the performance of some duties outside the UK[82] 'in a country whose laws or customs are such that the duties could not, or could not effectively, be performed by a woman'. The defence recognises that women may be culturally unacceptable for some jobs in some countries; there is no equivalent defence in the RRA 1976. A defence based on the racism of another country is not permissible; a defence based on the sexism of that self-same country may be. It is arguable that the legislation takes the view that racism is 'worse' than sexism and, perhaps, is easier to eradicate. There are no cases: it is assumed that the defence would apply to, for example, women seeking jobs as salespeople where the duties

---

[80] In *Dothard v Rawlinson* 433 US 321 (1977), the United States Supreme Court accepted the validity of just such a defence. A similar argument was rejected in *Secretary of State for Scotland v Henley* (1983), unreported, EAT, Case No: 95/83.

[81] Section 7(2)(f) is now repealed; see above, pp 220–23.

[82] If the work is to be done wholly or mainly outside the UK, the SDA 1975 is inapplicable by virtue of s 10.

involve travelling to some Middle Eastern countries or where a man would be unable to deal with female customers in similar situations. It would be difficult for an Employment Tribunal to gainsay an employer assertion that a particular job could not be effectively performed by a man or a woman, as the case may be. The lack of cases is probably more because of an absence of complaints than because this kind of discrimination does not occur.

Married couples

The final GOQ is s 7(2)(h), which provides a defence where the 'job is one of two to be held by a married couple'. As there is no general prohibition against discrimination against single people it is perfectly lawful to require a married couple to perform two jobs. It seems to follow that the only activity legitimated by this GOQ is to specify which of the couple is to perform which job.

GENERAL DEFENCES

There are two defences which are potentially of general application but are of particular relevance in the employment context. These concern acts done under statutory authority, and acts done for the purpose of safeguarding national security.

Statutory authority

Section 41 of the Race Relations Act 1976 provides that nothing shall:

> ... render unlawful any act of discrimination done:
>
> (a) in pursuance of any enactment or Order in Council; or
>
> (b) in pursuance of any instrument made under any enactment made by a minister of the Crown; or
>
> (c) in order to comply with any condition or requirement imposed by a minister of the Crown (whether before or after the passing of this Act) by virtue of any enactment.

Section 51A of the SDA 1975 is different, providing a defence in relation to 'any act done by a person if it was necessary for that person to do it in order to comply with a requirement of an existing statutory provision'. The key phrase is in sub-s 1(c): the defence applies to acts done 'in order to comply with' any statutory requirement, though in paras (a) and (b) the equivalent phrase is 'in pursuance of'.

Hampson v Department of Education and Science [1990] IRLR 202, HL[83]

A Hong Kong Chinese woman was refused qualified teacher status in England. She had taken a two year course in Hong Kong. Eight years later she took a third year. She came to England and claimed qualified teacher status. The Secretary of State had power to make regulations under which the key phrase was 'approved as comparable'. Her application was rejected on the grounds that her initial training was two rather than three years and because the content did not meet Department of Education standards.

She claimed that this rule was indirectly discriminatory on the ground of nationality. The EAT held that the Secretary of State had a defence under s 41(1)(b) by reason of being an act done 'in pursuance of any instrument made under any enactment by a minister of the Crown'. The Court of Appeal, by a majority, (Balcombe LJ dissenting) upheld this aspect of the EAT decision.[84]

The House of Lords allowed the appeal.

Lord Lowry (pp 305–07):

(1) The Act binds the Crown, which, apart from the prerogative, discharges its duties and exercises its powers by virtue of a multitude of statutes and regulations ...

(2) The acts not only of the Crown but of local authorities and a large number of statutory bodies, including the governing bodies of some (but not all) universities, would achieve virtual immunity under the wide construction.

(3) The most important weapons contained in Parts II and III of the Act would be irretrievably blunted and, indeed, would not make sense.

To adopt the Balcombe principle, if I may so describe it, will mean that racial discrimination is outlawed (or at least needs to be justified ...) unless it has been sanctioned by Parliament, whereas, if the respondent's argument were correct, a wide and undefined area of discrimination would exist, immune from challenge save, in very exceptional circumstances, through the medium of judicial review ...

[W]hen one reflects that almost every discretionary decision, such as that which is involved in the appointment, promotion and dismissal of individuals in, say, local government, the police, the NHS and the public sector of the teaching profession, is taken against a statutory background which imposes a duty on someone, just as the regulations of 1982 imposed a duty on the Secretary of State. It seems to me that to apply the reasoning of the majority here to the decisions I have mentioned would be to give them the protection of

---

[83] See, also, [1991] 1 AC 171; [1990] ICR 551; [1990] 2 All ER 513.

[84] Balcombe LJ, in reasoning subsequently approved by the House of Lords, said that Parliament 'could not have intended that the Secretary of State should be entitled to ignore altogether the racial implications of what he was doing ... If what is done is not necessary to comply with a statutory requirement, there is no valid reason why it should not have to be justified before an Industrial Tribunal'. [1989] IRLR 69, p 74.

s 41 and thereby to achieve results which no member of the Court of Appeal would be likely to have thought acceptable.[85]

Arguably, this is one of the most important decisions ever handed down on the interpretation of the discrimination legislation. It does not define discrimination or bring additional people within the scope of the legislation. What is does is to confirm that the legislation applies even where the activity challenged is founded upon statutory duties or powers. In other words, those acting under statutory authority are not immune from the general duty to take into account the anti-discrimination legislation in formulating policy and acting upon it. That this point should ever have been doubted may be a matter of some wonderment; that it was roundly rejected in *Hampson* was essential if the legislation was to have any significant impact at all in the public sector.[86]

So far as gender is concerned, acts purportedly done under statutory authority often involve health and safety legislation peculiar to women. The key decision is *Johnston v The Chief Constable of the Royal Ulster Constabulary*,[87] which held that Art 2(3) of the Equal Treatment Directive, which provides a defence for 'provisions concerning the protection of women, particularly as regards pregnancy and maternity' did not go wider than permitting special treatment for women because of the biological realities of pregnancy and childbirth.[88]

National security

Sections 52 and 42 respectively provide that nothing in the Act shall render unlawful an act done for the purpose of safeguarding national security. Section 52(2) of the SDA 1975, now repealed, provided that a ministerial signature was to be conclusive proof that an act was done for that purpose. The ECJ in *Johnston* held that the conclusive nature of such a certificate was contrary to Art 6 of the Equal Treatment Directive, which gives a right to 'all persons who consider themselves wronged by failure to apply ... the principle of equal treatment ... to pursue their claims by judicial process'. In other words, domestic law may not prevent an individual having access to the

---

[85] The same approach was adopted by the EAT in *General Medical Council v Goba* [1988] ICR 885; [1988] IRLR 425.

[86] It follows that, for areas to be excluded from the legislation, specific statutory provision must have been made. Immigration law and family law are obvious examples. The CRE recommends that, 'when new legislation is proposed, the Minister responsible should be expected to certify that the new measure is consistent with, and does not conflict with, the Race Relations Act. Where the Minister is not able to do so, she or he would be expected to explain, in a memorandum attached to the Bill, why the new measure should be enacted in its proposed form, despite being in conflict with the Race Relations Act', *op cit*, CRE, fn 7, p 11.

[87] Case 222/84 [1986] ECR 1651; [1987] QB 129; [1986] 3 All ER 135; [1986] IRLR 263.

[88] See above, pp 220–22.

courts, even on the purported ground of national security, as there is no national security exception within the terms of the Equal Treatment Directive.[89] The Fair Employment (Northern Ireland) Act has a similar defence, to which of course European Community law is irrelevant. Thus the blocking, on national security grounds, of a complaint that Catholics were refused public works contracts because of their religious beliefs or political opinions, is being challenged before the ECHR on the ground that it deprives the applicants of their right to 'a fair and public hearing ... by an independent and impartial tribunal' under Art 6 of the Human Rights Convention.[90]

SPECIAL CASES

There are two different categories of special cases: first, situations analogous to employment, such as agency workers, partnerships, employment agencies, etc; secondly, work or employment situations, such as barristers and the armed forces, which are specifically dealt with by one or both of the statutes.

Contract workers

The employer of contract workers is liable under s 6 of the SDA 1975 or s 4 of the RRA 1976 in the normal way. Sections 9 and 7 respectively deal with the liability of the principal for whom the work is actually performed, such as the business for whom an agency secretary is working, or a construction worker supplied to the site under a labour-only subcontract. The Acts apply by analogy, bearing in mind that the employer continues to control many aspects of selection, hiring and dismissal.[91] Thus the principal may not discriminate in relation to the terms of the employment; by not permitting the worker to carry on working; in relation to any benefits, facilities or services which are provided; and finally, the usual provision applies which prevents the imposition of any other detriment: here, this includes a duty on employers to prevent harassment by their own employees of agency workers. As like must be compared with like, the necessary comparison is with how the principal treats the complainant *as compared with other contract workers*. There are two important cases on the liability of principals: the first deals with the issue of who is a principal, and the second with what discrimination is prohibited.

---

[89] It followed that the only exceptions were those within the terms of the Equal Treatment Directive itself. The employers failed on Art 2(3), the pregnancy and maternity defence, but the Court held that the Art 2(2) defence, where the sex of the worker constitutes a determining factor for the job in question, was satisfied.

[90] See (1998) 79 EOR 11.

[91] Sections 9 and 7 will also apply if the person supplied to perform the work does so on a self-employed basis.

Harrods Ltd v Remick[92] concerned three employees of employers who had concessions to work within the Harrods store, a pen consultant, a cosmetics consultant and a florist. Such workers are required to have 'store approval'; in each case it was withdrawn, leading to their dismissal. They were held entitled to pursue claims of race discrimination against Harrods; what was done within the store amounted to doing 'work for' Harrods; the sub-section was not limited to situations where the principal had direct control over the work being done. In *BP Chemicals v Gillick and Roevin Management Services Ltd*[93] the applicant complained of discrimination when BP, the principal for whom she had worked for three years while the agency remained her direct employers, refused to allow her to return to the same job after maternity leave. Her claim succeeded on the basis that the prohibition against discrimination in s 9 is not limited to discrimination when the contract worker is actually working for the principal, but includes the decision on who will work for the principal and when. It follows that the principal can be liable if the selection from among the candidates supplied by the agency is carried out in a discriminatory manner. As such an employee has no direct rights under the 1996 Employment Rights Act in respect of a failure to permit return to work, she must argue that she is the victim of sex discrimination. Whether the courts would find in her favour on the basis of the 'protected status' of pregnancy, or whether they would require her to prove that a man off sick for a comparable period would have been treated more favourably, remains to be seen.

Partnerships

Under s 10 of the RRA 1976, partnerships are only covered by the legislation if they have six or more partners. The same was true of s 11 of the original SDA 1975, but following enforcement proceedings against the UK, the law was amended by s 2(2) of the SDA 1986 to cover all partnerships irrespective of the number of partners.[94] By parallel with the standard provisions on employment, the law covers arrangements for who should be offered a partnership, the actual offer, its terms, expulsion from a partnership, or any other detriment. The genuine occupational qualification defence applies by analogy. There is no justification for the fact that the RRA 1976 only covers partnerships with more than six partners; the law should be amended to cover partnerships of any size.

---

92 [1997] IRLR 583, CA.

93 [1995] IRLR 128, EAT.

94 The law was also amended, by SDA 1986, s 2(2), to take account, so far as partnerships were concerned, of the decision in *Marshall v Southampton and South West Hampshire AHA* Case 152/84 [1986] ECR 723; [1986] QB 401; [1986] ICR 375; [1986] IRLR 140, concerning discriminatory retirement ages.

Trade unions and employers' organisations

The relevant sections are s 12 of the SDA 1975 and s 11 of the RRA 1976. The law covers access to and conditions of membership[95] – as opposed to employment – as well as benefits, facilities and services conditional upon such membership, and expulsion and the imposition of any other detriment. Depending on its tactics in collective bargaining, a union might also be liable for pressure to discriminate or for aiding the unlawful acts of an employer. A union is normally vicariously liable for the actions of its *paid* officials, but as shop stewards are unpaid agents rather than paid employees, liability is dependent on general principles applicable to liability for the actions of agents – whether the actions of the shop stewards had been taken within the scope of the authority conferred upon them by the trade union.[96]

Unions may be placed in a difficult situation where an allegation of harassment is made by one union member against another, as occurred in *Fire Brigades Union v Fraser*.[97] The union chose to support the women who had complained of harassment and consequently declined to provide the complainant with assistance and representation in the disciplinary hearing. The majority of the EAT, over the dissent of the chair, held that the Industrial Tribunal held been entitled on the facts to hold that the failure to provide assistance was gender-related and thus unlawful on the basis that a woman accused of harassment would not have been treated in the same way. But in *Weaver v National Association of Teachers in Further and Higher Education*,[98] an allegation that a union had failed to investigate a complaint by a member against a fellow member failed, as the union was entitled to have regard to the inevitable conflict of interest that would have resulted.

There are two areas where it has been argued that unions have done less than they should have done to tackle discrimination and disadvantage. The first concerns enabling women to participate as members and officers. Union structures, even something as basic as the time and place of meetings, may discourage female participation, especially of part time workers. To counter these problems, unions are permitted to engage in two limited forms of positive action. Under s 48(2) of the SDA 1975 and s 48(3) of the RRA 1976,

---

[95] It used to be the case that obtaining a job might be dependent on being a member of a union. In *Record Product Chapel v Turnbull* (1984), unreported, EAT, Case No: 955/83, see 258 IRLIB 9, the union was liable for unlawfully excluding women cleaners from branch membership as they needed such membership to be eligible for a better job; similarly, the formal investigation into SOGAT '82 showed how segregating men and women into different chapels adversely affected women as all the best jobs came via the men's chapel; see *Formal Report: The Society of Graphic and Allied Trades*, 1987, Manchester: EOC.

[96] *Heatons Transport (St Helens) Ltd v T and GWU* [1973] AC 15; [1972] ICR 308, HL.

[97] [1997] IRLR 671, EAT.

[98] [1988] ICR 599, EAT.

unions may engage in training to assist and encourage members of under-represented groups to become union officials. Secondly, under s 49 of the SDA 1975 – there is no equivalent provision in the RRA 1976 – unions may reserve seats for women on any elected union committee. As with any forms of positive action, they are permissible rather than mandatory; even these steps are unlikely to be able to counter any continuing culture of male domination.

The second issue concerns the attention given in collective bargaining to what are sometimes disparagingly called 'women's issues' – maternity leave, flexible working, etc. Of course, this will itself partly depend on women's influence within the union. There is no legal obligation on the union to place these and other issues at the top of its collective bargaining agenda, and there may be problems in ensuring that policies agreed at national level are properly carried through at local level, where traditional attitudes of male dominance may continue to have greater influence. The effective application of equality policies in the workplace may significantly depend on union ability and willingness to police such policies. The attitude and behaviour of unions significantly influenced the way in which the EqPA 1970 was implemented at local level.[99] Union involvement and expertise in voluntary job evaluation is considered crucial in reducing scope for gender bias.[100]

Despite the overall decline in union membership and in collective bargaining in the last 20 years, it is still strongly arguable that effective equality polices at work are largely dependent on detailed union involvement and monitoring. Union polices may be crucial: the objective of seeking to maintain existing pay differentials may be in conflict with that of seeking to improve the lot of lower paid workers, a problem which may be exacerbated as unionism tends to be associated with higher paid, full time jobs, rather than the more typically female lower paid, part time jobs. On the other hand, the growth in female employment has been seen by some unions as a membership source to replace that from declining manufacturing industries. The overall picture is variable: it is certainly possible to argue that union attitudes, and the extent to which unions are enabled by law and by the economic situation effectively to press their claims, may have a greater impact on equality issues at work than legal developments.

Legally, the principles applicable to trade unions apply equally to employers' organisations, though these are bodies which may have a far looser relationship with their members than trade unions. In *National Federation of Self-Employed and Small Businesses Ltd v Philpott*,[101] it was held that

---

[99] Snell, M, Glucklich, P and Povall, M, *Equal Pay and Opportunities: a Study of the Implementation and Effects of the Equal Pay Act and the Sex Discrimination Act in 26 Organisations*, 1981, London: Department of Employment, p 66.

[100] See below, pp 423–24, 433–34.

[101] [1997] IRLR 340, EAT.

the appellants were 'an organisation of employers', even though it was partly a campaigning group and not all its members were employers. As a result, the tribunal had jurisdiction to hear the respondent's claim of expulsion from the organisation.

Qualifying bodies

Section 13 of the SDA and s 12 of the RRA deal with discrimination by bodies which confer authorisation or qualification necessary for entry into employment, such as the Law Society, the various Institutes of Professional Engineers, or sporting bodies such as the British Boxing Board of Control, a licence from whom is necessary in order to box professionally.[102] In parallel to the basic employment provisions, the sections cover the grant of the relevant qualification, its terms, and its withdrawal.

The concept of a qualifying body must be interpreted widely.[103] *British Judo Association v Petty*[104] concerned the refusal of the defendant to grant the female applicant a certificate to referee in men's judo competitions. They argued that their job was to uphold refereeing standards rather than to award a qualification. The EAT held that the issue is whether entry into the occupation was *in fact* facilitated – or not – by their activities, even if not specifically intended to do so, and on that basis the claim was permitted to proceed.

Jepson and Dyas-Elliott v The Labour Party [1996] IRLR 116, IT

The two plaintiffs were not considered for selection as Labour Party candidates because of the then existing policy of all-women shortlists. They brought a complaint under s 13 of the SDA 1975; it was argued that an MP is not a person in employment, and that Art 2(4) of the Equal Treatment Directive, the positive action provision, provided a defence.

The complaints were upheld.

Judgment (p 118):

[It is] not correct [to regard] s 13 as specifically restricted to employment as defined in s 82 of the Act ... It would have been quite easy for s 13 to be drafted in such a way as to have restricted its operation just to employment as so

---

[102] Refusing women such a licence was held to be unlawful in *Couch v British Boxing Board of Control*, unreported, IT, (1998) *The Guardian*, 31 March.

[103] However, in *Tattari v Private Patients Plan Ltd* [1997] IRLR 586, EAT, it was held that the rejection by the defendants, who underwrite private health care, of the plaintiff's application to be added to their list of accredited specialists, was outside s 12 of the RRA. The defendants were not authorising her to practise in her profession. They simply required that those wishing to enter commercial agreements with them should have a recognised UK qualification.

[104] [1981] ICR 660; [1981] IRLR 484, EAT.

defined ... As the section now stands it covers, and in our view was widely drafted as being clearly intended to cover, all kinds of professions, vocations, occupations and trades in which persons may engage, whether paid or unpaid, and whether they be in employment as defined by s 82 or not (for example doctors, lawyers and judges), including thereby persons who hold public offices.

Members of Parliament ... are engaged in an occupation which involves public service and for which they receive remuneration from public funds. It is immaterial so far as s 13 is concerned that a person seeking to be considered for approval as an official candidate for a major political party has further hurdles to overcome before he or she can achieve a position as an MP ... [H]e is no different position from a person denied approval by a body under s 13, who does not as yet have any particular work to do and who would need selection by others before obtaining such work.

Section 13(2) of the SDA 1975 – there is no RRA equivalent – requires such bodies, in assessing whether someone is of a proper character to enter the relevant profession, to take account of evidence that they have engaged in unlawful discrimination. It is not clear whether this covers both direct and indirect discrimination and how it might be enforced.

In *EC Commission v UK*,[105] it was held that s 13 failed to satisfy Art 4(b) of the Equal Treatment Directive, which requires Member States to ensure that the internal rules of qualifying bodies which fail to comply with EC law can be amended or declared void. Section 6(2) of the SDA now renders void such rules which would be unlawful under the provisions of the Act.[106]

Vocational training bodies

Section 14 of the SDA 1975 and s 13 of the RRA 1976 deal with discrimination by bodies which offer training to help fit people for employment. By analogy with the situation of employers, discrimination is prohibited in relation to offers, terms and terminations. However, there is an important exception, to deal with the fact that in some circumstances such bodies are permitted to offer special training to members of a particular race or gender in order to remedy under-representation.[107]

---

[105] Case 165/82 [1983] ECR 3431; [1984] 1 All ER 353; [1984] ICR 192; [1984] IRLR 29. The decision also applies to the internal rules of trade unions and professional bodies.

[106] See below, pp 432–34.

[107] See below, pp 547–51.

Employment agencies

These are defined as bodies which, whether or not for profit, 'provide services for the purpose of finding employment for workers or supplying employers with workers'. This definition includes the careers service of a school[108] and the activities of a trade union branch which supplies workers – if any still have that power. Under s 15 of the SDA 1975 and s 14 of the RRA 1976, discrimination is prohibited in relation to the terms and methods in which services are provided, and refusal to provide services, though there is a defence if the job falls within one of the exceptions or if the agency reasonably relies on that fact.

SPECIAL PROVISIONS FOR CERTAIN EMPLOYMENTS

The police

Under both statutes, the office of constable is treated as employment. Section 17(2)(a) of the SDA 1975 permits discrimination between men and women police officers 'as to requirements, relating to height, uniform or equipment ...'. This legitimates different height requirements, and prevents a claim that different uniforms are discriminatory. It would not prevent a claim, for example, that women but not men were required to wear uniforms in a particular context. It is the different rules which are protected, not necessarily the way in which those rules are operated. Different equipment is more problematic: *Johnston* only legitimated differential firearms rules in the particular context of Northern Ireland,[109] and any differentiation must be interpreted according to European law. It is submitted that equipment must be read as analogous to clothing rather than referring to special operational policing equipment. For example, it cannot be lawful under this provision to allow male but not female officers to drive specially modified police vehicles.[110]

---

[108] *CRE v Imperial Society of Teachers of Dancing* [1983] ICR 473; [1983] IRLR 315, EAT.

[109] See above, pp 220–22.

[110] Under the Pregnant Workers Directive (92/85/EEC), OJ L348/1, 1992, as incorporated into domestic law by the Employment Rights Act 1996, s 99(1), it is unfair to dismiss a woman 'for any reason connected with her pregnancy'. But as police officers may not complain of unfair dismissal, any such claim must be on the ground of unlawful discrimination rather than unfair dismissal.

The prison service

Unlike the police, the only specifically permissible discrimination concerns height requirements.[111] A challenge would still be permissible if the rules excluded disproportionately more men than women. The absence of reference to clothing means that differential rules must be tested according to the case law applicable to employment generally, which at present gives employers substantial discretion to impose different requirements,[112] so much so that the reference to clothing in the section on the police is probably redundant.

Religion

Employment by religious groups is excluded from the SDA 1975 'where the employment is limited to one sex so as to comply with the doctrines of the religion or to avoid offending the religious susceptibilities of a significant number of its followers'.[113] There is no parallel provision in the RRA: racist religious susceptibilities, where they exist, are not protected. The protection covers not only hiring but also the obtaining of relevant qualifications for the purposes of employment by that religious group. Such employment is not restricted to ministers. It could cover administrators and, for example, could permit teachers in a Muslim girls' school to be restricted to women. There have been no cases, but the law is vague, perhaps inevitably: it relies on the notoriously difficult problem of defining religion, and on establishing when enough followers have been adequately offended.[114]

Midwives

The original s 20 of the SDA 1975 permitted discrimination against men in the context of employment as a midwife. In *Commission of the European Communities v United Kingdom*,[115] the Court rejected the argument that this exception contravened the Equal Treatment Directive. It was stated that 'personal sensitivities may play an important role in relations between midwife and patient. In those circumstances ... the UK had not exceeded the limits of the power granted to the Member States by Art 2(2) ... which permits Member States to exclude from the application of the Directive occupational activities where the sex of the worker constitutes a determining factor'. In any event, the Government had already decided to change the law; men may now

---

[111] SDA 1975, s 18.

[112] See above, p 151–58.

[113] SDA 1975, s 19(1).

[114] On the issue of discrimination on the basis of religion, see above, pp 134–37.

[115] Case 165/82 [1983] ECR 3431; [1984] 1 All ER 353; [1984] ICR 182; [1984] IRLR 29.

become midwives on the same terms as women.[116] However, the defence of genuine occupational qualification relating to 'decency or privacy' may still be applicable. How many women must object, whether such objection would be reasonable, and indeed how many men are practising as midwives are all unclear.

The armed forces

Section 85(4) of the original SDA 1975 provided a blanket immunity as regards employment discrimination carried out by the armed services. Such justification could only relate, tenuous as it might be, to national security. *Johnston* made it clear that a defence of national security had to be tested according to the facts of individual cases – blanket exclusions were impermissible. As from 1995, s 85(4) only provides exemption for acts 'done for the purpose of ensuring the combat effectiveness' of the armed forces.[117] A case has recently been referred to the European Court where a female chef is challenging the policy of the Royal Marines not to permit women to serve. The Ministry of Defence is arguing that even chefs may have to serve in the front line and therefore s 85(4) provides a defence.[118]

Barristers

It became apparent that barristers fell outside the legislation because they work neither under a contract nor under a partnership agreement. In consequence, new sections have been inserted into the SDA 1975 and RRA 1976, s 35A and B, and s 26A and B respectively,[119] making the legislation applicable to barristers. Proceedings are, though, brought in county courts rather than before Industrial Tribunals.

Public bodies

Under s 75(5) of the Race Relations Act 1976, there is an exemption in relation to employment in the service of the Crown or certain public bodies which are permitted to restrict employment to persons of a particular birth, nationality, descent or residence. The number of such bodies has been greatly reduced by the Race Relations (Prescribed Public Bodies) Regulations 1994.[120]

---

[116] Sex Discrimination Act (Amendment of s 20) Order SI 1983/1202.

[117] Sex Discrimination Act 1975 (Application to Armed Forces, etc) Regulations SI 1994/3276.

[118] See (1997) 73 EOR 3.

[119] Inserted by the Courts and Legal Services Act 1990, ss 64 and 65.

[120] SI 1994/1986; see (1994) 54 EOR 7.

OTHER UNLAWFUL ACTS

Victimisation

It is clearly necessary to provide legal protection for people who take legal action under anti-discrimination law or assist others to do so.[121] The victimisation provisions, s 4 of the SDA 1975 and s 2 of the RRA 1976, are defined in the legislation as the third instance of discrimination along with direct and indirect discrimination. Defining victimisation in this way has caused problems as regards with whom the victimised applicant should be compared. As a matter of logic and policy it is more appropriate to consider victimisation as a self-standing unlawful act apart from the definition of discrimination.

The two Acts are similar.[122] Section 2 of the RRA 1976 provides:

(1) A person (the discriminator) discriminates against another person (the person victimised) in any circumstances relevant for the purposes of any provision of this Act if he treats the person victimised less favourably than in those circumstances he treats or would treat other persons, and does so by reason that the person victimised has:

   (a) brought proceedings against the discriminator or any other person under this Act; or

   (b) given evidence or information in connection with proceedings brought by any person against the discriminator or any person under this Act; or

   (c) otherwise done anything under or by reference to this Act in relation to the discriminator or any other person;[123] or

---

[121] 'In reality, adverse employer reaction is not uncommon, as is shown by [Leonard's] survey of the experiences of successful claimants undertaken by the EOC. The existence of the section on victimisation was not effective in preventing the fact of having taken action under the sex discrimination legislation from having an adverse effect on the careers and working experience of many of the applicants who had ... been successful in the tribunals, partly because the pressures to which they were subject were often subtle and informal.' Bourn, C and Whitmore, J, *Anti-Discrimination Law in Britain*, 3rd edn, 1996, London: Sweet & Maxwell, p 83. Furthermore, 'Jeanne Gregory in her study of 106 unsuccessful applicants found that more than half experienced a deterioration in working relationships, particularly with employers and managers, as a result of their bringing the case ... Forty five stated that their conditions of employment were adversely affected. Many reported that their chances of promotion had deteriorated to nil; some claimed that they had received smaller pay increases than their fellow workers and others that they were demoted ... Twenty applicants stated that they had left their job as a direct result of the case. Four made redundant said their selection was related to the case'. 'Victimisation is discrimination' (1990) 30 EOR 23, p 23.

[122] See, also, Art 8 of the Equal Treatment Directive.

[123] There must here be limits: hitting the discriminator or damaging his property is literally within the section but cannot amount to a protected act.

(d) alleged that the discriminator or any other person has committed an act which (whether or not the allegation so states) would amount to a contravention of this Act;

or by reason that the discriminator knows that the person victimised intends to do any of these things, or suspects that the person victimised has done, or intends to do, any of them.

It is necessary to prove, first, that one of the protected actions has been taken, and secondly that the complainant has been treated less favourably on the ground of having taken such action. Beyond the obvious examples of bringing a claim or giving evidence in support of a claim, the sections have also been held to cover reporting that particular employers were attempting to induce the Manpower Services Commission to discriminate, action held to be within sub-s 1(c), though not (a) or (b)[124] and the making of secret tape recordings in an attempt to establish discrimination by taxi drivers, which was covered by the same sub-section.[125] Sub-section (a) includes claims made if an employer has rejected an application for employment because the applicant has previously sued an employer for discrimination. It appears to be irrelevant that any allegation of victimisation is motivated by hostility or malevolence so long as the action is literally a protected act.

The Court of Appeal has taken a narrow approach to the question of what amounts to an allegation under sub-s 1(d) of a contravention of the Act.

Waters v Commissioner of Police of the Metropolis [1997] IRLR 589, CA[126]

Miss Waters, a police officer, alleged that she was the victim of a sexual assault by a fellow officer while they were both off duty. The claim was investigated but no action was taken against the alleged assailant. She claimed that she was victimised in that she suffered a detriment as a result of making the complaint in that her name was removed from the list of officers utilised for important police searches.

The EAT and the CA both rejected the complaint on the ground that she had not alleged that the act had been contravened.

Mummery J [1995] IRLR 531, p 534:

[There would not be] a contravention of the 1975 Act unless [the act] was done by the police officer 'in the course of his employment' ... As the tribunal decided that ... the alleged assault was *not* done in the course of the police officer's employment, the Commissioner is not treated as having done that act. It follows that Miss Waters has not alleged that the Commissioner has done an act which would amount to a contravention of the 1975 Act.

---

[124] *Kirby v Manpower Services Commission* [1980] 1 WLR 725; [1980] ICR 420; [1980] IRLR 229, EAT.

[125] *Aziz v Trinity Street Taxis Ltd* [1989] QB 463; [1988] ICR 534; [1988] IRLR 204, CA.

[126] See, also, [1997] ICR 1073.

Waite LJ (p 597):

[It was argued] that Parliament must have intended, if the prohibition against victimisation was to have any real value at all, that protection should arise from the making of the complaint, and should not depend on the terms in which it is articulated.

Charges of race or sex discrimination are hurtful and damaging and not always easy to refute. In justice, therefore ... it is vital that discrimination (including victimisation) should be defined in language sufficiently precise to enable people to know where they stand before the law. Precision of language is also necessary to prevent the valuable purpose of combating discrimination from being frustrated or brought into disrepute through the use of language which encourages unscrupulous or vexatious recourse [to the law]. The interpretation proposed ... would involve an imprecision of language leaving employers in a state of uncertainty as to how they should respond to a particular complaint, and would place the machinery of the Acts at serious risk of abuse. It is better, and safer, to give the words of the sub-section their clear and literal meaning. The allegation relied on need not state explicitly that an act of discrimination has occurred ... All that is required is that the allegation relied on should have asserted facts capable of amounting in law to an act of discrimination ... The facts alleged by the complainant in this case were incapable in law of amounting in law to an act of discrimination by the Commissioner because they were not done by him [and] because the alleged perpetrator was not acting in the course of his employment.

This conclusion is dubious on both policy and linguistic grounds. At the time complaint is made, it may be difficult for the complainant to know whether an allegation is protected. The policy should be to protect allegations whether or not they necessarily turn out to be well grounded, especially as the vast majority will never be brought to court. In addition, the phrase 'which would amount to a contravention' only appears in sub-s (d); in the other sub-sections there is no requirement that the claim needs to be well founded in order to form the basis of a successful victimisation complaint. It seems that the result may have been different had the complaint been, not under sub-s (d), but under sub-s (c), that the victimisation was for doing something 'under or by reference to' the Act 'in relation to the discriminator or any other person'. Finally, it is specifically provided in s 4(2) that the protection does not apply 'if the allegation was false and not made in good faith'; a false allegation which was made in good faith *will* thus be protected. It should make no difference whether the complaint failed on factual or on legal grounds.[127]

The second question is whether the complainant was treated less favourably for having done one of the protected acts. Two questions arise here: first, what is the relevant state of mind of the employer, and secondly, with whom should comparison be made for the purpose of establishing less

---

[127] See Townshend-Smith, R (1996) 2 IJDL 137.

favourable treatment. In *Nagarajan v London Regional Transport*,[128] it was held that for the protected act to constitute the reason for the alleged victimisation, conscious motivation is required. This will be a difficult test for applicants to satisfy, as it means they must show a subjective intention to victimise on the basis of the prior conduct. The next issue is whether the complainant can establish less favourable treatment. This clearly includes dismissal, refusal of promotion, harassment, and so on. But it is potentially far wider. In *Khan v Chief Constable of West Yorkshire*,[129] the first tribunal hearing held that the applicant had been victimised in not being provided with a reference, and the second hearing held that he had been further victimised in that he alone, of all the officers who gave evidence at the first hearing, was not treated as being on duty and thus had to take his attendance at the tribunal as holiday.

The final question is with whom should comparison be made. In *Kirby*, it was held that the employers would have dismissed anyone who disclosed confidential information and thus there was no less favourable treatment. The comparison should be between a person who had done a protected act and one who had done a similar but unprotected act. This reduced the protection of the law almost to nothing. It was soon rejected by the Court of Appeal.

Aziz v Trinity Street Taxis [1988] IRLR 204, CA[130]

The complainant was an Asian taxicab proprietor and a member of an association of taxicab operators. When the association required him to pay £1,000 to have a third taxi admitted to its radio system he felt he was being unfairly treated. He secretly recorded conversations with other taxi drivers, and also made an unsuccessful complaint to a tribunal about its imposition. It was as result of that complaint that the existence of the recordings was revealed. As a result he was expelled from the association on the ground that the making of the recordings was an unjustified intrusion and a serious breach of the trust which had to exist between members. He complained of victimisation.

Slade LJ (pp 210–11):

A complaint made in reliance on s 2 necessarily presupposes that the complainant has done a protected act. If the doing of such an act itself constituted part of the relevant circumstances, a complainant would necessarily fail to establish discrimination if the alleged discriminator could show that he treated or would treat all other persons who did the protected act with equal intolerance.

[The tribunal] said that the finding against him would have been the same even though his purpose in making the recording had nothing to do with the race relations legislation.

---

128 [1998] IRLR 73, CA.

129 Unreported, IT, Case Nos: 1800125/96 and 1802382/96, see 34 DCLD 5.

130 See, also, [1989] QB 463; [1988] ICR 534.

[I]t must be shown that the very fact that the protected act was done by the complainant 'under or by reference to the legislation' influenced the alleged discriminator in his unfavourable treatment of the complainant.

In our judgment para (c) no less than paras (a), (b) and (d) contemplates a motive which is consciously connected with the race relations legislation – here that fact did not influence them in expelling him.

The law is correctly stated but wrongly applied, because, in a similar fashion to *Kirby*, it provides an employer with a defence if it can be shown that the same action would have been taken against those who took the same action for different reasons. The complainant was attempting to obtain evidence that discrimination had occurred: that should have been protected even if, in other contexts, those who made secret tape recordings would have been disciplined or dismissed. A similar approach was adopted in *Cornelius v University College of Swansea*,[131] where the applicant failed because the employers would have treated applicants who brought proceedings under *any* statute in the same unfavourable way.

The provisions on victimisation are vulnerable to severe criticism as being both unduly technical and, even more important, as having failed to operate as an adequate deterrent. The CRE has recommended a revamp of the law, changing the definition so that a person would be protected from suffering any detriment whatsoever as a result of doing one of the protected acts. The EOC has proposed that, once less favourable treatment has been shown, the employer should be required to prove that the reason for the treatment was other than victimisation. They also propose that the minimum compensation for victimisation should be £1,000, that the widest publicity be given to the victimisation provisions in all documentation sent by courts and tribunals, and that the tribunal or court should automatically draw the attention of the parties to the provisions regardless of whether the complainant wins or loses. Their most recent reform proposal also recommends that there should be a fast track procedure to deal with cases of alleged victimisation under which tribunals could, in a similar fashion to some unfair dismissal cases, grant interim relief preventing action against the complainant until the tribunal hearing.[132]

The Public Interest Disclosure Act 1998 – designed to protect whistle-blowers – will provide new protection, though of course its coverage is far wider. The Act introduces a concept of 'qualifying disclosure' of which one example is a situation where a person has failed to comply with any legal obligation to which he is subject. This clearly covers breaches of the anti-discrimination legislation. Public disclosure is permitted where the worker reasonably fears that he will be subjected to a detriment if the disclosure is to

---

[131] [1987] IRLR 141, CA.

[132] *Op cit, Equality in the 21st Century*, fn 75, para 21.

the employer, and the worker has the right not to be subjected to any detriment at the hands of his employer on the ground of having made a protected disclosure. Unlike the victimisation provisions, this is a free-standing right, not requiring comparison with how anyone else was treated. However, it does not cover all cases of victimisation: the bringing of proceedings or giving evidence in proceedings may not fall within the definition, though information disclosed pre-hearing is likely to do so.

Employer responsibility for the actions of employees

Under s 41 of the SDA 1975 and s 32 of the RRA 1976, the employer is made liable for actions done by employees in the course of their employment.[133] As a result of *Jones v Tower Boot Co*,[134] the tort principles of vicarious liability are not determinative of this question, although it is not clear what principles, if any, are to replace them.[135] There is effectively automatic liability for the actions of a supervisor designed to have effect on the contract of employment of an employee, as only such supervisors have the authority to impact the contract in this way; thus the issue of employer liability is most likely to occur where action is taken which is not designed to have effect on the contractual terms and conditions of employment, especially, but not only, racial and sexual harassment. For this reason, the detailed discussion of the issue, and the defence that the employer has taken such acts as are reasonably practicable to prevent the discrimination from occurring,[136] are contained in Chapter 8.[137]

Instructions and pressure to discriminate[138]

If the person who is subjected to instructions or pressure does not comply, there will be no victim of discrimination who can bring an individual claim. In such cases, the Commissions have power to bring proceedings, and if they do so, they normally prove successful, as the tribunal will be able to rely on the evidence of the person subjected to the pressure or instructions. Such claims are frequently made in the same proceedings. For unlawful instructions, the instructor must either have authority over the person subject to the instructions, or the latter must be accustomed to act in accordance with his

---

[133] Sections 41(2) and 32(2) provide for the liability of a principal for the actions of an agent.
[134] [1997] ICR 254; [1997] 2 All ER 406; [1997] IRLR 168, CA.
[135] See above, pp 251–53.
[136] Sections 41(3) and 32(3) respectively.
[137] See above, pp 247–57.
[138] SDA 1975, ss 39, 40; RRA 1976, ss 30, 31.

wishes. For pressure, there must either be the provision or offer of a benefit, or the imposition or threat of a detriment.

In *CRE v Imperial Society of Teachers of Dancing*,[139] the defendant's secretary told a careers service that she would 'rather the school did not send anyone coloured'. It was held that there were no unlawful instructions to discriminate, as the secretary had no authority over the school, even though the school might normally have complied with her requests. However, pressure to discriminate was established because of the implied suggestion that the defendants would no longer deal with the school. It is a question of fact at what point a statement becomes an act of persuasion or inducement. For example, asking an employment agency whether the person being sent is black would probably not normally be sufficient to induce them to send someone else.

The person being instructed to discriminate may refuse. If disciplinary action is then taken on account of the refusal, that will amount to breach of the RRA 1976 but not the SDA 1975. Under the RRA it is unlawful to treat a person less favourably on the ground of *another person's* race.[140] However, under the SDA, the less favourable treatment must be on the ground of the gender of the actual complainant. It might nevertheless be possible to argue that there has been victimisation under s 4(1)(c) or (d). If one complains that one has been instructed to discriminate, that amounts to an allegation that an unlawful act has been committed. There is no requirement either that there must be a victim of the unlawful act or that the person victimised is aware that the act is unlawful.

Aiding unlawful acts

Section 32 of the RRA 1976 and s 42 of the SDA 1975 make it unlawful 'knowingly' to aid another person to do an act of unlawful discrimination. Under sub-s (2), the individual discriminator is deemed to aid the doing of the act by the employer. This means that individual liability for aiding an unlawful act depends upon the direct liability of the employer under s 31 or s 41 respectively. This is particularly problematic in harassment cases, as it means that the individual harasser can only be liable under anti-discrimination legislation if the employer is also deemed to be liable. Where the employer is liable, the individual employee may also be personally liable.[141] There is, however, a defence under ss 32(4) and 42(4) if the alleged

---

[139] [1983] ICR 473; [1983] IRLR 315, EAT.

[140] *Showboat Entertainment Centre v Owens* [1984] 1 WLR 384; [1984] ICR 65; [1984] IRLR 7, EAT. In *Weathersfield Ltd v Sargent* [1998] IRLR 14, EAT, it was held to amount to less favourable treatment on racial grounds where, in response to instructions not to rent vehicles to black people, the complainant quit the employment. See above, pp 143–44.

[141] *Read v Tiverton DC and Bull* [1977] IRLR 202, IT.

aider has reasonably relied on an assurance from the person alleged to be being aided that the act in question does not amount to unlawful discrimination.[142]

---

[142] Sections 39, 40 and 42 of the SDA 1975 only apply to contravention of that Act. It follows that it is not unlawful to instruct, pressure or aid a breach either of the Equal Pay Act or European law, eg, instructions to manipulate the outcome of a job evaluation study to favour male workers. In principle, this needs changing, although there is no evidence that problems have arisen.

CHAPTER 11

DISCRIMINATION OUTSIDE EMPLOYMENT

The employment provisions of the legislation have had the highest public profile and have been the subject of the bulk of the litigation. However, the Sex Discrimination Act 1975 and the Race Relations Act 1976 also contain very important provisions concerning discrimination in other spheres of life – some of which we have already come across in relation to the definition of discrimination itself.[1] The areas for discussion are, first, education; secondly, the provision of goods, facilities and services; and, thirdly, housing and premises. In addition, both acts contain a number of special provisions and exceptions which can most suitably be dealt with here.

EDUCATION

The history of education in Great Britain reveals the extent to which boys and girls have conventionally been educated both separately and differently. Yet the last 25 years have seen very rapid changes, as shown, for example, in the great increase in the number of girls entering universities, even though there remain huge variations between subject areas. Furthermore, girls are now achieving better examination and test results at most stages of the educational system. Indeed, concern is now being expressed at male under-performance, the explanations for which are various, though do not seem to include discrimination.

Issues of race in education are closely bound up with the fact that disproportionately large numbers of ethnic minorities live in inner city areas, where education achievement, at least if considered in terms of measurable outcomes, is often relatively low for *all* groups. Furthermore, there are noticeable differences in attainment between different groups, the causes of which are very hard to disentangle. It seems improbable that, except in rare cases, race impacts upon the education system in a way which is sufficiently precise and measurable to come within the legal definition of discrimination. Arguably, even more than in relation to employment, it would be folly to expect the anti-discrimination provisions to contribute more than marginally to the reduction of disadvantage. Where such hopes might legitimately be raised is in relation to disability: here, however, presumably because of the

---

1 See, eg, *James v Eastleigh BC* [1990] 2 AC 751; [1990] 2 All ER 607; [1990] IRLR 208; *Birmingham CC v Equal Opportunities Commission* [1989] AC 1155; [1989] 1 All ER 769; [1989] IRLR 173.

financial implications, the law eschews the principle of non-discrimination. No rights are given to individuals, the duties being imposed on public bodies concerned with the provision of education, and even these are very limited in scope.[2]

The educational provisions of the SDA 1975 have three main objectives: first, to define which actions are unlawful; secondly, to reconcile the non-discrimination principle with the fact that single-sex education remains relatively commonplace, and thirdly, to impose various duties on bodies concerned with the provision of education, such as local education authorities and funding councils. There is obviously no parallel to the second of these objectives in the RRA 1976.

Sex Discrimination Act 1975

s 22 It is unlawful in relation to an educational establishment ... to discriminate against a woman:

(a) in the terms on which it offers to admit her to the establishment as a pupil; or

(b) by refusing or deliberately omitting to accept an application for her admission to the establishment as a pupil; or

(c) where she is a pupil of the establishment:

(i) in the way it affords her access to any benefits, facilities or services, or by refusing or deliberately omitting to afford her access to them; or

(ii) by excluding her from the establishment or subjecting her to any other detriment.

Section 17 of the RRA 1976 is in substantially similar terms. Both sections deal only with discrimination in the way in which a particular educational establishment operates. No comparison is permitted between different schools or universities, even if the schools are within the same local education authority. The provisions apply equally to education providers in the public and private sectors.

Differential entry criteria are unlawful, whether directly or indirectly discriminatory. For that reason, the policy of Birmingham City Council that fewer grammar school places were available for girls, with the result that girls were required to achieve a higher entry standard, was held to be unlawful.[3] St George's Hospital Medical School at one time operated an admissions system with a deliberate built-in bias against women and ethnic minorities. A formal investigation by the Commission for Racial Equality uncovered this practice,

---

[2] See below, pp 611–12.

[3] *Birmingham CC v Equal Opportunities Commission* [1989] AC 1155; [1989] 1 All ER 769; [1989] IRLR 173.

which was enshrined in a computer programme and thus demonstrable.[4] Bias on the part of university admissions tutors or interviewers is clearly unlawful, but may be impossible to demonstrate in practice, especially as the UCAS form received by universities now contains no reference to the ethnic group of the applicant, the relevant information being retained by UCAS.

Entry criteria may have an indirectly discriminatory impact on ground of gender or race, though if they relate to academic performance they are very likely to be held to be justifiable.[5] Two CRE investigations provide examples. That into Watford Grammar Schools – which were non selective – revealed that the written case for admission made by parents had a significant influence, thereby disadvantaging those whose first language was not English. That into Calderdale LEA concluded that the English language test for admission to mainstream education, which was clearly indirectly discriminatory, was not justifiable, as those who failed the test were separated from other children and were exposed to a narrower curriculum.[6]

Differential provision within the individual educational establishment will automatically be unlawful if it is based on race, as racial segregation is conclusively proved to amount to discrimination.[7] Segregation of physical education lessons by race is unlawful. Similarly, the use of racial stereotypes to make educational decisions is likely to be unlawful, such as by assuming that black pupils are less likely to succeed with academic subjects. The application of differential criteria may be particularly problematic in the context of exclusions from school as there have been suggestions that a disproportionately high number of such exclusions are of black pupils. Schools will need to ensure that the criteria are applied even-handedly. This may require steps to ensure that, for example, there are no differences in the reporting rates of bad behaviour as between white and black pupils.

Some issues of sex discrimination are clearly similar: girls might be steered away from scientific and technical subjects; bad behaviour by boys and girls might not be dealt with in the same manner. There are, however, two areas of difference. The first springs from the fact that segregation by gender is not unlawful unless it results in less favourable treatment. Thus segregated classes, and other segregated school facilities, may be permissible in mixed schools. Secondly, s 44 provides that it is lawful to discriminate 'in relation to any sport, game or other activity of a competitive nature where the physical strength, stamina or physique of the average woman puts her at a

---

4   *Medical School Admissions: St George's Hospital*, 1988, London: CRE.

5   Cf *Mandla v Lee* [1983] 2 AC 548; [1983] ICR 385; [1983] IRLR 209, HL, where a requirement not to wear a turban was neither concerned with academic criteria nor a distinction unrelated to race, and therefore was not justifiable.

6   *Teaching English as a Second Language: Calderdale LEA*, 1986, London: CRE.

7   RRA 1976, s 1(2); see above, pp 141–42.

disadvantage to the average man'.[8] Not only does this legitimate, for example, teaching athletics in single-sex groups, it also appears to legitimate the common practice whereby boys are taught one sport while girls are taught another – football and hockey, basketball and netball are common examples.[9]

Section 26 of the SDA 1975 provides an exception for a single-sex educational establishment, with s 27 providing a parallel transitional exception for establishments which are in the process of becoming co-educational.[10] By s 26(2), it is further provided that a school which is not a single-sex establishment may nevertheless choose to offer boarding facilities and the benefits and services consequent upon such facilities to members of one sex only.

Section 23 of the SDA 1975 and s 18 of the RRA 1976 make it unlawful for a local education authority to do any act which constitutes discrimination.[11] This been extended to agencies which have responsibility for some aspect of educational provision, such as the Higher Education Funding Council, the Funding Agency for Schools and the Teacher Training Agency. This duty may, in effect, entail an obligation to take corrective measures to overcome disadvantage caused by the fact that, for example, specialist extra facilities are only available, within the LEA, in single-sex establishments.[12] It is by virtue of this section that Birmingham's provision of fewer grammar school places for girls was held to be unlawful.[13] Exclusive enforcement of these general duties

---

8   By the same logic, s 28 provides an exception for (a) a course in physical training, and (b) a course designed for teachers of physical training.

9   The argument is not clear cut: the section refers to 'any sport, game or other activity of a competitive nature'. It is arguable that this does not include situations, common in games lessons in schools, where the essence of the sport is being taught in a non-competitive manner. There is a strong case to be made that it is unlawful for school to deny girls the opportunity at least to try their hand at, eg, football, rugby and cricket; at present, there is a rapid increase in the female participation rate in all these sports. See, also, below, pp 384–85.

10   A 'single-sex establishment' is defined by SDA 1975, s 26(1), as one which 'admits pupils of one sex only, or which would be taken to admit pupils of one sex only if there were disregarded pupils of the opposite sex (a) whose admission is exceptional, or (b) whose numbers are comparatively small and whose admission is confined to particular courses of instruction or teaching classes'.

11   There are also more general duties under SDA 1975, s 25, and RRA 1976, s 19, to 'secure that facilities for education provided by [the authority], and any ancillary benefits or services, are provided without ... discrimination'. This section is mainly concerned with the educational planning duties of LEAs. In addition, RRA 1976, s 71, places a general duty, not restricted to education, on local authorities, inter alia, 'to promote equality of opportunity, and good relations, between persons of different racial groups'. See below, p 537.

12   Bourn, C and Whitmore, J, Anti-Discrimination Law in Britain, 3rd edn, 1996, London: Sweet & Maxwell, p 271.

13   In R v Cleveland CC ex p CRE (1992) The Times, August 25, CA, it was held that, where there was a conflict between this duty and the parental choice provisions of the education legislation, the latter prevailed. Thus the authority was bound to defer to parental choice of schools even where the latter was made on racial grounds; the authority was protected under RRA 1976, s 41, which protects acts done in pursuance of any enactment.

is placed in the hands of the Secretary of State for Education and Employment. To the extent that opting out of local authority control becomes more common, and if other steps are taken to reduce the influence of LEAs over educational provision, the impact and usefulness of these provisions will necessarily decline.

GOODS, FACILITIES AND SERVICES

Sex Discrimination Act 1975[14]

29(1) It is unlawful for any person concerned with the provision (whether for payment or not) of goods, facilities or services to the public or a section of the public to discriminate against a woman who seeks to obtain or use those goods, facilities or services:

(a) by refusing or deliberately omitting to provide her with any of them; or

(b) by refusing or deliberately omitting to provide her with goods, facilities or services of the like quality, in the like manner or on the like terms as are normal in his case in relation to male members of the public ...

(2) The following are examples of the facilities and services mentioned in sub-s (1):

(a) access to and use of any place which members of the public or a section of the public are permitted to enter;

(b) accommodation in a hotel, boarding house or other similar establishment;

(c) facilities by way of banking or insurance or for grants, loans, credit or finance;

(d) facilities for education;

(e) facilities for entertainment, recreation or refreshment;

(f) facilities for transport or travel;

(g) the services of any profession or trade, or any local or other public authority.

(3)[15] For the avoidance of doubt ... where a particular skill is commonly exercised in a different way for men and for women it does not contravene sub-s (1) for a person who does not normally exercise it for women to insist on exercising it for a woman only in accordance with his normal practice

---

[14] See, also, RRA 1976, s 20.

[15] There is no equivalent to this sub-section in RRA 1976, but the commencing words 'for the avoidance of doubt', imply that even without this provision there would be no unlawfulness.

or, if he reasonably considers it impracticable to do that in her case, to refuse or deliberately omit to exercise it.[16]

The public or a section of the public

This part of the legislation is concerned with activities which potentially lie at the margin of acceptable legal intervention. The law has to determine which activities should be controlled by law and which should remain unregulated in the interests of personal autonomy.[17] It would be too great an infringement of personal liberty to allow a claim of race discrimination if a black person was not invited to a birthday party.[18] A key way in which the laws seeks to avoid controls on essentially private behaviour is by insisting that the provision be to the public or a section of the public.

We should not be surprised to discover that the dividing line is not at all clear, and may be different in different contexts where regulation is under consideration. The leading case on the meaning of the phrase 'section of the public', *Charter v Race Relations Board*,[19] arose under the Race Relations Act 1968. The House of Lords held that a Conservative club was outside the scope of the legislation as membership was not offered to a section of the public.[20] The issue depends on whether the right to become a member is effectively automatic or whether genuine discretion is exercised in selecting candidates for membership. It is perhaps doubtful whether a court would today, after 30 years' experience of anti-discrimination legislation, adopt such a hands-off – and arguably complacent – approach. The point never arose, as s 25 of the RRA 1976 specifically brought such clubs with 25 or more members within the

---

[16] SDA 1975, s 50, and RRA 1976, s 40, bring within the legislation situations where defendants do not themselves provide the benefits, facilities or services, but where they facilitate access to them where the actual service is provided by another person.

[17] See Gardner, J, 'Private activities and personal autonomy: at the margins of anti-discrimination law', in Hepple, B and Szyszczak, E (eds), *Discrimination: The Limits of Law*, 1992, London: Mansell, Chapter 9.

[18] It makes no difference if the party is held, eg, in a hotel for which a room has been booked. The hotelier can only be liable if there is discrimination in the letting arrangements. Even if there is knowledge that there has been discrimination in the invitations, the hotelier is not liable: there has been no refusal or deliberate omission to provide the relevant service. It is for this reason that there is no breach of the legislation if facilities are provided to a known racist organisation.

[19] [1973] AC 885; [1973] 1 All ER 512, HL.

[20] By the same logic, in *Dockers Labour Club and Institute Ltd v Race Relations Board* [1976] AC 285; [1974] 3 All ER 592, HL, a working men's club was held to be outside the scope of the legislation even though there was a national organisation linking all the various such clubs.

ambit of *that* legislation.[21] Membership criteria may be directly or indirectly discriminatory; the equivalent to word of mouth hiring in the employment context is where applicants for membership are required to be sponsored by an existing member. On the assumption that such a practice would in most cases be *prima facie* indirectly discriminatory, the question arises whether such a practice could ever be justified. It is contended that the answer must be 'no', either if the club is comparatively large, or if it a local club with rather general purposes; the answer *might* – no more than might – be different if the club was a small one with specific objectives, such as to pursue an interest in war games or white-knuckle rides at theme parks around the country.

By contrast, private clubs whose membership is restricted by gender are not within the legislation.[22] While understandable, this may have unfortunate consequences. Such clubs may be nominally private, but given the degree of networking and decision making to which some are privy, they may be said to exercise a quasi-public function. Arguably, the law should cover such clubs unless, perhaps, their total membership is below a certain figure. This would bring, for example, London clubs and the Marylebone Cricket Club (MCC) within the legislation. In addition, certain clubs, of which some golf clubs are prime example, adopt differential membership criteria for men and women under which, for example, only men have the right to full voting membership and where only full membership carries a right to reciprocal membership of other such clubs. There can be no justification for such stereotyped differentiations which should be removed by law.

Charter held that club membership did not constitute a section of the public, a decision later reversed by legislation. By contrast, legislation removed the illegality following the decision in *Applin v Race Relations Board*[23] that children who had been taken into the care of a local authority were a section of the public and that therefore the provision of fostering facilities was covered by the legislation. In consequence, there could be no discrimination in the way in which fostering arrangements were organised, making it impermissible for foster parents to specify the race of the child they wished to foster. Section 23(2) of the RRA 1976 reverses this position, removing from the ambit of the act situations where someone 'takes into his home, and treats as if they were members of his family, children, elderly persons, or persons

---

21 Section 26 provides an exception where the main object of the club 'is to enable the benefits of membership ... to be enjoyed by persons of a particular racial group defined otherwise than by reference to colour ...'. This enables organisations to offer membership to groups defined by nationality, such as a Swansea Bangladeshi association or a London Welsh Society. As religious organisations are analogous to private clubs, and as religious discrimination may in some circumstances amount to race discrimination, there is thus a *de facto* exception for such organisations.

22 It goes without saying that such clubs may not discriminate in respect of their employees on grounds of race or gender. See, eg, *Hayes v Malleable Working Men's Club and Institute* [1985] ICR 703; [1985] IRLR 367.

23 [1975] AC 259; [1974] 2 All ER 73, HL.

requiring a special degree of care and attention'. The exception only covers acts of discrimination by the putative foster parents; it will thus only absolve actions by the local authority in so far as they respond to the declared wishes of potential fosterers. However, s 22 of the Children Act 1989 provides that racial origin should be taken into account by local authorities in making any decision involving a child in their care.

Goods, facilities or services

Most of the situations being aimed at by these sections are clear. A few examples will suffice. It is unlawful to treat men and women differently in relation to admission charges for, for example, stately homes, hotels or sporting facilities;[24] it is unlawful to refuse to serve women or black people when men or white people would be served;[25] it is unlawful to apply different rules of behaviour to men and women in places of public entertainment;[26] it is unlawful to apply different criteria to men and women, or black people and white people, in relation to the provision of facilities or services such as credit facilities or the offer of a mortgage.

It is unlawful to refuse the service on ground of race and gender, to grant the service on different conditions, and also if the service is not provided 'in like manner'. Harassment of a customer or client on ground of race or gender is unlawful by virtue of this provision. It might be easier to succeed in a claim than in the employment context, especially where the harassment concerns a single incident, as there is no requirement that the harassment be to the complainant's detriment, although that will clearly be relevant in assessing the degree of injury to feelings.

Section 29(3) of the SDA 1975 deals with the question of where the clientele for the service may be self-selecting on ground of gender: examples include a ladies' hairdresser or fashion shop. An equivalent example concerned with race might be a shop which sells food prepared according to the Muslim tradition or an organisation concerned with health problems peculiar to particular racial groups. It is clearly discrimination to refuse to

---

24 *James v Eastleigh BC* [1990] 2 AC 751; [1990] 2 All ER 607; [1990] IRLR 208. In *R v Secretary of State for Health ex p Richardson* Case C-137/94; [1996] ICR 471; [1996] All ER (E) 865 the European Court held that it was a breach of the Social Security Directive 79/7 to grant, on the ground of different pensionable ages, free medical prescriptions for women aged 60 whereas men only obtained the concession at age 65. The scope of the Directive is limited to matters concerning social security. The Transport Act 1985, s 93, specifically empowers local authorities to differentiate between men and women on the basis of pensionable age so far as free or reduced fares are concerned. The European Court held, in *Atkins v Wrekin District Council* Case C-228/94 [1996] All ER (E) 719, that such a scheme, lawful under domestic law, did not contravene Directive 79/7 as it was not primarily a social security scheme.

25 *Gill v El Vino Co Ltd* [1983] QB 425; [1983] 1 All ER 398; [1983] IRLR 206, CA.

26 *McConomy v Croft Inns Ltd* [1992] IRLR 561, High Ct of NI.

serve a person of a different race or gender from the usual clientele, but there is no obligation to alter the range of the services provided to make them more attractive to people of a different race or gender. In effect, the sub-section legitimises indirect discrimination in these contexts, as long as the discrimination concerns the nature of what is provided rather than the manner of its provision. While the line between the two may not always be clear, it is contended that there must be something in the nature of the service being provided which would indicate that it is likely to be especially attractive to members of a particular race or gender. A building society whose mortgage criteria mean that the houses on which they are prepared to lend money are outside the price range of the majority of black people could not have a defence based on this line of reasoning.[27] The sections assume that the services being provided are genuinely comparable. There is nothing to prevent, for example, differential pricing for male and female hair care, if it can be shown that there is a fundamental difference in the service being provided.[28] For reasons of commercial convenience, it is probably acceptable to have a single price for women which is higher than for men, even though in some particular instances the hair care being provided could not be regarded as involving a different service.

It is clear that commercial services provided by public bodies or local authorities are within the sections. The position with respect to non-commercial activities is much less straightforward. The answer to the question will determine the extent to which many of the major policy and administration functions of government are brought within the scope of the legislation. While judicial review *may* be available as an alternative, it is by no means automatic and under that route there is no possibility of compensation as a remedy. It seems clear that an activity of government which is primarily *detrimental* to individuals is outside the scope of the section. In *Savjani v Inland Revenue Commissioners*,[29] the Court of Appeal held that the Inland Revenue was not providing a service to members of the public in collecting tax from them. It is perfectly consistent to argue that some of the activities of the Revenue may be within the section: the giving of advice or information entails the provision of a service and must be carried out in a non-discriminatory fashion. Similarly, the prison department does not provide a service to the prisoners it incarcerates, but it does provide a service or a facility to prisoners in respect of work allocation within a prison.[30]

---

27 *Race and Mortgage Lending in Rochdale*, 1985, London: CRE.
28 *Waldock v Whitney and Prosser* (1984) unreported, county court.
29 [1981] QB 458; [1981] 1 All ER 1121.
30 *Alexander v Home Office* [1988] 2 All ER 118; [1988] ICR 685; [1988] IRLR 190. Work in a prison falls outside the statutory definition of employment; the case can only be argued on the basis of the provision of a facility or a service.

R v Entry Clearance Officer Bombay ex p Amin **[1983] 2 All ER 864**[31]

The plaintiff was a British Overseas Citizen whose right to enter the UK depended on a voucher scheme which, by assuming that men were normally the heads of households, discriminated between men and women. This was not a challenge to the operation of immigration legislation based on race, which is specifically excluded, but on ground of gender.

The majority of the House of Lords held that the scheme fell outside the provisions of s 29 of the SDA 1975.

Lord Fraser of Tullybelton (pp 872–73):

Section 29 as a whole seems to me to apply to the direct provision of facilities or services, and not to the mere grant of permission to use facilities ... The example in para (d) refers, in my view, to the actual provision of schools and other facilities for education, but not to the mere grant of an entry certificate or a special voucher to enable a student to enter the United Kingdom in order to study here ... In the present case the entry clearance officer in Bombay was in my opinion not providing a service for would-be immigrants; rather he was performing his duty of controlling them ...

[Section 85(1) of the 1976 Act] puts an act done on behalf of the Crown on a par with an act done by a private person, and it does not in terms restrict the comparison to an act of the *same kind* done by a private person. But in my opinion it applies only to acts done on behalf of the Crown which are of a kind similar to acts which might be done by a private person. It does not mean that the Act is to apply to any act of any kind done on behalf of the Crown by a person holding statutory office ...

Lord Scarman (dissenting) (p 879):

In my view the granting of leave to enter the country by provision of a special voucher or otherwise is the provision of a facility to a section of the public. Indeed, I have no doubt that some see it as a very valuable facility. Section 29(1) is wide enough, therefore, to cover the special voucher scheme which, in my judgment, is properly described as offering a facility to some members of the public, ie, United Kingdom passport holders, who seek access to this country for the purposes of settlement but have no lawful means of entering other than by leave.

If the first reason relied on by Lord Fraser is correct, it would mean that merely permitting someone to do something was outside the scope of the legislation. That cannot be right. It is much more natural to view *James v Eastleigh BC* as the granting of a permission through the issue of a ticket to use the swimming pool rather than, say, ensuring that the water was warm and germ-free. *Amin* itself is almost a case concerning the denial of a ticket or an equivalent facility. Furthermore, the need to restrict the meaning of the section to activities similar to those which might be provided by non-public bodies is

---

[31] See, also, [1983] 2 AC 818.

never explained. It cannot be the case that whether any activities of the prison department are covered depends on whether private prisons were in existence at the time of the alleged breach.

Gardner, J, 'Section 20 of the Race Relations Act 1976: "facilities" and "services"' (1987) 50 MLR 345, pp 347, 351:

[T]here is no necessary relationship between a person's primary function under statute and his subjection or non-subjection to s 20. Nor is there any necessary relationship between public conceptions of his role and his subjection or non-subjection to s 20. A government officer may conceive of himself as primarily an agent of control. The general public (even those who are successful in extracting some favourable decision from him) may also view him as an agent of control. Nevertheless, he may provide 'facilities' to the public for the purpose of s 20 if, for example, he accepts applications for some advantage or concession; he also provides 'services' by advertising the facility, advising on it, and accepting applications ...

[E]ven if it were plausible to claim that the 1975 Act and the 1976 Act only bind the Crown in respect of actions which are 'similar' to those of private persons, we need to provide a criterion of similarity. In some respects the process of considering an application for leave to settle is very similar to process of considering whether to grant a gratuitous licence to another to reside on one's land. In other respects the process of considering whether to grant leave *does* seem peculiar to governments. Unless the criterion of similarity is spelled out, we cannot tell whether Lord Fraser is right to treat the grant of a clearance voucher as being a purely governmental power. It is really only peculiarly governmental in the obvious sense in which all statutory powers of the Crown are peculiarly governmental.

The reversal of *Amin* is essential as a means to ensure that all activities of government departments and agencies are brought within the scope of the legislation. 'It is very particularly in areas such as the exercise of police powers, immigration controls, the treatment of prisoners and the licensing and enforcement functions of local authorities that discrimination can cause the greatest damage to race relations.'[32]

If discrimination on the ground of sexual orientation is held to contravene the SDA 1975, or European law, or becomes the subject of separate legislation, it is inevitable that issues will arise in respect of goods, facilities and services. Direct discrimination may occur, for example, if landlords refuse to rent to a gay couple, or hotels exclude openly gay parties.[33] Indirect discrimination on the ground of sexual orientation would probably be held to be present

---

[32] *Reform of the Race Relations Act 1996: Proposals from the Commission for Racial Equality,* 1998, London: CRE, p 12.

[33] Given the symmetry of British and European anti-discrimination legislation, it follows that for a gay bar to exclude non-gays would also become unlawful. Such a claim is perhaps unlikely, but, in the light of the rise of the so-called 'pink pound' it is clear that it would be unlawful, eg, to be prepared only to do business with other gays.

whenever the actual cause of the discrimination was HIV status. It may be held to be justified, based on normal insurance principles, to refuse life insurance or charge very high premia to someone who was HIV positive. However, to refuse facilities such as membership of a health club on the basis of a perceived health risk would almost certainly be unjustifiable.[34]

HOUSING AND OTHER PREMISES

Race Relations Act 1976

s 21(1) It is unlawful for a person, in relation to premises in Great Britain of which he has power to dispose, to discriminate against another:

(a) in the terms on which he offers him those premises; or

(b) by refusing his application for those premises; or

(c) in his treatment of him in relation to any list of persons in need of premises of that description.

(2) It is unlawful for a person, in relation to premises managed by him, to discriminate against a person occupying the premises:

(a) in the way he affords him access to any benefits or facilities, or by refusing or deliberately omitting to afford him access to them; or

(b) by evicting him, or subjecting him to any other detriment.[35]

The potential defendants under these provisions are primarily owners and managers; the likely plaintiffs, potential purchasers and potential tenants. Others involved in the transaction, such as estate agents and accommodation agencies, are covered by the section concerning the provision of facilities or services. Racial or sexual harassment of tenants by managers would come within this provision; harassment of an owner-occupier by neighbours would not do so. Individual owner-occupiers are exempt unless they either use the services of an estate agent or advertise in a discriminatory fashion.[36] It seems to follow that if the owner sexually or racially harassed a potential purchaser, there would be no liability under this section, but if the harassment was by an estate agent the situation would be different.

Section 22 of the RRA 1976 and s 32 of the SDA 1975 provide an exception from this provision for small dwellings. If the owner or a close relative lives in the premises, and shares a significant part of the premises with others, discrimination is permitted as long as no more than six people occupy the property in addition to the landlord's household. Thus a landlord or landlady

---

[34] Someone who is HIV positive but is not suffering from AIDS is outside the scope of the definition of disability in the Disability Discrimination Act 1995; see below, p 592.

[35] SDA 1975, s 30, is substantially identical.

[36] RRA 1976, s 21(3); SDA 1975, s 30(3).

who rents accommodation to students may not discriminate if the students are in exclusive accommodation, but may do so, on grounds either of sex or race, if the accommodation is shared. For example, a resident landlord may conclude that male students are rowdier than female, which is the kind of stereotyping which is normally unlawful. Discrimination should be restricted to situations where the resident landlady, for example, wishes to ensure that her tenants are female. But, 20 years after the passing of the RRA 1976, it is no longer acceptable that direct discrimination on the basis of race in the narrow sense is permissible, even in respect of tenants in one's private household. However, the wide exception does avoid problematic issues of indirect discrimination which may be to do with religion or lifestyle: arguably Muslims should be permitted to share their home with those who prepare food according to the same tradition, and, more generally, people may be thought to have a right to share only with those who follow the same religion.

In the light of the authority, discussed above, on the meaning of 'facilities and services', it had become unclear whether the planning functions of local and other authorities were within the scope of the legislation. For this reason, the Housing and Planning Act 1986 added a new section to the RRA 1976, s 19A, such that it is now unlawful for a planning authority to discriminate.

OTHER PROVISIONS

There are a number of other provisions where special or differential treatment is permitted under one or both pieces of legislation. Only the first two examples are covered by both the SDA 1975 and the RRA 1976.

Charities

Section 34 of the RRA 1976 legitimises discriminatory provisions in charitable instruments unless the ground of the discrimination is colour, in which case the restriction is disregarded, thereby bringing a wider class of beneficiary within the scope of the instrument. The effect is to exclude charities defined by race, but to permit those defined by nationality or religion. Section 43 of the SDA 1975 provides a similar exception for charitable instruments which only benefit members of one sex.[37] If the purpose of the charity is itself to provide employment, or, more likely, education – such as to the sons of Swansea solicitors – discrimination is permissible, but ss 78 and 79 provide a way of altering educational charities which discriminate on the basis of sex. Such charities may not, of course, discriminate as regards their own employees.

---

[37] See *Hugh-Jones v St John's College Cambridge* [1979] ICR 848, EAT.

Sports[38]

Section 44 of the SDA 1975, referred to above in the context of education, legitimises most unequal or discriminatory treatment in the context of the playing of sports and games, though not of course in relation to employment as teachers, coaches, physiotherapists, etc, unless the particular circumstances are covered by one of the genuine occupational qualifications.[39] Section 39 of the RRA 1976 legitimises discrimination on the basis of nationality, place of birth or length of residence for the purpose of selecting sporting teams, and for the purpose of eligibility to compete in a sporting competition. It is therefore permissible to pick only Welshmen or women to play rugby for Wales, and permissible to restrict eligibility to compete in the Welsh Junior Gymnastics Championships to those resident in Wales. In *The Football Association v Bennett*,[40] it was held to be lawful to refuse to register an 11 year old girl as a soccer player. It was irrelevant that *she* might have been under no disadvantage as compared with her opponents; the question was whether, taken as a whole, the average woman would be at a disadvantage. In *French v Crosby*,[41] the court rejected an argument that women would be at a disadvantage in playing snooker against men. While this case concerned casual snooker in a pub, in which context it is far more difficult to satisfy the defence than in a competitive context, it is far from clear what is the legal basis for continuing to differentiate between men and women in sports such as snooker, table tennis, bowls and darts. The defence is on its face permissive, that is, there is no *obligation* to segregate men and women for the purposes of sport, though if there were no such segregation it might be possible for a woman to argue that she had been treated less favourably than a man by being forced to compete against men.

A more liberal approach to discrimination in women's sports is reflected in *Couch v British Boxing Board of Control*.[42] It was held to be unlawful to refuse a licence to a female boxer to fight other women. It was held that there was no medical basis for regarding women's boxing as more dangerous to the

---

38 Title IX of the United States Education Amendments of 1972 provides that no 'person ... shall, on the basis of sex, be excluded from participation in, be denied the benefits of, or be subjected to any discrimination under any education programme or activity receiving federal financial assistance'. See Johnson, J, 'Title IX and intercollegiate athletics: current judicial interpretation of the standards for compliance' (1994) Boston UL Rev 553.

39 It was held in *British Judo Association v Petty* [1981] ICR 660; [1981] IRLR 484, EAT, that preventing a female judo referee from refereeing bouts between men was unlawful. Section 13 of the SDA 1975, which covers discrimination by qualifying bodies, applied; s 44 did not; that section only covers participants. It was irrelevant that such referees are not paid.

40 (1978), unreported, CA.

41 (1982), unreported, county court.

42 (1998) *The Guardian*, 31 March.

participants than male boxing, especially as one of the purported reasons for denying a licence was that, during menstruation, women would be too unstable to be permitted to box. The real reason was probably that a dead or seriously injured woman boxer might lead to unstoppable demands for the total outlawing of boxing.

Education and training

This exception only appears in the RRA 1976; it is closely linked with what positive action is permissible as discriminatory training.[43] Section 35 provides a defence 'for any act done in affording persons of a particular racial group access to facilities or services to meet the special needs of persons of that group in regard to their education, training or welfare ...'. This legitimises, for example, literacy campaigns targeted at immigrant groups, or assisting minority ethnic groups with housing or employment problems, assuming that the particular needs of the group targeted were sufficiently 'special'. Section 36 legitimises the provision of education or training to people not ordinarily resident in Great Britain and who do not intend to remain afterwards; language schools are the obvious example.

There are five exceptions peculiar to the SDA 1975.

The actuarial exception

Sex Discrimination Act 1975

s 45 Nothing ... shall render unlawful the treatment of a person in relation to an annuity, life insurance policy, accident insurance policy, or similar matter involving the assessment of risk, where the treatment:

(a) was effected by reference to actuarial or other data from a source on which it was reasonable to rely; and

(b) was reasonable having regard to the data and any other relevant factors.

This provision is unaffected by developments at the European level concerning pensions, which are primarily dependent on the interpretation of 'pay' in Art 119 of the Treaty of Rome.[44] In any event, the European Court has approved the use of actuarial tables in some forms of pension arrangements.[45] In *Pinder v Friends Provident Life Office*,[46] it was held to be reasonable for the defendants to charge a female self-employed dentist 50% more than men for

---

[43] RRA 1976, ss 37, 38. See below, pp 547–51.
[44] See Chapter 13.
[45] See below, pp 491–95.
[46] (1985) *The Times*, December 16; county court.

permanent health insurance. As the available statistics for private insurance lacked detail, considerable reliance was placed on National Insurance statistics, even though they had been prepared for a different purpose. Furthermore, the county court held that the 50% loading was reasonable, even though by its own admission it was on the high side. They considered the amount of the weighting to be in the end a matter of commercial judgment. There is no rigorous examination of the policy, great deference to the company being manifested. The lack of subsequent litigation on this issue is perhaps surprising and there is a strong case for the repeal of this provision.

Political parties

Section 33 of the SDA 1975 permits political parties to make 'special provision for one sex only in [their] constitution, organisation or administration'. Thus political parties may have special women's groups and may reserve places for women or, for example, the national executive of the party. Without this provision, many of the activities of political parties would come within the definition of 'facilities and services' in s 29. It appears to follow that black groups within a political party will normally be unlawful unless they can be regarded as meeting the special needs of that racial group under s 35 of the RRA 1976.

Voluntary bodies

There are three exceptions from the section concerning the provision of goods, facilities and services which closely mirror the defence of genuine occupational qualification for employment. Under s 34 of the SDA 1975, voluntary bodies may restrict their membership to persons of one sex only, and may likewise restrict the benefits or facilities which they provide. This provision is needed because many such bodies may cast their net sufficiently wide that their benefits are conferred upon a section of the public. For example, a centre for victims of female domestic violence is permitted to restrict employment to women under s 7(2)(e) of the SDA 1975 and may, under this provision, restrict its benefits to women.

Special facilities or services

This exception, which is closely linked with the previous one, enables the provision of single-sex facilities for 'persons requiring special care, supervision or attention', where the facilities are provided for members of one sex for religious reasons, and where segregation is needed for reasons of privacy.[47]

Communal accommodation

Section 46 of the SDA 1975 permits, for reasons or privacy or decency, discrimination in relation to the provision of communal accommodation. However, the providers of such accommodation must ensure that 'the accommodation is managed in a way which, given the exigencies of the situation, comes as near as may be to fair and equitable treatment of men and women'.

PROCEDURE AND REMEDIES

The normal procedure is that claims concerning the non-employment provisions of both pieces of legislation are heard in the county court, from which there is appeal to the Court of Appeal.[48] Unlike proceedings before Industrial Tribunals,[49] legal aid may be available for county court matters. But just as with employment matters, there is power in the CRE and EOC to assist individual claimants.

There are two major differences between employment and non-employment proceedings. First, the limitation period is six months rather than three,[50] although the power to accept a late application is the same. Secondly, the fact that such claims are heard in the county court means that it may be possible to obtain an injunction.

These points might suggest that the procedure and remedies might be more effective in non-employment cases than in employment cases. Experience indicates otherwise. The number of such cases is small, and, in those that are heard, the awards of compensation tend to be very modest. It is arguable that this branch of the legislation is even less suited to enforcement via the adversarial legal process than are the employment provisions. It would be unwise to anticipate that the non-employment provisions of the Disability Discrimination Act will be any more effective. In the light of these points, and

---

[47] SDA 1975, s 35.
[48] Under RRA 1976, s 67, only certain county courts have jurisdiction, the reason being that such courts may be provided with the assistance of assessors expert in the field of race relations.
[49] Now renamed employment tribunals by the Employment Rights (Dispute Resolution) Act 1998, s 1(1).
[50] SDA 1975, s 74(4); RRA 1976, s 65(4)

bearing in mind the essential similarity of all discrimination cases, the EOC considers that a separate division to hear non-employment cases should be established within the employment tribunal system.[51]

---

[51] *Equality in the 21st Century: a New Approach*, 1998, Manchester: EOC, p 36.

CHAPTER 12

THE LAW OF EQUAL PAY

INTRODUCTION

We have already examined the origins of equal pay legislation and the causes of the fact that, on average, women earn less than men. This chapter is concerned with the details and effectiveness of equal pay law. The Equal Pay Act 1970 enables a woman to claim equality with a man where she is engaged on 'like work',[1] work 'rated as equivalent' under a job evaluation scheme[2] and, since 1983, where her work is of equal value with that of her male comparator.[3] The employer has a defence where the difference in pay is 'genuinely due to a material factor which is not the difference of sex'.[4] In addition, both the Equal Opportunities Commission[5] and the European Commission[6] have recently launched Codes of Practice on equal pay.

The original s 3 of the EqPA 1970, which permitted a claim that a collective agreement was discriminatory, was repealed in 1986.[7] Article 119 of the Treaty of Rome guarantees the application 'of the principle that men and women should receive equal pay for equal work'.[8] The Equal Pay Directive[9] expands on this definition, declaring that 'the principle of equal pay' means equal pay 'for the same work or for work to which equal value is attributed'. In *Jenkins v Kingsgate (Clothing Productions) Ltd*,[10] the European Court held that the Equal Pay Directive did no more than re-state the content of Art 119. This meant that in effect the Equal Pay Directive was itself directly effective.[11] The European Court held in *Commission of the European Communities v United*

---

1 Equal Pay Act 1970, ss 1(2)(a), 1(4).
2 Equal Pay Act 1970, ss 1(2)(b), 1(5).
3 Equal Pay Act 1970, s 1(2)(c).
4 Equal Pay Act 1970, s 1(3).
5 *Equal Opportunities Commission Code of Practice on Equal Pay*, 1997, Manchester: EOC, in force 26 March 1997, see (1996) 70 EOR 36.
6 *A Code of Practice on the Implementation of Equal Pay for Work of Equal Value for Women and Men*, Commission of the European Communities COM(96) 336 final; see (1996) 70 EOR 43.
7 SDA 1986, s 9.
8 Under the draft Treaty of Amsterdam, yet to be formally ratified by the Member States, Art 119 is amended as to include a specific reference to work of equal value. See (1997) 75 EOR 30.
9 Directive 75/117/EEC, OJ L45/19, 1975.
10 Case 96/80 [1981] ECR 911; [1981] ICR 592; [1981] 1 WLR 972; [1981] IRLR 228.
11 Article 119 had been held directly effective in *Defrenne v SABENA (No 2)* Case 43/75 [1976] ECR 455; [1976] 2 CMLR 98; [1976] ICR 547.

Kingdom[12] that UK equal pay law failed to comply with Art 119 in that there was no provision whereby a complainant could argue that her work was of equal value to that of her chosen comparator. As a result, the Equal Pay (Amendment) Regulations 1983[13] purported to bring British law into line with the requirements of Art 119. Whether this has been successfully achieved will be considered subsequently. It is possible to mount a claim based on Art 119 even if the claim falls outside the provisions of the EqPA 1970; the procedural and remedial implications of such action will also be examined later.

RELATIONSHIP WITH THE SEX DISCRIMINATION ACT[14]

Despite the fact that the two pieces of legislation took effect on the same date in 1975, the relationship between them is unnecessarily complex and confusing.[15] While it is clear that as far as possible they are complementary and should be construed as one Code, courts have not always found this to be practicable or appropriate. Especially where the application of the principles of indirect discrimination are concerned, the approach under one Act will not always mirror that under the other.[16]

The Equal Pay Act is something of a misnomer. The Act governs 'terms (whether concerned with pay or not) of a contract under which a woman is employed ...'.[17] It follows that a claim may be brought in respect of inequality in any matter which is regulated by the contract of employment, such as hours, holidays, fringe benefits, etc. The SDA 1975 deals with matters not regulated by the contract, such as job offers (including promotions), dismissals, etc. It is therefore important for claimants to know whether or not a particular issue is part of the contract; it is especially important to bear in mind that contracts do not necessarily have to be in writing and that terms of

---

[12] Case 61/81 [1982] ECR 2601; [1982] ICR 578; [1982] IRLR 333.

[13] SI 1983/1794.

[14] Claims of victimisation under both statutes are dealt with by the SDA 1975, s 4.

[15] One of the main arguments contained in the recent EOC reform proposals is that a consolidating statute is urgently required. See *Equality in the 21st Century: A New Approach*, 1997, Manchester: EOC, paras 5–11.

[16] Thus in *Bhudi v IMI Refiners Ltd* [1994] ICR 307; [1994] IRLR 204, EAT, it was held that the claimant, in an indirect discrimination claim under the SDA 1975, had to establish that a requirement or condition was applied, thus adopting a different approach from that adopted in the equal pay context by the European Court in *Enderby v Frenchay AHA and Secretary of State for Health* Case C-127/92 [1993] ECR I-5535; [1994] ICR 112; [1994] 1 All ER 495; [1993] IRLR 591. Similarly, the approach to the defence of genuine material factor taken by the House of Lords in *Ratcliffe v North Yorkshire DC* [1995] ICR 837; [1995] 3 All ER 597; [1995] IRLR 439 differs markedly from the approach to justification in cases of indirect discrimination.

[17] EqPA 1970, s 1(2).

contracts may be derived from external sources, such as a collective agreement between employer and trade union.

If something is done under the contract of employment, whether the payment of money or the provision of other benefits, the first question is whether the EqPA 1970 applies.[18] If, for some reason, that Act does not apply, a claim may still be brought under the SDA 1975 *except* where the benefit consists of the payment of money.[19] An offer of a contractual term is governed by the SDA 1975 but the EqPA 1970 will apply when that offer is accepted and becomes part of the contract.[20] Thus an allegation of discrimination in relation to fringe benefits must first consider whether the case falls within the area of comparison mandated by the EqPA 1970; only if does not do so is a claim under SDA 1975 permissible.[21]

The determination of the issue under which Act a claim may be brought can be crucial. Under the SDA 1975 a claim may allege discrimination as regards how a man was or *'would have been'* treated. Under EqPA 1970, a claim may only proceed if there is an *actual* male comparator; the courts have rejected claims to permit comparison with the so called 'hypothetical man'.[22] In fact, the complexity of the interrelationship between the two statutes has not led to the litigation which might have been expected, but nevertheless the need for consolidation is impossible to oppose; the current distinction serves no practical purpose and is simply the result of the fact that the two pieces of legislation were passed separately, and that their origins and philosophy are significantly different from each other.[23]

CLAIMS UNDER THE ACT[24]

The permitted scope of comparison

The fact that comparisons are not permitted with a hypothetical man is a major limitation on the potential effectiveness of the Act. There is a close correlation between low pay and the proportion of female employees in a

---

18 SDA 1975, ss 6(2)(a), 8(5).
19 SDA 1975, ss 6(2), 6(5).
20 SDA 1975, s 8(3).
21 In *McKenzie-Wynne v Rowan Dartington and Co Ltd*, unreported, IT, Case No: 29293/96, see 32 DCLD 8, it was held that an allegation that discretionary non-contractual bonus payments were lower for women than for men should therefore be brought under the SDA 1975 and not the EqPA 1970.
22 See below, pp 408–09.
23 See above, pp 99–101.
24 The qualifying requirements mirror those under the SDA 1975. Under s 16(a), the definition of 'person employed' is the same; and both the applicant and her comparator must be employed at an establishment in Great Britain. See above, pp 321–24.

firm; in many of the lowest paying firms, the workforce is 100% female. In such firms, claims under the EqPA 1970 can effectively never be brought; therefore the Act cannot be viewed as the spearhead of an attack against poverty and low pay generally. For this, minimum wage legislation is a far more direct and immediate weapon. The government has calculated that the proposed minimum wage rate of £3.60 will benefit 1.4 million women and 1.3 million part time workers.[25]

There are other ways in which the potential radicalism of the Act is blunted from the start. Closely connected with the requirement for an actual comparator is the requirement that the comparison must be with a man who works for the same establishment.[26] Comparisons are thus not permitted between different firms, perhaps in different regions or simply because the other firm pays higher wages. I am not here necessarily arguing that such comparisons should have been permitted, merely that the scope of the Act is necessarily limited because they are not. A further restriction concerns the extremely limited impact which the law has over collective agreements. The original s 3 of the Act did give limited jurisdiction, but the fact that such jurisdiction was held to be limited to directly discriminatory collective agreements – in effect agreements which discriminated on their face – meant that such jurisdiction was of virtually no practical effect.[27] The replacement provisions dealing with collective agreements are both contorted and unhelpful. They are a deeply flawed and limited attempt to deal with collective problems in the guise of an individualistic legal framework. The Act as a whole is highly vulnerable to the charge that it pays no effective regard to the fact that pay is very often – still – negotiated collectively through trade unions, and that a solution to the problem of equal pay demanded a remedial regime which appreciated this collective reality rather than the current individualistic focus of litigation.

The choice of comparator

The claimant may choose with which employee she is claiming equality.[28] However, previous EAT authority that an employment tribunal[29] may not substitute a more suitable or 'representative' comparator[30] has had doubt

---

[25] Department of Trade and Industry Press Release, P/98/489, 18 June 1998.

[26] EqPA 1970, s 1(6).

[27] *R v Central Arbitration Committee ex p Hy-Mac Ltd* [1979] IRLR 461, DC.

[28] *Ainsworth v Glass Tubes and Components Ltd* [1977] ICR 347; [1977] IRLR 74, EAT.

[29] Industrial tribunals were re-named employment tribunals by the Employment Rights (Dispute Resolution) Act 1998, s 1(1).

[30] *Thomas v National Coal Board* [1987] ICR 757; [1987] IRLR 451, EAT.

upon it by a *dictum* of Balcombe LJ in *British Coal Corporation v Smith*.[31] He commented that it 'is necessary that the selected male comparator should be representative of the class, or group, of male employees from whom he is selected ...'.[32] He argued that this limitation is implicit in the somewhat more collective and less individualistic approach to issues of equal pay which has been taken by the European Court. This is especially the case where the claim is based on equal value, and true most of all where based on a difference in average pay between a group of men and a group of women. Here the selection of the appropriate group is crucial to the claim, and, according to the European Court in the *Royal Copenhagen*[33] case, must 'encompass groups each comprising all the workers who, taking account of a set of factors such as the nature of the work, the training requirements and the working conditions, can be considered to be in a comparable situation. [Such] comparison ... must cover a relatively large number of workers in order to ensure that the differences found are not due to purely fortuitous or short term factors or to differences in the individual output of the workers concerned'.[34] Even if an English court does permit a totally untrammelled choice of an individual comparator, use of a 'rogue' comparator may be of no avail to a female applicant, as the employer will normally be able to rely on the genuine material factor defence under s 1(3) to explain the inequality of pay.

It is possible to claim equality with more than one comparator at the same time; in theory losing a claim for equality with one comparator does not preclude a future claim utilising a different more appropriate comparator, but such a course is both practically and psychologically difficult. In *Hayward v Cammell Laird Shipbuilders Ltd (No 2)*,[35] the applicant claimed equality with a painter, a decorator and a thermal insulation engineer. This made practical and legal sense, as an applicant may have only a rough idea of what potential comparators earn, especially when fringe benefits are taken into account. It may be possible to use the discovery procedure to find out the details of the pay of comparators, but this can only be done after the commencement of a claim. In principle, even if a claim fails, there could be a further allegation involving the same comparator based on an argument that the nature of the work had changed since rejection of the first claim, but the tribunal will need to be convinced that there has been a significant change either in the work or in the pay and conditions of at least one of the two jobs being compared.[36] A

---

31 [1994] ICR 810; [1994] IRLR 342, CA. The case was subsequently reversed by the House of Lords [1996] ICR 515; [1996] 3 All ER 97; [1996] IRLR 404 (see below, pp 447–48) where the *dictum* was cited but not commented upon.

32 *British Coal Corporation v Smith* [1994] IRLR 342, p 358.

33 *Specialarbejderforbundet i Danmark v Dansk Industri (acting for Royal Copenhagen A/S)* Case C-400/93 [1995] IRLR 648.

34 *Specialarbejderforbundet i Danmark v Dansk Industri (acting for Royal Copenhagen A/S)* Case C-400/93 [1995] IRLR 648, p 658.

35 [1988] AC 894; [1988] 2 All ER 257; [1988] IRLR 257, HL.

36 *McLoughlin v Gordons (Stockport) Ltd* [1978] IRLR 127, EAT.

successful claim in relation to one comparator may generate subsequent claims seeking to use the successful claimant as the new comparator. The fact that there is, in theory, nothing to stop a series of leap-frogging claims, and nothing to guarantee the representativeness of the comparator chosen, demonstrates the need for collective rather than individualistic solutions.

An applicant may claim equality with a man employed at the same establishment[37] or employed by the same or an associated employer.[38] It has been held that local authorities or other public bodies fall outside this definition, thereby in effect confining the concept of control to corporate control, and excluding other forms of control such as political or managerial control.[39] However, in *Scullard v Knowles and Southern Regional Council for Education and Training*,[40] the EAT accepted that the employers in question were not 'associated employers'. However, it was held that Art 119 is wider. The court quoted from *Defrenne v SABENA (No 2)*[41] where the equal pay principle was held to apply to those employed in 'the same establishment or service, whether public or private'.[42] The form of control which is arguably relevant in many areas of the public service will be receipt of funds from the same funding body; how far this will in itself be sufficient remains to be seen.[43]

---

[37] The term is undefined; it has been suggested that 'the concept refers not to the business ... but to the place of work of an employee or group of employees. However, it may also cover a number of separate sites if they are linked by a common managerial structure or if they form part of a single unit for accounting or financial purposes. Thus a series of building sites owned by a single employer could, for this purpose, form a single "establishment"'. Deakin, S and Morris, G, *Labour Law*, 1995, London: Butterworths, pp 190–91.

[38] Section 1(6) provides that two employers are associated employers where 'one is a company of which the other (directly or indirectly) has control or both are companies of which a third person (directly or indirectly) has control'.

[39] *Gardner v London Borough of Merton* [1980] IRLR 472, CA; *Hasley v Fair Employment Agency* [1989] IRLR 106, NICA.

[40] [1996] ICR 399; [1996] IRLR 344. The applicant was a unit manager for one of 12 independent voluntary organisations which co-ordinate the work of Colleges of Further Education. She sought to compare her pay with that of unit managers employed by other councils.

[41] Case 43/75 [1976] ECR 455; [1976] 2 CMLR 98; [1976] ICR 547.

[42] [1976] ECR 455, p 476.

[43] The case was remitted to the Industrial Tribunal to consider in the light of this new approach the degree of interconnectedness. If she proved that the two employers were indeed associated employers under this wider approach, her claim could still only proceed if she proved that common terms and conditions were observed between the two establishments in question. It has been argued that the reference to 'the same service' directs attention to the nature of the work rather than the identity of the employer and thus could be used to mount an argument that, where work is contracted out, such workers will nevertheless be entitled to equality with those workers who are still employed by the original employer; see (1996) 67 EOR 45.

Utilising a comparator at a different establishments, even if clearly employed by the same employer, is only permissible if 'common terms of employment are observed between the two establishments'.[44]

Leverton v Clwyd County Council [1989] IRLR 28, HL[45]

A nursery nurse claimed that her work was of equal value to that of other staff employed by the local authority, none of whom worked at the same place as her, but whose pay was regulated by the same collective agreement.

The majority of the Court of Appeal held that the difference in working hours and holidays was a radical difference in the 'core terms' of the respective contracts of employment which prevented the comparison from satisfying the statutory test.

Lord Bridge of Harwich (pp 31–32):

It seems to me, first, that the language of the sub-section is clear and unambiguous. It poses the question whether the terms and conditions of employment 'observed' at two or more establishments ... are 'common', being terms and conditions of employment observed 'either generally or for employees of the relevant classes'. The concept of common terms and conditions of employment observed generally at different establishments necessarily contemplates terms and conditions applicable to a wide range of employees whose individual terms will vary greatly *inter se* ... Terms and conditions of employment governed by the same collective agreement seem to me to represent the paradigm, though not necessarily the only example, of the common terms and conditions of employment contemplated by the sub-section ...

The purpose [of the sub-section] is to enable a woman to eliminate discriminatory differences between the terms of her contract and those of any male fellow employee doing like work, work rated as equivalent or work of equal value ... With all respect to the majority view which prevailed below, it cannot in my opinion possibly have been the intention of Parliament to require a woman claiming equality with a man in another establishment to prove an undefined substratum of similarity between the particular terms of her contract and his as the basis of her entitlement to eliminate any discriminatory differences ...

[T]here is a sensible and rational explanation for the limitation of equality claims ... to establishments at which common terms and conditions of employment are observed. There may be perfectly good geographical or historical reasons why a single employer should operate essentially different employment regimes at different establishments ...

[The first example concerns an employer who operates two establishments, one in London and the other in Newcastle, where everyone in London earns

---

[44] In *Lawson v Britfish Ltd* [1988] IRLR 53, EAT, it was held that there is no need to show employment under common terms and conditions if the comparator works at the same establishment as the applicant.

[45] See, also, [1989] AC 706; [1989] 1 All ER 78.

more than their equivalent in Newcastle. 'The difference in pay is due not to sex but to geography'. The second example is where a factory with a long established collective agreement is taken over by an employer who operates a completely different pay structure at the other establishment.]

The effect of this undoubtedly correct decision is that the tribunal must ask itself whether the applicant would have been under the same terms and conditions of employment had she been doing her job at the comparator's establishment. The question then arose how great a degree of similarity must there be between the terms and conditions observed at the establishments in question for them to be regarded as 'common'.

British Coal Corporation v Smith [1996] IRLR 404, HL[46]

Canteen workers and cleaners claimed that they were employed on work of equal value with surface mineworkers and clerical workers. The claimants were employed at 47 different establishments, the comparators at 14. The Industrial Tribunal held that s 1(6) applied and the claim could proceed on the basis that, no matter at which establishment they worked, they were governed by national terms and conditions of employment. This was despite the fact that there were local variations resulting from differences in underground mineworkers' pay.

The House of Lords accepted this argument.

Lord Slynn of Hadley (pp 408–09):

It is accepted by the corporation that for the purposes of this appeal as between the different establishments common terms and conditions do in any event apply to the two classes of applicants, canteen workers and cleaners. What therefore has to be shown is that the male comparators at other establishments and at her establishment share common terms and conditions. If there are no such at the applicant's place of work then it has to be shown that like terms and conditions would apply if men were employed there in the particular jobs concerned.

The corporation contends that the applicants can only succeed if they can show that common terms and conditions were observed ... 'across the board'; in other words the terms and conditions of the comparators ... are 'common in substantially all respects' for such workers at her pit and at the places of employment of her comparators. This in effect means that all the terms and conditions must be common, ie, the same, subject only to *de minimis* differences.

The applicants ... contend that it is sufficient if there is a broad similarity of terms rather than that they are strictly coterminous ...

I do not consider that the s 1(3) inquiry [into the defence of genuine material factor], where the onus is on the employer, was intended to be excluded unless the terms and conditions of the men at the relevant establishment were

---

[46] See, also, [1996] ICR 515; [1996] 3 All ER 97.

common in the sense of identical. This seems to be to be far too restrictive a test.

In *Leverton*, the critical question was, between whose terms and conditions should the comparison be made? Here the question is, having established the persons between whom comparisons should be made, was there sufficient identity between the respective terms and conditions for them to be 'common'.

[The House of Lords went on to conclude that there was evidence which could properly support the tribunal's finding of fact that there was sufficient similarity between the different sets of terms and conditions, even though there were local variations concerning incentive bonuses and concessionary coal.]

The outcome is appropriate, adopting a far less technical approach than that which commended itself to the Court of Appeal. The House of Lords was not deciding that the claim should succeed, merely that it should not fail at the preliminary stage. The employer is still permitted to attempt to justify the pay differential. Yet such comparisons are only likely to prove possible where the employer operates a centralised collective bargaining structure. Plant bargaining, fragmented bargaining, or no collective bargaining at all are all likely to prevent cross-establishment comparisons being permissible.

The concept of pay

The coverage of the legislation has been transformed by European law. Article 119 provides:

For the purposes of this article, 'pay' means the ordinary or minimum wage or salary and or any other consideration whether in cash or in kind which the worker receives, directly or indirectly, in respect of his employment from his employer. Equal pay without discrimination based on sex means:

(a) that pay for the same work[47] at piece rates shall be calculated on the same unit of measurement;

(b) that pay for the same work at time rates shall be the same for the same job.

It is therefore clear that all fringe benefits are covered, such as mortgage interest allowance[48] and removal expenses.[49] But the effect of jurisprudence from the European Court has been to give the concept a far wider meaning. *Garland v British Rail Engineering*[50] extended the law in two ways. First, it

---

[47] It was held in *Royal Copenhagen* Case C-400/93 [1995] IRLR 648, p 657, that this provision applies to piece work in the context of an equal value claim, even though there the work is not the same. In such circumstances, the system 'must be objectively capable of ensuring that the total individual pay for workers in the two groups is the same'.

[48] *Sun Alliance and London Insurance Ltd v Dudman* [1978] ICR 551; [1978] IRLR 169, EAT.

[49] *Durrant v North Yorkshire HA* [1979] IRLR 401, EAT.

[50] Case 12/81 [1983] 2 AC 751; [1982] ECR 359; [1982] 2 All ER 402; [1982] IRLR 111.

applied the concept of pay to travel concessions granted after retirement to the dependants of male employees but not to the dependants of female employees. That the benefits were not received by the employee personally did not prevent them from being pay. Secondly, the benefits were granted by the employer as a concession rather than pursuant to a contractual obligation. Under English law that means that any claim would fall within the SDA 1975 rather than the EqPA 1970, but the European Court held that their non-contractual nature did not prevent them being pay within Art 119.

Payments made to third parties are an essential component of pension benefits, so *Garland* was a key step in the reasoning which eventually held that pensions were within the scope of Art 119. *Bilka-Kaufhaus v Weber von Hartz*[51] had decided that indirectly discriminatory rules governing membership of pension schemes were contrary to Art 119, and such holding had necessarily implied that the payment of benefits under such schemes amounted to deferred pay, an approach subsequently confirmed in *Barber v Guardian Royal Exchange*.[52]

There are many other components of a wage packet which clearly fall within the concept of pay.[53] Sick pay and maternity pay from the employer brook no argument.[54] This is true even if the rules under which such payments are made are regulated by statute rather than by collective agreement or employer decision.[55] Thus, in *Rinner-Kuhn v FWW Spezial-Gebäudereinigung*,[56] the fact that the German *statute* provided that sick pay

---

[51] Case 170/84 [1986] ECR 1607; [1986] 2 CMLR 701; [1987] ICR 110; [1986] IRLR 317.

[52] Case C-262/88 [1990] ECR I-1889; [1991] 1 QB 344; [1990] ICR 616; [1990] IRLR 240. In logic, the detailed rules on the application of Art 119 to pensions should be explored here, for they are significantly dependent on working out what is entailed in treating pensions as deferred pay. However, pension issues are complex and raise peculiar problems; for practical purposes it makes sense to consider them in a separate chapter.

[53] The criteria by which overtime pay, performance-related pay and piece rates are determined fall clearly within the scope of Art 119. See *Handels-og Kontorfunktionaerernes Forbund i Danmark v Dansk Arbejdsgiverforening* Case 109/88 [1989] ECR 3199; [1991] 1 CMLR 8; [1989] IRLR 532; *Stadt Lengerich v Helmig* Case C-399/92 [1994] ECR I-5725; [1996] ICR 35; [1995] IRLR 216; *Royal Copenhagen* Case C-400/93 [1995] IRLR 648.

[54] Similarly, the issue of payment for time off to attend training courses falls within the ambit of Art 119. See *Arbeiterwohlfahrt der Stadt Berlin Ev v Botel* Case 360/90 [1992] ECR I-3589; [1992] 3 CMLR 646; [1992] IRLR 423; *Kuratorium für Dialyse und Nierentransplanation Ev v Lewark* Case C-45/93 [1996] IRLR 637.

[55] *Clark v Secretary of State for Employment* [1995] ICR 673; [1995] IRLR 421, EAT, concerned the obligation placed on the State-financed Redundancy Fund to pay dismissed employees their due pay for a period of notice in situations where the employer was insolvent. It was held that, even though such payments were paid under a statutory obligation, they still constituted 'pay'.

[56] Case C-171/88 [1989] ECR 2743; [1989] IRLR 493.

from the employer need not be paid to those working less than 10 hours a week did not prevent the payment in question from constituting pay.[57]

Similar logic has led to the conclusion that redundancy pay is within Art 119, as held by the European Court in *Barber* and the House of Lords in *R v Secretary of State for Employment ex p Equal Opportunities Commission*.[58] This is clearly correct; even though the criteria are laid down by statute, the amount of the payment depends both on pay level and length of service. It is thus clearly referable to the employment in much the same way as pension provision. Whether the same approach can be taken with unfair dismissal compensation is more questionable.

Mediguard Services Ltd v Thame [1994] IRLR 504, EAT[59]

Morison J (p 507):

It seems to us quite clear that compensation for unfair dismissal is consideration received by the former employee, albeit indirectly, from his former employer in respect of his employment. The payment essentially fulfils the purpose stated in *Barber* ... namely a payment made with a view to enabling the former employee to adjust to the new circumstances arising from the termination of his employment ... There is, we think, a close connection between the contract of employment and the amount of compensation. The amount of compensation can truly be said to be determined by the content of the employment relationship in the sense that the compensation is based on an assumption that, but for the dismissal, the contract would have continued. Thus, in calculating the compensation, the Industrial Tribunal will take into account the amount of pay due under the contract and the value of any contractual fringe benefits. The amount of a redundancy payment is based on a specific multiplier of a week's pay which is limited in amount by statute. The latter is less determined by the content of the employment relationship than the former, as it seems to us.

R v Secretary of State for Employment ex p Seymour-Smith [1995] IRLR 464, CA[60]

Neill LJ (pp 470–71):

[I]t was submitted [for the Secretary of State] that there has to be an unseverable causal connection between pay and employment; that connection comes into existence when the employer makes a payment out of his own funds to workers whom he himself employs or has employed on account of

---

57 Maternity pay is pay. The problem is with whom should a comparison be made in order to show that its amount is discriminatory – a man still at work, or a man off work for another reason? In *Gillespie v Northern Health and Social Services Board* Case C-342/93 [1996] ICR 498; [1996] IRLR 214 (see above, pp 200–02), it was held to be not unlawful not to continue to pay a woman her normal salary while on maternity leave.

58 [1995] 1 AC 1; [1994] ICR 317; [1994] 1 All ER 910; [1994] IRLR 176.

59 See, also, [1994] ICR 751.

60 See, also, [1995] ICR 889; [1996] All ER (E) 1.

their work and therefore in respect of their employment. While it was conceded that such an unseverable causal connection exists in the case of redundancy payments which are 'earned' by the employee throughout the period of his employment it was submitted that no such connection exists between compensation for unfair dismissal and the services rendered by the ex-employee ... There are substantial differences, it was submitted ... between redundancy payments and compensation for unfair dismissal. They include the following.

(1) Redundancy payments are certain and assessable at the moment of redundancy, whereas compensation for unfair dismissal is not. [I]t is subject to the ... duty to mitigate ... loss and to possible reductions based on ... fault contributing to the dismissal ...

(2) A redundancy payment is the primary remedy for the former employee who has been made redundant whereas monetary compensation is only a remedy if reinstatement or re-employment ... does not occur ...

The House of Lords[61] did not consider the issue in any detail but, in referring the case to the European Court, posed as one of the questions whether unfair dismissal compensation does constitute 'pay' under Art 119.

The equality clause

The technique used to bring about equal pay is referred to an equality clause. Section 1(1) provides that if 'the terms of a contract under which a woman is employed ... do not include ... an equality clause they shall be deemed to include one'. Of course, the vast majority of contracts contain no such clause, so equal pay legislation operates by way of a compulsory modification of the contract of employment. There are now three situations where the equality clause is automatically included in the woman's contract: where she is employed on like work with a man, where she is employed on work rated as equivalent under a job evaluation scheme, and where she is employed on work of equal value. Section 1(2) provides that any term of the contract which is less favourable than the man's is modified to provide equivalence, and where there is no such equivalent term, such term is in effect created by the tribunal. This approach caused problems when the law was extended to enable a woman to claim that her work was of equal value to that of a man, as the terms and conditions of employment which had to be equalised might be very different, some more favourable to the man and some more favourable to the woman.

Hayward v Cammell Laird Shipbuilders Ltd [1988] IRLR 257, HL[62]

A canteen cook in a shipyard claimed equality with a painter, a joiner and an insulation engineer. The employers argued that there was no obligation to pay

61 [1997] ICR 371; [1997] 2 All ER 273; [1997] IRLR 315.
62 See, also, [1988] AC 894; [1988] 2 All ER 257.

the applicant the same basic pay as the men because she had a paid meal break, additional holidays and better sickness benefits which compensated for her lower basic pay. The issue was whether pay should be considered as a whole or whether there is entitlement to equality in relation to each and every term. The latter approach prevailed.

Lord Mackay of Clashfern LC (pp 260–61):

I am of opinion that the natural meaning of the word 'term' ... is a distinct provision or part of the contract which has sufficient content to make it possible to compare it from the point of view of the benefit it confers with similar provision or part in another contract ... It appears to me that it would be natural to compare the appellant's basic salary as set out in her contract with the basic salary determined under the men's contract. I think it would be natural to treat the provision relating to basic pay as a term in each of the contracts ... [T]he natural application of the word 'term' to this contract is that it applies, for example, to the basic pay, and that the appropriate comparison is with the hourly rate of basic pay ...

Lord Goff of Chieveley (pp 262–63):

If a contract contains provisions relating to (1) basic pay, (2) benefits in kind such as the use of a car, (3) cash bonuses, and (4) sickness benefits, it would never occur to me to lump all these together as one 'term' of the contract, simply because they can all together be considered as providing for the total 'remuneration' ... under the contract ...

I fully appreciate that this construction ... will always lead ... to enhancement of the relevant term in the woman's contract. Likewise, it will in the converse case lead to the enhancement of the relevant term in the man's contract ... I also appreciate that this may, in some cases, lead to what has been called mutual enhancement or leap-frogging, as terms of the woman's contract and the man's contract are both, so to speak, upgraded to bring them into line with each other. It is this effect which was found to be so offensive by the Employment Appeal Tribunal and the Court of Appeal. They viewed with dismay the possibility of equality being achieved only by mutual enhancement, and not by an overall consideration of the contractual terms of both the man and the woman ... considering that mutual enhancement transcended the underlying philosophy of the 1970 Act and that it could have a profoundly inflationary effect.

To these fears there are, I consider, two different answers on two different levels. The first answer is that ... the employer must, where he can, have recourse to s 1(3) [which] could ... have the effect, in appropriate cases, of preventing the mutual enhancement which was so much feared by the Court of Appeal ...

[T]he second answer ... is that, if the construction of s 1(2) which I prefer does not accord with the true intention of Parliament, then the appropriate course for Parliament is to amend the legislation ...

There is no doubt that the House of Lords reached the right result. Not only does it accord with the literal meaning of the statute,[63] but it also accords with the underlying policy of the legislation. It would be extremely difficult to assess the value of a fringe benefit as compared with basic pay; how great a reduction in basic pay would be appropriate to compensate for the granting of contractual sick pay? There could be no right answer and the issue would inevitably generate litigation. There has been no evidence since *Hayward* that leap-frogging claims have been a significant issue. The solution is for employers to create a unified and coherent pay structure so that different groups do not have their pay and benefits determined according to radically different criteria. Trends in pay determination are in this direction, and it is doubtful if *Hayward* is more than a gentle nudge towards a development that was occurring in any event.[64]

The meaning of equal pay may be unclear where part time workers are being compared with full time workers.

Stadt Lengerich v Helmig Case C-399/92 [1995] IRLR 216[65]

The collective agreement provided for an overtime supplement of 25% payable for any hours worked in excess of 38.5 in a week. The appellant's contract provided that her normal weekly working hours were 19.5. She regularly worked more than that, and claimed, on the basis of the principle that part time employees should receive equal benefits to full time workers on a *pro rata* basis, to be entitled to overtime pay for her extra hours.

Her claim failed.

Judgment (pp 222–23):

[I]t must be determined whether [the terms of the collective agreements] establish different treatment for full time and part time employees and whether that difference affects considerably more women than men ...

There is unequal treatment wherever the overall pay of full time employees is higher than that of part time employees for the same number of hours worked ...

In the circumstances considered in these proceedings, part time employees do receive the same overall pay as full time employees for the same number of hours worked.

---

63 A factor which concerned the House of Lords very much less in *Pickstone v Freemans plc* [1989] AC 66; [1988] 2 All ER 803; [1988] IRLR 357, which was decided around the same time.

64 Although s 1(3) might provide a defence to leap-frogging claims, it is only likely to do so in very limited circumstances, requiring the employer to show that one element in a compensation package has been specifically introduced to counterbalance a more favourable element granted to other employees, rather than, as is usually the case, the different packages having arisen through historical accident; see below, pp 441–44.

65 See, also, [1996] ECR I–5757; [1996] ICR 35.

A part time employee whose contractual working hours are 18 receives, if he works 19 hours, the same overall pay as a full time employee who works 19 hours ...

Consequently the provisions at issue do not give rise to different treatment as between part time and full time employees and there is therefore no discrimination ...

Here one version of a formal equality approach prevailed over substantive equality, under which it is arguable that the disadvantages of overtime working apply to any employee asked to work more than their normal contractual hours. The real question is not one of discrimination law but of the substantive rights which part time workers should have in this situation.

Arbeiterwohlfahrt der Stadt Berlin Ev v Botel Case C-360/90 [1992] IRLR 423

A part time worker attended six trade union training courses. As was required by German law, she was paid for her normal working hours (29.5) but, as the courses lasted longer than 29.5 hours, she claimed she should have been paid for the total number of hours spent on the courses. As they lasted less than 40 hours per week, full time workers received their normal salary.

The Court first held that the sums in question constituted 'pay' within Art 119.

Judgment (p 426):

[A]s regards the payment of compensation for participation in training courses, the application of legislative provisions such as those at issue ... give rise, in principle, to indirect discrimination against women employees ...

[T]he argument that compensation for participation in training courses ... is calculated only as a function of working hours not worked cannot alter the fact that the members of staff committees who are part time employees receive less by way of compensation than their counterparts who are full time employees, although ... the two categories of employees participate in exactly the same number of hours of training ...

[S]uch a situation is likely by its very nature to dissuade ... part time employees, of whom an undoubtedly larger proportion are women, from acting as a member of a staff committee or from acquiring the knowledge and skills required for that office, making the representation of this category of employees by qualified members of staff committees all the more difficult.

To that extent, the difference of treatment in question cannot be considered as justified by objective factors ... unless the Member State in question can establish the contrary before the national court.[66]

---

[66] The facts were very similar in *Kuratorium für Dialyse und Nierentransplantation Ev v Lewark* Case C-457/93 [1996] IRLR 637. Here, the complainant worked four days a week; the training course in question, for which the employers refused to pay, was on the fifth day. It was held that the national court might be able to conclude that the rule was justified; the court would have to balance the social policy objective of ensuring the independence of such representatives against the fact that the rule might make it more difficult to ensure adequate representation of part time employees. See above, pp 317–19.

Manor Bakeries Ltd v Nazir **[1996] IRLR 604, EAT**

The case concerned the pay a part time employee should receive to attend her union's annual conference. The Industrial Tribunal, following *Botel*, held that she was entitled to full pay. The EAT allowed the employer's appeal.

Judge Hull QC (pp 606–08):

> It is ... obvious that unless there is work, and pay for that work, Art 119 has no operation. It appears to us that the requirement for 'work' is frequently overlooked for the simple reason that employers are not in the habit of paying employees who are not doing any work. For similar ... reasons, the word 'pay' has been given a very wide meaning indeed, because employers frequently consider it in their interests to promote goodwill, enthusiasm and so on by giving bonuses, benefits in kind, and indeed promises of benefits in the future ... [W]e are obliged to enquire what the appellants were paying for, and in particular whether what Ms Nazir was engaged in can conceivably be described as 'work'...

> We should have thought that so far from ... being paid 'to attend the conference' she was being 'paid for time off' ...

> Underlying the entire decision ... in the *Botel* case, it appears to us that it is accepted that [her] work on the committee, and the special training required for her to do it properly, was a species of 'work' for which she was in receipt of 'pay' ... [S]taff committees are an important feature of German labour law, and their activities and training are specially provided for in the statute. It is this that enabled the Advocate General to say that the duties of a member of the staff committee promoted the social dialogue at the heart of the undertaking in which the employer himself had an interest.

> It appears to us that the activities of a staff committee under the German system have little in common, if indeed anything, with the annual conference of a British independent trade union.

Where the EAT went wrong was in applying the literal words of Art 119 without consideration of how they have been interpreted in other contexts. That definition extends to payment received from an employer, directly or indirectly, in respect of employment. It is difficult to see how payment from an employer to reimburse an employee for what has not been earned because the person concerned is not at work falls outside this definition of pay. Any money paid because of the attendance at the conference was paid because of the existence of the employment relationship. The fact that there is no direct benefit to the employer from making the payment is irrelevant: that is true of many fringe benefits, such as sick pay and holiday pay, where the employee receives 'pay' even though not actually 'at work'. Finally, the question at this stage is simply whether the payment is 'pay'; as in *Lewark*, the employer still has the opportunity to justify the disparity.

Like work

Section 1(4) provides that:

> A woman is to be regarded as employed on like work with men if, but only if, her work and theirs is of the same or a broadly similar nature, and the difference (if any) between the things she does and the things they do are not of practical importance in relation to terms and conditions of employment; and accordingly in comparing her work with theirs regard shall to be had to the frequency or otherwise with which any such differences occur in practice as well as to the nature of the differences.

This is the first and most obvious manifestation of the equal pay principle. It is also the most limited in its scope and impact. Unsurprisingly, there were, in the years immediately after the Act took effect, many cases under this section, as employers came to terms with the fact that they were no longer permitted to have separate men's rates and women's rates for people doing the same work. One response was to move either women or men to ensure that the like work provision could not be applied.[67] Pay inequalities continue, despite the fact that men and women routinely receive the same pay for the same work; the problem is that women do not routinely do the same work as men, and the work that women do may be undervalued compared with the work that men do.

In deciding whether there is 'like work', the first question is whether the jobs are broadly similar. The wording clearly shows that they are not required to be absolutely identical, and thus tribunals must disregard minor differences which are, in the real world, not likely to be reflected in different terms and conditions of employment.[68] The second stage, which is conceptually very close to the first and difficult to keep separate from it, is that the differences must be of practical importance in relation to terms and conditions of employment. Attention must be focused not simply on what the contract says but on what actually happens in practice. In *Shields v E Coomes (Holdings) Ltd*,[69] male employees in a betting shop were paid more because they had special responsibility for security in shops considered particularly vulnerable to burglary. This differentiation was unlawful for two reasons: first, all the men received the higher pay irrespective of whether in fact they carried out the additional function – they were paid for what the employers said would happen rather than for what actually happened in practice; secondly, the employers allocated the extra responsibilities to men simply because they were men. There was no proper individual selection of employees to exercise

---

67 Snell, M, Glucklich, P and Povall, M, *Equal Pay and Opportunities: a Study of the Implementation and Effects of the Equal Pay Act and the Sex Discrimination Act in 26 Organisations*, 1981, London: Department of Employment.

68 *Capper Pass Ltd v Lawton* [1977] QB 852; [1977] 2 All ER 11; [1976] IRLR 366, EAT.

69 [1978] ICR 1159; [1979] 1 All ER 456; [1978] IRLR 263, CA.

these functions and thus the whole payment structure was based on sex discrimination. The concept of what is done is to be viewed widely. For example, two employees may in a physical sense do precisely the same work, but one may be in a position of responsibility over the other. They are clearly not engaged on like work.[70] Flexibility and availability to do other work may also be relevant, depending on its frequency and duration.[71]

However, the time when work is performed is irrelevant to the like work issue.[72] The fact that the comparator works at night and the applicant works days is thus irrelevant *unless* the nature of the work changes if done at night, for example, because of greater responsibility or risks.[73] This does not mean, however, that people who work days earn as much as those doing the same job at night. While the work is like work, the fact of night work attracts and justifies an additional premium – often in the order of 20% – which constitutes a genuine material factor which is not the difference of sex and thus provides a defence to an equal pay claim. However, if the night shift premium is excessive, the tribunal can, according to the EAT in *Sherwin v National Coal Board*,[74] increase the applicant's basic pay so that the difference between her pay and that of her comparator becomes no more than an appropriate night shift premium would make permissible. The problem with this approach is that it may conflict with another principle: if the like work principle is not satisfied, there is no remedy, however great the pay disparity – if the jobs are 90% the same there is no entitlement to 90% of the pay. Arguably, if the night shift premium is excessive, the whole amount should be disallowed. The *Sherwin* approach virtually entails the tribunal acting as a rate fixing body, which is beyond their jurisdiction. In policy terms the outcome is undoubtedly correct and whether or not it can be supported by the strict wording of the Act matters less now that the European Court in *Enderby v Frenchay AHA*[75] has approved such an approach.

Under the Equal Pay Act, it is clear that a comparator must be a fellow employee of the applicant at the time the applicant was made.[76] Under European law, however, equality may be claimed with a predecessor in the job.

---

[70] *Eaton Ltd v Nuttall* [1977] ICR 272; [1977] 3 All ER 1131; [1977] IRLR 71, EAT.

[71] *Maidment v Cooper and Co (Birmingham) Ltd* [1978] ICR 1094; [1978] IRLR 462, EAT; *Electrolux Ltd v Hutchinson* [1977] ICR 252; [1976] IRLR 410, EAT.

[72] *Dugdale v Kraft Foods Ltd* [1977] ICR 48; [1977] 1 All ER 454; [1976] IRLR 368, EAT.

[73] *Thomas v National Coal Board* [1987] ICR 757; [1987] IRLR 451, EAT.

[74] [1978] ICR 700; [1978] IRLR 122, EAT.

[75] Case C-127/92 [1993] ECR I-5535; [1994] ICR 112; [1994] 1 All ER 495; [1993] IRLR 591.

[76] The fact that the comparator resigns before the hearing is irrelevant. *Sorbie v Trust House Forte Hotels Ltd* [1977] QB 931; [1977] 2 All ER 155; [1976] IRLR 371, EAT.

Macarthys Ltd v Smith **Case 129/79 [1980] IRLR 210**[77]

Mrs Smith, a stockroom manageress, discovered that the man who did the job before her had been paid £10 per week more. The Court of Appeal held that such a claim was not permissible under the Equal Pay Act but referred the case to the European Court for consideration of the effect of Art 119.

Judgment (pp 215–16):

In such a situation the decisive test lies in establishing whether there is a difference in treatment between a man and a woman performing 'equal work' ... The scope of that concept, which is ... exclusively concerned with the nature of the services in question, may not be restricted by the introduction of a requirement of contemporaneity.

[But] it cannot be ruled out that a difference in pay between two workers occupying the same post, but at different periods in time, may be explained by the operation of factors which are unconnected with any discrimination on grounds of sex.

The second question [is concerned with the submission] that a woman may claim not only the salary received by a man who previously did the same work for her employer, but also, more generally, the salary to which she would be entitled were she a man, even in the absence of any man who was concurrently performing, or had previously performed, similar work. The respondent ... defined this term of comparison by reference to the concept of what was described as a 'hypothetical male worker'.

It is clear that the latter proposition ... is to be classed as indirect and disguised discrimination, the identification of which ... implies comparative studies of entire branches of industry, and therefore requires, as a prerequisite, the elaboration by the Community and national legislative bodies of criteria of assessment. From that it follows that, in cases of actual discrimination falling within the scope of the direct application of Art 119, comparisons are confined to parallels which may be drawn on the basis of concrete appraisals of the work actually performed by employees of different sex within the same establishment or service.

It is also possible, though more problematic from an evidential point of view, to claim equality with a successor employee. In *Diocese of Hallam Trustees v Connaughton*,[78] a director of music was replaced, after a four month gap, at a salary of nearly double what she had been earning. Her complaint was upheld as it was clear that at least in the latter stages of her employment she was receiving lower pay than would have been the case had she been a man. It is a question of fact for the tribunal to decide over how long a period to permit such a comparison.[79] It is also for the tribunal to decide when a change of

---

[77] See, also, [1980] ECR 1275; [1981] QB 180; [1981] 1 All ER 111.

[78] [1996] ICR 860; [1996] IRLR 505, EAT.

[79] Under the EqPA 1970, compensation by way of back pay is limited to two years, a limitation which has been challenged as contrary to European law; see below, pp 460–61.

circumstances is sufficient to explain the difference in pay over time. Thus in *Albion Shipping Agency v Arnold*,[80] the question was whether her lower pay was due to a change in the trading position of the employers leading to a drop in profitability.[81]

These cases are a significant but relatively minor development of the law. The real significance of *Macarthys* lies in its rejection of the 'hypothetical man' argument. Given its potential radicalism and uncertain consequences, such rejection was hardly surprising. At present, equal pay law provides no benefit to women who work in sectors highly segregated by gender; moreover, that degree of segregation is a significant factor in explaining why such sectors are frequently low paid. Deciding what a man would earn where few, if any, men do a particular job would be a task fraught with difficulty, ill-suited to judicial resolution, and with uncertain consequences for employment and inflation. It would potentially involve bringing into the judicial arena all the factors which are alleged to contribute to the fact of women's lower average pay than men. The aim of such an approach is to tackle low pay; that is better done explicitly through a minimum wage rather than indirectly via a doctrine which would inevitably generate a mass of litigation.

However, there are situations where such claims may succeed. Discrimination in salary setting may contravene the SDA 1975, where of course comparison with how a man *would have* been treated *is* permissible. This might occur not only when a woman is paid less than a hypothetical man would be paid, but possibly also where the pay differential is not commensurate with the differences in the value of the work done by the man and the woman. In the American case of *County of Washington v Gunther*,[82] it was held to be unlawful to pay men 95% of their evaluated worth under a job evaluation study whereas the women were only paid 70%. In British terms, there is no question that the women were treated less favourably on the ground of their gender.[83] Proving that a pay structure was tainted by direct discrimination is never likely to be straightforward. Proving that it was tainted by indirect discrimination brings into play all the various factors which lead to the relative underpayment of women, and is conceptually very close to the entitlement to be paid equally for work of equal value. The issues will be considered in more detail below.

---

80 [1982] ICR 22; [1981] IRLR 525, EAT.

81 On the question of when economic factors can provide a defence to an equal pay claim, see below, pp 445–52. The Court in *Albion* made it clear that the employers would not have a defence simply because they were able to get a woman to do the job at lower pay than they would need to pay a man.

82 452 US 161 (1981).

83 Along similar lines, it has been argued that discrimination in collective bargaining and in resulting collective agreements is unlawful under the SDA irrespective of the position under the EqPA 1970. See Lester, A and Rose, D, 'Equal value claims and sex bias in collective bargaining' (1991) 20 Industrial LJ 163.

By the same token, it is not possible to compare one's pay with what employees doing the same work or work of equal value earn in other industries. This is inevitable, given the expressed policy that the courts should not become wage fixing bodies. Pay varies drastically between enterprises, and, while there is evidence that women work disproportionately in small firms, and that small firms on average pay less, a requirement of uniformity would entirely upset current pay structures. It would prevent profitability and other factors peculiar to the individual enterprise from continuing to be relevant to pay, and would impose a rigidity on pay issues which is entirely foreign to the British experience.

Work rated as equivalent

Under s 1(2)(b) of the Equal Pay Act 1970 an equality clause comes into operation if the woman's work has been 'rated as equivalent' to that of a man. What this means is defined by s 1(5):

> A woman is to be regarded as employed on work rated as equivalent with that of any men if, but only if, her job and their job have been given an equal value, in terms of the demand made on a worker under various headings (for instance effort, skill, decision), on a study made with a view to evaluating in those terms the jobs to be done by all or any of the employees in an undertaking or group of undertakings, or would have been given an equal value but for the evaluation being made on a system setting different values for men and women on the same demand under any heading.

The section raises two issues: what is meant by such a scheme, and when will two jobs be regarded as having been rated as equivalent.

Job evaluation is primarily a management technique used to relate jobs to one another, both to develop and implement a fair pay structure and to persuade the employees of the merits of the structure thus produced, in the hope, for example, of reducing employee discontent and turnover. The definition of value which is used is based on the input of the worker to the job, rather than any other possible criteria which might have been utilised.[84] The

---

84 The value of the job might have been assessed in at least three ways. First, market value might have been taken. This would consider the value of the job to be that which is actually paid for it in the market ... This is clearly not the meaning of value which is intended by the principle of "equal pay for work of equal value" ... though its relevance has not been rejected, as we shall see in examining the scope of the material factor defence.

A second idea of value is that of marginal productivity. What is the value which "the work adds to the total output of the enterprise"? An oversimplified example may help to explain the approach. Suppose that widgets are manufactured by first stamping them from sheets of widgetstock, then polishing them. A widget stamper and a widget polisher can each process 100 widgets per day. If widgetstock costs 10p per widget, and if stamped but unpolished widgets are worth 50p and if polished widgets are worth £3.00 each, the work of the polisher is worth £25 per day, and the work of the stamper is worth £4 per day. This method is not chosen, either, though, again, it is relevant as an aspect of the material factor defence. [cont]

same approach is used to the assessment of value where it is claimed that a woman's work is equal in value to that of a man. In *Eaton Ltd v Nuttall*,[85] the EAT, in an appendix to the decision, briefly summarised the principal methods of job evaluation.

Job ranking. This is commonly thought to be the simplest method. Each job is considered as a whole and is then given a ranking in relation to all other jobs. A ranking table is then drawn up and the ranked jobs grouped into grades. Pay levels can then be fixed for each grade.

Paired comparisons. This is also a simple method. Each job is compared as whole with other jobs in turn and points (0, 1 or 2) awarded according to whether its overall importance is judged to be less than, equal to or more than the other. Points awarded for each job are then totalled up and a ranking order produced.

Job classification. This is similar to ranking except that it starts from the opposite end; the grading structure is established first and individual jobs fitted into it. A broad description of each grade is drawn up and individual jobs considered typical of each grade are selected as 'benchmarks'. The other jobs are then compared with these benchmarks and the general description and placed in their appropriate grade.

Points assessment. This is the most common system in use. It is an analytical method which, instead of comparing whole jobs, breaks down each job into a number of factors – for example, skills, responsibility, physical and mental requirements and working conditions. Each of the factors may be analysed further. Points are awarded for each factor according to a predetermined scale and the total points decide a job's place in the ranking order. Usually, the factors are weighted so that, for example, more or less weight may be given to hard physical conditions or to a high degree of skill.

Factor comparison. This is also an analytical method, employing the same principles as points assessment but using only a limited number of factors, such as skill, responsibility and working conditions. A number of 'key' jobs are selected because their wage rates are generally agreed to be 'fair'. The proportion of the total wage attributable to each factor is then decided and a scale produced showing the rate for each factor for each key job. The other jobs are then compared with this scale, factor by factor, so that a rate is finally obtained for each factor of each job. The total pay for each job is reached by adding together the rates for its individual factors.

---

84 [cont] Instead a third method has been adopted ... which imposes an obligation to assess job content, ie, a form of job evaluation.' McCrudden, C, 'Equal pay for work of equal value: the Equal Pay (Amendment) Regulations 1983' (1983) 12 Industrial LJ 197, pp 201–02.

85 [1977] ICR 272; [1977] 3 All ER 1131; [1977] IRLR 71.

The first three methods can be summarised as being 'non-analytical' methods, the latter two as 'analytical'. The basic distinction is that non-analytical methods compare the whole job being assessed, whereas analytical methods break down the jobs into component elements. The next case explores the significance of this distinction.

Bromley v H and J Quick Ltd [1988] IRLR 249, CA[86]

Female clerical workers claimed that their work was equal in value to that of male managers. The employers claimed that the jobs in question had been given different values under a job evaluation study. If there had been such evaluation the tribunal would, under s 1(5) of the EqPA 1970, not have had jurisdiction to hear the equal value claim. The EAT held that such a scheme was not required to be analytical in nature.

The method used was a form of paired comparisons. The panel was permitted to change the ranking of the benchmark jobs on a 'felt fair' basis, ie, in accordance with the general level of expectation as to the value of the jobs.

The Court of Appeal reversed the decision of the EAT and held that only analytical schemes could satisfy the requirements of s 1(5).

Dillon LJ (pp 253–54):

One has to be a little careful ... in considering what is meant by 'objective' since ... there are no universally accepted external criteria for measuring how much of a factor or quality is involved in a particular job or for measuring what relative weights ought to be attached to different factors or qualities involved, to differing extents, in various jobs. Every attempt at job evaluation will ... inevitably at some stage involve value judgements, which are inherently to some extent subjective or 'felt fair' ...

In my judgment, [the word 'analytical'] conveniently indicates the general nature of what is required by the section, *viz*, that the jobs of each worker covered by the study must have been valued in terms of the demand made on the worker under various headings ... It is not enough ... that the 23 benchmark jobs were valued ... on the factor demand basis required by s 1(5) if the jobs of the appellants and their comparators were not.

Bromley reaches the correct result. A job evaluation study may be the basis of a successful claim under s 1(5) and may defeat an equal value claim under s 2A(2). No one contends that such studies are completely objective – a fact that Dillon LJ acknowledges – but that is no reason for not requiring them to be as objective as is reasonably possible. Analytical methods have a potential to do this in a way that non-analytical methods do not. Objectivity contributes to the attainment of appropriate and defensible results and, more particularly, to the avoiding of sex bias creeping into the way in which schemes operate, even though rooting out such bias is not straightforward even in relation to analytical schemes.

---

[86] See, also, [1988] ICR 623.

The second question is when can it be said that two jobs have been 'rated as equivalent'. In *O'Brien v Sim-Chem Ltd*,[87] it was held to be sufficient if the evaluations under the scheme had been completed. There was no need for the scheme to be implemented; complaints under this section are most likely to be because a completed scheme was, for some reason, not implemented. But, in *Arnold v Beecham Group Ltd*,[88] it was held that a scheme cannot be regarded as having been completed before it had been accepted by the parties. This must include the employer; whether it includes the union, where there has been union involvement in conducting the study, is unclear.[89]

Equal value

The purpose of a job evaluation study is to compare the value of different jobs. Section 1(5) only applies where the employer has voluntarily undertaken a job evaluation study; the law provided no compulsion and little impetus for this to occur, although general developments in the management of industrial relations meant that such schemes were being utilised more frequently.

The law was changed as a result of European developments. Article 119 itself originally made no reference to the concept of equal pay for work of equal value, though the draft Treaty of Amsterdam explicitly refers to work of equal value. The concept of equal value does appear in the wording of the Equal Pay Directive 75/117. However, the European Court held in *Jenkins v Kingsgate (Clothing Productions) Ltd*[90] that the Directive added nothing to the meaning of Art 119. Thus the concept of equal value was held to be inferentially contained within Art 119. Moreover, the Directive required Member States to introduce 'such measures as are necessary to enable all employees who consider themselves aggrieved by the non-application of the principle of equal pay to pursue their claims by judicial process'. Not surprisingly, the European Court held that the absence of an equal value law in Britain was contrary to Art 119.

---

[87] [1980] ICR 573; [1980] 3 All ER 132; [1980] IRLR 373, HL.

[88] [1982] ICR 744; [1982] IRLR 307, EAT.

[89] As long as the scheme satisfies s 1(5), it is not possible to argue that a different scheme would have produced a different result more favourable to the female applicant; see *England v Bromley London BC* [1978] ICR 1, EAT. The only exception is where it can be shown that there has been a fundamental error in operating the scheme, such as basing judgments on a wrong job description; see *Green v Broxtowe DC* [1977] ICR 241; [1977] IRLR 34, EAT. Given the complexity involved, it seems clear that only very significant errors would invalidate a scheme in this way.

[90] Case 96/80 [1981] ECR 911; [1981] ICR 692; [1981] 1 WLR 972; [1981] IRLR 228.

Commission of the European Communities v United Kingdom **Case 61/81**
[1982] IRLR 333[91]

Judgment (pp 339–40):

[T]he job classification system is, under the Directive, merely one of several methods for determining pay for work to which equal value is attributed, whereas under the provision in the Equal Pay Act ... the introduction of such a system is the sole method of achieving such a result.

Workers in the UK are ... unable to have their work rated as being of equal value with comparable work if their employer refuses to introduce a classification system ...

[W]here there is disagreement as to the application of [the concept of equal value] a worker must be entitled to claim before an appropriate authority that his work has the same value as other work and, if that is found to be the case, to have his rights under the Treaty and the Directive acknowledged by a binding decision. Any method which excludes that option prevents the aim of the Directive from being achieved ...

The UK has emphasised ... the practical difficulties which would stand in the way of implementing the concept ... [believing] that the criterion of work of equal value is too abstract to be applied by the courts.

The Court cannot endorse that view ... The Member States must endow an authority with the requisite jurisdiction to decide whether work has the same value as other work, after obtaining such information as may be required.

As a result of this judgment the Government, obviously reluctantly, introduced the Equal Pay (Amendment) Regulations 1983.[92] Because of the choice of parliamentary procedure, the Regulations had to be accepted or rejected *en bloc*, with no opportunity to propose amendments. The appalling complexity of the drafting – conceivably deliberate – renders the task of applicants, hard in the first place, all the harder. While the law is complex and hard to follow, what is perhaps more worrying is the fact that the *procedure* itself is complex, hard to follow and extremely lengthy. There is no question that the impact of the equal value law has been disappointingly slight; part of the failure must be attributable to the way in which it is drafted. In saying that, it must be remembered that there is a sense in which the then Conservative Government wanted the law to fail. Equal value law necessitates that a tribunal will in some circumstances be the determinant of wage levels, in total contradiction to the philosophy that holds that market forces should be the *only* factor which governs what people earn.

The Regulations added a new para (c) to s 1(2) of the Equal Pay Act 1970, under which an equality clause operates:

---

[91] See, also, [1982] ECR 2601; [1982] ICR 578.

[92] SI 1983/1794. The Regulations were supplemented by procedural changes which are now incorporated in the Industrial Tribunal (Rules of Procedure) Regulations 1993 SI 1993/2687. Much of the detail of the equal value law appears in these Regulations.

... where a woman is employed on work which, not being work in relation to which para (a) [like work] or (b) [work rated as equivalent] above applies, is, in terms of the demands made on her (for instance under such headings as effort, skill and decision) of equal value to that of a man in the same employment ...

The phrase in this section 'not being work in relation to which para (a) or (b) applies' proved troublesome. It was argued in *Pickstone v Freemans plc*[93] that the words prevented an equal value claim from being brought in any situation where a man was engaged on like work or work rated as equivalent with the female comparator, for in that situation there would be work to which (a) or (b) applied. This meant that a claim could not have been brought if there was *any* man engaged on like work with the applicant, however, much her work might have been undervalued in comparison with other men. There is little doubt that this is the best literal meaning of the phrase. Had it been accepted, the only women who could have utilised the procedure would have been those whose *job categories* were 100% female. Such a construction would undoubtedly have led to a finding of failure properly to implement the decision of the European Court. To avoid the problem, the House of Lords construed the section in a manner designed to achieve its avowed purpose, that a woman should be able to claim that her work was equal in value to that of *any* man in the same establishment. In a technical sense, this was achieved by notionally adding the words 'as between the woman and the man with whom she claims equality' *after* the words 'not being work to which para (a) or (b) applies'.[94]

As with other equal pay and discrimination cases, all claims must be referred to the Advisory Conciliation and Arbitration Service (ACAS) to investigate the possibility of a conciliated settlement, though in equal value claims such outcome is most unlikely. Assuming no settlement or withdrawal, there is a preliminary hearing before a tribunal at which the employer has the opportunity to contend that the case should be thrown out. If that argument fails, the employment tribunal either determines the equal value question itself or adjourns the hearing for a so called 'independent expert' to prepare a report on whether the applicant's work is equal in value to that of her comparator. The tribunal hearing is then reconvened, and the final decision made in the light of the expert's report and other evidence. In addition, the employer may argue that the pay difference was explained and justified by a genuine material factor.

The preliminary hearing

Section 2A (1) now provides:

---

[93] [1989] AC 66; [1988] 2 All ER 803; [1988] IRLR 357, HL.
[94] *Pickstone v Freemans plc* [1988] IRLR 357, p 362, *per* Lord Templeman.

Where ... a dispute arises as to whether any work is of equal value ... the tribunal may either:

(a) proceed to determine that question; or

(b) unless it is satisfied that there are no reasonable grounds for determining that the work is of equal value as so mentioned, require a member of the panel of independent experts to prepare a report with respect to that question,

and if it requires the preparation of a report ... it shall not determine [the equal value] question until it has received that report.[95]

Despite argument that such power was superfluous and should be removed, employment tribunals retain the power to throw out a claim at the preliminary hearing on the ground that the claim is hopeless. The language of both the amended and unamended version appears to place an even lower burden on the applicant than the need to show a *prima facie* case.[96] But, tribunals now have power to determine the equal value issue *without* first referring the claim to an independent expert. It remains to be seen how many tribunals will have enough confidence in their own abilities to resolve complex issues that they will feel reference to an expert is unnecessary.

Under reg 9(2E) the tribunal may, if it considers it appropriate to do so, hear evidence at the preliminary hearing concerning the defence of genuine material factor. If the defence succeeds at this stage, the complaint is dismissed with no reference being made to the independent expert. Following changes to the rules of procedure in 1993, if the defence fails at the preliminary hearing, the employer will not be permitted, apart from exceptional circumstances, to raise the defence once more at the reconvened hearing when the expert's report is considered. This reverses the previous position, where the defence could be argued both at the preliminary and reconvened tribunal hearings. There is a logically powerful argument that the employer should only be permitted to advance the defence after a conclusion that the work is of equal value. Such a finding may well influence the scepticism with which employer arguments are viewed; put the other way round, it may be easier to argue that a defence exists if the tribunal is in ignorance of the detailed facts against which such defence is necessary. However, the view prevailed that a defence which is strong enough to defeat the claim should be taken at the preliminary hearing in order to save the parties and the public the time and expense of the full, complex procedure.

---

95 The power in the tribunal to determine the claim for itself and not refer the case to an independent expert was introduced by the Sex Discrimination and Equal Pay (Miscellaneous Amendments) Regulations 1996 SI 1996/438, reg 3, and took effect as from 31 July 1996.

96 However, expert evidence is admissible at the preliminary hearing (*Dennehy v Sealink UK Ltd* [1987] IRLR 20, EAT) and it is not unknown for preliminary hearings themselves to last several days, thereby adding to delay, which the 1996 reforms attempt to reduce, and cost, the problem of which remains untouched and potentially ruinous to someone considering instituting a claim.

Job evaluation schemes

Under s 1(5), a complainant may allege that her job has been given the *same* rating as that of a man under such a scheme. Thus, the scheme provides the basis for a successful claim. Under s 2A(2), on the other hand, a job evaluation scheme where a man's job and a woman's job have been given *different* values may operate to defeat that woman's claim that her work is equal in value to that man's. Unfortunately, the convolutions of the drafting make unravelling the principles a grim task.

> s 2A(2) ... [T]here shall be taken ... to be no reasonable grounds for determining that the work of a woman is of equal value ... if:
>
> (a) that work and the work of the man in question have been given different values on a [job evaluation] study such as is mentioned in s 1(5) above; and
>
> (b) there are no reasonable grounds for determining that the evaluation contained in the study was (within the meaning of sub-s (3) below) made on a system which discriminates on ground of sex.
>
> (3) An evaluation ... is made on a system which discriminates on grounds of sex where a difference, or coincidence, between values set by that system on different demands under the same or different headings is not justifiable irrespective of the sex of the person on whom those demands are made.

What this contorted language is attempting to say is that discrimination in a scheme may exist either where the same demands have been given different values, or where different demands have been given the same value.

McCrudden, C, 'Equal pay for work of equal value: the Equal Pay (Amendment) Regulations 1983' (1983) 12 Industrial LJ 197, pp 207–08:

Suppose a JES has been set up and has resulted in different values for job x and job y. Suppose further that the factors, sub-factors, maximum points and weightings are as follows

Factors and Subfactors	Maximum Points
1 Responsibility	40
(i) Cost of replacement of machine	30
(ii) Amount of supervision required	10
2 Physical requirements	40
3 Mental requirements	30
4 Working conditions	40
(i) Outside work	20
(ii) Noise	20

The Regulations allow each of the elements in this scheme to be challenged. The different weightings for physical and mental requirements constitute a difference between values set by that system on different demands under different headings. The same weightings for responsibility and physical requirements constitute a coincidence between values set by that system on different demands under different headings. The different weightings given the responsibility subfactors constitute a difference in values set by that system on different demands under the same heading. The same weightings given the working conditions subfactors constitute a coincidence in valued set by that system on difference demands under the same heading. Last, the omission of a relevant factor, say 'skill', may be regarded as giving it a nil value and thus as constituting a difference in values set by that system on different demands under different headings.

Dibro Ltd v Hore[97] establishes, perhaps surprisingly, that the study relied on by the employer need not be in existence at the date of a claim. The employer may conduct and complete a study right up to the date of the reconvened hearing, and if it is a properly conducted analytical scheme, will have the effect of blocking the equal value claim 'provided it related to facts and circumstances existing at the time when the proceedings were initiated'. The policy behind this approach is that 'encouragement should be given to employers to carry out such schemes'. Such an approach has much to commend it: one argument is that a major purpose of the equal value law is to act as a spur to voluntary job evaluation. Whether the employer should be allowed to trump the applicant's claim with a belated scheme largely depends on the degree of confidence felt in the ability of tribunals to detect schemes which are tainted with discrimination or disadvantage. It is strongly arguable that employer schemes, whether conducted before or after the initiation of a claim, should *never* operate as a complete defence, but should be part of the evidence which the tribunal considers in deciding whether the jobs in question are indeed of equal value.

The employer has the burden of establishing that there is no basis for supposing that the scheme is tainted by discrimination. If there is any doubt, the case must go forward for the equal value issue to be resolved. In *Bromley v H and J Quick Ltd*,[98] Dillon LJ said that the employer must 'explain how any job evaluation study worked and what was taken into account at each stage ... [I]t must be possible to see through to what actually happened ... [The tribunal] may not be satisfied on the evidence in a particular case if the evidence offers no explanation of the basis on which some apparently wholly subjective decision was made ...'. [99] Employers will naturally contest vigorously any suggestion that the scheme has discriminatory elements. Such a finding will stigmatise a scheme and make it very difficult for the employer to continue its operation. The finding at this stage need not necessarily show that the scheme affected the complainant or her comparator in a discriminatory fashion; discrimination *anywhere* in the scheme's operation will

---

[97] [1990] ICR 370; [1989] IRLR 129, EAT.
[98] [1988] ICR 623; [1988] IRLR 249, CA.
[99] [1988] IRLR 249, p 254.

defeat the employer's argument. But, the resolution of the equal value issue will focus simply on the two individuals and will not necessarily resolve the doubts cast upon the scheme by the preliminary hearing.

There has been little litigation concerning job evaluation. The most significant case came before the European Court.

Rummler v Dato-Druck GmbH Case 237/85 [1987] IRLR 32[100]

The case concerned a job evaluation system at a German printing firm. The scheme provided for seven pay grades, with jobs classified according to previous knowledge required, concentration, effort and exertion, and responsibility. Her job was classed in pay grade III, requiring medium and sometimes high muscular effort. She claimed that she should be in grade IV, arguing that, *for her*, the job entailed heavy physical work.

Judgment (pp 33–34):

[The first] question ... is directed fundamentally at ascertaining whether a job classification system which is based on criteria of muscular effort and exertion and the degree to which the work is physically heavy is compatible with the principle of equal pay ...

The principle of equal pay ... requires fundamentally that the nature of the work to be done must be considered objectively ... If a job classification system is used in determining pay, then on the one hand it must be based on the same criteria regardless of whether the work is to be done by a man or by a woman, while on the other it may not be so designed overall as to lead in fact to general discrimination ...

It is compatible with the prohibition of discrimination to apply a criterion in setting differentiated pay grades which takes account of the objectively measurable level of physical strength needed to do the job or the objective degree to which the work is physically heavy.

Even if a particular criterion, such as that of the muscular exertion needed, may in fact favour male employees on the grounds that it may be assumed that they generally have greater physical strength than female employees, then that particular criterion should be considered along with the others which play a part in determining pay within the overall job classification system when assessing whether that criterion is discriminatory. A system is not discriminatory solely because one of its criteria is based on characteristics more commonly found among men. If a job classification system is not to be discriminatory overall and is to be in accordance with the principles of the Directive, it must, however, be so designed that, if the nature of the work under discussion so permits, it includes as 'work to which equal value is attributed', work in which other criteria are taken into account for which female employees may show particular aptitude.

---

[100] See, also, [1986] ECR 2101; [1987] ICR 774.

It is the task of the national courts to decide ... whether the ... system in its entirety permits fair account to be taken of all the criteria on the basis of which pay is determined ...

She argued that, in determining whether the work was 'heavy' work, account should have been taken of the fact of women's lower average strength. This was properly rejected for sound reasons of both principle and policy. She was seeking to *require* the employers to introduce an element of direct discrimination – in a sense affirmative action – into the scheme. Furthermore, if job evaluation is to have any chance of benefiting women it must operate and be seen to operate on objective criteria. The 'argument that typically female criteria are undervalued in some aspects of a scheme is not assisted by arguments that elsewhere in the scheme special allowance should be made for the fact that women score relatively badly. To say that an employer is not permitted to favour factors found more frequently in jobs of one sex is tantamount to saying that he is not permitted to value aspects of the job which he might legitimately regard as of value, simply because it happens that they are more associated with men's jobs than women's jobs'.[101]

But, *Rummler* does make clear that a scheme must be *representative* of the skills and attributes of both sexes. It must not be 'designed' to lead to discrimination and must take proper account of any different attributes of both sexes. In other words, a scheme can be challenged as being either directly or indirectly discriminatory. The concern here is with the outcomes which result from a scheme; challenge to the scheme at an earlier stage for being discriminatory in operation might also be possible.[102]

Facts which may indicate that a scheme is directly discriminatory might include deliberately misdescribing a job or placing it at too low a point in the salary structure;[103] manipulating the scheme if it became apparent that it would lead to drastic change to traditional pay relativities; or the union's persuading the employer to alter it for similar reasons. To prove direct discrimination it would have to be established that any such decision was based on sex; for this to be shown, the jobs either deliberately upgraded or downgraded must be significantly segregated by gender.

It will be rare that evidence will be forthcoming to establish direct discrimination in the establishment and operation of a scheme. More likely, any claim will be that the scheme *in practice* adversely affects women – an argument based on indirect discrimination. Such an argument is only possible where the job whose evaluation is challenged is substantially segregated, as otherwise the adverse impact cannot be on ground of gender.[104] There can be

---

101 Rubenstein, M, *Equal Pay for Work of Equal Value*, 1984, London: Macmillan, p 94.

102 See *op cit*, Lester and Rose, fn 83.

103 See *ibid*, Rubenstein, pp 89–90.

104 *Ibid*, Rubinstein, p 88.

no obligation on a claimant who seeks to establish that a scheme is tainted by gender to establish anything in the nature of a requirement or condition. Again, challenge could be to any stage of the process: on the way job descriptions are obtained, the choice of factors and their weighting, giving each job points under each factor, the process of totalling points and assigning pay levels, and any appeal procedure which is established.

The employer will have to justify both the substance of the scheme and the way it operates. The objective of creating a rational and acceptable pay structure will surely be an appropriate objective under the first part of the *Bilka* test of justification.[105] It is, however, contended that it would be inappropriate to impose too stringent a standard in relation to the next element, that the means chosen were appropriate and necessary in the light of that objective. Giving a maximum of 30 rather than 40 points for, say, physical effort, could never be said to be *necessary*. What is important is whether the employer has shown awareness of the way schemes may disadvantage women and taken steps to counter such potential problems. It is unlikely that tribunals would or should require an employer to do more than a reasonable employer aware of these issues would have done. It was held in *Handels v Danfoss*[106] – a case concerning a merit rating system – that the employer will not be able to justify using a pay structure unless its criteria and methodology are made clear.[107]

While the procedures are significantly different, there are close parallels between what is involved in voluntary job evaluation and the resolution of an equal value claim by an independent expert. It must be borne in mind that voluntary job evaluation costs an employer money; additional checks and balances in the interests of gender neutrality can only add to the costs, at least in the short term.

The first stage of voluntary job evaluation is to produce accurate descriptions of the jobs to be evaluated. This is not as straightforward as might be thought. The two main methods are questionnaire and observation. Both have their weaknesses. There is a tendency to exaggerate on a questionnaire – perhaps more a male tendency – and a tendency to behave untypically if observed. To improve accuracy, it may be necessary to have a trial run, which can be modified before embarking on the proper exercise.

But is it the next stage where most important issues arise. This encompasses the choice of factors, the assigning of a maximum score to each of those factors, and then deciding how much each job is worth on each of the

---

[105] See above, pp 294–96.

[106] Case 109/88 [1989] ECR 3199; [1991] 1 CMLR 8; [1989] IRLR 532.

[107] The EOC consider that it is 'unrealistic and unfair to expect an employee to be able to challenge effectively an employer's study for evidence of a sex-based system'. See 'Equal pay law: paradise for lawyers – hell for women' (1991) 35 EOR 30, p 31.

factors. The factors of effort, skill, responsibility and working conditions are those most frequently employed in schemes, and may be subdivided, such as into physical and mental effort. The evaluators must decide how important each of these factors is in the job to be evaluated, and then determine a maximum score for each factor. This is a matter of judgment and experience in which awareness of the possibilities of gender bias is vital. It is more likely that gender bias will be present in relation to the choice of factors and the maximum values attached to each rather than to the process of giving each job a value under each factor. The latter is so subjective that, unless gender differentiation has been explicitly mentioned, it will be very hard even to show reasonable suspicion that discrimination has occurred.

There is a danger that evaluators will overlook important characteristics of female-dominated jobs, especially those associated with skills needed to run a family. They may be regarded not as job-related skills but rather as qualities intrinsic to being a woman. Examples of characteristics of female jobs which are frequently ignored include doing the same job over and over for a long time; working around people who are sick and disabled with no hope of recovery; physically handling sick or injured people; showing new workers who make more money how to do their job. Working with mentally ill or retarded persons may be overlooked as a stressful working condition, while working with noisy machinery may not. Poor working conditions such as lifting heavy weights or working out of doors may be given a high point value, while the eye strain associated with working on VDUs may be entirely ignored; or, nurses who supervise employees and care for patients only receive points for supervision, because the way 'human relations know-how' is defined largely excludes skills necessary in working with people other than those supervised.

'Making the invisible visible: rewarding women's work' (1992) 45 EOR 23, p 28:

According to the [Ontario] Pay Equity Commission, the following are some of the job requirements frequently overlooked or ignored:

Skill

- operating and maintaining several different types of office, manufacturing, treatment/diagnosis or monitoring equipment;
- manual dexterity required for giving injections, typing, or graphic arts;
- writing correspondence for others, and proofreading and editing others' work;
- establishing and maintaining manual and automated filing systems, or records management and disposal;
- training and orienting new staff;
- deciding the content and format of reports and presentations to clients.

Effort

- adjusting to rapid changes in the office or plant technology;
- concentrating for long periods at computer terminals, lab benches and manufacturing equipment;
- performing complex sequences of hand-eye co-ordination in industrial jobs;
- providing service to several people or departments, working under many simultaneous deadlines;
- developing work schedules; and
- frequent lifting (office or medical supplies, retail goods, injured or sick people).

Responsibility

- caring for, and providing emotional support to children and institutionalised people;
- protecting confidentiality;
- acting on behalf of absent supervisors;
- representing the organisation through communications with clients and the public;
- supervising staff;
- shouldering consequences of error to the organisation;
- preventing possible damage to equipment; and
- co-ordinating schedules for many people.

Working conditions

- stress from noise in open spaces, crowded conditions; and production of noise;
- exposure to disease and stress from caring for ill people;
- dealing with upset, injured, irate or irrational people;
- cleaning offices, stores, machinery or hospital wards;
- frequent bending or lifting of office or medical supplies, retail goods;
- stress from answering complaints; and
- long periods of travel and/or isolation.[108]

---

[108] 'A particular problem with skill and knowledge factors is the emphasis on formal qualifications. There are many schemes ... whose measure of knowledge depend entirely on formal qualifications and take no account of knowledge obtained through experience either within the workplace or in, for example, the domestic environment ... Experience [factors may also] have an adverse impact on women. [Hastings] gave the example of a UK health service trust which has an experience factor with a number of levels which at the top level would suggest that there are jobs requiring 20 years of experience in order to perform them competently. What the factor is actually measuring ... is a particular career progression through the organisation, which is one usually followed by men ...' 'Making the invisible visible: rewarding women's work' (1992) 45 EOR 23, p 26.

It is impossible to say that one system of job evaluation or one conclusion as to the weight of appropriate factors can ever be found. The law must thus focus on the *procedures* rather than the *outcome*. Yet, the independent experts are given no detailed guidance as to how to go about their task and what factors to consider. All that is stated that is that they must compare the jobs 'for instance under the headings of effort, skill and decision'.

After the jobs have been evaluated and the points tallied, pay levels must be resolved. There is no necessary connection between job evaluation and high pay; indeed, job evaluation may be associated with an increase in differentials and, if this is the case, might even make the position of female employees worse. Pay levels need to be resolved by negotiation or other methods. There is no direct correlation between points score and amount of pay. If a job scored twice as much for responsibility than another job, it does not follow that in respect of that factor the former job would receive twice the pay of the latter. From an administrative perspective, it is sensible to have a wide spread of points. The normal practice is to band points for salary purposes, so that, for example, those who score 151–75 might be on a basic rate of £200 per week, those scoring 176–200 on a basic rate of £220.

A major practical problem with job evaluation concerns the process by which its results are implemented. A properly run gender-neutral scheme may conclude that some 'male' jobs should receive a pay cut. It is normal industrial relations practice not to cut the pay of any individual employees, whose pay will be protected or 'red-circled' until, by dint of annual increases elsewhere, their pay has found an appropriate level.[109] This may take some years. Furthermore, it is not unknown to stage increases due to female employees over a period.[110]

It is also important that job evaluation is conducted in a way which seeks to minimise gender effects. Training is important, as is the presence of female evaluators. Ghobadian and White found that the 'two forms of participation most closely linked to a higher likelihood of fair pay outcomes were trade union representation within the schemes and the presence of female as well as male representatives'.[111] It is rare that job titles are assigned to evaluation teams in a random fashion. Rather, a single team is likely to evaluate a total bargaining unit and, within that unit, to consider all jobs in a series together. Since most job series and even most bargaining units are sex segregated, this format for job evaluation significantly increases the likelihood of 'halo' effects in which the view taken in relation to one job will influence the view taken of

---

[109] It may be contended that this constitutes a genuine material factor justifying the refusal to implement equal pay immediately. See below, p 457.

[110] See *op cit*, 'Making the invisible visible', fn 108, p 27.

[111] Ghobadian, A and White, M, *Job Evaluation and Equal Pay*, 1986, London: Department of Employment, p 121.

succeeding jobs. 'Formality must be developed not only in the evaluation technique, but in the routine operation and control of the schemes, and in its periodic maintenance ... A balanced approach, which gives serious attention to organisation, procedures and participation by employees, is likely to be more effective in terms of equitable payment than reliance on even the most sophisticated techniques without proper supporting systems and practices.'[112]

As a means of determining pay, job evaluation is common and may be growing.[113] As a route towards greater pay equity, job evaluation holds out the hope of greater objectivity in pay determination, and equal value law, by charging the independent expert with the responsibility of using a somewhat attenuated form of job evaluation, heads in the same direction. However, the belief that traditional job evaluation will straightforwardly and automatically advance gender equality is naive and simplistic. Job evaluation needs to be redesigned with the specific interests of pay equity in mind.[114] How far independent experts, chosen at least in part for their familiarity with current techniques, can be expected to be sensitive to the issue of pay equity is unclear.

Moreover, there are dangers in relying too heavily on job evaluation, especially as the chances of mounting a successful legal challenge on the basis of the gender bias of a scheme are so slender. The first concerns its purpose. From an employer's perspective, the most vital characteristic of a good scheme is its acceptability. Very often, the purpose of job evaluation is to defend the status quo. There is a danger that the apparent scientific veracity of job evaluation may make pay discrimination 'more subtle, more covert and more difficult to prove'.[115] However scientific it might appear in its precise numerical ranking of jobs, these numbers ultimately rest on value judgments. 'Job evaluation derives these numbers from, rather than imposes them upon, the labour market ... The evaluation scheme serves to establish a decent level of coherence and equity within the internal labour market of the firm while at

---

[112] *Ibid*, p 154. In relation to the Australian experience, Burton has said that 'there needs to be a very detailed set of standards, guidelines and principles for the implementation of job evaluation in order to avoid the administrative "slippage" that can occur between the development of standards and the implementation of a system ... [Furthermore, the] proper application of a job evaluation system relies upon skilled practitioners and it relies upon implementers being willing, as well as able, to carry out the steps in the process so that the outcomes are consistent and fair. But, the overwhelming lack of expertise in the area, combined with the power relationships among, and the vested interests of, organisational players make this eventuality unlikely without some regulation or mechanism to enforce the meeting of standards'. See *op cit*, 'Making the invisible visible', fn 108, p 31.

[113] One study found that more than 50% of pay structures surveyed used some form of job evaluation. See 'Job evaluation and gender' (1991) 489 IRS Employment Trends 5.

[114] McColgan, A, *Pay Equity – Just Wages for Women*, 1994, London: Institute of Employment Rights, p 57.

[115] See *op cit*, 'Making the invisible visible', fn 108, p 25.

the same time respecting the real cost and recruiting constraints imposed by the external labour market ... If ... a major source of the disparity in male-female earnings is the fact that such female jobs as secretary or filing clerk have historically been underpaid relative to such male jobs as electrician or shop labourer, a job evaluation system that might use these existing wage relationships as a starting point for analysis becomes part of the problem, not part of the solution ...'[116] Furthermore, there may be difficulties for employers who wish to utilise job evaluation in some areas of their enterprise but not others. Equal value law appears to require the same pay criteria to be adopted throughout an organisation, in order to avoid the risk of claims by a woman in one area for equality of pay with a man in an area where pay is resolved entirely differently. While the employer may have a genuine material factor defence to explain the differential, the operation of that defence is not so clear-cut as to deter all claims. The law should not operate so as to discourage variety and innovation in pay setting.

Secondly, job evaluation may be 'associated with the growth of multinationals, moves away from collective bargaining and with the introduction of performance pay elements. These other conditions would be likely to offset any gains to women arising from a re-evaluation of their jobs. Thus the context under which job evaluation is being introduced must be regarded as a major factor influencing its likely impact on equal value'.[117] The law must consider various techniques by which the relative pay of women might be improved: the merits of job evaluation must be considered along with the merits of a national minimum wage, and the merits of encouraging trade unions and collective bargaining. Of course, more than one approach might be adopted. 'While job evaluation can and does have positive results, the pursuit of equal value-based job grading systems should not absorb all the energy available to promote women's pay. Equal attention must be paid to issues such as the transparency of the payment system, and above all the actual outcome in terms of gender pay ratios.'[118]

The report of the independent expert and the reconvened hearing

One of the major criticisms of the equal value procedure has been the time taken by experts to prepare reports. This has recently been tackled in two ways, first, by providing that tribunals may decide the issue for themselves, and secondly, by requiring tribunals to set a date by which the expert must have completed the report. The rules of procedure give the expert at least 42

---

[116] Weiler, P, 'The wages of sex: the uses and limits of comparable worth' (1986) 99 Harv L Rev 1728, p 1767.

[117] Rubery, J and Fagan, C, *Social Europe: Wage Determination and Sex Segregation in Employment in the European Community*, 1993, Luxembourg: Office for Official Publications of the European Communities, p 233.

[118] *Ibid*, p 205.

days to produce a report; in practice the average case takes around 20 months to complete, although this figure masks wide variations.

The only guidance given to experts is that the jobs shall be compared under such heads as 'effort, skill and decision'. This clearly mirrors a points factor job evaluation study. However, it focuses only on the applicant and the comparator or comparators, rather than attempting to fix the criteria for determining a more general pay structure. Experts must ignore the impact which a particular decision might have on pay elsewhere in the enterprise, especially if it is considered that a particular finding might generate consequential equal value claims. Furthermore, voluntary job evaluation aims at fixing a hierarchy of jobs. There is no claim under the equal value law if it is concluded that the jobs are not equal in value, however great the disparity in pay which ensues. The fact that the expert is directed to 'take no account of the difference of sex'[119] means that if the approach to the assessment of value was tainted by gender in any way, such as the potential defects identified earlier in connection with voluntary job evaluation, the tribunal may, at the reconvened hearing, decide not to admit the report.[120] Finally, the expert must compare the value of the jobs as they were at the date the claim was submitted rather than at the date they are observed or the date of the reconvened hearing. In contrast, a well designed voluntary job evaluation system will have procedures for dealing with changes in content over time, and always looks to the future rather than to the past.

At the reconvened hearing the tribunal may either admit the report into evidence, reject it, or commission a new one. In reaching this decision, the expert may be called for cross-examination, and each party has the right to call one expert witness to give evidence on the equal value question. The report must be admitted in evidence unless defective in one of a number of stated ways. These are procedural failings, such as not taking account of representations or not providing proper information to the parties,[121] reaching a conclusion which could not reasonably have been reached,[122] or that for some other material reason the report is unsatisfactory.[123]

The most likely reason for contending that a report should not be admitted is that it was prepared under a fundamental misapprehension of fact, such as that the work observed had changed significantly since the claim was submitted, or that one aspect of a job was either not taken into account or was over-emphasised. Given that it has been held that the report is not conclusive,

---

[119] Regulation 8A(3)(d).
[120] Regulation 8A(13).
[121] Regulation 8A(13)(a).
[122] Regulation 8A(13)(b).
[123] Regulation 8A(13)(c).

it is preferable, in order to avoid further delay, to admit the report and then reach a finding contrary to that of the expert.[124]

It is now clear that the findings of the independent expert are not conclusive. In *Tennants Textile Colours Ltd v Todd*[125] a laboratory assistant claimed equal value with technicians. The expert said that the work was equal in value with one of her chosen comparators. The tribunal decided to admit the report. The employers then sought an adjournment to obtain a report from their own expert witness. This was granted by the tribunal which, however, observed that the findings of fact contained in the expert's report would be binding as the report had already been admitted. On re-hearing, the tribunal held that once the report was admitted, the expert's conclusions should only be rejected if it were shown that they were so plainly wrong that they could not be accepted. The Northern Ireland Court of Appeal allowed the employer's appeal, holding that it was wrong to conclude that the findings of fact, once admitted, were binding on both parties, as although reg 8(2C) restricts the rights of parties, it does not prevent a party from making submissions to contradict the conclusions of the independent expert or inhibit the tribunal from asking questions. Furthermore, while the burden of proof is on the applicant, it does not become heavier if the report is against the applicant, nor is the burden of proof transferred to the employer if the report is in favour of the applicant. Finally, it was wrong to conclude that the report could only be rejected if the evidence were such as to show that it was so plainly wrong that it could not be accepted.

Aldridge v British Telecommunications plc [1990] IRLR 10, EAT[126]

Wood J (pp 13–15):

[T]he purpose of rr 7A(7) and (8) was to enable the tribunal in its discretion to refuse to accept the ... report in evidence ... if it discovered sufficient impropriety to make the findings of the report unsafe. The grounds have a common thread in that they strike at the essential validity of the report and whether it has been properly prepared. Those rules have no bearing on the way in which the tribunal approaches the weight to be given to the report once it has been admitted into evidence. There is no provision in the rules which gives the report, once admitted, any special status ... [T]he expert may be cross-examined and there is no provision restricting such evidence and such examination only to the preliminary issue of the admissibility of the report as evidence.

Due to the rigidity of the rules and the inevitable consequential delay if a fresh report is ordered, the most convenient course may well be for the tribunal to admit the report, and then to give it such weight as it deems fit in the final

---

[124] The procedures are discussed in more detail by Bourn, C and Whitmore, J, *Anti-Discrimination Law in Britain*, 3rd edn, 1996, London: Sweet & Maxwell, pp 245–51.

[125] [1989] IRLR 3, NICA.

[126] See, also, [1989] ICR 790.

weighing of the evidence. If the report is considered to be highly unsatisfactory, the weight would be small.

It is only after the admission stage that the facts on which the conclusion of the expert is based may not be challenged, but that does not prevent the tribunal, before reaching its conclusion, taking into account all the evidence including that given at the admission stage and subsequently.

The present restrictions on procedure imposed by the rules give rise to delays which are properly described as scandalous and to amount to a denial of justice to women seeking remedy through the judicial process. During these delays, women could be subjected to working in a most uncomfortable environment and with an unresolved grievance. To reverse the coin, there seems to be no limit on the number of successive applications which can be made with one or more different comparators, and the present procedures give scope for tactical use by applicants, which amongst other things may involve employers in substantial expenditure.

It is arguable that there is no need for independent experts and that tribunals should be able to determine all claims.[127] The relatively new power to resolve claims without reference to the expert can be seen as an experiment along these lines. Yet the Equal Opportunities Commission is worried about the potential effects.

'Equal pay law: paradise for lawyers – hell for women' (1991) 35 EOR 30, p 32:

First, an equal value case involves the measurement of work against a variety of factors, which in the EOC's view cannot be 'carried out sensibly during a tribunal hearing'. Secondly, the measurement of work inevitably involves skill and experience in work measurement techniques. Thirdly, independent experts are completely detached from the responsibility to present the case for either party. Finally, the EOC fears that applicants could find themselves in a very difficult position in practice as regards the burden of proof if independent experts are removed from the proceedings. 'In the absence of an independent expert, and given the choice of competing evaluations commissioned by the parties, where both evaluations seem reasonable we consider that an Industrial Tribunal would very probably be driven to dismiss a claim, particularly in the light of the special nature of equal value, namely its tendency to challenge and upset established pay arrangements.'

---

127 Beddoe, R, 'Independent experts' (1986) 6 EOR 13, an article written soon after the procedure came into effect, highlighted instances where experts had failed to follow best practice: (a) by highlighting unreal differences between jobs, which would be unlikely to have any practical impact in the real world; (b) by failing to provide adequate definitions of the factors taken into account; (c) by providing inadequate job descriptions; and (d) by insisting on 100% parity in a way which would be unlikely to occur in the real world. It is probable that since 1986 matters have improved somewhat. However, given the inevitable delay and cost which the independent expert procedure entails, it is only defensible if the outcomes are more reliable than would occur if tribunals decided the matter for themselves. There is little reason for believing this to be the case. See, also, 'Evaluating the work of independent experts' (1989) 24 EOR 17.

The meaning of equal value

The applicant needs to establish that her work is of equal value to that of her comparator. She also succeeds if she establishes that her work is of *greater* value than his.[128] It is a question of fact whether relatively minor points differences will at the end of the process support a conclusion that the work is not of equal value. Two Industrial Tribunal decisions point in different directions. In *Wells v F Smales and Son (Fish Merchants)*,[129] the tribunal held that applicants who scored between 79% and 95% of the comparator's score were employed on work of equal value as the differences were too small to be material and substantial. But, in *Brown and Royle v Cearns and Brown*,[130] a different tribunal found that an applicant who was scored at 95% of her comparator's score was not employed on work of equal value. Given that a percentage difference in score cannot be translated into a percentage pay difference, this tribunal was surely relying on technical and minor differences which most employers would regard as of no practical relevance.

Assessment of the equal value law[131]

In principle, equal value claims have a radical potential. That is why the American doctrine of comparable worth was subject to concerted attack both academically and in the courts. But the way it has operated has been a deep disappointment. The question must be considered whether it is the particular form the law takes which is the problem, or whether the issue is more deep rooted. Such debate is especially pertinent given that the EOC urged the European Commission to take action against the UK Government on the basis that the current law fails to meet European equal pay requirements. However, the Commission decided in late 1996 that no action would be taken.

Delay

'Industrial Tribunals have now ruled on equal pay following referral to an independent expert in 39 cases ... The total average time taken is 20 months, ranging from five months to 49 months.'[132] Where issues needed to be resolved by appeal courts before the expert even started work, some cases have taken more than a decade to resolve.[133] The EAT in *Aldridge* said that the delays were scandalous. The reasons for delay are various and cumulative. The preliminary procedure, the time needed to marshal facts, the time spent

---

128 *Murphy v Bord Telecom Eireann* Case 157/86 [1988] ECR 673; [1988] ICR 445; [1988] IRLR 267.

129 (1985), unreported, Hull IT.

130 (1985), unreported, Liverpool IT.

131 See Gregory, J, 'Dynamite or damp squib – an assessment of equal value law' (1997) 2 IJDL 167.

132 'Equal value update' (1997) 76 EOR 18, p 19.

133 *Ibid*.

by independent experts, as well as the very complexity of cases, contribute to delay. Delay is especially damaging in this context because the law does no more than take a snapshot of the pay relationship between an applicant and a comparator at one moment. A proper picture of pay structures requires a moving picture to take account of inevitable changes over time and a broad screen to include a fully representative group of workers.

The legal system

Legal aid is unavailable and the cases are far too complex, lengthy and expensive to allow for individual representation. Without union assistance claims will be few and far between. Yet for unions the law is only one weapon in an overall pay strategy, and the *threat* of legal action may carry more weight than the action itself. Unions do not and should not focus on the individual whose right has been infringed but on the best tactics to advance the interests of the union membership as a whole. Whether an equal value claim will serve union strategy depends on many factors. These include the likelihood of success, but also the extent to which the union is attuned to the interests of women members in general and the potential gender bias of pay systems in particular. 'Because of the complexity of the cases, it is a necessary condition of effective access to judicial protection and remedies that claimants should be represented by expert and specialist lawyers. The need for legal representation and the protracted nature of the claims means that equal pay cases are costly. According to the EOC, the average cost of an equal value case which is not appealed is over £6,500. In cases which have been appealed, the applicant's costs frequently exceeded £50,000. Complainants who do not have the support of the EOC or their trade union are in practice denied access to court.'[134]

Lack of impact

A further strand in the EOC's case that the UK law has failed properly to implement the Directives lies in the fact that the pay gap remains substantial. In particular, it is argued, the abolition of Wages Councils removed the only method available to protect very many employees in low paid industries from being victims of pay discrimination. Such abolition, it is claimed, had an adverse impact on women in that women were over-represented among those employees who previously benefited from Wages Council protection.[135]

The numerical impact of the law has been tiny. In the period 1984–96, only 27 equal value claims were upheld by tribunals, 16 failed before tribunals, while 108 were either settled or withdrawn.[136] The impact has been bitterly

---

[134] 'EOC looks to Europe for action over UK equal pay laws' (1993) 52 EOR 20, p 22.
[135] *Ibid*, p 23.
[136] *Op cit*, 'Equal value update', fn 132, p 19.

disappointing, even allowing for the fact that settlements have on occasion produced substantial benefit for women.[137] As a result, 'few managers, let alone workers, [have] anything but a hazy idea of what equal value [means] or how it might be implemented. However, it could also be argued that until equal value has ideological legitimacy, it is unlikely to be widely implemented'.[138]

Technical limitations

The EOC has argued that the abolition of Wages Councils is indirectly discriminatory against women. They are forced to this argument partly because of the technical limitations of equal value law, which is concerned with equal pay, not low pay.[139] The need for a male comparator in the same establishment means that the law cannot be used where segregation is most entrenched and where pay is lowest. Indeed, the 'establishment' requirement may even be an incentive to subcontract areas of work and thereby prevent the possibility of a claim,[140] though this may be over-theoretical, as the small numbers of employers who have lost equal value cases hardly indicates a need for employers to alter their pay structures in consequence.

> The problem of sex-based wage discrimination ... is not susceptible to some quick legal cure. Change will come slowly, because wage rates are 'sticky', with wage differentials particularly resistant to change. This 'stickiness' exists because once wage rates for jobs are set in a labour market and differentials between jobs become established, these differentials are accepted in terms of normative social values. Thus, even though changes in the supply and demand for employees in certain occupations may occur, wage rates do not change according to a model of perfect competition in the labour market. Wage differentials are remarkably stable, because both young persons and persons already in the labour market make career decisions based on existing differentials and they resist adjustments in differentials that would be detrimental to them. As a result, the ability of courts to hasten the rate of change is severely constrained.[141]

---

[137] Over 1,500 school catering workers settled their claim for a total in excess of £4 million; *ibid*, p 21. Nearly 400 school meals staff employed by Bedfordshire County Council settled claims for a total of £1.5 million, see (1998) 78 EOR 4. To these figures the additional year-on-year costs should properly be added.

[138] Rubery, J, *The Economics of Equal Value*, 1992, Manchester: EOC, p 39.

[139] This is dramatically indicated through the experience of local authority manual workers. Their job evaluation exercise has been held up as a model of what voluntary job evaluation can do to reduce gender bias in payment structures (see 'Local authority job revaluation' (1987) 13 EOR 21). Yet Rubery, *op cit*, fn 138, p 30, shows how the same group lost out in *absolute* pay, not just compared with private sector workers, which might have been expected, but with other *public* sector workers. Equal value law is simply incapable of resisting general upward or downward labour market trends.

[140] *Op cit*, Rubery, fn 138, p 25.

[141] Bellace, J, 'Comparable worth: proving sex-based wage discrimination' (1984) 69 Iowa LR 655, p 699.

Equal pay and collective bargaining

The story here is an unhappy one, both in a technical legal sense and in a policy sense. It is a story of total failure to get to grips with the issues.[142]

The Equal Pay Act 1970 originally contained, in s 3, a limited provision aimed at remedying discrimination in collective agreements. If a provision of an agreement referred 'specifically to men or women only' it could be referred to the Central Arbitration Committee, which had the power to alter the terms of the agreement so as to eliminate discrimination. By virtue of the normal contractual effect of collective agreements, any such amendment would have become incorporated into the contract of employment of the individual employee. The problem with the law, of course, was that the likelihood of finding agreements which referred *expressly* to men or women only rapidly disappeared once the Act came into force. The *real* equality issue came to be seen as agreements which had a discriminatory effect, in particular where occupational segregation meant that different agreements *in practice* applied to women or men only. The CAC took jurisdiction over such situations, but, in *R v Central Arbitration Committee ex p Hy-Mac*,[143] the Divisional Court held that such activity and activism was beyond their powers. The decision in effect made s 3 a dead letter.

The original s 77 of the SDA 1975 provided that any contractual term which required a contracting party to perform an act of unlawful discrimination should be void. This was assumed to be irrelevant to British collective agreements, which are normally not enforceable as contracts.[144] However, the European Court held in *Commission of the European Communities v United Kingdom*[145] that s 77 was in breach of the Equal Treatment Directive because it provided no means of regulating discriminatory clauses in collective and other agreements which were *not* enforceable as contracts.

Section 6 of the Sex Discrimination Act 1986 repealed s 3 of the 1970 Act and amended s 77 of the 1975 Act by extending it to non-binding collective agreements. A discriminatory non-binding collective agreement is void. However, the section cannot be invoked by an individual claimant. The legal

---

[142] 'Women are more likely to fall outside the net of collective bargaining for several reasons. First, these agreements may exclude some atypical workers where women are dominant (homeworkers and short part time work); second, in some countries agreements exclude certain feminised occupations such as clerical or cleaning work (by omission rather than design in some cases, but this itself is evidence of the invisibility of women in the collective bargaining system); third, women are often over-represented in industries where enforcement of collective agreements is weak, for example in textiles and clothing, retail and catering.' *Op cit*, Rubery and Fagan, fn 117, p 100.

[143] [1979] IRLR 451, DC.

[144] Trade Union and Labour Relations (Consolidation) Act 1992, s 179; *Ford v AEF* [1969] 2 QB 303, QBD.

[145] Case 165/82 [1983] ECR 3431; [1984] ICR 192; [1984] 1 All ER 353; [1984] IRLR 29.

effect of declaring a non-binding provision to be void is nil, and, perhaps more important, provides no deterrent against discriminatory terms in such collective agreements. Once such an agreement becomes a part of an individual contract, there will be a normal EqPA 1970 claim, but such claims are not automatically extended to all members of the group covered by the same agreement, which is the great procedural advantage of taking action in respect of the agreement itself. The 1993 Trade Union Reform and Employment Rights Act added a new sub-section 6(4A) into the 1986 Act. An individual may now claim before an employment tribunal that a term of a collective agreement[146] is discriminatory against her. Further, the tribunal may take action, not simply against rules which have a present discriminatory effect, but also against those which may have such effect in the future, even though they bring about no present detriment which would support a claim under s 6 of the SDA 1975.[147]

It remains the case that there is no mechanism whereby the outcome of a successful equal pay claim can be automatically extended to all other employees in the same position as the successful applicant. As a matter of practice, though, employers are likely take such a step in order to avoid consequential claims from being brought. Perhaps more important, there is no mechanism for bringing about the amendment of a collective agreement which is discriminatory in its effects. However, in *Kowalska v Freie und Hansestadt Hamburg*,[148] the European Court held that employees covered by a discriminatory collective agreement are entitled to the terms and conditions of employment that they would have had if the agreement had not been discriminatory. There is thus an argument that current English law is defective in failing to provide a specific mechanism to enable this to be done.

Section 77 appears to be geared towards direct discrimination. However, in *Meade-Hill v British Council*,[149] it was held to be potentially applicable to an indirectly discriminatory clause in a collective agreement which had been incorporated in the applicant's contract of employment, in this case a mobility clause which might potentially require employees to serve anywhere in the UK. However, for it to be void, it would have to be shown that there were no possible circumstances in which the application of such a clause to the applicant could be justified. Proving a negative such as this is likely to be an almost impossible task.

The role of trade unions in securing genuine equality is very significant. The prosecution of a successful equal value case is unlikely without union

---

[146] The provision also applies to rules made by employers, trade unions, employers organisations, professional organisations or qualifying bodies.

[147] *Meade-Hill v National Union of Civil and Public Servants and British Council* [1995] ICR 847; [1996] 1 All ER 79; [1995] IRLR 478, CA.

[148] Case C-33/89 [1990] ECR I-2591; [1992] ICR 29; [1990] IRLR 447.

[149] *Meade-Hill v National Union of Civil and Public Servants and British Council* [1995] ICR 847; [1996] 1 All ER 79; [1995] IRLR 478, CA.

support; the decision whether the union will support a case may be made on grounds which have little to do with the intrinsic merits of a case. More important, even a successful case is only a snapshot of a pay problem involving two employees at one moment. Pay structures are continually changing, and no legal system could provide the kind of detailed monitoring that is possible for a trade union. This requires time, money and expertise, which in turn requires a union to devote its resources to equal value issues. Research, perhaps now a little dated, is not particularly encouraging.

'Bargaining for equality' (1990) 29 EOR 22, pp 23:[150]

Women are under-represented at the bargaining table ... As a result it is ... no surprise ... that the bargaining agenda is so conservative ... [S]ensitivity to women's interests, a concern for eliminating sex discrimination and 'equality aware bargaining' are all less likely to be found when women are absent from the table.

The importance for women's interests of having women in the negotiating team can, says the report, be seen in terms of informational input and in ensuring that women's interests are pursued effectively ...

However, the mere presence of women may not be enough to generate 'equality awareness' because of the constraints imposed by notions of what is a 'good negotiator' and 'proper bargaining'. The researchers found that the accepted roles for a good negotiator and proper bargaining were defined by men. If female shop stewards attempted to push forward the interests of their members, they were accused of sectionalism ...

Issues of particular importance to women were perceived as minority or special interests rather than members' interests. This applied not only to childcare and working time but was also reinforced by job segregation, so that particular occupational interests were categorised as women's interests and then marginalised or ignored.

In contrast, the researchers found that serving men's interests and upholding existing structures and arrangements which favour men tended to be equated not with sectional interests but with serving members' interests.

THE DEFENCE OF GENUINE MATERIAL FACTOR

It is clear that people who do the same work do not always receive the same pay. Seniority systems, bonus payments and individual merit payments are examples. Section 1(3) of the Equal Pay Act provides a defence in the following terms:

An equality clause shall not operate in relation to a variation between the woman's contract and the man's contract if the employer proves that the

---

[150] This article identifies the main conclusions of Colling, T and Dickens, L, *Equality Bargaining – Why Not?*, 1989, Manchester: EOC.

variation is genuinely due to a material factor which is not the difference of sex and that factor

(a) [where the claim is based on like work or work rated as equivalent] must be a material difference between the woman's case and the man's; and

(b) [in equal value claims] may be such a material difference.[151]

The operation of the defence assumes that the applicant has proved that she is employed on like work, work rated as equivalent or work of equal value. It was held in *Davies v McCartneys*[152] that there was no limit on the range of factors which could be considered as relevant to the defence.[153] This goes too far: matters relevant to the question whether there is a *prima facie* case of equal pay, such as relative job content, cannot logically be relevant to this defence, which is concerned with distinctions apart from the nature of the jobs themselves.[154] It is especially important that tribunals bear this in mind where the defence is being considered in a preliminary hearing before consideration of the equal value question.

The basis of the defence

The explanation for the difference in wording between (a) and (b) is only comprehensible in the light of judicial decisions on the interpretation of the sub-section before the equal value amendment was introduced. It is nevertheless a good example of legislation aimed at giving rights to and imposing obligations on ordinary people which is expressed in a manner which in most cases will be quite beyond their capacity to grasp. The wording is a disgrace.

---

[151] The equivalent authority for European equal pay cases is *Bilka-Kaufhaus v Weber von Hartz* Case 170/84 [1986] ECR 1607; [1986] 2 CMLR 701; [1987] ICR 110; [1986] IRLR 317, where it was held that the practice or policy being challenged must 'meet a genuine need of the enterprise', must be 'necessary for that purpose' and must be 'suitable for attaining the purpose pursued' (see above, pp 294–96). European law thus imposes the same test for discrimination cases as for equal pay cases. As English law has two different tests, the interrelationship between English and European law is far from straightforward.

[152] [1989] ICR 707; [1989] IRLR 439, EAT.

[153] Such factors must continue to operate at the time the claim is made. In *Benveniste v University of Southampton* [1989] ICR 617; [1989] IRLR 122, CA, because of financial constraints, she was appointed on a salary scale below that to which her age and qualifications entitled her. After the constraints ended she was awarded normal annual increments but remained underpaid for a lecturer of her age and qualifications. It was held that the defence failed as, when the constraints ended, she should have been placed in the salary position in which she would have been had they never existed.

[154] Cf *McGregor v GMBATU* [1987] ICR 505, where the EAT wrongly accepted the view of the tribunal that the pay difference was attributable to the man's skills, knowledge, responsibilities and experience. This totally confuses factors relevant to the nature of the job with personal factors relevant to the establishment of the defence.

Its origin is the decision of the Court of Appeal in *Clay Cross (Quarry Services) Ltd v Fletcher*.[155] The question was whether it was a defence that a male employee hired to do the same job as an existing female employee could be paid more than her, as otherwise he would not have been prepared to accept the job. As Lord Denning MR pointed out: 'If any such excuse were permitted, the Act would become a dead letter. Those are the very reasons why there was unequal pay before the statute. They are the very circumstances in which the statute was intended to operate.' However, rather than holding that the employer failed because the difference alleged was in reality a difference of sex, Lord Denning concentrated on the words 'between her case and his' and held that only distinctions based on differences between the 'personal equation' of the woman and the man could provide a defence. Market forces, such as relied on here, were outside the personal equation and thus no defence.

The approach taken by Lord Denning failed to survive for two reasons. First, it proved impossible to decide what was part of the personal equation and what was not. After all, the fact that the man would not work for less pay was very personal to him and arguably within the concept. Secondly, the European Court in *Bilka-Kaufhaus* held that business efficiency considerations, which *Fletcher* had held to be outside the scope of the defence, were potentially justifiable. In consequence, the House of Lords in *Rainey v Greater Glasgow Health Board*[156] refused to follow *Fletcher*.

These developments occurred after the passing of the equal value amendment, the philosophy of which clearly permits challenges to wage levels set by the principles of market economics. The Government had been forced by European developments to concede the applicability of the equal value principle, but were anxious to ensure that market forces should remain a potential defence where two jobs were held to be of equal value, contrary to the view of Lord Denning in *Fletcher*. The wording applicable to equal value claims was that the defence 'may' relate to the personal equation, but by implication need not do so. Following *Bilka* and *Rainey*, the distinction ceases to be relevant; the remainder of this section assumes that there is now no practical difference between s 1(3)(a) and s 1(3)(b).

The explanation for the pay differential must be 'genuine', 'material' and 'not the difference of sex'. 'Genuine' means that the employer's purported reason for the pay differential must be the real reason. As the employer will never put forward gender as the explanation for the pay differential, an ungenuine explanation will often be one that is directly discriminatory. But a reason which is 'not the difference of sex' may also be one which operates to

---

[155] [1979] 1 All ER 374; [1979] ICR 1; [1978] IRLR 361.
[156] [1987] AC 224; [1987] 1 All ER 65; [1987] IRLR 26.

the practical disadvantage of women even if not intended to do so. Thus a genuine material factor may be a factor which operates to justify what would otherwise be an indirectly discriminatory pay criterion.

However, different views have been expressed as to whether the employer must establish that the difference in pay was objectively justified even in situations where it was not tainted with discrimination. It is possible to have pay differences which are in no way due to sex discrimination but which cannot be justified according to the *Bilka* criteria. For example, if the employer proves that the pay difference is because the man receives too much pay owing to an administrative error, the difference will be proved to be not the difference of sex, but will not be a justified difference.[157] The House of Lords has now resolved the issue.

Strathclyde Regional Council v Wallace [1998] 1 All ER 394

The nine female applicants were teachers who were doing the work of principal teachers. They claimed equality with men who were *employed* as principal teachers and thus were paid more. However, the pay difference was not because of sex. Most of the 134 unpromoted teachers doing the work of principal teachers were male. The reason for the disparity was the interaction of a statutory promotion structure with financial constraints. The House of Lords held that it was sufficient to show that the pay disparity was genuinely due to a material factor which was not the difference of sex; there was no need to show that it was justified according to the *Bilka* test.

Lord Browne-Wilkinson (pp 400–01):

The words of the sub-section indicate no requirement of such a justification inherent in the use of the words 'material factor'. It has long been established ... that a factor is material if it is 'significant and relevant', a test which looks to the reason why there is a disparity in pay, not whether there is an excuse for such disparity. To my mind decisively, if one were to accept [the plaintiff's] submission, that would be to turn the Equal Pay Act into a 'fair wages' Act requiring the elimination of disparity in wages even though the disparity had nothing to do with sex discrimination ...

[I]f a difference in pay is explained by genuine factors not tainted by discrimination, that is sufficient to raise a valid defence ... [I]n such a case there is no further burden on the employer to 'justify' anything. However, if the factor explaining the disparity in pay is tainted by sex discrimination (whether direct or indirect), that will be fatal to a defence ... unless such discrimination can be objectively justified.

---

[157] In *Yorkshire Blood Transfusion Service v Plaskett* [1994] ICR 74, EAT, the court accepted that such a defence amounted to a genuine material factor, whereas in *McPherson v Rathgael Centre for Children and Young People* [1991] IRLR 206, NICA, the opposite result was reached. *McPherson* was overruled in *Wallace*. Other cases to adopt a similar approach to *Plaskett* are *Tyldesley v TML Plastics Ltd* [1996] ICR 356; [1996] IRLR 385, EAT; and *Barber v NCR Manufacturing* [1993] IRLR 95, EAT.

The conclusion is not self-evident. The section requires the employer to establish that the defence is 'material' and that it is not a difference of sex. The House of Lords assumes that any difference not the difference in sex will be material, and thus fails to give the two concepts separate meanings.[158] If the word 'material' is to have a separate meaning, as normal principles of statutory interpretation would demand, the question arises whether it means objectively material or merely material in the mind of the employer. In *Tyldesley* and *Wallace*, it was held to mean 'a significant influence' which amounts to no more than a requirement to show that the factor *caused* the difference in pay. In *Rainey*, on the other hand, 'material' was held to mean 'significant and relevant' which, while not completely free from doubt, suggests a more objective interpretation. It might be countered that this imposes an undue burden on the employer; after all, anyone can make mistakes. This argument is especially strong where the mistake benefits one man among many doing the same work, where the danger of citing a 'rogue' comparator is especially acute. *Wallace* holds that absolute objectivity in pay is not required in all cases. But such a conclusion must be accompanied by a rigorous examination of the facts to establish whether any element of direct or indirect discrimination is present.[159]

The question whether the distinction between direct and indirect discrimination should be incorporated into equal pay law is not free from difficulty.

Ratcliffe v North Yorkshire County Council **[1995] IRLR 439, HL**[160]

School catering assistants claimed equal pay with men in jobs such as road sweepers and gardeners, with whom they had been rated as equivalent under the local government revaluation scheme. Because of compulsory competitive tendering, they were given notices of dismissal and re-employed at lower rates of pay, being told that unless the rates were lower, the authority would have lost the school meals contract to a cheaper private contractor.

The Court of Appeal allowed the defence. The employers did not directly discriminate against women. Further, the 'material factor' which led to the

---

[158] See Kilpatrick, C, 'Deciding when jobs of equal value can be paid unequally: an examination of s 1(3) of the Equal Pay Act 1970' (1994) 23 Industrial LJ 311.

[159] 'What is the most common reason for unequal pay for equal work or work of equal value? It is that the employer genuinely thought that one job was worth more than the other and paid the two jobs accordingly. That reason is non-discriminatory on its face (though it may rest on some difficult to prove sexist stereotypes about the value of work done by women as compared with the value of work done by men). If this kind of good faith defence discharges the burden of proof under s 1(3), it will place a major constraint on the future potential of the Equal Pay Act. The fact is that employers have often defended equal pay claims on the basis of some unconvincing, and ultimately unsuccessful, justifications precisely because they have been advised that a defence that they genuinely believed the man's job to be worth more was not strong enough.' (1998) 78 EOR 52.

[160] See, also, [1995] 3 All ER 597; [1995] ICR 837.

lower pay was genuinely due to the operation of market forces and the need to compete with a rival bid. It was not in any way based on the difference of sex.

The House of Lords allowed the appeal.

Lord Slynn of Hadley (p 442):

In my opinion the Act of 1970 must be interpreted ... without bringing in the distinction between so called 'direct' and 'indirect' discrimination.

By a majority [the Industrial Tribunal] were satisfied that the employers had failed to show that the [defence was made out] ... In my opinion it is impossible to say that they were not entitled on the evidence to come to that conclusion ...

The women could not have found other suitable work and were obliged to take the wages offered if they were to continue with this work. The fact that two men were employed on the same work at the same rate of pay does not detract from the conclusion that there was discrimination between the women involved and their male comparators. It means no more than that the two men were underpaid compared with other men doing jobs rated as equivalent ...

The fact that [they] paid women less than their male comparators because they were women constitutes direct discrimination and *ex hypothesi* cannot be shown to be justified on grounds 'irrespective of the sex of the person' concerned.

This is a difficult case, not least because of the brevity of the single judgment. The House found it unnecessary to 'review the many [decided cases ... [nor] to consider Art 119 of the Treaty of Rome and the decisions of the European Court on that article ...'. It is not clear what the case *did* decide. While rejecting the relevance to the issue of 'genuine material factor' of the distinction between direct and indirect discrimination, the House stressed that here, the employers were guilty of direct pay discrimination. Even if they were not, the tribunal were entitled to conclude that the defence had not been made out. As no reference is made to other cases, one can only guess at the appropriate criteria for establishing the defence. It is contended that where it is alleged that a salary structure on average operates to disadvantage women, it will be impossible to resolve such a claim without reference to the concepts of adverse impact and justification.

One may also question the conclusion that the facts established direct discrimination. For that, the reason they were paid less must be on the ground of gender. The fact that all but two of those who were underpaid were female is evidence of that fact, but it is not conclusive evidence. In *Bullock v Alice Ottley School*[161] the fact that all the female employees had to retire at 60 did not establish that they were victims of discrimination: they retired at 60 not because of their gender but because of the job they did. That logically impeccable reasoning seems equally applicable here. The House of Lords

---

[161] [1993] ICR 138; [1992] IRLR 564, CA.

accepted the reasoning of the tribunal that the pay differential arose 'out of the general perception ... that a woman should stay at home and look after the children and if she wants to work it must fit in with that domestic duty and a lack of facilities to enable her, easily, to do otherwise'. But the perception and lack of facilities do not affect all woman; it would have been preferable to analyse this as a situation where the utilisation of market forces failed to operate in a gender-neutral way and so was unjustifiable on that basis. It *would* have been theoretically possible to argue that the way in which the tendering process operated was tainted by gender, but as the tendering requirement applied to all manual jobs, such argument would be hard to establish.

It is not being contended that the claim should have failed, rather that the sketchiness of the judgment both glosses over the issues and decides the case on an inappropriate basis. What was at issue was a clash between the values of public service, which emphasises national pay rates covering a wide range of different types of job, and the values of pure market forces, where employers may pay no more than is necessary in order to attract workers and remain in business. Of course that process affects many women in a qualitatively different way from men, but the real issue is the extent to which reliance on market forces can be justified. It would have better for the future had the House's commendable awareness of the problems lower paid part time women face in the labour market been translated into suitably sceptical rules on when employers are permitted to rely on market forces.

Despite *Ratcliffe*, it is clear from the decisions of the House of Lords in *Rainey* and the European Court in *Enderby*[162] that indirect discrimination doctrine is applicable to pay as well as other areas of discrimination, and the House of Lords in *Wallace* took the view that *Ratcliffe* went too far in denying the relevance of the distinction. However, Lord Browne-Wilkinson also stated that 'where the variation [in pay] is genuinely due to a factor which involves the difference of sex, the employer can still establish a valid defence ... if he can justify such discrimination, whether the differentiation is direct or indirect'.[163] The suggestion that direct discrimination can be justified is contrary to principle, has the capacity seriously to undermine the Equal Pay Act, was unnecessary to the decision in the case, and should not be regarded as binding.

Given that indirect discrimination analysis is applicable to equal pay law, an immediate problem is whether the SDA 1975 principle of needing to show a 'requirement or condition' is applicable here. There is no such specific rule in the EqPA 1970 and in any event European law is less restrictive both as regards equal pay and equal treatment.

---

[162] *Enderby v Frenchay AHA* Case C-127/92 [1993] ECR I-5535; [1994] ICR 112; [1994] 1 All ER 495; [1993] IRLR 591.
[163] [1998] 1 All ER 394, p 400.

Enderby v Frenchay AHA and Secretary of State for Health Case C-127/92 [1993] IRLR 591[164]

Speech therapists claimed that they were employed on work of equal value with male principal grade pharmacists and clinical psychologists whose salary exceeded theirs by about 60%.

The EAT held that no statutory provision in UK or EEC law provided that there was a presumption of unlawful indirect discrimination where the applicant is a member of a predominantly female group paid less than her male comparator doing work of equal value (or presumed equal value). The unlawful discrimination must come about as a result of a requirement or condition. The ECJ rejected this argument.

Judgment (p 595):

If the pay of speech therapists is significantly lower than that of pharmacists and if the former are almost exclusively women while the latter are predominantly men, there is a *prima facie* case of sex discrimination, at least where the two jobs in question are of equal value and the statistics describing that situation are valid.

It is for the national court to assess whether it may take into account those statistics, that is to say, whether they cover enough individuals, whether they illustrate purely fortuitous or short term phenomena, and whether, in general, they appear to be significant.[165]

In *British Road Services Ltd v Loughran*,[166] it was argued that the fact that a group was 75% female rather than 'almost exclusively female' was insufficient to trigger the *Enderby* presumption, which would require the employer to explain the variation in average pay. In rejecting this argument, the court held that interpreting the statistics is a matter for the tribunal, and that, as long as the numbers involved are sufficiently large and the figures quoted not short term or fortuitous, the tribunal would be entitled to conclude that a *prima facie* case had been made out.[167]

The next question is what facts the employer must establish in order to explain the variation in pay. However, payment structures and levels have often developed piecemeal and it may be difficult or impossible for the

---

[164] See, also, [1993] ECR I-5535; [1994] ICR 112; [1994] 1 All ER 495.

[165] In *Royal Copenhagen* Case C-400/93 [1995] IRLR 648, however, the Court held that, if the difference in average pay concerns employees paid on piece rates, such difference only gives rise to a *prima facie* of discrimination where 'it is not possible to identify the factors which determined the rates or units of measurement used to calculate the variable element in the pay ...' ([1995] IRLR 648, p 657). The Court appears to hold that *Enderby* decided that the burden of proof *may* be shifted rather than *must* be shifted. Whether this more cautious approach will become the norm remains to be seen.

[166] [1997] IRLR 92, NICA.

[167] The decision in *Enderby* and especially the opinion of the Advocate General led to the argument, rejected in *Bhudi v IMI Refiners Ltd* [1994] ICR 302; [1994] IRLR 204, EAT, that the need in the SDA 1975 for a requirement or condition was inconsistent with European law. See above, pp 266–68.

employer to show the extent to which particular factors contribute to overall pay. It is this fact which explains and justifies the approach of the European Court in *Enderby*: it may be impossible to explain *why* women are paid less than men by a particular employer but the differential average in effect raises a case to answer that the factors are discriminatory.

Byrne and Others v The Financial Times Ltd [1991] IRLR 417, EAT

In an equal value claim the employer's defence relied on factors such as different responsibilities, different hours of work or rotas, total flexibility, red-circling, and collective bargaining.

The applicants sought a breakdown of the difference between their salaries and those of their male comparators and an allocation of a specific sum or a specific fraction of that difference to a particular fact in the work record or history of each comparator.

The tribunal chair refused the application for discovery: 'The pay of the woman and the pay of the comparator have got to be looked at as one sum – it is not permissible to split them.'

The EAT dismissed the appeal.

Wood J (p 418):

[The lay members] stress that in realistic industrial situations, it was impossible to attribute a particular weight to a particular factor when fixing a wage ... [T]he situation quite often occurs where it is impossible to attribute a particular percentage or amount to a specific part of the variation and that more than the variation may ultimately be proved.

This does not even require the employer to show that it is impossible to break down the pay so that a particular sum of money cannot be applied to a particular factor; it assumes this to be the case and denies the employee the information necessary to disprove it. The burden of lack of knowledge falls entirely on the employee;[168] this cannot be consistent with *Handels-og Kontorfunktionaerernes Forbund i Danmark v Dansk Arbejdsgiverforening (acting for Danfoss)*,[169] where the European Court held that 'where an undertaking applies a pay system which is characterised by a total lack of transparency, the burden of proof is on the employer to show that his pay practice is not discriminatory, if a female worker establishes that, by comparison with a relatively high number of employees, the average pay of female workers is lower than that of male workers'.

---

168 '[I]t is difficult to see how equal value proceedings can be fairly disposed of without revealing information that may hitherto have been regarded by the employer as confidential.' *Op cit*, Rubenstein, fn 101, p 68.

169 Case C-171/88 [1989] ECR 3199; [1991] 1 CMLR 8; [1989] IRLR 532.

Townshend-Smith, R, 'Economic defences to equal pay claims', in Hervey, T and O'Keeffe, D (eds), *Sex Equality Law in the European Union,* **1996, Chichester: John Wiley, pp 42–43:**

[T]he law should exercise reasonable deference to the payment *choices* made by employers, even those which have an adverse impact on women, though the *degree* of adverse impact will be significant. A key caveat to this point is that they should indeed be choices. The labour market is characterised by ill-thought out and ill-planned behaviour, where payment strategies may simply reflect long standing tradition or what other similarly situated employers habitually do. It is central to the operation of an appropriately balanced equal value law that employers are not permitted to engage in *ex post facto* rationalisations or justifications for their payment strategies.[170] Deference should be paid to choices, but the employer should face the burden of showing that such a choice was indeed made. This approach prevents women from continuing to be victims of historically discriminatory structures reproduced without thought, while at the same time permitting innovative approaches to pay.

Employers should therefore be required to produce evidence of how such decisions were taken and why. That this may require them to disclose the internal workings of the firm, internal memoranda, etc, is inevitable. This goes beyond ... *Danfoss*, which concerned openness in the implementation of decisions rather than in the prior decision to utilise particular criteria. Indeed, greater openness in pay is essential to enable courts to make, and to be seen to make, a fair assessment of an equal value claim, given that in the end such decisions are impressionistic rather than scientific or purely logical. The detailed facts on pay are necessary for a strict scrutiny, in a literal sense, to occur.

McColgan, A, 'Legislating equal pay: lessons from Canada' (1993) 22 Industrial LJ 269, p 271:

The existing law requires a woman to perceive a disparity between her wages and the wages of a man who is engaged in work of equal value to hers. Given the secrecy which surrounds the issue of wages, particularly in non-unionised workplaces, many potential complainants will have no idea what other employees earn. Further, even if such information were available, a woman must choose as a comparator a man engaged in work of less than or equal value to hers. The evaluation of jobs is an immensely complex task from which fortunes have been made by firms of management consultants. Such evaluation is impossible without detailed analyses of the skill, knowledge and responsibilities demanded by each job, and the working conditions under which it is performed. This information is not readily available to fellow

---

[170] It is for this reason that, in *Hayward v Cammell Laird Shipbuilders Ltd* [1988] AC 894; [1988] 2 All ER 257; [1988] IRLR 257, HL, the House of Lords rejected the argument that the woman's greater fringe benefits adequately compensated for her lower rate of basic pay. As the distinction was based on history, the employers would not have been able to produce evidence to show that the one was introduced specifically to compensate for the other.

workers; nor can they know the weights which an expert might ascribe to each category under which value could be assessed. To attempt to redress the collective underpayment of women by requiring such improbable feats from individuals, and by failing to ensure the extension of any wage increase to those performing the same or similar work to the claimant, is to condemn the whole enterprise to failure.

The *Byrne* approach is especially problematic for an applicant where an employer proves the existence of a factor which explains *some* but not necessarily all of the variation.[171] In *Enderby*, the EAT held that, where market forces account for some of the difference in pay, the whole of the difference is justified, as to hold otherwise would involve the tribunal in a wage fixing role.[172] A similar approach was adopted in *Calder v Rowntree Mackintosh Confectionery Ltd*,[173] where Balcombe LJ observed that 'the fact that some indeterminate part of the shift premium was attributable to unsociable hours did not mean that the IT was in error in finding that the difference in pay was due to a genuine material factor'. The court felt able to reach this conclusion despite the fact that the employer abandoned reliance on the other factors which had been put forward to explain the differential, namely, market forces and collective bargaining. Thus even though the employer all but admitted that the whole of the differential was *not* attributable to the unsocial hours premium, the defence nevertheless succeeded. The deference shown to employer reasoning processes on pay – or lack of them – is quite inconsistent with *Enderby* and *Danfoss*. To say that it cannot *always* be established precisely how a pay level is made out does not mean that employers should be not required to make the attempt, to be as transparent as is reasonably practicable, and to justify the components which can be observed, even if such justification, as in *Sherwin*, can be no more than what is commonplace.

The defence in operation

In Chapter 9 we considered, *inter alia*, the question of when first, seniority, and secondly, part time work, can justify unequal pay. We now turn to other specific examples of the defence in operation.

---

[171] In *Sherwin v National Coal Board* [1978] ICR 700; [1978] IRLR 122, EAT, it was held that the differential for night shift work was too great, that 20% was appropriate, and that the applicant's basic pay should be increased so that the remaining differential was appropriate. While this approach permits analysis of the components which make up total pay, the court is not deciding that 20% is the appropriate differential for night shift work for any other reason than that is what is conventionally paid.

[172] This approach was criticised by the Advocate General in *Enderby* but not specifically discussed in the judgment of the Court.

[173] [1993] ICR 811; [1993] IRLR 212, CA.

Market forces/collective bargaining cases

Cases where market forces are put forward as a defence are critical for the conceptual aim and practical effectiveness of equal pay – especially equal value – legislation. There is a clear philosophical clash between determining wages according to the input of the individual worker – equal value – and determining them according to the operation of supposedly impersonal and external market forces. If the latter is permitted to trump the former, the potential cutting edge of the law will be severely blunted.

We examined earlier[174] the causes of pay inequality and concluded, first, that the market, being no more than a sum of its component actors, does not operate in an impersonal and gender-neutral fashion, and, secondly, that there are ideological, historical, structural and organisational explanations for women's lower average pay than men.

Townshend-Smith, R, 'Economic defences to equal pay claims', in Hervey, T and O'Keeffe, D (eds), *Sex Equality Law in the European Union*, 1996, Chichester: John Wiley, pp 40–42:

The concept of the market is fundamentally ambiguous. At one level it refers to those factors regarded by employers as worthy of reward, such as seniority, qualifications and individual performance. In a sense there is a 'market' in these qualities, yet the second meaning relates to the supply of and the demand for workers, irrespective of their personal qualities. A third meaning, hardly discussed in litigation but significant in governmental thinking, relates pay to the employer's ability to pay, which may be affected by profitability or by cash limits. Each argument may become the defence to an equal pay claim, and each must be tested by the objective standard outlined above. Labelling a defence based on 'market forces' does not change the applicable legal rules, both because the very concept is ambiguous and because in policy terms the defence should be tested by the same standard.

The unspoken assumption appears to be that there is a uniformity in the way wages are fixed based on the universal, immutable economic laws of supply and demand. In reality, systems vary at three levels at least, between Member States, within Member States, and within individual enterprises.

First, payment strategies tend to differ between Member States. For example, Germany tends to value qualifications, while France places greater weight on seniority.[175] The concept of the single market in goods and services entails that the market should operate in the same way, valuing the same features, in each Member State. Even if that could be attained for the labour market, it is not self-evident that such objective is desirable for payment structures, given the variation in the social meaning of wage structures between different countries. Equal value law needs to work within such social expectations and not against them.

---

[174] Above, Chapter 2.

[175] *Op cit*, Rubery and Fagan, fn 117, pp 111–13; *op cit*, Rubery, fn 138, p 68.

Not only are there differences between countries, there are also significant differences within countries, even between similar employers. One employer might operate an internal labour market characterised by high investment and training and a well established career structure; another might invest less in training and prefer to 'buy in' already trained employees.[176] At a level of individual litigation it would be inappropriate to describe one policy as better than the other.

Thirdly, employers frequently have different approaches to pay covering different areas of the workforce. 'Most organisations have several different pay structures and each pay structure tends to be dominated by either male or female-dominated jobs.'[177] Again it is contended that it is both undesirably interventionist and beyond the objective of equal value legislation to require uniformity of approach. For this reason, enterprise-wide job evaluation schemes, even gender-sensitive ones, are not a universal panacea.

Enderby v Frenchay AHA Case C-127/92 [1993] IRLR 591[178]

The EAT held that either market forces or the existence of different collective bargaining structures could amount to a defence. The standard of justification imposed was relatively lax, and included 'objectively justified grounds which are other than economic, such as administrative efficiency in a concern not engaged in commerce or business'.

Judgment (p 595):

The fact that the rates of pay at issue are decided by collective bargaining processes conducted separately for each of the two professional groups concerned, without any discriminatory effect within each group, does not preclude a finding of *prima facie* discrimination where the results of those processes show that two groups with the same employer and the same trade union are treated differently.

The state of the employment market, which may lead the employer to increase the pay of a particular job in order to attract candidates, may constitute an objectively justified economic ground ...

If ... the national court has been able to determine precisely what proportion of the increase in pay is attributable to market forces, it must necessarily accept that the pay differential is objectively justified to the extent of that proportion. When national authorities have to apply Community law, they must apply the principle of proportionality.

Advocate General (pp 599–600):

If a *pro rata* justification is to be permitted, the effect of the objective criterion on the level of pay must be quantifiable. The EAT, the UK and the defendant were all of the opinion that a series of factors go to determine the level of pay and it is not possible to ascribe a particular amount of pay to any one of those

---

[176] *Op cit*, Rubery, fn 138, p 41.

[177] *Op cit*, Rubery, fn 138, p 104.

[178] See, also, [1993] ECR I-5535; [1994] ICR 112; [1994] 1 All ER 49.

factors. But elsewhere it is asserted that the requirements of the labour market justify a difference in pay of at most 10%. On that basis it would appear to be quantifiable. The very fact that several factors influence the level of pay ought to make it possible to ascribe part of the pay to each of the factors.

[If] it can also be established that only part of the difference between job A and job B is attributable to the need to attract suitable candidates to job B, only that part of the difference which is attributable to the need to attract suitable candidates to job B is objectively justified.[179]

British Coal Corporation v Smith [1994] IRLR 342, CA[180]

The defence was based on separate wage structures and a policy of removing the link between the pay of mineworkers and all other workers for economic reasons ... [O]ver the years some ancillary workers had been transferred to the category of surface – all such employees were male.

The Court of Appeal rejected the defence.

Balcombe LJ (pp 300–02):

[D]oes the appellant show that a group which is predominantly female is treated less favourably than a group doing like work or work of equal value, of whom a majority are men? If so, then the burden shifts to the employer to show the difference is 'objectively justified' on a non-discriminatory basis ... If 'market forces' are relied upon, [the employer] must show that these are gender-neutral.

The canteen workers and the cleaners are predominantly female – thus [there is] a *prima facie* case of discrimination within *Enderby*. But if they should be regarded as part of the larger group of ancillary workers, no such case is made out, because there is no preponderance or even a majority of women employees in that larger group.

The appellants are separately classified as regards their terms and conditions of employment, and the fact that their classes form part of a larger group does not alter that fact ...

[T]he variation in the rates of pay ... is the result of separate collective bargaining processes which themselves are untainted by sex.

The question is not whether the policy of disassociation was capable of objective justification [we agree that it was], but whether its application to these particular classes of employees was shown to be objectively justified.

The tribunal said that they were not satisfied that there was any economic justification for paying surface mineworkers – some of whom did work which on a superficial comparison was no more arduous, strenuous or difficult than the work of cleaners – at a higher rate.

---

[179] The original complaint was lodged in March 1986. Following a government concession, it was finally settled in April 1997. See (1997) 73 EOR 2.

[180] See, also, [1994] ICR 810.

It seems to us likely that the difference was due to an ingrained approach based upon sex, which meant that women, whatever they did, would not be classed or categorised as surface mineworkers.

[The House of Lords[181] dismissed the appeal on this point, without examining the legal issues in great detail. They accepted that the existence of separate bargaining structures was not in itself a defence, reasoned that the question was primarily one of fact for the tribunal and concluded that the employers had not discharged their burden of proof.]

It is clear from *Enderby* and *Smith* that neither market forces nor the existence of separate collective bargaining units is, in itself, a defence. It is equally clear that they may, if operated in a gender-neutral fashion, amount to a defence. But the law on the precise circumstances in which this may occur, and the precise details of what employers must establish, is still in its infancy, as the European Court routinely holds that the question of whether the *facts* establish justification is for the national court to determine. *Enderby* was a relatively straightforward case, in that the different amounts for different components was generally agreed. In *Smith*, the different wage structures were the product of long standing tradition, not having been developed to meet a specific need of the undertaking, as required by *Bilka*. In *Ratcliffe*, the House of Lords accepted the view of the tribunal that there was direct discrimination because male employees were treated differently.

There are few cases where the facts have been subject to a detailed examination to show when market forces may be a defence. In *Lord v Knowsley BC*,[182] the pay of home carers, almost all women, was reduced in order to compete with outside contractors. Male refuse drivers and school caretakers, on the other hand, continued to be paid at the same local government rate. The Industrial Tribunal rejected the employers' market forces defence. The employers were in effect saying to the women: 'Yours, we realise, is work predominantly done by women. We need to compete against others who pay less than we do for it. We will therefore pay you less.' The tribunal concluded that it is the vulnerability of women workers such as these in the labour market outside the local government service that enabled them to pay less to home carers. That was not 'a factor which is not the difference of sex. The women were paid less than the men because their equivalent work attracts lower pay for the women who do it elsewhere'. Thus the 'market forces' defence failed: it was not operated in a gender-neutral fashion, both because the same criteria and approach were not applied to male employees and because the application of market forces had a disparate impact on women which could not be justified.

---

[181] [1996] 3 All ER 97; [1996] ICR 515; [1996] IRLR 404, HL.
[182] Unreported, Liverpool IT – see (1996) 70 EOR 23.

Rainey v Greater Glasgow Health Board [1987] IRLR 26, HL[183]

It was decided to set up an NHS prosthetic service in Scotland and to discontinue the existing arrangement under which prosthetic services were provided by private contractors. Private sector prosthetists who wished to transfer to the new service were able to remain on the rates of pay and service that they were then receiving, subject to future changes as negotiated by their union. However, new entrants were paid at significantly lower rates based on the Whitley scale for ancillary health service staff. The 20 prosthetists previously employed by private contractors were all men. Female new entrant prosthetists claimed equal pay with these men, there being no question that they were employed on like work.

Lord Keith of Kinkel (pp 28–31):

The Secretary of State for Scotland decided, as a matter of general policy. that the Whitley Council scale ... was appropriate. It was also decided that the appropriate part of the scale ... was that applicable to medical physics technicians ...

[W]here there is no question of intentional sex discrimination, whether direct or indirect (and there is none here) a difference which is connected with economic factors affecting the efficient carrying on of the employer's business or other activity may well be relevant.

I consider that, read as a whole, the ruling of the European Court [in *Bilka*] would not exclude objectively justified grounds which are other than economic, such as administrative efficiency in a concern not engaged in commerce or business ...

[A] new prosthetic service could never have been established within a reasonable time if [they] had not been offered a scale of remuneration no less favourable than that which they were then enjoying. That was undoubtedly a good and objectively justified ground for offering ... that scale of remuneration.

[As far as paying the women less is concerned] from the administrative point of view it would have been highly anomalous and inconvenient if prosthetists alone ... were to have been subject to a different salary scale and different negotiating machinery ... There is no suggestion that it was unreasonable to place them on the particular point on the Whitley Council scale ... It was not a question of the appellant being paid less than the norm but of [the comparator] being paid more. He was paid more because of the necessity to attract him and other privately employed prosthetists into forming the nucleus of the new service.

Rainey is an important and controversial case. Even though the only beneficiaries were men, it is correctly argued as a case of indirect discrimination; there was no intention to treat women less favourably. It purported to apply an objective standard and carefully analysed the facts in

---

[183] See, also, [1987] AC 224; [1987] 1 All ER 65.

the light of that standard before upholding the defence, yet the outcome was to perpetuate a substantial pay differential. There is no question that the employer's objective was valid, it is probably the case that the men would not have transferred but for the higher payments, so that the means chosen were necessary to achieve the end. It may be that the court accepted the employer's evidence too blithely: they felt that the alleged anomaly was 'easy to see' and that the employer had 'objectively justified administrative reasons'. The case in the end depends on the principle of proportionality: were the means chosen appropriate? On the one hand, the difference was substantial and would last for a substantial period; on the other, all new entrants would be paid at the same rate, it must be right that to pay NHS prosthetists more than other similar NHS employees would be inappropriate. However, to grant courts the task of determining the importance of eliminating discrimination as compared with other valid social objectives will necessarily produce uncertainty.[184]

The *general* operation of market forces cannot be a defence, as the fact of women's lower average pay is the mischief at which the law is aimed. The defence must be confined to situations where it is argued that, in a *particular* job situation, pay levels need to be *above* the rate paid for a job of equal value in order to counteract, for example, staff shortages. It is this approach which leads, for example, to offering higher pay to teachers of mathematics and physics than English and French. The operation of the defence is necessary to prevent other groups of employees comparing themselves with the higher paid group. Employers who seek to use market forces as a defence must, as a minimum, show how they discover the market rate. They must also show that the same criteria are applicable to grades which are predominantly female as well as to grades which are predominantly male. 'An employer who pays 10% above the market rate for all jobs except those mainly occupied by women may be said to be treating the women less favourably on grounds of sex.'[185]

Objective proof from employers is most unlikely to be forthcoming in this kind of case. 'Let us take a defence that a group of men are paid above their assessed value to meet a staff shortage in that job. The legitimate business objective of the differential ... presents no problem. But taken to its logical conclusion, a test requiring the employer to show that the variation in pay ... was in fact reasonably necessary ... would require the employer to show evidence that the purpose had in fact been achieved (that is, the vacancies had been filled) and was not simply still an aspiration; that it was the extra pay for the men's jobs that was responsible for the purpose being achieved and, by implication, that it could not have been achieved had there not been the variation in pay ... Few employers would be able to produce such

---

[184] Davies, P and Freedland, M 'The impact of public law on labour law 1972–97' (1997) 26 Industrial LJ 311, pp 329–34.

[185] 'Market forces and the equal value material factor defence' (1986) 5 EOR 5, p 8.

evidence.'[186] On policy grounds, the test should be less stringent. Given the difficulty in measuring outcomes, the law should be concerned largely with process: how was the decision to utilise market forces reached and implemented? This is especially important as so many payment systems are products of tradition, not rationality. If they are clearly and consciously introduced to deal with a specific problem, that will be strong evidence that they are justifiable. Counterevidence will include the degree of the differential, the numbers affected, its duration, and the extent to which the employer is relying on general labour market inequality between men and women rather than responding to a specific immediate need.

'The system of collective bargaining has a dual role in the determination of gender pay differentials: it provides a form of protection against low pay and is the major vehicle through which changes in gender pay differentials have been achieved; yet it acts to codify and reinforce customary payment practices, including gender pay differentials.'[187] It is clearly no defence for an employer to argue that he had to pay a male bargaining group more than a female group because of the former's greater industrial strength. The employer is responsible for the pay outcome and, just as under the SDA 1975, cannot hide behind discriminatory behaviour or attitudes, direct or indirect, manifested by the workforce. Unions have traditionally been more successful in recruiting men and in serving their interests. There may be no difference of substance between a market forces defence and one based on the operation of collective bargaining. It is unclear when a collective bargaining outcome, jointly negotiated by employer and union, could ever satisfy the defence.[188] It is tentatively suggested that one example might be where the employer operates collective bargaining in one part of the enterprise and, say, job evaluation in another. A successful claim might thus cause stresses and dissatisfaction with the differing pay structures. The difficulty is the extent to which a court will permit any comparison across payment structures. This may depend partly on the degree of occupational segregation within the enterprise and the degree of pay disparity between primarily male and primarily female grades.

Many argue that an important way forward for pay equity is to increase the number of women in trade unions and the coverage of collective bargaining. However, strong and effective bargaining has been associated with the widening of gender differentials.[189] Typically, male workplaces may

---

[186] Op cit, 'Market forces', fn 185, p 12.

[187] Op cit, Rubery and Fagan, fn 117, pt V.

[188] In Royal Copenhagen Case C-400/93 [1995] IRLR 648, the Court held that collective bargaining 'may be taken into account' in determining whether differences in average pay can be explained by objective factors. This approach is less stringent than that adopted in Enderby, but no specific examples were given.

[189] Op cit, Rubery and Fagan, fn 117, p 99.

be easier to organise, and atypical workers, predominantly female, may fall outside the coverage of collective bargaining. On the other hand, women benefit through their over-representation in the public sector as collective bargaining there is both wider in its coverage and more regulatory in its nature, especially where the bargaining is conducted nationally.

Premium and merit payments

We are concerned here with controls over decisions to base pay on individual factors, such as payments based on qualifications, merit or productivity. Like other payment systems, they may operate to the advantage or disadvantage of women, depending on the criteria and the way in which they are operated, and they are most unlikely to be justifiable if any attempt is made to apply the stringent *Bilka* criteria. The advantage for women is that performance within the current job may be recognised and rewarded, and that performance pay may be associated with less emphasis, so far as pay is concerned, on position in a job hierarchy. The disadvantage is clearly that reliance may be placed on subjective criteria and managerial discretion. In addition, performance pay often benefits most those in higher grades, which might widen differentials between average pay of men and women. It may also be used as a signal to attract men, and the emphasis on competition rather than co-operation may also benefit men.[190]

Equal Opportunities Commission Equal Pay Code of Practice Bonus/premium rates/plus elements

29(a) *Problem*

Female and male manual workers receive the same basic pay but only jobs mainly done by men have access to bonus earnings and those mainly done by women do not.

Recommended action

Check the reason why. Does this reflect real differences, for example, in the value of the work or in productivity? Can it be justified objectively on grounds unrelated to sex?

(b) *Problem*

Where shift and overtime work is available and paid at a premium rate, fewer full time women employees have access to this higher rated work.

Recommended action

Check that women and men have equal access to this work and, if not, can it be justified objectively ...

(d) *Problem*

Average female earnings under a variable payment system are lower than average male earnings ...

---

[190] *Op cit*, Rubery and Fagan, fn 117, p 149.

Recommended action

Review the design and operation of the variable payment system. Do these genuinely reflect the demands of the job and the productivity needs of the organisation?

The same rather bland generalisations are reproduced in relation to such matters as why performance pay may be applied largely to employees of one sex, and why women might receive lower average performance ratings than men. The European Commission Code is similar in its lack of detail.

Handels-og Kontorfunktionaerernes Forbund i Danmark v Dansk Arbejdsgiverforening (acting for Danfoss) **Case 109/88 [1989] IRLR 532**[191]

The relevant collective agreement allowed the employer to make additional payments to individuals within a grade on the basis of the employee's 'flexibility', which was defined to including an assessment of their capacity, quality of work, autonomy of work and responsibilities. In addition, pay could be increased on the basis of the employee's vocational training and seniority. The average pay of women was 6.85% less than that of men.

Employees did not actually know what were the criteria for the increases which applied to them and how they were applied. They were only informed of the amount of their increased wages, without being able to determine the effect of each of the criteria for the increases. Those who came within a particular pay grade were, therefore, unable to compare the different components of their pay with those of the pay of their fellow employees within the same grade.

Judgment (pp 536–37):

[W]here an undertaking applies a pay system which is characterised by a total lack of transparency, the burden of proof is on the employer to show that his pay practice is not discriminatory, if a female worker establishes that, by comparison with a relatively high number of employees, the average pay of female workers is lower than that of male workers.

In order to demonstrate that his pay practice is not systematically unfair to female workers, the employer is bound to show how he has applied the incremental criteria, thereby making his pay system transparent.

[A] distinction is to be made according to whether the criterion of flexibility is used to reward the quality of the work carried out by the employee or whether it is used to reward the adaptability of the employee to variable work schedules and places of work.

In the first case, the criterion of flexibility is indisputably totally neutral from the point of view of sex. Where it results in systematic unfairness to female workers, that can only be because the employer has applied it in an abusive manner. It is inconceivable that the work carried out by female workers would

---

[191] See, also, [1989] ECR 3199; [1991] 1 CMLR 8.

be generally of a lower quality. The employer may not therefore justify the use of the criterion of flexibility so defined where its application shows itself to be systematically unfavourable to women.

If it were understood as referring to the adaptability of the worker to variable work schedules and places of work, the criterion of flexibility may also operate to the disadvantage of female workers who ... may have greater difficulty than male workers in organising their working time in a flexible manner.

[To such a result the *Bilka* test applies.]

The employer may justify payments for such adaptability by showing that it is of importance in the performance of the specific duties entrusted to the worker concerned.

[T]he employer may justify rewarding specific vocational training by demonstrating that that training is of importance for the performance of the specific duties entrusted to the worker.

This approach is clearly inconsistent with and preferable to prior English authority. In *Reed Packaging Ltd v Boozer and Everhurst*,[192] hourly paid employees earned more than those on staff grades. It was held that there were 'objectively justified administrative reasons' for the distinction, despite the fact that the majority of hourly paid workers were men. It should be impossible to justify a scheme such as this, which originates in tradition and convenience. If jobs are of equal value, their being placed in different grades may be due to different bargaining structures, or simply to the fact that the employer considered one employee to be more worthy than another. Neither defence can provide objective justification in the face of a finding that jobs are of equal value.

The *Danfoss* approach requires the employer to explain and justify the criteria used to reward individual performance. On the facts, if this led to a lower average pay for women than men that would be clear evidence of discrimination, at least where the numbers were sufficiently large to eliminate the possibility of chance results. Flexibility defined by reference to adaptability, and vocational training, are both potentially justifiable.

Townshend-Smith, R, 'Economic defences to equal pay claims', in Hervey, T and O'Keeffe, D (eds), *Sex Equality Law in the European Union*, 1996, Chichester: John Wiley, p 45:

[T]he employer must show that employees knew the applicable criteria in advance in order to establish a correlation with increased performance. Beyond that, there must be a system for measuring performance which is both objectively and consistently applied, which may cause problems especially in relation to higher level jobs where accurate measurement of performance is often not possible. Employers should be required to produce statistics where

---

[192] [1988] ICR 391; [1988] IRLR 333, EAT. A similar approach based largely on the fact that subjectively there was no intention to discriminate exonerated the employer in *Calder v Rowntree Mackintosh Confectionery Ltd* [1993] ICR 811; [1993] IRLR 212, CA.

these are logically relevant. If it is claimed that productivity would be improved, the methods used for its assessment must be demonstrated. Similarly, the employer should be required to show how, for example, qualifications and work performance, or bonus payments and absenteeism, are linked. To reiterate, this cannot be done at a scientifically satisfactory level of proof, but, where appropriate, the reasonable effort must be made. It is especially important in relation to performance-related pay, which carries an obvious risk that subjectivity may perpetuate gender pay inequalities.

However, if this approach were applied literally, employers would be unable to introduce changes to their payment systems which had an adverse impact until those changes had been shown to be effective in attaining the required purpose. This is to impose an unrealistic, often impossible, standard. Reference to the experience of other employers is neither necessary nor sufficient proof of the causal connection. Employers must be permitted to innovate, without proof of effectiveness, if the possible adverse impact is considered and if it can be shown that the attainment of the objective is a reasonably plausible consequence.

Rubery, J and Fagan, C, *Social Europe: Wage Determination and Sex Segregation in Employment in the European Community*, 1993, Luxembourg: Office for Official Publications of the European Communities, p 43:

It may ... be possible to state, as an argument against its introduction, that performance-related pay causes the pay structure to become opaque: the pay structure may therefore be protected from an examination as to whether the principle of equal value has been implemented ... It is, however, much more difficult to argue that a firm must adopt a detailed job evaluation system and detailed pay grading by job in order to implement equal value, if it is at the same time moving towards more flexible deployment of labour. Equally, it is difficult to maintain that a firm should not relate pay to the qualifications of its employees and only to their current jobs, when it wishes to encourage employees to acquire qualifications.

Red-circle cases

The *principle* of what has come to be known as red-circling is entirely fair. It is commonplace that a person who, for example, is unable to continue with a job for reasons of illness or redundancy, but for whom there is an alternative job in the workplace, nevertheless continues to be paid at the old rate so that no reduction in pay is experienced. Furthermore, it is normal for the 'red-circled' employee, at least in sickness cases, to receive the pay increases that would have been received in the old job had that been continuing. A particular problem with the practice from an equal pay perspective is that a successful claim of equality with a red-circled employee may lead to a substantial increase for the applicant, and consequential claims from those on like work or work of equal value with that applicant, claims which may undermine a whole pay structure. Red-circling may be good industrial relations, but it could never be described as necessary in the sense required to satisfy the *Bilka* test; it is sufficiently commonplace that it will not be automatically outlawed even where there is an adverse impact on women, such as where the majority of those whose wages are protected in a redundancy situation are men.

It must be shown that the employee received the higher rate because he had been red-circled and not because it was the rate for the job. This may be problematic where some jobs have a tradition of being filled by those who, for health reasons, are unable to continue in their old job.[193] It should also be permissible for an applicant to argue that she is doing like work or work of equal value with the job the comparator would have been doing but for the red circle. This may be important if there is no other potential comparator, though comparing the value of the applicant's job which has disappeared through redundancy may not be straightforward.[194]

Like any other pay practice, there must be no direct discrimination in the way in which it operates.

Snoxell v Vauxhall Motors Ltd; Charles Early and Marriott (Witney) Ltd v Smith and Ball [1977] IRLR 123, EAT[195]

In the first case a male warehouseman was transferred to the lesser paid job of ticket writer. In the second case, the employers had graded men and women on separate wage scales, but in 1970 they reorganised their pay structure, and machine part inspectors in a protected all-male grade were red-circled. No women had been in the protected grade and no women were red-circled.

In both cases the defence failed.

Phillips J (pp 126–29):

[I]t is relevant to consider: whether the red-circling is permanent or temporary, being phased out; whether the origin of the anomaly enshrined in the red-circling is to be found in sex discrimination; whether the group of red-circled employees is a closed group; whether the red-circling has been the subject of negotiations with the representatives of the workpeople, and the views of the women taken into account; or whether the women are equally with the men able to transfer between grades.

[The argument is that] although the immediate cause of the discrimination lay in the fact that the male inspectors were red-circled whereas [the applicants] were not, and although they were red-circled to preserve their status for reasons unconnected with sex, it was necessary to look to see why [the applicants] were not also within the red circle. The answer was that, because they were women, they were not able to enter grade X2, and so did not qualify.

---

[193] *Methven and Musiolik v Cow Industrial Polymers Ltd* [1979] ICR 613; [1979] IRLR 276, EAT; [1980] ICR 463; [1980] IRLR 289, CA.

[194] As this is not a claim of current equal value, it would be more appropriate for the tribunal to resolve the claim directly rather than refer it to an independent expert; there may not even be power to do the latter.

[195] See, also, [1978] 1 QB 11; [1977] 3 All ER 770.

[T]he employer can never establish ... that the variation ... is genuinely due to a material difference ... when it can be said that past sex discrimination has contributed to the variation.

Does it make any difference that the red-circling is continued, even continued indefinitely? In principle, we do not see why it should. Assuming that there are no additional factors, and that in other respects affairs are operated on a unisex, non-discriminatory basis, the situation will continue to be that the variation is genuinely due to a material difference other then the difference of sex. The red circle will persist, ageing and wasting until eventually it vanishes.

The defence failed because the history of discrimination prevented women from having access to the red-circled grade. However, the defence should be satisfied if the employer's criteria for red-circling have no adverse impact on female grades.

But this relaxed approach to the defence is problematic where the reason for the red-circling is pay protection following downgrading by a job evaluation scheme. It is not uncommon to protect the pay of those downgraded by keeping them at the same pay, awarding no annual increases, until the pay of the grade they should be on has caught up. This is done to make the job evaluation exercise more acceptable to the employees and the unions. In principle, this should never be a defence. The red circle has its origin in discrimination, albeit perhaps not direct discrimination, and it is no defence to an employer that he was forced or persuaded to discriminate by the union or the employees. Nevertheless, if this defence is never to be allowed in any circumstances, it has the potential to act as a significant deterrent which may dissuade employers from conducting job evaluation. On the other hand, especially where turnover is low, it may in practice perpetuate the very inequality the evaluation was designed to remove. Sometimes an additional policy is adopted, whereby the employer awards pay increases in stages to those who would otherwise have received a substantial pay increase through regrading. It is contended that this is never justifiable, though the chances of a female applicant who will have received some sort of pay increase being willing, in effect, to sue for more, are not high, especially as the union may well have been partly instrumental in the staging of the increases and so be unwilling to assist with such a claim.

Snoxell and *Outlook Supplies v Parry*[196] make it clear that there is no rule requiring the elimination of a red circle as soon as is practicable, though its duration is an element in the decision on its acceptability. It is especially problematic where the beneficiaries receive pay increases which would have been received had they continued in their old job. If there is no discrimination in such a policy apart from the fact that the applicant is receiving lower pay than a man on like work or work of equal value, the employer should have

---

[196] [1978] ICR 388; [1978] IRLR 12, EAT.

the burden of establishing that giving the increases in this manner accorded with good industrial relations practice.

EQUAL PAY REMEDIES

Section 2(4) of the Equal Pay Act provides that '[n]o claim ... shall be referred to an employment tribunal ... if [the woman] has not been employed in the same employment within six months preceding the date of the reference'. Section 2(5) of the Equal Pay Act provides that a woman 'shall not be entitled ... to be awarded any payment by way of arrears of remuneration or damage in respect of a time earlier than two years before the date on which the date on which the proceedings were instituted'. The question has arisen of the compatibility with European law of both of these domestic rules. The normal rule of European law is that *national* rules of procedure and limitation apply to cases based on Community law.[197] However, there is a crucial exception where the effect of such domestic rules is to make it impossible in practice to exercise Community law rights. This exception has been used to challenge the validity both of the six month limitation period and the two year back pay restriction, especially, but not only, in the context of decisions holding that it was unlawful to exclude part time workers from membership or full membership of pension schemes on the same basis as full time workers.[198]

In *Preston v Wolverhampton Healthcare NHS Trust*,[199] the House of Lords had to consider the effect of the above rules on the pension rights of some 60,000 employees. In addition, the House held that, under s 2(4), a claim had to be commenced within six months of the termination of any particular contract to which an equal pay claim related. The effect was that, where an employee was employed on a succession of fixed term or temporary contracts, equal pay claims would have to be brought separately in respect of each separate contract. Unlike the general law of continuity of employment, therefore, the employee may lose rights owing to a break in continuity, the significance of which the employee may have been unaware. The disadvantage and unfairness of this construction is such that it is clearly arguable that it operates to frustrate the effectiveness of rights under European law. The House therefore referred the issue of the compatibility of s 2(4) with Art 119 for resolution by the European Court of Justice.

Two further arguments were put by the appellants in *Preston*. In *Emmott v Ministry of Social Welfare and AG*,[200] it was held that time limits are not

---

[197] *Rewe-Zentralfinanz Eg v Landwirtschaftshammer für das Saarland* Case 33/76 [1976] ECR 1989.

[198] See below, pp 486–99.

[199] [1998] 1 All ER 528; [1998] IRLR 197, HL.

[200] Case C-208/90 [1991] ECR I-4629; [1991] IRLR 387.

unreasonable if they are no less favourable than those relating to similar actions under domestic law. The Court of Appeal held in *Preston* that six months was the appropriate period for claims brought under Art 119, and that it could not be said that the period was too short to enable the right to be effectively exercised. The gist of the claim was not so much that such a period was in itself inappropriate, but rather when in this case should the period be deemed to commence. It is this issue which has potentially far-reaching consequences so far as retrospective membership of pension schemes was concerned. The applicants contended that it started in May 1995, which was the date that English domestic law first provided a remedy for someone who had been unlawfully excluded from membership of an occupational pension scheme. The defendants countered that time started to run in 1986, which, according to the European Court in *Vroege*[201] and *Fisscher*,[202] was the date the law was made clear by the judgment in *Bilka*. The fact that no one was aware at the time of the breach which gave rise to the potential remedy did not mean that enforcement of Community law was at that time impossible. The limitation period did not commence only upon awareness of the breach in question.[203] The reason for the holding, of course, is the complexity and expense which would be entailed in granting retrospective rights to become a member of an occupational pension scheme. The House of Lords in *Preston*, however, decided that *Magorrian and Cunningham v Eastern Health and Social Services Board*,[204] a case on retrospective *membership* of pension schemes, had placed the issue in sufficient doubt that reference to the European Court was necessary.

Biggs v Somerset County Council[205] concerned a similar issue, that of the limitation period for an unfair dismissal claim, which under domestic law is normally three months. The *Equal Opportunities Commission* case decided that the exclusion of part time workers from the right to claim unfair dismissal contravened Art 119. The applicant, who was dismissed in 1976, nevertheless contended that time only began to run when that decision was handed down. The Court of Appeal rejected the submission, holding that the judgment of the House of Lords had simply declared what the law had always been and thus

---

[201] *Vroege v NCIV Institut voor Volkshuisvesting BV and Stichting Pensioenfonds NCIV* Case C-57/93 [1994] ECR I-4541; [1995] ICR 635; [1994] IRLR 65.

[202] *Fisscher v Voorhuis Hengelo BV and Stichting Bedrijfspensioenfonds voor de Detailhandel* Case C-128/93 [1994] ECR I-4583; [1995] ICR 635; [1994] IRLR 662.

[203] The court also held that the applicants were unable to rely on the proviso in *Emmott* that a 'State is not able, in contending that a claim is time barred, to rely on its own failure to implement properly the requirements of Community law'. In that case, time only begins to run when the State has properly implemented Community law. Technically, this applies to failure to implement a directive, and not to a Treaty provision, and it is limited to claims where the State is defendant.

[204] Case C-249/96 [1998] IRLR 86.

[205] [1996] ICR 364; [1996] 2 All ER 234; [1996] IRLR 203, CA, criticised by Hervey, T and Rostant, P (1998) 3 IJDL 68.

there was no legal reason why a claim should not have been initiated within three months of her dismissal in 1976. While the claim was not against the State, it was the State which was responsible for the fact that applicants were misled as to the true legal position, and there was a case for applying *Emmott* by analogy, even though the claim concerned a Treaty provision rather than a Directive. The applicant was hamstrung by previous authority that the Equal Pay Directive conferred no rights additional to those conferred by Art 119 itself.[206]

The claim in *Biggs* remained a domestic law claim with no direct parallel in European equality legislation. It followed that it was governed by the provision that the Industrial Tribunal only had jurisdiction to hear a complaint out of time if it was not reasonably practicable for the claim to have been brought within the statutory time limit. The equivalent provision in the SDA 1975 merely requires that it be 'just and equitable' to extend the limit. *British Coal Corporation v Keeble*[207] concerned a voluntary redundancy scheme which was thought to be lawful when implemented in 1989, but which turned out to be unlawful in the light of *Barber* the following year. It was held to be just and equitable to allow the claim to be commenced when the effect of *Barber* was appreciated. Under the Equal Pay Act 1970 there is no discretion to extend the six month limitation period, so the solution adopted in *Keeble* was unavailable in *Preston*.

The second issue concerns the extent of the available remedy. The effect of the equality clause is to bring about future pay equality; this issue therefore concerns the applicant's entitlement for past failure to be granted equality. It was held in *Marshall (No 2)*[208] that s 6 of the Equal Treatment Directive requires that compensation shall be adequate and effective as a deterrent. It is arguable that, by analogy, a restriction to two years' back pay falls foul of the *Marshall* reasoning. On the other hand, in social security cases, equivalent limitations have been held to be compatible with Community law.[209]

The argument centres on whether s 2(5) is better viewed as a limit on damages or a time limit on the retrospective effect of a claim. If the former, it contravenes *Marshall (No 2)*; if the latter, it is compatible with *Johnson (No 2)*. In *Preston*, both the EAT and the Court of Appeal were clear that the latter was the appropriate analogy. However, in *Levez v TH Jennings (Harlow Pools)*

---

206 By the same 'logic', a part time employee who initiated and then withdrew a claim for a redundancy payment having been advised that she did not have sufficient hours of service was held to be unable to reopen her claim when the true legal position became known. *Barber v Staffordshire County Council* [1996] IRLR 209, CA.

207 [1997] IRLR 336, EAT.

208 *Marshall v Southampton and South West Hampshire AHA* Case C-271/91 [1993] ECR I-4367; [1994] AC 530; [1993] CMLR 293; [1993] IRLR 445.

209 *Steenhorst-Neerings v Bestuur van der Bedrijfsverereniging* Case C-338/91 [1993] ECR I-5475; [1994] IRLR 244; *Johnson v Chief Adjudication Officer (No 2)* Case C-410/92 [1994] ECR I-5483; [1995] ICR 375; [1995] IRLR 157; discussed by de Burca, G (1995) 1 IJDL 185.

Ltd,[210] the lay members of the EAT, over the dissent of Mummery J (who took the same view as he had in *Preston*), considered that, as the mechanism of the equality clause is a contractual mechanism, the appropriate analogies are with claims for back pay arising from a breach of contract or claims under the SDA 1975 or the RRA 1976. In consequence, the issue was referred to the European Court.[211] In the light of this reference, and in the light of the prior decision of the European Court in *Magorrian*, it was clearly appropriate for House of Lords in *Preston* to refer effectively the same issue to the European Court.

CONCLUSION: THE FUTURE FOR EQUAL PAY LAW[212]

At certain points we have identified specific weaknesses with current equal pay law, especially the way in which equal value law operates in practice. Change in these areas is needed, but such changes would leave the basic framework untouched. To argue for more fundamental changes requires consideration of their purpose, whether to improve the lot of the low paid generally or to attempt to ensure that the concept of equal pay for work of equal value has a real impact on the way pay structures are determined. To achieve the latter outcome, a combination of legal remedies with Codes of Practice may be required, though it is far less easy to produce effective and meaningful Codes on pay than on other aspects of equality. To an extent, the approach taken to avoid discrimination in recruitment will be applicable in any recruitment situation. The same is not true of pay systems, which are both more variable and more complex. In consequence, the Codes recently prepared by the EOC and the European Commission are in rather general and aspirational terms. It remains to be seen the extent to which they will influence the behaviour of employers and tribunals.

The most serious defects of current equal pay law are, first, its failure to recognise the collective element in pay determination and, secondly, the fact that employers may wait for a claim to be brought rather than being under an obligation to take positive steps in the direction of equal value. As the legislation in force in Ontario purports to deal with both these issues, it provides a possible model for future British developments.

---

[210] [1996] IRLR 499.

[211] It has been argued that there is no logical distinction between discrimination in dismissal and discrimination in pay, and that social security cases arguably raise different considerations because they involve issues of government funding of schemes, an issue irrelevant to *Levez*. See (1996) 69 EOR 56.

[212] See, also, McColgan, A, *Just Wages for Women*, 1997, Oxford: Clarendon.

McColgan, A, 'Legislating equal pay: lessons from Canada' (1993) 22 Industrial LJ 269, pp 273–77, 283:

The aim of Ontario's legislation is far from unique. What differentiates it from legislation in the UK and in the rest of Europe is the method chosen to achieve that aim. Rather than ... leaving it to individual employees to complain of perceived wage inequalities, the Act goes a step further and obliges employers to take the initiative in eliminating sex-based wage differentials. Employers are required to determine the relative value of female and male 'job classes' within each 'establishment' and to correct any disparity between female and male job classes of equal or comparable value, unless the disparity is shown to result from one of a number of permissible factors, such as a formal non-discriminatory seniority system or a skills shortage in a particular area. A 'job class' is defined as 'those positions ... that have similar duties and responsibilities and require similar qualifications, are filled by similar recruiting procedures, and have the same compensation schedule, salary grade or range of salary grades'. A job class is 'female' where 60% or more of its incumbents are female or where it has been designated 'female' by the employer, through collective bargaining or by the Pay Equity Commission. Gender predominance may also be determined by reference to the historical incumbency and gender stereotype of work ...

Once a suitable job comparison system has been chosen and applied, the Act requires that public employers and private employers of 100 or more workers post a 'pay equity plan' for the establishment or, where one or more unions are recognised, for each bargaining unit within the establishment and for the non-unionised workforce. The plans must describe the comparison system chosen and its application to the job classes covered by the pay equity plan, and detail the pay equity adjustments to be made, together with a timetable for necessary wage adjustments in accordance with the Act. No more than 1% of the previous year's payroll need be spent on pay equity adjustments in any year, although the adjustments must be continued until each female job class has the same job rate as that of its chosen comparator ...

The potential of Ontario's legislation lies in its effective reversal of the burden of proving discrimination. Rather than encouraging employers to ignore issues of equal pay save in the unlikely event of an individual's complaint, the Pay Equity Act obliges them, in co-operation with any bargaining agent, to scrutinise their own pay practices for evidence of discrimination and eliminate it. The success of the Act, then, must depend in the first instance upon the good faith of the employers and the strength and commitment to pay equity of any bargaining agent, and thereafter upon the effectiveness of any enforcement mechanisms ... The legislation takes a 'self-managed' approach, providing for intervention by the Commission generally only upon the request of one of the parties. This approach is most apparent in the failure of the legislation to provide for the systematic monitoring of pay equity plans, making it possible that many employers who claim to have 'done' pay equity are in fact very far from having eradicated the effects of gender discrimination on their compensation practices. The 'self-management' ethos is perhaps one of the reasons why the impact of pay equity in Ontario has been rather more in the nature of a whimper than a bang ...

There is a strong argument ... for legislation to support unions in bargaining for better pay for women, and to prod into action those unions which might otherwise not place pay equity high on their bargaining agenda. Even unions which are committed to improving women's pay have to deal with the conflict thrown up by male members who fear that such an improvement will damage their own earnings. The potentially inflationary effects of equalising men's and women's pay are enormous, the relatively low costs of the legislation in Ontario being proof of the inadequacies of the Pay Equity Act rather than of the possibility of achieving true pay parity without a significant increase in the wage bill. Employers in the UK are unlikely to capitulate readily to union demands for action unless those demands have strong legislative backing. The cost of achieving equal pay cannot be viewed as a valid argument against it, but renders legislation necessary. To use an argument borrowed from one leading proponent of pay equity: 'If one were honestly to believe economists and employers who cry out that equal value will be disastrous for the economy, causing inflation and widespread unemployment, then it appears that the ongoing health of the Canadian economy depends mainly on the exploitation of working women ... I cannot think of any other area of human rights legislation where it is a legitimate point of discussion to debate whether society can afford the costs of eliminating discrimination.'

No one knows the true cost of a full commitment to equal value principles. Even if a legislative commitment to such equality were introduced, other factors may militate against a significant reduction in the male/female pay gap.

Rubery, J and Fagan, C, *Social Europe: Wage Determination and Sex Segregation in Employment in the European Community,* **1993, Luxembourg: Office for Official Publications of the European Communities, p 43:**

The principle of equal value requires a systematic evaluation of jobs, a removal of systematic gender bias in the evaluation of jobs and greater integration of pay structures between and within organisations. Some of the problems in Britain in the implementation of these principles arise from the general movement in institutions away from these principles to more fragmented pay between organisations and between workers within organisations. Other problems relate to the fact that, in some societies or organisations, pay determination based on training, qualifications, or potential skill might be considered to be as valid as payment according to current job content; however, where there are gender differences in the acquisition of training, experience and qualifications, such systems may in fact be used to evade the implications of the equal value principle. Until, or unless, there is institutional or legal change, the only effective way of implementing equal value within a specific organisation may be to engage in detailed job evaluation. This is the conclusion that unions have tended to reach in Britain and the USA, despite all the inherent problems of job evaluation and despite the fact that there are many other ways in which pay structures can be formulated.

Given the inevitable problems involved in the effective use of the law, can voluntary Codes of Practice be expected to contribute to reducing the pay gap? Here again, proactive steps are needed; whether employers can be encouraged or persuaded to take the steps which the Equal Opportunities Commission would like to see must be regarded as dubious.

EOC Code of Practice on Equal Pay
Review of pay systems for sex bias

25(a) Pay arrangements are frequently complicated and the features which can give rise to sex discrimination are not always obvious. Although pay systems reviews are not required by law, they are recommended as the most appropriate method of ensuring that a pay system delivers equal pay free from sex bias.

(b) A pay systems review also provides an opportunity to investigate the amount of information employees receive about their pay. Pay systems should be clear and easy to understand. Where they are not and where pay differentials exist, these may be inferred to be due to sex discrimination ...

(c) The Equal Opportunities Commission recommends that a pay systems review should involve the following stages:

Stage 1

Undertake a thorough analysis of the pay system to produce a breakdown of all employees, which covers, for example, job title, grade, whether part time or full time, with basic pay, performance ratings and all other elements of remuneration.

Stage 2

Examine each element of the pay system against the data obtained in stage 1.

Stage 3

Identify any elements of the pay system which the review indicates may be the source of any discrimination.

Stage 4

Change any rules or practices including those in collective agreements which stages 1 to 3 have identified as likely to give rise to discrimination in pay. It is recommended that this should be done in consultation with employees, trade unions or staff representatives where appropriate. Stages 1 to 3 may reveal that practices and procedures in relation to recruitment, selection and access to training have contributed to discrimination in pay; in that event, these matters should also be addressed.

Stage 5

Analyse the likely effects of any proposed changes in practice to the pay system before implementation, to identify and rectify any discrimination which could be caused.

Stage 6

Give equal pay to current employees. Where the review shows that some employees are not receiving equal pay for equal work and the reasons cannot be shown to be free of sex bias, then a plan must be developed for dealing with this.

Stage 7

Set up a system of regular monitoring to allow checks to be made to pay practices.

Stage 8

Draw up and publish an equal pay policy with provision for assessing the new pay system or modification to a system in terms of sex discrimination. Also, in the interests of transparency provide pay information ... where this is not already usual practice.

Finally, it should be remembered that pay is only one aspect of gender inequality; the jobs that women do and their position in the hierarchy are equally significant. Real change requires these different aspects to be confronted in a coherent overall strategy.

Rubery, J and Fagan, C, *Social Europe: Wage Determination and Sex Segregation in Employment in the European Community*, 1993, Luxembourg: Office for Official Publications of the European Communities, pp 151, 192:

[N]either performance nor seniority pay, even if it operates according to non-discriminatory principles, can be regarded as full substitutes for promotion, as they provide the pay but without the status and visibility attached to higher level job positions. What is required for the implementation of equal value is a three pronged approach to the creation of better promotion opportunities: the creation of more rungs in the job ladder in feminised areas; the development of promotion opportunities linked to skills, experience or expertise and not necessarily to an hierarchical authority structure; and policies to reduce discrimination in the promotion of women to higher level jobs ...

[T]here are two separate influences on pay levels: position in the occupational and skill hierarchy and the characteristics of the industry or organisation in which the job is located. Traditional positive action programmes for women have tended to concentrate on the former issue, that of moving women up the skills hierarchy. Equal value programmes have concentrated on changing the hierarchy of skills within organisations. However, the analysis of the institutional system of wage determination suggests that the impact of the industry or organisation on the level of pay should not be neglected. Improving women's position within the skill hierarchy, either by desegregation or by raising the evaluation of women's jobs, will not be effective in closing the gender pay gap if women are disproportionately represented in low paying industries or in unregulated and low paying organisations. Closing the gender pay gap will depend on three factors: moving women up within the skills and jobs hierarchy; changing the position of women's jobs within the hierarchy; and ensuring that these gains are not offset by widening differentials and changing wage structures.

CHAPTER 13

RETIREMENT AND PENSIONS

INTRODUCTION

Pensions law is exceedingly complex but of fundamental importance in relation to issues of equality and to the more general issue of maintaining a proper standard of living for the growing proportion of the population which has ceased to work. For many years, it was conventional in the UK for men to retire at 65 and women to retire at 60. The original Sex Discrimination Act adopted the conservative stance of not wishing to upset these traditional arrangements, and thus s 6(4) permitted discrimination 'in relation to death or retirement'. The Court of Appeal in *Garland v British Rail Engineering Ltd*[1] held that the section should be interpreted widely, and consequently any discrimination in pension provision and retirement ages continued to be lawful despite the SDA 1975.

The fact that women conventionally retired earlier than men was perhaps slightly curious given that women, on average, live longer than men. It followed that women would, on average, be contributing towards pension provision for a shorter period and yet receiving benefits for a longer period than men. As a result, on average, it costs more to provide the same periodic pension for women than for men. In the same way, schemes which accumulate a capital sum which is used on retirement to purchase an annuity which will cover the period between retirement and death will, if averages are used, necessarily lead to a man's annuity being larger than a woman's. This use of average behaviour goes against the general thrust of the Sex Discrimination Act.[2] It is, however, fundamental and essential to the operation of any pension scheme, for the amount of contributions which must be collected depends on an actuarial assessment of the amount of benefits which must one day be paid out, which in turn depends on the average life expectancy of the beneficiaries under the scheme. There is, however, no *logical* need for a scheme to differentiate between men and women; it might be equally rational to differentiate, say, between smokers and non-smokers. The attraction of differentiation by gender is that it is cheap and, unlike smoking, for example, cannot be faked and does not normally change over time.

---

1   [1979] ICR 558; [1979] IRLR 244. The case subsequently went to the European Court, Case 12/81 [1982] ECR 359; [1983] 2 AC 751; [1982] 2 All ER 402; [1982] IRLR 11.

2   SDA 1975, s 45, permits insurance companies to quote different rates for men and women, provided that these derived from appropriate and commonly used statistics.

There are also difficulties in determining what is meant by equality. To allow a woman to retire earlier than a man may look like discrimination against the man; to *require* her to retire at 60 where a man may work until 65 and thus, among other things, earn a higher pension, may look like discrimination against her.[3] In practice, because so many people nowadays take early retirement, the terms of which will be more beneficial the closer to pension age at which it occurs, increasing women's pension age from 60 to 65 will disadvantage large numbers of women.

Pension arrangements in the UK are divided between occupational pensions and the State retirement pension scheme. Every employee is entitled to a flat rate State pension on reaching retirement age.[4] For employees who are not members of an occupational scheme, the State Earnings Related Pension Scheme (SERPS) provides additional benefits. Occupational schemes, however, require the approval of the Occupational Pensions Board, and in that sense even a private-sector scheme requires an element of State authorisation. The existence of an occupational pension scheme means that SERPS no longer applies, as approval is conditional on providing benefits at least as beneficial as those under SERPS, and in practice the benefits provided are likely to be substantially superior.[5]

The conservative, non-interventionist stance of the original SDA 1975 has been totally transformed and swept aside by EC law. The current law remains in some aspects problematic, as regards the precise legal rules currently in place, as regards the procedures to enforce them, and as regards the extent to which they will bring a substantial improvement in the financial position of women – and maybe some men – post-retirement.[6]

---

[3] 'Soaring unemployment and compulsory early retirement has meant that the lower pension age for women has come to be seen as a coveted advantage. Currently, as many as 43% of men and 68% of women have already retired by the age of 60. Pension age crucially affects the terms of such retirement: redundancy within sight of pension age usually attracts a more advantageous package than a redundancy earlier on in a worker's life.' Fredman, S, 'The poverty of equality: pensions and the ECJ' (1996) 25 Industrial LJ 91, p 96.

[4] For the ways in which the assumption of men as workers and women as dependants led to the State scheme operating to women's disadvantage, see Fredman, S, *Women and the Law*, 1997, Oxford: Clarendon, pp 336–39.

[5] There are two types of occupational pension scheme. In final salary schemes, the level of pension is normally a defined fraction of the final salary, such as one-sixtieth or one-eightieth, for each year of service. In money purchase schemes, the contributions are put into a fund which is used, on retirement, to purchase an annuity. Both types of schemes may be contributory, where the fund is built up from contributions from both employer and employee, or non-contributory, where the employer provides the whole income for the scheme.

[6] The changes wrought by European law have in many respects been consolidated by the Pensions Act 1995, though the primary purpose of this act was to reform the general operation of pensions law in the light of the Maxwell scandal.

RETIREMENT AGE

Marshall v Southampton and South West Hampshire AHA (Teaching) Case
152/84 [1986] IRLR 140[7]

This was a straightforward allegation that to require women to retire at 60
whereas men could work until 65 contravened the Equal Treatment
Directive,[8] even though it was clearly permitted by the SDA 1975. The case
concerned the dismissal as such rather than the financial consequences of that
dismissal such as pensions. The defence was that such a differentiation
depended on the difference in State pension age which continued to be lawful
under the Social Security Directive.[9]

Judgment (p 148):

The Court observes in the first place that the question ... does not concern
access to a statutory or occupational retirement scheme, that is to say the
conditions for payment of an old age or retirement pension, but the fixing of an
age limit with regard to the termination of employment pursuant to a general
policy concerning dismissal. The question therefore relates to the conditions
governing dismissal and falls to be considered under Council Directive 76/207
EEC.

[A]n age limit for the compulsory dismissal of workers pursuant to an
employer's general policy concerning retirement falls within the term
'dismissal' ... even if the dismissal involves the grant of a retirement pension ...

[I]n view of the fundamental importance of the principle of equal treatment ...
Art 1(2) of Directive No 76/207, which excludes social security from the scope
of that Directive, must be interpreted strictly. Consequently, the exception to
the prohibition of discrimination on grounds of sex provided for in Art 7(1)(a)
of Directive No 79/7 applies only to the determination of pensionable age for
the purposes of granting old age and retirement pensions ...

[W]hereas the exception contained in Art 7 of Directive No 79/7 concerns the
consequences which pensionable age has for social security benefits, this case
is concerned with dismissal within the meaning of Art 5 of Directive No
76/207.

[A] general policy concerning dismissal involving the dismissal of a woman
solely because she has attained the qualifying age for a State pension, which
age is different under national legislation for men and for women, constitutes
discrimination on grounds of sex ...[10]

Had the facts been treated as a matter of social security, the discrimination
would have been permissible. It was the construction of the situation as

---

7   See, also, [1986] ECR 723; [1986] 1 QB 401; [1986] ICR 335.
8   Directive 76/207/EEC, OJ L39/40, 1976.
9   Directive 79/7/EEC, OJ L6/24, 1979.
10 See, also, *Beets-Proper v Van Lanschot Bankiers NV* Case 262/84 [1986] 2 ECR 773; [1986]
ICR 706.

concerning working conditions that brought the case within the Equal Treatment Directive. In British terms, the consequence of that decision was the Sex Discrimination Act 1986, as a result of which it is now unlawful to discriminate against a woman in relation to retirement with regard to access to opportunities for promotion, transfer or training, or by subjecting her to any detriment, demotion, or dismissal. The employer is no longer permitted, therefore, to discriminate in relation to employment on the basis of retirement age. This is true even though the State retirement provision is still based on a man retiring at 65 and a woman at 60. The Government has opted to equalise the State pension age at 65 by the year 2025;[11] this will mean that women who would previously have retired at 60 will take substantially less by way of pension than would formerly have been the case.

PENSION PROVISION

The main legal issues which need to be addressed are as follows:

(a) To what extent do pension arrangements constitute 'pay' within the meaning of Art 119 of the Treaty of Rome and to what extent may pension provision be outside the scope of Art 119 and governed by the Social Security Directive?

(b) If pensions constitute pay, do the rules governing equality in pension schemes apply only to employer and employee, or will they apply to others, such as the employee's spouse, and the scheme trustees, who may be affected by the operation and administration of the scheme?

(c) If pensions are in principle within the scope of equality law, which discrimination is prohibited? In particular, does the law apply to access to schemes and to benefits under schemes?

(d) Given that for many years it has been the accepted practice that differentiation between men and women was permissible in relation to pension provision, a belief which was fortified by the provisions of the Occupational Social Security Directive,[12] should there be transitional arrangements before full equality becomes mandatory?

(e) How should the law deal with the issue of equality so far as pensionable age – as opposed to retirement age – is concerned and should it continue to be permissible to take account of the fact that, on average, women live longer than men?

---

[11] *Equality in State Pension Age*, White Paper, Cm 2420, 1993, London: HMSO.

[12] Directive 86/378/EEC, OJ L225/40, 1986. This directive was subsequently amended by Directive 96/97/EEC, OJ C218/5, 1997.

(e) What remedies should be available for the failure to provide past equality in pensions?

Are pensions pay?

Article 119 provides that 'pay' is 'the ordinary minimum wage or salary and any other consideration which the worker receives, directly or indirectly, in respect of his employment from his employer'. In the context of pension provision, the wording has received an extremely broad interpretation, an interpretation which has been the basis of the dramatic changes in the law wrought by the European Court.

Bilka-Kaufhaus v Weber von Hartz **Case 170/84 [1986] IRLR 317**[13]

Under the company's occupational scheme, part time employees could obtain pensions only if they had worked full time for 15 out of a total period of 20 years. The claim was that to differentiate in this way was indirectly discriminatory against women. Breach of Art 119 could only be established if the employer's pension arrangements fell within the definition of 'pay'.

Judgment (pp 319–21):

In *Defrenne v Belgium* [Case 80/70 [1971] ECR 445 the Court took] the view that, although pay within the meaning of Art 119 could in principle include social security benefits, it did not include social security schemes or benefits, in particular retirement pensions, directly governed by legislation which do not involve any element of agreement within the undertaking or trade concerned and are compulsory for general categories of workers. [The contributions to such a scheme are] determined less by the employment relationship between the employer and the worker than by considerations of social policy, so that the employer's contribution cannot be regarded as a direct or indirect payment to the worker ...[14]

[T]he occupational pension scheme at issue [here], although adopted in accordance with the provisions laid down by German legislation for such schemes, is based on an agreement between Bilka and the staff committee representing its employees and has the effect of supplementing the social benefits paid under national legislation of general application with benefits financed entirely by the employer ... Benefits paid to employees under the scheme therefore constitute consideration received by the worker from the employer in respect of his employment, as referred to in the second paragraph of Art 119.

[The Court went on to hold that the exclusion of part time workers was indirectly discriminatory against women, and to lay down criteria against which national courts should judge whether such policy could be justified.]

---

[13] See, also, [1986] ECR 1607; [1986] 2 CMLR 701; [1987] ICR 110.

[14] In *Defrenne v Belgium*, entitlement did not depend on the particular employment, and benefit did not depend on the level of employer contributions.

[The applicant also argued] that the disadvantages suffered by women because of the exclusion of part time workers ... must at least be mitigated by requiring the employer to regard periods during which women workers have had to meet family responsibilities as periods of full time work.

[T]he scope of Art 119 is restricted to questions of pay discrimination between men and women. Problems relating to other conditions of work and employment, on the other hand, are covered generally by other provisions of Community law ... with a view to the harmonisation of the social systems of Member States and the approximation of their legislation in that area.

The imposition of an obligation such as that envisaged ... goes beyond the scope of Art 119 and has no other basis in Community law as it now stands.[15]

What is critical about this case is that denial of *access to* the pension scheme is held to be pay discrimination by treating it as equivalent to discriminatory *benefits under* the scheme.[16] The case decides that, in principle, Art 119 may be applicable to occupational pension schemes. The exclusion of part time employees will normally be unlawful, at least where the number of hours worked per week is substantial.[17] But qualification rules for pension schemes will be subject to the normal rules concerning justification of an indirectly discriminatory practice. Assuming that they will have a disparate impact – which is by no means self-evident – the employer may have to justify, for example, requiring employees to work for a year to qualify for a pension scheme, or excluding temporary and fixed term workers. In no sense does the case establish a universal right to join a pension scheme. Nor is an employer required to extend pension provision to all grades of employee, even if the lower grades are predominantly female. In fact, it is arguable that *Bilka* might encourage employers to abandon pension provision for lower grade employees where a substantial proportion of such employees work part time. High turnover might well be accepted as a justification for not establishing pension provision for particular grades, and high turnover is associated with lower grade employment.

---

[15] In response to this, Fredman, *op cit*, fn 3, p 110, observes that 'structural considerations such as the division of labour within the family are explicitly disregarded. The refusal to neutralise the effects of breaks in continuity of employment leaves uncorrected a crucial factor contributing towards women's disadvantage in old age'.

[16] See, also, *Worringham v Lloyds Bank Ltd* Case 69/80 [1981] ECR 767; [1981] ICR 558; [1981] IRLR 178; *Liefting v Directie van het Academish Ziekenhuis* Case 23/83 [1984] ECR 3225.

[17] The reasoning in *R v Secretary of State for Employment ex p Equal Opportunities Commission* [1994] ICR 317; [1995] AC 1; [1994] 1 All ER 910; [1994] IRLR 176, HL, might suggest that an eight hour threshold would not be regarded as too high. *Dietz v Stichting Thuiszorg Rotterdam* Case C-435/93 [1996] IRLR 692 concerned a claim for retroactive membership of a scheme by a female cleaner who had worked seven hours a week for 18 years. The Court held that the limitation in *Barber v Guardian Royal Exchange Insurance Group* Case C-262/88 [1990] ECR I-1889; [1991] 1 QB 344; [1990] ICR 616; [1990] IRLR 240 to claims from the date of judgment onwards did not apply to the denial of access to a scheme, and did not consider whether on the facts such denial might have been justified.

It remained unclear after *Bilka* precisely which schemes were subject to Art 119, especially as the nature of schemes varies so enormously among the Member States. *Defrenne v Belgium*[18] decided that pure social security schemes were outside the scope of Art 119. The ECJ has recently had to consider a scheme where the degree of legislative control was far greater than in *Bilka*.

Bestuur van het Algemeen Burgerlijk Pensioenfonds v Beune Case C-7/93 [1995] IRLR 103[19]

This case concerned the applicability of Art 119 to the Dutch Civil Service pension scheme (ABPW) and its interrelationship with the general State old age pension scheme (AOW). The applicant, a married man, retired in 1988, having worked in the public service for 40 years. The set off from his ABPW pension was 16,286 guilders per year. Had he been a female civil servant with the same length of service the set off would have only been 11,300 guilders per year.

A key question was whether the Civil Service scheme was governed by Art 119 or Directive 79/7.

Judgment (pp 116–17):

On the basis of the situations before it, the Court has developed, *inter alia*, the following criteria: the statutory nature of a pension scheme, negotiation between employers and employees' representatives, the fact that the employees' benefits supplement social security benefits, the manner in which the pension scheme is financed, its applicability to general categories of employees and, finally, the relationship between the benefit and the employees' employment ...

[T]he possibility of relying on Art 119 before a national court cannot depend on whether the unequal treatment in respect of pay allegedly suffered by the employee derives from legislation or regulations or from a collective agreement.

It follows that in classifying pension schemes, the Court has not confined itself to a formal finding of statutory origin. It has given precedence to the criterion of whether there is an agreement rather than the criterion of statutory origin ...

However, the negotiation between the employers and the employees' representatives must ... be such as results in a formal agreement. In most of the Member States, even in the Civil Service, there are various kinds of consultation between employers and employees, which take different forms and are more or less binding on the parties, without thereby necessarily culminating in agreements properly so called ...

No doubt a pension fund like the Netherlands fund is almost entirely funded by contributions paid by the various Civil Service employers and deductions from civil servants' salaries and is managed independently in accordance with rules similar to those applicable to occupational pension funds. But those

---

[18] Case 80/70 [1971] ECR 445.
[19] See, also, [1994] ECR I-4471.

characteristics do not substantially distinguish it from certain social security schemes covered by Directive 79/7 which, under laws or regulations governing contributions and benefits, may also be funded by contributions from employers and employees and be managed jointly by employers and employees.

Moreover ... by contrast with the scheme in *Ten Oever*[20] ... the ABP may, exceptionally, have recourse to the budget of the Netherlands State if the pension fund is unable to discharge the obligations imposed on it by the ABPW. It is also apparent that the scheme reimburses to the ABP the additional costs associated with the elimination of discrimination between widows and widowers. The scheme is not therefore financed exclusively by the public employers and their employees ...

[C]onsiderations of social policy, of State organisation, of ethics or even budgetary preoccupations which influenced, or may have influenced, the establishment by the national legislature of a scheme such as the scheme at issue cannot prevail if the pension concerns only a particular category of workers, if it is directly related to the period of service and if its amount is calculated by reference to the civil servant's last salary. The pension paid by the public employer is therefore entirely comparable to that paid by a private employer to his former employees.

This apparently arcane case is of great significance.[21] Much of the judgment, focusing on the State involvement in legislative and even in fiscal terms, appears to be pointing to a conclusion that Art 119 would not apply. Yet the final section of the judgment shows that these considerations do not prevail, because the scheme concerned only particular categories of worker, and the benefits were related to length of service and final salary. It follows that schemes, however established, which relate only to the employees of a particular employer – even if that employer is the Civil Service – will be within the scope of Art 119. It may even follow that the result in *Defrenne v Belgium* would be different today, although in that case there was no element of consultation with the workers concerned. It is unclear whether agreement is necessary or whether it is sufficient that the scheme covers workers employed by one particular employer.

Barber v Guardian Royal Exchange Insurance Group Case C-262/88 [1990] IRLR 240[22]

The employer's non-contributory pension scheme provided that employees should receive a pension but the payment of the pension was deferred until a man reached the age of 62 and a woman 57. A number of employees were

---

[20] *Ten Oever v Stichting Bedrijfspensioenfonds Voor het Glazenwassers – en Schoonmaakbedrijf* Case C-109/91 [1993] ECR I-4879; [1995] ICR 74; [1993] IRLR 601.

[21] See, also, *Moroni v Firma Collo GmbH* Case C-110/91 [1993] ECR I-6591; 1995] ICR 137; [1994] IRLR 130.

[22] See, also, [1990] ECR I-1889; [1991] 1 QB 344; [1990] ICR 616.

being made redundant and the severance terms agreed provided for an immediate pension if the employee made redundant was a man aged 55 or a woman aged 50. The employee was compulsorily made redundant at the age of 52 and therefore he was only entitled to a deferred pension under the scheme, whereas a woman of the same age would have received an immediate pension.

The questions for the ECJ were whether benefits received under a private, contracted out, non-contributory scheme by a group of employees made compulsorily redundant were 'pay'; whether the principle of equal pay was infringed if a man and a woman of the same age were made redundant but only the woman received an immediate pension, or the total value of the benefits received by the woman was greater than the man's.

Judgment (pp 257–58):

[T]he fact that certain benefits are paid after the termination of the employment relationship does not prevent them from being in the nature of pay ...

[T]he schemes in question are the result either of an agreement between workers and employers or the result of a unilateral decision taken by the employer. They are wholly financed by the employer or by both the employer and the workers without any contribution being made by the public authorities in any circumstances. Accordingly, such schemes form part of the consideration offered to workers by the employer.

[S]uch schemes are not compulsorily applicable to general categories of workers. On the contrary, they apply only to workers employed by certain undertakings, with the result that affiliation to those schemes derives of necessity from the employment relationship with a given employer. Furthermore, even if the schemes in question are established in conformity with national legislation and consequently satisfy the conditions laid down by it for recognition as contracted out schemes, they are governed by their own rules ...

[I]t is contrary to Art 119 to impose an age condition which differs according to sex in respect of pensions paid under a contracted out scheme, even if the difference between the pensionable age for men and that for women is based on the one provided by the national statutory scheme ...[23]

---

[23] In *Burton v British Railways Board (No 2)* Case 19/81 [1982] ECR 554; [1982] 1 QB 1080; [1982] IRLR 116, the employers had offered early retirement to all employees within five years of normal retirement age, so women were eligible for early retirement at 55 while men had to wait until they were 60. It was held by the ECJ that the case concerned discriminatory working conditions and was therefore governed by the Equal Treatment Directive 76/207 rather than Art 119. Had this approach been adopted in *Barber* the Directive would not have had direct effect, as the defendant was a private employer. In *Barber*, the Advocate General distinguished the cases on the basis that *Burton* concerned differential ages for dismissal, and so no issue of pay was involved; see *Barber v Guardian Royal Exchange Insurance Group* Case C-262/88 [1990] IRLR 240, pp 248–50. No mention was made of *Burton* in the judgment of the Court in *Barber*.

> [G]enuine transparency, permitting an effective review, is assured only if the principle of equal pay applies to each of the elements of remuneration granted to men or women.[24]

Whereas *Bilka* had implied that benefits under occupational schemes were 'pay', this case decided the point. And it did so in the face of the fact that the differentiation here depended on the differential retiring age for women and men, which itself depended on the different State pension age. Furthermore, it did so in the face of Art 9 of Directive 86/378 EEC – the Occupational Social Security Directive – which provided that 'Member States may defer compulsory application of the principle of equal treatment with regard to: (a) determination of pensionable age for the purposes of granting old age or retirement pensions, and the possible implications for other benefits ...'.[25] Not surprisingly, this had been taken to authorise the continued payment of different benefits where these were dependent on the different pensionable age under State social security systems – a different issue from that in *Bilka*. However, the Court decided that the principle of equal pay enshrined in Art 119 took precedence over Directive 86/378; the exception contained in that Directive was therefore of no application.

Equality in pension provision

The case gave rise to three major issues: first, who may claim and against whom; secondly, what is meant by equality in the provision of benefits; and, thirdly, to what extent did the decision have retrospective effect?

Who may claim and against whom?

In determining what is meant by equality in pension arrangements, the first question concerns who is entitled to claim equality and against whom may equality be claimed. A wide interpretation has consistently been given to these issues. First, in *Barber* itself it was stated that the 'interpretation of Art 119 is not affected by the fact that the private occupational scheme in question has been set up in the form of a trust and is administered by trustees who are technically independent of the employer, since Art 119 also applies to consideration received indirectly from the employer'.[26] In *Coloroll Pension*

---

[24] The case was decided on 17 May 1990. Subsequent cases showed that rights in respect of benefits accruing after that date differed from those in respect of benefits accruing before that date. See pp 484–89 below.

[25] The temporary derogation for social security schemes found in Directive 79/7, Art 7(1)(a) was mirrored in this provision for occupational schemes.

[26] [1990] IRLR 240, p 258.

Trustees Ltd v Russell[27] the Court held that 'employers and trustees cannot rely on the rules of their pension scheme, or those contained in the trust deed, in order to evade their obligation to ensure equal treatment in the matter of pay. In so far as the rules of national law prohibit them from acting beyond the scope of their powers or in disregard of the provisions of the trust deed, employers and trustees are bound to use all the means available under domestic law to ensure compliance with the principle of equal treatment, such as recourse to the national courts to amend the provisions of the pension scheme or the trust deed.'[28] Furthermore, *Coloroll* also decided that 'in the event of the transfer of pension rights from one occupational scheme to another owing to a worker's change of job, the second scheme is obliged, on the worker reaching retirement age, to increase the benefits it undertook to pay him when accepting the transfer so as to eliminate the effects, contrary to Art 119, suffered by the worker in consequence of the inadequacy of the capital transferred, this being due in turn to the discriminatory treatment under the first scheme, and it must do so in relation to benefits payable in respect of periods of service subsequent to 17 May 1990'.[29]

The second issue was also clarified in *Coloroll* where the Court held that 'since the right to payment of a survivor's pension arises at the time of the death of the employee affiliated to the scheme, the survivor is the only person who can assert it. If the survivor were to be denied this possibility, this would deprive Art 119 of all its effectiveness so far as survivors' pensions are concerned'.[30]

The meaning of equality

The second aspect of equality concerns the issue of what is meant by equality in the context of pensions, and how that equality is to be achieved. There are two issues: equality as regards access to a scheme, and equality as regards the benefits under the scheme.

---

[27] Case C-200/91 [1994] ECR I-4389; [1995] ICR 179; [1994] IRLR 586. See, also, *Fisscher v Voorhuis Hengelo BV and Stichting Bedrijfspensioenfonds voor de Detailhandel* Case C-128/93 [1994] ECR I-4583; [1995] ICR 635; [1994] IRLR 662.

[28] [1994] IRLR 586, p 596. As a result of this ruling trustees were given powers, by the Pension Act 1995, s 65, to make alterations to pension schemes, in defined circumstances, in order to ensure conformity with the principle of equal treatment.

[29] [1994] IRLR 586, p 600. This ruling has led to the widespread practice in the pensions industry of refusing to accept such transfers. See McCrudden, C, 'Third time lucky? The Pensions Act 1995 and equal treatment in occupational pensions' (1996) 25 Industrial LJ 28, p 39.

[30] [1994] IRLR 586, p 596. The same point was made in *Ten Oever*, Case C-109/91 [1993] ECR I-4879; [1995] ICR 74; [1993] IRLR 601. Fredman, *op cit*, fn 3, p 99, comments that these decisions mean that the 'assumption of men as providers and women as dependants [is] punctuated. It is worth noting, perhaps cynically, that this is one context in which men are the direct beneficiaries of equality for women'. This is because the decisions hold that pension schemes must provide for *women's* survivor-dependants on the same terms as *men's*.

Smith v Advel Systems Ltd **Case C-408/92 [1994] IRLR 602**[31]

Until 1 July 1991 the employers' normal retirement age was 65 for men and 60 for women. At that date the age for women was increased to 65. This change was applied both to benefits earned in respect of years of service after 1 July 1991 and service before that date. This reduced the pension payable to women retiring between 60 and 65 by up to 20%, as if a woman were to retire at age 60, her pension would be reduced by 4% per year for each year that her retirement preceded age 65, whereas previously she would have received a pension at the full rate. The same rule was applied to benefits earned in a previous pensionable employment on the basis that retirement would be at 60. Furthermore, if she were to leave the scheme before age 65, the pension rights which could be transferred or used to purchase an insurance policy would be calculated on the basis that her normal pension date was her 65th birthday.

It was claimed that all three of these rules contravened Art 119.

Judgment (pp 614–15):

[O]nce the Court has found that discrimination in relation to pay exists and so long as measures for bringing about equal treatment have not been adopted by the scheme, the only proper way of complying with Art 119 is to grant to the persons in the disadvantaged class the same advantages as those enjoyed by the persons in the favoured class.

Application of this principle to the present case means that, as regards the period between 17 May 1990 [the date of the *Barber* judgment] .... and 1 July 1991 the pension rights of men must be calculated on the basis of the same retirement age as that for women ...

As regards periods of service completed after the entry into force, on 1 July 1991, of rules designed to eliminate discrimination, Art 119 of the Treaty does not preclude measures which achieve equal treatment by reducing the advantages of the persons previously favoured ...

[T]he step of raising the retirement age for women to that for men, which an employer decides to take in order to remove discrimination in relation to occupational pensions as regards benefits payable in respect of future periods of service, cannot be accompanied by measures, even if only transitional, designed to limit the adverse consequences which such a step may have for women ...

Even assuming that it would, in this context, be possible to take account of objectively justifiable considerations relating to the needs of the undertaking or of the occupational scheme concerned, the administrators of the occupational scheme could not reasonably plead, as justification for raising the retirement age for women [during the period between 17 May 1990 and 1 July 1991] financial difficulties as significant as those of which the Court took account in the *Barber* judgment, since the space of time involved is relatively short and

---

[31] See, also, [1994] ECR I-4435; [1995] ICR 596.

attributable in any event to the conduct of the scheme administrators themselves.[32]

This judgment provides that equality may be brought about by the process of so called 'levelling down' – benefits for the advantaged group may be *reduced* so long as equality is attained. This is despite the fact that the Court in *Defrenne v SABENA (No 3)*[33] held that Art 119 necessitated raising the lower salary to the level of the higher 'in view of connection between Art 119 and the harmonisation of working conditions while maintaining improvement'. Not only that, the Court requires that this notion of equality be achieved immediately, with no transition period permissible to cushion those disadvantaged by the change.

This approach is a fundamental challenge to the view that anti-discrimination legislation is designed to improve the living standards of previously disadvantaged groups rather than simply concerned with a formal notion of equality.

Fredman, S, 'The poverty of equality: pensions and the ECJ' (1996) 25 Industrial LJ 91, pp 96–97:

While the earlier cases demonstrate a clear commitment to the improvement of living and working standards, the Court has rapidly moved away from the notion that equality is allied to distributive justice. Instead, a formal conception has emerged, one which is fully satisfied by consistent treatment, even if this means depriving women of their existing benefits or vested expectations. Indeed, the Court has gone further and insisted that, once a decision has been made to 'level down', equality requires that this be achieved immediately and without any transitional measures protecting women's vested interests. Only in cases where women have already received benefits does equality require the extension of such benefits to men. The result is a notion of equality which is fully consistent with an increase in disadvantage ...

It was only in respect of discrimination between the date of the *Barber* decision and the equalisation of pensions that it was necessary to extend women's benefits to men. Three factors seem to have influenced this limiting choice of 'levelling up': a practical recognition of the impossibility of withdrawing benefits already granted to women; the fact that the financial consequences for employers would be limited and well defined; and a gesture towards fault-based fairness, which requires that compensation be payable because the employer was at fault in failing to introduce equality speedily.[34]

---

[32] The Court ruled in the same way in *Van den Akker v Stichting Shell Pensioenfonds* Case C-28/93 [1994] ECR I-4527; [1995] ICR 596; [1994] IRLR 616. These cases do not overturn the principle that changing the terms of a employee's pension may give rise to remedies against the employer for breach of the employment contract; it is also possible that there may be remedies in trust against the trustees.

[33] Case 149/77 [1978] ECR 1365; [1978] 3 CMLR 312.

[34] According to the 1993 survey conducted by the National Association of Pension Funds, at least 90% of UK occupational pension schemes had equalised pensionable ages by that date, of which 63% had chosen equality at 65.

Interaction with State schemes

Because of the fact that State pension arrangements – as well as ages – often differentiated between male and female benefits, it is not uncommon for occupational pension schemes to make adjustments in an attempt to ensure overall fairness. While equality of benefits is now mandatory for benefits applicable to periods of service after the date of the Barber judgment, these cases raise the problem of whether consideration of equality permits the level of benefits under the State scheme to be taken into consideration.

Birds Eye Walls Ltd v Roberts Case C-132/92 [1994] IRLR 29[35]

Mrs Roberts retired at 57 on grounds of ill-health after 17 years service. She received an annual pension of £383 from the Unilever Superannuation Fund. In addition, she received £919 (making a total of £1,302) as a 'bridging pension' from a discretionary scheme operated by companies in the Unilever Group.

These additional payments were made where the employee was not yet entitled to a State pension and where the entitlement to an occupational pension was at a reduced rate. The objective was to place the employees in the position they would have been in had they not been forced to retire. The additional sum was paid to make up the difference between what was actually received by way of pension and what would have been received had the employee continued at work until the State pension age.

Thus, until age 60, there was no substantial difference between the bridging pension paid to women and to men, since neither qualified for a State pension. From the age of 60, however, the bridging pension for a woman was reduced by the amount of the State pension she received or was deemed to have received, but no such reduction was made in respect of a man until age 65. Her pension was reduced by £749 (£919 to £170) from age 60 when it was assumed that she would start to receive an old age pension from the State. She argued that a man in her position would have been entitled to receive the pension at the full rate until age 65.

An Industrial Tribunal rejected her claim on the basis that the difference in payment stemmed from the difference in State pension provision.

Barber was decided after that decision. Allowing her appeal, the EAT held that by deducting her State pension from her occupational pension, the employers would be depriving her of her entitlement to the same 'pay' from her employer as a man would receive, even though the result would be that she would receive, when the State provision was added on, £749 per year more in total than a male comparator between 60 and 65.

---

[35] See, also, [1993] ECR I-5579; [1994] ICR 338.

Judgment (pp 31–32):

While sharing Mrs Roberts' view as to the existence of direct discrimination, the Commission considers, however, that this does not mean that because the discrimination is direct it cannot be justified, since the very concept of discrimination, whether direct or indirect, involves a difference of treatment which is unjustified ... Birds Eye Walls is attempting to achieve substantive equality between the sexes by compensating for an inequality arising from the difference in pensionable ages in a particular set of circumstances where such inequality would cause considerable hardship ...

[A]lthough until the age of 60 the financial position of a woman taking early retirement on grounds of ill-health is comparable to that of a man in the same situation, neither of them as yet entitled to the payment of the State pension, that is no longer the case between the ages of 60 and 65 since that is when women, unlike men, start drawing that pension. That difference as regards the objective premise, which necessarily entails that the amount of the bridging pension is not the same for men and women, cannot be considered discriminatory.

What is more, given the purpose of the bridging pension, to maintain the amount for women at the same level as that which obtained before they received the State pension would give rise to unequal treatment to the detriment of men who do not receive the State pension until the age of 65 ...

It is not contrary to Art 119 ... when calculating the bridging pension, to take account of the full State pension which a married woman would have received if she had not opted in favour of paying contributions at a reduced rate ...

This case purports to focus on the justice of the substantive outcome rather than on a more formal notion of inequality. Normally, such a process of reasoning might be thought to favour women. It is ironic that what is said to be substantive equality here reduces the total amount of post-retirement income available to women. Moreover, the case assumes entitlement to a State pension, even though the plaintiff was not entitled to one since she had elected to pay National Insurance contributions at the reduced married woman's rate. Her decision and the consequences flowing from it were said to depend on her free choice and could not affect the Court's reasoning.

However, the Court took a different, more formalistic, approach, in *Bestuur van het Algemeen Burgerlijk Pensioenfonds v Beune*.[36] Here, when equality was introduced into the Dutch Civil Service pension scheme, it was decided to protect the expectations of married women rather than opt for absolute immediate equality. The upshot was that the operation of the State scheme caused married men to face a greater deduction from their occupational scheme than did married women. A male plaintiff was successful in his argument that he should be treated no less favourably than a woman. *Roberts* decided that an occupational scheme may take into account

---

[36] Case C-7/93 [1994] ECR I-4471; [1995] IRLR 103.

the benefits received under a statutory scheme in order to ensure overall equality. It is the only recent case in which differentiation in private pension arrangements dependent upon a different State pensionable age has been found compatible with European law. There may be a distinction in that in *Roberts* there was no differentiation as to the age at which benefits became payable; rather, the differentiation concerned the level of such benefits; on the other hand, in *Beune* it seems that the differentiation was based upon and perpetuated the permitted distinction in State pensionable ages. Whether or not this is convincing – it may simply be that the cases are in conflict – it is clear that *Roberts* is out of line with the trend of recent authority.

> **Whiteford, E, 'Occupational pension schemes and European law: clarity at last?', in Hervey, T and O'Keeffe, D (eds), *Sex Equality Law in the European Union*, 1996, Chichester: John Wiley, pp 32–33:**
>
> [The Court in *Roberts* appeared] to acquiesce in account being taken of sources of income (the statutory pension) falling outside the scope of Art 119. The total income received from both sources may well have been equal as a result of the scheme operated by Birds Eye Walls, but the 'pay' (the amounts paid by the occupational scheme) of male and female employees between the ages of 60 and 65 was different. A discrimination in the statutory scheme which is generally seen to favour women was used in this case to justify a discrimination in the occupational scheme which favours men, because the outcome was seen to be neutral. Two wrongs do apparently make a right.

The EqPA requires equality only where there is a male comparator; the SDA permits comparison with a hypothetical man. The Pensions Act 1995 adopts the equal pay model. This has both advantages and disadvantages so far as applicants are concerned.[37] The main disadvantage is that there can be no claim for a pension – by either a full time or a part time female employee – if there are no men in the same employment doing work of equal value.[38] These are of course the main areas of very low pay. Equal pay legislation is generally of no value in this situation, so it is vain to anticipate a more constructive approach to pension inequality. On the other hand, it is possible that the decision of the House of Lords in *Ratcliffe v North Yorkshire CC*[39] means that there appears no longer to be a need to establish indirect discrimination in order to succeed with an equal pay claim. If that is correct, it would not be necessary to show, in the particular employment context involved, that, for example, a substantially lower proportion of women than men work full time. There is plenty of scope for disputes over statistics, especially where women

---

[37] The Occupational Pension Schemes (Equal Access to Membership) Regulations SI 1995/1215 confirms that indirectly discriminatory exclusions are unlawful, as well as those which are directly discriminatory.

[38] See *Coloroll* [1994] IRLR 586, p 600.

[39] [1995] 3 All ER 597; [1995] ICR 837; [1995] IRLR 439.

predominate in both part time and full time capacities – teaching has been suggested as an example.[40]

The effect of maternity or family leave

McCrudden, C, 'Equal treatment and occupational pensions: implementing European Community law in the United Kingdom following the post-*Barber* judgments of the European Court of Justice' (1995) 46 Northern Ireland LQ 376, pp 391–92:

Section 63(3) of the 1995 Act provides that an equal treatment rule has effect subject to paras 5 and 6 of Sched 5 to the Social Security Act 1989 ... Under these provisions, a period of paid maternity leave is to be treated as though it were a period of 'normal employment' for the purpose of access to scheme membership and the entitlement to and calculation of benefits. 'Unfair maternity provisions' are overridden and the woman on such leave is treated as if she had worked normally throughout the period of paid absence, and had received the remuneration likely to have been paid for doing so. Full pension rights accrue, even if the maternity leave is paid at less than the normal remuneration. The rule applies to paid maternity leave.

Under para 5 of Sched 5, pension rights will not accrue to women who take unpaid maternity leave beyond their statutory or contractual maternity leave. However, under the provisions of the Trade Union Reform and Employment Rights Act 1993 ... a woman is entitled to a maximum of 14 weeks' maternity leave, during which her contract of employment continues. During this time, she must benefit from all the terms and conditions (including any relating to pensions, but excluding pay) which would have applied had she not been absent. A woman who has a contractual right to belong to an occupational pension scheme would appear to be entitled to continue to have the employer's pension contribution paid as if she had not been absent on maternity leave.

Under para 6, unfair family leave provisions are prohibited. These are terms which treat scheme members differently when they are away from work on paid family leave compared with how they would be treated if they were working normally. Unlike the broader provisions regarding maternity leave, benefits payable to someone who has taken family leave, in so far as they are determined by reference to earnings, need only be calculated on the basis of 'the remuneration in fact paid to him for that period', not the remuneration likely to be paid for working normally. Pension entitlement is based on the actual level of pay during the period of family leave.

---

[40] *Op cit*, Fredman, fn 3, p 100. '[S]tatistical gymnastics can simply disguise the real detriment suffered by part time workers, the vast majority of whom are women, simply because they work in a female-dominated profession ... [F]ar simpler and more effective would be a package which protects part time workers as such', *op cit*, Fredman, fn 3, p 110. For an example of the problem, see *Staffordshire County Council v Black* [1995] IRLR 234, EAT.

The temporal limitation

Barber v Guardian Royal Exchange Insurance Group **Case C-262/88 [1990] IRLR 240; [1990] ECR I-1889; [1991] 1 QB 344; [1990] ICR 616, p 259:**

[M]ember States [are authorised] to defer the compulsory implementation of the principle of equal treatment with regard to the determination of pensionable age for the purposes of granting old age pensions and the possible consequences thereof for other benefits ...

In the light of [the provisions of the Occupational Pensions Directive] the Member States and the parties concerned were reasonably entitled to consider that Art 119 did not apply to pensions paid under contracted out schemes and that derogations from the principle of equality between men and women were still permitted in that sphere.

In those circumstances, overriding considerations of legal certainty preclude legal situations which have exhausted all their effects in the past from being called in question where that might upset retrospectively the financial balance of many contracted out pension schemes. It is appropriate, however, to provide an exception in favour of individuals who have taken action in good time in order to safeguard their rights. Finally, it must be pointed out that no restriction of the effects of the aforesaid interpretation can be permitted as regards the acquisition of entitlement to a pension as from the date of this judgment.

It must therefore be held that the direct effect of Art 119 of the Treaty may not be relied upon in order to claim entitlement to a pension with effect from a date prior to that of this judgment, except in the case of workers or those claiming under them who have before that date initiated legal proceedings or raised an equivalent claim under applicable national law.

In other words, the *Barber* decision was only to apply as from the date of the judgment, 17 May 1990. But given the fact that pension entitlement builds up gradually over a period of years, it was unclear what was the precise effect of this temporal limitation. There were four possible views as to the persons who could rely on *Barber*:

(a) those who began to contribute to a pension after 17 May 1990 (a very narrow interpretation);

(b) those in receipt of pension benefits which were applicable only in respect of periods of employment after 17 May 1990 (arguably a middle position and the one eventually adopted);

(c) those beginning to receive pension benefits after 17 May 1990, whether referable to periods of employment before or after that date (a fairly wide interpretation);

(d) those receiving any pension payment after 17 May 1990, whether referable to periods of employment before or after that date (the widest interpretation).

Moore, S, 'Justice doesn't mean a free lunch': the application of the principle of equal pay to occupational pension schemes' (1995) 20 EL Rev 159, pp 165–66:

The financial balance of a pension scheme depends upon a number of premises, including pension lifetimes and the survival probabilities of men and women but, in particular, upon the correlation between the pension contributions paid in respect of a period of pensionable service and the subsequent pension benefit which is derived from that same period of service. An interpretation of *Barber* which had raised pension benefits in respect of service before 17 May 1990 would therefore have led to an increase in liabilities without a corresponding change in assets and thereby upset the financial balance of the scheme. It would also have failed to respect the legitimate expectations of the parties by imposing upon the pension funds, and/or the employer, retrospective liabilities.

[T]he actual cost to the industry and the reserves which it had on hand to meet that cost were a matter of fierce controversy. For example, the estimated bill ranged from £45 billion, on the part of the UK Government, to £6–12 billion spread over a period of 10–15 years ... Furthermore, it was argued that the real cost of implementing *Barber* pursuant to the third or fourth interpretation was less than the pension industry claimed because it was necessary to deduct the costs of payments made to men aged 60–65 which would no longer have to be made if men were to receive pensions at the same age as women. Two benefits identified as yielding reductions were death-in-service benefits and ill-health pensions. In addition, it was suggested that it was legitimate to take account of the extent to which pension schemes had built up a surplus of capital assets over the years which could be used to fund the cost of equalisation.

[The] Court has held on many occasions that Art 119 is intended to guarantee a fundamental right ... The Court has also consistently recognised that it is appropriate to draw inspiration from international treaties designed to protect human rights and from the constitutional traditions of Member States in order to determine what constitutes a fundamental human right ... Any restriction on the temporal effect of Art 119 should therefore have taken account of the fundamental nature of the rights guaranteed by Art 119 and should have been construed as narrowly as possible with due regard to the social policy which it reflects.

There was widespread unease at the potential width – which really means cost – of Barber. As a result, before the European Court clarified the law, a protocol was attached to the Treaty of European Union – the Maastricht Treaty:

For the purposes of Art 119 ... benefits under occupational social security schemes shall not be considered as remuneration if and in so far as they are attributable to periods of service prior to 17 May 1990, except in the case of workers or those claiming under them who have before that date initiated legal proceedings or raised an equivalent claim under applicable national law.

In any event, the issue soon came before the European Court.

Ten Oever v Stichting Bedrijfspensioenfonds Voor het Glazenwassers – en Schoonmaakbedrijf **Case C-109/91 [1993] IRLR 601, p 603**[41]

[I]t must be made clear that equality of treatment in the matter of occupational pensions may be claimed only in relation to benefits payable in respect of periods of employment subsequent to 17 May 1990, the date of the *Barber* judgment, subject to the exception prescribed therein for workers or those claiming under them who have, before that date, initiated legal proceedings or raised an equivalent claim under the applicable national law.[42]

Coloroll Pension Trustees Ltd v Russell **Case C-200/91 [1994] IRLR 586, p 598**

[T]he national court asks whether, and how, the limitation of the effects in time of the *Barber* judgment applies to benefits payable under occupational social security schemes which are not linked to length of actual service ... such as a lump sum payment in the event of an employee's death during his employment.

Since such a benefit is payable solely by reason of an employment relationship existing at the time of the event triggering payment of the benefit, irrespective of the length of previous periods of service, the limitation of the effects in time of the *Barber* judgment applies only where the operative event occurred before 17 May 1990. After that date, such benefits must be granted in accordance with the principle of equal treatment without any need to distinguish between periods of service prior to the *Barber* judgment and periods of service subsequent to that judgment.

Thus equal treatment was required in respect of one-off payments such as a death-in-service lump sum, whereas benefits which were dependent on length of service accrued over time would only be equalised gradually as the period since *Barber* increased.

Vroege v NCIV Institut voor Volkshuisvesting BV and Stichting Pensioenfonds NCIV **Case C-57/93 [1994] IRLR 651**[43]

From 1 May 1975, the applicant worked 25.9 hours per week for NCIV. Until 1 January 1991, their pension scheme rules allowed only men and unmarried women working at least 80% of the normal full working day to be members, a rule which excluded the applicant. From 1 January 1991, when the rules were changed, she began to accrue pension rights. However, under the transitional arrangements adopted, she was not allowed to purchase years of membership in respect of her service prior to 1991.

She claimed that the fund rules contravened Art 119 in that she had no right to be a member of the scheme in respect of periods of service prior to 1

---

[41] See, also, [1993] ECR I-4879; [1995] ICR 74.

[42] The same approach was adopted in *Neath v Hugh Steeper Ltd* Case C-152/91 [1994] ECR I-6935; [1995] ICR 118; [1994] IRLR 91.

[43] See, also, [1994] ECR I-4541; [1995] ICR 635.

January 1991. She claimed membership with retrospective effect as from 8 April 1976, the date of the decision in *Defrenne v SABENA*, in which the ECJ held that Art 119 had direct effect.

The argument was based on *Bilka-Kaufhaus*, which held that an hours requirement for membership of a pension scheme was indirectly discriminatory against women. The UK Government argued that the terms of the post-*Barber* Protocol were sufficiently wide that *Bilka* was impliedly overruled and that therefore retrospective membership of schemes could not be claimed in respect of periods before the *Barber* judgment. The ECJ disagreed.

Judgment (p 661):

[T]he limitation of the effects in time of the *Barber* judgment concerns only those kinds of discrimination which employers and pension schemes could reasonably have considered to be permissible owing to the transitional derogations for which Community law provided and which were capable of being applied to occupational pensions.

It must be concluded that, as far as the right to join an occupational scheme is concerned, there is no reason to suppose that the professional groups concerned could have been mistaken about the applicability of Art 119 ...

[I]f the court had considered it necessary to impose a limit in time on the rule that the right to be a member of an occupational pension scheme is covered by Art 119, it would have done so in the *Bilka* judgment.

Protocol No 2 [of the Maastricht Treaty] ... relates only to benefits – being all that is mentioned in Protocol No 2 – and not to the right to belong to an occupational social security scheme.

This decision gave the right to retrospective pension schemes, in theory back to 1976. Its enormous potential was, however, significantly curtailed by the following case.

Fisscher v Voorhuis Hengelo BV and Stichting Bedrijfspensioenfonds voor de Detailhandel Case C-128/93 [1994] IRLR 662[44]

Here again a part time worker claimed retrospective membership of the relevant scheme.

Judgment (p 665):

[A] worker cannot claim more favourable treatment, particularly in financial terms, than he would have had if he had been duly accepted as a member [when he started work].

[T]he fact that a worker can claim retroactively to join an occupational pension scheme does not allow the worker to avoid paying the contributions relating to the period of membership concerned.

---

[44] See, also, [1994] ECR I-4583; [1995] ICR 635.

To obtain retrospective membership of a contributory scheme the worker will have to pay the contributions which would have been paid during the relevant period. Thus the employer avoids having to pay contributions in respect of any previous years the backdated contributions for which the employee cannot now afford to buy. The decision has been the subject of powerful criticism, in terms both of its reasoning and its practical impact.

Fredman, S, 'The poverty of equality: pensions and the ECJ' (1996) 25 Industrial LJ 91, p 105:

[*Fisscher* held that contributions were payable retrospectively by the women.] In practice ... this functions as an effective bar to married or part time women making use of their rights to retrospective membership, given the fact that employee contributions are worth an average of £550 per annum. This is a good example of the fluidity of equality justifications: a focus on the requirement to pay contributions yields a diametrically opposite decision to a focus on whether pension benefits will in fact be available. Moreover, the Court in this case takes a static view of equality, ignoring the very real continuing effects of past discrimination. Instead, the Court has clearly been influenced by the expense likely to be incurred by employers to make good their denial of membership.

Whiteford, E, 'Lost in the mists of time: the ECJ and occupational pensions' (1995) CML Rev 801, pp 813–15:

It appears to have been considered beyond doubt by the parties to the [*Fisscher*] litigation that where an individual wishes to claim retroactive membership the employer will be bound to pay the backdated retroactive contributions. However, merely requiring that employer and employee to pay the contributions which they would have had to pay in the past will not suffice to ensure that the level of benefit obtained by the wrongfully excluded employee is equal to that which has been accrued by the formerly advantaged employee. This is because pensions are funded not only through employer and employee contributions, but the funds invest their income which, in turn, all being well, yields investment income which also funds the future benefits. So in ensuring that all the consequences of the past discrimination are eradicated, someone must pay the interest. It is suggested that the employer must be held responsible for making good any interest which has been lost ...

If an employer chooses to require that someone in Ms Fisscher's position pay all backdated contributions in one lump sum – which does not appear to be precluded by the Court's judgment – the financial barrier to the individual seems likely to prove insurmountable in most cases.

Magorrian and Cunningham v Eastern Health and Social Services Board Case C-246/96 [1998] IRLR 86

The appellants alleged that, as part time workers, they were deprived of additional pension benefits to which they would have been entitled had they worked full time, benefits which would have been payable without any requirement to make additional contributions. The question was whether the remedy should be backdated to 1976, the date of the *Defrenne* decision, or 1990, the date of *Barber*.

Judgment (p 99–100):

As regards the right to receive benefits additional to a retirement pension under an occupational scheme ... the Court finds that, even if the persons concerned have always been entitled to a retirement pension under the superannuation scheme, nevertheless they were not fully admitted to that contributory scheme ...

[E]ntitlement to a retirement pension under an occupational scheme [is] indissolubly linked to the right to join such a scheme.

The same is true where the discrimination suffered by part time workers stems from discrimination concerning access to a special scheme which confers entitlement to additional benefits ...

[A]pplication of a procedural rule ... whereby, in proceedings concerning access to membership of occupational pension schemes, the right to be admitted to a scheme may have effect from a date no earlier than two years before the institution of proceedings would deprive the applicants ... of the additional benefits ... to which they are entitled to be affiliated ...

However, it should be noted that, in such a case, the claim is not for the retroactive award of certain additional benefits but for recognition of entitlement to full membership of an occupational scheme ...

Consequently, unlike the rules at issue in [*Steenhorst-Neerings*[45] and *Johnson*],[46] which in the interests of legal certainty merely limited the retroactive scope of a claim for certain benefits and did not strike at the very essence of the rights conferred by the Community legal order, a rule such as before the national court in this case is such as to render any action by individuals relying on Community law impossible in practice.

PROCEDURES AND REMEDIES IN RETROSPECTIVE CLAIMS

It was held in *Fisscher* that the national rules governing time limits for bringing claims apply to workers who are claiming retrospective membership of an occupational scheme, 'provided that they are not less favourable for that type of action than for actions of a domestic nature and that they do not render the exercise of rights conferred by Community law impracticable in practice'. In the UK, such claims are, by regulation, treated as equal pay claims and thus governed by the six month limitation period and the two year limit on back pay contained in the Equal Pay Act 1970.[47] Reasoning by analogy

---

[45] *Steenhorst-Neerings v Bestuur van der Bedrijfsvereeniging* Case C-338/91 [1993] ECR I-5475; [1994] IRLR 244.

[46] *Johnson v Chief Adjudication Officer (No 2)* Case C-410/92 [1994] ECR I-5483; [1995] ICR 375; [1995] IRLR 157.

[47] Occupational Pension Schemes (Equal Access to Membership) Regulations 1995 SI 1995/1215.

with the decision in *Biggs v Somerset CC*[48] would lead to the conclusion that employees have only six months to make a claim following termination of the employment which they are arguing should have been pensionable.[49] This logic prevailed in the lower courts in *Preston v Wolverhampton Healthcare NHS Trust*,[50] where large numbers of claimants were alleging that the historic exclusion of part time workers from pension schemes – or failure to give credit for periods of part time service – was unlawful, and that claims could be made back to 1976 – the date of the judgment in *Defrenne v SABENA*. However, the House of Lords[51] considered that it was arguable that the six month rule made it excessively difficult or impossible in practice for the applicants to enforce their rights under Community law, and referred the issue for resolution by the European Court.

The second procedural problem is that the Equal Pay Act 1970 limits claims to a maximum of two years' back pay. This type of limitation has been upheld by the ECJ in the context of social security.[52] The lower courts in *Preston* held that those denied membership of a pension scheme could only claim in respect of the two years service immediately prior to the claim being brought. In *Levez v TH Jennings (Harlow Pools) Ltd*,[53] it was argued that the two year limit was contrary to EC law in failing to ensure full compensation for losses suffered as a result of sex discrimination in pay, and on the ground that the limitation is less favourable than procedural rules applicable to similar domestic actions such as breach of contract. The lay members of the EAT thought that these arguments were sufficiently compelling to justify a reference to the European Court, though the chair, Mummery J, thought that European law has consistently left matters such as this to be determined by national law, and thus there was no possibility of the claim succeeding. The House of Lords in *Preston*, hearing the case after *Magorrian* had been decided, asked the ECJ to determine what was effectively the same issue as in *Levez*.

It is unclear if the decision in *Magorrian* means that both issues referred in *Preston* must necessarily be decided in favour of the plaintiffs. The distinction between denial of full access to membership of a scheme and mere inequality of benefits under a scheme is exceptionally thin. If *all* situations are classed under the former approach, it will always be the case that the six month period to make a claim and the limitation of back pay to two years will make

---

48   [1996] ICR 364; [1996] 2 All ER 234; [1996] IRLR 203, CA.

49   The Pensions Act, s 63(4), applies the same approach under the new statutory framework by making claims under the Act subject to the procedural provisions of the Equal Pay Act.

50   [1997] ICR 899, CA.

51   [1998] 1 All ER 528; [1998] IRLR 197, HL.

52   See, eg, *Johnson v Chief Adjudication Officer (No 2)* Case C-410/92 [1994] ECR I-5483; [1995] ICR 375; [1995] IRLR 157.

53   [1996] IRLR 499, EAT.

it effectively impossible to enforce Community rights. In such a way the temporal limitation laid down in *Barber* has the capacity to be outflanked. The trend of recent decisions would suggest that both *Preston* and *Levez* will be decided in favour of the applicants. Even if this proves correct, however, the value to women of retrospective membership is severely weakened by the decision in *Fisscher* that women have to pay backdated contributions. Women without a comparable man still have no entitlement to an occupational pension. On the other hand, many part time workers now have rights to membership. However, given that such employment is typically of rather short duration, the value of such pension rights is itself frequently dependent on the ease and value of transfer rights.

ACTUARIAL CONSIDERATIONS

The issue is the extent to which it is permissible for pension arrangements to take into account the fact that, on average, women live longer than men. This could be done by increasing female employee contributions relative to men, or by differentiating between employer contributions in respect of male and female employees. There is no *logical* need to do either of these: the total potential liabilities of a scheme may be calculated actuarially, but the level of contributions could be averaged out between men and women. The issue is also relevant to the level of benefits to be reimbursed to an early leaver from a scheme.[54]

Neath v Hugh Steeper Ltd Case C-152/91 [1994] IRLR 91[55]

The applicant was employed from January 1973 to 29 June 1990, when he was made redundant when aged 54. He was a member of a pension scheme where employee contributions were the same for men and women. A woman could retire on full pension at 60, whereas a man could not do so until 65. The method of calculating the pension varied according to the sex of the worker and the circumstances of the case. An employee could retire early and take a reduced pension at any time after age 50, with the consent of the employee and the trustees. The reduction took account of the length of the period between actual retirement date and normal retirement date. If the employer and the trustees did not consent to early retirement, a member leaving the

---

[54] Under Directive 86/378, money purchase schemes were permitted different benefit levels where this represented actuarial differences, employee contributions had to be equal after 30 July 1999 – a point rendered irrelevant by *Barber* – but employer contributions could continue to differentiate. Final salary schemes required equal benefits, equal employer contributions, and equal employee contributions after 30 July 1999.

[55] See, also, [1994] ECR I-6935; [1995] ICR 118.

scheme after 50 was entitled only to a deferred pension or a transfer payment to another scheme. The transfer payment varied according to the sex of the worker based on actuarial factors. As the cost of providing a pension for a woman was greater than for a man, the transfer value for a woman's accrued pension contributions was therefore considered to be greater than for a man.

The applicant was allowed to take an immediate pension when made redundant. He was offered the choice of a deferred pension or a transfer payment; if he opted for the latter, its value would be £30,672.59. This calculation was based on the assumption that he received his pension at 65, except as regards benefits attributable to his period of employment after 17 May 1990, in relation to which the calculation was based on a retirement age of 60 in accordance with one view of the effect of *Barber*. If he was assumed to have a normal retirement age of 60 in relation to his entire pensionable service, the transfer payment would have been £39,934.56 using male actuarial factors and £41,486.25 using female actuarial factors.

He also argued that he would have to wait five more years than a woman in order to receive a deferred pension, but also that if he then wished to exercise his right to exchange part of his pension for cash, he would receive £17,193.94 rather than the £21,029.02 that would be received by a woman in similar circumstances. That difference was also based on actuarial tables.[56]

Judgment (pp 94–95):

The employer's contributions ... vary over time, so as to cover the balance of the cost of the pensions promised. They are ... higher for female than for male employees.

This variability and inequality is due to the use of actuarial factors in the mechanism for funding the scheme. The aim of an occupational retirement pension scheme being to provide for the future payment of periodic pensions, the scheme's financial resources, accrued through funding, must be adjusted according to the pensions which, according to the forecasts, will have to be paid. The assessments needed to give effect to this system are based on a

---

[56] The Advocate General, in his opinion in *Smith* and *Van den Akker* [1994] IRLR 616, pp 610–13, argued that the use of actuarial factors should not be permitted, first, on the ground of principle that average differences in life expectancy do not determine how long any individual will live, and that anti-discrimination legislation does not normally allow use to be made of averages; and secondly, on the ground that the financial balance of pension schemes will not be upset if schemes do not distinguish between men and women in their *external* relations with their members. He quoted from the American case of *City of Los Angeles v Manhart* 435 US 677 (1978) that '... when insurance risks are grouped, the better risks always subsidise the poorer risks. Healthy persons subsidise health risks for the less healthy; unmarried workers subsidise the pensions of married workers; persons who eat, drink or smoke to excess may subsidise pension benefits for persons whose habits are more temperate. Treating different classes of risk as though they were the same for the purposes of insurance is a common practice which has never been seen as inherently unfair. To insure the fit and flabby as though they were equivalent risks may be more common than treating men and women alike; but nothing more than "habit" makes one subsidy seem less fair than the other'.

number of objective factors, such as the return on the scheme's investments, the rate of increase in salaries and demographic assumptions, in particular those relating to the life expectancy of workers.

The fact that women live on average longer than men is one of the actuarial factors taken into account in determining how the scheme in question is to be funded. This is why the employer has to pay higher contributions for his female employees than for his male employees ...

It must be determined whether transfer benefits and lump sum options constitute pay ...

The Commission claims that this is indeed the case and that consequently any difference in treatment based on sex would be permissible only if it were objectively justified. Statistical data based on the life expectancy of the two sexes do not, in its view, constitute an objective justification because they reflect averages calculated on the basis of the entire male and female population, whereas the right given to equal treatment in the matter of pay is a right given to employees individually and not because they belong to a particular class ...

The assumption underlying this approach is that the employer commits himself, albeit unilaterally, to pay his employees defined benefits or to grant them specific advantages and that the employees in turn expect the employer to pay them those benefits or to provide them with those advantages. Anything that is not a consequence of that commitment and does not therefore come within the corresponding expectations of the employees falls outside the concept of pay.

In the context of a defined-benefit occupational pension scheme such as that in question ... the employer's commitment to his employees concerns the payment, at a given moment in time, of a periodic pension for which the determining criteria are already known at the time when the commitment is made and which constitutes pay under Art 119. However, that commitment does not necessarily have to do with the funding arrangements chosen to secure the periodic payment of the pension, which thus remain outside the scope of application of Art 119.

The amount of contributions must be the same for all employees, male and female, which is indeed so in the present case. That is not so in the case of the employer's contributions, which ensure the adequacy of the funds necessary to cover the cost of the pensions promised, so securing their payment in the future, that being the substance of the employer's commitment. It follows that, unlike periodic payment of pensions, inequality of employer's contributions paid under funded defined-benefit schemes, which is due to the use of actuarial factors differing according to sex, is not struck at by Art 119.

Coloroll Pension Trustees Ltd v Russell Case C-200/91 [1994] IRLR 586, pp 599–600[57]

The essence of the High Court's fourth question is whether Art 119 precludes actuarial factors ... from being taken into account in occupational pension

[57] See, also, [1994] ECR I-4389; [1995] ICR 179; [1994] IRLR 586.

schemes and, if so, how the limitation of the effects in time of the *Barber* judgment applies in this context.

Article 119 applies to all benefits payable to an employee by an occupational pension scheme, irrespective of whether the scheme is contributory or non-contributory. Whether contributions are payable by the employer or the employees has no bearing on the concept of pay when applied to occupational pensions ...

However, the situation is different in the case of additional voluntary contributions paid by employees to secure additional benefits such as, for example, an additional fixed pension for the member or the member's dependants, an additional tax-free lump sum or additional lump sum benefits on death.

The order for reference shows that these additional benefits are calculated separately, solely on the basis of the value of the contribution paid, which are credited to a special fund managed by the trustees as a distinct fund ...

[S]uch benefits cannot be regarded as pay ...

Thus, the situations in which the use of actuarial factors remains permissible are: first, in respect of the transfer value of a scheme or its conversion into a capital sum; secondly, in respect of additional voluntary contributions; and, thirdly, where a reduced pension is paid on early retirement, where the reduction is due to actuarial factors. The device used to ensure their continued lawfulness is to exclude them from the definition of 'pay' in Art 119.

Moore, S, 'Justice doesn't mean a free lunch: the application of the principle of equal pay to occupational pension schemes' (1995) 20 EL Rev 159, p 176:

The rationale [of *Neath*] appears to be [that] since contributions made by the employer do not fall within Art 119, differences in those contributions due to actuarial factors are not prohibited by Art 119 and, consequently, differences in benefits payable under the scheme which are the direct result of the differences in the contributions paid by the employer are not prohibited by Art 119 either. If this is indeed the reasoning behind the judgment, it is surprising that the Court did not distinguish between differences in the *funding arrangements* which are due to actuarial factors and similar differences in the *benefits* paid ... [Such benefits are clearly pay and] there is no reason why Art 119 should cease to apply to discriminatory benefits simply because the discrimination is the result of the funding arrangements chosen by the employer to operate the scheme. First, as a matter of practice, there seems to be no necessity for an employer to use sex-based actuarial factors to calculate his liabilities ... Secondly ... a prohibition of the use of sex-based actuarial tables to calculate benefits paid out under a pension scheme would not have affected the ability of the pension fund to acquire an accurate picture of the life expectancy of the scheme members in order to assess outstanding and future liabilities because the internal actuarial methods of administration, used to calculate the funds needed in order to maintain a financial balance between contributions and benefits, does not, in any event, fall within Art 119.

This permitted continued use of actuarial factors arises from the interpretation given by the Court to Art 119.[58] This interpretation was confirmed by the wording of the amended Directive 96/97/EC. An exception is provided for defined-contribution schemes which may continue to take account of actuarial factors based on sex.[59] In the case of funded defined-benefit schemes, certain elements may continue to be unequal where such inequality is dependent upon actuarial factors.[60] Examples given in an annex to the Directive include the conversion into a capital sum of part of a periodic payment, the transfer of pension rights, and a reduced pension where the worker opts to take early retirement. In other words, the case law of the ECJ, which gave a limited green light to the continued use of actuarial factors, is confirmed by subsequent legislation. It is arguably permissible for employers to grant their employees low basic occupational pensions which are then topped up with substantial additional contributions, voluntary in theory but perhaps less so in practice, to which, because they are outside the definition of 'pay', Article 119 is inapplicable. Such schemes may continue to utilise gender-based actuarial factors.

CONCLUSION

The overall effect of the approach of the European Court of Justice is to allow the phasing in of equality in pension arrangements. Totally equal pensions at the same pensionable age will only finally be provided approximately 40 years after the supposedly seminal judgment in *Barber*, and a similar approach is being taken by the UK Government to the issue of the State pension age. But it is true to say that pension rights for current employment are now being accrued under conditions of equality, so to that extent the change wrought by European law is of very considerable significance. It is also true to say that there is no *right* to an occupational pension, and women continue to be employed in jobs where pension provision may be the exception rather than the rule.

---

[58] The Pensions Act 1995, s 64(3), allows for the continued use of actuarial factors when calculating the level of employer contributions, and thus may conflict with Directive 86/378.

[59] Article 6(1)(h).

[60] Article 6(1)(i).

CHAPTER 14

ENFORCEMENT OF ANTI-DISCRIMINATION LEGISLATION

The effectiveness of any law depends on the way in which it is administered and enforced. While we have seen that there are major criticisms of the substantive anti-discrimination law, many of the most severe criticisms have been directed at the procedural and remedial weapons at the disposal of victims. There are significant practical barriers in the path of potential plaintiffs, and the remedies available are limited in scope – although the removal of the maximum limit on compensation has undoubtedly had an impact, the extent of which it is still too early to assess. The limitations of reliance on individual enforcement of anti-discrimination law were appreciated when the legislation was passed. In consequence an elaborate system of administrative enforcement was designed, with leading roles to be taken by the Equal Opportunities Commission and the Commission for Racial Equality. However, the operation of these powers, especially that of formal investigations, has been a dismal failure. These were originally conceived as a mechanism for overcoming the individualistic stance of the traditional common law approach. However, a combination of conceptual naivety, bad drafting and unsympathetic judges combined severely to weaken these powers.

Effective implementation of anti-discrimination legislation requires, first, a system of procedural law which readily permits the presentation of serious claims; secondly, a definition of unlawful practices which includes those which actually bar job progress; thirdly, remedies which provide incentive for voluntary compliance and effective means for change; and fourthly, the availability of adequate resources both in the legal profession and in the government to implement the law.[1] Lustgarten in effect adds a fifth: that the judiciary must show a sensitivity to the underlying moral force of the legislation.[2] All but the second criterion focus on procedure and remedies, and they provide a helpful framework by which to evaluate the procedural and remedial provisions of the legislation.

Under the Race Relations Act 1968, individuals were unable to bring an action directly against an employer or other defendant. Rather, all claims had to be channelled through the Race Relations Board. If, for whatever reason, the Board declined to take action, that was the end of the matter. It was clearly a source of potential grievance that individuals might thereby be deprived of

---

1   See Chambers, J and Goldstein, B, 'Title VII: the continuing challenge of establishing fair employment practices' (1986) 49 Law and Contemporary Problems 9.
2   Lustgarten, L, 'The new meaning of discrimination' [1978] PL 178, p 198.

their 'day in court'. At the same time, it was recognised that reliance on individual litigation was likely to prove an inefficient and haphazard method of promoting social change. As discriminatory practices tend to occur for structural reasons, they are unlikely merely to affect isolated individuals. It was for this reason that there is, under the Sex Discrimination Act 1975 and the Race Relations Act 1976, a twin track enforcement approach: individual enforcement and administrative enforcement.

INDIVIDUAL CLAIMS BEFORE INDUSTRIAL TRIBUNALS

Before the hearing

Under the SDA 1975 and the RRA 1976 individuals may complain to an Employment Tribunal of a breach of the employment part of the legislation.[3] We have already considered the procedure under which a potential applicant may question the employer concerning the alleged discriminatory acts.[4] Legal aid is not available for representation at tribunal hearings. Many have argued that it should be, but such a reform would achieve little without a radical re-appraisal of the purpose and limits of legal aid provision. Applicants may be supported by their trade union, possibly in rare cases by a pressure group, or may represent themselves.

Commission assistance

Both the CRE and the EOC have the legal power to assist applicants with individual cases. There are far more requests for assistance with proceedings than can be met from available resources, but the Commissions provide some forms of preliminary and general assistance in many other cases.[5] The requests that are received are necessarily dependent on the applicant's knowing that such a power exists. This cannot be taken for granted. The statutory criteria for deciding whether or not to provide assistance are if:

(a) the case raises a question of principle; or

(b) it is unreasonable, having regard to the complexity of the case or the applicant's position in relation to the respondent or other person involved or any other matter, to expect the applicant to deal with the case unaided; or

---

3   Non-employment matters go to county courts. See above, pp 387–88.

4   See above, p 168.

5   'As regards representation at tribunal or in the county court and higher, the EOC is only able to assist approximately 100 individuals per year. Several thousands of individuals, however, are given information and advice.' *Equality in the 21st Century: a New Approach*, 1998, Manchester: EOC, para 92.

(c) by reason of any other special consideration.[6]

The forms of assistance may include:

(a) giving advice;

(b) procuring or attempting to procure the settlement of any matter in dispute;

(c) arranging for the giving of advice or assistance by a solicitor or counsel;

(d) arranging for representation by any person including all such assistance as is usually given by a solicitor or counsel in the steps preliminary or incidental to any proceedings ...[7] [This may include taking over a case at the appeal stage.]

It is not normal practice for the Commissions to give reasons for refusing to provide assistance in any given case. As a matter of *logic*, refusal says nothing about the merits of the case. But in practice such refusal is frequently followed by abandonment of the claim, for financial or other reasons. 'Applicants who are granted assistance by the CRE have a substantially better chance of success than other claimants under RRA 1976, for at least three reasons: first, the CRE tries to select the stronger cases; secondly, it is likely to provide more effective advice and representation than any other body; thirdly, and perhaps more important, it provides moral support to the applicant throughout the earlier stages, thus greatly reducing the chance that he or she will withdraw. Because the minority of applicants who are granted CRE assistance have a substantial advantage, the determining factor becomes the CRE's decision about whether or not to assist. This means that the CRE retains a dominant and quasi-judicial function. Another consequence is that there has been no development of campaigning organisations which sponsor individual complaints.'[8]

Time limits

The normal rule in sex and race discrimination cases[9] is that an application must have been presented within three months of the commission of the acts of discrimination of which complaint is made.[10] The tribunal has discretion to

---

6   SDA 1975, s 75(1); RRA 1976, s 66(1).

7   SDA 1975, s 75(2); RRA 1976, s 66(2).

8   McCrudden, C, Smith, D and Brown, C, *Racial Justice at Work: Enforcement of the Race Relations Act 1976 in Employment*, 1991, London: Policy Studies Institute, p 155.

9   For time limits in equal pay cases, see above, pp 458–60.

10   SDA 1975, s 76(1); RRA 1976, s 68(1). If the original complaint is, eg, of victimisation, it is possible subsequently to add a complaint of indirect discrimination, so long as the addition or amendment does not unfairly prejudice the defendant; *Quarcopoome v Sock Shop Holdings Ltd* [1995] IRLR 353, EAT. This principle does not apply, however, if the amendment or addition is *never* made; eg, if the complaint is only of direct discrimination, the tribunal may not uphold the complaint on the basis of indirect discrimination; *Chapman v Simon* [1994] IRLR 124, CA.

permit a claim which is out of time 'if, in all the circumstances of the case, it considers that it is just and equitable to do so'.[11] There are two linked problem areas with the limitation period: first, when does the act of discrimination occur so as to start time running; and, secondly, when will the tribunal exercise its discretion to permit a claim to proceed, despite more than three months having elapsed.

As the tribunal's power is discretionary, appeal against the manner of its exercise is highly unlikely to succeed. In *Hawkins v Ball and Barclays Bank plc*,[12] an applicant only presented a claim of sexual harassment five months after an incident of verbal harassment, having originally been advised by a solicitor that the incident was trivial. The EAT held that in the circumstances it was just and equitable to permit the claim to proceed. Similar cases reaching a different outcome under the more stringent unfair dismissal law were of no relevance.

In relation to the first issue, it is provided that:

(a) where the inclusion of any term in a contract renders the making of the contract an unlawful act, that act shall be treated as extending throughout the duration of the contract; and

(b) any act extending over a period shall be treated as done at the end of that period; and

(c) a deliberate omission shall be treated as done when the person in question decided upon it ...[13]

There is a difference between a continuing act of discrimination and a single act of discrimination with continuing consequences. This distinction may be crucial in determining when the three months' limitation period commences. It is not at all easy to determine which side of the line a particular case falls.

Barclays Bank plc v Kapur [1991] IRLR 136, HL[14]

The case concerned East African Asians who had come to the UK in the early 1970s and had become employees of predecessors of the defendants. The bank had refused to take account of previous service with East African banks in computing their pension entitlement. The question was whether the complaints were time barred; this depended on whether the refusal was viewed as an act of one-off or of continuing discrimination.

Lord Griffiths (pp 138–39):

The applicants ... say that the term upon which they are credited with a pension is to be classified as an act extending over a period, namely the length

---

[11] SDA 1975, s 76(5); RRA 1976, s 68(5). This is a more lenient test than that which normally applies in Industrial Tribunal proceedings, such as unfair dismissal and redundancy payment claims, where the tribunal must be satisfied that it was not reasonably practicable for the complaint to be presented within the three month period.

[12] [1996] IRLR 258, EAT.

[13] SDA 1975, s 76(6); RRA 1976, s 68(7).

[14] See, also, [1991] 2 AC 355; [1991] 1 All ER 646.

of their employment, and therefore to be treated as done at the end of the period of employment ...

Calder v James Finlay Corporation[15] [concerned the] refusal of a mortgage subsidy. The EAT said that there was continuing discrimination against her so long as she remained in their employment. The rule of the scheme constituted a discriminatory act extending over the period of her employment and is therefore to be treated as having been done at the end of her period of employment.

[The position is the same here. In substance here there is no] real difference to the continued payment of lower wages.

On the other side of the line are cases such as a regrading or downgrading which will have continuing consequences in the form of lower pay and benefits, but is not in itself an act of continuing discrimination.[16] But, an act extends over a period of time if it is sufficiently entrenched in the organisation to amount to a practice or policy which governs decisions on a particular issue.[17] Which side of the line a particular case falls may not be at all obvious. Furthermore, there may be problems both in identifying precisely when an individual act of discrimination has occurred and whether there is a single act of discrimination or more than one such act.

In *Cast v Croydon College* [1997] IRLR 14, EAT; [1998] IRLR 318, CA, the applicant, after becoming pregnant, was refused permission to return to work after the birth on a part time basis. She did in fact return on what was theoretically a full time basis, but accrued holiday entitlement meant that in practice she only worked part time. Further requests to transfer to a part time contract were refused and eventually she resigned. The EAT held that the only act of discrimination occurred before she went on maternity leave and thus the complaint of discrimination following her eventual resignation was out of time. The fact that she repeated the request did not convert it into an act of continuing discrimination.

Before the appeal to the Court of Appeal, *Rovenska v General Medical Council* [1997] IRLR 367, CA, was decided. This case concerned repeated requests for registration as a doctor. Following her final request and refusal, the CRE wrote on her behalf, but the defendants wrote back confirming the refusal. It was held that each refusal was a separate act of discrimination and that the letter to the CRE was itself a refusal constituting an act of discrimination.

While each case depends on own facts, there is little doubt that *Rovenska* made it easier for the Court of Appeal to allow the applicant's appeal in *Cast*. It was held that the application of a discriminatory policy here amounted to

---

[15] [1989] ICR 157; [1989] IRLR 55.

[16] Eg, *Sougrin v Haringey HA* [1992] ICR 650; [1992] IRLR 416, CA.

[17] *Owusu v London Fire and Civil Defence Authority* [1995] IRLR 574, EAT.

an act extending over a period, so that the effects of the first decision were continuing. In addition, each subsequent refusal was a separate act of discrimination; further consideration was given to the matter rather than mere reference back to the prior decision.

There is no doubt that the Court of Appeal's decision is right both in law and policy. The effect of the EAT decision was to require her either to make a complaint of discrimination right around the time the baby was born, or to make the request on return from maternity leave, in which case the employer might be able to argue that there was insufficient advance warning to be able to accede to the request. Neither in a satisfactory outcome.

A somewhat similar issue arises in relation to internal procedures. If the employee is dismissed, and an appeal against such dismissal fails, it can either be concluded that the confirmation of the dismissal is a separate act of discrimination, or that the original dismissal is the only act of discrimination, but that in such circumstances it would be just and equitable to extend the time limit. In *Littlewoods Organisation plc v Traynor*,[18] the employee complained of racial abuse, was promised by the employer that the situation would be remedied, but in the event nothing happened. The claim was brought more than three months after the original incident. While the claim was correctly permitted to proceed, the argument, that there was here a continuing act of discrimination, fails to convince. While the employer might have been liable for the abuse, failing to remedy it is discrimination of a different form from the original discrimination, and is more appropriately regarded as a 'deliberate omission'.

It has proved remarkably difficult to determine when a single 'act' of discrimination occurs. In *Clarke v Hampshire Electro-Plating Co Ltd*,[19] it was not the date when the applicant was told he was not the person wanted for the job – the date on which he *felt* he had suffered discrimination – but the subsequent date on which someone else was appointed, because only then could it be said that the cause of action had 'crystallised'. In *Swithland Motors plc v Clarke*,[20] it was held that the act of discrimination occurred not when the decision was made, but when it was communicated to the employees concerned which, in the peculiar circumstances of that case involving a receivership, did not occur for two to three weeks. But as in some instances, such as a failure to upgrade, discrimination can occur with no communication with the victim, it would have been preferable to conclude that the discrimination occurred when the action was taken, but to extend the time limit on the basis that it was just and equitable to do so.

---

[18] [1993] IRLR 154, EAT.
[19] [1992] ICR 312; [1991] IRLR 490, EAT.
[20] [1994] ICR 231; [1994] IRLR 275, EAT.

These cases are highly technical but highly important. The three month period is so short that any problem with its application has potential for injustice. While tribunals have discretion to extend the time limit, they cannot be guaranteed to exercise it appropriately. Many potential complainants may be disadvantaged by the shortness of the period; there is a strong case for its extension.

Conciliation

As with other Industrial Tribunal matters, individual claims of discrimination are referred to the Advisory, Conciliation and Arbitration Service in an attempt to promote settlement.[21] Conciliation may be problematic in unfair dismissal cases, but the consensus is that it is even more problematic in the field of discrimination, so much so that it is arguable that it may do more harm than good.[22] First, 'conciliation officers will pursue a settlement. That is their goal. They will not be deflected by the broader issues of principle which an application raises, for it is the immediate interests of the person before them which they have to address'.[23] It is not their function to determine what a case is worth or to point the applicant in the direction of independent expert legal advice. Secondly, there is no guarantee whatever that a monetary settlement will reflect what an applicant might have been awarded had the case reached a tribunal; a significant offer inevitably generates pressure to settle and thereby avoid the psychological and financial costs of proceeding to a hearing. Thirdly, an intransigent employer who refuses all suggestion of settlement may convey the message that fighting on is unwise and thereby lead to withdrawal; this may partly explain the surprisingly high proportion of claims which are initiated but withdrawn in advance of a hearing. Fourthly, it may be more difficult than in a relatively straightforward unfair dismissal case for the employer to accept the possibility that there has been unlawful discrimination; a finding of unlawful discrimination implies a moral condemnation possibly absent from a finding of unfair dismissal. Fifthly, the

---

[21] SDA 1975, s 64; RRA 1976, s 54. The normal rule is that a contractual term which attempts to prevent an employee utilising the legislation is void; SDA 1975, s 77(3); RRA 1976, s 73(3). This rule does not apply to a proper settlement drawn up under the auspices of a conciliation officer, to settlements achieved without such assistance as long as the applicant has received legal advice, nor to cases where a dispute is settled by arbitration; see SDA 1975, s 77(4A)–(4C); RRA 1976, s 72(4A)–(4C), inserted by the Trade Union Reform and Employment Rights Act 1993 and amended by the Employment Rights (Dispute Resolution) Act 1998, s 8.

[22] See, especially, Graham, C and Lewis, N, *The Role of ACAS Conciliation in Equal Pay and Sex Discrimination Cases*, 1985, Manchester: EOC. Like much of the research into the workings of the legislation, this work is now somewhat dated. It is the best we have, but it is impossible to be sure that the conclusions are equally valid today. Eg, we have no knowledge of whether the removal of the maximum limit on compensation has affected the level of settlement where ACAS promotes a conciliated settlement.

[23] *Ibid*, Graham and Lewis, p 61.

variations in the level of compensation mean that it is more difficult to predict what a case would be 'worth' should it go to tribunal, especially as such a high proportion of compensation is for injury to feelings; this makes the process of conciliation more uncertain.[24] Sixthly, 'compared with unfair dismissal ... discrimination complaints are more likely to lead to considerable argument over the facts. When this is combined with less access to hard evidence on the part of the complainant, it is harder to give sensible advice while abstaining from giving an opinion on the merits of the case'.[25]

In 1995–96, of 6,108 discrimination and equal pay cases that were registered, 1,997 were settled and 2,620 were withdrawn. In other words, 75% never proceeded to a hearing. Of those that did, 109 race discrimination cases were successful and 453 failed; 218 sex discrimination cases succeeded and 356 failed; and 36 equal pay cases succeeded and 46 failed.[26] It is hard to draw clear *conclusions* from these figures. The most noteworthy observations concern, first, the high rate of settlement and withdrawal and, secondly, the greater success rate in gender cases than in race cases: 38% as compared with 19%.

EMPLOYMENT TRIBUNAL HEARINGS

Employment Tribunals – formerly known as Industrial Tribunals – are statutory bodies established to resolve disputes concerning the individual employment relationship. They are locally based, and consist of a panel of three people, a legally qualified chair, and two lay people. Appointments to serve as panel members are taken from lists supplied by employers' organisations and trades unions, though it cannot be said that the panel members directly *represent* their constituency. The tribunals were established in 1964 to handle disputes about levies under the Industrial Training Act of that year, a jurisdiction long since disappeared. Their powers were extended to deal with, *inter alia*, disputes under the Redundancy Payments Act 1965 and claims of unfair dismissal under the Industrial Relations Act 1971; since then, unfair dismissal cases have always formed the bulk of their case load.[27] It was seen as inevitable that employment discrimination cases should be resolved in the same way, partly because the same facts might generate a claim of unlawful discrimination and unfair dismissal. There was, however, little

---

[24] *Op cit*, McCrudden *et al*, fn 8, p 190.
[25] *Op cit*, McCrudden *et al*, fn 8, p 190.
[26] See (1997) Labour Market Trends, April 1997.
[27] The statutory basis of these jurisdictions is now the Employment Rights Act 1996, Pts XI and X respectively.

planning or forethought as to the way in which the tribunals would operate.[28] In particular, it was assumed that the normal 'judicial' accusatorial approach would operate, rather than an 'administrative' inquisitorial approach. This assumption has done no favours for the enforcement of anti-discrimination law. Tribunals are rightly perceived as courts, albeit lacking some of the pageantry and formality. Cases proceed by the normal method of examination and cross-examination of witnesses, so legal and forensic skills are hugely significant. The degree of assistance which the tribunal chair will provide to an unrepresented applicant is variable but tends to be very limited, because the impartiality and distance of the court are key features of the distinction between inquisitorial and accusatorial techniques. The assumption, which may be an *ex post facto* rationalisation rather than the original notion, that tribunals will provide a cheap, speedy and relatively informal dispute resolution mechanism, is highly dubious throughout their jurisdiction. It is at its weakest in relation to anti-discrimination law, where the cases tend to be factually and legally complex, often to the tribunal as well as to the parties and their representatives.[29]

Leonard researched the effectiveness of the tribunals in dealing with sex discrimination and equal pay cases.[30] Her study revealed very serious inadequacies in the system. But as she surveyed tribunal decisions in the years 1980–82, the current relevance of the findings is questionable.[31] She particularly identified lack of tribunal expertise as a problem, partly due to the relative rarity of discrimination cases as compared with tribunals' standard work load of unfair dismissal. Thus it was recommended that a full time chair should be assigned to every discrimination case, and that there should be a woman on the panel for every sex discrimination or equal pay case.[32]

The other major problem concerned the availability and quality of legal advice and representation, lack of which may often lead to basic but fatal errors, such as failing to file a claim within three months, and a failure to present a claim in the most effective manner. Not surprisingly, legal representation or the lack of it – on both sides – has been shown to be

---

[28] Davies, P and Freedland, M, *Labour Legislation and Public Policy*, 1993, Oxford: Clarendon, pp 161–64.

[29] The Employment Rights (Dispute Resolution) Act 1998, Pt II, gives ACAS powers to draw up a scheme the aim of which is that more claims should be settled by arbitration and fewer proceed to a tribunal hearing. The scheme will apply in the first instance to unfair dismissal and so will exclude discrimination claims. It is unclear what will happen where both are alleged.

[30] Leonard, A, *Judging Inequality: the Effectiveness of the Tribunal System in Sex Discrimination and Equal Pay Cases*, 1987, London: The Cobden Trust. For similar material in relation to race, see *op cit*, McCrudden *et al*, fn 8, Chapter 5.

[31] It is especially likely that tribunals have improved in their knowledge of the current legal standard to be applied. See *ibid*, Leonard, pp 29–37.

[32] Her study was not concerned with race cases; an analogous recommendation might be harder to accomplish.

significantly correlated with success at tribunal.[33] McCrudden's research concluded that prospects for 'success are considerably better for applicants with legal representation than others; while this is partly due to selection effects (strong cases attract representation) it does probably indicate that legal representation gives applicants better chances of success. Indeed, legal representation seems to be almost a prerequisite of a successful outcome: at only 12% of full hearings that upheld the applicant's case was the applicant not represented by a lawyer, compared with 32% of hearings where the applicant was not successful'.[34] This is undoubtedly still a major problem, despite growing expertise among specialist practitioners.[35] However, access to affordable and effective legal services is hardly a problem confined to discrimination law: it may be that since Leonard's research, there is no longer a significant gap in that availability between discrimination and other branches of law. In the absence of more recent research, conclusions on these issues are necessarily tentative. However, no apology is made for referring to this material. It is important to see that the effectiveness of the legislation depends at least as much – probably more – on access to law and on the quality of decision making than on the technical legal definitions of what is prohibited. The EOC recommends that all discrimination cases, both employment and non-employment, should be heard by a specialist division within the Industrial Tribunal system.[36]

It is however arguable that some form of alternative dispute resolution procedure would prove preferable to the parties, especially applicants, and a more effective means of enforcing anti-discrimination legislation.[37]

Hunter, R and Leonard, A, 'Sex discrimination and alternative dispute resolution: British proposals in the light of international experience' [1997] PL 298, pp 304–11:

[A] major advantage of mediation as opposed to adjudication – or arbitration – is its potential for enabling parties to work out a mutually acceptable solution rather than submit to a decision in favour of one or the other of them. Moreover, the range of outcomes that may be agreed in mediation is much

---

[33] *Op cit*, Leonard, fn 30, pp 88–90.

[34] *Op cit*, McCrudden *et al*, fn 8, p 147.

[35] '[U]se of the law involves skills which large-scale employers may be expected to command far more readily than complainants ... [This] goes a long way towards explaining both the relative ease with which discrimination claims have been defeated, and also the fact that individual complainants are more likely to be successful if they obtain aid from the CRE ... The element of skill also means that each potential loophole will be explored in depth ... delaying tactics adopted, and the like. This is standard practice for good lawyers ... [y]et short of forbidding discriminators to defend themselves in a legal forum, these tactics cannot be curbed.' Lustgarten, L, 'Racial inequality and the limits of law' (1986) 49 MLR 68, pp 77–78.

[36] *Op cit*, *Equality in the 21st Century*, fn 5, para 96.

[37] See, also, Thornton, M, 'Equivocation of conciliation: the resolution of discrimination complaints in Australia' (1989) 52 MLR 733.

broader than is available in the ITs or the county court, or that might result from arbitration. For example, terms of settlements agreed in the [Equal Employment Opportunity Commission] mediation pilot programme and in the conciliation of Australian sex discrimination complaints included, in addition to compensation: apologies; the provision of references; assistance in searching for a new job; reconsideration for a position; making a casual employee permanent; promotion; adjustment to seniority; transfer to a different position; the provision of training; an employee responsible for discrimination penalised or removed from the workplace; the clarification of duties or policies; review of management structure; a voluntary departure package; and the dropping of criminal charges against the complainant. In some ... cases ... respondents also agreed to institute an EEO programme and/or EEO training.

[But the authors highlight several potential problems with private forms of dispute resolution. The first is the removal of issues from the public agenda, so that the educational/deterrent impact of the law is weakened, as well as reducing the scope for the clarification of legal rules and responsibilities. They continue.]

A second potential problem with mediation of sex discrimination cases is that it fails to even out, and therefore reproduces, financial, informational, skill, status and personal power imbalances between the parties. There are suggestions in the literature that alternative methods of dispute resolution work best when the parties are in more or less equal power positions. When this is not the case, outcomes of mediation will be the product of power relations rather than of the free agreement of each party ...

If power imbalances are to be addressed ... the role played by the mediator becomes crucial. A mediator who remains strictly impartial, who sees his or her role as merely to facilitate negotiations between the parties, and who is prepared to accept any outcome the parties agree, can only reflect power imbalances, not rectify them.

[If these disadvantages can be overcome, the advantages of mediation are considerable].

[M]ediation may be very attractive to sex discrimination complainants who cannot produce documentary or other strong evidence to support their claim ... Early referral of weaker cases to mediation might also help to reduce the withdrawal rate for sex discrimination cases, which to date has remained around 30% ...

[M]any disputes are largely factual ... These kinds of differences might again be suitable for mediation, where the parties are encouraged to listen to each other's point of view rather than harden their own position about what did or did not occur and what it did or did not mean ...

In the US mediation pilot project, 21% of settlements included changes in employer policies and practices ... The lowest figure [in Australia] came from the agency which was most determinedly neutral as to the outcomes agreed by the parties, while the highest figure came from the agency which included institutional change as one of the objectives of conciliation ...

Mediation as a method of dispute resolution must be integrated with the substantive provisions of the SDA. It must reflect the aims of and ensure compliance with the legislation. The Act must be treated not merely as a set of guidelines within which parties may or may not choose to operate, but as a source of binding behavioural norms, legal rights and entitlements ... We would argue that the experience of conciliation by ACAS and by Australian complaint-handling agencies illustrates the limitations and inappropriateness of an interest-based approach – [where parties are assisted to arrive at a solution which enhances their mutual interests] – to the resolution of discrimination cases. Arbitration based on general industrial relations standards of fairness ... would also fail to achieve the aims of sex discrimination legislation.

By contrast, rights-based mediation would be an appropriate dispute resolution method for sex discrimination cases. This model prioritises legal rights and the elimination of discrimination. It also intervenes in the power balances between the parties by allowing an otherwise less powerful complainant to assert legal entitlements which have 'an existence and legitimacy separate from the relationship' between herself and the respondent. This model of mediation ... involves certain requirements about the role of the mediator and/or other professionals.

INDIVIDUAL REMEDIES

There are three remedies available to the tribunal if a claim succeeds: a declaration, an award of compensation, and a recommendation for action.[38] The remedies apply only to the successful applicant, reflecting the individualistic philosophy of the legislation. The failure to make the remedies more collective and wide ranging is one of the major failings of the legislation, and contrasts sharply with the class action procedure available in the USA.[39]

Declaration

A declaration is 'an order declaring the rights of the complainant and the respondent in relation to the act to which the complaint relates'.[40] Such an order follows naturally upon a conclusion that the complaint is well founded, but in most cases is accompanied by one or both of the other available remedies, both of which are of more direct practical significance.

---

[38] SDA 1975, s 65; RRA 1976, s 56.

[39] See Pannick, D, *Sex Discrimination Law*, 1985, Oxford: OUP, pp 284–301.

[40] SDA 1976, s 65(1)(a); RRA 1976, s 56(1)(a).

Compensation

The method of assessment is the same as it would be in a tort case; in a sense, therefore, unlawful discrimination is a species of statutory tort. It is, however, specifically provided that 'for the avoidance of doubt ... damages ... may include compensation for injury to feelings ...',[41] a head of damages not normally recoverable in tort.

Limits on compensation

The original legislation provided for a maximum limit of compensation, which, when *Marshall (No 1)* was decided, was no more than £8,500, a figure subsequently increased to £11,000.[42] The rationale for the limit was never explained; it was simply lifted from the parallel unfair dismissal provisions, where the rationale is also unclear. *Marshall* successfully argued that such a maximum limit contravened the Equal Treatment Directive.

Marshall v Southampton and South West Hampshire AHA (No 2) **Case C-271/91 [1993] IRLR 445**[43]

The Industrial Tribunal assessed the loss resulting from the imposition of a discriminatory retirement age at £19,405, which included interest of £7,710. The tribunal ignored the statutory limit on compensation. The issue was referred to the European Court, which held that such a limit contravened the Equal Treatment Directive.

Judgment (pp 449–50):

> [T]he objective is to arrive at real equality of opportunity and cannot therefore be attained in the absence of measures appropriate to restore such equality when it has not been observed ... [T]hose measures must be such as to guarantee real and effective judicial protection and have a real deterrent effect on the employer.

> Such requirements necessarily entail that the particular circumstances of each breach of the principle of equal treatment should be taken into account. In the event of discriminatory dismissal contrary to Art 5(1) of the [Equal Treatment] Directive, a situation of equality could not be restored without either reinstating the victim of discrimination or, in the alternative, granting financial compensation for the loss and damage sustained.

> Where financial compensation is the measure adopted to achieve the objective indicated above, it must be adequate, in that it must enable the loss and

---

[41] SDA 1975, s 66(4); RRA 1976, s 57(4).

[42] As from 1 April 1998, the maximum compensatory award for unfair dismissal has been increased to £12,000; Employment Rights (Increase of Limits) Order 1998 SI 1998/924. The government is now proposing abolition of the limit. See *Fairness at Work* Cm 3968, 1998, London: The Stationery Office, para 3.5.

[43] See, also, [1993] ECR I–4367; [1994] AC 530; [1993] 4 All ER 586; [1994] ICR 242.

damage actually sustained as a result of the discriminatory dismissal to be made good in full in accordance with the applicable national rules.

[T]he fixing of an upper limit of the kind at issue ... cannot, by definition, constitute proper implementation of Art 6 ... since it limits the amount of compensation *a priori* to a level which is not necessarily consistent with the requirement of ensuring real equality of opportunity through adequate reparation for the loss and damage sustained.

[Furthermore] full compensation ... cannot leave out of account factors, such as the effluxion of time, which may in fact reduce its value. The award of interest, in accordance with the applicable national rules, must therefore be regarded as an essential component of compensation for the purposes of restoring real equality of treatment.[44]

The immediate effect of the decision was to disallow reliance on the maximum limit in actions where the defendant was an organ of the State. However, to maintain a distinction on compensation according to the status of the defendant would have been indefensible, as well as potentially giving rise to *Francovich* claims for failing to amend domestic law in line with European law.[45] In consequence, the statutory limit was removed by the Sex Discrimination and Equal Pay (Remedies) Regulations 1993.[46] Had the law been left there, there would have been an anomaly between gender cases and race cases. In consequence, the statutory limit in race cases was removed by the Race Relations (Remedies) Act 1994. This is an excellent example of the piggybacking effect of European law in relation to race discrimination.

It is a general principle of Community law that matters of procedure and remedies are for the Member States to resolve. The European Court has distinguished between a limit on the *amount* of compensation, and a limit on the *period* in respect of which such compensation may be claimed. In the British context, this distinction is especially relevant to limits of the amount of

---

[44] The decision in *Marshall* had been foreshadowed by that in *Von Colson and Kamann v Land Nordrhein-Westfalen* Case 14/83 [1984] ECR 1891; [1986] 2 CMLR 430, where the Court had held that the Equal Treatment Directive requires that any sanction must guarantee real and effective protection and must have a real deterrent effect, and that any award of compensation must be adequate to remedy the damage sustained. In *Draehmpaehl v Urania Immobilien Service ohg* Case C-180/95 [1997] IRLR 538 the Court held, first, that a Member State may not make an award of compensation in a sex discrimination case dependent on showing fault on the part of the employer; secondly, it is impermissible to place an upper limit of three months' salary where the applicant establishes that she would have been appointed but for the act of unlawful discrimination, but that such a limit is permissible where it is established that the applicant would not have been appointed. Such a limit may apply to any financial losses which are established, but is only permissible where the national law gives no better remedies for breaches of analogous provisions of domestic law. Finally, it was held unlawful to establish a limit on total compensation where there is more than one victim of discrimination in relation to the same recruitment exercise.

[45] See above, pp 94–96.

[46] SI 1993/2798. It was held in *Harvey v The Institute of the Motor Industry* [1995] IRLR 416, EAT, that the regulations applied to an award made after they came into effect even if the act of discrimination preceded that date.

retrospective compensation which may be awarded in an equal pay or social security case.[47] In *Johnson v Chief Adjudication Officer (No 2)*[48] it was held that a rule of national law which limited arrears of benefit to 12 months was not incompatible with Community law. The issue in *Levez v TH Jennings (Harlow Pools) Ltd*,[49] which has been referred to the European Court, is whether the two year limit on arrears of pay in an equal pay case is more akin to *Johnson* and thus lawful, or more akin to a limit on damages and thus unlawful.

Compensation for indirect discrimination

Both the SDA 1975 and RRA 1976 originally provided that, in the context of indirect discrimination, 'no award of damages shall be made if the respondent proves that the requirement or condition was not applied with the intention of treating the claimant unfavourably ...'.[50] As a result of recent amendments to the law, there is now a difference between gender and race cases.

It was clearly arguable after *Marshall* that s 66(3), which was designed to make compensation for indirect discrimination the exception rather than the rule, contravened European law. This view was accepted by some Industrial Tribunals, but of course could only be utilised in an action against an emanation of the State. The approach of these tribunals now seems eminently justified in the light of *Draehmpaehl*, where it was held that compensation may not be made to depend on proof of fault. The consequence was the Sex Discrimination and Equal Pay (Remedies) Regulations 1993,[51] which amends s 65 of the SDA 1975. Basically, the same test applies as in a direct discrimination case: it must be just and equitable to make an award of compensation. However, it is spelt out that the tribunal must be satisfied that the power to make a declaration and a recommendation are not in themselves an adequate remedy in the circumstances. The impact of the change in the law remains to be seen. As the bulk of so many awards include compensation for injury to feelings, it is possible that awards may be low on the basis that the tribunal considers that the injury to feelings induced by indirect discrimination is relatively insubstantial.

The statutory change applies to gender but not to race cases. However, the interpretation to be placed on s 57(3) of the RRA 1976 has recently undergone a radical rethink.

---

[47] See above, pp 458–61.
[48] Case C-410/92 [1994] ECR I-5483; [1995] ICR 375; [1995] IRLR 157.
[49] [1996] IRLR 499, EAT. The same issue was referred to the European Court in *Preston v Wolverhampton Healthcare NHS Trust* [1998] 1 All ER 528; [1998] IRLR 197, HL.
[50] SDA 1975, s 66(3); RRA 1976, s 57(3).
[51] SI 1993/2798.

JH Walker Ltd v Hussain [1996] IRLR 11, EAT[52]

A complaint of indirect discrimination arose after 18 employees were disciplined for taking a day off work to celebrate Eid, a Muslim holy day, in breach of a new rule that non-statutory holidays would no longer be permitted during the company's busiest months – May, June and July.

The tribunal held that the requirement was not justifiable and awarded each applicant £1,000 compensation for injury to feelings.

EAT dismissed the appeal.

Mummery J (p 15):

The burden of proof under s 57(3) [to show that the requirement or condition was not applied with the intention of treating the claimant unfavourably on the ground of race] is on the company.

'[I]ntention' in this context signifies the state of mind of a person who, at the time when he does the relevant act ...

(a) *wants* to bring about the state of affairs which constitutes the prohibited act of unfavourable treatment on racial grounds; and

(b) *knows* that the prohibited act will follow from his acts.

In our view, s 57(3) is not concerned with an inquiry into the motivation of a respondent, that is, the reason why he did what he did. It is concerned with the state of mind of the respondent in relation to the consequences of his acts.

[A] tribunal may infer that a person wants to produce certain consequences from the fact that he acted knowing what those consequences would be [for example, continuing to apply a requirement or condition after it had been declared unlawful], even though his *reason or motive* for persisting in the action was one of business efficiency.

The tribunal took account of the company's knowledge of the consequences of its acts and made an inference that it wanted to produce those consequences. The company knew that Eid was important to its Muslim employees, that they were the only employees affected by the application of the condition or requirement, and that they were required to work on that day ... The fact that the company's reason or motive in adopting or applying the holiday policy was to promote its business efficiency does not, in our view, either displace the company's knowledge of the consequences ... or prevent the Industrial Tribunal from inferring that the company wanted to produce a state of affairs in which the applicants were in fact treated unfavourably on racial grounds.[53]

The impact of this decision is unclear. Intentional indirect discrimination may be easier to establish in gender cases than in race cases. In such cases, indirectly discriminatory requirements often have an obvious, general and

---

[52] See, also, [1996] ICR 291.

[53] Likewise, in *London Underground Ltd v Edwards* [1995] ICR 574; [1995] IRLR 355, EAT, a gender case decided before the change in the law, it was held that compensation was payable for indirect discrimination as the employers were aware of the adverse impact of the new rostering arrangements even though they had not been drawn up with the purpose of treating women unfavourably.

well documented adverse impact, knowledge of which employers would be hard put to deny. This point is still relevant despite the change in the law, for the purpose of the requirement and the knowledge of its adverse impact will remain factors in the tribunal's determination of whether it is just and equitable to award compensation for indirect discrimination, and in the amount so awarded. The same may be true of race cases, but not so frequently. *Walker* was a case of direct religious discrimination which the lack of a religious discrimination law meant could only be argued as an indirect discrimination case. It would be relatively easy for a tribunal which was so minded to distinguish the case and hold that no compensation was payable because of the employer's lack of knowledge of adverse impact.

Extension of compensation to indirect discrimination is extremely important. Its absence was based on a quasi-criminal notion that a requirement to pay compensation was only 'just' if the employer was in some way blameworthy. Such an approach entirely loses sight of the functions of compensation, both as a deterrence mechanism and as an incentive to initiate legal action. While victims may sue in order to prevent the discrimination happening to others in the future, the absence of any financial incentive to bring an indirect discrimination case has surely contributed to its lack of use. While the change brought about by legislation and by *Walker v Hussain* will not transform the effectiveness of this area of the law, it was a very necessary step in that direction.

Heads of compensation

Compensation may be obtained for pecuniary losses, non-pecuniary losses in the form of injury to feelings, and aggravated damages. In the current state of the law, exemplary damages may not be awarded.

Pecuniary losses

The principles are the same as in tort; the application of the principles may be far from straightforward, especially where it is unclear whether, but for the discrimination, the applicant would have been appointed to the job in question. As discrimination may be in the 'arrangements' for determining who should be appointed, it may be all but certain that the victim would not have been appointed in any event.

If the tort principles were applied properly and thoroughly, the approach to compensation for loss of earnings should be as follows. First, the tribunal should determine the net annual loss for the job in question. Secondly, it should estimate a reasonable period into the future in which the employee would be performing the job. This is similar, but may be even more difficult than, the process of determining the likely effect of future possible ill-health and redundancy on the plaintiff's earning capacity. Thirdly, the tribunal should make any deduction which is appropriate if the plaintiff has failed to mitigate her loss. Fourthly, the tribunal may have to discount for the chance that the employee would not have been appointed or would not have remained in the job.[54] This approach based on 'loss of a chance' was held applicable to past pecuniary losses in *Ministry of Defence v Cannock*[55] and the same logic must apply to the assessment of future losses. Estimating the chance will be a process fraught with difficulty, and appears rarely, if ever, to be attempted in discrimination cases, but there is no doubt in principle that it *ought* to be attempted. For the applicant to convince a tribunal that he or she might well have been appointed in the face of employer denial will, however, almost never be straightforward. Finally, there should be deducted whatever has been earned in the period up to trial, and whatever it is calculated will be earned in the period for which damages are being calculated.

In practice, cases of future loss of earnings most frequently arise where the allegation is of a discriminatory dismissal, and the claim may be combined with one of unfair dismissal. The principles governing compensation for loss of earnings in unfair dismissal are, with certain modifications, transferable to discrimination cases, and double compensation for the same element is not possible.[56] It should also be borne in mind that discrimination, perhaps especially in a case of harassment, may cause ill-health and thus pecuniary loss. Here the analogy with personal injury cases is closest.[57]

In most cases, pre-trial losses will be both modest and fairly easy to calculate, as the period of such losses is normally fairly short. The exception concerns cases where the losses potentially extend back to the date when the

---

[54] It was held in *Ministry of Defence v Wheeler and others* [1998] IRLR 23, CA, that any deduction for what was or would have been earned in the armed forces, and any deduction for failure to mitigate, should be carried out before the issue of loss of a chance is considered.

[55] [1994] ICR 918; [1995] 2 All ER 449; [1994] IRLR 509, EAT.

[56] Claiming discrimination may be advantageous. Unlike the present law of unfair dismissal, there is no qualification period and no limit on compensation, though as seen earlier (above, pp 509–11) the limit on compensation is to be removed and the qualification period reduced from two years to one. Furthermore, compensation for injury to feelings is very limited in unfair dismissal cases. On the other hand, a dismissal may be unfair without the applicant being able to prove that it was discriminatory; there is no power under the SDA 1975 or the RRA 1976 for the tribunal to order reinstatement, which in unfair dismissal law is an important, albeit rarely used power; and unfair dismissal compensation includes a 'basic award' calculated on length of service which is not dependent upon measurable financial loss. If the dismissal is both discriminatory and unfair, it is possible to add together the most favourable elements of each of the compensation packages, as long as that solely attributable to unfair dismissal does not exceed the statutory maximum. In *D'Souza v London Borough of Lambeth* [1997] IRLR 677, EAT, it was held that additional compensation for failing to comply with a reinstatement order following a discriminatory unfair dismissal was therefore not subject to the statutory limit on unfair dismissal compensation.

[57] In *Thomas v London Borough of Hackney*, unreported, IT, Case No: 42961/93, see 34 DCLD 10, the compensation awarded for racial abuse and physical attack included £10,000 for the severe depression and anxiety which resulted, an element separate from that for injury to feelings.

UK Government should have complied with a European Directive.[58] It is for this reason that the awards of compensation to pregnant women dismissed from the armed forces were so large[59] In most discrimination cases, these hypothetical questions will not be relevant. But the approach to what been lost is of general application. It is simply that the contingencies are much less likely to arise, as the period in respect of which compensation is being assessed is so much less.

Just as in tort, expenses are recoverable, though these are likely to be modest. For example, the applicant may have undergone considerable expense in applying for a job or in travelling to an interview at which discrimination occurred.

Injury to feelings

The EAT has held that there should be an award under this head in virtually all cases.[60] It is clear that the right amount cannot be fixed with any degree of precision. It is a question of fact and impression for the Industrial Tribunal. In *Coleman v Skyrail Oceanic Ltd*,[61] Lawton LJ said that an appellate court can only interfere with an award if the tribunal 'have acted on a wrong principle of law or have misapprehended the facts or for other reasons have made a wholly erroneous estimate of the damage suffered'. Nevertheless, some principles emerge from the cases.

Alexander v Home Office [1988] IRLR 190, CA[62]

A black prisoner's initial assessment was littered with racist comments and stereotypes. On transfer to a new prison he was given work in the press shop where he would normally have stayed for a minimum of three months. On four occasions he was rejected for a job in the prison kitchen and once for a cleaner's job.

It was found that the comments in the initial assessment had resulted in less favourable treatment. The county court awarded £50 for injury to feelings.[63]

The Court of Appeal increased the award to £500.

---

58 It was held in *Emmott v Ministry of Social Welfare and AG* Case C-208/90 [1991] ECR I-4629; [1993] ICR 8; [1991] IRLR 387, that the limitation period for making a claim only started to run from the time that the Directive had been properly implemented in domestic law.

59 See *Ministry of Defence v Cannock* [1994] ICR 518; [1995] 2 All ER 449; [1994] IRLR 509, EAT; Arnull, A, 'EC law and the dismissal of pregnant servicewomen' (1995) 24 Industrial LJ 215.

60 *Murray v Powertech (Scotland) Ltd* [1992] IRLR 257.

61 [1981] ICR 864; [1981] IRLR 398, CA.

62 See, also, [1988] ICR 685; [1988] 2 All ER 118.

63 Work in prison is not 'employment' under the Act. Rather, he was denied access to 'goods, facilities or services'.

May LJ (p 193):

[T]he objective ... is restitution. Where the discrimination has caused actual pecuniary loss, such as the refusal of a job, then the damages referable to this can readily be calculated. For the injury to feelings, however, for the humiliation, for the insult, it is impossible to say what is restitution and the answer must depend on the experience and good sense of the judge and his assessors [or, in employment cases, the Industrial Tribunal]. Awards should not be minimal, because this would tend to trivialise or diminish respect for the public policy to which the Act gives effect. On the other hand, just because it is impossible to assess the monetary value of injured feelings, awards should be restrained. To award sums which are generally felt to be excessive does almost as much harm to the policy and the results which it seeks to achieve as do nominal awards. Further, injury to feelings, which is likely to be of a relatively short duration, is less serious than physical injury to the body or mind which may persist for months, in many cases for life.

[C]ompensatory damages may, and in some cases should, include an element of aggravated damages where, for example, the discriminator may have behaved in a high-handed, malicious, insulting or oppressive manner ...

[I]f the plaintiff knows of the racial discrimination and that he has thereby been held up to 'hatred, ridicule or contempt', then the injury to feelings will be an important element in the damages.

While the general approach set out in *Alexander* still represents the law, the amount awarded was modest by current standards. The case also confirmed that aggravated damages are best regarded not as a separate head of compensation, but as factors which increase awards for injury to feelings.

In *Noone v North West Thames RHA*,[64] the Court of Appeal, while rejecting a contention that £1,000 should be the normal maximum, reduced an award from £5,000 to £3,000 on the basis that, in fixing the appropriate figure, tribunals would need to bear in mind the statutory maximum (£7,500 at the time) and reserve that award for the worst imaginable case. Inevitably, the issue arose whether the removal of the statutory limit affected the level of compensation awarded in cases well below the worst imaginable.

Orlando v Didcot Power Station Sports and Social Club [1996] IRLR 262, EAT

The tribunal awarded £750 for injury to feelings in the case of the dismissal of a part time bar worker when she became pregnant.

The EAT held that no error of law had been committed.

Morison J (pp 263–64):

Essentially, on behalf of the appellant, three submissions were advanced.

(1) [that the Industrial Tribunal paid too much attention to *Noone*, which was decided before the cap was lifted. Without the cap the award would have been higher];

---

[64] [1988] ICR 813; [1988] IRLR 195.

(2) [that the tribunal erred] in having regard to the fact that [she worked] part time. Being a part timer is not relevant to the level of award for injury to feelings ...;

(3) [that the award was perversely low and should have been between £1,000 and £2,000.]

We are not persuaded that the Court of Appeal [in *Noone*] was so linking the amount of an award for injury to feelings to the then limit on compensation that it can legitimately be argued that, without the limit, the award would have been higher ...

On the statistical material available, for what it is worth, Industrial Tribunals have not thought it right to increase awards for injury to feelings simply because of the removal of the cap. If the appellant's argument were correct, presumably every such award would be wrong in law. We disagree.

The relevant circumstances to which a tribunal must have regard will include the nature of the lost employment. A person who unlawfully loses an evening job may be expected to be less hurt and humiliated by the discriminatory treatment than a person who loses their entire professional career. That will not always be so; partly because of the principle that a wrongdoer must take a victim as he or she is. A vulnerable person who has lost what might have appeared at first sight to be an easily replaced evening job may suffer more hurt than a resilient person who loses a career. But it is going too far, we think, to suggest that this is not a relevant circumstance, although we emphasise that the compensation is based on the discrimination rather than the loss of the job *per se*, for which other compensation is available. The tribunal did no more than refer to the fact that she had been humiliated in the context of being dismissed from her part time job. They noted her evidence that she loved her job, was good at it and made many friends through it. All these were matters the tribunal was properly entitled to take into account, and in our judgment the tribunal has made no generalised assumptions: rather, it has applied its mind to the particular facts of the case before them. We should add that in assessing the injury to feelings the willingness of the respondent to admit that he has acted in breach of the discrimination legislation may well help to reduce the hurt which is felt ... [Here she was] spared the indignity and further hurt of having to rehearse the nature of her treatment by the club.

***Armitage, Marsden and HM Prison Service v Johnson* [1997] IRLR 162, EAT**

The plaintiff, an auxiliary prison officer, was ostracised by his colleagues and subjected to a campaign of 'appalling treatment' after objecting to the treatment of a black prisoner.

The tribunal upheld his complaint and awarded a total of £28,500, including £20,000 for injury to feelings and £7,500 aggravated damages.

The EAT dismissed the appeal.

Smith J (pp 165–67):

[The appellant] referred us to the bracket of awards recommended by the Judicial Studies Board for cases of post-traumatic stress disorder. The most severe cases, resulting in an inability to work, attract awards in the region of

£25,000 to £30,000. Moderately severe cases where some recovery has occurred or is anticipated attract damages between £10,000 and £20,000. Cases described as 'moderate' attract awards in the region of £3,000 to £7,000 ...

We summarise the principles:

(1) Awards for injury to feelings are compensatory. They should be just to both parties. They should compensate fully without punishing the tortfeasor. Feelings of indignation at the tortfeasor's conduct should not be allowed to inflate the award.

(2) Awards should not be too low, as that would diminish respect for the policy of the anti-discrimination legislation ... On the other hand, awards should be restrained, as excessive awards could ... be seen as the way to untaxed riches.

(3) Awards should bear some broad general similarity to the range of awards in personal injury cases ...

(4) In exercising their discretion, tribunals should remind themselves of the value in everyday life of the sum they have in mind ...

(5) Finally, tribunals should bear in mind ... the need for public respect for the level of awards made ...

The award of £21,000 is larger than any other reported award ... We do not say it is the worst possible case, but it is certainly a very serious case. It does not seem to us that this award is grossly or obviously out of line with the general range of personal injury awards [or with awards for injury to reputation] ...

We consider that, as a matter of principle, aggravated damages ought to be available ... for the statutory torts of race and sex discrimination. Damages are at large and, at least as far as direct discrimination is concerned, the torts may be sufficiently intentional as to enable the plaintiff to rely upon malice or the defendant's manner of committing the tort or other conduct as aggravating the injury to feelings ... [T]his award is not outside the bracket of reasonable awards and is not so high as to permit us to interfere.

This case sets a benchmark for the proper approach. It is the first appellate decision to attempt to relate discrimination awards to awards in other areas of law. Awards for post-traumatic stress disorder are the most appropriate comparison, not least because discrimination – especially harassment perhaps – might lead to this condition. The EAT also referred to *John v Mirror Group Newspapers Ltd*,[65] where the Court of Appeal attempted to lay down guidelines with the intention of cutting back on some of the more outlandish awards in defamation cases. I wrote in 1989 that 'however deliberate and egregious the discrimination, most employers need fear no more than an award of damages of a few thousand pounds, compared with a maximum of around half a million in defamation cases'.[66] Whatever else has happened, the change in that comparison has been significantly in the right direction.

---

[65] [1997] QB 586; [1996] 2 All ER 35.

[66] Townshend-Smith, R, *Sex Discrimination in Employment: Law, Practice and Policy*, 1989, London: Sweet & Maxwell, p 208.

Compensation in *Orlando* was lower than might have been the case because the employer 'pleaded guilty'. The conduct of the employer is significant in three ways: first, an apology is likely to reduce the injury to feelings, especially as many victims are interested in an apology above all else; secondly, the employer who fights a bad case tooth and nail will increase the injury to feelings, part of which is the stress of the case itself; thirdly, a campaign of victimisation or malice will probably lead to an element of aggravated damages in the award for injury to feelings. In *McConnell v Police Authority for Northern Ireland*,[67] a case under the Fair Employment Act but governed by the same basic principles as to compensation, it was confirmed that the element of aggravation goes to increase the award for injury to feelings rather than being a separate head of damages. However, the fact that the employers did not admit discrimination was not in itself held to be an element of aggravation. Although *Orlando* shows that admission and apology might reduce the injury to feelings, this case shows that an honest defence which is rejected on its merits is not a ground of aggravation. While the distinction is clear and correct in principle, it tends over-optimistically to assume that there is a clear starting point for awards for injury to feelings, which can then be increased or decreased accordingly.

Exemplary damages

At present, these may not be awarded in a discrimination case, despite the decision to the contrary in *City of Bradford Metropolitan Council v Arora*.[68] In a review of the general principles applicable to exemplary damages, the Court of Appeal held in *AB v South West Water Services Ltd*[69] that such damages can only be awarded in respect of torts where they were awardable before the 1964 decision of the House of Lords in *Rookes v Barnard*.[70] Subsequently, the EAT in *Deane v London Borough of Ealing*[71] accepted the inevitable, that such damages cannot be awarded in a discrimination case. It was further held in *Ministry of Defence v Meredith*,[72] one of the armed services pregnancy cases, that Community law imposes no requirement that exemplary damages be available. Claims under the Equal Treatment Directive are analogous to those under the SDA 1975 and the same rule of non-availability applies.

There is a clear argument that such damages are potentially appropriate in discrimination cases, an argument accepted by the Law Commission.[73] Such

---

[67] [1997] IRLR 625, NICA.
[68] [1991] 2 QB 507; [1991] 3 All ER 545; [1991] IRLR 165, CA.
[69] [1993] QB 507; [1993] 1 All ER 609.
[70] [1964] AC 1129; [1964] 1 All ER 367.
[71] [1993] ICR 329; [1993] IRLR 209.
[72] [1995] IRLR 539, EAT.
[73] *Aggravated, Exemplary and Restitutionary Damages*, Law Commission Report No 247, 1997, London: The Stationery Office. This is a general survey into their appropriateness as tort remedies.

damages should be awardable where there is 'deliberate and outrageous disregard' of the complainant's rights, and where 'the other remedies awarded would be inadequate to punish the defendant'. An example given is where an employer ignores, and effectively connives in, a campaign of sexual or racial harassment.

Interest

Marshall (No 2) held that, where applicable, interest must be included as an element of compensation. Both the SDA 1975 and the RRA 1976 were amended in the light of this decision.[74] Interest is normally payable on the injury to feelings element from the date of discrimination to the date of decision. For other losses, the interest runs from a date *halfway* between discrimination and calculation date. In addition, the Industrial Tribunals (Interest) Order 1990[75] makes interest payable on awards of compensation as from the date of the award, except that no interest need be paid if the award is paid in full within 14 days.

Current levels of compensation

'Compensation awards up' (1997) 74 EOR 13

The average award increased in 1996 by 21% to £6,799, from £5,617 the previous year; and the median award increased from £2,615 to £3,614 ... Such figures hide the wide range of awards. At the upper end stand record-breaking awards of just under £114,000 and just over £80,000 ... and at the lower end, awards of £100.

Around 14% of awards were in excess of the current limit on compensation awards in unfair dismissal cases and one in 10 were for £20,000 or more ... At the other end of the scale, just under 15% of all awards were for less than £1,000; and three out of five were for less than £5,000 ...

Analysing the awards in race and sex discrimination cases separately, we found that ... victims of race discrimination, on average, are likely to be paid around two-thirds more than victims of sex discrimination ...

Awards for injury to feelings ... accounted for just over 40% of the total compensation awarded. The average award increased by a fifth, from £2,426 in 1995 to £2,916 in 1996 ... The median award also rose, from £1,500 to £1,750 ...

Tribunals awarded an average of £4,170 compensation for injury to feelings in race discrimination cases compared with an average of £2,565 to victims of sex discrimination ... 14% of race awards for injury to feelings (included aggravated damages) were for £10,000 or more compared with just under 6%

---

74 Sex Discrimination and Equal Pay (Remedies) Regulations SI 1993/2798; Race Relations (Interest on Awards) Regulations SI 1994/1748.

75 SI 1990/479.

of sex awards. At the bottom end, around a third of awards in sex cases were for less than £1,000, compared with 16% of race awards.

The highest *awards* in 1996 were, as indicated above, of £114,000 and £81,000. The former was a race case involving a local authority valuer who was forced into early retirement. The main elements in the award were approximately £64,000 for past and future loss of earnings, £25,000 for injury to feelings, including aggravated damages, and £16,000 interest.[76] The latter case concerned discrimination against a female bond dealer as regards access to promotion. Here, £56,000 was for financial loss, £20,000 for injury to feelings and £8,000 interest. However, 1996 also saw a compensation *settlement* of £200,000 in a case where a female firefighter won her claim on the merits following a five year campaign of sexist abuse from her male colleagues.[77] The tribunal observed that her 'personality and self-confidence have been totally destroyed ... Her daily life was a misery. Her career was shattered'. The award of £358,000 in *D'Souza v London Borough of Lambeth*[78] was so high largely because of the long delay between the finding of discrimination and the hearing as to remedies, which resulted in an exceptionally high award for past and future loss of earnings and for interest. Apart from the interest element, the highest award is of £234,000, the bulk of which was for past and future loss of earnings, to a former senior local government officer.[79]

Recommendations

If it considers it just and equitable to do so, a tribunal may make 'a recommendation that the respondent take within a specified period action appearing to the tribunal to be practicable for the purpose of obviating or reducing the adverse effect on the complainant of any act of discrimination to which the complaint relates'.[80]

The drafting of this power is seriously defective. First, it is limited to making a recommendation affecting the complainant. Those in a similar position are untouched. This utterly fails to grasp that discrimination, by its very nature, may very well occur more than once, in similar or not-so-similar situations. There is no power even to recommend that the employer revises its hiring or promotion procedure. It would be possible to give tribunals power to recommend that employers consult with and take advice from the

---

[76] In 1997, a tribunal awarded £25,000 for injury to feelings and £8,000 aggravated damages for a series of denials of promotion which were held to be on racial grounds; *Qureshi v University of Manchester*, unreported, IT, Case No: 01359/93, see 35 DCLD 6.

[77] See (1997) 71 EOR 2.

[78] [1997] IRLR 677, EAT.

[79] See (1997) 77 EOR 2.

[80] SDA 1975, s 65(1)(c); RRA 1976, s 56(1)(c).

appropriate Commission in order to avoid the recurrence of discriminatory practices. Moreover, a recommendation cannot be made if the employee has another job, where any action by the defendant can have no effect *on that particular plaintiff*. The claimant may even have used evidence of discrimination against others as part of the case, but still no recommendation affecting those others or those like them may be made.[81] There is thus little scope for making recommendations in either recruitment or dismissal cases where the complainant either never has been or is no longer an employee of the defendant.

The way in which the power has been interpreted has not helped. In *Noone v North West Thames RHA (No 2)*,[82] it was held that there is no power to make a recommendation that the victim be hired in the future. The case may not be of general application, first, because a statutory hiring procedure exists for consultant posts, which appointing her directly would necessarily have entailed abandoning, and, secondly, the degree of specialisation involved arguably weakens the argument that they should be, in effect, required to hire her. In consequence, however, the recommendation had no more practical effect than to require the employers to avoid discriminating against her in the future. If it is demonstrated that, but for the discrimination, the applicant would have been appointed, logic and justice demand that she be placed in the position she should have been in.

The fact that the power is merely to recommend is typical of the timidity of UK employment law to the issue of remedies. The law will not specifically enforce a contract of employment and thus will not force an employer to hire an employee against his will. In the law of unfair dismissal, where the tribunal has power to 'order' reinstatement or re-engagement, failure to comply with such an 'order' merely leads to increased compensation. Breach of a court order is here not treated as contempt of court. The point is ever clearer in the context of anti-discrimination legislation; the power is to *recommend* not issue an *order*, and thus the remedy for failure to comply can be no more than increased compensation.[83]

---

[81] 'It seems to be the case that the legislators contemplated the race and sex Commissions following up individual cases to deal with the wider implications, either by promotional work ... or by use of the formal investigation power.' Bourn, C and Whitmore, J, *Anti-Discrimination Law in Britain*, 3rd edn, 1996, London: Sweet & Maxwell, pp 263–64.

[82] [1988] IRLR 530, CA.

[83] SDA 1975, s 65(4); RRA 1976, s 56(4). In one respect, discrimination plaintiffs may be in a better position than their unfair dismissal counterparts, as even the increased award for refusing to comply with a reinstatement order is subject to a statutory maximum. See *O'Laoire v Jackel* [1990] ICR 197; [1991] IRLR 70, CA.

AFTER THE HEARING

The impact of litigation is of course highly variable. Some plaintiffs, both successful and unsuccessful, are victimised.[84] But even successful applicants who are not victimised may find it impossible to remain with their employer,[85] and bringing a case may harm job prospects. The victimisation provisions may need strengthening, perhaps by making it a criminal offence or by setting a minimum amount of compensation, even though this would not transform the situation, both because the pressures which cause people to leave may be too subtle to fall foul of the law, and because it is asking a great deal of an applicant who has finished a law case to commence another shortly afterwards. The extension of remedies in appropriate cases to other similarly situated members of a group would assist in countering the current problem of the isolation and the individuation of victims' experiences.

The impact of litigation on employers is uncertain and largely unresearched. But the CRE has taken steps to utilise the outcome of individual litigation in a strategic manner.

'Life after the tribunal: the CRE and follow-up work' (1997) 76 EOR 13, pp 13–15:

There are basically two types of follow-up work. The first focuses on the individual respondent to ensure that it takes the necessary steps to prevent further breaches of the Race Relations Act, and ensure equality of opportunity ... The second type of follow-up takes a much broader perspective, extending beyond the individual firm to the relevant sector or class of organisation ... For example, following an Industrial Tribunal finding ... that the employer's failure to take prompt action to protect and support a black probation officer exposed to racism from clients was unlawful discrimination, the [CRE] wrote to all probation services, local authorities and health authorities and trusts, giving advice on the decision and its implications for action.[86]

The letter also included the following four recommendations made by the tribunal:

- Clients expressing racist views about staff should receive prompt written advice making it clear that this behaviour is unacceptable.

- Clients objecting on racially prejudiced grounds to the allocation of their case to a particular officer should receive prompt written advice firmly rejecting their attempt to influence the choice of officer.

---

[84] See above, pp 362–63.

[85] *Op cit*, Leonard, fn 30, pp 22–25. *Op cit*, Graham and Lewis, fn 22, p 48, found that only half the applicants employed at the time of lodging their complaint were still employed there six months later.

[86] See *Jeffers v North Wales Probation Committee*, unreported, IT, Case No: 61385/93, see 31 DCLD 5.

- Effective steps should be taken to safeguard the personal safety of officers at risk from racially prejudiced clients.

- Policies on racial equality should be specific in this regard ... and provide for the training of managers in this area.

Employers are not legally bound to collaborate with follow-up work, so why do they? ... [E]mployers realise 'that Industrial Tribunal cases are embarrassing and cost time and resources, they realise it makes business sense to prevent discriminatory practices happening in the first place' ... 'Progress has been most marked with public sector bodies such as local authorities and colleges and with some large national companies.' The most resistant employers ... have been medium sized and smaller firms in the private sector.

STRATEGIC ENFORCEMENT OF THE LEGISLATION

The Equal Opportunities Commission and the Commission for Racial Equality are the bodies charged both with enforcement of the legislation and with acting in various ways on behalf of their constituencies.[87] The statutory duties which they have in common are to work towards the elimination of discrimination, to promote equality of opportunity and to keep the working of the legislation under review, a task which entails the making of reform proposals.[88] In addition, the CRE has the duty to 'promote good relations between persons of different racial groups ...'.[89] For this duty there is no EOC equivalent.[90]

The statutes define and limit the various powers vested in the Commissions. We have already looked at the power to issue Codes of Practice,[91] the duty to assist individuals to enforce the legislation,[92] the duty

---

[87] Especially in the light of incorporation of the European Convention on Human Rights, it has been argued that the CRE and EOC should be merged, the new Disability Commission included, and other human rights responsibilities incorporated into one overarching Human Rights Commission. Whatever the merits of this proposal, there would be a risk of diluting the expertise and specialisms within the CRE and EOC. It is not surprising that the proposal has been put on hold until some experience of the Human Rights Act has been obtained. See (1997) 76 EOR 3. However, a recent Government White Paper has proposed that, in Northern Ireland, the Fair Employment Commission, the EOC (NI), the CRE (NI) and the Disability Council (NI) should be merged to form one over-arching Equality Commission. There are concerns that such a commission would inevitably prioritise issues of religious discrimination, perhaps at the expense of the other issues. See *Partnership for Equality*, 1998, London: The Stationery Office, paras 4.12–4.14.

[88] SDA 1975, s 53; RRA 1976, s 43.

[89] RRA 1976, s 43(1)(b).

[90] For discussion of the structure and functions of the CRE, see *op cit*, McCrudden *et al*, fn 8, pp 49–56.

[91] See above, pp 167–68.

[92] See above, pp 498–99.

to take enforcement action in relation to pressure and instructions to discriminate,[93] and discriminatory advertising.[94] The main emphasis here is on the Commissions' power to conduct formal investigations. In addition, two further ways in which the Commissions may take legal action in their own name will be examined: the power to deal with persistent discrimination and the taking of judicial review proceedings.

How the Commissions operate

The Commissions are quangos; they are nominally independent of government but are funded by government money. A potential conflict of interest is immediately apparent. The Commissions may fund individual actions or formal investigations against the government as an employer, and may seek judicial review against the government. Not only are the Commissions funded by the government; the government 'appoints the Commissioners, approves additional Commissioners for formal investigations, approves the decision making arrangements internally, frequently sends in review teams, provides observers to sit in on chief executive appointments, and reviews the papers for Commission meetings'.[95] Some of the Commissioners are directly chosen by the government, others nominated by the TUC or CBI. There is no necessity for prior experience in matters of discrimination or equal opportunity. The pattern of membership of one-third employer, one-third union and one-third government has its genesis in the corporatist approach to industrial relations epitomised by the Labour Government of the 1970s. It assumes that all sides can work towards a consensus. There are two particular problems with this model: first, to assume that union representatives necessarily represent the interests of women and minority ethnic groups fails to appreciate the conflicts between different groups that may arise within unions and the role that unions have had in maintaining unequal structures; secondly, this approach conceptualises employment discrimination as an industrial relations issue, rather than as a human rights or civil liberties issue, underestimating the cost which the elimination of discriminatory practices may have for *both* sides of industry. Arguably, British industrial relations law and practice has frequently been hampered by a search for a non-existent consensus; the basis of the work of the Commissions may fall into the same trap. In America, the Equal Employment Opportunities Commission, which covers both race and gender discrimination, is a pressure group as well as a law enforcement agency. This is probably due to the fact that powerful statutory agencies, such as the

---

[93] See above, pp 367–68.
[94] See above, pp 324–26.
[95] *Op cit*, Bourn and Whitmore, fn 81, p 291.

Federal Communications Commission and the Securities and Exchange Commission, are part of the American legal and administrative tradition. It has not been easy for the Commissions to develop a sense of identity and a high public profile. There has been internal tension between the legal/conflict approach to their duties and the consensus/bridge building approach. The Commissions encourage employers to take a more proactive approach to equal opportunities and advise them how to do so; at the same time they may be involved with legal action against the same employers.

It is virtually impossible to know how far these somewhat theoretical points actually affect their everyday work.[96] Many staff are committed to a human rights/legal intervention approach and there have been many instances of the Commissions using the law extremely effectively. Many problems that have arisen have more to do with the law as drafted and interpreted than the structure and organisation of the Commissions.

Formal investigations[97]

In most situations the Commissions have no power to institute proceedings directly against an employer suspected of discrimination. The route laid down by the statutes is that of a formal investigation (FI) which may lead to the issue of a non-discrimination notice (NDN). The model for this remedial approach is health and safety law, where inspectors have power through a prohibition notice to order the immediate ceasing of a dangerous practice. The expert agency investigates the facts through an administrative process, and if it finds that unlawful behaviour has occurred, it has the power to order it to stop. The model has two perceived advantages: first, the courts are removed from the day to day task of determining whether discrimination has occurred; not only does this have procedural advantages, but it vests fact-finding in the hands of an expert agency presumed to be more sensitive to the subtleties and nuances of discriminatory behaviour; secondly, the remedy effectively extends beyond an individual complainant to embrace those who are also victims and those who might be in the future. The individualistic thrust which bedevils the English law of remedies is thereby sidestepped.

> **Applebey, G and Ellis, E, 'Formal investigations: the Commission for Racial Equality and the Equal Opportunities Commission as law enforcement agencies' [1984] PL 236, pp 273–75:**
>
> [F]ormal investigations provide the best remedy in five situations:
>
> (1) Cases of 'victimless' discrimination ... where discriminatory attitudes have existed for a long time and are well known so that, for example, women do not apply for jobs ... and no specific act of discrimination therefore occurs.

---

96 The Annual Reports of each Commission are a useful indicator of the balance of different types of work within the Commissions.

97 See *op cit*, McCrudden *et al*, fn 8, Chapters 3 and 4.

(2) Situations where many people are affected, too many for the courts to handle, and where there would be a waste of resources if everyone had to pursue an individual claim.

(3) Where the practices are very complicated and require the ascertainment of facts which are beyond the capacity and resources of an individual.

(4) Where the individual who has been discriminated against is in fact a member of a clearly defined group and the Commission feels it essential to investigate further in the interests of the remaining members of the group.

(5) Where references are made to the Commissions to investigate matters believed to be in the public interest.

To understand why this vision of an effective enforcement agency has been shattered is far from straightforward.

Re Prestige Group plc [1984] IRLR 166, HL[98]

In September 1978, the CRE wrote to the company that they had decided to conduct an FI into the employment by the company and its subsidiaries of different racial groups. At that time the Commission had no specific belief that the company might have committed acts of discrimination. After the FI, the CRE told the company that, having considered the information obtained during the FI, the Commission were minded to conclude, subject to any representations that might be made, that there had been discriminatory practices contrary to RRA 1976, s 28. In November 1981, an NDN was served.

The company claimed that the entire FI was *ultra vires* and void *ab initio*.

Lord Diplock (pp 168–70):

[T]he terms of reference [of the FI] contained no statement that the CRE believed that Prestige had committed acts of racial discrimination of any kind and the CRE, at the time when they gave notice to Prestige of the holding of the FI with those terms of reference, did not, in fact, believe that Prestige might have committed *any* [such] unlawful acts ...

In essence the contention of the CRE ... is that even if the CRE had no such belief when they started on the FI, any invalidity there might have been initially was cured by the subsequent formation by the CRE of such a belief during the course of the investigation, and that this was so notwithstanding that no notice of the formation of the belief was given to Prestige and that no revision was made of the terms of reference of the FI ...

[S]ections 49 and 50 disclose a clear dichotomy between a named-person investigation and an investigation ... which is not confined by its terms of reference to the activities of persons actually named in it. The crucial difference between these two types of FI is that in a general investigation, the Secretary of State, who is answerable to Parliament, retains control of any exercise by the CRE of coercive power to require persons to give oral information or to produce documents; whereas over a named-person investigation he has none.

---

[98] See, also, [1984] ICR 473; [1984] 1 WLR 335.

The discretion of the CRE, who are not answerable to Parliament, as to whether these coercive powers shall be exercised and, if so, how, is quite unfettered ...

In contrast to a named-person investigation, in which the terms of reference must confine it to 'activities' of persons named in them, the only limitation upon the subject matter of a general investigation is that it must be for a purpose connected with the carrying out of the duties of the CRE ...

[T]he nature [of a named-person investigation is] accusatory in the sense that it is directed to determining whether or not there is justification for pre-existing suspicions of the CRE that the person to whose activities the named-person investigation is confined [had committed unlawful acts] ...

Hillingdon London BC v CRE [1982] IRLR 424, HL[99]

The council had the responsibility of housing immigrant families who arrived at Heathrow with nowhere to live. The council felt that national government, rather than the local council, should bear this financial burden and they protested to this effect. The CRE inferred that the council might be discriminating in their provision of housing. They drew up terms of reference under s 49 with a view to an FI, stating that they believed that the council had done or might be doing unlawful acts.

The council sought *certiorari* to quash the CRE determination; the Commission expressly admitted that at no time had they any real belief that the council might be doing unlawful acts.

Lord Diplock (pp 427–30):

It is a condition precedent to every FI embarked upon by the Commission on their own initiative that terms of reference for the investigation should have been drawn up by them, and where the terms of reference are confined to the activities of named persons it is also, in my view, a condition precedent to the drawing up of any terms of reference for an investigation of this kind ... that the Commission should have formed the belief, and should so state in the terms of reference, that the named persons may have done or may be doing discriminatory acts ...

[T]he Commission's belief *as stated in the terms of reference* defines and limits the scope of the full investigation and thus of the information which the Commission may lawfully demand ... [F]airness demands that the statement in the terms of reference as to the kinds of acts which the Commission believe the persons named may have done or may be doing should not be expressed in any wider language than is justified by the genuine extent of the Commission's belief.

The purpose of the preliminary inquiry is to give the persons named in the terms of reference an opportunity of making written or oral representations or both, with regard to the proposal to embark upon a full investigation of unlawful acts of the kinds specified in the terms of reference ...

---

[99] See, also, [1982] AC 779.

The right of a person to be heard in support of his objection to a proposal to embark upon an investigation of his activities cannot be exercised effectively unless that person is informed with reasonable specificity what are the kinds of acts to which the proposed investigation is to be directed and confined. The Commission cannot 'throw the book' at him; they cannot, without further particularisation of the kinds of acts of which he is suspected, tell him no more than that they believe that he may have done or may be doing *some* acts that are capable of amounting to unlawful discrimination ... if their real belief (which is a condition precedent to embarking upon a belief investigation at all) is confined to a belief that they may have done or may be doing only acts of one or more particular kinds ...

To entitle the Commission to embark upon the full investigation it is enough that there should be material before the Commission sufficient to raise in the minds of reasonable men, possessed of the experience of covert racial discrimination which has been acquired by the Commission, a suspicion that there may have been acts by the person named of racial discrimination of the kind which it is proposed to investigate.

If they are of opinion that, from individual acts which raise a suspicion that they may have been influenced by racial discrimination, an inference can be drawn that the persons doing those acts were also following a more general policy of racial discrimination, the Commission are entitled to draw up terms of reference wide enough to enable them to ascertain whether such inference is justified or not. But such is not the instant case; the Commission never did draw any inference of this kind, nor did they suspect the council of doing any acts of discrimination upon racial grounds except in relation to that particular section of the public which consisted of immigrant families newly arrived at Heathrow airport who claimed to be homeless.

At each stage of the procedure, there are difficulties and problems for the Commissions:

(a) A non-discrimination notice can only be issued if the Commission is satisfied, through an FI into the activities of a named person, that unlawful discrimination has occurred.[100] It follows that the judicial hamstringing of the FI procedure directly impacts upon the utility of NDNs.

(b) Prestige decides that there can be no general investigation into the activities of a named person. The EOC may not, for example, conduct a general investigation into whether a university is guilty of gender discrimination in its hiring practices. Only an 'accusatory' investigation is possible into the activities of a named person.[101] This decision should be reversed, enabling a formal investigation to occur without specific evidence of discriminatory activities. But, even were this to occur, the

---

[100] SDA 1975, s 67; RRA 1976, s 58.

[101] This contrasts with general investigations into an area of activity, such as entry into the profession of chartered accountancy, and equal opportunities at a shopping centre. The impact of a general investigation is purely persuasive; an NDN cannot result.

history of the Commissions' work would suggest that such investigations are most unlikely to form the centrepiece of their activities which was originally envisaged.

(c) To embark on a named-person investigation, there must be belief that such person may have committed specific unlawful acts (*Hillingdon*), although *Prestige* held that *some* grounds for belief will be adequate. It seems both safe and sensible to assume that statistical evidence of gross disparity such as is relevant in individual cases would be sufficient to provide evidence of belief. But such information would need to be in the public domain to start with. There is no legal right in the Commission to obtain information in order to determine if adequate grounds for a belief in discrimination exist. The investigation may not be to see if there is such information: that would be a general investigation into the activities of a named person, which is not permissible. One of the reasons for the Courts' requiring the Commissions to show evidence of discrimination before embarking on a named-person investigation is that such an investigation carries with it considerable powers to obtain information from the person being investigated.

(d) The Commissions must give notice to the 'named person' that an investigation is contemplated, state what are the proposed terms of reference and offer an opportunity to make representations.[102] Legal representation is permissible at preliminary hearings, at which the employer may argue that the FI should not proceed or that the terms of reference should be modified. Such preliminary hearings have been expensive and lengthy, as employers have fought to prevent FIs from being started. Not only that, if during the conduct of an FI the Commission discovers evidence of discrimination not covered by the original terms of reference, it must draw up revised terms of reference and hold *another* preliminary hearing providing an opportunity for representations to be made on the revised terms of reference.

The Commissions must issue a formal report concerning the findings of an FI. If the evidence discloses that unlawful discrimination has occurred, or if there has been a finding of breach of the EqPA 1970, SDA 1975 or RRA 1976, the appropriate Commission may serve a non-discrimination notice.[103] This requires the employer not to commit unlawful acts, and, in appropriate cases, to inform both the Commission and other persons concerned what changes to practices and procedures have been made to prevent a recurrence of discrimination.[104] As with the conduct of an FI, there are detailed procedural requirements. The employer must be informed that an NDN is contemplated,

---

[102] SDA 1975, s 58(3A); RRA 1976, s 49(4).
[103] SDA 1975, s 67; RRA 1976, s 58.
[104] SDA 1975, s 67(2) (3); RRA 1976, s 58(2)(3).

on what grounds, and an opportunity to make representations offered.[105] If it is nonetheless issued, there may be an appeal within six weeks to an Employment Tribunal. It is provided that where it is considered that 'a requirement [of an NDN is] unreasonable because it is based upon an incorrect finding of fact or for any other reason, the court of tribunal shall quash the requirement'.[106] Moreover, the EAT has the power to rewrite the NDN as it thinks fit.

Commission for Racial Equality v Amari Plastics Ltd [1982] IRLR 252, CA[107]

The company appealed on the ground that the findings in the non-discrimination notice were contrary to the weight of the evidence.

The EAT held that all facts forming the basis of the requirements in an NDN were open for consideration on an appeal under s 59. The CRE argued that challenge should be permitted only to findings of fact which were relevant to the reasonableness of the Commission's requirements in the NDN, and hence which bore on such matters as the cost or feasibility of compliance with the requirements.

The court dismissed the CRE appeal.

Lord Denning MR (pp 254–55):

[O]n the wording of the statute, it seems to be that it is only on the appeal that the company can get a proper hearing. The appeal to the Industrial Tribunal is the first time that the company are able to put their case. It is the first time they can say that the findings of fact are wrong. It is the first time that they can be heard by an impartial tribunal ... The foundation of the whole NDN is those findings of fact already made by the Commission themselves.

This case shows that the machinery of the Act is extremely cumbersome. This case has taken four years already, from 1978 until now. It is still only at a stage in which further particulars have been ordered to be given by both sides. That will take some time. Then there is to be a hearing. Goodness knows when it will take place. The machinery is so elaborate and so cumbersome that it is in danger of grinding to a halt. I am very sorry for the Commission, but they have been caught up in a spider's web spun by Parliament, from which there is little hope of their escaping.

Griffiths LJ (pp 255–56):

There is no doubt that before a NDN is served, the Commission have carried out a searching inquisitorial inquiry to satisfy themselves of the truth of the facts upon which the notice is based and have given at least two and probably three opportunities to the person to put his case, either orally or in writing ... This is necessarily an expensive and time consuming process ... I can understand the frustration the Commissioners must feel if the Act requires that their findings of fact are liable to be reopened and reversed on appeal.

---

[105] SDA 1975, s 67(5); RRA 1976, s 58(5).
[106] SDA 1975, s 68; RRA 1976, s 59.
[107] See, also, [1982] 1 QB 1194; [1982] 2 All ER 409.

[T]he Commission submit that it cannot have been the intention of Parliament that the findings of fact at which they have so painstakingly arrived in the course of an FI should be reopened on appeal. They submit that Parliament has constituted them as the fact-finding body for the purpose of an anti-discrimination notice, subject only to the safeguard that if they do not conduct the investigation properly and fairly, it can be challenged by ... judicial review. If it were not for the plain wording of s 59(2), I should be most sympathetic to the Commission's argument ...

There is little doubt that the concept of an NDN is potentially very effective in requiring employers to revise procedures and thereby deal with discrimination at a structural level.[108]

Coussey, M, 'The effectiveness of strategic enforcement of the Race Relations Act 1976', in Hepple, B and Szyszczak, E (eds), *Discrimination: The Limits of Law*, 1992, London: Mansell, pp 38–39:

The strategic investigations carried out ... before *Prestige* ... were chosen with reference to the broad labour market position. It was decided to carry out a rolling programme of general inquiries into the extent of inequality in a number of representative industries located in areas of significant ethnic minority population. In this way it would be possible to build up a range of models, demonstrating in practical terms how discrimination operates ... [While many] aims were not fulfilled because many of the early strategic investigations had to be abandoned after the *Prestige* decision ... the experience gained was the basis for many of the recommendations in the Code of Practice ...

Many potentially discriminatory practices were identified. These included informal word-of-mouth recruitment ... and the application of geographical preferences ... Discriminatory selection criteria were also found, such as informal oral or written English tests which had little relation to the standards needed for the work ... Subjective criteria, acceptability criteria and stereotypical judgments were widespread ...

None of the companies involved in these pre-1984 investigations had taken steps to introduce equal opportunities polices. The discriminatory practices could flourish unchecked, as there were no records of the ethnic origins of applicants or employees. Ironically, in the absence of such data, it was difficult for the Commission to find sufficient evidence of discriminatory practices. The alternative was to rely on employers' records of reasons for rejection or their accounts of selection practices. Not surprisingly, the evidence gleaned from this was often too weak to justify the use of enforcement [a problem made worse by *Amari*].

---

[108] Eg, the NDN in relation to Dan-Air required them to cease banning men from employment as cabin staff, to change their recruitment practices, and to provide the EOC with information to enable the changes to be monitored: *Formal Investigation Report on the Recruitment and Selection Policy and Practice of Dan-Air Services Ltd*, 1986, Manchester: EOC. The NDN served on SOGAT '82, as well requiring the provision of information to members and to the EOC, required recognition that seniority in the women's branch counted equally with seniority in the women's branch: *Formal Report: the Society of Graphic and Allied Trades*, 1987, Manchester: EOC.

It is all the more disappointing that the procedural barriers now provide serious disincentives to embarking on the long and expensive procedure that *might* lead to the issue of such a notice. At every stage, from the preliminary hearing, through the investigation, to the question of whether an NDN should be issued and in what form, employers have ample opportunity for challenging the Commissions and for delaying tactics. In consequence, the Commissions, badly stung by their experiences with the courts in the three cases above, have largely abandoned the FI, at least as the centrepiece of their strategy for enforcing the employment part of the legislation.[109] For reasons of tactics and reasons of resource, the preferred approach is now to deal with employers on a voluntary basis, using their expertise to conduct what becomes in effect a voluntary investigation.[110] Under such an approach, the legal technicalities become irrelevant, and undue delay is avoided. Yet such a strategy, for all the evident advantages, is dependent on employer goodwill for its success.[111] A recent example is the agreement between the CRE and the Ministry of Defence to promote racial equality practices in the armed forces.[112] In return for abandoning the possibility of seeking a non-discrimination notice, the CRE persuaded the MoD to introduce detailed measures to recruit more ethnic minority servicemen and women, and to take steps to counter harassment. The agreement contains specific numerical targets for minority recruitment.[113]

Nevertheless, if the agreement is not adhered to, the only powers of the CRE are persuasive and political. There is a strong argument that the Commissions should have powers to seek and enter into legally binding undertakings, breach of which would give them power to go to court or tribunal, where victims of such discrimination would be entitled to be awarded compensation.

Coussey, M, 'The effectiveness of strategic enforcement of the Race Relations Act 1976', in Hepple, B and Szyszczak, E (eds), *Discrimination: The Limits of Law*, 1992, London: Mansell, pp 46–47:

There has as yet been no full scale evaluation of the effectiveness of strategic enforcement ... We do not know whether progress has been faster in those industries which have had sustained experience of strategic Commission activity. Changes in levels of ethnic minority unemployment seem to be due to

---

[109] The point is less true of the non-employment parts of the legislation, but here the emphasis has been more on general investigations which do not have the capacity to lead to an NDN.

[110] For discussion of the way in which the FI procedure changed following the judicial decisions, see *op cit*, McCrudden *et al*, fn 8, pp 78–85.

[111] *Op cit*, McCrudden *et al*, fn 8, pp 94–95, 111–14.

[112] See 'Partnership for equality: agreement between the CRE and the armed forces' (1998) 79 EOR 44.

[113] See below, p 562.

economic factors and owe little to the law. We have seen an increase in the number of employers with equal opportunities policies, but few of these can show a change in ethnic minority participation rates, especially at higher levels.

Experience in the United States suggests that employers begin to take voluntary action when they see it as to their advantage to do so. In order to create this perception, six conditions are necessary. First, the standard must be established by law. Where standards are not so established, employers will change or waive them for economic or professional reasons ... Arguably, the employment Code has such an authority and sets standards for carrying out certain employment practices, but these are not legally enforceable and so fail as regulatory standards.

The second condition for self-regulation is that there must be a vigorous enforcement programme, one in which there is significant risk of serious consequences to employers who flout the standards ...

The third condition is that the results achieved must be objectively measurable ...

The fourth condition is that the law should provide for liability to individuals, so that even where an organisation is carrying out equal opportunity programmes which may protect them from State regulatory action, an individual is free to litigate. This condition does apply in this country ...

The fifth condition is that employers should be better off after voluntary compliance. There must be a regulatory inspection, or other periodic reporting requirements, of voluntary affirmative action plans.

The final condition is that there must be sufficient and organised public concern. Given that there has never been an effective independent civil rights movement in Great Britain, arguably no such condition exists here.

Enforcement in Britain meets only one of these tests, that of private access to litigation.

Persistent discrimination

After an NDN has been issued, or following a tribunal finding of breach of the law, the Commissions have the power to seek a county court injunction at any time within five years if further acts of discrimination are likely to be committed.[114] After such an injunction is issued, further breaches are contempt of court, which could lead to severe sanctions.

Discriminatory practices

In most discrimination cases there will be an identified victim who must establish that a detriment has been suffered. Where there is no such victim,

---

[114] SDA 1975, s 71; RRA 1976, s 62.

action may be taken by the appropriate Commission. A discriminatory practice is an indirectly discriminatory practice where there is no identifiable victim.[115] There is no power to take immediate action before an Industrial Tribunal; the Commission can only act through a non-discrimination notice, having first completed a formal investigation.

Reform

Lustgarten, L, 'Racial inequality and the limits of the law' (1986) 49 MLR 68, pp 72–73:

Discrimination law is hampered in several ways by individuation, but in none so important as the restrictions on the scope of remedies. These may be backward looking (compensation) or forward looking (changes in discriminatory polices and practices). Because all members of the minority group will have been identically affected by the discrimination, it is reasonable that all such persons adequately qualified and shown to be affected be accorded the same remedy as the individual who won his particular case. In the United States, this is accomplished by means of the class action, but there is nothing magical about this particular procedural device: it is quite conceivable that the representative action could be adapted to achieve the same result. The practical consequence is that an American employer adjudged to have discriminated will face a large bill for compensation to all those within the law. It therefore often becomes cheaper and easier to obey the law: the employer is forced to bear the true cost of his illegality because its effect is fully taken into account rather than measured only in relation to the individual who has had the courage, persistence and patience to bring an action. This cost-maximising deterrence is not possible under English law and its absence, by making discrimination cheap, virtually ensures the ineffectiveness of the rights approach.

It is worthwhile summarising the main criticisms of the current remedial structure. Formal investigations may only occur where there is specific suspicion of discrimination. An appeal against a non-discrimination notice may reopen the whole factual premise on which it is based. An NDN cannot require particular changes as opposed to merely requiring discrimination to cease, as there is no power in the Commissions to accept legally binding undertakings as an alternative to the NDN procedure. The Commissions have very few powers to instigate proceedings in their name, such as where patterns and practices of discrimination have been identified, and to seek remedies on behalf of a group of similarly situated victims. While the law on compensatory damages has improved, there is no current power to award exemplary damages, and the tribunal's power to make recommendations is

---

[115] SDA 1975, s 37; RRA 1976, s 28. The provisions do not apply to directly discriminatory practices.

feeble in the extreme. There is nothing which comes anywhere close to an injunctive power.

Furthermore, the two approaches of individual remedies and Commission enforcement have virtually no points of contact with each other. As a result, the advantages of the one system are unavailable to the other. For example, no award of compensation is payable to victims of compensation identified during the course of a formal investigation, and a recommendation may only concern the applicant, there being no power to extend its effects to similarly situated employees. This 'iron curtain' seriously weakens the enforcement arm of the legislation. The Commissions should be given a far greater role as regards individual enforcement, such as by representing in their own name a group of applicants, a power which might be especially useful in equal pay claims. At the same time, tribunals should have power to order that compensation be payable to other victims of similar discriminatory acts, and to require employers to post a plan concerning what steps employers will take in order to prevent a recurrence of such discrimination.

JUDICIAL REVIEW

It is specifically provided that the remedial structure of the legislation 'does not preclude the making of an order of certiorari, mandamus or prohibition'.[116] Thus judicial review may be an alternative method of enforcing obligations under the legislation, assuming that the body charged with having behaved unlawfully is a public body. In *R v Secretary of State for Employment ex p Equal Opportunities Commission*,[117] it was held that the Commission had *locus standi* to allege the incompatibility with European law of the qualifying requirements to claim unfair dismissal or a redundancy payment. The basic requirement for such standing is that the applicant has sufficient interest in the matter, and, after this case, this is unlikely to be a hard task for the Commissions, given that they have a statutory function to work towards the elimination of discrimination. Furthermore, individuals may themselves seek judicial review of an unlawful policy, as in *Seymour-Smith*,[118] and, in the cases where it was eventually conceded that the armed forces pregnancy policy was unlawful, two individual nurses and the EOC each sought judicial review.

---

[116] SDA 1975, s 62(2); RRA 1976, s 53(2).

[117] [1995] 1 AC 1; [1994] ICR 317; [1994] 1 All ER 910; [1994] IRLR 176, HL.

[118] *R v Secretary of State for Employment ex p Seymour-Smith* [1996] All ER (E) 1; [1995] ICR 889; [1995] IRLR 464, CA; referred to ECJ by HL [1997] 2 All ER 273; [1997] ICR 371; [1997] IRLR 315.

SECTION 71 OF THE RACE RELATIONS ACT 1976

This provides that 'it shall be the duty of every local authority to make appropriate arrangements with a view to securing that their various functions are carried out with due regard to the need (a) to eliminate unlawful racial discrimination; and (b) to promote equality of opportunity, and good relations, between persons of different racial groups'.[119] Judicial review is available to contend that a council has acted beyond its powers under this section. In *R v Lewisham London BC ex p Shell UK Ltd*,[120] the council boycotted Shell products because of their continuing ties to South Africa. This was held to be unlawful, because one of the main objectives of the policy was to exert pressure on the company to pull out of South Africa. It was contended that such an outcome would result in improved race relations in Lewisham, but, as Shell had done nothing unlawful, it was held to be beyond the scope of s 71 to seek to persuade Shell to withdraw from South Africa. They could not use their powers under the section to punish a company which had done nothing contrary to English law. Similarly, in *Wheeler v Leicester CC*,[121] the council was held to be acting beyond its powers in withdrawing use of a recreation ground for one year in order to punish a rugby club, three of whose members had chosen to tour South Africa. The club itself had done nothing wrong, its members for this purpose being private citizens. But both these cases make clear that the section does empower councils to have regard to the wider race relations implications of their decisions, even though on the facts their actions were unlawful.[122] Whether it would ever be possible to obtain judicial review based on an argument that a council had *failed* in its duty under s 71 is doubtful, not because it is unavailable in principle, but because the generality of the statutory language would make it hard to establish breach of the section.

---

[119] This provision mirrors one of the functions of the CRE and, as in that context, there is no gender equivalent.

[120] [1988] 1 All ER 938, DC.

[121] [1985] AC 1054; [1985] 2 All ER 105, HL.

[122] For discussion of the particular issue of contract compliance after the Local Government Act 1988, see below, pp 563–66.

CHAPTER 15

AFFIRMATIVE ACTION

It has long been argued that the mere avoidance of discrimination carries with it little prospect of significant overall improvement in the socio-economic position of disadvantaged groups. For that reason, it is contended, more proactive measures are essential, aiming positively to redress such disadvantages, especially in the field of employment. Such action may be undertaken by employers and those concerned with employment, and also, in a more general sense, by the government. Affirmative action is, potentially, legally and politically controversial, especially when it raises the spectrum of a less well qualified person being preferred for a job over a better qualified person. However, whether or not one considers this type of action to be appropriate or permissible, it is important to see that most affirmative action falls far short of such an ultimate step.

The chapter is divided into five main sections. First, the definition of positive or affirmative action will be considered;[1] secondly, we will examine the limited case law on the topic; thirdly, we will consider the areas under the statute where positive action is specifically permitted; fourthly, we will examine lawful steps which may be taken by employers under a voluntary equal opportunities policy; finally, it is necessary to consider whether broader and more radical steps should be either mandatory or permissible. This involves consideration of the theoretical and practical arguments for and against affirmative action, which itself entails some examination of legal developments both in the USA and in the context of religious discrimination legislation in Northern Ireland.

However, it is also argued that one of the most effective reforms of positive action is a commitment by Government to take proper account of equality issues in all their activities.[2] Equality needs to be made a permanent priority and obligation for Government and all public bodies. All public bodies should be under a duty to work positively to promote equality, and to report annually on their achievements in this regard.[3] The mainstreaming of equal opportunity issues is central to real, measurable social progress. It is perhaps beginning to happen as regards gender issues, as is shown by the

---

[1] For the purposes of this chapter, I shall use the terms positive action and affirmative action interchangeably; in general the former is the more common British usage and the latter the more common American usage.

[2] See, also, Chapter 17.

[3] See *Reform of the Race Relations Act: Proposals from the Commission for Racial Equality*, 1998, London: CRE, pp 11–15; *Partnership for Equality*, 1998, London: The Stationery Office, paras 4.1–4.11, which proposes similar measures for Northern Ireland.

Government's concern to present its 1998 budget as 'family-friendly'; there is little or no evidence of a parallel development in the field of racial equality.

DEFINITION

The definition of positive or affirmative action is potentially problematic. There are at least three interrelated types of objective. First, many policies are directed towards the identification of policies and practices which may disadvantage women and black people in the workplace. This is usually a major objective of workforce monitoring, but is really no more than taking action to ensure that there is no direct or indirect discrimination. Such steps are very important, but hardly merit being described as affirmative action. A second type of positive action concerns the organisation of work and the workplace. This category includes the development of policies to reconcile home and work, such as maternity and childcare policies, career break schemes, etc. Anti-harassment policies can also be classified under this heading, though there is clearly the additional element of the prevention of unlawful behaviour. To some extent, these issues are dealt with elsewhere, though they are frequently and properly included in a company equal opportunity policy. The third focus, often the source of the greatest controversy, is on positive action to overcome the fact that, in many jobs, black people and women are under-represented.[4] This may vary from outreach programmes designed to increase the number of applicants from members of groups perceived to be disadvantaged, through the provision of training designed to promote competition on a level playing field with white males, to programmes which take account of the actual numbers performing such jobs, whether in the form of aims or targets, or in the form of quotas whereby a particular proportion of jobs in a particular grade is reserved for women or black people. This final example might be referred to as reverse discrimination, as it permits the hiring of a person with fewer qualifications for the position than an unsuccessful candidate, and is clearly unlawful under English and European law.

The above classification is not the only possible approach.

McCrudden, C, 'Rethinking positive action' (1986) 15 Industrial LJ 219, pp 223–25:

Five types of action appear to come under the rubric of what positive action *might* include, not in the sense of what is legally permissible, but in the sense of how the term appears to be used in common parlance.

---

4   Logically, the same approach could be taken to the issue of the under-valuation of typically female jobs; it is purely for convenience that positive action in relation to that issue is considered in the equal pay chapter.

Eradicating discrimination ... Employers should be encouraged to consider it necessary to review regularly the steps taken to eradicate unlawful discrimination, assess the effectiveness of the steps taken, and consider what more needs to be done to achieve the objective ...

Facially neutral but purposefully inclusionary polices. Such policies seek to increase the proportion of members of the previously excluded or currently under-represented group ... Thus, for example, the status of being unemployed or living in a particular geographical area might be stipulated as a relevant condition ... with the knowledge that a greater proportion ... are members of the under-represented group than the majority group.

Outreach programmes ... Outreach programmes are designed to attract qualified candidates from the previously under-represented group. They do so in two ways: first, by bringing employment opportunities to the attention of members of the group who might not previously have been aware of them and encouraging them to apply ... second, by providing members of the under-represented group ... with training the better to equip them for competing when they do apply.

Preferential treatment in employment ... This ... involves a plan to reduce under-representation ... more directly ... by introducing what has sometimes been called reverse discrimination in favour of members of the group ... There may be different aspects of the employment relationship covered, with some programmes involving preferences only in hiring while others extend to promotion and redundancy. A second difference relates to whether race or gender is merely a relevant consideration among others (eg, where minority status is a positive factor to be considered in evaluating the applications of minority applicants) or whether it is the sole consideration (eg, where a predetermined number of new hires is reserved for qualified minority applicants).

Redefining 'merit'. This ... differs from the previous four in that it alters substantially the qualifications which are necessary to do the job by including race, gender or religion as a relevant 'qualification' in order to be able to do the job properly ... Positive action has been defended, for example, as a means of encouraging the recruitment of more social workers from minority groups ...

CASE LAW

Because affirmative action is voluntary, it can never be contended that employers are under an obligation to engage in it, or that courts should order it as a remedy for proven acts of unlawful discrimination. Rather, the cases concern situations where it is alleged that more has been done than is legally permissible. That there are so few may imply the relative rarity of such action.

Hughes v London Borough of Hackney (1986), unreported, London Central Industrial Tribunal, see 7 EOR 27.

A job advertisement stated that 'Blacks and ethnic minorities are heavily under-represented in the [authority's] Parks and Open Spaces Services ... We would therefore warmly welcome applications from black and ethnic minority people for the two [gardening] apprenticeships.

The applicant was rejected by letter which stated that 'you cannot be considered for these posts as they are only open to black and ethnic minority people as was indicated in the advertisement'.

The tribunal upheld his claim of unlawful discrimination. The phrase 'access to facilities and services' [in s 35 of the RRA 1976] is not wide enough to encompass the provision of job opportunities ... '[E]ncouraging' [black people to apply] does not extend to providing job opportunities for one section of the community. If Parliament had intended to provide immunity for a discriminatory act in the circumstances of the present case, clear and precise language would have been used.

The case thus reflects and upholds the clear statutory policy of distinguishing between, on the one hand, positive action in the sense of encouraging people to apply for jobs and enabling them to be appropriately qualified for such jobs and, on the other hand, restricting jobs to members of one race or one gender, or, by logical extension, requiring lower qualifications for women or black people.

Jepson and Dyas-Elliott v The Labour Party [1996] IRLR 116, IT

This case concerned the then policy of the Labour Party of requiring certain constituencies to draw up all-female shortlists for parliamentary candidates in order to increase the number of women MPs.

The policy was challenged by the two applicants on the ground that s 13 of the SDA 1975, which deals with discrimination by qualifying bodies, applied to local constituency Labour Parties.

Judgment (pp 117–18):

It may well be that many would regard [the aim of the policy] as a laudable motive but that is of no relevance to the issue of whether the arrangement ... results in direct unlawful sex discrimination ...

As [s 13] now stands it covers, and in our view was widely drafted as being clearly intended to cover, all kinds of professions, vocations, occupations and trades in which persons may engage, whether paid or unpaid and whether they be 'employment' as defined in s 82 or not ... including thereby persons who hold public offices ...

[W]e can see no reason why what we perceive to be the deliberately drawn wide ambit of s 13 that for the applicants to be seeking the approval of the Labour Party or the constituency Labour Party to their being selected as prospective official Labour Party candidates with a view to that facilitating possible future engagement in the occupation of being a Member of Parliament should not be regarded as falling within s 13.

At one level, this is a purely technical decision as to the correct interpretation of s 13 and of no general import. At another level, it reveals and epitomises the fact that the merits of such policies are irrelevant. The reason, of course, is that the general policy of the legislation protects white people and men in precisely the same way as black people and women. The symmetry of the anti-discrimination principle denies the legality of any of the more radical forms of affirmative action – though, in saying that, the degree of radicalism inherent in the Labour Party policy was hardly extreme. The rejection of policy discussion is also manifested in *Hughes*: a policy to increase the number of black people or women doing a particular job does not prevail over the *individual's* right not to be discriminated against, that is to be treated on the basis of merit. The reasoning in the leading case on the definition of direct discrimination, *James v Eastleigh BC*,[5] is itself dependent on a rejection of the contention that a good motive may be a defence to a claim of unlawful direct discrimination. While this is crucial as necessitating rejection of what might generally be regarded as bad motives, such as cost and customer preference, the decision treats all motives, good and bad, in the same condemnatory fashion. However, to entrust decisions as to the validity of motives to Employment Tribunals – or any courts – would itself be problematic. Such decisions would inevitably draw courts and tribunals into issues of great political sensitivity, as has happened in the USA. It is arguable that decisions as to the permissible scope of affirmative action are, so far as possible, more appropriately taken by legislatures than by the judiciary.

European law grants the same primacy as English law to the principles of symmetry and the individual's right to be free of discrimination. Until recently, the only pronouncements of the European Court in relation to positive action concerned the specific issues of pregnancy and maternity, areas which do not concern the question of the scope of permissible positive action in relation to recruitment. The next case, where the positive action was extremely limited, reveal deep-rooted judicial hostility at the European level to the very concept. Such hostility is especially apparent from the opinion of the Advocate General, whose philosophy was wholeheartedly endorsed in the much briefer judgment of the full Court.

Kalanke v Freie Hansestadt Bremen **Case C-450/93 [1995] IRLR 660**

The case concerned promotion to the position of section manager in the Parks Department. After determining that the two candidates were equally qualified, the employers gave preference to the woman under the Bremen public service law, which required such preference where the candidates were equally qualified and where women were under-represented, defined as where women 'do not make up at least half the staff ... in the relevant personnel group ...'.

---

5   [1990] 2 AC 751; [1990] 2 All ER 607; [1990] IRLR 208, HL.

Judgment (pp 667–68):

A national rule that, where men and women who are candidates for the same promotion are equally qualified, women are automatically to be given priority in sectors where they are under-represented, involves discrimination on grounds of sex.

It must, however, be considered whether such a rule is permissible under Art 2(4) [of the Equal Treatment Directive], which provides that the Directive 'shall be without prejudice to measures to promote equal opportunity for men and women, in particular by removing existing inequalities which affect women's opportunities'.

That provision is specifically and exclusively designed to allow measures which, although discriminatory in appearance, are in fact intended to eliminate or reduce actual instances of inequality which may exist in the reality of social life ...

It thus permits national measures relating to access to employment, including promotion, which give a specific advantage to women with a view to improving their ability to compete in the labour market and to pursue a career on an equal footing with men.

National rules which guarantee women absolute and unconditional priority for appointment or promotion go beyond promoting equal opportunities and overstep the limits of the exception in Art 2(4) ...

Advocate General (pp 663–64):

To my mind, giving equal opportunities can only mean putting people in a position to attain equal results and hence restoring conditions of equality between members of the two sexes as regards starting points. In order to achieve such a result, it is obviously necessary to remove the existing barriers standing in the way of the attainment of equal opportunities between men and women ...

It seems to me to be all too obvious that the national legislation at issue in this case is not designed to guarantee equality as regards starting points. The very fact that two candidates of different sex have equivalent qualifications implies in fact by definition that the two candidates have had and continue to have equal opportunities; they are therefore on an equal footing at the starting block. By giving priority to women, the national legislation at issue therefore aims to achieve equality as regards the result or, better, fair job distribution simply in numerical terms between men and women. This does not seem to me to fall within either the scope or the rationale of Art 2(4) of the Directive ...

Article 2(4) ... does enable intervention by means of positive action, but ... only so as to raise the starting threshold of the disadvantaged category in order to secure an effective situation of equal opportunity. Positive action must therefore be directed at removing the obstacles preventing women from having equal opportunities by tackling, for example, educational guidance and vocational training. In contrast, positive action may not be directed towards guaranteeing women equal results from occupying a job, that is to say, at points of arrival, by way of compensating for historical discrimination. In sum, positive action may not be regarded, even less employed, as a means of remedying, through discriminatory measures, a situation of impaired equality in the past.[6]

Such quotas are relatively commonplace in Germany and their lawfulness a matter of some political significance.[7] However, the operation of the system apparently left no room for leeway as under-representation was not merely *a* relevant factor; rather, if under-representation was established, and two candidates were held to be equally qualified, the law required automatic preference to be given to women, so, for example, a man repeatedly rejected on this basis would have no ground for complaint.[8] Furthermore, the 'target for women's representation in the public service chosen by the Bremen legislature was notably crude. Women may represent 50% of the population, but because of family responsibilities, women do not represent 50% of the economically active population. There was no attempt by Bremen to measure women's availability in the labour market or the proportionate numbers with qualifications for particular posts or grades. Thus, to give preference to women until they form 50% of each post and grade bore little relation to what the position would be in the absence of sex discrimination'.[9]

The reaction to *Kalanke* was almost universal hostility, especially from the European Commission, which itself operated a scheme not unlike that which the European Court had condemned and thus had a vested interest in the issue. The Commission, in a communication sent to the European Parliament and the Council,[10] stated that the decision was only meant to condemn automatic quota systems which preventing the taking into account of individual circumstances. Unsurprisingly, the European Court had a second look at the issue.

Marschall v Land Nordrhein-Westfalen Case C-409/95 [1988] IRLR 39

The plaintiff was a teacher who applied for promotion. The relevant rule stated that where 'there are fewer women than men in the particular higher grade post in the career bracket, women are to be given priority for promotion in the event of equal suitability, competence and professional performance, unless reasons specific to an individual [male] candidate tilt the balance in his favour'. The plaintiff's application was rejected by virtue of the operation of this rule. In this case the Court took a significantly softer attitude than in *Kalanke*.

Judgment (p 48):

[E]ven where male and female candidates are equally qualified, male candidates tend to be promoted ... particularly because of prejudices and

---

6   For comment, see Szyszczak, E, 'Positive action after *Kalanke*' (1996) 59 MLR 876.
7   See Shaw, J, 'Positive action for women in Germany: the use of legally binding quota systems', in Hepple, B and Szyszczak, E (eds), *Discrimination: The Limits of Law*, 1992, London: Mansell.
8   See (1996) 65 EOR 31.
9   *Ibid.*
10   COM(96) 88 final.

stereotypes concerning the role and capacities of women in working life and the fear, for example, that women will interrupt their working lives more frequently, that owing to household and family duties they will be less flexible in their working hours, or that they will be absent from work more frequently because of pregnancy, childbirth or breastfeeding.

For these reasons, the mere fact that a male candidate and a female candidate are equally qualified does not mean that they have the same chances.

It follows that a national rule, in terms of which, subject to the application of the saving clause, female candidates for promotion who are equally as qualified as the male candidates are to be treated preferentially in sectors where they are under-represented may fall within the scope of Art 2(4) if such a rule may counteract the prejudicial effects on female candidates of the attitudes and behaviour described above ...

[S]uch a national measure specifically favouring female candidates cannot guarantee absolute and unconditional priority for women in the event of a promotion without going beyond the limits of the exception laid down in [Art 2(4)] ...

[A] national rule which contains a saving clause does not exceed those limits if, in each individual case, it provides for male candidates who are equally as qualified as the female candidates a guarantee that the candidatures will be the subject of an objective assessment which will take account of all criteria specific to the individual candidates and will override the priority accorded to the female candidates where one or more of the criteria tilts the balance in favour of the male candidate.

'Limited positive discrimination allowed' (1998) 77 EOR 38, pp 39–40:

Positive action is the engine of progress for women in many Member States. Lacking a tradition of litigation by individuals to enforce the right not to be discriminated against such as has developed in the UK, women in countries such as Germany, Austria, the Netherlands and Scandinavia have focused on measures increasing group representation ... [R]ules mandating preferential treatment where women are under-represented are often the main way in which equal opportunities are implemented in practice ...

The reasoning [in *Marschall*] is undistinguished. It is extremely difficult to see how this kind of positive discrimination can be said to fall within the scope of the derogation from the principle of non-discrimination allowed by Art 2(4) for 'measures to promote equal opportunity' ... The intention of the rule-maker, however, should have been of little weight; all positive discrimination measures are intended to reduce inequality, including the measure held unlawful in *Kalanke*. The relevant issue is not intent, but whether the rule properly falls within the description of a 'measure to promote equal opportunity' ...

[O]peration of the rule does not require any prior assessment of how likely it is that women would be equally represented in the grade if there had been no discrimination by the employer. In many jobs, the proportion of women is a function of sex discrimination in education or vocational training, or of occupational choice by women, not of sex discrimination in recruitment by the employer. An employer can appoint 20% of all female applicants and 20% of all male applicants, but if there are 10 times as many men as women applying, there will be far fewer women than men in the post. Does this mean that women are 'under-represented' and should be given preferential treatment? ...

The practical impact of the case is highly dependent on when two people can properly be regarded as equally qualified. In the wide range of jobs where personal factors play a part in a hiring decision, it will not be difficult to justify a conclusion that there was no equality. It may be, however, that in Germany candidates were sometimes treated as equally qualified just so as to trigger the operation of the tie-break provision. In *Marschall*, the employer stated that 'a man would tend to be appointed over an equally qualified woman ... because he is likely to be older and to have had longer service ...'.[11] In Britain the experience of the respective candidates would normally feature as one of the qualifications for the job. If such qualifications prove unnecessary, they may be challenged on the basis of indirect discrimination. While the reasoning in the case can be criticised, it is clear that the European Court will not countenance any form of positive discrimination which is more extensive in scope than that at issue in *Marschall*. That necessarily constrains the ability of the UK Government to amend domestic law to widen the scope of permissible action even – and this seems most unlikely at present – were they minded to do so.

DOMESTIC LEGISLATION[12]

Both the RRA 1976 and the SDA 1975 spell out certain forms of permissible positive action. It is vital to grasp that these are not the *only* steps which may be taken. Positive action is only unlawful if it results in an individual becoming the victim of unlawful discrimination. Most action under employer equal opportunity policies concerns general policies and practices which do not result in the creation of any individual victims. Indeed, much of what is specifically spelled out in the legislation and the Codes of Practice as permissible may strictly speaking be legally unnecessary, but to do so is of importance symbolically and as an encouragement to the taking of voluntary action.

There are two types of permissible positive action under the legislation, one designed to persuade more of the disadvantaged group to apply for the job in question, and the other to equip members of such groups with the skills to enable them effectively to compete for such jobs.

The objective of positive action is to increase the numbers of women and black people doing a particular job. There is no such need if the numbers

---

[11] (1998) 77 EOR 38, p 40.
[12] See 'Achieving equal opportunity through positive action' (1987) 14 EOR 13.

doing the job in question are approximately proportionate to numbers in the general population. Thus, to trigger the legislation, 'under-representation' must be shown. Under s 47(1) of the SDA 1975, this applies where 'at any time within the 12 months immediately preceding the doing of the act there were no persons of the sex in question doing that work or the number of persons of that sex doing the work was comparatively small'.

The RRA 1976 definition in s 37(1) requires either:

(a) that there are no persons of the racial group in question among those doing the work at that establishment; or

(b) that the proportion of persons of that group doing that work at that establishment is small in proportion with the proportion of persons of that group:

(i) among all those employed by that employer there; or

(ii) among the population of the area from which that employer normally recruits persons for work in his employment at that establishment.

Under s 47 of the SDA 1975, what matters is the numbers of women *as a whole* doing the kind of work in question.[13] It makes no difference whether there is such under-representation in the employment of the particular employer. An enlightened employer may thus continue with such policies even after there is adequate representation at that particular enterprise. Section 48 is different, focusing on the issue of whether there is under-representation among women doing the particular job for the particular employer.[14]

There is no authority on the meaning in this context of 'comparatively small'.[15] Two suggestions are offered. First, it must mean comparatively small in relation to the total number of women in the population rather than in relation to the proportion of women employed in similar positions by other employers. Secondly, without offering any figure, it is suggested that the provisions will not be triggered by any under-representation short of equality. One of the problems with the approach adopted by the employers in *Kalanke* was that under-representation was defined as any figure short of 50%. One of the difficulties with legal intervention, perhaps inevitably, is that there is no sliding scale of what is permissible. The *degree* of under-representation has no effect at all on the scope of the permitted positive action. In policy terms, the greater the degree of under-representation, the greater and more varied the steps an employer should be encouraged and permitted to take.

---

[13] Section 48(2) provides that the definition of under-representation may be satisfied for an area within Great Britain even if it is not satisfied for the country as a whole.

[14] For discussion of the meaning of under-representation in the context of the Fair Employment (Northern Ireland) Act, see McCrudden, C, 'Affirmative action and fair participation: interpreting the Fair Employment Act 1989' (1992) 21 Industrial LJ 170, pp 186–90.

[15] See Sacks, V, 'Tackling discrimination positively', in Hepple, B and Szyszczak, E (eds), *Discrimination: the Limits of Law*, 1992, London: Mansell, pp 376–78.

The RRA 1976 definition of under-representation is different in two main ways. First, it focuses on the numbers employed by the particular employer, rather than looking at the statistics more broadly.[16] Secondly, in determining whether there is under-representation, attention must be directed to the labour market area from which the employer normally recruits.[17] The former point may in part be due to the difficulty in obtaining information about the numbers of ethnic minorities doing particular jobs; it is certainly more straightforward to focus on an individual employer. It may be shown that there is under-representation in one job compared with other jobs in the same employment – a comparison between supervisory and lower level jobs might be appropriate. It may also be shown that there is under-representation compared with the employer's normal labour market. In *Hughes v Hackney*, 9% of gardeners were of ethnic minority origin compared with 37% of the borough's population. However, as only 58% of recruits came from within the borough, the Court held that the employer's defence failed, as there was no evidence of where the remaining recruits came from or what percentage of that group were from minority ethnic groups.[18]

Sacks, V, 'Tackling discrimination positively' in Hepple, B and Szyszczak, E (eds), *Discrimination: The Limits of Law*, 1992, London: Mansell, p 376:

Of the organisations researched, none of the smaller ones had sought the statistical evidence required, and indeed a significant number of them were either totally unaware of this requirement or somewhat hazy as to the precise conditions. Most had taken an impressionistic approach and had set up courses without regard to the need for a precise statistical base. Apart from the obvious fact that this part of the Act is little known or understood, difficulties would have lain in wait even for those more legally aware. Statistics are not collected by the Department of Employment on a trade by trade basis: for example, the numbers of people employed in the construction industry are collected on the basis of whether they are managerial, administrative or manual, and not on the basis of skills such as welders, plumbers, bricklayers, etc. Thus for many occupations, compliance with the letter of the Act is not possible.

If under-representation is established, s 47(1) of the SDA 1975 permits an employer to do acts '(a) affording women only, or men only, access to facilities for training which would help to fit them for that work; or (b) encouraging women only, or men only, to take advantage of opportunities for doing that work ...'. Section 47(3) specifically provides that the special need for training may be 'by reason of the period for which [the recipients] have been

---

[16] Section 38(1).

[17] Section 38(2).

[18] While literally s 38(2)(b)(ii) appears to refer to the area from which the employer normally recruits for any job in his establishment, it is clearly sensible in policy terms to focus on the labour market from which the employer recruits for the particular job under consideration; this was the approach adopted by the IT in *Hackney*.

discharging domestic or family responsibilities to the exclusion of regular full time employment'. This section entitles employers to target training courses for women, assuming that the general provision for under-representation is met. For example, training bodies may organise courses designed to familiarise women with technical changes which occurred during their period of absence from the labour market. The employer providing the training may well have a majority or even an entirely female workforce, especially if an organisation dedicated to the provision of such training.[19] Section 37 of the RRA 1976 grants the same permission to training opportunities which discriminate on grounds of race.[20]

There is no question that the restriction of training opportunities to members of a particular race or gender would, in the absence of specific provision, be unlawful. This is not necessarily true of other practices mentioned in the statutes. In particular, encouraging only women to apply for a job does not entail discrimination against any individual man in the arrangements made for determining who is to be offered a job. It is thus permissible to state in advertisements that applications from women or black people will be particularly welcome because of under-representation. It may be lawful to adopt such a policy even where the specific under-representation provisions are not satisfied, but an employer would need to show that, despite the statement, there was no discrimination in the arrangements made for determining who should be employed. To make such a statement otherwise than in specific accord with the statutory provisions would be a high-risk strategy for an employer.

Other forms of acting to increase the number of female or black applicants are also permissible. For example: advertising not only in traditional outlets but also in black newspapers; sending careers information specifically to schools with a substantial black population; notifying employment agencies that applications from women or black people are particularly welcome. It is here hard to see that there is any male or white victim of discrimination, especially if the targeting is not exclusively aimed at black or female recipients.[21] If male or white applicants have in the past predominated, taking action to increase the number of female or black applicants does not involve

---

[19] Sacks, *op cit*, fn 15, p 379, found that about one-quarter of the training organisations surveyed employed only women tutors. The general view was that it was 'vitally important for the trainees to be with women who could serve as role models and who would be more sympathetic and understanding'. Such a practice may well be unlawful: it is doubtful whether the provision of such courses could come within the 'personal services' genuine occupational qualification in SDA 1975, s 7(3).

[20] It was formerly the case that such training could only lawfully be provided by bodies designated as being permitted to offer such training. The need for designation was, in the context of gender, removed by the SDA 1986, and, for race, by the Employment Act 1989.

[21] To take a different but parallel example, that Oxford and Cambridge universities might attempt to encourage more applicants from comprehensive schools certainly implies no discrimination against applicants from private schools.

any less favourable treatment, and no requirement or condition, however widely that be interpreted, is imposed. Furthermore, it is only if the targeting is exclusively aimed that the statutory sections apply and thus need to be satisfied. Employers might wrongly be led to believe that the only permissible encouragement is that falling within the precise wording of the statute.

Section 48 of the SDA 1975 and s 38 of the RRA 1976 apply similar principles to encouragement and training provided by employers in relation to work in their employment. This is of especial significance in relation to career development, promotion, etc. If women or black people are under-represented in supervisory or management positions, it is lawful to run training courses to equip them for such positions, and specifically to encourage applications from members of these groups. The relevance and effectiveness of such policies depend on the reasons for the under-representation. 'There is a real risk that special training schemes will be set up to cater for ethnic minorities and women when the real problem is not that they lack training, but that there was a reluctance to appoint them to supervisory positions because of their race or sex. If the persons on such training schemes look to be already well qualified, the chances are that the organisation concerned has expected ethnic minority or women managers to be better qualified than whites or men ...'[22]

By far the most important point concerning these provisions is that they are in all circumstances permissive rather than mandatory, unlike the law on affirmative action which applies to Northern Ireland. British employers are *never* under a positive obligation to engage in any form of affirmative action, from the mildest forms of encouragement upwards. The sections themselves are complex and ill understood. Lack of detailed knowledge of the law may cause employers both to fear legal challenge and to underestimate the scope of what is lawful. Many employers have implemented voluntary equal opportunities policies, but it is contended that these sections have rarely been central to such decisions.

EQUAL OPPORTUNITIES IN PRACTICE

It has been argued that affirmative action is widespread in the USA for four main reasons: (a) the public availability of the requisite statistics; (b) the potential imposition of extremely high damages; (c) the powerful position of the Equal Employment Opportunities Commission in conciliating and monitoring out-of-court settlements; and (d) the power and willingness of the

---

[22] Bourn, C and Whitmore, J, *Anti-Discrimination Law in Britain*, 3rd edn, 1996, London: Sweet & Maxwell, pp 146–47.

courts to make positive action orders.[23] None of these four criteria apply to the current British situation. Why, then, should any British employer seek to engage in positive action? Many, if not most large employers have, in recent years, introduced equal opportunities policies. These may include communicating to employees the steps which are necessary to avoid breach of anti-discrimination law, the use of voluntary measures to increase female and black representation in the workplace[24] and, in much rarer cases, the use of numerical targets by which such increases may be judged.

The motivations for such policies are variable and not always clear. There is no doubt that, especially in the public sector, some employers have manifested an altruistic desire to attract more women and black people, such motivation not being primarily concerned with increasing the operational effectiveness of the employing enterprise. Other explanations are more functional: employers have sought to improve the quality of their workforce by seeking to attract and retain highly qualified female employees, partly in response to a perceived shortage of skilled labour. While for such enterprises issues of race have taken a back seat, image factors may mean that they cannot be entirely ignored.

> **Jenkins, R, 'Equal opportunity in the private sector: the limits of voluntarism', in Jenkins, R and Solomos, J (eds), *Racism and Equal Opportunity Policies in the 1980s*, 1987, Cambridge: CUP, pp 113–15:**
>
> [T]here are at least seven factors which may lie behind the initial organisational decision to adopt an [equal opportunities] policy ...
>
> In the first place, an EO policy may represent a straightforward response to a 'race' problem, such as, for example, pressure from the Commission for Racial Equality, an unfavourable [legal] decision, or a 'race'-related industrial relations problem. Second, the formulation and implementation of an EO policy may be an attempt at a pre-emptive strike, to prevent [such] difficulties ... happening in the future ... Third, such an initiative may be nothing more than a public relations strategy, aimed at improving the organisation's standing in the eyes of a particular constituency, be that its employees, its customers, or its paymasters. Looked at together, these three factors may be categorised as *defensive* or *reactive*. Impressionistic evidence leads one to believe that, certainly in the private sector, they are among the most characteristic reasons for EO policy formulation and implementation.
>
> Coming now to the public sector in particular, a fourth factor which may underlie EO initiatives – one which is not unrelated to the public relations strategy discussed above – is the *political* appeal of such a problem. This is particularly the case in local government and especially in those cities with a concentration of the black vote ...

---

[23] Atkins, S and Hoggett, B, *Women and the Law*, 1984, Oxford: Martin Robertson, p 55.

[24] Many such policies also deal with discrimination on other grounds, such as sexual orientation and disability. Discussion of their operation in these areas will be found in the appropriate chapter.

A fifth reason relates to the fact that the equal opportunity issue has become part of the professionalising rhetoric of personnel management specialists, an integral component of the profession's claim to the custodianship of employment policy and legal issues ... There are two dimensions of the professional personnel model of 'best practice' ... : one, it offers a *technical* rationale for formal 'rational' employment procedures, that is, in this manner the best possible recruits are selected and the optimum utility derived from manpower resources; and two, it is also a *moral* rationale, that is, that such an approach serves to ensure the fairness of the process ... [25]

Related to this is a sixth factor: the use to which individuals ... can put an EO policy in their personal mobility strategies within or between organisations ...

[The final factor] is the impact of *external* organisational policy. This can take three forms. The first is found in multinational organisations; here one may find policy imperatives and even, in some cases, the *minutiae* of policy and procedural detail ... being imported by an American or European controlling organisation and imposed on its UK subsidiaries ... Second, policy may be formulated by management in the UK, although more with an eye to satisfying the requirements of top management elsewhere ... Third, even in wholly UK-owned organisations, policy may be developed centrally at a senior corporate level and passed down to, or imposed upon, subsidiary organisations ...

At the one extreme there are those organisations who express a public commitment to 'equal opportunity', in their job advertisements for example, but make no further moves towards the operationalisation of such a commitment ... At the other end of the spectrum, however, there are highly elaborate policies which include a wide variety of topics from training, promotion and recruitment, to the provision of special facilities for particular minority groups, to systems for the detailed ethnic and gender monitoring of the workforce.

That an employer has an equal opportunities policy, even one whose wording approximates to the ideal, is no guarantee that such a policy will make a real practical difference to the employment opportunities of women and black people – while at the same time it might cause a significant deterioration in the employment lives of those who have to operate it in the sense of increased

---

[25] Thus, eg, the Equal Opportunities Commission Code of Practice, paras 34–35, states that an 'equal opportunities policy will ensure the effective use of human resources in the best interests of both the organisation and its employees. It is a commitment by the employer to the development and use of employment procedures and practices which do not discriminate on grounds of sex or marriage and which provide genuine equality of opportunity for all employees ... An equal opportunities policy must be seen to have the active support of management at the highest level. To ensure that the policy is fully effective, the following procedure is recommended:

(a) the policy should be clearly stated and, where appropriate, included in a collective agreement;

(b) overall responsibility for implementing the policy should rest with senior management;

(c) the policy should be made known to all employees and, where reasonably practicable, to all job applicants'.

bureaucracy and paperwork. Thought must be given on how to ensure both that the wording of a policy is faithfully observed by the workforce, and how to ensure that a real difference ensues. Different aspects of policies will be considered, and the pitfalls analysed.

Monitoring

Monitoring is the obtaining and keeping of records relating to the race, gender and, in Northern Ireland, religious affiliations of employees or prospective employees. It is the foundation stone without which any voluntary employer attempts at promoting equal opportunities are likely to be of little practical significance. It is logically inescapable that, if change is to measurable, statistics must be kept. Obtaining such statistics may enable conclusions to be drawn as to the progress or otherwise which a firm is making in relation to equal opportunities. There are three major issues so far as monitoring is concerned: why monitor, how should the monitoring be conducted, and what should be the policy impact of the results of monitoring?

From a statistical perspective, monitoring may seek to obtain information in a number of different areas. For example, a comparison may be made between the number of black people or women in a local labour market as compared with the number of applications received for particular jobs; a similar comparison may be made of current holders of those jobs as compared with the local labour market; and the relative success rate of candidates according to race and gender may be examined, both for new entrants to the organisation and in relation to promotions.[26]

The reasons for such monitoring are to identify patterns of disadvantage, presumably with a view to their alteration. The objectives are to determine *who* is being disadvantaged and by what practices and procedures. It may be necessary to determine what changes to recruitment, promotion and other procedures are needed to overcome the effects of such disadvantage, and also whether any special training might be needed to that end. It should never be thought that monitoring can be an end in itself; it is the necessary first step towards the identification of problem areas and the development of policies aimed at remedying them.

The question of how to monitor differs first, between gender and race and, secondly, between the existing workforce and job applicants. The production of statistics on gender, at least in relation to the current workforce, is reasonably straightforward and few additional steps may be needed to

---

[26] See *op cit*, McCrudden, fn 14, pp 186–89.

convert what is currently done into an equal opportunities exercise.[27] Furthermore, the maintenance of such statistics has not normally been conceived as in any sense stigmatising. Monitoring by race is a very different matter, raising issues of how the classification should be carried out and perhaps even appearing as a threat. It is a reasonably straightforward technical exercise to include in a job application pack an ethnic monitoring form, but, even if the recipients are broadly in sympathy with the object of the exercise, it is impossible to ensure a very high level of returns, in which case the figures may be too unreliable to form the basis of policy changes.

Racial Equality Code of Practice
Monitoring equal opportunity

1.33   It is recommended that employers should regularly monitor the effects of selection decisions and personnel practices and procedures in order to assess whether equal opportunity is being achieved.

1.34   The information needed for effective monitoring may be obtained in a number of ways. It will best be provided by records showing the ethnic origins of existing employees and job applicants ...

1.35   It is open to employers to adopt the method of monitoring which is best suited to their needs and circumstances, but whichever method is adopted, they should be able to show that it is effective. In order to achieve the full commitment of all concerned, the chosen method should be discussed and agreed, where appropriate, with trade union or employee representatives.

1.37   The following is the comprehensive method recommended by the CRE.

Analyses should be carried out of:

(a) the ethnic composition of the workforce of each plant, department, section, shift and job category, and changes in distribution over periods of time;

(b) selection decisions for recruitment, promotion, transfer and training, according to the racial group of candidates, and reasons for these decisions.

1.38   Except in cases where there are large numbers of applicants and the burden on resources would be excessive, reasons for selection and rejection should be recorded at each stage of the selection process, for example, initial shortlisting and final decisions.

1.40   This information should be carefully and regularly analysed and, in order to identify areas which may need particular attention, a number of key questions should be asked.

---

[27] It is common to provide job applicants with a monitoring form which is to be returned in a separate envelope and will not be seen by anyone involved in the hiring process for that particular job.

1.41   Is there evidence that individuals from any particular racial group:

(a) Do not apply for employment or promotion, or that fewer apply than might be expected?

(b) Are not recruited or promoted at all, or are appointed in a significantly lower proportion than their rate of application?

(c) Are under-represented in training, or in jobs carrying higher pay, status or authority?

(d) Are concentrated in certain shifts, sections or departments?

There are also difficulties in achieving a high response rate when monitoring the current workforce, especially as 'the fears which people have about the confidentiality of racial details ... and the use to which the information will be put, are very deep rooted'.[28] It may require considerable expenditure in both time and money to ensure that a monitoring exercise is not all but futile. Time may need to be spent in explaining to a possibly suspicious workforce what is the purpose of the exercise, and effort taken, by follow-up letters and so on, to seek to bring about as high a response rate as possible. The less that management appears to be acting for reasons of principle and the more because it is expected of them, the less effective a monitoring exercise is likely to be.

Following up a monitoring exercise is crucial. Monitoring the workforce may need to be a regular, though not necessarily an annual, event. Analysis of the results, which should be the precursor to action, requires sensitivity to the ways in which discriminatory practices may be reproduced.

Jewson, N and Mason, D, 'Monitoring equal opportunities policies: principles and practice', in Jenkins, R and Solomos, J (eds), *Racism and Equal Opportunity Policies in the 1980s*, 1987, Cambridge: CUP, pp 125–26:

Monitoring is ... almost always conceived as a statistical exercise; that is, the keeping of records concerned with applications for jobs, shortlisting, appointments, promotions and progress and the like. It is generally suggested that such record keeping has two functions. First, as a diagnostic tool which may reveal *prima facie* evidence of discrimination. Secondly, as a means of charting the subsequent progress of black or women workers ... There is a potential confusion here. Progress towards greater representativeness has clearly on occasion been taken as an indicator of the provision of equality of opportunity ... The presence or absence of equality of outcomes becomes the yardstick by which the provision of equality of opportunity is measured ... The intended beneficiaries of the policy may feel cheated but unable to identify the means by which the deception has been perpetrated. Sections of management may feel aggrieved at being the object of continuing and intensified accusations of discrimination, despite having developed employment procedures which appear, at least, to be scrupulously fair ... [I]n our research

---

[28] 'Ethnic monitoring: issues and practice' (1986) 7 EOR 6, p 8; Blakemore, K and Drake, R, *Understanding Equal Opportunities Policies*, 1996, Hemel Hempstead: Prentice Hall, pp 114–17.

company an elaborate policy had been developed ... which was widely regarded, inside and outside the company, as embodying fair procedures. Nevertheless, a significant body of black and women workers on site claimed that it could not possibly be fair because black people and women were still under-represented in skilled and supervisory positions.

Lest we be misunderstood ... we are not arguing that statistical monitoring is · an inappropriate procedure. Nor would we deny that it may be essential to reveal some forms of disadvantage and/or discrimination. However, we believe that, taken on its own, it may both create the potential for misunderstanding and fail effectively to ensure policy implementation. Moreover, both the wider literature and our research indicate that statistical monitoring is neither widespread nor easy to carry out ... [T]his should not be allowed to become an excuse for a lack of political will in the pursuit of equality of opportunity ...

The major difference between British law and Northern Irish law under the Fair Employment Act 1989 is that, for most employers in Northern Ireland, monitoring is compulsory. All public sector employers and private sector employees with at least 10 employees must monitor the religious affiliations of their workforce and submit annual returns to the Fair Employment Commission. All public sector employers and private sector employers with at least 250 employees[29] must, in addition, monitor and submit returns on job applicants. It is the imbalances, the existence of which may be revealed by monitoring, which then trigger the obligation to engage in affirmative action. The link between information and subsequent action is fundamental. Compulsory workforce monitoring is one of the most needed amendments to British anti-discrimination law.

Managing equal opportunities policies

The mere announcement of an equal opportunities policy, however detailed, provides no guarantee of any real change in the organisation, let alone change which is measurable by outcome. In this context it is helpful to view equal opportunities as an issue of management design, asking what are the criteria which determine whether success has been achieved. For example, if an 'organisation manages its business without written policies and procedures in every other area, it is unlikely to manage the issue of equal opportunity [any differently]. If the organisation does act out of character and issue a formal policy, it is unlikely to work. Managers will conclude that the written policy is merely a public relations exercise, because from their experience they know that when the company really wants change it goes about it in a different

---

[29] It is now proposed to extend this obligation to all private sector employers with more than 10 employees and to extend its coverage so as to include part time workers. See, *op cit, Partnership for equality*, fn 3, paras 5.11–5.14.

way'.[30] Thus mere generalities that discrimination is to be avoided may achieve little or nothing, as it is 'particularly easy for employees to ignore general statements [which do not] positively tell individual employees what they should do, only what is to be avoided'.[31] Equal opportunity, if it is to mean anything, is about the achievement of social change against a background of discrimination and disadvantage. One cannot expect an employer's policy manual to 'change attitudes and assumptions about blacks and women that were acquired unconsciously as part of the process of growing up'.[32]

An effective equal opportunities plan entails a number of elements. There must be awareness and commitment to the removal of those aspects of employment which erect barriers for women and minorities, including the subtle and covert ways in which discrimination often operates. Employers must examine the numerical profile of their workforce and seek to determine which of their policies and practices produce that profile, especially where it results in under-representation of women and black people. Once identified, of course, there needs to be a determination that change needs to occur, where possible change that is measurable in numerical terms. For employers to do this successfully requires continuous demonstrations of commitment and allocation of adequate resources. There is no necessity that all change be undertaken from a belief in the moral or ethical value of equal opportunity or diversity; it is possible that employers may be convinced of the practical financial value of such a course of action. Genuine equality of opportunity means, in theory, that employers have greater access to potentially better employees; a diverse workforce may prove better at dealing with customers and clients, etc. The danger with this kind of argument, though, is that employers may need to be convinced that the economic benefits of change outweigh the inevitable costs. But the cynical view, one which accepts severe limitations on the role of law as a producer of social change, is that equal opportunities policies can only become effective when employers see it as in their own interests to make them effective.

Sawyer, M, 'The operation of labour markets and the economics of equal opportunities', in Rubery, J (ed), *The Economics of Equal Opportunities*, 1995, Manchester: EOC, pp 50–51:

Equal opportunities polices are often seen as involving significant costs, especially for employers, and hence resisted on these grounds. Extra costs for employers may include higher wages, provision of nursery facilities, maternity leave, and so on. The cost calculus of equal opportunities policies is rather complex, however, and initial appearances may be deceptive.

---

[30] Wainwright, D, *Discrimination in Employment*, 1979, London: Macmillan, p 208.
[31] *Ibid.*
[32] *Ibid.*

First, even when employers appear to bear the cost, they may not do so, in that they can shift the cost on to others. There is, for example, extensive literature suggesting that employers' social security contributions are not ultimately borne by employers but passed on to consumers or back to employees. In a similar vein, any costs of equal opportunities policies may be shifted on to employees and consumers.

Second, what appears as costs to one party (such as wages to the employer) are benefits to another party (wages to the employee). If higher wages stimulate higher productivity ... then no extra costs would be involved. However, it may take some time before the higher productivity comes through. If the higher wages represent a correction of previous underpayment, then in effect the costs of non-equal opportunities are borne by the disadvantaged.

Third ... equal opportunities policies can represent a redistribution of costs rather than the creation of new costs. As an example, take a policy which permitted a parent to take paid absence from work to care for a sick child. At present the costs of such care are borne by the parents and to an extent by the child; a policy as outlined would shift some of the costs on to the employer ...

Holterman, S, 'The costs and benefits to British employers of measures to promote equality of opportunity', in Rubery, J (ed), *The Economics of Equal Opportunities*, 1995, Manchester: EOC, pp 140–41, 151:

Corporate image is an important consideration. Some companies gain praise and esteem by being able to show that they are good equal opportunities employers. However, benefits of this kind may be almost impossible to quantify. How does an organisation measure and value the gain from having this kind of corporate image? Does a good record on equal opportunities improve profit by generating customer or supplier loyalty? Does it increase the value of shares through greater demand from ethical investment trusts that use equal opportunities policy as one of their criteria? Is it a matter of the personal satisfaction and self-image of the employers?

Employee productivity is another benefit which is hard to measure. Employers work with greater commitment and goodwill for organisations that they respect and trust to treat them supportively ... But it is difficult to quantify exactly what part of productivity or industrial peace can be attributed to equal opportunities policies ...

Cost savings are a major factor. Some benefits to employers may accrue in the form of reduced costs of employing labour [such as] the benefits ... of family friendly employment practices. Labour turnover may be lower because of higher retention of women employees ... There may also be lower rates of unofficial absence from work, thereby reducing the costs associated with absence – disruption of work programmes, lost output, the extra cost of temporary workers and their relatively low productivity, and so on.

The final aspect is employment costs. Equal opportunities measures may have direct costs. Workplace nurseries, for instance, require substantial capital and running costs; the wages and salaries of parents on leave must be met and other workers paid to do their work ... There are also indirect costs: when parents take leave, for example, employers must carry a vacancy or employ a temporary worker, who will need induction and training and may be in the job for too short a time to reach full productive potential ...

Is it acceptable from the point of view of equal opportunities policy for measures that have a favourable cost-benefit ratio for employers to be given priority? The risk is that while the more expensive type of measure may stay on an organisation's agenda for social responsibility, they will be repeatedly pushed to the bottom of the list because there is insufficient financial reward to the employer. There is a danger of a shift in attitude towards a position where equality of opportunity is no longer seen primarily as a matter of social justice, desirable in its own right, but merely as something that can be pursued if, and only if, it coincides with the employing organisation's own self-interest.

It does, however, have to be accepted that there are situations where a gain in equality of opportunity can only be made by individual employers incurring some net cost, and there is a trade-off between competing objectives: ... equality of opportunity [and] cost efficiency ...

It is precisely [here] that there is greatest need for the government, which has a wider set of objectives than individual employers, to introduce (and enforce) national minimum standards.

The content of such policies is variable. The first aspect will normally reflect the provisions of the Codes of Practice concerned with avoiding discrimination in recruitment. For example, a job specification may state that time out of the labour market may be treated as valuable experience, or that overseas qualifications are accepted as equivalent to British ones. One key aspect of policies is normally an attempt to impose greater formality on the recruitment process in order to reduce the scope for direct or indirect discrimination. This may be done by ensuring that all decisions involve more than one person, that interviewers are trained in the avoidance of discrimination and that, so far as possible, interview questions are standardised. This approach suggests that equal opportunities may be no more than ensuring that the appropriate procedures are in place.

Jenkins, R, 'Equal opportunity in the private sector: the limits of voluntarism', in Jenkins, R and Solomos, J (eds), *Racism and Equal Opportunity Policies in the 1980s*, 1987, Cambridge: CUP, pp 118–19:

[A] purely technical approach to equal opportunity misses an important – indeed crucial – aspect of the issue: attacking discrimination and promoting equal opportunity, both for women and black workers, are political measures whose legitimacy ... cannot by any stretch of the imagination be regarded as secure or consensual ...

As the people who profess the skills in the field of employment procedures, employee relations and the law, the personnel profession is the obvious, or indeed perhaps the only, custodian of an EO policy within most organisations. Having recognised this, however, one must then also acknowledge the inescapable fact that within the political networks of the majority of organisations the personnel function has limited influence, authority or resources. Furthermore, the commitment of many personnel managers and officers to the professional personnel model of equity and equal opportunity is, to say the least, lukewarm. These factors conspire together to ensure that, if equal opportunity is left in the care of the personnel profession, the prospects for women and black workers are likely to remain gloomy.

Jewson, N and Mason, D, 'Monitoring equal opportunities policies: principles and practice', in Jenkins, R and Solomos, J (eds), *Racism and Equal Opportunity Policies in the 1980s*, 1987, Cambridge: CUP, pp 136–37:

The fact that the principles of individualism and collectivism are simultaneously involved in both positive discrimination and positive action to some extent explains the frequent confusion between the two and the mistaken assumptions that the policy measures derived from one type can achieve the policy objectives of the other. It also explains the extreme hostility which proposals for positive discrimination often invoke, since they simultaneously involve the imposition of a collectivist conception on a sphere of social life usually associated, in capitalist societies, with extreme individualism and, at the same time, they reverse the principles of legitimation normally applied at the point of individual selection.

Those who see the goal of equal opportunities policy as completely equal distribution should recognise that the logical implication is positive discrimination ... This indeed may account for the fact that people in our research examples frequently perceived the introduction of an equal opportunities policy as the prelude to positive discrimination. For example, we have come across a situation in which white employees refused to fill in ethnic self-classification forms because they believed this to be the prelude to the dismissal of some workers in order to increase the number of black employees. We have also come across the case of a senior local government officer who believed that the confusion between equality of opportunity and equality of outcome was leading to pressure on him to engage in positive discrimination. This was because only an increased proportion of black and female workers was regarded by his political superiors as satisfactory evidence of his operation of the equal opportunities policy.

The second aspect to such policies concern the restructuring of work in the interests of, usually, women. There are many ways in which workplaces need to be made more amenable to those who wish to combine work and family life. Some of the more obvious include increased promotion opportunities for part time workers, the opportunity to work part time after childbirth without damaging one's career prospects, maternity pay and leave provisions superior to the statutory minimum, improved childcare provision (although the extent to which this should be the responsibility of the employer rather than the State is open to question), and the opportunity to take time out of the workforce for family reasons without irretrievably damaging one's career. While these concentrate on improving the position of employees already in work, and may be introduced because of the potential costs to employers of having to replace such employees, they also benefit potential employees who will be attracted to employers with such policies, and thereby increase female representation.

Targets

There may be nothing as specific as the absence of family friendly policies to explain the under-representation of minority ethnic groups. In addition, such policies may do nothing to ensure appropriate representation of women in the higher echelons of an organisation. In most situations, it is impossible to point to changes in policy or practice which will rapidly and inevitably increase black and female representation. It is thus very strongly arguable that the only way to bring about real change is to ensure that policies can be measured for their effectiveness in terms of numerical outcomes. This can be done in one of two ways: targets or quotas. There is a crucial difference between the two: targets are aspirational in nature and do not predetermine the outcome of any given selection decision – the merit principle is thereby retained; quotas, on the one hand, may require the hiring of a less qualified individual. The preferred approach depends substantially on how far one accepts that jobs both are and should be allocated on the basis of merit.

The ostensible objective of a target is to increase within a given period the numbers of black people or women employed in particular positions. If the target is not met, that should lead to analysis or explanation of the reason. But there is a very important distinction between a target directed at the number hired and one directed at the total number of employees. For example, a bank which is committed to equal opportunities for women may set a target that, over a five year period, at least 30% of promotions to bank manager should be female.[33] A target that after five years 30% of *all* managers should be female would be far more difficult to achieve. For a job classification with relatively low turnover, even the successful achievement of a target may have no more than a minor impact on the overall gender or race distribution. There is no doubt that in America, where attainment of affirmative action targets might be a measure of individual or corporate achievement, the incentive to set hard targets may be correspondingly reduced. In addition, the setting of targets makes far more sense where the numbers being hired are substantial, where the outcomes can less convincingly be attributed to chance factors.[34] Where an employer rarely, if ever, hires large numbers for any one job grade, it may be necessary to group jobs together, such as unskilled manual jobs. But as with any statistical exercise involving the employment of black people, attention

---

[33] '[S]uppose that an employer aims to recruit 1,000 unskilled staff in a travel-to-work locality known to have a 25% black population of working age. It is reasonable to suppose that somewhere around 250 of those appointed will be black, and that figure could be set as a target. If only 50 black people are appointed, some very searching questions should be asked; if 220 or 280, so be it.' *Op cit*, Bourn and Whitmore, fn 22, p 122.

[34] The recent agreement between the CRE and the MoD has targets for recruitment of ethnic minorities into the armed forces, 2% for 1998–99, rising by 1% per year and reaching 5% in 2001–02. See 'Partnership for equality: agreement between the CRE and the armed forces' (1998) 79 EOR 44.

must be given to the size of the labour market from which the employer is expecting to recruit, the size of the economically active minority ethnic population within that area, and whether any distinctions should be drawn between the different minority ethnic groups.

Setting targets is a complex activity and fraught with potential problems for employers. It is therefore not surprising that few employers have voluntarily followed that route. Furthermore, it is naive to suppose that target setting can overcome the legacy of employment disadvantage. Most importantly, it does nothing to overcome a lack of women or black people with the qualifications and training for more senior positions. In addition, hiring women or black people to positions where they are pioneering employees may prove unsuccessful because of the pressures thereby imposed, whether overt or covert. The forced or apparently forced hiring of women or black people, however competent, may give rise to problems from current employees, especially if the new recruits are isolated individuals. It is problematic for equal opportunities policies to achieve lasting results without the support, or at least tolerance, of the workforce. Indeed, in such circumstances they may be almost harmful: if minorities quit in the face of such opposition, that will merely reinforce stereotypes about the unsuitability of groups of workers for particular jobs.[35]

Contract compliance

One problem with positive action is that there may be little or no incentive for its implementation, which is why so many of the more extensive policies are in the public sector, where the rationale for their introduction may be at least partly ideological. Contract compliance policies are procedures adopted by government agencies to ensure that those contractors with whom they do business are themselves pursuing equal opportunities policies. Given the amount of business which is placed by government, there is considerable potential to encourage the taking of steps which contractors might not have adopted on a purely voluntary basis. It provides a means of putting economic pressure on employers to set targets. Under contract compliance, though, the sanction for failure is removal from the list of firms with which the government agency will do business, thereby providing an economic incentive for compliance.[36] Essential to the American experience of contract

---

35 Aitkenhead, M and Luff, S, 'The effectiveness of equal opportunities policies', in Firth-Cozens, J and West, R (eds), *Women at Work – Psychological and Organisational Perspectives*, 1991, Milton Keynes: OU Press, Chapter 3.

36 For discussion of contract compliance in the USA, see *op cit*, Bourn and Whitmore, fn 22, pp 316–17; Stamp, P and Robarts, S, *Positive Action for Women*, 2nd edn, 1986, London: NCCL, pp 106–09.

compliance is that employers must set goals and timetables so that the results of efforts to counter under-representation may be measured.[37]

In the UK, the now abolished Greater London Council was at the forefront of attempts to introduce and promote contract compliance, though it utilised a less rigid system than is commonplace in America. In effect, the Contract Compliance Equal Opportunities Unit encouraged employers to implement the provisions of the Codes of Practice, and in its first year of operation, 77 out of 106 companies instituted equal opportunities policies.[38] How many additional women or minorities were hired in consequence is not known.[39]

Until 1988, there were no specific legal controls over the way in which local authorities operated contract compliance policies. In that year the Conservative Government, whose commitment to the free market and to low wages overrode any concern for equal opportunities, effectively made contract compliance unlawful so far as gender is concerned.[40] This was done by making it the duty of local authorities, a duty enforceable by judicial review, to disregard 'non-commercial matters' as regards their supply and work contracts. Section 17(5)(b) provides that non-commercial matters includes 'the terms and conditions of employment by contractors of their workers or the composition of, the arrangements for the promotion, transfer or training of ... their workforces'. In *R v London Borough of Islington ex p Building Employers Confederation*,[41] it was held that, despite the fact that they were not specifically mentioned in s 17(5)(b), the phrase 'workforce matters' included issues relating to recruitment and dismissal of the workforce. Furthermore, it was not even permissible for council contracts to contain a term specifically requiring employers to comply with the provisions of the SDA 1975, with the implied threat that the contract may be lost if they did.

Section 71 of the Race Relations Act 1976 places a duty on local authorities to promote good race relations and to work towards the elimination of unlawful discrimination. For that reason, and perhaps because racial issues were perceived as more politically sensitive than gender issues, the 1988 Act authorises a limited form of contract compliance where it is reasonably

---

[37] 'In developing goals for women and ethnic minorities the [Office for Federal Contract Compliance Programmes] requires employers to look at population, local unemployment, the local labour force, skill levels, recruitment possibilities, availability of training externally, promotion potential of existing employees and training availability within the company. The results of this analysis should produce a realistic figure for the employment of women and minorities.' *Op cit*, Stamp and Robarts, fn 36, pp 108–09.

[38] Fredman, S, *Women and the Law*, 1997, Oxford: Clarendon, p 388.

[39] See 'Equal opportunities and contract compliance' (1986) 8 EOR 9.

[40] Local Government Act 1988, s 17(1). However, under the Fair Employment (Northern Ireland) Act 1989, ss 38–43, both government contracts and government grants may be withdrawn in the case of persistent unlawful discrimination.

[41] [1989] IRLR 382, DC.

necessary to do so in order to comply with s 71.[42] Local authorities may take account of issues affecting the workforce or their contractors in discharging this duty and, in addition, may ask prospective contractors six approved questions[43] on race matters and may include in contracts terms relating to matters of race.[44] 'Around half of all local authorities [had] incorporated the approved questions in their pre-tender questionnaires to contractors, according to Commission estimates in 1992. Just over a quarter [included] racial equality terms in their contracts.'[45]

The future of contract compliance is uncertain. The EOC considers that a duty equivalent to s 71 of the RRA 1976 should be included in the SDA 1975, whereby 'all bodies carrying on a service or undertaking of a public nature [would be required to] work towards the elimination of unlawful discrimination and to promote equality of opportunity'.[46] By the same token, it is hard to gainsay the view that the myopic economism of s 17 of the Local Government Act is wrong; contract compliance in relation to gender issues should once again be permissible. On the other hand, the scope for contract compliance, which is essentially a duty imposed on public authorities to monitor their contractors, has been seriously weakened by privatisations.[47] However, the impact of compulsory competitive tendering has been that many functions of government are now provided by the private sector; these are most often in low paid jobs, often in small firms fully segregated by gender – the type of firm where the direct impact of anti-discrimination

---

[42] See *op cit*, Bourn and Whitmore, fn 22, pp 320–25.
[43] (1) Is it your policy as an employer to comply with your statutory obligations under the Race Relations Act 1976 ...?

(2) In the last three years has any finding of unlawful racial discrimination been made against your organisation ...?

(3) In the last three years, has your organisation been the subject of a formal investigation by the Commission for Racial Equality ...?

(4) If the answer to question (2) is in the affirmative or, in relation to question (3), the Commission made a finding adverse to your organisation, what steps did you take in consequence of that finding?

(5) Is your policy on race relations set out:

(a) in instructions to those concerned with recruitment, training and promotion;

(b) in documents available to employees, recognised trade unions or other representative groups of employees;

(c) in recruitment advertisements or other literature?

(6) Do you observe as far as possible the ... Code of Practice ...?

The two main problems with the questions are, first, their limited scope, as no question is permitted on workforce monitoring; and, secondly, authorities may only seek supporting evidence in relation to question (5), so that in relation to the key questions (1) and (6), answers of 'Yes' will satisfy the statutory requirements.
[44] See 'Contract compliance in the 1990s' (1994) 54 EOR 11.
[45] *Ibid*, 'Contract compliance', p 12.
[46] *Equality in the 21st Century: a New Approach*, 1997, Manchester: EOC, para 52.
[47] See 'Best value, best equality' (1998) 79 EOR 20.

legislation is likely to be at its smallest, and where firms are least likely to implement voluntary equal opportunities policies. Here, contract compliance may be virtually the only way to secure any appreciation of anti-discrimination legislation. Once more, though, minimum wage legislation and the direct protection of labour standards may be more beneficial, especially as such low paid, poor condition jobs are disproportionately performed by women and minority ethnic groups. From a cost-benefit analysis, contract compliance is one of the greatest stimuli which can be placed on employers, especially given the relatively low risks of litigation and the limited amounts of compensation payable. It should be placed on a statutory footing as a matter of urgency.

Quotas

The limitation of targets, whether voluntary or mandated through contract compliance, is that the employer remains free to hire the 'best' person for the job; the merit principle remains sacrosanct. If a disadvantaged educational and social background – which itself may be racist – leads to black people having lower qualifications and experience, the higher unemployment rate and fewer numbers in senior positions can be rationalised as their own fault. This explanation can appear especially disingenuous in the light of the perceived lack of real change despite 20 years of anti-discrimination legislation. In the face of such explanations, it is not surprising that there have been demands for a far more interventionist approach to the sharing of the economic cake between different racial groups by insisting that job allocation should be proportionate to membership of different groups.[48] Such approach is clearly unlawful under both the SDA 1975 and the RRA 1976, which protect white people and men on the same symmetrical basis as black people and women, an approach also adopted by the European Court of Justice, a fact which would seriously constrain any government minded radically to reform the law. In some circumstances, however, the American courts have been prepared to countenance what look like quotas, though often in language which appears to deny that is what is being done. For example, in *United Steelworkers v Weber*,[49] it was held to be lawful to reserve for black people 50%

---

[48] Whether one accepts this argument must in the end be a matter of opinion and dependent on one's views about the importance of reducing comparative economic disadvantage between different racial, gender and religious groups.

[49] 443 US 193 (1979).

of the places in a company training programme. The justification for this approach, both philosophically and pragmatically, is highly controversial.[50]

The problem with quotas is that they are assumed to work to the disadvantage of white males; the issue is whether it is appropriate to override their interests in the interests of members of historically disadvantaged groups. The main arguments are based on compensation, on redistribution, and on a rejection of the validity of the merit principle.

Wasserstrom, R, 'Racism, sexism and preferential treatment: an approach to the topics' (1977) 24 UCLA L Rev 581, pp 617–18:

The racial quotas and practices of racial exclusion that were an integral part of the fabric of our culture ... were pernicious. They were a grievous wrong and it was and is important that all morally concerned individuals work for their eradication from our social universe. The racial quotas that are a part of contemporary affirmative action programmes are, I think, commendable and right ... [But] even if contemporary schemes of racial quotas are wrong, they are wrong for reasons very different from those which made quotas against blacks wrong ... Programmes which excluded or limited the access of blacks and women ... were wrong both because of the direct consequences of these programmes on the individuals most affected and because the system of racial and sexual superiority of which they were constituents was an immoral one in that it severely and without any adequate justification restricted the capacities, autonomy and happiness of those who were members of the less favoured categories.

Whatever may be wrong with today's affirmative action and quota systems, it should be clear that the evil, if any, is not the same. Racial and sexual minorities do not constitute the dominant social group. Nor is the conception of who is a fully developed member of the moral and social community one of an individual who is either female or black. Quotas which prefer women or blacks do not add to the already relatively overabundant supply of resources and opportunities at the disposal of white males. If racial quotas are to be condemned, or if affirmative action programmes are to be abandoned, it should be because they will not work well to achieve the desired result. It is not because they seek either to perpetuate an unjust society or to realise a corrupt ideal.

---

[50] The literature is immense. Apart from the material cited, some of the key writings include Edwards, J, *When Race Counts: The Morality of Racial Preference in Britain and America*, 1995, London: Routledge; Abram, M, 'Affirmative action: fair shakers and social engineers' (1986) 99 Harv L Rev 1312; Goldman, A, *Justice and Reverse Discrimination*, 1979, Princeton: Princeton UP; Merritt, D and Reskin, B, 'Sex, race and credentials: the truth about affirmative action in law faculty hiring' (1997) 97 Columbia L Rev 199; Duncan, M, 'The future of affirmative action: a jurisprudential/legal critique' (1982) 17 Harv CR CL LR 503; Rutherglen, G and Ortiz, D, 'Affirmative action under the Constitution and Title VII: from confusion to convergence' (1988) 35 UCLA L Rev 467; Rosenfeld, M, 'Affirmative action, justice and equalities: a philosophical and constitutional Appraisal' (1985) Ohio State LJ 845.

Fredman, S, 'Reversing discrimination' (1997) 113 LQR 575, pp 575–79:

Affirmative action denotes the deliberate use of race- or gender-conscious criteria for the specific purpose of benefiting a group which has previously been disadvantaged on grounds of race or gender. Its aims range from providing a specific remedy for invidious discrimination to the more general purpose of increasing the participation of groups which are visibly under-represented in important public spheres ... At its most controversial, it requires that individual members of the disadvantaged group be actively preferred over others in the allocation of jobs, university places and other benefits.

[T]he 'symmetrical' approach rests on three basic propositions. First, justice is characterised as an *a priori* concept, formulated independently of its historical or political contexts, and unaffected by the distribution of benefits and disadvantages in any particular society. The principle that it is unjust to discriminate on the basis of race or sex therefore applies in the same way whether the discrimination causes detriment to a disadvantaged or an advantaged group. Secondly, the symmetrical model asserts the primacy of the individual. This individualism has two dimensions: merit and fault. The 'merit' principle requires that an individual be treated according to her or his own personal characteristics. Merit is assumed to be objective and unquantifiable, to which race and gender are deemed irrelevant. The fault principle requires that individuals should only be responsible for their own actions, not for others. Thus no individual should be required to compensate for social ills which are not directly his or her fault. Affirmative action contravenes both merit and fault, according to this argument, by excluding a white person or a man from a benefit on grounds unrelated to merit, and even though he or she is not responsible for the history of discrimination against black people or women. Finally, the 'symmetrical' principle assumes that the State should be neutral as between its citizens, favouring no one above any other. The proposition that a group should be favoured on account of gender or race, even in a remedial sense, is therefore anathema ...

All three of these propositions are challenged by the 'substantive' model. First, it is argued, formal justice substitutes the ideal for the reality. Because race and sex ought not to affect the individual, it is assumed that they do not. However, it is impossible to deny the continuing effects of discrimination against ethnic minorities or women in society. Justice therefore necessitates an asymmetric vision ...

Similarly, the substantive approach rejects as misleading the aspirations of individualism ... [I]t insists that fairness take into account the extent to which opportunities are determined by individuals' social and historical status, which includes their race and gender. The argument extends to both merit and fault. In portraying merit as objective and quantifiable, it is argued, opponents of affirmative action are concealing the inherent subjectivity of decision making processes and therefore making it difficult to root out prejudicial assumptions ... The fault principle is also seen to be flawed. Discrimination, on this fault, is not merely a result of personal fault; it is deeply embedded in the structure of society. Thus the responsibility for correcting institutional discrimination should not only lie with those to whom fault or causality can be

attributed; all members of the privileged class share the duty and may be
expected to bear some of the cost of remedy ...

Finally, the 'substantive' approach challenges the possibility of a neutral State
... [viewing it] as an emanation of the democratic process, the aim of which is to
function as a conduit for or resolution of the cross-currents of social power ...
The 'substantive' approach maintains that the State has a duty to act positively
to correct the results of discrimination.

One particular question is whether quotas should only be permissible where
the employer has been shown to be a discriminator.

**Sullivan, K, 'Sins of discrimination: last term's affirmative action cases'
(1986) 100 Harv L Rev 78, pp 91–92, 95, 96–97:**

Casting affirmative action as penance for particular sins of discrimination ...
has appeal at first glance. Limiting affirmative action to those who have
specifically wronged blacks or other racial minorities in the past neatly steers
between two courses: that all must pay or none. It rejects any notion that the
original sin of American slavery so taints everyone in our current society that
no defence to affirmative action could ever be raised. But it likewise rejects the
notion that all must be equally absolved. Only some – those who have
themselves been guilty of race discrimination – may be permitted the *mea culpa*
of voluntary affirmative action, or be prescribed such measures as a penance
by a court.

Visiting affirmative duties to integrate only upon past wrongdoers also makes
racial preferences seem more like corrective or retributive justice than like
social engineering. It thus helps to rebut charges that racial balancing has
become an end in itself. If just any employer were free to become an avenging
angel, using affirmative action to right a diffuse and generalised history of
racism in society at large, the racial composition resulting in that employer's
workplace might appear arbitrary. But if the employer discriminated in the
past, its extension of preferential treatment to blacks can now be understood as
simply creating a racial balance that might have existed anyway, but for the
discrimination.

Making sins of past discrimination the justification for affirmative action,
however, dooms affirmative action to further challenge even while
legitimating it. As a practical matter, it subjects affirmative action plans to
potentially protracted litigation over the 'factual predicate' for adopting them:
how much past discrimination is enough? And having to ask that question
may deter implementation of voluntary affirmative action at all. To admit guilt
for past discrimination is against employers' and unions' self-interest, and,
indeed, may invite race discrimination lawsuits by non-whites ... [T]he task of
self-judgment and self-condemnation in *any* form casts a chill over efforts to
implement affirmative action voluntarily.

More fundamentally, viewing affirmative action as penance for past
discrimination invites claims that the focus on that discrimination should be
sharper. True, viewing affirmative action that way saves it from the charge that
it aims only at racially balanced *results* by making it seem instead a matter of
corrective or retributive justice, compensating for or punishing earlier racial

wrongs. But because corrective justice focuses on victims, and retributive justice on wrongdoers, predicating affirmative action on past sins of discrimination invites claims that neither non-victims should benefit, nor non-sinners pay ...

If casting affirmative action as compensation invites protests about windfalls to non-victims, casting it as punishment invites protests about unfairness to non-sinners. Viewed through the lens of retributive justice, a focus on sin begets claims p innocence. Making an employer or union atone for *its* past discrimination would be all very well, these claims go, but that is not what affirmative action does. For it is not the errant management that 'pays' for affirmative action, but 'innocent' white workers. And retribution breaks down when aimed at innocent targets. Dead bosses' guilt cannot taint live workers' jobs. Nor are employees on the rank and file responsible for the ongoing racial wrongs committed by their management or union leadership ...

Public and private employers might choose to implement affirmative action for many reasons other than to purge their own past sins of discrimination ... improving their services to black constituencies, averting racial tension over the allocation of jobs in a community, or increasing the diversity of a workforce, to name but a few examples. Or they might adopt affirmative action simply to eliminate from their operations all *de facto* embodiments of a system of racial caste. All of these reasons aspire to a racially integrated future, but none reduces to 'racial balancing for its own sake'.

If such aspirations for the future rather than past sin, would white claims of 'innocence' count for less? They should, for it is easier to show that displacing 'innocent' whites is narrowly tailored to goals that turn on integrating institutions now than it is to show that doing so is narrowly tailored to purging past sins of discrimination that the displaced whites did not themselves 'commit' ...

[V]oluntary affirmative action is as defensible as the architecture of a better future as it is as a remedy for the sins of discrimination past. And by turning to such forward looking justification, the Court might more effectively quiet protests about windfalls to non-victims and injustice to innocents than it has by treating affirmative action as penance for past sins.

If affirmative action is seen as having a redistributive aim, it is vulnerable to the criticism that its beneficiaries are likely to be the relatively well qualified members of previously disadvantaged groups. For this reason, it is vital to emphasise the potential role of the State in countering disadvantage, for the State can attack the causes of disadvantage in a more wide ranging fashion than is within the capacity of an individual employer. Forcing affirmative action on employers can, in political terms, be no more than a cheap way of passing the buck.

Pitt, G, 'Can reverse discrimination be justified?', in Hepple, B and Szyszczak, E (eds), *Discrimination: The Limits of Law*, 1992, London: Mansell, p 199:

The major objection [to the compensation justification] is that the real victims of discrimination are the earlier generations living in a society when discrimination was allowed. Compensation now will benefit the wrong people. To this it may be answered that present generations are still disadvantaged because their forbears were relegated to the lowest positions in society. This argument is obviously more convincing in relation to race discrimination than to sex discrimination, and more convincing in relation to race discrimination in the United States than in the United Kingdom ...

Even if present generations do continue to suffer disadvantage, the position is not really redressed by reverse discrimination, which benefits only *some* members of the group, who are likely to be those who have suffered least from the effects of past discrimination. They have at least managed to get themselves into the position of being serious candidates for the desirable opportunity ... [Furthermore] there is no necessary correlation between those of the majority group who are receiving wrongful benefits and those who will not get jobs if wrongful discrimination is permitted ...

A different kind of compensation argument ... claims ... that the institutional framework of society is so stacked against women and members of ethnic minorities that even though discrimination is now prohibited it still occurs and is bound to continue to occur. Reverse discrimination is a counterbalancing measure, attempting to compensate for the inherent bias in the system. It is a crude remedy, but then social rules can rarely be made to apply with precision ... [T]his is essentially the principle on which the United States' Supreme Court has permitted reverse discrimination ...

The theoretical arguments which support the use of quotas are strong if not conclusive. Whether they are defensible on utilitarian grounds – whether they would actually work in practice in the best interests of black people and women – is equally, if not more, problematic.

Fredman, S, 'Reversing discrimination' (1997) 113 LQR 575, pp 596–600:

Proponents of affirmative action ... need to face at least four interrelated questions. First, what is the aim of such action? Secondly, is it effective in achieving that aim? Thirdly, what role should merit play? Finally, are the costs fairly spread?

Of the various aims suggested ... the least controversial is the narrow remedial role, which permits affirmative action only to compensate for demonstrable past discrimination by the actor in question. However, to restrict the permissible goals so severely is to risk rendering affirmative action programmes largely ineffective ... Instead of demonstrable fault, it should be sufficient to prove that there is a visible disparity in participation rates between races or genders; a disparity which the State has a responsibility to counteract.

A move away from individualism also permits consideration of so called non remedial aims, such as diversity and role models ... [But] the desire for diversity must be seen as part of the wider remedial aim of achieving greater participation by black people and women in areas from which they have traditionally been excluded or absent. A student body or workforce which includes members of the disadvantaged group will be an arena in which prejudicial attitudes of the dominant group are challenged and bridges built. It is similarly misleading to classify the provision of role models as a non-remedial aim. A long history of discrimination can lead to the internalisation of inferiority ... Visible success by other members of the same group helps to dispel such lack of confidence and feelings of inferiority.

Chief Justice Dickson [in the Canadian case of *Action Travail des Femmes v Canadian National Railway Co* (1987) 40 DLR (4th) 193] identified at least three ways in which [an employment equity programme] is likely to be more effective than one which simply relies on equal opportunities or the proscription of intentional prejudice. First, the insistence that women be placed in non-traditional jobs allows them to prove that they really can do the job, thereby dispelling stereotypes about women's abilities. Secondly, an employment equity programme helps to create a 'critical mass' of women in the workplace, overcoming the problem of tokenism, which would leave a few women isolated and vulnerable to sexual harassment or accusations of being impostors. It would also generate further employment of women, partly by means of the informal recruitment network and partly by reducing the stigma and anxiety associated with strange and unconventional work. Finally, a critical mass of women forces management to give women's concerns their due weight and compels personnel officers to take female applications seriously ...

The ECJ in *Kalanke* was correct in pointing out that numerical equality can be illusory if not accompanied by equality of opportunity. But ... equality of opportunity can itself be illusory unless it goes far beyond merely formal measures. A fully fledged equal opportunities policy requires a radical reshaping of the world of paid and unpaid work to accommodate the combination of paid and family work for both men and women. It also requires a sea change in both the quantity and quality of education and training available to ethnic minorities and women. Equalising the starting points therefore demands not only careful thought and planning but a high level of resource input reflecting a strong political commitment. The combination of such an equal opportunities strategy and carefully targeted affirmative action programmes could begin to yield the kind of progress not yet generated by anti-discrimination legislation.

NORTHERN IRELAND[51]

The most striking fact about the Northern Irish legislation is that it exists.[52] The political will was and is present, which has been absent in relation to race and gender issues in Great Britain. Catholic unemployment remains significantly higher than Protestant unemployment, the reasons being complex and multifaceted.[53] The two key political factors which led to

---

[51] See *op cit*, McCrudden, fn 14; Hepple, B, 'Discrimination and equality of opportunity – Northern Irish lessons' (1990) 10 OJLS 408.

[52] For proposed changes to strengthen the legislation, see *op cit, Partnership for Equality,* fn 3.

[53] *Ibid*, Hepple, p 410.

legislation were the link with possible violence if action were not taken, and also the threat to economic investment, especially from North America. The legislation thus has a symbolic significance as well as a real practical impact.

We have already examined the system of compulsory monitoring. If that reveals a significant imbalance, a duty to engage in affirmative action is triggered. It is up to the employer to determine what steps should be taken to redress the imbalance, an obligation which is subject to the overriding review powers of the Fair Employment Commission. This obligation may require determining appropriate goals and timetables for the securing of an improvement.[54] This obligation is *not* dependent on the employer being shown to have discriminated in the past, but merely on a significant imbalance in representation being revealed. To that extent, the process is results-orientated and not dependent on any showing of guilt or responsibility on the part of the employer – a very important concession to redistributive thinking, at least in terms of the procedures which must be put in place.[55]

But because the legislation had to treat a narrow political tightrope, such affirmative action may not override individual interests in a substantive sense. McCrudden argues that the Act is redistributive in its objective, but that employers and the Commission are limited in the means which may be employed to secure that objective.[56] Employers are not permitted to give training to members of one religion only, a limitation which the recent White Paper proposes should be removed, nor may the merit principle be jettisoned at the point of hiring. The compulsory review to ensure that employers do nothing to hinder the achievement of fair participation in practice is essentially procedural. The law thus has limited weapons against the deeper causes of disadvantage. 'We know ... that there is a connection between lack of educational and skill qualifications and belonging to the Catholic community. The appeal to "merit" must appear disingenuous to members of the disadvantaged community who are rejected as "unsuitable".[57]

In one respect the causes of discrimination in Northern Ireland are different. The degree of segregation of housing and employment is far greater than in almost all areas of Great Britain.[58] Employment disadvantage is about far more than skills and qualifications. For that reason the emphasis in the legislation on outreach measures and the encouragement of applicants from different communities is important both symbolically and practically. The

---

[54] For the enforcement and review powers of the Fair Employment Commission, see *op cit*, McCrudden, fn 14, pp 173–76.
[55] *Op cit*, McCrudden, fn 14, pp 178–79.
[56] *Op cit*, McCrudden, fn 14, p 184.
[57] *Op cit*, Hepple, fn 51, p 413.
[58] On the extent to which desegregation is part of the concept of fair participation, see *op cit*, McCrudden, fn 14, pp 192–94.

steps to reduce sectarian harassment are a further essential step.[59] But any reduction in disadvantage which results from anti-discrimination law surely pales into insignificance compared with the potential impact of a lasting political settlement.

CONCLUSION

The utilitarian arguments for affirmative action depend greatly on the way it is operated. Quotas run the risk that *all* women and black people who are hired will be treated as not having got the job on the basis of merit. Affirmative action runs the risk of creating of a backlash, not least because the notion of merit and desert in job allocation is so deeply rooted in our culture. Whether ordinary people accept this is unclear, but those in positions of power have a vested interest in the defence of the merit principle. A problem with *imposed* affirmative action, either by government fiat or court order, is that it may tend either to inflexibility or to blandness, both of which need to be avoided if greatest effectiveness is to be achieved. It may be true to say that affirmative action can only succeed if it has the basic approval of employers charged with operating it, but the premise underlying the need for such action was the relative failure of both the law and voluntary measures. A partial answer is that the views of organisations are not frozen in time; the development of family friendly employment policies demonstrates this. It may be that court-ordered affirmative action would lead employers to appreciate the benefits of voluntary action, but, especially in relation to race, it might equally lead to a backlash and to political polarisation.

The effects of affirmative action in the USA are unclear, not least because of the problem of determining the extent to which social changes are its *result*. There has been a significant increase in the numbers of black people in more senior and prestigious positions.[60] At the same time, the problem of black unemployment, crime and drugs is well documented. Some social problems can only be tackled, if at all, by governments. Affirmative action can make no more than a modest contribution to improvements in socio-economic conditions, improvements which will primarily be felt by those who are relatively well qualified. Affirmative action by *employers* will do little to overcome weaknesses in the education system. We return here to the first chapter, because the more one thinks that black under-achievement is caused by directly racist practices and structures, the more it is in theory able to be attacked by affirmative action, while if the causes are more deep rooted, the emphasis must be far more on governmental action.

---

[59] See 'Sectarian harassment guidelines' (1997) 71 EOR 32.

[60] Eg, there is in America a real concern for the proportion of university law teachers who are black, which is utterly foreign to the British experience.

CHAPTER 16

DISCRIMINATION ON THE GROUND OF DISABILITY

After many years of political pressure, the anti-discrimination principle was finally extended to disabled people through the Disability Discrimination Act 1995.[1] The Act is similar in many ways to the Sex Discrimination Act 1975 and the Race Relations Act 1976, and its procedural and remedial provisions are almost identical.[2] The major differences of substances are, first, that direct discrimination is potentially justifiable and, secondly, there is no explicit outlawing of indirect discrimination; rather, there is a duty to make reasonable adjustments to the needs of disabled people, a duty which fulfils many of the same functions as the concept of indirect discrimination. Another difference is that far more details of the law are, and will be, in the form of Regulations and Guidance. The reason is that the many different forms and varying severity of disabilities make it more difficult to deal with every issue through primary legislation.

BACKGROUND TO THE LEGISLATION

It is straightforward to discover the number of women in Britain, and reasonably straightforward to discover the numbers in each ethnic or national group. In the vast majority of cases one's gender and racial status is clear and immutable. The concept of disability is far more fluid. It is problematic both to discover the number of disabled people in Britain and to define disability in a clear and comprehensive manner for the purposes of the legislation.

Doyle, B, *New Directions Towards Disabled Workers' Rights*, 1994, London: Institute of Employment Rights, pp 3–6:

Using a broad definition, the [Office of Population Censuses and Surveys] found a disabled adult population in Britain of 6.2 million people, of whom 5.7 million were living in private households ... Some 42% of disabled adults living in private households were of working age (16–64 years old), compared with 74% of adults in the general population ... The [Social and Community

---

[1] See Doyle, B, 'Enabling legislation or dissembling law? The Disability Discrimination Act 1995' (1997) 60 MLR 64.

[2] There are at present no enforceable in European law granted to disabled people, although the new Art 6a of the Treaty of Rome, inserted by the draft Treaty of Amsterdam, provides that disability is one of the grounds of discrimination upon which legislative action is permissible. On the prospects for such action, see Whittle, R, 'Disability discrimination and the Amsterdam Treaty' (1998) 23 EL Rev 50.

Planning Research] study, using a narrower definition of disability (by reference to employability) estimated that 22% of adults of working age had a health problem or disability, and so measured the disabled adult population at 7.3 million persons ... [The researchers concluded] that disabled workers who are occupationally handicapped and economically active (in work or seeking work) represented nearly 4% of the population ...

Seventy eight per cent of disabled adults are mobile without assistance and 92% with assistance if necessary, but [it was found] that disability placed some restrictions on mobility in terms of frequency and distance. Transport difficulties, lack of assistance, problems in affording mobility and obstacles to access were frequently cited to explain this picture ... Closely linked with mobility questions is the need of disabled persons for aid, equipment or adaptations. The OPCS researchers estimated that nearly 70% of disabled adults used some sort of equipment to assist or relieve their disability, while some 24% required domestic adaptations in order to sustain independent living ...

Whereas 69% of the population under pension age are working, only 31% of disabled adults are similarly situated ...[3]

Disabled workers are nearly twice as likely as non-disabled workers to lack formal educational qualifications, while manual occupational status and low levels of qualifications tended to be associated with an increased incidence of disabled unemployment. When in employment, disabled employees are likely to be under-represented in the professional and managerial occupations or non-manual jobs, but disproportionately represented in manual, semi-skilled and unskilled employment ...

The OPCS researchers found that the gross weekly earnings of disabled adults in full time employment [in 1988] averaged at £156.70 for men and £111.20 for women ... [T]his compared unfavourably with weekly earnings of £192.40 and £126.40 for men and women respectively in the general population ...

Weiss identified a number of problems faced by disabled workers in attempting to enter employment ... First, they must surmount physical and vocational obstacles during rehabilitation and training. Second, disabled persons must overcome the barriers confronted in architectural designs and transportation systems. Third, they will encounter resistance by employers to hiring persons with disabilities. Fourth, disabled jobseekers experience self-doubt as a product of previous prejudice. Fifth, they must master the tests created by inflexible medical examinations, which many employers use without questioning their value and utility.

---

[3] '[T]he official unemployment rate for disabled people is 20%, compared to 9% for able bodied people. In fact, the unemployment rate is much higher. Two-thirds of disabled people do not work, and [OPCS] found that half of these wanted to work, given the right circumstances.' Gooding, C, *Disabling Laws, Enabling Acts*, 1994, London: Pluto, p 6.

Gooding, C, *Disabling Laws, Enabling Acts,* **1994, London: Pluto, p 6:**

[T]he majority of people with impairments become disabled during the course of their lives. For these people, disability frequently leads to the loss of a job. Only one-third of people who were in employment at the time they became disabled retained their jobs.

The causes of discrimination and disadvantage

There are two rather contradictory attitudes to the employment of disabled people. On the one hand there is evidence that employers who do employ disabled people testify to a high level of satisfaction with their work performance.

Doyle, B, *New Directions Towards Disabled Workers' Rights,* **1994, London: Institute of Employment Rights, p 7:**

It was found that among employers employing disabled workers, one in 10 rated their level of performance as better than other employees, while seven in 10 thought such workers to be comparable with other employees. These employers reported that disabled employees' attendance records were about the same or better than their non-disabled workers, although nearly a quarter thought that their disabled personnel took more time off than their comparators.

On the other hand a 1993 survey of a broad range of employers found that 42% of employers had no disabled employees.

Gooding, C, *Disabling Laws, Enabling Acts,* **1994, London: Pluto, pp 7–8:**

One of the most frequently cited reasons for this was that there were no suitable jobs ... within the organisation ... [I]t is highly unlikely that the respondents truly had no posts which could be filled by anyone with any degree of disability ... The researcher comments: 'Many of the perceived difficulties are associated with somewhat stereotypical views of the range of difficulties likely to be encountered.' Thus, one of the commonest explanations for the unsuitability of the work was its 'physical nature'. And yet ... a higher proportion of disabled people work in manual jobs than do able bodied people ... [A]nother common reason given by employers ... was the lack of accessible premises. These employers equate disability with wheelchairs, and yet only 5% of disabled people use wheelchairs.

To an extent some of these 'reasons' are simply an excuse for discrimination. Some employers are blatant in their attitudes: 6% of employers ... said that they would not employ disabled workers under any circumstances. A survey of disabled solicitors found that 21% thought that their careers would be affected by prejudice. A further 8% said that they experienced 'appearance problems'. 'What clients would think' was the commonest reason for rejection given by potential employers ...

If the stereotyping and underestimation of disabled people's abilities is one half of the equation, the other half is a distorted sense of what abilities are required to carry out a job. A ... survey of employers' attitudes found that 65% thought that being able to climb stairs was 'vital for work in management' ... 75% thought that good eyesight was 'vital' for management work. Thirty one per cent stated that ability to walk fairly long distances was vital for a career as a business professional.

Doyle, B, *New Directions Towards Disabled Workers' Rights*, 1994, London: Institute of Employment Rights, p 6:

Discrimination against disabled persons often takes the form of prejudice. Prejudice is manifested in attitudes that distort social relationships by over-emphasis upon the characteristic of disability. Prejudice feeds the stereotypical, stigmatised view of disabled persons, exaggerates the negative connotations of impairment, and excludes or devalues other measures of social worth or attributes. The view of disabled persons as lesser individuals poisons their chances of full participation in employment opportunities. The assumption is that *disability* means *inability* and consequently many jobs are assumed to be beyond the capacity of disabled workers.

Previous legislation

The previous legal framework regulating the employment of disabled people was provided by the Disabled Persons (Employment) Act 1944. The Act required all employers employing 20 or more employees to have a quota whereby 3% of employees should be registered disabled. Employing a non-disabled person where an employer was below quota was a criminal offence. Two classes of employment, passenger electric lift attendant and car park attendant, were reserved for registered disabled people.

There is no doubt that the quota system failed to meet the aspirations and expectations of disabled people, and by the time of its abolition it had come close to falling into disuse. The Act allowed for employers to apply for a permit exempting them from responsibilities under the quota legislation; permits were issued straightforwardly in bulk, an approach which contributed to the view that, in effect, compliance was voluntary. Evidence suggested that employer awareness of the scheme was low and did not in practice influence employment decisions.[4] Only those who were registered as disabled counted towards fulfilment of quota; registration was voluntary and, for many disabled people, unnecessary and stigmatising. It became mathematically impossible for all employers to achieve their quota requirements. In these circumstances, perhaps not surprisingly, enforcement was so lax that there were only eight successful prosecutions throughout the operational period of the quota legislation.

---

[4] Doyle, B, *New Directions Towards Disabled Workers' Rights*, 1994, London: Institute of Employment Rights, p 11.

Thus the scheme failed for practical reasons. Whether it is objectionable in principle and whether a different approach is appropriate is less obvious. The advantages are a potential guarantee of employment opportunities irrespective of the individual merit of a disabled applicant, a recognition that it is society's responsibility through employers to provide meaningful work for disabled people, and the possibility of linking a quota system with employment subsidies. But the disadvantages are many. First, it provides no guarantee of employment at a level commensurate with the abilities of the individual, and indeed the two jobs reserved for the disabled only served to entrench a view that low-level menial tasks were the best that could be aspired to. Secondly, it imposes a solution on the disabled, rather than empowering individuals by the granting of rights, and it is thus paternalistic in nature. Thirdly, the enforcement mechanisms are taken out of the hands of individuals and given to some kind of enforcement agency. Experience with this kind of regulatory legislation suggests that there will always be a great willingness to find reasons not to prosecute. Finally, a quota system reinforces a belief that the disabled are an entirely separate category from the able bodied and pays no heed to the fact that what is regarded as a disability depends in large measure on society's response to particular situations.

Progress towards legislation

Even if the view is taken that a quota system is inappropriate, it does not follow that anti-discrimination legislation is the right solution. Throughout most of the 1970s and 1980s the preferred government response was an entirely voluntary approach by way of education and assistance, both of employers and the disabled, in the belief that goodwill towards the disabled was present, with only the means to implement it lacking.[5]

The pressure for anti-discrimination legislation, strong as it was in its own terms, developed a momentum from the fact that other jurisdictions, especially the USA and Australia, had themselves enacted such legislation.[6] In America, legislation was a response to the growing political power and social awareness of disabled people, especially disabled war veterans, who were able to argue that the cause of their disability imposed obligations of fair treatment on the State, and who were able to extend that reasoning to other groups of disabled people.

There are two pieces of American legislation which influenced the British debate: the Rehabilitation Act 1973 and the Americans with Disabilities Act 1990. Section 504 of the former Act outlawed disability discrimination by any

---

5   *Op cit*, Doyle, fn 4, pp 13–17.

6   See Doyle, B, *Disability, Discrimination and Equal Opportunity: a Comparative Study of the Employment Rights of Disabled People*, 1995, London: Mansell.

programme which received federal government funding, and s 501 required the federal government as employer to engage in affirmative action in relation to disabled employees. Section 503 imposed a similar requirement on organisations which did business with the federal government.[7] The limitations of the legislation are apparent: it was restricted to employees of the federal government and those doing business with the federal government and so had no direct impact in the private sector; and did not in terms give individual rights to the disabled themselves. However, granting some rights but not full rights itself became a spur to the political mobilisation of disabled people.[8] The 'rights-based approach ... was itself a stimulus to the unification of different groups of disabled people. Historically, organisations sought to represent the interests of groups based upon a common medical condition ... and these groups then competed against each other for resources from the State. However, once the common experience of discrimination was recognised, this formed the basis for united action'.[9]

Given that the Civil Rights Act provided direct rights to women and black people, and that the Rehabilitation Act was a significant but limited step towards the protection of disabled people, pressure to enact further legislation was both inevitable and powerful. The Americans with Disabilities Act 1990 outlaws discrimination on the ground of disability in relation to employment, housing, public accommodation, education, transport, communications, recreation, institutionalisation, health services, voting and access to public services. In a precursor of British developments, employers are required to make reasonable accommodation for the needs of qualified disabled people, subject to a defence based on the concept of undue hardship.

Proponents of anti-discrimination legislation had to face up to the fact that the experience of the SDA 1975 and the RRA 1976 was somewhat disappointing, a fact that many critics attributed to the individualism of the legislation, with the enforcement emphasis firmly based on the victim's claim before the Industrial Tribunal.[10] Some, indeed, regarded the emphasis on individual rights as wholly misplaced and as apt to deflect attention from the real political and social changes necessary to improve the lot of women and ethnic minorities. Gooding answered the argument in the following terms.

Gooding, C, *Disabling Laws, Enabling Acts*, 1994, London: Pluto, p 43:

[A] rights-based discourse has a great capacity for empowering disabled people and for beneficially shaping broader social discourse ... [While] rights

---

7   *Op cit*, Doyle, fn 4, pp 24–27.
8   *Op cit*, Gooding, fn 3, p 25.
9   *Op cit*, Gooding, p 25.
10 Re-named employment tribunals by the Employment Rights (Dispute Resolution) Act 1998, s 1(1).

do not resolve problems [their value is] in transposing the problem into one which is defined as having a legal solution ...

[T]he subordination of disabled people has been located by society in the incapacities of their own bodies. Casting access requirements in the framework of rights discourse locates disabled people's subordination in the public rather than the private sphere. It therefore promotes a sense of collective identity among disabled people who, despite the vast differences in their individual disabilities, share a common experience of exclusion and stigmatisation by society ...

[T]his contradicts the common argument that because law reduces people to isolated individuals it runs counter to the only possible basis for radical change – collective action. Rights discourse promotes the development of an individual's sense of self and a group's collective identity most powerfully through the process in which these rights are asserted. The act of claiming a right is itself an assertion of moral self-worth. The advocacy process itself, for a group like disabled people who have historically been excluded from public life, combats this exclusion ...

It is a paradox, in no way unique to disabled people, that the anti-discrimination approach requires that in order to assert their right to full and equal participation in society, they must continue to assert their differences. The price of being heard, and achieving some control over the consequences of disability, is to accept the label.

But, to accept that rights are appropriate does not resolve the question of what kind of rights. Disability may have an impact upon capacity and qualifications, especially in relation to work, that race and gender do not have. That there are a few exceptions to this point, in the form of the genuine occupational qualification defences under the SDA 1975 and the RRA 1976, does not destroy its main thrust. It is further arguable that disabilities vary so greatly in their nature and impact that to the utilisation of one overarching anti-discrimination principle is flawed in theory and unworkable in practice.

These points can be answered. There is a clear parallel with the historical exclusion of women, which, while often purporting to be for physical reasons, in reality had a social explanation. Arguments that there are 'real' differences between the disabled and the able bodied collapse in the face of social explanations in much the same way as explanations that there are differences between men and women. They collapse even more obviously, as disability is clearly not a status, but a relative position on a sliding scale of different abilities. The fact that there are exceptions within the SDA 1975 and the RRA 1976 merely demonstrates that rights are rarely absolute. That the DDA 1995 accepts the possibility of a defence to the employer based on excessive cost – adjustments need only be 'reasonable' – does not destroy the argument based on rights, but merely indicates that the employer has rights as well, albeit of a different nature. After all, cost may be relevant under the SDA 1975 and the RRA 1976 as a potentially relevant factor to the question of justified indirect discrimination. Finally, we have already stressed the symbolic importance of rights. Discrimination is now generally acknowledged to be 'wrong'; this attitude, while a huge generalisation, has been wrought by previous legislation. For both symbolic and practical reasons, it is appropriate for those wishing to counter disadvantages experienced by the disabled to utilise the anti-discrimination strategy.

But, just as in relation to women and race, it should not be assumed that this is the only strategy. For women, direct rights, such as a national minimum wage or maternity benefits, may be of greater practical importance than the SDA 1975. For black people, improved educational opportunities may do more than the RRA 1976. The same logic applies to the disabled. For the disabled, major structural changes entailing significant expense, for example, to buildings or to public transport, may be better achieved through direct legislative requirements than through the principle of non-discrimination. While making individual adjustments is essential, they can only be provided when someone has actually applied for a job. Unlike direct legislation, the non-discrimination principle cannot require adjustments to be made in the hope or expectation that disabled people will apply in the future. Furthermore, the principle works best in relation to employers, as is revealed by the small number of non-employment cases under the SDA 1975 and the RRA 1976, and by the fact that in its first year of operation 40 non-employment DDA cases were commenced, compared with 1,400 employment cases.[11] In many such cases, the amount of loss is likely to be limited and hard to measure, both factors thereby discouraging litigation. For example, compensation for being refused entry to a cinema on a single occasion, however demeaning, is likely to be considerably less than for denial of a job. The non-discrimination principle may be little used in relation to goods, facilities and services. In relation to education and transport, the legislation grants no individual rights. The effectiveness of those parts of the legislation will depend almost entirely on future regulations.

The legislation was passed by the Conservative Government, a fact that might be thought somewhat surprising. The explanation is that, having ensured that a previous – and arguably stronger – Private Member's Bill – was prevented from passing through Parliament, the Government felt under a moral obligation to legislate. Two Codes of Practice have been issued: one concerned with employment,[12] and the other with the provision of goods, facilities and services.[13] While their legal effect is the same, they are noticeably

---

[11] Of those 1,408, 568 were completed. Of those, as many as 53% were settled and 29% withdrawn, leaving 102 that proceeded to Tribunal. See 'Vast majority of DDA cases settled or withdrawn' (1998) 79 EOR 10.

[12] *Code of Practice for the Elimination of Discrimination in the Field of Employment Against Disabled Persons or Persons who have had a Disability*, 1996, London: HMSO.

[13] *Code of Practice: Rights of Access; Goods, Facilities, Services and Premises*, 1996, London: HMSO.

more comprehensive and detailed than the equivalent race and gender Codes, because of the greater variety of situations with which disability issues are concerned. The detail provided in the Codes, and especially the many specific examples, suggest that tribunals may be encouraged to refer to and rely on this Code more than has been the case with the gender and race Codes.

THE DEFINITION OF DISABILITY[14]

Because of the nature of the issue, the definition of who is protected by the legislation – the definition of disability – is more complex than in relation to gender and race, and is logically the first legal issue to consider.

Gooding, C, *Disabling Laws, Enabling Acts,* **1994, London: Pluto, 15:**

To understand the full operation of discrimination on disabled people's lives we need to extend our understanding of that process to include the socio-economic and political forces which shape not only our attitudes towards disability but also the very meaning of that term. In a very real sense society disables individuals by constructing a disabled identity into which individuals are fitted ... [For example] the labels 'blind' or 'deaf' are relative ones, based on the percentage of 'full' vision' which a person possesses ...

[C]lassifications of disability have varied historically. In part, these historical variations result from shifts in technology and the social conditions in which that technology is disseminated ... [For example] visually impaired people ... by wearing glasses can possess a 'normal' range of vision. Often these people would be unable to read or distinguish objects without their visual aids. Yet they will not be considered 'disabled' both because this impairment is sufficiently widespread not to be stigmatised and because in our society such corrective aids are readily available.

The technological level of society can reduce disabilities by 'curing' physical impairments or by reducing their impact ... However it can also, paradoxically, increase them. Medical advances can increase the numbers of disabled people, prolonging the lives of people who would previously have died. Less positively, society can disable more individuals by increasing the level at which individuals are expected to function in society, and hence magnifying the disabling effects of impairments. One example of this is the invention of the telephone, which has had a detrimental effect on the ability of deaf people to function socially ...

Stone suggests that the concept of disability has been used to resolve the issue of distributive justice. This issue is created by the presence in the modern world of two distributive systems – one of which distributes on the basis of waged labour and the other on the basis of need. There is a potential conflict between the two systems, since if people can acquire goods through the need

---

[14] See 'Interpreting the DDA – part 1: the meaning of disability' (1998) 79 EOR 13.

system they will not need to engage in waged work ... This conflict has historically been resolved by the creation of rigid categories of need – the elderly, children, the disabled – to determine who will be allowed to claim public assistance. Hence, disability becomes synonymous with dependence and inability to work.

The definition of disability is key to the scope of the legislation, even though the vast majority of claimants or potential claimants will be disabled under any definition. Unlike under the SDA 1975 and the RRA 1976, the boundary between the protected and unprotected groups is unclear. 'The definition of disability must be both inclusive and exclusive: embracing individuals outside the limited popular perception of "disability", yet excluding idiosyncrasies, human traits and transient illness. A distinction must be drawn between chronic or handicapping conditions and temporary or minor maladies.'[15] The statutory definition adopted oscillates between a medical and a social model of disability, and is highly complex. It is to be found in the main text of the statute, as amplified by Sched 1. In addition, the meaning is further expanded by Regulations[16] and Guidance[17] on matters to be taken into account in interpreting the definition.

Section 1(1)   Subject to the provisions of Sched 1, a person has a disability for the purposes of this Act if he has a physical or mental impairment which has a substantial and long term adverse effect on his ability to carry out normal day to day activities.

There are four criteria which must be satisfied: there must be a physical or mental impairment, it must affect ability to carry out everyday activities, and such effect must be both substantial and long term.

Impairment

Schedule 1, para 1(1):

Mental impairment: includes an impairment resulting from or consisting of a mental illness only if the illness is a clinically well recognised illness.

Regulations

3(1)   Subject to para (2) below, addiction to alcohol, nicotine or any other substance is to be treated as not amounting to an impairment for the purposes of the Act.

(2)   Paragraph (1) above does not apply to addiction which was originally the result of administration of medically prescribed drugs or other medical treatment.

4(1)   For the purposes of the Act the following conditions are to be treated as not amounting to impairments:

---

15   Doyle, B, 'Employment rights, equal opportunities and disabled persons: the ingredients of reform' (1993) 22 Industrial LJ 89, p 91.

16   Disability Discrimination (Meaning of Disability) Regulations 1996 SI 1996/1455.

17   *Guidance on Matters to be Taken into Account in Determining Questions Relating to the Definition of Disability*, 1996, London: HMSO, issued under Sched 2, para (3).

(a) a tendency to set fires;

(b) a tendency to steal;

(c) a tendency to physical or sexual abuse of other persons;

(d) exhibitionism; and

(e) voyeurism.

Guidance

10 In many cases there will be no dispute whether a person has an impairment. Any disagreement is more likely to be about whether the effects of the impairment are sufficient to fall within the definition. Even so, it may sometimes be necessary to decide whether a person has an impairment ...

11 It is not necessary to consider how an impairment was caused, even if the cause is a consequence of a condition which is excluded. For example, liver disease as a result of alcohol dependency would count as an impairment.

12 *Physical or mental impairment* includes sensory impairments, such as those affecting sight or hearing.

13 *Mental impairment* includes a wide range of impairments relating to mental functioning, including what are often known as learning disabilities ...

There are a number of problems with this definition. First, there must be an actual impairment.[18] Someone who is wrongly perceived as having an impairment is not within the statutory definition. This excludes, for example, a person who is misdiagnosed as being dyslexic or as suffering from a mental illness. It also appears to exclude someone who does have an impairment, but one which has no substantial effect on everyday activities. This might apply to cases of epilepsy or mild mental illness, where the prejudiced employer might still wish to exclude employees. In such cases, though, the tribunal might find it rather easy to conclude that there was a substantial degree of impairment. It also follows that there can be no claim if a person is dismissed because, for example, a relative has become disabled and the employer fears that too much time off will be taken to care for the relative, or if an employee is sacked because other employees object to the bringing of a severely disfigured partner to out-of-office functions. The definition is governed by the medical

---

18 In *Howden v Capital Copiers (Edinburgh) Ltd* (1997), unreported, IT, Case No: S/400005, 33 DCLD 1, it was held that severe abdominal pain was an impairment even though its exact cause could not be diagnosed; in *O'Neill v Symm and Co Ltd* (1997), unreported, IT, Case No: 2700054, 33 DCLD 2, ME, was held to be a disability on the basis that it is classified by the World Health Organisation as a separate and recognisable disease of the central nervous system. The employer's successful appeal to the EAT, [1998] IRLR 233, did not contradict the correctness of this conclusion, though it was stressed that all will depend on the applicant's particular impairments.

model of disability rather than the social model.19 Secondly, mental illness is only covered if it is a clinically well recognised illness. There are potential problems both in defining what is meant by an 'illness' and in deciding how much recognition is needed for an illness to be well recognised. The recent controversy in criminal law as to whether 'battered woman syndrome' amounts to an 'abnormality of mind' for the purposes of the law of diminished responsibility shows that 'new' mental illnesses remain discoverable or classifiable. Thirdly, the exclusion of substance addictions and conditions with extreme anti-social or criminal consequences shows a desire to exclude conditions for which the individual is responsible and which, if within the definition, carry the potential for bringing the law into disrepute. Smokers, for example, will not be able to claim that they are victims of discrimination if a no-smoking policy is introduced in their workplace. Disability is in this context treated as an unfortunate occurrence thrust on us rather than something we bring on ourselves. This approach is applied to mental conditions; it is not carried through to physical conditions. If somebody becomes physically disabled as a result of a failed suicide attempt they are clearly within the statutory definition.

Normal day to day activities

Schedule 4(1)

An impairment is to be taken to affect the ability of the person concerned to carry out normal day to day activities only if it affects one of the following–

(a) mobility;

(b) manual dexterity;

(c) physical co-ordination;

(d) continence;

(e) ability to lift, carry out or otherwise move everyday objects;

(f) speech, hearing or eyesight;

(g) memory or ability to concentrate, learn or understand; or

(h) perception of the risk of physical danger.

Regulations

6 [W]here a child under six years of age has an impairment which does not have [a relevant] effect ... that impairment is to be taken to have a

---

19 'In the US, the protected class includes a person whose disability represents no handicap to employment but is treated by employers as if it did; or whose disability *is* a handicap to employment but only as a result of attitudes of others towards it; or who has no disability at all but is erroneously treated by employers as disabled. As the Supreme Court has explained in *School Board of Nassau County, Florida v Arline* 480 US 273 (1987): an impairment might not diminish a person's physical or mental capabilities, but could nevertheless substantially limit that person's ability to work as a result of the negative reactions of others to the impairment ... Congress acknowledged that the society's accumulated fears about disability and disease are as handicapping as are the physical limitations that flow from actual impairment.' *Op cit*, Doyle, fn 15, p 93.

substantial and long term adverse effect ... where it would normally have a substantial and long term adverse effect on the ability of a person aged six years or over to carry out normal day to day activities.[20]

Guidance

C2 The term 'normal day to day activities' is not intended to include activities which are normal only for a particular person or group of people. Therefore ... account should be taken of how far [an activity] is normal for most people and carried out by most people on a daily or frequent and fairly regular basis.

C3 [It] does not, for example, include work of any particular form, because no particular form of work is 'normal' for most people. In any individual case, the activities carried out might be highly specialised. The same is true of playing in a particular game, taking part in a particular hobby, playing a musical instrument, playing sport, or performing a highly skilled task. Impairments which effect only such an activity and have no effect on 'normal day to day activities' are not covered ...

C6 Many impairments will, by their nature, adversely effect a person directly in one of the [relevant] respects ... An impairment may also indirectly affect a person in one or more of these respects, and this should be taken into account when assessing whether the impairment falls within the definition. For example:

- medical advice: where a person has been professionally advised to change, limit or refrain from a normal day to day activity on account of an impairment or only to do it in a certain way or under certain conditions;

- pain or fatigue: where an impairment causes pain or fatigue in normal day to day activities, so that the person may have the capacity to do something but suffer pain in doing do; or the impairment might make the activity more than usually fatiguing so that the person might not be able to repeat the task over a sustained period of time.

C7 Where a person has a mental illness such as depression, account should be taken of whether, although that person has the physical ability to perform a task he or she is, in practice, unable to sustain an activity over a reasonable period.

The Guidance lists examples of day to day activities, which are specifically stated not to be exhaustive. Included are examples of activities which it would be reasonable to regard as having a substantial adverse effect, and those which it would not. For example, in relation to mobility, ability to walk is not mentioned because it is obvious; rather, the examples of a substantial adverse effect which are given include 'inability to walk other than at a slow pace or with unsteady or jerky movements' and 'difficulty in going up or down stairs,

---

20 While this has little if any relevance to employment discrimination, it has potential application where there is discrimination in the provision of goods or services.

steps or gradients'; those not having such effect are 'difficulty walking unaided a distance of about ... a mile without discomfort or having to stop ...' and 'inability to travel in a car for a journey lasting two hours without discomfort'.[21] It is, though, important to note that indirect effects are included, as where an employee can no longer perform a day to day activity because of medical advice or where such activity causes abnormal pain or fatigue.

The most important, and, arguably, most illogical exclusion is that of work. Despite the legislation being concerned with employment discrimination, work is not treated as a normal day to day activity. The explanation is to prevent an argument that someone is disabled merely by virtue of the fact that they are unable to pursue a particular occupation. It follows that if an impairment is only manifest in a workplace environment, its victim will be outside the scope of the legislation. For example, if a back condition prevents someone from performing a job involving heavy lifting, the definition of disability would only be satisfied if their ability to lift ordinary objects outside work is also affected.[22]

Long term effects

Schedule 1

2(1) The effect of an impairment is a long term effect if:

    (a) it has lasted at least 12 months;

    (b) the period for which it lasts is likely to be at least 12 months; or

    (c) it is likely to last for the rest of the life of the person affected.

2(2) Where an impairment ceases to have a substantial adverse effect ... it is to be treated as continuing to have that effect if that effect is likely to recur.

Guidance

B2 It is not necessary for the effect to be the same throughout the relevant period. It may change, as where activities which are initially very difficult become possible to a much greater extent. The main adverse effect might even disappear – or it might disappear temporarily – while ... other effects ... continue or develop. Provided the impairment continues to have, or is likely to have, such an effect throughout the period, there is a long term effect.

B3 Conditions which recur only sporadically or for short periods (for example, epilepsy) can still qualify [see para 2(2) above] ... *Regulations specifically exclude* ... hayfever ... except where it aggravates the effect of an existing condition.

B5 Likelihood of recurrence should be considered taking all the circumstances of the case into account. This should include what the person could

---

[21] This exercise is repeated for each of the specifically listed day to day activities; there is not the space to discuss them all in detail. See 'Disability Discrimination Act Regulations and Guidance' (1996) 68 EOR 29, pp 36–38.

[22] *Op cit*, 'Interpreting the DDA', fn 14, p 15.

reasonably be expected to do to prevent the recurrence [for example, avoiding substances to which there is an allergy] ... In addition, it is possible that the way in which a person can control or cope with the effects of a condition may not always be successful because, for example, a routine is not followed or the person is in an unfamiliar environment. If there is an increased likelihood that the control will break down, it will be more likely that there will be a recurrence. That possibility should be taken into account when assessing the likelihood of a recurrence.

The most problematic issue here concerns fluctuating conditions. It seems that there must be a likely recurrence *after* 12 months has elapsed for the condition to be regarded as long term. The ability to control the condition is also relevant to the question of likelihood of recurrence, and when such recurrence may be expected.

In *Clark v Novacold Ltd*,[23] the Tribunal stressed that the likelihood of its lasting 12 months must be determined when the alleged act of discrimination occurred and not retrospectively at the time of the tribunal hearing. Furthermore, this issue is not the same as whether the employee is likely to be able to return to work within 12 months, as effect on ability to work is different from effect on day-to-day activities.

Disfigurements

Schedule 3(1)

An impairment which consists of a severe disfigurement is to be treated as having a substantial adverse effect ...

Regulations

5   For the purposes of para 3 ... a severe disfigurement is not to be treated as having a substantial adverse effect ... if it consists of:

   (a) a tattoo (which has not been removed); or

   (b) a piercing of the body for decorative or other non-medical purposes, including any object attached through the piercing for such purposes.

Guidance

A17 Examples of disfigurements include scars, birthmarks, limb or postural deformation or diseases of the skin. Assessing severity will be mainly a matter of the degree of the disfigurement. However, it may be necessary to take account of where the feature in question is (for example, on the back as opposed to on the face).

This is the clearest example of the 'social' model of disability; it is premised on the assumption that such disfigurements may cause no functional impairment but may lead to social disadvantage or discrimination, although the effect of the disfigurement must be long term. That employers or anyone else do not refer to it or make decisions based on it is irrelevant to the question whether

---

[23]   IT, unreported, Case No: 1801661/97.

the person is disabled, but will be relevant to the subsequent question whether any less favourable treatment was connected with the disability.

Substantial adverse effects

The statute contains no definition on what this concept entails, as in most instances it will be a question of fact. It is fleshed out through examples given by way of guidance.

Guidance

A1 A 'substantial' effect is more than would be produced by the sort of physical or mental conditions experienced by many people which have only minor effects ...

A2 The time taken by a person with an impairment to carry out a normal day to day activity should be considered when assessing whether the effect of that impairment is substantial ...

A4 An impairment might not have a substantial effect on a person in any one [of the relevant respects], but its effects in more than one of these respects taken together could result in a substantial adverse effect ...

A5 For example, although the great majority of people with cerebral palsy will experience a number of substantial effects, someone with mild cerebral palsy may experience minor effects ... which together could create substantial adverse effects ... fatigue may hinder walking, visual perception may be poor, co-ordination and balance may sometimes cause difficulties. Similarly, a person whose impairment causes breathing difficulties may experience minor effects in a number of respects but which overall have a substantial adverse effect ... For some people, mental illness may have a clear effect in one ... respect ... However, for others ... there may be effects in a number of different respects which, taken together [amount to a substantial adverse effect].

A6 A person may have more than one impairment, any one of which alone would not have a substantial effect. In such a case, account should be taken of whether the impairments together have a substantial effect overall ... For example, a minor impairment which affects physical co-ordination and an irreversible but minor injury to a leg which affects mobility, taken together, might have a substantial effect ...

A7 Account should be taken of how far a person can reasonably be expected to modify behaviour to prevent or reduce the effects of an impairment ...

A10 Whether adverse effects are substantial may depend on environmental conditions which may vary; for example, the temperature, humidity, the time of day or night, how tired the person is or how much stress he or she is under may have an impact ...

This last point is significant: if the impairment is only manifest in particular environmental conditions found in a particular workplace, there is no protection, for 'work' is not within the definition of day to day activities. It follows that, where an employee becomes unable to continue work in unpleasant working conditions, but suffers no serious adverse consequences outside work, there is no obligation to make an attempt to find alternative work, as the employee does not satisfy the definition of a disabled person.

There are four situations for which the law makes specific provision.

Effect of medical treatment

6(1) An impairment which would be likely to have a substantial adverse effect ... but for the fact that measures are being taken to treat or correct it, is to be treated as having that effect.

(3) Sub-paragraph (1) does not apply:

    (a) in relation to a person's sight, to the extent that the impairment is, in his case, correctable by spectacles or contact lenses ...

Guidance

A11 [The effect of Sched 1, para 6 is] that where an impairment is being treated or *corrected* the impairment is to be treated as having the effect it would have without the measures in question.

A12 This applies even if the measures result in the effects being completely under control or not at all apparent.

A13 For example, if a person with a hearing impairment wears a hearing aid the question ... is to be decided by reference to what the hearing level would be without the hearing aid. And in the case of someone with diabetes, whether or not the effect is substantial should be decided by reference to what the condition would be if he or she was not taking medication.

A14 [But with sight impairments] the only effects ... to be considered are those which remain when spectacles or contact lenses are used.

It should thus be clear that a person may be within the definition even if there are no current adverse effects. It is the potential for such effects in the absence of the controls which provides the foundation for satisfaction for the definition. Apart from diabetes and hearing impairments mentioned in the Guidance, other examples might be asthma and epilepsy. This may be particularly significant for those suffering from mental illness which is controlled by medication; the test is what would be the effects of the condition in the absence of that medication.

Those previously in the register of disabled persons

The legislation abolished the previous protection available through the quota system. While such protection was very limited, it was considered to be inappropriate to exclude anyone who might previously have been classified, rightly or wrongly, as disabled, but who, but for this section, would fall outside the new definition. The effect of s 7 is to grant the protection to those who were registered as disabled both in January 1995, when the Bill was introduced, and in December 1996, when the employment provisions came into effect. Such protection will last for an initial period of three years.

Progressive conditions

8 (1) Where:

- (a) a person has a progressive condition (such as cancer, multiple sclerosis or muscular dystrophy or infection by the human immunodeficiency virus),
- (b) as a result of that condition, he has an impairment ...; but
- (c) that effect is not (or was not) a substantial adverse effect,

he shall be taken to have an impairment which has such a substantial adverse effect if the condition is likely to result in his having such an impairment.

Guidance

A15 Where a person has a progressive condition, he or she will be treated as having an impairment which has a *substantial* adverse effect from the moment any impairment resulting from that condition first has *some* effect ... The effect need not be continuous and need not be substantial.

The effect of this provision is that the sufferer is protected as from the moment that there is any effect on normal day to day activities as defined. It follows that someone diagnosed as HIV positive is *not* protected merely by virtue of that fact;[24] the protection only comes into effect when some symptom of the illness is manifest. In consequence of this approach, the definition excludes someone who is wrongly thought by the employer to be disabled when in fact there is no actual impairment. Equally, those with a genetic disorder which is latent are outside the statutory protection. It is thus not permissible to discriminate against someone who has a diagnosed impairment, even though the currents effects may be relatively minor, whereas it is lawful to discriminate against someone who is likely to develop precisely the same condition in the future.

Past disabilities

A person is treated as being presently disabled if he or she is at present symptom-free but such symptoms are likely to recur. This does not include someone who has recovered from a past disability. This is particularly important as regards mental illness, even though the person will still be treated as *currently* disabled if the condition is only controlled rather than cured. Paragraph 2 to Sched 2 therefore provides that references to a disabled person 'are to be read as references to a person who has had a disability'. This important provision allows for consideration of potentially long term social consequences of disability as well as its current effects. In addition, someone with a fluctuating condition, such as arthritis, which has at any time in the past met the definition, is treated as within the definition even during symptom free periods, as long as the disabling effects are likely to recur.

---

[24] On HIV generally, see Napier, B, 'AIDS, discrimination and employment law' (1989) 18 Industrial LJ 84.

Evaluation

The complexities of the definition are inevitable: disability is far less clear cut a concept than either race or gender. The Guidance notes spell out, for example, examples of when a lack of manual dexterity would normally be regarded as sufficient to constitute a disability and when not; and examples of when inability to learn, concentrate or understand are sufficiently serious to amount to disability. But bringing a claim involves self-definition as a person with a disability, and thus in the vast majority of cases litigated the disability will immediately be apparent. 'American employers seldom challenge a plaintiff's claim to be a disabled person. As in personal injury litigation, marshalling expert evidence to undermine a claimant's contentions will cause employers to measure the costs against the benefits of doing so. Defendants will not wish to lose the sympathy of the court by aggressively attacking the plaintiff's disability status',[25] especially as they are very likely to have alternative defences available. Whether this attitude will eventually prevail is unclear, but in early cases 'it has been become commonplace for employers to challenge whether or not an applicant with an impairment meets the DDA's test of a disabled person'.[26]

DISCRIMINATION IN EMPLOYMENT

The most important point concerning the coverage of the legislation is that the employment provisions apply only to employers who had 20 or more employees at the time of the alleged discriminatory act.[27] Section 7 of the Act allows for a statutory instrument to reduce, but not to increase, the threshold, although it may only be reduced to two employees rather than abolished altogether, which would require fresh legislation. If the threshold were reduced to two employees, the Government has calculated that the number of employers covered would increase from 90,000 to 720,000.[28] The numbers of employees covered would increase from 12 million to 16.1 million.[29] The Government has set up a task force, one of the tasks of which is to consider whether the current threshold should be retained, or whether it should be reduced to 15, 10, 5 or 2 employees.[30]

---

[25] *Op cit*, Doyle, fn 15, p 94.
[26] *Op cit*, 'Interpreting the DDA', fn 14, p 13.
[27] DDA 1995, s 7.
[28] *The Employment Provisions and Small Employers – a Review*, 1997, London: The Stationery Office.
[29] *Ibid*.
[30] See 'Review of small firm DDA opt-out' (1998) 77 EOR 9.

Apart from being objectionable in principle, as being an unnecessary and unfair carrot which was thrown to the small business sector, application of the provision will not always be straightforward. It is not always obvious precisely clear when a discriminatory act occurs. While part time, temporary and casual workers come within the Act's definition of employment and so must be counted, the same is not true where work is contracted out. Even an employee working for an enterprise may be unsure of the exact employment status of some workers; for a rejected applicant the problems are even greater. It may be necessary to expend considerable time and money in order to rebut an employer's defence that at the relevant time there were fewer than 20 employees on the books. Employers may move in and out of the legislation as circumstances change.

The qualifications provisions are similar to those under the other anti-discrimination statutes. 'Employment' has the same extended meaning, not being restricted to those employed under contracts of service. It follows that the Act applies to those who hire contractors to do work, and, strictly speaking therefore, the duty to make reasonable accommodation applies also. It is difficult to imagine that a tribunal would often impose such a duty where the person being hired was genuinely self-employed.

Section 4(6) excludes employment outside Great Britain, although in contrast with the other statutes, the DDA 1995 applies directly in Northern Ireland rather than having specific separate legislation. There are significant exceptions from the coverage of the legislation: the police are excluded, as they have no contract, and there is no specific inclusion as is the case with the SDA 1975 and RRA 1976; prison officers, fire fighters, employment in the armed services, and employment on board a ship, hovercraft or aeroplane are also excluded. While it is clear that many people with particular categories of disability would be unable to perform some such jobs, blanket exceptions are unnecessary and unacceptable. Many jobs in the services are desk jobs, and many disabilities would not hinder combat effectiveness; the legislation would permit airlines to refuse to employ cabin staff with disfigurements or who require a hearing aid. Once again, the instinctive reaction of government appears to have been to exclude its own employees rather than to give a lead to the private sector.

Section 13 covers discrimination by trade organisations – trade unions,[31] employers' organisations, etc – in similar terms to that prohibited by the RRA 1976 and the SDA 1975. The duty to make reasonable adjustments also applies. This is potentially a source of considerable expense for unions. Meetings may need to be at a time and place suitable for those with mobility impairments, and union literature will need to be accessible to those with

---

[31] See 'Trade Unions and the DDA' (1998) 77 EOR 23.

visual impairments.[32] How this should be done is problematic: it would be imposing a heavy burden to require all such literature to be in Braille; it is arguable that a large print version should be provided as a matter of course, but this would be expensive and not adequate for all visually impaired members. The needs of disabled members who wish to attend training courses or stand for election might also need to be considered. The overall question of how much money non-profit making bodies such as trade unions should be required to spend is not at all clear. There is, however, no specific prohibition, as in the other legislation, against discrimination by partnerships, qualifying bodies, bodies concerned with vocational training and employment agencies, although in many situations employment agencies will be covered by the provision concerning discrimination against contract workers. In many of these examples reliance could be placed on the prohibition of discrimination in relation to the provision of goods and services.

With one exception, other unlawful acts are regulated by the DDA 1995 in much the same way as under the SDA 1975 and the RRA 1976. Victimisation is outlawed by s 55, s 58 provides the same test for the liability of the employer for acts of employees, and s 57 prohibits the aiding of unlawful acts. There is no equivalent to the sections dealing with instructions to discriminate and pressure to discriminate. The different approach concerns discriminatory advertising; under the SDA 1975 and the RRA 1976 the Commissions have responsibility for enforcement. The absence of an equivalent Commission necessitated a different approach. A discriminatory advertisement is not itself unlawful; it merely becomes evidence of unlawfulness once a complaint has been presented to a tribunal. The effect of s 11 is little more than empowering the tribunal to take account of a discriminatory advertisement as part of the evidence relevant to the question of whether the applicant has been discriminated against. This requires a disabled applicant who sees a discriminatory advertisement nevertheless to proceed with an application; this will only happen in the rarest of cases. Even where it does, it will be open to the employer to argue that the discriminatory tone of the advertisement was justified by the nature of the job. One of the immediate symbolic effects of the SDA 1975 and the RRA 1976 was the virtual disappearance of overtly sexist or racist advertising. Partly because of the nature of disability discrimination and partly because of the absence of a disability Commission, it is most unlikely that the DDA 1995 will have the same impact.[33]

Section 4 of the DDA 1995 directly parallels the equivalent provisions of the SDA 1975 and the RRA 1976, making it unlawful to discriminate before someone obtains a job, while they are in employment, and also discrimination

---

32 *Op cit*, 'Trade Unions', fn 31.
33 It has been recommended that a Disability Rights Commission should be established; see below, p 607.

in relation to dismissal.[34] The specific reference to subjecting an employee to a detriment means that harassing someone on the basis of their disability will be unlawful on the same basis as racial and sexual harassment. By the same token it casts the onus on employers to ensure that their anti-harassment policy makes specific reference to the issue of disability; an employer whose policy referred to race and gender but not disability might have difficulty convincing a tribunal that all reasonable steps had been taken to prevent harassment from occurring.

If a person is dismissed because of absence from work, and the reason for that absence is a disability within the definition, that should be sufficient to establish that the reason for the dismissal is connected with the disability. But this sensible approach was not adopted by the EAT in O'Neill v Symm and Co Ltd.[35] It was held that the dismissal would only be connected with the disability if the employer was aware that the applicant had an illness which came within the statutory definition. This cannot be right. The definition is objective and it is for the tribunal to determine if it is satisfied. Further, it would be impossible to resolve how much knowledge of each component of the definition was required by the employer.[36]

THE MEANING OF DISCRIMINATION

Under the RRA 1976, a white person may claim to have been the victim of discrimination; under the SDA 1975 a man may claim to have been the victim. But under the DDA 1995, a non-disabled person does not have the right to make a claim. Conceptually, this is a very important difference, for it means that positive action to benefit disabled people will normally be lawful. Quotas, special training and so on are all presumptively lawful; this is inevitable and correct given that the foundation stone of the act is the duty to make reasonable accommodation for the needs of disabled people. But the general point is subject to two exceptions. First, a disabled person may argue that he or she has been treated less favourably *than another disabled person* has or would have been treated. It thus appears that positive action beyond that mandated by the reasonable accommodation principle may not be targeted at any particular group of the disabled. Section 10(2)(a) protects those who

---

[34] DDA 1995, s 12, covers discrimination against contract workers. The duty of reasonable adjustment may therefore be placed on the principal/hirer rather than, or in addition to, the employer of the contracted worker. However, what that duty requires will vary greatly according to the circumstances, especially where the hiring is only for a short period.

[35] [1998] IRLR 233.

[36] See (1998) 79 EOR 50–52.

provide 'supported employment'[37] for a particular group of the disabled – such as Workshops for the Blind – from falling foul of the anti-discrimination principle. But what might be described as open market employers may not specifically target particular groups of the disabled. This may be especially problematic where reasonable accommodation is provided in advance, so as to encourage and enable particular groups to apply for and perform a job. A person from another group may have a case that such accommodation was only provided on a selective basis. Secondly, the Local Government and Housing Act 1989, which precludes local authorities from acting on a non-commercial basis, requires appointments to be made on merit. The previous exception requiring such authorities to employ their quota of disabled persons is of course no longer applicable. However, the merit principle only applies after the duty of reasonable accommodation has been worked through; the duty is to decide on merit between the able bodied applicant and the disabled applicant for whom reasonable adjustment has been or could be made.

Section 5(1) provides that:

an employer discriminates against a disabled person if:

    (a) for a reason which relates to the person's disability, he treats him less favourably than he treats or would treat others to whom that reason does not or would not apply; and

    (b) he cannot show that the treatment in question is justified.

(2) [A]n employer also discriminates against a disabled person if:

    (a) he fails to comply with a s 6 duty [the duty to make reasonable adjustments] imposed on him in relation to the disabled person; and

    (b) he cannot show that his failure to comply with that duty is justified.

(3) [F]or the purposes of sub-s (1) treatment is justified if, but only if, the reason for it is both material to the circumstances of the particular case and substantial.

(4) For the purposes of sub-s (2), failure to comply with a s 6 duty is justified if, but only if, the reason for the failure is both material to the circumstances of the particular case and substantial.

This definition shows that the structure of the DDA 1995 is fundamentally different from that of the SDA 1975 and RRA 1976. There is no formalised distinction between direct and indirect discrimination and, furthermore, direct discrimination is potentially justifiable. Nevertheless the differences may be more apparent than real. The functional equivalent of indirect discrimination is the s 6 duty to make reasonable adjustments. Failure to make such adjustments means that unnecessary and unjustifiable barriers are being placed in the way of equal employment opportunities for disabled people in

---

[37] This is defined by s 10(3) as where there are 'facilities provided, or in respect of which payments are made, under s 15 of the Disabled Persons (Employment) Act 1944'.

much the same way as unjustifiable employment conditions may disadvantage women and minority ethnic groups.

It is sufficient if the reason 'relates' to disability. There are five points of importance here. First, the process of comparison is not necessarily with a person who is not disabled; it could be with a person who suffers a different disability. Secondly, it need not be shown that disability was the whole or main reason for the less favourable treatment, merely that it was a significant element in the decision. Nor will it be possible to argue that the real reason for a rejection was not disability but inability to perform the job. Issues of proof may therefore be somewhat easier than under the RRA 1976 or the SDA 1975, though tribunals will still need to be willing to draw adverse inferences from employer conduct. In race and gender cases, it has taken many years even to approach an appropriate degree of such willingness. There is a danger that the same experience could be repeated as tribunals grapple with new legislation in a context where they may be unwilling to impose significant adjustment costs on employers. Thirdly, when coupled with the prohibition in s 4 on 'standards, criteria, administrative methods, work practices or procedures that adversely affect a disabled person' it seems clear that many practices which are indirectly discriminatory, in the sense that they disproportionately disadvantage the disabled, are nevertheless directly discriminatory against those particular groups of disabled people who may effectively be totally excluded by the requirement. A job requirement to take the mail downstairs to the basement is indirectly discriminatory against the disabled as a whole but directly discriminatory against some with impaired mobility, who may effectively be excluded by the requirement. Were indirect discrimination specifically included, the issue of who should be compared with whom would become impossibly complex; the hybrid solution seems appropriate. Fourthly, there is no specific provision, as in the RRA 1976, that segregation amounts to less favourable treatment. It may do so, but it has been suggested that in some circumstances such segregation may be the only way to make reasonable adjustments.[38] Finally, utilising health-related criteria for employment decisions such as redundancy – which would normally be attacked through indirect discrimination – may sufficiently relate to disability to be challengeable if they operate to the disadvantage of a disabled person.[39] As disability clearly may impact on many aspects of job performance in a way that race and gender normally do not, cases where claimants seek to explain as related to disability what would otherwise be seen as personal failings will undoubtedly cause problems for the interpretation and application of the legislation.

---

[38] Bourn, C and Whitmore, J, *Anti-Discrimination Law in Britain*, 3rd edn, 1996, London: Sweet & Maxwell, p 98.

[39] 'Disability Discrimination Act 1995' (1996) 65 EOR 31, p 39. See, eg, *Morse v Wiltshire County Council* [1998] IRLR 352, EAT.

The defence of justification

Unlike race and sex discrimination, direct discrimination on ground of disability is potentially justifiable. We are not here concerned with a situation where a disabled person is not appointed on merit, for in that case no less favourable treatment will have occurred.[40] Rather, the legislation contemplates that, despite merit, there may still be circumstances where it is permissible to discriminate. It is specifically provided that this defence cannot succeed where the employer has failed to make a reasonable adjustment as required by s 6 but, in circumstances falling outside the scope of that section, justified discrimination is a possibility.

The less favourable treatment may be justified if it is both material and substantial.[41] The wording of the defence owes something to the defence of genuine material factor under the Equal Pay Act 1970. For a defence to succeed, an employer will need to rely on facts relevant to the individual circumstances of the particular case; stereotypes as to the average performance of those with a particular disability will not suffice. Even apart from the duty to make adjustments, a requirement will only be 'material' to a job if it is reasonably central to the performance of the job and not something so incidental that it could easily be performed by another employee. Safety is another factor which is relevant to materiality: a requirement necessary for the safe performance of a job will be material. It may well be that safety factors, read broadly, will be the commonest purported justifications advanced by employers.[42] This remains true even though safety issues are also subject to the duty to make reasonable adjustments.[43]

Whether a requirement is substantial will necessitate the tribunal to make a value judgment. It has been pointed out that, in the context of the definition of disability, a stringent test of when adverse effects are substantial might operate to the disadvantage of an applicant, whereas a stringent test applied here might be of benefit to the same person. It is impossible to predict whether

---

40 In *Fozard v Greater Manchester Police Authority*, unreported, IT, Case No: 2401143/97, see 33 DCLD 2, a person with learning difficulties applied for a job as a word processor operator, but was rejected as the application form contained a number of errors. The tribunal held that the rejection was related to her disability, but was justified, as accuracy in written work was an important element in the job.

41 For specific examples, see Code of Practice, para 4.6.

42 In *Smith v Carpets International UK plc*, unreported, IT, Case No: 1800507/97, see 34 DCLD 2, it was held to be justified on safety grounds to suspend an epileptic from work which involved driving a fork-lift truck. However, a similar defence in a case of a labourer working in a forge was rejected in *Holmes v Whittingham and Porter*, unreported, IT, Case No: 1802799/97, see 34 DCLD 4, as specialist medical advice should have been taken before the employee was dismissed rather than relying on the recommendation of a general practitioner.

43 See below, pp 602–06.

tribunals would take the same approach to the same word in the two different contexts.[44] It does seem clear that, for a reason to be substantial, it must be substantiated: that is, the test should require the employer to produce some objective evidence of the need for the requirement, rather than base a decision on unsubstantiated assertions. The reason must also be the actual reason why the less favourable treatment was imposed; an after the fact explanation cannot amount to a substantial reason.

The duty to make adjustments

This section is the key to the legislation. It imposes a duty to take positive action in a way entirely unknown to the SDA 1975 and the RRA 1976, reflecting the truths that disabilities do affect ability to perform a job, but to a far lesser extent than is often supposed and in a way which can often be overcome with effort and imagination.

Section 6(1)   Where:

(a) any arrangements made by or on behalf of an employer; or

(b) any physical feature of premises occupied by an employer,

place the disabled person concerned at a substantial disadvantage in comparison with persons who are not disabled, it is the duty of the employer to take such steps as it is reasonable, in all the circumstances of the case, for him to have to take in order to prevent the arrangements or feature having that effect.[45]

(3) The following are examples of steps which have to take ... in order to comply with sub-s (1):

(a) making adjustments to premises;

(b) allocating some of the disabled person's duties to another person;

(c) transferring him to fill an existing vacancy;

(d) altering his working hours;

(e) assigning him to a different place of work;

(f) allowing him to be absent during working hours for rehabilitation, assessment or treatment;

(g) giving him, or arranging for him to be given, training;

(h) acquiring or modifying equipment;

(i) modifying instructions or reference manuals;

(j) modifying procedures for testing or assessment;

---

[44] See *op cit*, 'Disability Discrimination Act 1995', fn 39, p 39.

[45] In *Morse v Wiltshire County Council* [1998] IRLR 352, EAT, it was held that this covered the making of reasonable adjustments so as to avoid the need to dismiss an employee who would otherwise have been dismissed, in this case on ground of redundancy.

(k) providing a reader or interpreter;

(l) providing supervision.[46]

(4) In determining whether it is reasonable for an employer to have to take a particular step ... regard should be had, in particular, to:

(a) the extent to which taking the step would prevent the effect in question;

(b) the extent to which it is practicable for the employer to take the step;

(c) the financial and other costs which would be incurred by the employer in taking the step and the extent to which taking it would disrupt any of his activities;

(d) the extent of the employer's financial and other resources;

(e) the availability to the employer of financial or other assistance with respect to taking the step.

(5) In this section 'the disabled person concerned' means:

(a) in the case of arrangements for determining to whom employment should be offered, any disabled person who is, or who has notified the employer that he may be, an applicant for that employment;

(b) in any other case, a disabled person who is:

(i) an applicant for the employment concerned; or

(ii) an employee of the employer concerned.

(6) Nothing in this section imposes any duty on an employer in relation to a disabled person if the employer does not know, and could not reasonably be expected to know:

(a) in the case of an applicant or potential applicant, that the disabled person is, or may be, an applicant for the employment; or

(b) in any case, that the person has a disability and is likely to be affected in any way mentioned in sub-s (1).

A claim may be based either on less favourable treatment in the sense familiar under the SDA 1975 and the RRA 1976, or on a failure to make adjustments. An employer may refuse to hire a disabled person, either out of pure prejudice or from a lack of belief that a disabled person could be competent to do the job, or the rejection might be on the basis that, while disabled people are considered on merit, in the circumstances it would be impracticable for the particular applicant to perform the job. At the outset, the basis of claim may be unclear: it will frequently be sensible to argue both alternatives. The duty is triggered where the disabled person is placed at a 'substantial disadvantage'. This includes factors affecting the actual performance of the job, factors affecting safe access to and from the place of work, and any other factor

---

[46] For specific examples of how these might operate, see Code of Practice, paras 4.7 and 4.20.

affecting the safe performance of the job. If a reasonable adjustment would enable the job to be performed safely, the duty may be triggered.

The duty is personal in nature, being triggered by some action on the part of an individual disabled person. It follows that there is no general obligation to make a workplace more accessible or work practices more amenable to disabled people. It would be extremely difficult for an employer to predict in advance the wide range of disabilities in respect of which prospective adjustments would otherwise have to be made.[47] However, where the disability is relatively commonplace, and where clear steps to overcome it are possible, failure to plan ahead may constitute failure to make reasonable adjustments.[48]

The duty only arises when the employer has sufficient knowledge as to the situation of the disabled applicant or potential applicant. This may include current employees, for while the employer may normally be expected to be aware of the current situation of members of the workforce, many people become disabled while in employment – whether or not through a workplace incident. In the past, it might have been in the interests of disabled people to conceal their situation from the employer; that is no longer the case. One of the practical and psychological difficulties with the legislation is that a disabled person will be best advised to be as frank and explicit as possible. There is a fine line between giving information necessary to trigger the employer's duty to make reasonable adjustments, and making the situation appear so bad as to suggest that no adjustment may be practicable.[49]

The duty can only arise where the employer has become aware of the disability. Under normal principles, knowledge held by any employee should be imputed to the employer. For example, if an employer instructs a secretary to discard application forms of applicants without degrees, and on checking the forms, the secretary becomes aware that an applicant without a degree has a disability, the employer will be treated as aware of that fact. If the form is discarded before anyone appreciates that the applicant is disabled, no duty can arise – subject of course to any informal communications between applicant and employer – but once there is any knowledge of a disability, the

---

[47] However, para 3.4 of the Code of Practice states that 'when planning for change it could be cost-effective to consider the needs of a range of possible future disabled employees and applicants. There may be helpful improvements that could be built into plans. For example, a new telecommunications system might be made accessible to deaf people even if there are currently no deaf employees'.

[48] Eg, in *Williams v Channel 5 Engineering Services Ltd*, unreported, IT, Case No: 2302136/97, see 34 DCLD 3, the employers were held liable for organising a training course which included a video with no subtitles, which meant that the deaf complainant was unable to complete the course.

[49] See, also, Code of Practice, paras 4.57–4.63.

employer must be taken to be aware of all the information contained in the form concerning any necessary adjustments.

The example itself shows the limitations, inevitable perhaps, of the legislation. While reasonable adjustments must be within the scope of the employer, the question of what is reasonable is an objective one for the tribunal, upon which it is legitimate and, in some cases, necessary for the tribunal to substitute its own view of what is reasonable for that of the employer.[50] However, employers cannot be expected to make up for the fact that the applicant's disability may have contributed to educational underachievement or lack of experience. An employer is still permitted to require applicants to possess an engineering degree, even though, on average, this may operate to the disadvantage of disabled people. The requirement itself cannot be challenged as being indirectly discriminatory, and nothing by way of adjustment could reasonably be expected of all but the very biggest employers. Furthermore, maintenance of pay levels is not required by way of reasonable adjustment: if an employee becomes disabled, even in a workplace accident, such that the old job becomes impossible, the employer is under a duty to make reasonable efforts to find alternative work, if necessary by making adjustments to that work, but there is no obligation to keep paying the employee the same pay as was being earned before the disability struck.[51]

Sub-section (3) shows how potentially wide the duty may be. There is a large body of knowledge and experience as to what adjustments are *capable* of being made in the interests of a disabled person, and disabled people themselves are often the best sources of what can be done in the most cost-effective manner. The key issue, however, is what degree of adjustment will tribunals consider to be reasonable.[52]

Adjustments to the job application process can be used as an example.

'Adjusting the workplace: employers' duty under the Disability Discrimination Bill' (1995) 61 EOR 11, p 13:

The Cornell Program on Employment and Disability in the USA [has given the following] examples of possible accommodation to the selection process:

---

50 *Morse v Wiltshire County Council* [1998] IRLR 352, EAT

51 The obligation to transfer a disabled employee provides greater protection than is provided by the law of unfair dismissal provides to victims of ill-health, even apart from the fact that the latter has at present a two year qualifying period and the DDA 1995 none at all. Victims of long term ill-health will receive greater protection if the problem can be classed as a disability. It is contended that most such cases will be within the definition.

52 See 'Adjusting the workplace: employers' duty under the Disability Discrimination Bill' (1995) 61 EOR 11; also, the Code of Practice, paras 4.21–4.34.

- For people with cognitive disabilities: simplifying and minimising wording on the job applications; clarification and assistance in completing information needed on the job application; describing job requirements clearly, concisely and simply and showing the person the job; adjustment of the length of interview to maximise a person's ability to remain attentive and decrease stress level.

- A person who does not see well enough to read an application form may be discouraged from applying for a job, even if the job itself requires minimal vision. Ask the applicant how he or she would prefer to meet the requirements of the process. If you require applicants to complete an application form, ask which would be the most convenient; mail the application to the candidate who requests it; offer the walk-in applicant the opportunity to take the form, have someone help complete it, and return it by mail or in person; offer the services of someone in the office to assist in completing the form.

- For applicants who are deaf or hard or hearing: minimally, interviews should be sensitive to the range of communication abilities of [such] persons ... Simple accommodations may include conducting the interview in a quiet, well lit environment that minimises visual distractions. The interviewer must be willing to use the interviewee's assistive listening device, if one is used ... Avoid sitting in front of bright lights or windows which make it difficult to speech read. If requested, use an effective professional sign language interpreter.

[T]he 'simplest' strategy is to ask the applicant what appropriate accommodations are needed.

It will also be necessary for employers to review any tests or examinations to ensure that they do not discriminate against disabled people. In the USA, the ADA requires that tests be given to people who have sensory, speaking or manual impairments in a format that does not require the use of the impaired skill, unless that is the job-related skill the test is designed to measure. The EEOC gives as an example: 'An applicant who has dyslexia, which causes difficulty in reading, should be given an oral rather than a written test, unless reading is an essential function of the job. Or, an individual with a visual disability or a learning disability might be allowed more time to take a test, unless the test is designed to measure speed required on the job.'

'Disability Discrimination Act' (1996) 65 EOR 31, p 41:

Section 6(4) sets out the key criteria of 'reasonableness'. Lord Henley explained the criteria as follows: 'The first is the extent to which the step would prevent the effect in question. For example, if the only adjustments possible could make no more than a small improvement to the output of someone who was significantly under-productive, then they might not be reasonable if they were costly or disruptive.

[On the second - practicability: it] might not be reasonable for an employer needing an employee urgently to have to wait for an adjustment to be made to allow a disabled person to be employed ... Also, an adjustment would not be reasonable if it is impossible because the employer would be in breach of health or safety or fire laws were it to be made.

[On the third, cost. This] includes the use of staff and other resources and disruption, as well as direct money costs ...

[Fourth, the employer's resources.] Although the size of a business is not necessarily an indication of the resources available, it is more reasonable for an employer with considerable resources to make an adjustment with a significant cost than for an employer with few resources. Also, it would not normally be reasonable for an employer to spend fewer resources on retaining a disabled person than on recruiting a replacement.

Finally, there is the availability ... of financial or other assistance ... A step is not unreasonable if the availability of help from an outside organisation or from the disabled person would compensate for the factors that would have made it unreasonable. For example, it might be unreasonable on grounds of cost for a particular employer to provide a laptop computer with a Braille keyboard. However, if a suitable one could be loaned or borrowed when needed, for example under the Access to Work Scheme, of if the individual has a suitable one he could provide, then the employer could not successfully claim that provision of the laptop was unreasonable because of the cost.'

There is no doubt that employers fear the cost of enforced adjustment.

'Adjusting the workplace: employers' duty under the Disability Discrimination Bill' (1995) 61 EOR 11, pp 17–18:

The findings from the September 1994 survey [conducted by the US-based Job Accommodation Network] indicate that around half (52%) of accommodations had cost $200 or less ... In 68% of cases the accommodations had cost less than $500 ... It is also notable that nearly a third of employers claimed to have saved more than $15,000 by making the accommodations. Such savings arise through avoiding costs such as termination payments, recruiting and training a new employee, and increasing the employee's productivity through the accommodation. JAN currently estimates that for very $1 spent on making the accommodations, an employer receives $27 of benefits ...

According to the [British-based] Contributions Agency, the cost of the adaptations it has introduced has been quite low. 'It is remarkable how one or two relatively cheap items can make a real difference to someone's comfort and efficiency at work. Several of the aids we provided – such as footrests, magnifiers and cushions – cost under £20. The most expensive items were an electric wheelchair which cost just over £3,000, and an electric scooter, which was £2,226. This sort of equipment virtually pays for itself in terms of increased output from staff who are less tired.'

Particular problems may arise concerning modification to buildings. The Regulations provide that an employer does not have to alter the physical characteristics of any building which was constructed in accordance with the part of the Building Regulations concerned with access and facilities which was in force at the time of construction. Paragraph 8(2) provides that 'it is never reasonable for an employer to have to take steps ... to the extent that this would involve altering any physical characteristic to which this regulation applies'. If this provision is interpreted literally, it takes precedence however minor the adjustment which is contemplated, and would drastically curtail the capacity of the law to mandate physical alterations to buildings in the interests of disabled people.

A further problem with adjustments to buildings arises from the fact that many employers do not own the building where they operate, but lease it. Where the lease provides that consent is necessary to any alteration 'it is always reasonable for the employer to have to take steps to obtain that consent and it is never reasonable for the employer to have to make that alteration before that consent is obtained'.[53] If the proper procedures are followed, however, the employer must make the adjustment if the landlord has unreasonably refused consent, but is under no such obligation if the refusal is reasonable.[54] In the case of unreasonable refusal, the landlord may be joined as party to the proceedings and may be ordered to pay compensation directly to the applicant.

OCCUPATIONAL PENSION SCHEMES AND INSURANCE SERVICES

While s 4 already covers the actions of employers as regards membership and terms of pension schemes, s 17 imposes an obligation on the trustees and managers of a scheme not to discriminate against disabled people, and s 17(1) implies a non-discrimination rule into the terms of such schemes. The purpose of the provisions is to ensure that decisions relating to pension schemes are taken in the light of the particular health, personal circumstances and life expectancy of the individual – as will continue to be permissible – rather than on the mere fact of that person's disability, a fact which may carry no necessary consequences for pension scheme membership.

Section 18 adopts a similar approach to situations where the employer arranges with a private insurer for the provision of benefits – such as private health insurance – for employees. The insurance company will be acting unlawfully if it acts in a way that would be unlawful in the case of the provision of such services to members of the public. Again, the objective is to ensure that the criteria adopted relate to health, etc, and not to the mere fact of being disabled.

The duty of reasonable adjustment does not apply either to occupational pension schemes or to private insurance arrangements. 'Therefore, neither the

---

[53] Regulation 10(1).

[54] See the Code of Practice, regs 11–15 and paras 4.40–4.48.

employer nor the scheme's trustees or managers will need to make any adjustment for a disabled person who will be justifiably denied access either to such a scheme or to a benefit under the scheme. Nor will they receive an adjustment for someone receiving less benefit because they justifiably receive a lower rate of pay.'[55] However, the employer may need to make an adjustment in order to ensure that an insurance company would continue to provide cover, for example, where an epileptic person is removed from contact with valuable items so that the insurance company will continue to provide cover in respect of those items.[56]

EMPLOYMENT PROVISIONS – ENFORCEMENT AND REMEDIES

Before the DDA 1995 was passed, it was argued that it was 'essential for a strong statutory body, representative of disabled people's views, to be created ... In general terms the legislation will fail unless its provisions become widely known and understood and those who decide to register complaints of discrimination are supported and encouraged to do so. It is already hard enough to find lawyers able and willing to deal with discrimination legislation. What if, in addition, the potential client finds the solicitor's office, Legal Aid Board, and county court all unadapted to accommodating their disability? Many such forms of discouragement will arise immediately and the Commission's role must be to seek to redress them where possible.'[57] The Act, though, was passed without a Commission equivalent to the EOC and the CRE, so that there was no power to assist complainants or to conduct formal investigations, though the fact that there are far more voluntary bodies concerned with disability issues than is the case for race and gender will provide some assistance to individual complainants. However, the task force which has been set up to consider the small employer exception was also charged with considering whether there should be a Commission. Not surprisingly, the Disability Rights Task Force has recommended the setting up of a Disability Rights Commission whose powers and duties would be effectively identical to those of the Equal Opportunities Commission and the Commission for Racial Equality.[58] The Government's response is still awaited; implementation of the recommendations would require primary legislation.

---

55 Code of Practice, para 6.16.
56 Code of Practice, para 6.18.
57 Bynoe, I, Oliver, M and Barnes, C, *Equal Rights for Disabled People: the Case for a New Law*, 1991, London: Institute for Public Policy Research, p 69.
58 See 'Disability Rights Commission recommendations' (1998) 79 EOR 41.

The enforcement provisions and available remedies are effectively identical to those under the SDA 1975 and the RRA 1976. Three comments may be made. First, the power to make recommendations may be expected to be of greater importance than has been the case in race and gender cases. Despite the Code, much discrimination may be expected to arise out of ignorance of what can be done, and done at a reasonable cost. In such circumstances, a recommendation may be expected. This will be of potential benefit where the case concerns discrimination against an existing employee, but of less use where an applicant was refused employment perhaps many months before the tribunal hearing. Where an employee is dismissed having become less able to perform a job because of a disability there is, as usual, no power to order reinstatement. The familiar limitations on the effectiveness of recommendations are equally applicable here. Secondly, the highest awards for injury to feelings under the RRA 1976 and the SDA 1975 apply where there is clear evidence of hostility. To the extent that disability discrimination is due to ignorance it may be surmised that awards may be somewhat lower.[59] On the other hand, awards for loss of future earnings may tend to be higher, especially where an employee becomes disabled and loses a job in consequence, for tribunals may need little convincing that another job may be hard to come by. Thirdly, the assumption that employment tribunals are a suitable forum for resolution of these disputes can be questioned. The legislation would have provided an ideal opportunity at least to experiment with alternative forms of dispute resolution. If many such cases arise through ignorance, forcing the parties into the confrontation arena of a courtroom may be inappropriate. Such a forum imposes stresses and pressures on all applicants, but perhaps to an even greater extent where the applicant is disabled. In addition, monetary compensation seems even less appropriate here than in race and gender cases; many applicants might prefer an apology and a belated adjustment to the discriminatory practice. This is not to deny that there may be circumstances where none of these three points is true, where the publicity and formality of a tribunal hearing is entirely appropriate; what is being contended is that a different remedial route to which the parties might have opted should have been provided.

---

[59] The highest award, of £103,000, was made in *Kirker v British Sugar plc*, IT, unreported, Case No: 2601249/97, see 35 DCLD 1. The bulk of the compensation was for future loss of earnings, £3,500 being awarded for injury to feelings.

NON-EMPLOYMENT DISCRIMINATION AGAINST THE DISABLED

For many disabled people, discrimination and disadvantage in employment are but one of a litany of problems that may be experienced. A substantial proportion of the disabled do not seek work: many are over retiring age and others will be unable to work in other than sheltered surroundings. And even if discrimination in employment is removed, a non-driving disabled person may either be unable to use public transport or be greatly restricted as to the physical range of employment opportunities. It is not being suggested that the non-employment provisions of the SDA 1975 and the RRA 1976 are unimportant – though they have been litigated relatively little – but the non-employment provisions of the DDA 1995 may in time develop a higher public profile.

Goods, facilities and services

Section 19 deals with discrimination as regards goods, facilities and services and in this regard is similar to the RRA 1976 and the SDA 1975, in particular the need for the service to be provided to 'members of the public'. By contrast with the employment provisions, the provisions apply even if the service provider has fewer than 20 employees. The section applies whether or not the service is paid for.[60] The two most important exceptions, as compared with the lists under the other Acts, are education and transport, which are regulated, arguably inadequately, by separate parts of the Act.

As with employment, discrimination may take the form either of less favourable treatment or of a failure to make reasonable adjustments. The Act specifically covers offering the disabled a lower standard of service than is offered to other people. The Code of Practice observes that '[a]busive behaviour towards disabled customers, especially the use of insulting language about their disability, is very likely to be used as evidence that they

---

[60] Section 19(3) provides that the 'following are examples of services ...

    (a) access to and use of any place which members of the public are permitted to enter;

    (b) access to and use of means of communication;

    (c) access to and use of information services;

    (d) accommodation in a hotel, boarding house or other similar accommodation;

    (e) facilities by way of banking or insurance or for grants. loans, credit or finance;

    (f) facilities for entertainment, recreation or refreshment;

    (g) facilities provided by employment agencies ...

    (h) the services of any profession or trade, or any local or other public authority.

have been provided with a worse standard of service'.[61] However, this duty 'does not mean that you have to change the service you provide to overcome the effects of the disability. Nor do you have to stock special products for disabled people'.[62]

In this part of the Act, what amounts to justification is specifically spelled out.

Section 20

(3) ... [T]reatment is justified only if:

    (a) in the opinion of the provider of the services, one or more of the conditions satisfied in sub-s (4) is satisfied; and

    (b) it is reasonable, in all the circumstances of the case, for him to hold that opinion.

(4) The conditions are that:

    (a) in any case, the treatment is necessary in order not to endanger the health and safety of any person (which may include that of the disabled person);[63]

    (b) in any case, the disabled person is incapable of entering into an enforceable agreement, or of giving an informed consent ...[64]

    (c) [in a case of refusal to provide the service] the treatment is necessary because the provider of services would otherwise be unable to provide the service to members of the public;[65]

    (d) [in a case relating to the standard or manner of the service or the terms on which it is provided] the treatment is necessary in order for the provider of services to be able to provide the service to the disabled person or to other members of the public;

    (e) [in a case relating to different terms of service] the difference in the terms on which the service is provided to the disabled person and

---

61 Code of Practice, para 3.6.

62 Code of Practice, para 3.7.

63 Eg, a 'landlord refuses to let a third floor flat to a disabled person living alone who is clearly unable to negotiate the stairs in safety or use the fire escape or other routes in an emergency. *This is within the law.*' Code of Practice, para 5.5.

64 'A landlord refuses to let a flat to a person with a severe learning disability who does not understand that rent would have to be paid. *This is within the law.*' Code, para 5.8. 'Unless there is clear evidence to the contrary, you should assume that a disabled person is able to enter into any contract.' Code of Practice, para 5.9.

65 'These conditions will justify less favourable treatment only where not treating the disabled person less favourably would effectively prevent other customers or the disabled person from using the service. They cannot be used to justify refusal simply because other people would be inconvenienced or delayed.' Code of Practice, para 5.13. The Code of Practice distinguishes between refusing to serve a deaf person in a post office in order to avoid delaying other customers, and not allowing an unaccompanied wheelchair user on a guided tour as the extra time needed would prevent the tour being completed in the time allocated.

those on which it is provided to other members of the public reflects the greater cost to the provider of the services in providing the service to the disabled person.[66]

The emphasis placed on the opinion of the service provider means that there is a risk that courts might be too deferential to arguments based on subjective considerations. This should not happen for two reasons. First, the reason given to the court for the discrimination must be the actual reason that operated at the time and not a subsequent rationalisation; secondly, the duty to make reasonable adjustments in s 21 to some extent requires a proactive approach to the provision of services to disabled people.

The duty to make adjustments applies where there is a 'practice, policy or procedure which makes it impossible or unreasonably difficult' for a disabled person to make use of a service; and where 'a physical feature (for example, one arising from the design or construction of a building or the approach or access to premises)' has the same effect. Discrimination may be avoided by removing the feature, altering it, providing a reasonable means of avoiding it, or providing an alternative means of making the service available to disabled people.

Much of what is required in practice will be subsequently spelt out by Regulations. In particular, it is envisaged that a maximum limit will be set on necessary expenditure under this section, thereby avoiding county courts having to decide what is appropriate to spend to make such services more user friendly for disabled people; no such limit has yet been set and many of the details of the practical implementation of these provisions remain to be finalised. The impact of these sections will depend on the content of the Regulations and the extent to which the sections receive a sympathetic judicial interpretation.[67]

Education

The Act confers no individual right to claim unlawful discrimination in relation to education – although employment in an educational institution is of course covered. The basic obligations, imposed on schools by s 29 and institutes of further and higher education by s 30, are no more than to publish information concerning their polices in relation to the education of disabled persons. 'The disability statements regime will be policed, if at all, by a subtle mixture of parental pressure, market forces, and adjustments to funding

---

66 'Charging more can be justified only where the service is individually tailored to the needs of the customer and the disabled person's particular requirements increase costs ...' – the example given is that of an orthopaedic bed. Code of Practice, para 5.14.

67 The enforcement provisions in s 25 are effectively identical to those contained in the equivalent provisions of the SDA 1975 and the RRA 1976.

formulae. One cannot be optimistic that a new era of disabled educational opportunity is about to be ushered in.'[68]

Transport

The 'use' of means of transport is excluded from the general principle of non-discrimination in relation to the provision of services. In consequence, the range of facilities provided to the public, such as information about times, waiting rooms, etc, are covered under s 19, and, again, the employment provisions clearly apply to transport operators in the same way as to other employers.

Considering that accessible public transport is such a vital need for disabled people – not to mention the need for it to be frequent, reliable, and go where it is wanted – the legislation is hugely disappointing.[69] Aircraft and sea-going vessels are excluded from the Act altogether. The basic principle, which applies to taxis, buses and trains, gives the Secretary of State power to make regulations to control the design, manufacture and mode of operation of such vehicles, as well as to ensure that they comply with standards of accessibility for those who are disabled. The main problem is that the provisions are intended to apply to new, rather than existing vehicles, which means that a substantial period will elapse before the provisions begin to have a noticeable impact. Furthermore, no firm timetable has yet been set for the promulgation of the relevant Regulations.

The sections dealing with education and transport show that, while there are serious problems with an individual rights focus, the alternatives are feeble by comparison. This is partly due to the lack of imagination shown by English law in developing any effective alternative to a rights approach. We may scout around for alternative remedies and for alternative methods of adjudication, but the fact remains that, if individual rights are not granted, the effect of legislation is significantly weakened, if only from an educational and a symbolic perspective. The message sent to employers is that something has to be done, and that efforts must be made to find out what that is; the current message sent to educational institutions and transport operators is that voluntary action is commendable, but rapid change unnecessary.

---

[68] *Op cit*, Doyle, fn 1, p 71.

[69] There could be no claim parallelling the Australian case of *Waters v Public Transport Corporation* (1991) EOC 92-390 (see Thornton, M, 'Domesticating disability discrimination' (1997) 2 IJDL 183, p 190) where the Court upheld a claim of indirect discrimination against a transport company which had, *inter alia*, removed conductors from trams and introduced 'scratch' tickets. The claim was brought by nine individuals and 29 community groups, which represented people suffering a wide range of physical and intellectual impairments.

CRITICISMS AND LIKELY EFFECTS OF THE LEGISLATION

Many of the points have already been made. The exclusion of small employers, uncertainties as to when discrimination will be justified and when adjustments will be reasonable, and reliance for enforcement on individual litigation all have the potential to weaken the impact of the legislation. In addition, the non-employment provisions, where individual enforcement is even more problematic, are likely to prove of little impact unless supplemented with strongly drafted regulations.

What are considered here are alternative strategies for enforcement of the employment provisions plus brief consideration of the impact of the Americans with Disabilities Act. First, there is no contract compliance scheme similar to the American example contained in the Rehabilitation Act 1983. Employers may sit tight and wait for litigation rather than take proactive steps for fear of losing valuable business;[70] they will be protected from the fear that taking action themselves will increase labour costs and reduce competitiveness. Any attempt at introducing contract compliance, though, has to deal with the objection that the penalty for non-compliance, loss of the contract, is so drastic that in practice it is never utilised.[71]

The legislation provides no requirement for effective statistical monitoring of the workforce to identify disabilities and thus needs. While many employers are monitoring voluntarily as a result of the Act, it remains to be seen how widespread this will be and how effective. There must be doubts as to whether a straightforward questionnaire technique will result in full disclosure in every case. In connection with race and sex, most researchers argue both that equal opportunities policies are essential and that they are difficult to operate in such a way as to make them effective; exactly the same points apply here.[72]

The legislation aims, first, to grant enforceable rights to disabled individuals and, secondly, to increase the numbers of disabled people in meaningful employment. The experience under the SDA 1975, RRA 1976 and ADA 1990 indicates that the former may be easier to achieve than the latter. The major effects of the American legislation has been some increase in the

---

70   See *op cit*, Doyle, fn 6, pp 42–43.
71   See above, pp 563–66.
72   See *op cit*, Doyle, fn 6, pp 43–44.

degree of integration in employment,[73] while at the same time there was little improvement in the position of those not previously employed in integrated settings.[74] It is the most disabled, especially those with little or no history of independent employment, who are least likely to benefit from the employment provisions of the DDA 1995. Those who are most likely to benefit are those who become disabled while at work. In America 'the most common type of ... claim filed ... involves the discharge or termination of individuals with back or spine impairments. Roughly another one-third of claims involve a mental or neurologic disability. In contrast, a smaller percentage of claims involve sensory disabilities ... or serious life-threatening conditions'.[75] It is unrealistic to expect the UK legislation to transform the life prospects of large numbers of disabled people, and, while the legislation could no doubt be strengthened, for many people the expenditure of government money is potentially far more significant than the granting of legal rights concerned with employment. For that reason the absence of effective legal rights in so many of the non-employment provisions is the most serious criticism of the Act.

---

[73] Although over time the majority of individuals remain in the same type of employment, one-third are employed in more integrated and competitive settings ... From 1990 to 1994, the majority of individuals show no change in their employment category (56%), while one-third (34%) improve and approximately one-tenth (11%) regress in their employment category ... [I]ndividuals in integrated employment ... show higher capabilities and qualifications ... reflected in better job skills ... and health status ... [T]hose in integrated employment are more likely to reside independently in the community ... This finding supports the view that independent living is central for full inclusion into society for many persons with disabilities. In addition, those in integrated employment are most satisfied with their jobs and daily life activities ...' Blanck, P, 'Empirical study of the Americans with Disabilities Act: employment issues from 1990 to 1994' (1996) 14 Behavioural Sciences and the Law 5, p 7.

[74] 'Most participants not employed or employed in non-integrated settings in 1990 remain in these settings in 1994 ... The black hole trends reflect the problems of chronic unemployment and under-employment faced by many qualified persons with disabilities. Enhanced strategies are needed to assist the millions of qualified persons with disabilities entering the workforce. Job retention and advancement strategies are needed to help people with disabilities keep jobs and achieve their full potential.' Op cit, Blanck, fn 73.

[75] Ibid.

CHAPTER 17

CONCLUSION

Discrimination and inequality are moral issues. This is true whether one's personal focus is on human rights or on redistribution of economic benefits. The objective is to alter society for the better in the interests of justice and/or fairness. A belief in the need for legislation reflects a 'moral ideal of the equality of human beings which affirms that, although we are unequal in our skill, intelligence, strength and virtue, we are morally equal because of our common humanity'.[1] For that reason, a study of discrimination law and its effects which is politically and ethically neutral is unattainable and pointless. To conclude the study, we will briefly focus on ways in which the law itself might be improved, the inherent limitations of such a reform strategy, and the broader social and economic context into which any such reform strategy must be placed. Most of the points have already been made; the purpose of the conclusion is to collect the arguments in a simplified but coherent form. Of course, one's view about reform depends on whether one's individual focus sees anti-discrimination law as concerned primarily with individual rights or as a mechanism for significant redistribution of economic and political power.

It is naive to suggest that law reform by itself can transform society. It is, nevertheless, a significant first step. Law needs to be as well written and effective as possible to enable it to operate in conjunction with other social and political measures. With this in mind, there are three broad areas in which anti-discrimination law might profitably be strengthened: the protected groups; the coverage and wording of current discrimination legislation; and the available remedies.

WHO SHOULD BE PROTECTED

There are many groups who have a claim that anti-discrimination legislation should justly be extended to them. Discrimination on the grounds of sexual orientation, religion and age should be unlawful throughout the UK. Religious discrimination has been unlawful in Northern Ireland for more than 20 years, but is not unlawful in Great Britain. Despite the problems of definition and of defining permissible exceptions, the symbolic and moral argument for extending anti-discrimination legislation to cover religion is

---

1   Lord Lester, 'Making discrimination law effective: old barriers and new frontiers' (1997) 2 IJDL 167, p 168.

overwhelming. The history of colonialism and its association with a particular form of Christianity has meant that certain Western manifestations of the Christian religion have come to be associated with racism and oppression. Furthermore, even the white population of the UK is no longer predominantly Christian. Finally, it is frequently impossible to disentangle notions of race and racism from issues of religious intolerance and discrimination. The case is surely almost self-evident.[2]

Sexual orientation discrimination is, at the time of writing, not *per se* unlawful,[3] though in some circumstances it might be possible to bring it within the scope of the Sex Discrimination Act 1975, especially where gay men are treated differently from gay women. The Government has recently issued a consultation paper with proposals that discrimination against transsexuals should be made unlawful. Such a limited reform would only serve to highlight the apparent injustice of excluding gay people from the scope of the legislation. Some would argue, however, that while discrimination on the basis of sexual orientation should be unlawful where it concerns actual job performance – issues of hiring, promotion, dismissal, etc – it does not follow that the law should treat gay relationships in precisely the same way as heterosexual relationships. On this basis, it might be contended that discrimination in relation to those fringe benefits which affect not simply the employee but also that employee's partner should not necessarily be unlawful.

Discrimination on the basis of age is not unlawful, unless the way in which age conditions are operated entails discrimination on the basis of, usually, gender. The moral strength of the argument for age discrimination legislation is not as compelling as that concerning race and gender. However, the average age in society is increasing, the proportion of jobs requiring physical strength is decreasing, while at the same Western societies do not accord the same respect and status to age and experience as did previous generations. These factors provide strong arguments for the extension of the legislation to cover discrimination on the ground of age.[4]

There is also a strong case for a consolidating anti-discrimination statute. The law at present is a mass of primary, amending and secondary legislation, which must be read together with European Community law. The law needs consolidation to be made far more user friendly, one aspect of which is, so far as possible, to apply the same criteria to each of the unlawful grounds of discrimination.[5] The current law has been described as 'an incoherent mess of

---

2   See above, pp 134–36.
3   See above, pp 117–28.
4   See above, pp 129–34.
5   See *op cit*, Lester, fn 1, pp 174–76.

piecemeal legislation'.[6] It is clearly plausible to argue that the overall impact of the law would be greater if all protected groups were brought under the same basic legislative umbrella, both because utilising such a law would be easier for applicants and their advisers, and because of the more powerful moral message that such a law might be thought to send. However, even if one accepts this somewhat speculative argument so far as the substantive law is concerned, it does not necessarily follow that the umbrella enforcement agency is appropriate for the entire ambit of anti-discrimination legislation. First, that might deflect attention away from less high profile areas and, secondly, the wider the range of protected groups within the jurisdiction of the same enforcement agency, the greater the scope for internal and external conflict concerning objectives, strategy and resources.

THE DETAILS OF CURRENT LEGISLATION

A strategy which seeks to focus on the similarities between discrimination on different grounds also encompasses the second necessary change: to many of the details of the current sex and race discrimination legislation. Most of the points have already been covered; it is here sufficient merely to highlight the most significant. First, equal pay law needs amendment. The differentiation between the Equal Pay Act 1970 and the Sex Discrimination Act 1975 is outdated, confusing and unnecessary. It may cause problems in knowing under which statute a particular issue arises. The legal rules under the two statutes, while normally dovetailing, do not always do so, especially as regards the operation of indirect discrimination and the applicable remedial structure. Claims under the SDA 1975 permit comparison with how a hypothetical man would have been treated, while under the EqPA 1970 an actual male comparator is required.[7] My own view is that, in pay cases heard before Employment Tribunals, hypothetical comparisons are frequently inappropriate as they would necessitate the tribunal acting in effect as a wage setting body. However the same would not be true if an arbitration body were given jurisdiction over collective equal pay claims, though even here I am entirely unconvinced that equal pay law is the appropriate tool for tacking the problem of low pay and gender segregation, especially in the part time service sector. The law undoubtedly needs amendment to incorporate a collective dimension to equal pay claims. Without such a change, the complexity, delays, and expense involved in bringing an equal value claim are indefensible and in urgent need of simplification, despite the recent modest changes, the impact of which is likely to be no more than marginal.

6   'Improving equality law: the options' (1997) 72 EOR 28.
7   See above, pp 407–09.

There are other changes to the legislation that are required. That indirect discrimination necessitates the establishment of a requirement or condition which has been interpreted as a 'must' means that the law is far too narrow.[8] That decisions on justification are held to be matters of fact for each Employment Tribunal has hindered the development of a coherent body of law on the importance to be attached to the elimination of indirectly discriminatory practices, taking clearly and explicitly on board the doctrine of proportionality.[9] The definition of victimisation is narrow and has been routinely interpreted in a fashion so as to make it narrower still;[10] in addition, the evidence suggests that it fails to act as a real effective deterrent against the victimisation of claimants and others. There is an urgent need for a separate statute – or at least a separate section within a statute – on sexual and racial harassment.[11] Despite recent legislation, the law on maternity rights is desperately technical and confusing and may therefore deprive ordinary people of the practical benefit of their rights.[12] Many of the exceptions, especially these in the SDA 1975, need to be drawn more tightly, not least so as to ensure conformity with European law.[13] Outside employment, the decision in *R v Entry Clearance Officer Bombay ex p Amin*[14] that the prohibition on discrimination in relation to the provision of goods and services only applies to governmental activities which are analogous to market activities is a quite unacceptable restriction on the scope of the legislation.[15]

PROCEDURES AND REMEDIES

These are examples; others might have been quoted. It remains true, however, that the vast majority of practices which ought to be unlawful do come within the scope of the legislation.[16] It is arguably of even greater significance to focus on the procedures and remedies available for the enforcement of the legislation. Even here, we should not expect miracles. There can hardly be an area of law whose objective is to increase the rights of ordinary people which does not face problematic issues of procedure and remedies. Problems of

---

8 See above, pp 266–72.
9 See above, pp 291–96.
10 See above, pp 362–67.
11 See above, pp 257–58.
12 See above, Chapter 7, especially pp 200–07.
13 See above, pp 336–50.
14 [1983] 2 AC 818; [1983] 2 All ER 864.
15 See above, pp 378–82.
16 In the same way, while the definition of disability under the Disability Discrimination Act 1995 can be subject to severe criticism, the vast majority of those who ought to be within the definition are within the definition.

access to legal advice, the costs involved, the trauma of going to law, and other factors, can never be entirely eliminated. Even alternative dispute resolution, which should certainly be explored as a means for resolving at least some such disputes, can never completely remove the practical disadvantages of a law-based system, and may bring in its wake its own disadvantages, such as the reduction of publicity as a factor in deterring unlawful behaviour.[17] Legal aid for discrimination cases is the ideal, but one most unlikely to be implemented, and in any event the legal aid criteria would exclude most potential applicants. It is too much to expect sufficient additional funding to enable the Commissions significantly to increase the proportion of cases that can receive their financial backing. There remains a great need for pressure groups and voluntary bodies to bear some of this load, as occurs so successfully in the USA, and which may develop under the DDA 1995. Such a development, though, can hardly be provoked by legal compulsion.

While the quality of decision making in tribunals and higher courts may well have improved somewhat since the weaknesses of the period so clearly documented by Leonard,[18] there is no room for complacency, and there remains a strong argument for the establishment of a specialist tribunal to hear all discrimination cases. Nevertheless, it is plausible to contend that the higher profile and greater visibility of discrimination cases – the mainstreaming of discrimination law – will have contributed to a greater willingness, subconsciously perhaps, in tribunal members to be sympathetic to and find in favour of applicants.

There are, though, many changes to the available remedies which would assist in strengthening the legislation. A significant start was made with the removing of the maximum compensation limit in both race and gender cases.[19] The DDA 1995 has no maximum limit, and it is now proposed that the limit should be removed in unfair dismissal cases not involving issues of discrimination. It is clear that such a maximum limit significantly weakens the deterrent impact of the law.

The powers of the Commission for Racial Equality and the Equal Opportunities Commission are heavily circumscribed both by legislation and judicial interpretation. One of the justifications for the Commissions is to counteract the individualism that bedevils English law in general and anti-discrimination law in particular, to provide a mechanism for tackling entrenched practices of discrimination rather than confining the law to isolated pathological acts. The formal investigation procedure was envisaged as the main method of transposing this ideal into a practical means of tackling

---

17 See above, pp 506–08.
18 See above, pp 504–06.
19 See above, pp 509–10.

discrimination. It is thus imperative that these powers are given a new lease of life, by removing the procedural handcuffs placed around the Commissions.[20] The Northern Ireland Fair Employment Commission may investigate any organisation, whether or not it suspects that discrimination may have occurred, and may recommend action which should be taken to promote equality of opportunity. The Great Britain Commissions should have similar powers. In addition, the DDA 1995 should be amended so as to *create* a Disability Commission, whose powers should be along the lines here indicated.

This should not be all. It is strongly arguable that the Commissions should have the power to represent groups of individuals similarly situated, thereby providing a mechanism somewhat akin to the US class action procedure which has been so instrumental in bringing about high profile cases. But on its own, such a power of representation would be of limited impact: it needs to be accompanied by a right in tribunals to make an award of compensation to any victim of equivalent discrimination who has become a party to the proceedings. In this way, the collective element in discrimination would be recognised, the rights of victims vindicated, and the potential additional compensation might provide a significant element of deterrence against patterns and practices of unlawful behaviour.

Further changes to the remedial powers of tribunals are also appropriate, though there is no logic in confining such reforms to anti-discrimination law and not extending them, in particular, to unfair dismissal law. The three types of change worthy of serious consideration are to enable awards of exemplary damages to be made, to give tribunals power to *order* appointment, promotion, reinstatement, etc, and to bolster the very limited powers to deal with persistent or recurrent discrimination.

The final area of much-needed legal reform straddles issues of substantive and remedial law. At present employers have no legal incentive to take the initiative to promote equality, but may choose to sit back and await allegations of discrimination, which statistically are unlikely to be successful. Employers should be placed under a positive duty, similar to that under the Fair Employment (Northern Ireland) Act 1989, to monitor their workforce by ethnic origin and gender, and, where significant differences are found, there should be a concomitant duty to take positive steps to reduce such disparities.[21] Where such information is not available or provided on request, the appropriate Commission should have the legal power to require action by the employer, backed up by the possibility of an injunction. The situations in which positive action is permissible should be extended, clarified and publicised, though it is presumed that European law will continue to set strict

---

[20] See above, pp 526–34.
[21] See above, pp 554–57.

boundaries on what is permissible in relation to gender.[22] Finally, contract compliance should once more be lawful in relation to gender and its availability clarified in relation to race.[23] Here, though, perhaps the more important issue is the willingness or otherwise of government and its agencies to take equality issues seriously, to ensure that equal opportunities becomes a mainstream political issue.

LAW, GOVERNMENT AND SOCIAL POLICY

It is naive to expect dramatic social changes merely from improved laws.[24] There are at least two reasons for this. First, anti-discrimination laws, especially concerning employment, can do little or nothing to counteract social disadvantages which prevent women and black people competing on an equal playing field with white males. If the goal is redistribution, other policies may have greater benefit than anti-discrimination laws. Putting adequate resources into inner city education may benefit far more black people than any improved Race Relations Act. Tackling racism within the criminal justice system may have similar benefits.[25] So far as gender is concerned, it is readily apparent that law cannot alter the fact that the majority of low paid part time jobs in the service sector are held by women. Deeply entrenched ideological assumptions and practical considerations contribute to this situation, which, as Fredman notes, even drastically increased male unemployment has done nothing to shift.[26] That such a social situation is in no sense natural or inevitable does not mean it is easy to alter. The Government does appear to be committed in some small ways to policies attempting to reconcile the dichotomy between work and home. However, such policies are tempered by an unwillingness to impose significant costs on employers or on taxpayers, and appear to be purely aimed at women. Apart from a few days' paternity leave,[27] there is little or no social policy commitment aimed at enabling men – or successful, highly paid career women – the more easily to reconcile domestic and employment spheres. The

---

22 See above, pp 543–47.

23 See above, pp 563–66.

24 The CRE's belief that we 'have it in our power as a society to eliminate racial discrimination, to ensure equality of opportunity, to reject prejudice and xenophobia and to embrace tolerance and inclusivity' (*Reform of the Race Relations Act: Proposals from the Commission for Racial Equality*, 1998, London: CRE, p 5) is, as befits their role, highly aspirational, but runs the risk of leading to disappointment by ascribing too great a power to law and policy to achieve social change.

25 See Lustgarten, L, 'Racial inequality, public policy and the law: where are we going?', in Hepple, B and Szyszczak, E (eds), *Discrimination: The Limits of Law*, 1992, London: Mansell Publishing, pp 458–62.

26 Fredman, S, *Women and the Law*, 1997, Oxford: Clarendon, p 414.

27 See above, pp 207–08.

trend of the last 20 years has been towards greater workloads on those in permanent jobs combined with higher unemployment and insecurity for those without. The gender implications of this development are apparent, but the further implications are increasing economic inequality and possibly a weakening of family ties and commitments. In this area, policies which benefit women thus stand to benefit the whole of society. In the immediate future, however, women may have to be content with the limited impact of a national minimum wage set at £3.60 per hour. Welcome as the development is, a social transformation it is not.

A lead from government is therefore vital. This might be achieved in a number of ways. The CRE has recommended that racial equality should be 'a permanent priority and obligation for government and all public bodies'.[28] Not only should the State act as a model employer, but there should be an obligation to consider the implications for racial equality of *all* aspects of government policy. Where a policy might be expected to have significant adverse impact on racial minorities, 'the public body would be expected to consider alternatives to the proposed policy or action'.[29] Ethnic monitoring and contract compliance would be an essential feature of such a proactive approach, the basic framework of which could equally be applied to gender and disability.

But the second barrier concerns the current ideological framework within law and society. Lustgarten identifies a lack of faith in egalitarianism and redistribution, a growth in consumerism and a trust in market solutions, and a declining faith in public institutions as a solvent of social problems.[30] Women, black people, gay people, and the disabled become pressure groups like any others. There is no over-arching value system by which to evaluate social policy. In such a context, individual rights can be presented as part of the consumerist society. Rights may thus deflect attention from economic redistribution and issues of group equality. That is why it is so vital to stress once again the *moral* dimension to anti-discrimination law and policy. So often the argument is heard that the market demands particular solutions or that redistribution is not affordable. For this reason, the argument that equality policies may benefit employers by increasing the pool of available talent, while frequently correct, is ideologically problematic. Anti-discrimination law and policy must be about using the resources of the State, legal and otherwise, to benefit individuals and groups in our society who are disproportionately excluded from access to economic, social and political power. As the law itself has so frequently been a means of maintaining, rather than challenging,

---

[28] Op cit, *Reform of the Race Relations Act*, fn 24, p 11.
[29] Op cit, *Reform of the Race Relations Act*, fn 24, p 13.
[30] Op cit, Lustgarten, fn 25, p 462

existing power relationships, especially in the field of gender, law cannot be expected to *transform* society.

But it is appropriate to end on a note of qualified optimism. Law can achieve limited benefits for disadvantaged groups, as is shown by the impact of European law on gender equality. An approach utilising rights, rather than the complexities of the anti-discrimination approach based on comparisons, will frequently be more productive. There *have* been improvements, both in the content of the law and the way in which it is administered, and the pressure to extend anti-discrimination law into new areas, while it may take time, is probably irresistible.

But law can never be more than a small part of an overall strategy. Outside employment, the impact of anti-discrimination law has been rather marginal. Even a shift towards legal recognition of group rights will do little or nothing to overcome structural patterns of social disadvantage, especially in education and housing, and in gender relations within work and family. Government needs to take the lead, both in terms of public expenditure and issues such as taxation and social security policy. Social change has occurred and is continuing to occur, especially as regards some aspects of gender issues. It is arguable that legal change is more a reflection of this social change than its cause. At the same time, the social and economic position of minority ethnic groups has improved no more than marginally. Improved law is a vital tool in seeking to increase the speed of such change, but political, social and cultural developments have the capacity to bring about more significant improvements. The task requires committed lawyers as well as other groups in society. If this book has encouraged some students to take an active role in seeking to use the law in a positive and proactive way in the interests of disadvantaged groups, it will have achieved its objective.

INDEX